I AM YOUR DUST

The Olamot Series in the Humanities and Social Sciences translates recent and innovative books by Israeli scholars with the goal of making them more widely available to English-speaking audiences. The series aims to reflect the originality and diversity of Israeli scholarship by publishing books on a range of topics in Israel and Jewish Studies from antiquity to today. The series encourages scholarship that broadens its particular field from perspectives that have not been sufficiently explored or brought into dialogue heretofore.

Irit Dekel, Jason Mokhtarian, and Noam Zadoff, Series Editors

I AM YOUR DUST

Representations of the Israeli Experience in Yiddish Prose, 1948–1967

Gali Drucker Bar-Am

Olamot Series in the Humanities and Social Sciences
Published in association with Indiana University Press

Indiana University Press

This book is a publication of

Indiana University Press
Office of Scholarly Publishing
Herman B Wells Library 350
1320 East 10th Street
Bloomington, Indiana 47405 USA

iupress.org

Manufactured in the United States of America

First Printing 2024

Cataloging information is available from the Library of Congress.

ISBN 978-0-253-07150-7 (hdbk.)
ISBN 978-0-253-07151-4 (pbk.)
ISBN 978-0-253-07152-1 (web PDF)

Cover credit: © Micha Bar-Am, Shikun Chadash Neve Sharet, Israel, 1968.

In memory of the beloveds
My Bundist grandmother, Sara-Khashke Novodvorski
(Novi-Dvor 1907–Ramat Eliyahu 1995)
My Zionist mother, Esther Drucker Novodvorski
(Buenos Aires 1947–Ramat Eliyahu 2012)

Contents

Acknowledgments ix

Introduction 1

Part I: Yiddish in Israel: A Cultural History, 1948–1967

1 Tel Aviv after the Holocaust: A Yiddish Metropolis? 31

2 May the Place Comfort You: Memory, Space, and Consolidation of National Identity in the Yiddish Press 120

Part II: The Israeli Experience in Yiddish Prose, 1948–1967

3 The Nostalgic Paradox of Yiddish Prose 159

4 Israeli Spaces in Yiddish Prose 179

Conclusion: The End of Yiddish Culture and the Invention of an Israeli Jewish Identity 267

Appendix A: Biographical Details of Yiddish Writers and Journalists in Israel 275

Appendix B: Global Centers of Yiddish Culture, 1948–1967 279

Notes 285

Bibliography 345

Index 371

Acknowledgments

The book that you are holding has had several incarnations. The first incarnation was an academic work researched and written at the Hebrew University of Jerusalem in 2013. I thank Avraham Novershtern, as well as Avner Holzman, Natan Cohen, Eli Lederhendler, Dalia Ofer, and my Yiddish teacher Ester Rozhanski for their essential guidance and support throughout my studies. And I thank my dear colleagues Laura Jockusch, Michal Aharoni, and Ella Florsheim for their long-standing friendship and good advice.

I am grateful to institutions and organizations that found my research worthy of support: to the Mandel Foundation and its Scholion Center for three years spent in a vibrant intellectual incubator as part of the "Jews and Cities" research group, Beit Sholem Aleichem, the Mandel Institute of Jewish Studies and the Harman Institute of Contemporary Judaism at the Hebrew University of Jerusalem, the Rachel Yanait Ben Zvi Foundation of the Center for the Study of Eretz Yisrael and Its Yishuv at Yad Izhak Ben-Zvi, the Memorial Foundation for Jewish Culture, the Lerner Fund, the Genya and Itzik Manger Foundation, the Jacob Groper Foundation, and the "Targum Shlishi" Foundation.

Throughout my research, I was fortunate to receive an outstretched hand from several people who were its subjects: I wish to express my deep thanks to Tsvi Ayznman; to the Luden family—Ester, Yitskhok, Hanna, and Urit; to Shura Turkov, Pesya Portnoy, and Aleksander Shpiglblat for sharing with me memories of their rich culture and insights about it, generously, warmly, and painfully; to Aviva Halamish, Lea Marom, Ruth Maron, and Edna Nachshon, who shared with me memories of their parents—Mordechai Halamish, Moyshe Grosman, Khaye Elboym-Dorembus, and Dovid Eydlman—and of their childhood in the Yiddish cultural circles of Tel Aviv; to Hila Zur and the staff of the Gnazim Archive; to Leo Greenbaum and Gunnar Berg of the YIVO Archive in New York; and to Oded Steklov for essential help with data processing.

The research for this book received the Giora Yoel Yashinski Award for Outstanding Doctoral Research; the Yad Vashem Prize for Graduate Students from the Rokhl Oyerbakh and Mala Zimetbaum Funds; the Moritz and Charlotte Warburg Research Prize in Jewish Studies, the Hebrew University of Jerusalem; and the Simon Wiesenthal Prize for study in the field of Holocaust research, the Harman Institute of Contemporary Judaism at the Hebrew University of Jerusalem. My deep gratitude is extended to these institutions.

A soft landing from the "Eden" of graduate studies was made possible thanks to a fellowship from "Da'at haMakom": Center for the Study of Cultures of Places in the Modern Jewish World (founded by I-Core—the Israeli Centers for Research Excellence) at the Hebrew University of Jerusalem. I wish to thank Eli Lederhendler and Richard (Richie) Cohen for their ongoing and stimulating support during the process of adapting this work into a book. My heartfelt thanks are extended to my students, my listeners, and interlocutors at the Hebrew University, Tel Aviv University, Beit Sholem Aleichem, and Arbeter ring (Worker's Alliance), and to those from ultra-Orthodox communities and Israeli settlements. The conversations with them helped me understand how to turn the dry academic study into a book.

The Hebrew edition of this book was published by Yad Izhak Ben-Zvi. I am deeply grateful to the staff of the publishing house for their friendly and attentive support throughout the process of bringing the book to press: to Yaakov Yaniv, Yael Dinovitsh, Amnon Ramon, and Liat Oshri. Thank you to Beit Sholem Aleichem, to the World Union of Jewish Studies, and to Haim Goldgraber and Rafi Weichert, whose crucial help made the book's publication possible. Rafi's grandfather, Michał Weichert, contributed to Yiddish culture in Israel and is mentioned in this book. I am grateful to Rafi for his friendship.

Special thanks to those who contributed photographs to the book: the Micha Bar-Am Archive; Gnazim Archive—the Hebrew Writers' Association; Yad Vashem Photo Archive; Arbeter ring Tel Aviv—Beit Sholem Aleichem; and my dear khaver Eran Turbiner, Esther Luden and Ruth Maron, Tzvika Palchinski of the Novi-Dvor Hometown Association, and Ami Yechieli and Eti Reuveni of the Vilna Hometown Association, who helped find family photos among the members of the associations.

In its Hebrew incarnation, the book won two awards: the Nathaniel and Erika Lorkh Prize from the Center for the Study of Eretz Yisrael and Its Yishuv at Yad Izhak Ben-Zvi, for the best academic book in 2018–2021 on the history of Israel; and the Shapiro Prize for the best book in Israel studies in 2021, awarded by the Association for Israel Studies (AIS). My sincere thanks to the award committees for finding my book worthy of these nominations.

The book's final (for now) incarnation is this English edition. I am deeply grateful to the wonderful staff of the Olamot Center: to Irit Dekel, Noam Zadoff, and Jason Mokhtarian for their warm and sensitive accompaniment of the book into the English-speaking realm. I wish to thank the center for its generosity in financing the book's translation into English and for giving me the opportunity to work on the English edition with the master translator Natalie Melzer. Natalie's grandfather, the poet, editor, and translator Shimshon Melzer, made a substantial contribution to Yiddish culture in Israel and to the importing of

Yiddish culture into Hebrew culture in Israel. Her work is suffused with the cultural breadth of her lineage, and to this she adds sensitivity, patience, thoroughness, and intelligence. I am deeply grateful to her.

Thank you to my love, Nimrod, a worker of truth whose work is truth. And special thanks to our son, our treasure, Orian-Sholem, by whose light all of it is done.

I AM YOUR DUST

Introduction

1. Prelude: The "Return to Zion" of a Yiddish-Writing Refugee

One of the guests who arrived in Israel for the celebrations of the ten-year anniversary of its establishment (1958) was the prominent Yiddish poet Itzik Manger (1901–1969). It was his first visit to Israel.[1] His arrival received wide coverage in the Hebrew press and especially in the Yiddish papers and periodicals. The editors of these publications marked the occasion by referencing one of his well-known poems, "Kh'hob zikh yorn gevalgert [in der fremd]" (For years I wandered [in Foreign Lands]), from which the title of this book is borrowed. Avrom Sutzkever, editor of the prominent literary magazine *Di goldene keyt* (*The golden chain*), greeted the honorable guest in his magazine with these words: "Now that you have come 'to wander at home'—let us bow to that. May you be blessed, Itzik Manger, you wandering prince."[2] And Moyshe Grosman, editor of the periodical *Heymish* (homey), wrote in a cover piece devoted to the event, "For years, Itzik, you wandered in foreign lands, now come here, to wander at home."[3]

In modern Jewish culture, Manger is known as "the troubadour of Yiddish poetry." The troubadour is, of course, the traveling, homeless singer. The rootlessness and wandering of the Jewish troubadour are considered prominent features of Yiddish culture as a whole, given that it developed in "exile," in a hostile, threatening environment. The arrival of such a troubadour in Israel on the occasion of the ten-year anniversary of its establishment was thus widely perceived as a quintessential symbol of the return of the exilic Jew to his home, of the end of two thousand years of exile and hardship in the Diaspora. His poem "Kh'hob zikh yorn gevalgert" embodies many layers of experience of the return to Israel of Eastern European Jewry and of the culture they brought with them. These layers are the subject of this book.

Manger's poem centers on the figure of a Jew who after long years of travel arrives in his country, the land of his forefathers. By virtue of this image, which merges the universal archetype of the prodigal son who returns, perhaps too late, to his destination, with the Jewish archetype of the end of exile, and by virtue of its intimate, personal, and elegiac tone, the poem became a kind of anthem (an ironic one, as we will soon see) that expresses the sentiments of many of the Yiddish-speaking Eastern European Jews who migrated to Israel after the Holocaust (and viewed themselves as *sheyres-hapleyte*, "the surviving remnant"). Many of them saw in this poem the story of their own return, and some even thought it was written especially for this first visit and in honor of Israel's ten-year anniversary.[4] In fact, it had already appeared as the final poem in his collection *Lid un balade* (Poem and ballad), which appeared in 1952 in New York. In September of the same year, the poem appeared there in the daily Yiddish press.[5] This fact is interesting because it suggests that, for Manger, writing the poem was not an expression of his personal excitement over the upcoming meeting with Israel, as if he were standing on the deck of a ship and chronicling his thrilled anticipation as the ship approached the shores of the promised land. Rather, it was an imagined meeting with Israel from afar, and perhaps even a substitute for an actual encounter with it—his own encounter or that of his readers. The choice to seal *Lid un balade* with this poem, however, also underscores its conspicuous significance as an "end of the road" poem, a poem that brings an era to its conclusion.

Manger was not the only great Yiddish writer to visit Israel in the first years after its establishment. Among the prominent visits were those of H. Leyvik (in 1950 and 1957) and of Yoysef Opatoshu (in 1952).[6] But Manger's visit differed from theirs insofar as it marked the first time (and the only time in the state's first two decades) that a representative of Yiddish culture was received warmly not only by the Yiddish-speaking public in Israel but also by the Hebrew press and the Israeli establishment. The minister of education and culture, Zalman Aran, and the chairman of the Jewish Agency, Zalman Shazar, gave their patronage to the festive reception in his honor, held by the World Jewish Congress and the Y. L. Peretz Library at the Ohel Shem Hall in Tel Aviv.[7] Israeli president Izhak Ben-Zvi hosted Manger in his residence along with Speaker of the Knesset Yosef Sprinzak and Secretary General of the Histadrut (the General Organization of Hebrew Workers) Pinhas Lavon. Nor did the Hebrew cultural elite remain indifferent to the visit: at his reception, theater actors (like Hanna Rovina, who read Manger's aforementioned poem), authors, playwrights, and poets writing in Hebrew (including Avraham Shlonsky), as well as Hebrew writers who in Israel had returned to writing in Yiddish (like Uri Zvi Greenberg), mingled with their colleagues from the Yiddish cultural scene in Israel: authors, journalists, actors, directors, and playwrights.[8] After the reception, a party to celebrate Manger at the famous Café Kasit drew the country's top poets, including the man regarded as the country's "national poet," Nathan Alterman.[9] The (Hebrew) Press Association also held a reception for Manger at Beit Sokolov in Tel Aviv.[10]

This warm welcome by the hegemonic Hebrew culture at Israel's ten-year celebrations did not reflect a recognition of the contribution of modern Yiddish culture to the birth of Israel, to the very crystallizing of the national idea and its realization in the context of a rich and multilayered Jewish-national culture, a recognition of the country's moral obligation to preserve the culture of the

Holocaust survivors after the reparations agreement with Germany, or a recognition of the importance of the cultures that the various groups of migrants brought with them to Israel and of their decisive contribution to the development of a rich and varied Israeli culture. The warm welcome, rather, served the hegemonic culture as a means of bolstering the commonly accepted hierarchy that posited the "exilic" cultures imported by the "mass migration," and primarily Yiddish culture, as inferior to the hegemonic culture and even as reprehensible—a view that in turn had dictated a discriminatory distribution of budgetary recourses in education and culture. The Hebrew press described Manger as a popular, folk poet who portrayed the old home with nostalgia. He was presented in these journalistic descriptions as an unthreatening symbol of a ruined Diaspora, the last of the weary survivors of a bygone folklore tradition, someone whose poetry sums up and seals an old traditional world that no longer exists; someone doomed to write in a forgotten, almost mute language, which in any case is destined to disappear; someone living in the past and clinging to it; someone who is not a bona fide Zionist (because of his support of Yiddish language and culture) but who is also not an anti-Zionist, as he cannot help being taken in by the charms of the new Hebrew state, its landscapes, and its people. He was also described as a tired old man, socially uprooted and lonely, roaming the globe; as overwhelmed by the generous honors and affections with which he was showered in Israel; and even as someone who had arrived in Israel carrying only a single, last remaining copy from among all of his books (a copy of *Lid un balade*), which, it was reported, he hoped to bequeath to the president if the latter would deign to invite him to his residence (as if every part of his visit were not already planned in advance).[11] These were the typical trappings that in those days made it possible for the Hebrew consensus to show sympathy for a Yiddish poet. His culture and his language were given a place by his Israeli audience at the cost of accepting them as a (reprehensible) attribute of survivors, as something to be played down, a symbol of the sorrowful Diaspora, its weaknesses and illnesses, a Diaspora associated with a bygone world and with the "shtetl" provinciality from which the new Sabra who "rose from the sea" (or from the sand dunes) had sought to distance himself.[12] A common moniker for the surviving remnant in Israeli society of those days was *Sheyres-hablote*, a polite translation of which is "the remnant of mud" or the "remnant of filth."

A diametrically opposed impression is gained by reading Manger's poem. It exposes the full scope of the innovativeness and boldness of the Yiddish body of work written after the Holocaust, as well as the emotional and cultural complexity it sought to express. The poem became an anthem of sorts for many of the surviving-remnant migrants not because it offered, as anthems typically do, a simplistic, catchy myth that replayed canonical images and popular symbols that organized the world of those who recited it around simple, stable, and homogenous binary categories of "them" and "us," "Zion" and "the Diaspora," "hardship" and "overcoming"; but precisely because it succeeded in expressing a complexity bordering on disorientation with respect to the meaning of such symbols, and because this complexity-to-the-point-of-disorientation echoed the inner experience of his readers. This, I believe, is perhaps the most important feature of the Yiddish fiction of surviving-remnant migrants explored in this study and a chief source of the great interest it holds.

The central position in Manger's poem, as mentioned, is that of the Jewish vagabond who imagines the impending end of an arduous journey looking out at the various mythical landscapes of the promised land: he sees himself, in his mind's eye, standing before the Sea of Galilee and the desert. These scenes coalesce into the poem's refrain, in which the speaker boldly announces to the Land of Israel, in a tone that combines pain and apology with unmistakable defiance, that he does not intend to kiss its soil:

> Kh'vel nisht kushn dayn shtoyb vi yener groyser poet,
> Khotsh mayn harts iz oykh ful mit gezang un geveyn.
> Vos heyst kushn dayn shtoyb? Ikh bin dayn shtoyb.
> Un ver kusht es, ikh bet aykh, zikh aleyn?
>
> I'll not kiss your dust as that great poet did
> Though my heart, like his, is filled with song and grief
> How can I kiss your dust? I am your dust.
> And how, I ask you, can I kiss myself?[13]

The work is constructed as a contrast to a familiar epic scheme in which a pilgrim to the holy land, poised at the culmination of a journey filled with hardship, and out of gratitude for the opportunity afforded him, falls to his knees and kisses its soil. In particular, Manger chose to contrast the speaker in his poem with the speaker in Judah ha-Levi's poem "Tsiyon halo tishali" ("Zion, Won't You Ask").[14] The hymn was written between 1125 and 1141 and was known as the "Song of Songs for Zion" (and because it is a poem of love for a mythical homeland that stands destroyed, it has become one of the traditional lamentations recited on **Tisha be-Av** in services commemorating the destruction of the First and Second Temples).[15] This ode to Zion created a subgenre of liturgical poems that followed in ha-Levi's footsteps and were called "Zionist" poems. Ha-Levi imagined his protagonist prostrating himself on the soil of Zion and kissing it ("I'd fling myself down on the ground and treasure / your stones and favor your dust").[16] The speaker in his poem tours the Land of Israel and sees it in its emptiness and destruction. Nonetheless, his heart rejoices over the very fact of this overwhelming encounter and is emboldened by it, and he prays for the land's redemption. Ha-Levi's hymn is read as a religious and spiritual message of encouragement, as consolation and an expression of the pain of waiting for the long-tarrying redemption. The pilgrim's imagined arrival at his destination in and of itself offers some measure of comfort and compensation, a realization of the writer's yearning to bolster his hope for the building of the Land of Israel and "consummate" his love for it, embodied in the act of the kissing.

Thus, we have before us two encounters between lovers: imagined encounters by Jewish writers with their promised land, two imagined realizations of a dream ("When the LORD brought back those that return to Zion, we were like unto them that dream" [Psalms 126:1]), or two responses to its imagined realization—the first is canonical and traditional, written in Hebrew; the second is modern and secular, written in Yiddish. Both describe an imagined roaming in the Land of Israel and the speaker's response to the imagined encounter with its landscape. In both works the speakers are astonished by its breathtaking and heartbreaking sceneries.[17] But here the analogy ends and the contrast begins. Manger's poem is a wonderfully articulated protest against ha-Levi's hymn. Ha-Levi's speaker opens the poem with a gentle taunting of his beloved for the fact that she does not inquire after the well-being of those who love her in the Diaspora, but the speaker does not develop this complaint against his object of love, which is but another expression of the pain of separating from her. He does not pause over her indifference but quickly moves on to descriptions of the longing of her lovers, of her beauty, and of their hope for her redemption. By contrast, in Manger's poem, the pained apology for the impossibility of realizing the protagonist's love for his country becomes a protest, which he repeats in three of the poem's five verses, a protest that gradually gains in intensity and is essentially the work's central pillar. In the second verse, he says,

> Kh'vel nisht kushn dayn shtoyb . . .
> Vos heyst kushn dayn shtoyb? Ikh bin dayn shtoyb.
> Un ver kusht es, ikh bet aykh, zikh aleyn?
>
> I'll not kiss your dust[18] . . .
> How can I kiss your dust? I *am* your dust.
> And how, I ask you, can I kiss myself?

And in the fourth verse he says again,

> Kh'vel nisht kushn dayn blo . . .
> Vos heyst kushn dayn blo? Ikh bin dayn blo
> Un ver kusht es, ikh bet aykh, zikh aleyn?
>
> I'll not kiss your blue . . .
> How can I kiss your blue? I *am* your blue.
> And how, I ask you, can I kiss myself?

The height of the reproof and protest appear in the fifth and final verse:

> Kh'vel nisht kushn dayn zamd, neyn un tsen mol neyn.
> Vos heyst kushn dayn zamd? Ikh bin dayn zamd.
> Un ver kusht es, ikh bet aykh, zikh aleyn?
>
> I'll not kiss your sand. No, and ten times no.
> How can I kiss your sand? I *am* your sand.
> And how, I ask you, can I kiss myself?

The speaker's persistent and repeated refusal to kiss the soil of the Land of Israel has a cumulative effect: the more time he spends in Israel, the more he realizes that he, and not she, is the promised land; he is all that is beautiful and sacred in Jewish tradition. And just as the promise, in his view, is the beholder, so too is the sanctity: since he, the speaker, is the dust and the blue of the sacred land, he realizes that he, the eternal wanderer, is none other than the final destination of his travels; that is to say, he is the essence of Judaism, and not the land or the return to it. In ha-Levi, the pain over the land's destruction is alleviated by the myth—and the union with the divinity is made possible by the union with the land and with the dream of its redemption.[19] In Manger, the same pain, symbolized by two thousand years of exile, has rendered the immigrant returning to his mythological homeland not only the protagonist of a pilgrimage but also its true destination: the meeting with himself, and more precisely with his "creative self," is the purpose of the "pilgrimage," of his existence as a Jew.

The endings of the two poems also demonstrate the fundamental difference between them. Ha-Levi's poem ends on a note of consolation, in light of his unwavering confidence and belief in the religious-messianic redemption of Zion: "Blessed is he who stands and waits, and sees / your light rising as dawn breaks over him, and beholds / the wealth of your chosen, and rejoices / in your joy when you regain the vigor of your youth." In Manger's poem, the speaker does not look up to the heavens and does not seek the redemption outside of himself; instead, he looks into his own soul, where he finds "the blue," the royal color of inspiration and creativity (which for him is clearly modern), as well as the color of sorrow, of course. Manger's poem ends with a minor consolation—a secular, partial consolation whose essence lies in the ability to meet the myth head-on, to look on it as an adult, who understands its part in the illusion and its complex role in the power that his cultural heritage has to enchant him.[20] Manger's "wander-song" observes all of these themes:

> K'vel shteyn fartrakht far dayn midber groys,
> un hern di doyres-alte keml trit,
> vos vign af zeyere hoykers ibern zamd
> Toyre un skhoyre un dos alte vander lid

vos tsitert iber di zamdn heys-tseglit,
shtarbt op, dermont zikh, un vil keyn mol nisht fargeyn.

Musing, I'll stand before your great desert,
And hear the camels' ancient tread as they
Sway with trade and Torah on their humps.
I'll hear the age-old hovering wander-song
That trembles over glowing sand and dies,
And then recalls itself and does not disappear.

Within this objection by the speaker to the act of merging with the long-awaited land is contained a bold statement that the historical link between a man and his country differs from the mythological love tale in which the lovers end up uniting. It even contains an implied claim that the essence of Judaism is not the return to the Land of Israel and its settlement, but the Jewish way of being and Jewish culture as these were shaped over two thousand years of exile, and including, perhaps, as an inherent part, an exile that is irremediable. In Yiddish, in certain cases words whose origin is in biblical and Mishnaic Hebrew takes on an entirely different meaning. The words *'olam* (world) and *sviva* (environment) are examples of this phenomenon: in Yiddish, *oylem* means "the public," and *svive* refers to the "human society/milieu" in which the individual lives. In Yiddish culture, man is to a large extent "the mold of the social landscape" in which he lives, to paraphrase Shaul Tchernichovsky. The destruction of the Jewish society in Eastern Europe, in which were formed cultural and ideological movements like Hasidism, Jewish enlightenment, and Jewish nationalism (that is where they developed and gained influence), may render meaningless the attempt to connect the remnants of this society with the physical-geographical sviva of Israel. It is this possibility that holds the painful tension so unique to Manger's poem, the tension between two different experiences of Judaism that clashed within the poet's soul and in the souls of his Yiddish-speaking readers in Israel and beyond.

Manger is known for his extensive use of materials drawn from the Jewish tradition and primarily from the Bible. In a poem he wrote shortly after the establishment of Israel, and perhaps under the influence of this seminal event, there is no dominant reference of this kind (like a mention of the kings of Israel or the ancient conquest of Canaan). Instead, he chose to juxtapose his poem with a lamentation written by a (Spanish) Diaspora poet. With this choice he underscored the place of Yiddish culture in the experience of the return to the Land of Israel as a culture that was shaped in an exilic context. He underscores the resemblance and the difference between Yiddish culture in the Eastern European realm and the culture of Jews in Spain. Yiddish culture emerges even more clearly as inherently rootless and alien to its environment (the figure of "the wandering Jew" was created by Christians to distinguish and denounce the Jews living among them as people who would never be able to assimilate).[21] And indeed, even in Israel, which is supposed to symbolize the end of its wandering, Yiddish culture does not find its "home." On the contrary, it is precisely facing the landscapes of Israel that Yiddish culture realizes that it has carried its home on its back and in its heart all along. And since not-belonging is the fundamental experience of every wanderer, the constant foreignness became the home of this culture. With this realization, which leads to a catharsis, Manger was specifically relating to the historical period in which the historical moment of the establishment of Israel as a national home was celebrated. It amounts, then, to the admission that the exile of Yiddish culture will never reach its end.

Finally, it is noteworthy that Manger's choice of ha-Levi's poem as a fundamental contrast for his own work afforded him a subtle reference to the Holocaust without any mention of it. In Yiddish the Holocaust is known as *khurbn*, the "destruction," and ha-Levi's poem, as I mentioned, has been added to the traditional **Tisha be-Av** prayers in which the Jews lament the destruction of their temple. Thus, a further meaning is attached to Manger's claim that Judaism is only the mold of the psychic landscape of the Eastern European Jew, since the destruction of the temple becomes one with the destruction of Eastern European Jewry. The word *bayit* ("home") in the Hebrew phrase *hurban bayit* ("destruction of the home," referring to the Temple's destruction) is suddenly cast in a new light. The refusal of the speaker in Manger's poem to kiss the soil of Israel appears like a new incarnation of the traditional Jewish custom of evoking the destruction at the moments of joy and redemption: after the destruction of Eastern European Jewry, even the joy and relief that attend the return to Zion are lined with mourning. After the destruction of their home, the surviving remnant became "the dust and the blue" of Judaism, the last remnant, which is also its essence. In a kind of variation on the wandering Jew, who has carried the curse of rootless travels ever since he was witness to the crucifying of the Christian savior, the surviving-remnant refugees, who witnessed the destruction of Eastern European Jewry and the murder of their families and communities and survived, were doomed, in their lives and their creative work, to combine the two constitutive experiences—to "continue to wander" even in their new "national home": "K'hob zikh yorn gevalgert in der fremd / itst for ikh zikh valgern in der heym" ("For years I wandered in foreign lands / Now I am wandering in my own home").

Thus, those who saw Manger as representing a nostalgic form of literature, tired and conservative, that was behind the times because it did not incorporate the critical changes that Judaism underwent from the time of the enlightenment up to the height of the Zionist movement and the establishment of Israel, clearly failed to note the potential embodied in the rich dialogue that writers like Manger conducted with their cultural past. The label "traditional" is often wrongly understood as denoting a kind of stagnant conservativeness (religious or ethnic), a lack of innovativeness and critical perspective, or a static and simplistic stance. Many champions of the enlightenment mistakenly believed in the possibility of a stance free of all tradition, one that sprang abruptly out of pure reason, with no cultural past, language, or historical affiliation. This mistake took on a unique shape in the opinion of many of Israel's Hebrew-speaking Jewish residents about themselves. But even innovativeness is possible only against the backdrop of the tradition out of which it grows, and it can exist and have an impact only as a conversation with this tradition and with those who share the tradition. The label "popular" is often rightly understood as denoting mediocrity and crudeness in culture, a low and superficial taste. There is truth to this insofar as high culture is inherently elitist. But popularity is not a sign of lesser quality: the quality of the works of Hayim Nahman Bialik and Yehuda Amichai, Sholem Aleichem and Manger, is not diminished by the popularity of their writings. And the ability to say truthful and worthwhile things to a wide audience, to bring out the best in such an audience and awaken in it the will to transform its daily existence, is an art at least as high and rare as the ability to touch the refined and sophisticated readers, the select few, and it is not necessarily the opposite of enlightenment. On the contrary, it is the notion of the lone genius writing for the select few that is quintessentially romantic. The sense of belonging to a group is also a basic and essential need of all individuals. The sentiment, in itself, is neither low nor high. What makes Manger's writing unique is precisely the ability to transform such basic emotions into great art that offers his readers a subversive, complex message in the guise of simplicity.

The wandering Jew is a fascinating and unusual instantiation of the basic mythical archetype of the trickster, which recurs in different times and incarnations in various cultures. It is an incarnation of the protagonist who crosses boundaries (geographical, temporal, moral, and cultural) and who is often found unintentionally bridging gaps. He is an agent of change who enables movement within the mythical worlds that he crosses and between which he mediates.[22] The Yiddish-speaking surviving-remnant refugees are a kind of "trickster" of this sort: their literature forces its reader to reexamine dichotomous perceptions that were received and became fixed among the general public and in scholarship about Israeli society in the first decades of its existence.

2. Background Information and Basic Terminology

The surviving-remnant refugees, or *'olim* (more later on this ideologically loaded term), are the protagonists of this book. In the many lectures I have given on the topic of Yiddish in Israel, I have had the privilege of meeting face-to-face with some of them and mainly with their children, who were born after the end of World War II, in Israel or en route to it, and who grew up in the young state. Whether or not the lectures were delivered in an academic setting, the works

I read in Yiddish triggered in my audiences deep and genuine emotion: love and longing for their parents who have passed away, alongside guilt, regret, and even insult over the lack of an intergenerational transmission of Yiddish and its culture. Our joint love of Yiddish and its culture, as well as the similarities in our biographies (I was born on the eve of the Yom Kippur War to a family that emigrated from Poland to Buenos Aires in the 1930s and came to Israel in the mid-sixties), allowed us to share these feelings, to observe them, and to contemplate their nature. The study of Yiddish and its culture sometimes enables a certain healing of the ongoing relationship with deceased family members. My audiences share with me their memories and personal stories. My own contribution to our conversation consists in proposing a historical, demographic, and cultural context that often is unfamiliar to the bearers of the memories. When the two perspectives intertwine, my audience and I share the grace that is born of this multidimensional understanding of history and culture—the nectar of the victors is mixed with the pain of those who paid its price. The aim of this book is to serve as a foundation for the continuation of these fruitful meetings, conversations, and discussions. Therefore, the professional terminology and information are presented here in simple language that is as far as possible jargon-free.

The topic of the book lies at the intersection of several fields of research: it is a chapter in the history of the Yiddish-speaking surviving-remnant refugees in Israel but also a study of its literary products, and especially those literary works that describe the encounter with Israel in the first two decades after its establishment. By virtue of its interdisciplinary nature, the study uses basic terminology from the disciplines of sociology and history, which I present later so that they may serve as a basis for our discussion. I also clarify and explain several imprecise uses of common terminology in these fields.

"Yiddish is the language of exile." This is the first claim I hear from my Israeli students and audiences in every course or lecture on modern Yiddish culture, and all the more so about Yiddish culture in Israel, and thus it is the first notion that needs to be corrected. Jewish culture in the Land of Israel and beyond it was in all times bi- and even multilingual,[23] so that Hebrew too was (and still is) the language of "exile." And in any case, Judaism itself is a religion that evolved and took shape also in exile. The false dichotomy between Hebrew and Yiddish and between Israel and exile was formed and occupied a central place in the thought of some of the Zionist movements and organizations, especially in the early decades of the twentieth century. But it is important to note the gap between the ideological rhetoric (however justified and influential) and the cultural and historical reality: critical attitudes toward the Jewish existence in Eastern Europe were not the exclusive purview of Hebrew-writing thinkers or authors. They drew inspiration from the Yiddish writings of Mendele Moykher Sforim (S. Y. Abramovich) and his predecessors, the enlightenment writers. And obviously, favorable attitudes toward the Zionist ideas and toward the Land of Israel were not the exclusive purview of Hebrew-writing Zionist thinkers and writers. The first language of most of the fathers of Zionism, which as we know was born in "exile," was Yiddish, and in this language they took their first steps as writers. Yiddish was the language spoken at most of the Zionist Congresses, and many Yiddish authors across the world supported the Zionist ideas (the most well-known among them is Sholem Aleichem).[24]

The term *Sheerit hapletah* or *Sheyres hapleyte* in Yiddish (surviving remnant) is used here in its broad sense, as shaped in current and canonical research.[25] Historian Israel Gutman has defined the *'oley sheyres hapleyte* as "those Jews who after the war refused to rebuild their lives in the countries of destruction and insistently demanded to be allowed to emigrate to other countries, and especially demanded for themselves the right to make *'aliya* to the Land of Israel."[26] After World War II, these Jews gathered as refugees in transit towns or refugee camps (mostly in Germany but also in Austria and Italy). Most of them, as Gutman notes, specifically chose Israel as their next destination. Until the 1970s, the scholarship regarded the 'oley sheyres hapleyte as a fractured, silent, and passive group, "*avak adam*" (human dust). Accordingly, studies focused mostly on the ideological and national influences on these refugees. In recent decades, an important shift has taken place in this perception: attention has been turned to the impressive and politically diverse activeness of the members of this group, already during the war and in its immediate aftermath (in areas like managing educational and cultural institutions in the displaced persons [DP] camps, establishing farms for agricultural training, and more).[27] Hagit Lavsky documented their activity and argued that it was not the product of passive, victim-like behavior on the part of those who (as the common assumption would have it) underwent political indoctrination at the hands of Zionist organizations and other elements. She argues that the national and Zionist tendencies of the Surviving Remnant were not formed as a result of the manipulative effort on the part of external elements nor even thanks to a built-in ideology, but rather resulted from a spontaneous process that took place among the survivors themselves. They did not turn their back on their heritage in exile, to the Yiddish language and its literature and to the heritage of Israel. On the contrary, they aspired to merge the Zionist agenda with this heritage of theirs, which was cornerstone of their Jewish national consciousness.[28]

Ze'ev Mankowitz's research also supported this view; it emphasized that "any attempt to present the people of Surviving Remnant as the helpless objects of history is misleading and regrettable. Regrettable because it runs counter to the facts, and misleading because these kinds of patronizing interpretations damage our ability to see clearly, for in several important respects the members of the Surviving Remnant were indeed ahead of their time."[29]

This book joins this perspective as it traces the story of the institutional organization of 'oley sheyres hapleyte in Israel. In particular, I hope to help remedy the widespread misconception according to which the Holocaust survivors who came to Israel were silent about their experiences in the Holocaust. What appears or is often portrayed as silence is shown to be a lack of attentiveness on the part of the public and the scholarship to things that they in fact expressed in a clear voice, through many different channels, and incessantly, in their own language.[30] Clearly, this abundant and intensive speech was intended not for the ears of their young girls and boys but for their peers, and it was therefore conducted in Yiddish—"di kinder zoln nisht farshteyn" (so that the children won't understand), as the popular saying went. Ella Florsheim, who studied the culture of the surviving remnants in the DP camps, has pointed out a paradox that characterizes the scholarly literature about this group: there is, she argued, a commendable interest in the "voice" of the surviving remnants but still not in their language—Yiddish.[31] Even in the few cases in which studies deign to mention their language or quote from it, it is treated as a folkloric remnant and not as a cultural asset that offers access to further cultural treasures. This book aims to listen to 'oley sheyres hapleyte in their voice and in their language, and indeed to emphasize the importance of their language as a fundamental feature of their modern identity as individuals and as a public. In the very reference to the large group of refugees that arrived from Eastern Europe after the war as the "surviving remnant" lies a risk that we will underestimate the value of the *longue durée* of their cultural essence.[32] By focusing excessively on the fact that they are Holocaust survivors, we might forget that they are the sons and daughters of a multifaceted culture with a rich past, which they sought to preserve and develop even after arriving in their new land.

The term *'olim* (literally: those who ascend) appears frequently in the book to denote these immigrants, and it requires explanation. Researchers today avoid using the term *'ole* (someone who ascends) to describe Jewish immigrants to Israel (and indeed openly criticize the term), instead preferring either *immigrant* or *refugee*.[33] This preference is grounded in a justified caution about the all-too-common mixture of ideological language with the neutral language of academic research. But this caution is misplaced in the case at hand. Those who are described here as 'oley sheyres hapleyte were different from the immigrants and refugees who came to Israel before them. The fact that they came after the destruction of Eastern European Jewry is a central characteristic of their communal identity. This loss imposed on them two loyalties that today seem almost contradictory: first, they felt a weighty cultural responsibility to preserve and sometimes even revive the last remains of their culture, which only a decade or two earlier had reached the height of its creative powers; and second, the Holocaust had led many of them to a "spontaneous Zionism," which for many of them was a prominent (and often enthusiastic) motive for choosing Israel as their destination. In this sense they were indeed ʻolim. Thus, of all the various titles used in the scholarship, none is less suitable than the title *immigrants*—that is, those who left their homeland for economic reasons and chose their destination country for similar reasons. A central observation of this study is that the national ideological position of ʻoley sheyres hapleyte did not force them to cut themselves off from the Diaspora or its language, culture, and tradition. On the contrary—these were the building blocks of their unique national identity. Of course, this is not to say that all ʻoley sheyres hapleyte came to Israel purely for ideological reasons. Unifying families was a strong urge after the Holocaust, and there were also those who were indifferent to the ideological question. Yet even these were not immigrants in the usual sense of the term. The term *ʻoley sheyres hapleyte* is therefore an oxymoron, but it aptly captures the inherent tension that characterizes the subjects of my study.

The ʻoley sheyres hapleyte form part of the "great ʻaliya"/ "mass ʻaliya." In the canonical research on the mass ʻaliya, two main biases are conspicuous: a bias in the sources on which it draws and a bias in the point of view from which the phenomena are observed (and therefore in the narrative that emerges from this point of view). The study of the mass ʻaliya draws almost exclusively on sources produced by and affiliated with the absorbing establishment (sources written in Hebrew, of course) and not on sources of the absorbed (in their languages). The focus of the absorbing institutions is almost always on the physical and local aspects of the absorption of individuals (who, for the absorbing institutions, embodied problems to be solved). This book proposes to explore the phenomenon of the mass ʻaliya from an opposite perspective—that of the absorbed, in the long-term collective and cultural aspects of their absorption, based on the sources they produced in their own language, Yiddish, during the period of the absorption. In literature, too, the response of the ʻolim has thus far been explored through literature written in Hebrew *about* them, and only in rare cases was this literature written by the ʻolim themselves (for instance, by the Iraqi-born Israeli writer Shimon Balas). Yet even these rare cases involve works that appeared in Hebrew at a late stage of the absorption processes, after the writers had become skilled in writing Hebrew and in distancing themselves from the events they describe. In both cases, the processes of adaptation of the Eastern European Jews and their absorption occupy a marginal place in both the literature and the academic research about the mass ʻaliya. Both corpuses appear clearly to be based on the assumption that their absorption in Israel was fast and easy relative to that of other groups, perhaps because a large part of the "veteran" receiving public was itself made up of Jews of Eastern European origin and even Yiddish speakers.[34] Moreover, the scholarship tended to focus on the absorption of Jews from Islamic countries and indeed on a single aspect of it: the permanent and self-reinforcing power relations between these ʿolim and the establishment, a focus accompanied often either by a justification of the policy of the absorbing establishment or by firm criticism of it.[35] This is partly because the well-known works by the "absorbed" were written by this group of ʿolim, and in them they describe the ways of coping with the trauma of immigration.[36] The Eastern European Jews, by contrast, in the rare cases when they are mentioned in the works of literature and research, are described simultaneously as representatives of the Ashkenazi hegemony (who in our days are considered undeserving of encouragement because of their long-standing hegemony) and as representatives of a rejected exilic culture, shameful and contemptible, as silent Holocaust survivors whom the founders of the prevailing Israeli ethos wished to repress, to forget and cause others to forget so as to enable Israeli culture to be established on a new, solid, and at the same time rootless foundation. Researchers have tended to underscore the advantages (real or imagined) of their predicament relative to that of Jews from Islamic countries—for instance, the fact that, on average, they spent less time in the refugee absorption camps in Israel (*Ma ʿabarot*)—while ignoring the fact that Eastern European Jews had been refugees for some ten years before their arrival in Israel, during which time they gained experience in conducting themselves vis-à-vis aid groups and institutions. They similarly ignored a long-standing tradition of membership in grassroot mutual-aid associations that emerged in the communities of Eastern European Jews (as early as the late nineteenth century). Like other groups of ʿolim who came to Israel in the years of the mass ʿaliya, many Eastern European Jews also faced expressions of the imperviousness and rigidness of the establishment, as well as expressions of arrogance and a patronizing attitude on the part of Israel's veteran residents (who were themselves typically Yiddish speakers of Eastern European origin). Like other groups, they too showed clear signs of the struggle to preserve their language, their culture, and their heritage in Israel, since the establishment's policy of cultural absorption of the ʿolim, known as the "melting pot" approach, was of course applied also to them.[37]

The literature they wrote therefore allows us to expand the corpus of "ʿolim literature" both linguistically and thematically and to expand the ways in which it is read. The readings I offer here explore the phenomenon of the mass ʿaliya as comprising different kinds of trauma (trauma of immigration, trauma of refugeehood and of the Holocaust) while challenging the commonly accepted distinction, the "traditional" and seemingly homogenous distinction that in fact was imposed from above on the ʿolim of the mass ʿaliya, between "Ashkenazi" and "Mizrahi" Jews, along with the power relations that derive from this division.

Mizrekh-eyropeishe yidn (the Jews of Eastern Europe) and *yidishe yidn* (the Yiddish Jews) are the common terms that ʿoley sheyres hapleyte used to define themselves. The vague and misleading term *Ashkenazim* was attributed to

Eastern European Jews in Israel (just as the term *Edot ha-Mizrah*—communities of the East—was attributed to Jews from Islamic countries) by the receiving establishment and the veteran residents. It was adopted uncritically by both the public and the scholarship. The label "Ashkenazi" (whose parallel is "Sephardic") is religious in origin and is mistaken for a historical, cultural characteristic of the Jews of Eastern Europe in the modern era. While the roots of Yiddish culture are indeed in Western Europe (Ashkenaz) of the Middle Ages, from the sixteenth century and on a unique Jewish culture developed in the eastern part of the continent. The Yiddish spoken and written by the Jews of Eastern Europe gradually distinguished itself from that of Western Europe, which eventually died out. The Yiddish spoken in Western Europe in the nineteenth and twentieth centuries was an eastern Yiddish brought over by the Eastern European Jews who immigrated to the western parts. The differences between the communities of Jews in Western and Eastern Europe were apparent on all levels: social, economic, and cultural. To mark these significant differences, which became more and more conspicuous with the rise of secular modern Yiddish culture beginning in the mid-nineteenth century, Max Weinreich described this period as "Ashkenaz II."[38] The label "Ashkenazim" obliterates these significant cultural differences, and with them also the sociological fact that the Jews of Western Europe (many of whom are of Eastern European origin) went to great lengths to externalize their difference from the Jews of Eastern Europe. It preserves the sense of superiority of the Jews of Western Europe over those of Eastern Europe, denies the fact that most of the Jews in the modern era lived and were culturally formed in Eastern Europe and that modern Judaism was born and developed primarily in Eastern and not Western Europe, and therefore erases Eastern European Jewry's enormous contribution to the emergence of the national identity, the Zionist movement, and modern, secular Jewish culture. Using the term *Ashkenazim* to describe the Jews of Eastern Europe therefore casts this Jewry back to the Middle Ages along the Rhine river and portrays it as a small collection of premodern religious communities—as if the only alternative to the religious and premodern Jewish identity is the Hebrew-Zionist identity.

3. On the Topic of This Study and Its Sources

A certain artificiality is involved in almost every act of defining a timeframe for a study that describes historical processes. The period between 1948 and 1967 was chosen because it encompasses the impressive rise and fast fall of a modern and secular Yiddish cultural center established in Israel by 'oley sheyres hapleyte, a center on which the supporters of Yiddish culture the world over pinned many hopes. The year 1948, of course, marks the establishment of Israel and the beginning of the legal and massive migration to it. Throughout the 1950s, 'oley sheyres hapleyte in Tel Aviv founded richly active cultural institutions, whose story I recount in chapter 1. The 1960s were the years in which many of these institutions became more established and succeeded in some of the central battles they waged for the recognition and status of Yiddish in Israel (some of these achievements are described in this study). Ironically, the process in which these cultural institutions became more firmly established coincided with a decline in the number of Yiddish speakers and consumers of its culture, as well as a lessening of the cultural threat that the establishment saw in them. The latter half of 1967, after the Six-Day War, was in many ways the euphoric height of "Israeliness," of the Israeli experience, and thus also the height of its influence on 'oley sheyres hapleyte. Over the two decades of their lives in Israel, the members of this public became integrated into Israeli society in most of its echelons. As was the case with Yiddish in its cultural centers all over the world, in Israel too (and perhaps especially), the Yiddish speakers converted their collective loyalty from the ethnic group to the national one. The Israeli ethos of the melting pot and the policy it dictated—which prevented Jews (who are not ultra-Orthodox) from operating Yiddish-speaking kindergartens and Yiddish-speaking public schools—combined with the strong desire of 'oley sheyres hapleyte to assimilate into Israeli society and adopt its values, had the result that Yiddish ceased to serve its speakers and lost the material and symbolic capital it had accumulated from the mid-nineteenth century to the mid-twentieth. This "bankruptcy" was already felt in the late 1960s, in the absence of a new and young generation of speakers in the culture and in the institutions in which it was created.

This study focuses on prose. It presents and examines novels, novellas, short stories, travel memoirs, and feuilletons written by 'oley sheyres hapleyte in Israel. This category of works was chosen because of the distinct advantage of fiction over other forms of literature and art as a detailed source for describing the experience of the encounter with a new society and an unfamiliar geography. Fiction, in contrast to poetry, is characterized by clarity and a descriptive "long haul." What poetry tends to shape with great density, which is often timeless, fiction typically describes expansively, thereby inviting an open and straightforward mode of grappling with the place and the time, with the human and physical landscape. Poetry can be written in a "dead" language (it is no coincidence that the first steps of Jewish literature were taken in this genre), and it is written almost always for a limited audience. Prose, by contrast, reflects a daily experience of life and requires a spoken language. The use of prose testifies to the vitality of the community of speakers of a given language and of its institutions. Benedict Anderson noted the novel and the newspaper as two forms through which the national character of a community is imagined.[39] Thus, examining the novels written in Yiddish in Israel allows us to uncover the unique character of the 'oley sheyres hapleyte's perception of nationality. Writing realist prose is a particular challenge for the victims of trauma. Dominick LaCapra argued that one of the dangers of trauma is the collapse of temporal, spatial, and personality distinctions.[40] The traumatized person is haunted by a past that seeks a presence in the present and to govern his future. Because of the compulsive return of the traumatic experience, he struggles to develop a continuing storyline, one that is expansive and evolving, whether it is the story of his own life or the story of another. The fiction written by ʻoley sheyres hapleyte is especially fascinating in this respect; it allows us to explore the attempts they made to process their trauma and the cultural, social, and political implications of their choice by describing the experience of their absorption in Israel.

Of all the fiction written by ʻoley sheyres hapleyte in Israel, I chose that which describes the encounter with Israel, its society and landscapes, and the act of setting up home in it. I focus on their experiences as newcomers, in depopulated Palestinian villages, refugee absorption camps, neighborhoods of refugee housing, the Kibbutzim, and Tel Aviv. These sites reflect both the different waves of mass ʻaliya and different periods in the preparation for them. Obviously, ʻoley sheyres hapleyte also settled in all the other Israeli cities; but their literary works suggest clearly that Tel Aviv held particular interest for them as the first modern Hebrew metropolis. The vast majority of Yiddish cultural institutions were established there. And even in the works devoted to describing the lives of the ʻolim in other cities, towns, and settlements, Tel Aviv (more than other cities) is prominently present as the modern-cultural and economic horizon of life in Israel and as a central motif in shaping the characters and the plot.

The topic of my research dictated clear criteria for my choice of sources; in this book I do not discuss the works of important Yiddish writers who lived in Israel but did not describe daily life in it (for example, the prose of Sutzkever, Leyb Rokhman, and A. M. Fuchs) or works that do deal with the experiences of survivor-ʻolim in Israel's first years but were published after 1967. The stories published by Ka-Tsetnik in the journal *Di goldene keyt* in 1979–1993 are a clear example. The book also does not deal with the work of veteran Yiddish writers who emigrated to the United States before the Holocaust and came to Israel toward the end of their lives (like Dovid Pinski, Zalman Shneur, Sholem Asch, and Manger). And finally, you will find no reference here to ʻoley sheyres hapleyte literature written by writers who belong to ultra-Orthodox religious communities in Israel, whose language was Yiddish[41] (or to descriptions of these communities by secular Yiddish writers like Yisroel Kaplan).

Traditionally, ultra-Orthodox culture and modern Yiddish culture are treated as separate areas of research. While in Eastern Europe and also in Israel's first years the differences and boundaries between the communities were not as deep and clear-cut as they are today, even in Eastern Europe the two cultures differed in the role they ascribed to Yiddish: whereas the ultra-Orthodox Jewish communities adopted Yiddish to set themselves apart from the secular and national modern culture in which they lived, for the creators and consumers of modern Yiddish culture, the language served as way to assimilate. Ultra-Orthodox Judaism thus regarded Yiddish as a means and not an aesthetic or scholarly end in itself. Therefore, the Orthodox communities produced no "high" literature. The themes with which the literatures of these two sectors deal are also different: for instance, the religious refugee as protagonist, by the very fact of his faith, copes differently with trauma (insofar as it poses a challenge also to his religious belief), and the range of possibilities available to him for coping is different. The secular protagonist, by contrast, typically seeks to acknowledge the meaninglessness of his life, and thus of his suffering, and come to terms with it as far as possible, with no comforting redemption. And finally, the attitude of the Israeli establishment to these two Yiddish-speaking communities, the ultra-Orthodox and the secular, was completely different. The Orthodox public was the only sector permitted by the state to operate primary schooling in Yiddish in the 1950s and 1960s (indeed, it was subsidized by the state), an achievement attributable to the political cohesiveness of the Orthodox community, its negligible size in the state's first years, and its self-isolating and exceptional nature. For these reasons, it was not perceived as threatening to the dominant Hebrew culture.

The aim of this study is to paint a broad historical picture of the Yiddish literature written in Israel and of the organizational aspects involved in its writing and consumption. The canonical scholarship on the relations between Yiddish literature and Hebrew literature, by Benjamin Harshav, Itamar Even-Zohar, Gershon Shaked, and Dan Miron, which I discuss in what follows, describes a period of linguistic diglossia in Eastern Europe until the period of the revival, and after it a separation and establishment of two rather independent and almost entirely disconnected cultural "multi-systems." According to these scholars, this separateness reached its height in Israel, where, so they argue, only one cultural multi-system existed—Hebrew. Yiddish, the maintain, was attached to the Hebrew like an appendage and became absorbed in it, and its visibility is mostly in "low," noncanonical cultural forms: the joke, the folktale, and entertainment and traditional song skits. This picture overlooks the fact that, at least in the state's first two decades, an entire cultural multi-system in Yiddish existed alongside the Hebrew one, including "high" and canonical cultural products in addition to the "low," noncanonical culture. This oversight is especially surprising in the case of Harshav, who was himself an active participant in the high branches of this multi-system.

The main sources on which this study is based are the Yiddish newspapers and periodicals published in Israel (and abroad) in 1948–1967. As a source of information about cultural activity, the press has certain unique characteristics. On the cultural level, the press typically contrasts with canonical literature (i.e., the high literature that was consciously written and intentionally published as such) and complements it, to form a multi-system. Other central sources of this study are the personal archives of Yiddish authors and journalists, since the cultural institutions whose stories I tell here typically did not establish official archives, and if attempts were made to establish them, they were not successful. Here the distinction between research "from above" and "from below" is paramount: the information gleaned from institutional archives, even information about a particular writer, undergoes processes of sorting, selection, and classification that are laden with an often-hidden agenda, one that requires separate reconstruction, and sometimes this agenda expresses an ignoring of various broader contexts. Studying family archives and newspapers of the same timeframe has afforded me, I hope, a different and complementary perspective. Unlike institutional archives, a newspaper typically has a known editor with declared goals, even if they change over time. These goals are reflected not only in editorials and opinion pieces but even in the placement and size of news items in the paper. The newspaper, of course, has not only news sections and literary and culture supplements but also letters to the editor, various advice columns, and advertisements, including social advertisements; each of these sections may include details that are relevant to our overall assessment of a given cultural event. A paper's political affiliation is obviously another important tool for reconstructing the cultural context of any piece of information. Many of the works of prose on which this study is based were published first in newspapers and periodicals and only later as books, and the difference between these platforms is also crucial to understanding the distinction between high and low literature—in other words, even high literature, when it appears in the context of the daily press, plays a different kind of role, which deserves to be unpacked. Thus, by examining the Yiddish press published in Israel, I hope to shed light on the contribution of this culture to the consolidation of the main components of Israeli culture, such as the national time and national space.[42] The photographs I chose for this book also reflect my overall aim to contribute to the completion of a cultural history "from below" of my subjects: here you will find not only official, canonical images of the kind you find hanging on the walls of institutions, behind the desks of the managers, but also, and deliberately, photographs taken by the "little people," documenting daily personal episodes in the context of the cultural institutions through which they ran their lives.

4. Theoretical Background

A major theoretical backdrop to this work consists of studies in the history and sociology of modernity. From the second half of the nineteenth century, Eastern European Jewry (like all European nations) was shaped by (and against) the "culture of modernity."[43] The main general characteristics of this culture were the processes of secularization and urbanization, the rise of national ideologies and of the capitalist economy, and, following these developments, a collapse of the authority of traditional institutions and a disintegration of traditional communities. Modern Yiddish literature can hardly be discussed without considering these developments, as they are one of its central themes. Even when they are not a central or explicit subject of a given work, they are almost always a backdrop that is essential to understanding it. Modern secular Judaism is an identity riddled with tensions and contradictions. Secular Jews who refused to embrace the Zionist idea on the one hand, but on the other hand refused to be assimilated into the nationalism of the country in which they lived, faced a fundamental dilemma. The choice to stay secular Jews in the Diaspora, whether it was calculated or a default, brought those who made this choice face-to-face with very basic conflicts, which characterized their daily existence as human beings, their taste and culture as men and women of society, and their literature. They had to decide to which parts of their Jewish tradition they would remain loyal out of a sense of identification with those who shared the tradition with them. When ʿoley sheyres hapleyte arrived in Israel, they brought along a cultural identity that was shaped in these conditions. Even though after the Holocaust many of those who had opposed Zionism or been indifferent to it found themselves supporting it as "spontaneous Zionists" (in Lavsky's accurate phrase), all the other characteristics of their pre-Zionist culture remained intact and were essential to their identity. In this book you will find descriptions of their encounter with those who from the outset had identified the core of secular Judaism with the establishment of Israel and the act of ʿaliya—alongside encounters with those who emigrated to Israel but did not regard its establishment as the heart of secular Judaism. The special historical circumstances that characterized these cultural encounters set Israel apart as a unique cultural arena in that time. It brought together (at least) two different ideals of the modern secular Jew: on the one hand, the supporters of secular Yiddish and its culture, and on the other hand, supporters of Hebrew and secular Israeli culture. The ʿoley sheyres hapleyte regarded Yiddish and Hebrew as complementary languages that represented complementary aspects of their personal and national identity. They saw their "exilic" past as an integral part of their rich heritage and sought to shape their autonomous-national present in Israel in light of it. And they believed that the way in which the speakers of Yiddish and the centers of its culture were destroyed in the Holocaust added moral weight to this view, that Israel had an obligation to preserve their unique culture and encourage it.[44]

The loyalty of many Yiddish-speaking members of the ʿoley sheyres hapleyte to their language clearly went beyond the built-in slowness of immigrants to become assimilated in their new country and learn its language, and it should also be clearly distinguished from notions of "linguistic chauvinism"[45]—that is, the tendency of speakers of a certain language to regard their language and the culture it embodies as superior to others (and thus to advocate and organize politically to eradicate competing languages and cultures). In fact, the only linguistic chauvinism in the meeting of cultures and languages that took place in Israel in the years that concern this study was on the part of the Hebrew supporters. This linguistic chauvinism is neither "linguistic loyalty" nor "linguistic utilitarianism." The notion of linguistic loyalty describes situations in which the use of a language requires a conscious intention on the part of its speakers, meaning institutional and communal effort and organization, and especially when they are an absorbed minority. In other words, this kind of linguistic loyalty is performed out of an emotional commitment and sometimes also out of an ideological commitment to the language and the culture it embodies. This loyalty forms the basis for a personal and communal identity; it dictates preferences—social, cultural, and sometimes even political—and is linked to social and organizational activity. Linguistic utilitarianism, by contrast, is an opposite linguistic policy: it expresses the wish to exploit the linguistic cohesiveness of a public for essentially political ends. The use of Yiddish in the enlightenment movement, for example, was utilitarian because advocates of the enlightenment ultimately sought to get rid of Yiddish and of the isolationism that its use expressed and created, but they deliberately utilized it as a tool to achieve their goal. In chapter 1, I discuss cases in which political organizations in Israel used Yiddish in this kind of utilitarian way. I emphasize this fact here mainly because its implication is that some cultural products written in Yiddish in Israel fall outside the purview of this study, because they are not an expression of loyalty to Yiddish.

Another important distinction is between two phases of linguistic assimilation in a population of new immigrants. In the first phase, the unilingual phase, only the language of the immigrant is used—and in the case of the Jews, the languages of the immigrant, since they always had more than one origin language. In the second phase, a bi- or multilingual existence begins to take shape, combining the language of the absorbed with language of the absorbing population. These are typically regarded as transitional stages leading up to a new unilinguality, which symbolizes the immigrants' assimilation. Eli Lederhendler cautions us against adopting this simplistic picture. He shows that adopting the language of the absorbing population does not necessarily distance the absorbed minority from its primary language and its culture, and in some cases even strengthens them. This is the scenario that 'oley sheyres hapleyte Yiddish-supporters hoped to realize in Israel. Obviously, they did not seek to make Yiddish the state's official and exclusive language. Moreover, life alongside the Hebrew language enriched the Yiddish, just as Hebrew culture had absorbed the richness of Yiddish culture. I disagree with Even-Zohar's claim that Yiddish literature and Hebrew literature "severed contact with each other" from the moment the state was established and Hebrew became its official language.[46] The two languages, I explain here in detail, in fact continued to coexist in Israel, and their speakers created, mediated, and consumed complementary literatures. Linguistic loyalty to Yiddish in Israel, then, does not mean a rejection of Hebrew as Israel's national language but rather refers to the attempts of 'oley sheyres hapleyte to challenge and expand the notion that the nation-state in the Land of Israel must base its culture on a single Jewish language.

Modern Yiddish literature is typically discussed in the scholarship as a "minor" and "marginal" culture (after all, it developed among the nations of Europe, in which the Jews were a minority).[47] But the writers of Yiddish from among 'oley sheyres hapleyte who came to Israel did not regard themselves or their culture as minor—that is to say, as the culture of a powerless minority whose work was created in a language that was aware of its own ethnic and religious foreignness, in defiance of the dominant, established culture and with the intention of undermining its foundations. In any event, it seems that in the 1950s the self-perception of many of them was just the opposite: they felt themselves to be a majority in the country, ethnically and culturally, but a majority that was perceived as the "masses" by the dominant elitist culture. As noted, 'oley sheyres hapleyte were a clear majority among the immigrants who came to Israel in the first years of the mass migration and a public that could not be overlooked among Israel's Jewish inhabitants. Their literature was written not in defiance of the literature produced in Hebrew in those years (and many of them were barely familiar with it) but rather in reference to Yiddish literature, both earlier and contemporaneous, and in reference to its readers and its critics. In recent years, attempts have been made to free the way we think about the interactions between "major" cultures and the cultures of minorities from the bonds of the dichotomous discourse that locks each of them into a homogenous and stable identity as either a victimizing oppressor or an oppressed victim and into the fixed power relations that derive from these identities, and instead to understand them in a more fruitful framework as a multidirectional process of reciprocal influences in which the influenced party is simultaneously also an active agent of influence.

The research presented in this book drew inspiration from two theoretical perspectives that in the last several decades have been enriching the study of Jewish culture: the "cultural turn" and the "spatial turn."[48] These perspectives explore the experiences of the study's subjects, their memories and the meanings they give to their lives, their culture, and their environment. The story in this book therefore unfolds from the bottom up (that is, from the point of view of 'oley sheyres hapleyte) and not from the top down (the point of view of the absorbing establishment), and also "from within": it is based on sources that the surviving-remnant immigrants created in their language and in which they expressed their wide-ranging experiences of the Israeli space and the ways in which they created and shaped this space in light of their memories and their culture.

One of the book's premises is that the Israeli space, with all its typical "sites"—the depopulated Palestinian village, the ma'abara (emigrant and refugee absorption camps), the Kibbutz, the immigrant housing project, and the city—was not created only from above by the hegemonic institutions that gave these sites to the residents by force of their power and authority. This space and these sites were also, equally, created from below by force of the daily performance of those who lived their lives there. They created and shaped this space out of their experiences and memories, which were forged and buried in it, and out of the horizon of their hopes and the abyss of their suffering.

5. Toward a Multilingual Study of Israeli Literature

The study of nationality and nationalism in recent decades has tended to focus on the transition of multilingual traditional societies into unilingual modern societies. It is evident that this focus is somewhat essentialist and ideological, since such processes by nature never actually reach an end point. The Land of Israel and Israel were examined in this framework primarily as a space in which a "war of languages" was waged.[49] In this "war," as we know, Hebrew "defeated" Yiddish as well as other Jewish languages. Its victory is described and analyzed primarily as reflecting the success of the sustained and focused melting-pot policy applied by state and pre-state institutions and organizations. The scholarship's focus on wars and victories (which is important from moral, political, and theoretical perspectives) overshadowed the fact that wars in general and cultural wars in particular drown out our attention to the more multifaceted and subtle processes that take place alongside them. An excessive focus on the power of the absorbing institutions was expressed, as I already noted, in insufficient attention to the voice of the absorbed, even when historians and sociologists sought to tell their story. The scholars of literature were similarly biased. Gershon Shaked, for example, divided what he described as "'olim literature"—namely, the literature that describes the experiences of those who came in the mass immigrations of the 1950s—into that written by "the absorbers" (those writers born in Israel, who are described as active) versus that written by "the absorbed" (in the passive formation),[50] which he addressed only when it was written in Hebrew (that is, only when the immigrants had attained sufficient command of the Hebrew language).[51] In this, Shaked expressed the tendency of literary scholars to focus on the linguistic aspect as the primary and even exclusive determinant of the culture of their field. And yet Israel of those days was a multilingual space that expressed a cultural polyphony. Even today it is a space that is in many ways multinational, multilingual, and multicultural, since its Arabic-speaking population, for example, creates a rich literature in Arabic, and so does its Russian-speaking population in Russian. To make these observations is not to call for a replacement of the standardly drawn identity between nationality, language, and culture (a practice that underlies the accepted paradigm of writing literary history) but to call attention to the fact that this identity does not accurately characterize the geopolitical space of Israel, and that literary scholars stand to enrich their understanding of the culture they are studying if they recognize the different voices of the polyphonic space in which the studied literature was created. This is especially true of cultures created in immigration countries in general, and in particular when such immigration is at its height.[52] At such key moments, it is both appropriate and beneficial to expand the standard principle for selecting works.[53] In this way, the study of Israeli literature is able to enrich the study of Hebrew literature on the one hand and of Yiddish literature on the other.

Why is it, actually, that in the study of nationalism it is an accepted premise to regard linguistic and cultural multiplicity as unnatural to the nation-state? The accepted premise, based on the observation that language is a powerful tool for social differentiation, is to a large extent well suited to the nation-state of the late nineteenth century, but not to the European nation-states of our day. Scholars studying a literature written in the mid-twentieth century will likely notice this if they focus not only on the regular activity of the systems of the national establishment but also on the active force of the masses, whoever and wherever they are. Scholarship that seeks to take a step toward the literature of a geopolitical space must be based on a consideration of the sociology and history of that space. For instance, the frequent use (in literary theory as well) of the term *hegemony* might lead us to forget that this is not the only term that does not denote a fixed and homogenous category, not at a given moment in time and certainly not over a period of time. The same is also true of civilian agency. The ability of individuals and groups to act within a nation-state is the result of a perpetual and ongoing negotiation, in which the multitude seeks expression for its inherent variety, while the institutions of government (in most cases) seek to unify it. I have found that the battle between these opposing forces defines modernity better than a focus on each of these opposing forces separately. The battle of the Yiddish loyalists in Israel for recognition of the diversity they expressed will therefore stand out to the scholar who seeks to focus on their experience as a multitude encountering a new country, more than to a scholar whose selection of works is dictated purely by a linguistic principle, and also more than to the scholar who focuses primarily on hegemony, its policy, and its mechanisms. The scholar who focuses on the multitude in a new land is exposed first of all to the fascinating phenomenon of a polyphony of voices searching for its own shape and organization in the face of an unfamiliar environment. In following this phenomenon, she is exposed to a wide range of references on the part of different groups within the multitude toward a particular official policy, in addition to noting the range of policies that various institutions have attempted to implement in various periods. And thus, she is exposed to conspicuous gaps between the declared policy of various mechanisms of power and its implementation, and gaps between the attitude of official national institutions and that of independent cultural institutions that do not implement the hegemonic policy, not necessarily out of opposition to it.

One of the results of Hebrew's "victory" in the "war of languages" is that there are panoramic studies of the Hebrew literature written in Israel, whereas there are no parallel studies about Yiddish literature written in the Israeli space. The existing studies on the poetics of works and authors whose language is Yiddish and who wrote or were written in Israel are therefore noteworthy,[54] as are the more comprehensive studies about Yiddish literature and culture produced in the geographic space of Israel before its establishment.[55] There are also studies that deal with other aspects of Yiddish culture in Israel, like the teaching of Yiddish in universities, the politics of languages, and Yiddish theater.[56] This book aims to add to these studies and contribute its part to creating a panoramic picture of Yiddish, its literature, and its culture in Israel.

6. Translations, Transliterations, and Use of Special Terms

- "Arabs" / "depopulated Palestinian villages." In the literature reviewed in this study, the Palestinian residents of Israel are referred to as "Arabs" and their villages as "abandoned." These terms appear in quotes from these works. In the discussions of these works, I use the terms *Palestinians* and *depopulated villages.*
- *Yiddish* as an adjective. When the noun *Yiddish* functions as an adjective in that language, it has two meanings: "Jewish" and "Yiddish." This can sometimes make it hard to understand the straightforward meaning of a text. The meaning of the terms *Yidishe* (Jewish/of Yiddish) and *Yidishkeyt* (Jewishness) is not limited to the Jewish religion but encompasses all aspects of the way of life and the cultural life that developed in the Jewish communities of Eastern Europe.
- Israel and not "the State of Israel." Israel's name is "Israel," just as France's name is "France" and Germany's, "Germany." The combination "the State of Israel" harbors a complicated and problematic ideology of which most users of the phrase are not even aware.
- Translations and transliterations. Quotations from poetry in Yiddish are given in the original and in translation. Quotations from Yiddish prose are given in translation. Translations from Yiddish are my own unless otherwise noted. In footnotes, the titles of works, books, and periodicals are given in the original (transliterated), followed by an English translation. The transliteration of names (of people, places, published works, and so on) from Yiddish into English follows YIVO guidelines or their

Itzik Manger visiting the *Letste nayes* offices in Tel Aviv, 1958.
Seated in the front row, from the right: Mordkhe Yofe, A. Volf Yasny, Itzik Manger, Mordkhe Tsanin, Leyzer Aykhnrand, Dr. A. Sh. Yuris. *Standing in the second row, from the right*: Dovid Eydlman, Yitskhok Berst, Yitskhok Luden, Eliezer Rubinshteyn, Avrom Karpinovitsh, [unidentified]. Gnazim Institute, Tsanin Archive 504.

spelling in the *YIVO Encyclopedia* or at the JewishGen communities database.

- The transliteration of names used here follows (in accordance with the guidelines of the Academy of the Hebrew Language) common English use (Kibbutz, Shamir, etc.), whereas the transliteration of titles of works from Hebrew into English follows (again, in accordance with the guidelines of the Academy of the Hebrew Language) strict phonetic notation.
- Marks and symbols that appear in quoted excerpts. Yiddish words that appear in square brackets are my own additions, essential to understanding the original, or a correction of the grammatical form that appears in the original. My own translation clarifications appear in square brackets, [thus]. The mark [expression] indicates that a certain translated combination of words is an expression in Yiddish, whose meaning goes beyond the literal translation of the words that make it up. In translating expressions, I tried as much as possible to convey this "extra" meaning.
- Monikers and pen names. Writing under monikers and pen names was a very common practice in modern Yiddish journalism and literature. The reasons for this are many and have changed throughout history,

from shame at the fact of writing in Yiddish to self-protection from a hostile regime. In Israel, a new reason was added: the Hebraization of the original names. Wherever I was able to trace the name of an author who signed his or her work with a moniker, the name appears in brackets, thus: Y. Darin [Mordekhe Tsanin]. Where I was not able to trace the writer's identity, the symbol [M] follows the moniker—for example, Tsila bat David [M].

- Citations. The first time I cite a work of secondary literature in each chapter, full details are provided in the footnotes, and subsequent references to that work are abbreviated, providing the author's last name and a shortened version of the work's title.
- Common abbreviations in the book: AR, Arbeter ring; *DGK*, *Di goldene keyt*; *LN*, *Letste nayes*; *LF*, *Lebns fragn*; SA, State Archive.

Part I

Yiddish in Israel: A Cultural History, 1948–1967

1

Tel Aviv after the Holocaust

A Yiddish Metropolis?

In 1959, while visiting Montreal (a vibrant center of Yiddish culture at the time), Avrom Sutzkever, one of the most important poets in Yiddish (and one of the most important modern poets)[1] as well as editor of the leading Yiddish literary magazine *Di goldene keyt* (*The golden chain*), wrote a letter to a fellow Yiddish writer in Tel Aviv, Mordekhe Tsanin, editor of *Letste nayes* (*Latest news*), Israel's only Yiddish daily newspaper and the most popular publication in the language worldwide: "But now I am beginning once again to be convinced of how important is our Yiddish-work in Tel Aviv. Our shtetl, Tel Aviv, must and will become the metropolis of Yiddish."[2] Sutzkever referred to Tel Aviv as a "small town" on the world map of Yiddish culture—"Yiddishland"—and expressed his faith that thanks to their activities Tel Aviv would be transformed from a peripheral small town on this map to its throbbing center.

On what was this optimism based? What were the growth factors of the young center of Yiddish culture in Tel Aviv, what were its advantages over other centers of Yiddish culture in the world at that time, and what were the unique challenges facing Yiddish-culture activists in Israel as compared to those of other centers? In this chapter, I offer some answers to these questions.

1. Modern Yiddish Cultural Centers in Historical Context

In modern Yiddish culture, the term *Yiddishland* designates the transnational linguistic realm that served as a cultural common ground for Yiddish speakers worldwide. Until the Holocaust, Yiddish had a much greater number of speakers worldwide than Hebrew: four of every five Jews in the world were of Eastern European origin, and the vast majority of them spoke Yiddish, whether as their primary language or in the background of whatever new or old immigration language they had acquired alongside it. Yiddish was typically their mother tongue and the language of their childhood, and often the language in which they had grown up and lived and in which they created, studied, loved, and died—they, as well as many of their cultural heroes. So, from a quantitative point of view, we must conclude that the bulk of Jewish culture prior to World War II was created and consumed in Yiddish, or at least with its accompanying presence.

Modern Yiddish culture was born in the cities of Eastern Europe, and with the mass migration to North and South America, from the end of the nineteenth century and throughout the twentieth, centers of Yiddish culture developed there as well.[3] One of the paradoxes that characterize modern Yiddish culture, then, is embodied in the gap between its image as the culture of a homogenous, traditional "Jewish small town" (the shtetl) and the fact that it was actually created far from such places, in the big cities, the cradle of modernity. These cities offered their inhabitants a variety and plurality—professional, religious, ethnic, social, intellectual, and ideological—that influenced the cultures and identities that were shaped within them. In modern culture, big cities symbolize the site in which the individual is made and shaped,[4] an individual who sometimes becomes an artist, who in his work creates a new and imagined national collective (gesellschaft) and attributes to it old and traditional characteristics (gemeinschaft).[5] So, too, in the modern Jewish culture in Yiddish and in Hebrew: big cities like Odesa, Moscow, Warsaw, and New York were new environments for Jewish immigrants and offered them opportunities to shed old loyalties (religious, communal, familial) and create new social and familial identities and connections.[6] As I noted earlier, in modern Yiddish culture (unlike modern Hebrew culture), these modern identities and connections were paradoxically described as traditional and folkloric.

Modern Yiddish culture was created and shaped by its press, its literature, its cultural and educational institutions, and its ideological and political organizations.[7] The larger the city, the richer and more varied was its cultural scheme: it featured more Yiddish newspapers, which were more frequently published and of a wider range of quality; more types of formal education institutions in Yiddish (kindergartens, elementary schools, high schools, and teachers' seminaries) and informal ones (youth organizations and sports associations); and more theater groups, ideological and political movements, publishing houses, and public libraries. Over the years, new elements were added, including (particularly in the Americas) radio, cinema, and television. Thus, the cities of America and Eastern Europe offered the young Jews who migrated to them occupational opportunities that would support intellectual growth and artistic creation (like teaching in the Jewish schools or writing or editing in the Jewish press), alongside a wide human variety, both Jewish and non-Jewish, exposure to which and interactions with which provided inspiration for their creative work and nourished it. It is not for nothing that Dr. Yisroel Isidor Elyashiv, known as Bal-Makhshoves ("the Thinker"), declared in the early twentieth century that the future of the Jews was in the big cities.[8]

Unlike modern Hebrew culture, which was characterized by a fundamental tension between Palestine/Eretz Yisrael and the cultural centers that emerged outside of it in "exile," modern Yiddish culture was created and consumed all over the world.[9] The multiplicity of centers in which this culture was created gave

Yiddish writers, journalists, editors, actors, teachers, and various operators and promotors many avenues of livelihood and enrichment. However, this unique cultural realm maintained a distinct character of center and periphery. The periphery was not just the remote Eastern European towns from which young men and women had set out to the big cities of Europe and America in the hope of gaining financial and sometimes even cultural standing. From the start of the twentieth century and up to the 1930s, lively debates were waged on the questions of where the best conditions for the continuation of this culture existed, where its new great authors were emerging, and where its readers were located.[10] Warsaw, of course, had a special status among Eastern European–born producers and consumers of Yiddish culture across the world. Many of them regarded it as the "trunk"—the seat of Yiddish culture—whereas the other centers, even the dense, rich, and established ones like New York, they saw as the "branches," a periphery. New York did of course enjoy a place of honor thanks to the number of Jews living in it and their cultural, social, and financial activity, which to a large extent enabled the cultural activity in Warsaw and the other centers in Eastern Europe during the years of World War I and thereafter. For Moscow, leaders of Yiddish culture held high expectations because of the Soviet institutional support of Yiddish culture, which allowed writers and other creators to earn a living from their art, allowed them to establish cultural and research institutions, and mostly allowed them an unprecedented participation in the hegemonic culture, a dynamic that had no parallel in other centers across the world. So it was at least until 1929, when the Soviet regime began to limit the freedoms of producers of Yiddish culture and even to persecute them. The Great Depression that broke out in the same year in the United States severely hit the Yiddish writers working there, as well as the readers and the cultural organizations, which were increasingly hard put to support the Yiddish cultural centers in Eastern Europe. Indeed, as early as 1924, the cultural growth in New York began showing signs of slowing, with the implementation of the Immigration Act making it much harder to immigrate to the United States. This prevented both leaders of Yiddish culture and its consumers from coming over from Eastern Europe and injecting new force into the New York Yiddish center. Nor did these quotas stop the decline of Yiddish culture in Eastern Europe: throughout the 1920s and 1930s, communities continued to dwindle in favor of other destinations in the world (in Western Europe, South America, South Africa, and Australia). In Warsaw, New York, and Moscow, fewer and fewer Jews spoke Yiddish and consumed its culture. The golden age of modern Yiddish culture, then, between the two world wars, occurred largely by force of the bitter realization that the fate of this culture in Eastern Europe, and perhaps even throughout the world, was in fact sealed.[11]

Modern Yiddish culture enabled its producers (the "intelligentsia") and consumers (the Jewish public) to participate in the modern, mostly national societies without losing their ethnic and cultural uniqueness. But in the interwar years, a growing number of Jews, in Eastern Europe and beyond it, chose to prepare their children to integrate into the society of the countries in which they lived by adopting the hegemonic language and culture and thus effectively abandoned their ethnic-cultural uniqueness. Progressive ideas about protecting this cultural identity whose language is Yiddish (ideas that were given the problematic and misleading name "diasporic nationalism" and that are enjoying a popularity and even mythicization among present-day Jewish American researchers)[12] remained largely theoretical: they were held by a minority, mostly among the intelligentsia (most prominently by Simon Dubnow, Ber Borokhov, and Max Weinreich), were never adopted by the masses, and barely received any support outside of Warsaw and Vilna, and attempts to ground the aspiration to preserve this unique culture in legal civil rights in Poland and Lithuania met with little success.[13] In the United States, where the producers and consumers of Yiddish culture enjoyed civil rights guaranteeing cultural and religious freedom, a vibrant modern Yiddish culture was maintained, as I described, through the extensive press, varied literature and theater, educational systems, social organizations for mutual aid, and more.[14] But in the United States especially—because of the social and economic mobility it afforded in the interwar years—the more the masses became integrated in the general culture, the more their involvement in their original ethnic culture declined.[15] Even preserving ethnic uniqueness among the Jews of the United States in the interwar years was a means of integration into the general immigrant society, a manner of expressing a general American spirit. The thin stratum of the creators of modern Yiddish culture in the United States gradually distanced itself in those years from the universal-liberal and secular ethos of their culture, which was embodied by the big city, and became more attached (or else "returned") to its religious-traditional and ethnic elements, embodied in the image of the Eastern European "ghetto"—an imagined one, since until the Holocaust, Jews there did not live in ghettos.[16]

After the Holocaust, centers of Yiddish culture continued to exist in various big cities. A look at the map of Yiddish culture centers across the world after the Holocaust, according to the Yiddish press published in them (App. B), shows that the important centers were New York, Buenos Aires, Paris, and Montreal. As Sutzkever's letter quoted at the beginning of the chapter attests, the creators of Yiddish culture and its agents continued to move between the centers, to distribute their work personally and meet face-to-face with their varied public of consumers (adults and the pupils of Yiddish schools). These trips were challenging, financially and physically, for both the guests and the hosts. But the fact that they were undertaken, and not just by prominent figures like Sutzkever but also by young and minor writers and other artists of this culture, testifies to the relatively strong economic status of the institutions and of their supporters, which still allowed them to finance these trips. Yet the main cultural institutions in the large and most established centers of Yiddish culture in New York and Buenos Aires—the daily press, the educational networks, the social organizations—were already showing signs of aging and weakening in the late 1950s, when Sutzkever visited the Jewish communities in America. He had undoubtedly noticed the stagnation that afflicted the Yiddish organizations, whose activities were directed primarily at the first generation of immigrants. For the youth of the second (or third) generation of immigrants, they were not able (and perhaps did not even try) to offer a current and attractive Jewish identity that would prevent assimilation into the country's dominant culture. These communities had hoped to absorb the Holocaust survivors, who were the last generation to grow up in the Yiddish cultural centers of Eastern Europe. But because of the harsh immigration policies of the United States and Argentina, only a third of them were absorbed in the Jewish communities in these countries. Their small number relative to the absorbing community (the Jewish communities); the dramatic economic gap between the absorbers, who were typically established, and the absorbed, who were refugees; and the defective internal politics that prevailed in most of the veteran Yiddish culture organizations in these communities prevented the Holocaust survivors from being active within them and leaving their mark. By contrast, those two-thirds of the surviving remnant, most of them Yiddish speakers, who came to Israel transformed it from a distant and remote periphery of the worldwide Yiddishland into an important center on this map.

What were the internal growth factors that contributed to the rise of a center of Yiddish culture in Israel? What were the challenges this growing center faced in the Israeli environment? And what were the factors that slowed its growth and eventually led to its wilting and demise? To answer these questions, I examine these processes as they were manifested across the four elements that are essential to the life of any cultural center: (a) the public—a critical mass of addressees, who make up a community that shares a common cultural and linguistic identity; (b) a class of intelligentsia—a group that constitutes a cultural leadership and assumes the responsibility and burden involved in such leadership; (c) a network of media outlets and financial organizations that allow the producers of the culture and its agents to make a living, support their activity, and disseminate it to the consumers; and (d) a shared past, present, and future—the cultural leadership must define its immediate environment in a way that evokes in the public a desire to belong to the community and be active within it and that gives it a sense of common and desired identity and direction. In general, after the Holocaust, the hubs of Yiddish culture experienced themselves as a periphery with no center or a bereaved periphery that had lost its center—Jewish Eastern Europe, which had been the emotional, creative, and spiritual source of their vitality.[17] According to Dubnow, "For every period in the life of a dispersed nation there rises one

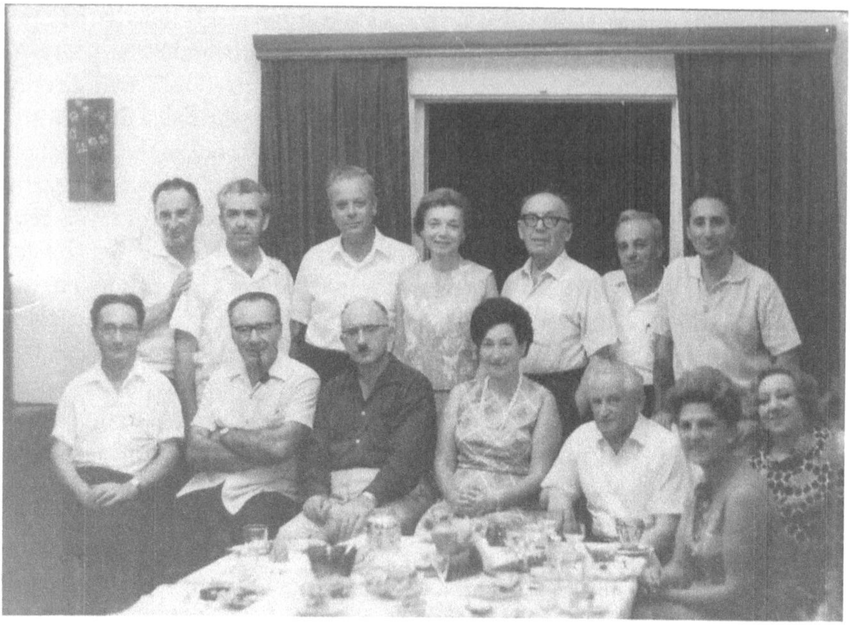

Party at the home of Hana and Mordechai Halamish, Tel Aviv, 1966. *Seated, from the right*: Rita Karpinovitsh, Dora Tsanin, Y. Stolarski, Mrs. Stolarski, Avrom Sutzkever, Mordekhe Tsanin, Binem Heler. *Standing, from the right*: Avrom Karpinovitsh, Avraham Sharon, Moyshe Gros-Tsimerman, Ida Leyvik, Daniele Leyvik (the daughter-in-law and son of the writer H. Leyvik), Mordechai Halamish, Yitskhok Turkov-Grudberg. Gnazim Institute, Tsanin Archive 504, Halamish Collection 507.

main center, and sometimes two centers, which by virtue of their autonomous rule and high culture are the leading speakers in the Diaspora of Israel in their generations. . . . In the period of the lack of a political center in Israel, from the Second Destruction onward, the division is inevitably geographic, in accordance with the changing hegemony of various centers in the life of the nation."[18] How did the establishment of Israel influence this characteristic dichotomy of center and periphery in modern Yiddish culture?

2. Israel's Yiddish Culture Center: A Portrait

A. *The Masses*

"Israel is the most Yiddisher country in the world," observed the economist and historian Jacob (Yankev) Leshtshinski in 1960: "Yiddish is (after Hebrew) the second language that roams the country and the second language in terms of the press and literature."[19] And in the same vein, in 1957, the educator and editor

Shmuel Rozhanski of Buenos Aires reported at a reception held in his honor in New York after his return from a visit to Israel, "In no country is Yiddish spoken as much as in Israel."[20] "Here Yiddish is spoken more than in any country abroad,"[21] wrote the literary critic Leo Kenig of Kibbutz Hatzerim to the readers of the New York–based Yiddish magazine *Di Tsukunft* in 1955. Another aspect of the linguistic choice of the *'oley sheyres hapleyte* (surviving-remnant refugees) appears in the following report from Tel Aviv, delivered in 1964 by the envoy of the fundraising organization Keren Hayesod, the literary critic and editor Moyshe Gros-Tsimerman:

> Many of the Jews who survived came to Israel, speaking the foreign, frightened and terrified languages with which they were left after their many difficult trials—like Polish and Romanian. In the past, in the romance of assimilation, these languages held the promise of a new beginning—but here, in the housing projects of Tel Aviv, Jerusalem and Haifa, in Beer-Sheva, Kfar Saba, Netanya, Hadera, among scaffoldings and complaints, among new neighbors, from whom one borrows a pair of pliers or a watering can, here the language anyway becomes Yiddish [though it absorbs into itself such words as:] "lift" . . . , "lishkat-haAvoda" [the employment bureau] . . . , "Kupat holim" [HMO]. One reads the morning paper, as one once used to read *Haynt*, and when one disagrees [with something], one writes a letter to the editor—as usual: in Yiddish.[22]

Gros-Tsimerman ties the linguistic choice of the immigrant-survivors to the national choice: their earlier choices to speak the languages of the countries in which they lived expressed their aspiration to integrate and become equal citizens there. Yet these countries failed to protect their Jewish citizens in World War II, and they became refugees. In Israel, they went back to speaking Yiddish as part of the process of establishing their new social and national identity.

Just how widespread was the choice of Yiddish among 'oley sheyres hapleyte, and what was its influence on the general Israeli society? In 1946–1951, 152,000 'oley sheyres hapleyte arrived in Israel. For the sake of comparison, consider that during those same years only 66,000 survivors came to the entire American continent.[23] By 1956, approximately two-thirds of all surviving remnants had come to Israel, in three waves.[24] Their number is estimated in the scholarship at between 383,000 and 500,000 people.[25] 'Oley sheyres hapleyte, as noted earlier, were part of a mass migration to Israel that took place between 1948 and 1953, after the provisional government lifted all restrictions on the immigration to Israel in May 1948. On the eve of Israel's independence, the total population of Jewish residents in Palestine/Eretz Yisrael stood at 670,000. By the end of 1952, this "Yishuv" had absorbed 717,923 citizens ("new 'olim")![26] The demographic meaning of these numbers is central to our present concern: it implies that in those years, more new immigrants lived in Israel than veterans. Between 1948 and 1950, 'oley sheyres hapleyte made up approximately 70 percent of all the "mass immigration" immigrants,[27] and in the decade 1946–1956 their estimated percentage among all immigrants was forty-three.[28] A decisive number of them spoke Yiddish or understood it (as did a considerable number of veterans). And given that Yiddish, like any language, is not just a means of communication but a whole set of cultural attributes, this was a population with a cultural presence that could not be ignored.

The exact number of Yiddish speakers among 'oley sheyres hapleyte is hard to determine. It was not the language of all of them—immigrants from the Czech Republic, Yugoslavia, Bulgaria, and most parts of Hungary typically did not speak Yiddish. In practice, the situation was more complicated, and the full data is not always available: first, between the two world wars there was a significant movement of Jews from Eastern Europe to Central and Western Europe, so that some of the Jews who immigrated to Israel supposedly from non-Yiddish-speaking countries actually came to those countries as immigrants or refugees from countries in which Yiddish was the spoken language among Jews; and second, the national definitions of various regions and the borders of European countries underwent many changes in the interwar years, so that Jews listed as having arrived from a country in which Yiddish was not spoken, in fact often came from areas in which it was common. It is agreed that the vast majority of 'oley sheyres hapleyte were originally from Poland and Romania.[29] These immigrants typically spoke Yiddish, often as their first language.[30] Thus, we can generalize and say that Yiddish was the language of most of the 'oley sheyres hapleyte. Other languages that were common among this group of immigrants include (in descending order of use) Polish, Romanian, Hungarian, German, Ladino, Russian, and Bulgarian.

Studies that examined the languages spoken in Israel in the 1950s reveal that the percentage of Yiddish speakers was indeed very high, as the picture I portrayed suggests. Roberto Baki studied the use of Hebrew in the years 1917–1954 and found that in 1948, Yiddish speakers constituted 47 percent of all non-Hebrew speakers in Israel.[31] In 1950, Yiddish was one of the three most spoken languages in Israel other than Hebrew.[32] He notes that "Jews of Eastern European origin in Israel tend to use Yiddish; in fact, the percentage of their use of Hebrew in family circles is low, and in their social life it is also relatively not high; moreover, they make rather significant use of other languages besides Hebrew to satisfy their cultural needs."[33] He added, "Some of the immigrants from countries such as Russia, Poland, Romania, Hungary, the Czech Republic and others continue to speak Yiddish or return to this language . . . The transition to Hebrew or the continued use of Yiddish—or return to it—result in many cases from ideological factors."[34]

So, did the choice of 'oley sheyres hapleyte to speak Yiddish imply an opposition to Zionism and Hebrew? It turns out that just the opposite is true. The common ideological stance among ʻoley sheyres hapleyte ʻolim in Israel was essentially Zionism as it was perceived at the time—that is, as a claim to establish a national home for Jews in Israel and, after its establishment, dedication to the task of building it as part of the realization of Judaism in the new sense, which was inspired by the modern national movements and, like them, rested on ancient mythical values or drew inspiration from them. Understood in these ways, Zionism characterized many of the ʻoley sheyres hapleyte ʻolim who before the war had not regarded themselves as Zionists. As Israel Gutman noted, this Zionism was not essentially "persuasion and ideological consideration, but mostly the consequence of harsh and cruel experience."[35] Hagit Lavsky described their position as "spontaneous Zionism."[36]

The "loyalty" of the Yiddish-speaking ʻoley sheyres hapleyte to the language and culture they brought with them was part of their Jewish tradition, which was multilingual in nature,[37] and they did not see it as in any way contradicting their ideological Zionist position. On the contrary, they saw it as complementing their national-cultural Jewish identity and as a natural extension of the new Israeli Jewish identity that they sought to help shape. This position did not receive attention and recognition from the absorbing public and the establishment. And thus, the fascinating cultural encounter that took place in Israel was in fact between ʻoley sheyres hapleyte's Zionism and the "Sabra" (native Israeli) Zionist ideal that Israel reflected. In the local Zionist ethos of the time, ʻoley sheyres hapleyte were perceived as the polar opposite of the Sabra: old, physically weak, with an exilic "ghetto mentality," and Yiddish-speaking (like the image attributed to Itzik Manger at the beginning of this book). But in truth, most of the ʻoley sheyres hapleyte who came to Israel were young men and women,[38] with young families,[39] and their formal education typically fell slightly below that of the Israeli-born Jews. They had professional training in various manual labors and industrial jobs and in administration and clerical work. Before the war, the large majority of them had lived in more or less urban towns or big cities. In Israel, most of them preferred this housing and living pattern so far as it was up to them. Because they had arrived in Israel on the eve of its establishment, the receiving establishment was not yet prepared to absorb them in an organized manner, so at first, they settled independently in depopulated Palestinian villages, and later, with the gradual organization of the absorbing establishment, they were sent to the refugee transit camps. Their move to these immigrant neighborhoods erected on the fringes of various Israeli cities was carried out through a combination of independent organization on the part of the immigrants and help from the absorbing establishment. A minority settled in Kibbutzim and moshavim (cooperative agricultural communities).[40] Hanna Yablonka described their absorption in Israel as "individual absorption": they were not initially absorbed by organized official bodies because Israel was in the early stages of consolidating itself as a state. In the absence of an organized absorbing system, ʻoley sheyres hapleyte took care of various aspects of their absorption in Israel on their own.[41]

The waves of migration that fall under the category of the "mass migration" to Israel are typically divided into four subperiods. This division is not merely numerical; it also reflects the ways in which the immigrants were absorbed and the fundamental experiences of their encounter with Israel.[42] The first period is typically called "the period of the refugee camps" (May 1948 to mid-1950); the second, "the period of the Maʻabarot" (mid-1950 to mid-1952); the third (mid-1952 to mid-1954) is characterized by a decline in the number of incoming immigrants and preparations by the establishment to improve the absorbing process of future immigrants; and the fourth is dubbed "from the boat to the village" (August 1954 to mid-1956). According to Moshẹ Lissak, this period differs from the earlier ones in that the establishment absorbed the immigrants in an organized, efficient manner. According to his estimates, between May 1948 and the end of 1954 some 740,000 Jews immigrated to Israel, and 690,000 of them settled there.[43] Those who came during the period of the immigrant transit camps were persecuted refugees who had suffered personal and social hardships. Their arrival in Israel reflected a decision by the leadership in Israel that it was imperative to bring them to the country as soon as possible, and in some cases they were brought over as entire communities. Among those who came to Israel during that time were the refugees held in the camps in Cyprus, those living in the displaced persons (DP) camps and in transit camps in various European sites, the Jews of Bulgaria, the Jews of Yemen (in Operation Magic Carpet), the Jews of Libya, and the Jews of Iraq (in Operation Ezra and Nehemiah). The Jews of Romania and Morocco also began to immigrate to Israel during these years, but their immigration was gradual and spanned a longer time. In this first period of immigration, 330,000 Eastern European Jews came to Israel—97 percent of all European immigrants to the country in the 1950s.[44]

Gila Menahem and Efraim Yaʻar argue that when the scholarship of the mass migration addressed the issue of ʻoley sheyres hapleyte, it treated them as immigrants and not as refugees—that is to say, as having experienced trauma of one particular sort, that of immigration only. This, despite the fact that the suffering they endured in the Holocaust years made them an extreme case of refugeehood.[45] According to Menahem and Yaʻar, the social-economic achievements of ʻoley sheyres hapleyte after thirty years of life in Israel (in 1983) were significantly lower than those of immigrants who came before the war, in terms of education, profession, and income, and this was all the more conspicuous in light of the fact that they were of the same origin as the dominant and veteran group in Israel.[46] They attribute this to the war and its scars. According to Menahem and Yaʻar, the gaps between ʻoley sheyres hapleyte and Israeli natives, especially in education, were reduced in the second generation despite restrictions that had been placed on them as the children of refugees: they were directed mostly toward vocational education but still managed to obtain high school diplomas and find their way into white-collar jobs and even academia. The children of ʻoley sheyres hapleyte even reached higher incomes than those of veteran Israelis in these professions. According to Menahem and Yaʻar, this attests to their investment of great personal effort in social and economic mobility. Yablonka points out the paradox that even though most ʻoley sheyres hapleyte were young and married when they arrived, the rate of population growth among this group came to a halt after the immigration to Israel.[47] In their children, who represented the healing of the wounds and the promise of continuity, ʻoley sheyres hapleyte instilled the need for security and the drive to succeed socially and economically.

ʻOley sheyres hapleyte, then, were mostly young, with young families, traumatized, and typically lacking any possessions or financial means, and most of them spoke Yiddish. Studies have shown that among immigrants, group identity is a significant factor in the choice of language. The choice of language functions as a mark of their group identification.[48] The process of absorbing an immigrant is described as a resocialization that involves internalizing new values, creating new channels of communication, integrating into new primary groups, and expanding one's range of activity beyond the original primary groups.[49] But the testimonies I present here (in chap. 2) show that the fact that in the Holocaust many of the survivors lost their original primary groups (i.e., their nuclear families) drove them to create alternative primary groups. One of the principal ways to achieve intimacy among their members was the common language of the lost primary groups—namely, Yiddish. This kind of loyalty to a language that is not the language of the country admittedly dooms those who adhere to it to a certain marginality, but it can actually help them integrate themselves into the country's hegemonic culture in an organized way: Eli Lederhendler has shown that organized activity among culturally marginal groups can help their integration into the general sociopolitical system.[50]

It is no wonder, then, that when Mordkhe Tsanin wrote to Prime Minister Ben-Gurion in 1963 seeking to know, apparently (as I did not find a copy of his letter to the PM in his archive), how many Yiddish speakers lived in Israel in its early years, he received a very partial answer. Ben-Gurion did answer the letter, quoting the results of the 1948 population census (according to which 121,414 people from among the country's total population—11.9 percent—spoke Yiddish). The letter opens with the sentence, "These are the numbers (which I'm sure you will be pleased with)."[51] But Tsanin would certainly have been more pleased had the prime minister divulged the additional data he possessed but chose not to include in his reply: in the 1950 census, 13.4 percent of the Jewish population spoke Yiddish, and by the end of 1953, a third of the Jewish population in Israel,[52] natives and immigrants, understood the language.[53]

B. Cultural Leadership: The Yiddish Intelligentsia

Among the 'oley sheyres hapleyte were several dozen Holocaust survivors who made up the leadership of Yiddish culture in Israel. Sutzkever and Tsanin were the most prominent, and alongside them functioned several editors (Y. Artuski, Moyshe Grosman); journalists (A. Volf Yasny, Yitskhok Luden, Yitskhok Paner); writers, who wrote about the encounter with Israeliness and the Israeli way of being (Rokhl Oyerbakh, Tsvi Ayznman, Khaye Elboym-Dorembus, Shloyme Berlinski, Yekhiyel Granatshteyn, Avrom Karpinovitsh, Yishaye Shpigl); and cultural activists (like Yoisef Rotnberg), as well as poets, theater actors, and teachers.[54] They chose to come to Israel and not to the older, more established centers of Yiddish culture in New York or Buenos Aires, where they could have carried out their professional and creative lives more easily and comfortably. Relative to these centers, Israel in the late 1940s was, as I described earlier, a remote corner on the global map of the Yiddishland, and living there meant they had not only to face rehabilitating their own private lives but also to take upon themselves the challenge of building organizations and other frameworks that would sustain their culture. What were the factors that drew them, of all places, to Israel, which was known in the Jewish world of Eastern Europe and America for its problematic attitude toward Yiddish?[55]

The scholarship has proposed several possible explanations for this phenomenon, such as that other immigration destinations outside of Europe, primarily the United States, made it very hard for Jewish refugees to enter their territories, and that intensive ideological and educational Zionist activity in the DP camps and in Cyprus influenced the decision of many refugees to immigrate to Israel. These explanations attribute the active factor, the agency, to establishments (in Israel and outside of it). The other side, the survivors, are described as passive subjects devoid of any ability to decide their own fate and whose consciousness these establishments supposedly shaped however they wished. And above all, the survivors are described as a single homogenous unit, with no class of cultural leadership. What, then, was the explanation that leaders of Yiddish culture gave for their decision to settle in Israel? I found a fascinating, detailed description in an essay, with the handwritten note "Jaffa, July 1950," written by Rokhl Oyerbakh—one of the only female literary editors in Yiddish culture, an esteemed author, a member of the team of the important Ringelblum Archive (known by the code name Oyneg Shabes) that operated in the Warsaw Ghetto (and one of the group's few surviving members), and in later years, in Israel, one of the earliest Holocaust historians[56]: "We are living in a Jewish state. In the very midst of the Jewish people. Simply—among Jews. . . . A [Yiddish] writer has to be where the masses are. For Yiddish writers who come to Israel to stay here for better or worse, [under] good fortune or [under] a curse, to share the Jewish fate in all of its forms—there is no doubt about this."[57]

According to Oyerbakh, the proper place for a Yiddish writer is among "his people," among the Yiddish-speaking masses. A similar position was presented five years earlier by the leading Yiddish literary critic of the time, Shmuel Niger. As early as March 1945, before the liberation of Europe, the New York–based *Di Tsukunft* (the world's leading journal of Yiddish culture) held a symposium on the topic of "Jews after the War." Niger spoke about the "creative-spiritual" forces in post-Holocaust Jewish society, which have the power to lead Yiddish culture to the cusp of a new beginning. According to him, "The divine spirit of contemporary Yiddish culture can dwell only within the life of masses of Jews. . . . An insufficiently large Jewish population in a country or region will significantly limit or even render impossible the life of Yiddish culture, [the] creation of Yiddish culture—and therefore also the existence of a Jewish/Yiddish intelligentsia. . . . Yiddish life and Yiddish culture will have to continue to be built in the Land of Israel. And we must be part of this building."[58]

This sympathy on the part of Yiddish cultural leaders toward the Yiddish-speaking masses was not at all obvious, contrary to the widespread public perception of Yiddish culture as one that was created "from below," by and for the masses. The social and intellectual phenomenon known as "intelligentsia" is tied to the ideas of mid-nineteenth-century German romantic idealism and to the rise of nationalism and the nation-states.[59] These opened up new professional and educational possibilities for the middle classes in their bureaucratic institutions. And these possibilities, in turn, increased the social mobility of members of the middle classes and created a new class, which included journalists, writers, publishers, editors, translators, librarians, educators, and more, and which was characterized by, among other things, its loyalty to the state and government. When it reached Eastern Europe (Poland and Russia), this phenomenon took on other characteristics. There, it designated a social class marked by a sense of commitment to guide and lead society "from below," and not to control it by means of the state, as in the Western European model. In some cases, the Eastern European intelligentsia was identified with revolutionary and avant-garde elements. The education received by members of this class was regarded as a resource that ought to be channeled back into the development of society in general and especially of the lower classes, who had been weakened and had their political consciousness oppressed by the state. To this end, the intelligentsia took upon itself to establish alternative social and cultural institutions to the state-supported institutions, like the press, public libraries, and reading rooms, and through them to bolster democratic and pluralistic values in the modern society.

The Jewish intelligentsia that evolved in Eastern Europe in the nineteenth century was similar in character to the Russian one. According to Jonathan Frankel, the best way to understand the politically conscious and politically active intelligentsia, which after 1881 became the new force in the Jewish world, is to regard it as one of the branches of the Russian intelligentsia (and that which underwent a process of Russification),[60] because the Jewish intelligentsia in Eastern Europe, too, was a social-cultural leadership; it, too, saw in advancing the modernization of all parts of society, including the weak ones, an important goal that would advance society as a whole, and to achieve this, it too set up organizations, associations, new social and cultural institutions, and political parties. But there were also important differences: the Jews had significantly reduced possibilities relative to their Russian (and Polish) counterparts to influence the general society on the social and political level. Their access to higher education in the universities of the Russian Empire was highly limited due to a discriminatory policy, for academic reasons (inability to meet the entry requirements because of gaps between the Jewish and the general education systems), or for financial reasons (most Jewish families could not afford to send their children to high school, let alone to university, which typically required traveling to Central or Western Europe). The result was that only a few of the members of the Jewish intelligentsia received university training (these include a small number of thinkers who were among its leaders, like the aforementioned Bal-Makhshoves, Dr. Khaym Zhitlovski, and Dr. Max Weinreich). Most members of the Jewish intelligentsia, therefore, were autodidacts and not "specialists." They were not part of the bourgeoisie, since Eastern European Jewry did not develop any real middle class (unlike Western European Jewry)[61] but rather belonged to the ranks of the small merchants and craftsmen (a prominent example is Ber Borokhov).[62] Even those who did receive an academic education were typically unable to make their way into state institutions (except in the Soviet Union). And intellectual, cultural, political, or professional collaborations with private liberal elements from among the general intelligentsia also typically did not work out well, causing the Jewish intelligentsia to turn its focus inward on Jewish society itself.

Jewish society, then, did not display the gap that typically exists between most members of an intelligentsia and the masses in terms of institutional-cultural capital and symbolic capital, as it existed in German, Russian, or Polish societies, and therefore the Jewish intelligentsia's access to the masses was greater than that of the Russian intelligentsia to the *narod* ("people" in Russian). The vast majority of the Jewish intelligentsia in Eastern Europe did not need to "go to the people," as the Russian slogan urged; they were "the people." To stress this particular characteristic of the Eastern European Jewish intelligentsia, Frankel called it the "polu-intelligentsia" (half-intelligentsia).[63] Its attitude toward the masses changed and varied across the different periods and realms in which it existed. In Eastern Europe, before the 1881–1882 anti-Jewish pogroms in the Russian empire (known as *Sufot Ba-Negev*, "the storms in the South"), the harbingers of the intelligentsia sought to distinguish themselves from "the uneducated Jewish masses," to distance themselves from them and sometimes even ignore them altogether.[64] But after this violent turning point, many of them embraced the idea of "going to the Jewish people" (in Frankel's fitting wording),[65] adopted the language and culture of the masses, and placed them at the base of their artistic and ideological-political commitment. Through this adoption, they succeeded in getting close to the masses while at the same time establishing a certain distance from them, small but crucial to establishing their own distinct self-definition. And indeed, it is they who developed the ethos of the "Jewish mass" (*Yidishe folksmasn*), of the "man of the people" (*folksmentsh*), and of Yiddish literature as a "literature of the people." Yet it is important to note the elitist threads that run through supposedly populist central phenomena of modern Yiddish culture, like certain imageries and the work of the great classic writers of this culture (Mendele Moykher Sforim, Sholem Aleichem, and Y. L. Peretz), the YIVO Institute, and the Jewish People's Party (*folkspartey*).[66] In other words, modern Yiddish culture, too, like every other modern culture, was created by the intelligentsia, even if the culture it created had a distinct populist inclination.

In New York in the interwar period, a greater distance opened up between the polo intelligentsia of Yiddish culture and the masses, who were perceived by the former as holding back the culture's development.[67] According to members of the intelligentsia, the inferior taste of the masses and their demand for "low" products caused a vulgarization of the culture and prevented the emergence of a subtle and "high" body of work. Yiddish writers in New York (and especially the poets) adopted an elitist attitude toward the masses, influenced in part by the contemporaneous English and American literature, in response to (and as compensation for) the painful fact that their work had almost no readers. Jews who held socialist and communist views tended to distance themselves from the Jewish ethnic identity and sought to join internationalist movements and parties, and in general, according to Avraham Novershtern, "the presence of the modern Jewish ideologies and parties was felt much more strongly in Warsaw than in New York, to say nothing of the pressure exerted on them in the Soviet Union."[68] Thus, the populist position expressed by Shmuel Niger attests more than anything else to the impact of the Holocaust on Yiddish culture in the United States.[69] In its aftermath, the gap between the polo intelligentsia and the masses appeared to be closing and perhaps even to have closed, and with it also the gap between the Jewish society created and consolidated in Eastern Europe and the one that was gradually consolidating in the United States. But was this really so?

A group of Yiddish authors and journalists who chose to come to Israel after the Holocaust is notable for its high variety (see App. A). They were born in different places in Eastern Europe; before the Holocaust, they belonged to different political and ideological movements: left and right wing, secular (most of them) and religious, or "religious Zionist" (a minority). During the Holocaust, they lived through very different war experiences: refugeehood in the Soviet

Union (Dovid Eydlman, Tsvi Ayznman, Y. Artuski, Shlyome Berlinski, Moyshe Grosman, Mendl Man, Malsha Mali, Khave Slutska-Kestin, Levi Papiernikov, Yitskhok Perlov, Mordekhe Tsanin, Shimen Kants, Avrom Karpinovitsh, Avrom Rubinshteyin) but also imprisonment and forced labor in the ghetto (Rokhl Oyerbakh, Khaye Elboym-Dorembus, Rivke Kviatkovski-Pinkhasik, Avrom Sutzkever, Yishaye Shpigl), labor camps, concentration camps, and death camps (Shmaye Avni, Yitskhok Paner, Rivke Kviatkovski-Pinkhasik), life in rural hiding (Leyb Rokhman) or under a fake identity in the city (Khaye Elboym-Dorembus), fighting as partisans (Yekhiel Granatshteyin, Avrom Sutzkever), and fighting in the Russian or Polish armies (Mendl Man, Shimen Kants). Some of them came to Israel alone, after losing their family, and others came with a young family. Most of them arrived first at a processing camp known as Sha'ar Ha-'Aliya (Gate of Immigration) and from there on navigated the process of their absorption on their own (that is, with the help of relatives or of societies of immigrants from the same hometown), living in depopulated Palestinian neighborhoods and villages (Jabaliya [later Giv'at 'Alyia], Sheih Munis [Ramat Aviv], Yazur [Azor], Beit Dagan [Beit Dagan]) and immigrant housing projects on the outskirts of cities (for example, Yad Eliyahu and Hadar Yosef [Tel Aviv], Ramat 'Amidar [Ramat Gan], Kiryat Motzkin, Bnei Brak). Some of them first arrived at the Ma'abarot and from there moved to these immigrant neighborhoods thanks to savings they were able to accumulate during the years of displacement and bring with them to Israel, or thanks to loans from the hometown societies or other social aid organizations. A minority arrived at Kibbutzim (Yagur, Gvat), and even fewer settled in Tel Aviv proper, because the policy of population dispersion applied at the time of their absorption restricted the development of Tel Aviv but encouraged building in its peripheries: Jaffa, Giv'atayim, Ramat Gan, and the neighborhoods north of the Yarkon River.[70] And indeed, most of them managed to improve their housing conditions and by the end of the 1960s had once again moved into larger apartments. A small number of them left the country.

Alongside the diversity, this group had certain features in common: most of its members were born in the first and second decades of the twentieth century to traditional families, typically low-class, in Polish towns and cities. Their childhood and young adulthood took place in a new national environment—that of the independent Poland (1918–1939). This environment "immeasurably accelerated the penetration of the modern era into the lives of Jews, and especially the lives of the young generation."[71] An important factor in this process was the compulsory education act (for boys and girls alike), which was passed in 1922 and required seven years of schooling, between the ages of seven and fourteen. Its impact was felt in the transition from traditional educational systems to new systems of a more national and secular character.

The traditional Jewish society and its institutions had already disintegrated and split into various secular and modern ideological camps when this generation of the writers and journalists of the future was born. The ideological environment in which they lived largely dictated the linguistic one. The establishment of Jewish secular educational systems in Yiddish between the two world wars played a central role in shaping their generation: most of them received primary education in (private) Jewish institutions whose principal teaching languages were Yiddish and Polish and, to a lesser degree, Hebrew.[72] Compared with previous generations, the Jewish education this generation received was highly variegated, since their schools had been established mostly by political parties—from the Mizraḥi (in whose institutions Rivke Kviatkovski-Pinkhasik had studied, for example) to TSYSHO (Di Tsentrale Yidishe Shul-Organizatsye, the Central Yiddish School Organization, a collaboration of the Bund, Po'ale Zion Left, and the Folkists, whose schools were attended by Tsvi Ayznman and Yitskhok Luden). These schools applied new and advanced educational methods designed to cultivate in their students not only verbal skills but also skills of movement, labor, arts, and more.

Most of the journalists and writers whose works I survey here received their primary education in Jewish schools (unlike most of the Jewish children who grew up in Poland between the world wars, who studied in the traditional *heder* only till age seven, after which most of them attended primary Polish state schools, some of which were designated specifically for Jewish children). A minority from among the journalists and writers who came to Israel had attended secondary school at Polish gymnasiums. A few had studied at schools whose teaching language was Yiddish or Hebrew, or in yeshivas.[73] In any case, even those who received a high school education typically did not succeed in completing their studies and earning a matriculation certificate or professional diploma (mostly for financial reasons—the need to provide for themselves and help provide for their families; but also due to antisemitism), and they became autodidacts.

In this reality, nonformal education played an important role in the life of the young generation that would become the journalists and writers who immigrated to Israel. The various Jewish youth movements (from Beitar and 'Akiva to the Bund's Tsukunft and the communist movement, which operated underground) were established beginning in the first decade of the twentieth century, like the new Jewish educational institutions.[74] The youth movements sought to cultivate in their members a "collective consciousness"—that is to say, a strong connection to such "imagined communities" as a people, nation, class, or even the whole of humanity—in part by reading and discussing Jewish and general press and literature. This consciousness very often led to direct involvement with political parties that were identified with the youth movements. The movements that were prevalent among the future journalists and writers were either Zionist (Yosl Birshteyn and Mendl Man—Hashomer Hatzaʿir; Moyshe Grosman—the youth movement of Poʿale Zion Left; Malsha Mali—Dror; Rivke Kviatkovski-Pinkhasik—Gordoniya) or Bundist (Tsvi Ayznman, A. Volf Yasny, Khave Levkovitsh, Yitskhok Luden).

During the youth years of the Yiddish journalists and writers who came to Israel after the Holocaust, modern secular Yiddish culture reached its height. Many of them were exposed to Yiddish journalism, literature, and theater. All the Yiddish journalists and writers mentioned here were multilingual: in addition to the Jewish languages, they used the language of the countries in which they were schooled (primarily Polish but also Russian and German). They were exposed to their literatures and shaped by them. Some of them abandoned Yiddish in their teens because their education, as I noted earlier, typically took place in institutions whose language of study was the language of the state. The later choice of Yiddish as their creative language was therefore a declarative act of self-aware traditionalism, after some of them had already taken their first literary steps in other languages.[75] Most of them began to publish works of literature in Yiddish on the eve of World War II.

During the Holocaust years, the creators of Yiddish culture continued to write works of literature, hold literary evenings, and so on.[76] Alongside their writing, writers like Sutzkever in the Vilna Ghetto, Oyerbakh in the Warsaw Ghetto, and Shpigl in the Lodzh Ghetto held various roles (sometimes prominent) in the cultural life of the ghettos.[77] In Eastern Europe during the years of the Holocaust and in its aftermath, Jews who before the war had adopted the state culture "returned" to Yiddish culture, as an expression of their disappointment in the European states' treatment of the Jews after the latter had assimilated into their cultures.[78] This "return" occurred because of their life among Jews in the ghettos and camps, and also thanks to the rich Yiddish cultural activities that took place in some of them. Some of the writers encountered modern Yiddish language for the first time in the ghettos and camps and even began to produce literary writing in Yiddish. So testified the writer Rivke Kviatkovski-Pinkhasik of Lodzh: "In school I learned Polish as an everyday language. At home we spoke Yiddish. But with Yiddish as a language of artistic creation I was not sufficiently familiar, and until I arrived in the ghetto, I had not studied Yiddish literature. In the ghetto I met a group of writers. . . . I was not a Yiddish writer, nor did I have, shall we say, the consciousness to describe myself as such."[79]

By contrast, most of the Yiddish writers who came to Israel and began writing during the Holocaust years had been familiar with modern Yiddish literature prior to the war, in part from studying in Jewish schools or from the youth movements. In the DP camps in Germany and internment camps in Cyprus, the Yiddish cultural activity continued.[80] The Yiddish writers and journalists

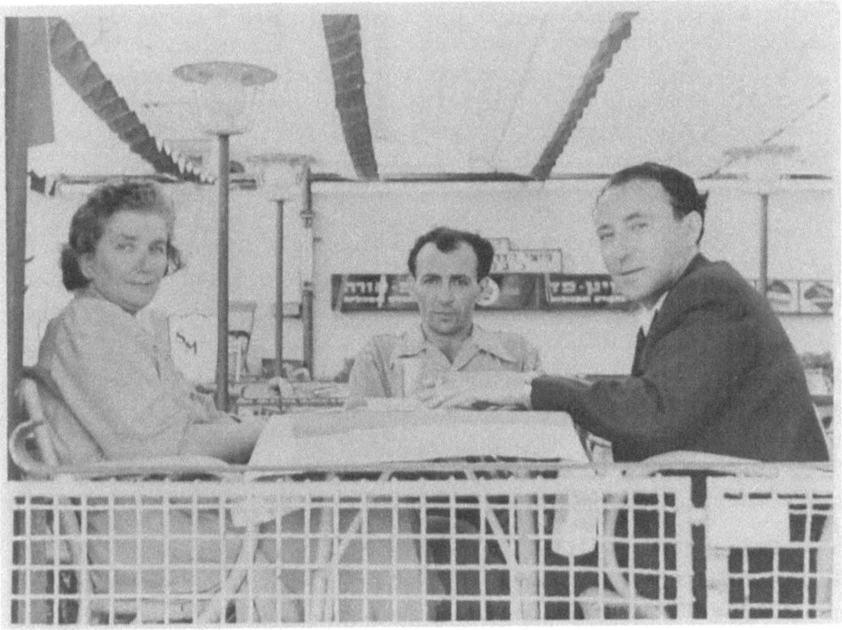

Rokhl Oyerbakh, Café Ginati-Yam in Tel Aviv, May 18, 1950. Yad Vashem, Rokhl Oyerbakh Collection P-16\2\00005.

continued to supply the growing demand for cultural literature in this language and printed their works in the pages of the periodicals published there, and also as books through publishing firms in Europe. Alongside their creative activities, the writers organized, establishing organizations such as Shrayber Farband fun Sheyres Hapleyte (the Association of Surviving Remnants Writers) in Munich, whose members were writers who immigrated to Israel, including Shloyme Berlinski, Shloyme Varzoger, Mendl Man, Yitskhok Perlov, Yisroel Kaplan, and Ruven Rubinshteyn. One of the important tasks of the association was to help the writers leave Europe. In an undated letter sent by the writer Mendl Man to the Rescue Fund for Jewish Refugee Writers, in New York, he pleads, "I write to you, honored friend, with the impassioned request to help me. . . . First: **to leave the blood-soaked German land**."[81] Israel, then, promised the Yiddish writers and journalists a safe haven with a large and receptive reading public as well as a vibrant literary community. The lack of this kind of literary environment was mentioned as one of the main difficulties that faced young Yiddish writers in the DP camps in Germany.[82] And indeed, according to Oyerbakh's description, it was above all in Israel that the masses continued to demand Yiddish cultural products:

> The Jewish mass and the Jewish people are not necessarily measured in numbers. The intention is on activity! On essence! . . . Here in Israel . . . the same small Israel in which the death of Yiddish was declared so many times, the same number of books is bought from Yiddish publishers as in the United States. . . . And as for Yiddish. . . . Since the end of the war I have visited several big cities in Europe, with a large Jewish population. They do not speak as much Yiddish there as they do here![83]

The revival of Yiddish culture after the Holocaust, then, hinged on the ability of a class of cultural leaders to meet the demand of the masses for culture. This is how Niger put it in the 1945 symposium mentioned earlier: "The primary and most important role of the Yiddish/Jewish intelligentsia must now be—to . . . begin to rebuild the life of Yiddish culture, the Yiddish/Jewish institutions, meaning the Yiddish schools, Yiddish Press, Yiddish publishing firms, Yiddish theatre, etc."[84]

C. Yiddish Cultural Institutions in Tel Aviv

Until 1948, the Po'ale Zion Left party ran several modest operations of Yiddish culture in Tel Aviv: a biweekly titled *Nayvelt: Vokhnshrift far politik un kultur* (New World: Weekly writings on politics and culture) and a small and dwindling network of public libraries for Yiddish books in various cities across the land. In addition to these, there was a small number of political party journals and literary journals, all short lived.[85] And then, toward the end of 1948, Tel Aviv saw the establishment, one by one, of newspapers and literary journals that published original Yiddish literary works; publishing firms that printed Yiddish poetry books, short-story collections, novels, memoirs, and books of testimony and research; and institutions founded by ideologically varied organizations of Yiddish speakers, such as libraries and culture clubs, which hosted vibrant activities that made Tel Aviv ("the first Hebrew city"), and later all of Israel, a rising and promising center on the global Yiddishland map (at least until the latter part of the 1960s).[86] In the words of Khone Shmeruk, this growth took place because "the surviving remnant of Eastern Europe brought to Israel a significant public that had a need for Yiddish literature, and with it a large group of writers, whose immigration had in any case already been driven by a decision to continue creating in Yiddish in Israel."[87] But this is only part of the explanation. The "surviving remnant of Eastern Europe" brought with them not only personal savings from their years as refugees but also eligibility for reparations from Germany—money that they invested in the rehabilitation of their culture—as well as connections with Jewish organizations in the United States that provided financial support.

On the eve of the founding of Israel, Tel Aviv was a thriving cultural, political, and financial center of the hegemonic culture—Hebrew culture. The prominent newspapers were based there, as were many of the important literary journals and book publishers. According to Dov Schidorsky, "in the eyes of its residents, it was the heir of Jewish culture, in which the vision of building the new spiritual center had been realized."[88] As I described earlier, most of the activists and leaders of Yiddish culture did not live in the center of Tel Aviv (at least not in their first years in Israel), but when it came to the cultural institutions they established, they chose to situate them in the heart of the city. Thus, contrary to the common perception, Tel Aviv was not "given" to 'oley sheyres hapleyte "from above" (i.e., from the hegemonic institutions); rather, they managed to carve out a place for themselves in the city despite the establishment's opposition, thanks to the alternative institutions they themselves established "from below." The cultural, political, and financial centrality of Tel Aviv made it very attractive to the advocates and creators of Yiddish culture.[89] To them, their Jewish-modern culture was not peripheral or minor in their Jewish state but rather deserved to take center stage. Tel Aviv was the place in which a modern and secular identity could be imagined and even sustained to a certain degree (with the mobility, anonymity, and cultural, linguistic, and ethnic variety and foreignness that the city enabled) within the new nation-state, which had been founded on religion and religious hegemony.

In his story "Tsvishn tsvey berg" ("Between Two Mountains"), Y. L. Peretz described the loaded and complex relationship between the Hasidic rebbe of Biyale and the rabbi of Brisk, a *misnaged* (opponent of Hasidism).[90] These two "mountains" represented the two poles of a mythical spiritual realm from which their disciples drew sustenance. This same "topography" can also serve to describe the realm of Yiddish culture created in Tel Aviv, the city that represents the new "place" in modern Jewish history. Sutzkever and Tsanin, whose correspondence opened this chapter, stand for the two poles of the realm of Yiddish culture in Israel. As we will see, they differed in almost every respect: intellectually, culturally, and ideologically. They were attributed opposite cultural value: Sutzkever was considered a creator of "high culture" as a poet and elitist editor whose work targeted a select few; Tsanin, by contrast, was considered a creator of "mass culture" as a journalist, editor, and populist writer who wrote and created for a mass audience. The two men also hailed from different realms and different traditions in modern Yiddish culture: Sutzkever's home base, both actual and mythical, was Vilna, and Tsanin's—Warsaw. Considering these two men face-to-face allows us also to notice their commonalities: they shared a deep loyalty to Yiddish and its culture, both established cultural institutions that spearheaded the center of Yiddish culture in Israel, and both were considered its representatives (in the eyes of consumers and creators of Yiddish both in Israel and abroad). They were opposites also in their attitude toward the hegemonic establishment: whereas Sutzkever collaborated with the establishment ideologically, politically, and financially, Tsanin did not hesitate to clash with it as part of the various battles he initiated—to bring the state to recognize its obligation to preserve the cultural heritage of those killed in the Holocaust, for the freedom of expression and of cultural occupation of its survivors, and for the just allocation of state funds for culture and education. Juxtaposing these two opposite approaches allows us to observe the space that unfolds between them, within which various other people acted, establishing interesting cultural institutions and waging fascinating battles for their survival.

The Daily Press: *Letste nayes* and Its Editor Mordkhe Tsanin

The press, as noted earlier, and most prominently the daily press, played an important role in establishing a center of Yiddish culture.[91] One of the criteria for determining the prominence or marginality of centers is the frequency with which its periodicals were published. In Warsaw alone, eleven daily newspapers in Yiddish appeared between 1935 and 1937.[92] And though Warsaw was an important and particularly vibrant center, it was not the only center in Eastern Europe and beyond: almost all the big and midsize Eastern European cities with a Jewish population teemed with cultural activity in Yiddish. A "big" cultural center, therefore, is a place in which a newspaper is published daily (the more daily newspapers appear in it, the bigger a center is considered) and alongside it a variety of different periodicals at lower frequencies of publication. By contrast, in a "marginal" center of Yiddish culture, publications appeared less frequently (weekly or less). In the history of modern Yiddish culture from its inception until after the Holocaust, the press also played a significant role in the development of the literature, since, as Shmeruk observed, "the rise of Yiddish press created an economic foundation for the modern intelligentsia and the Yiddish writer."[93]

The newspaper is a product of modern culture and one of its quintessential symbols. Its emergence followed developments in the fields of economy, technology, communications, and education. It unified its readers into an imagined national community, in part by representing the dimensions of national time and national space.[94] From the end of the nineteenth century, the various corners of the Yiddishland enjoyed a rich Yiddish press that was varied in terms of its areas of interest, target audiences, and ideologies. This press was at once local/national and transnational because Yiddish was not the unique national language of any modern nation-state, and its readers and creators were scattered all over the world. Thus, as a modern cultural phenomenon, Yiddish embodies some of the basic tensions that underlay and shaped modernity and that were expressed in the gap between the mass migrations that occurred during this period and the establishment of nation-states: the tension between a local national identity and an ethnic transnational identity, and between the masses, who typically sought to integrate into their local and national environment, and the intelligentsia, which sought to preserve its unique linguistic and cultural identity, even at the cost of distancing itself from its local/national environment, and to establish a transnational "literary republic."[95]

Letste nayes: Umparteyish blat far gezelshaft, politik, virtshaft un kultur (Latest news: A non-partisan daily paper on society, politics, economy, and culture) was the youngest daily in Yiddish and the last one to be printed anywhere in the world (see App. B).[96] Throughout the 1950s, it was a private paper unaffiliated with any political party, which addressed the mass public, "all the people of Israel" (in the 1960s it was semiprivate, on which more later). In those years, the daily papers in the world's major centers of Yiddish culture (New York and Buenos Aires) were already veteran, established institutions: they were founded between the end of the nineteenth century and the end of World War I. The antisemitism in Eastern Europe in the 1930s brought a new wave of refugees to South America, which launched daily press activity in Uruguay as well. Jewish refugees who arrived in Paris in those years propelled a growth in the press that operated there. ʿOley sheyres hapleyte in Israel had facilitated *Letste nayes* (*LN*) and stimulated its publication. In the years of its establishment and expansion, the rest of the Yiddish press across the world gradually diminished.

The *LN*'s first issue appeared on November 3, 1949.[97] Its editor was Tsanin,[98] and his partners were Yisroel Khadash (a Yiddish journalist and member of Poʿale Zion Left) and Matzliah Zeytuni (owner of Ha-Carmel Press in Tel Aviv). Yiddish newspapers titled *Letste nayes* had also appeared in Vilna (1916) and Warsaw (1919), the city in which Tsanin came of age. The Warsaw *LN* was a sensationalist afternoon paper published by the cooperative Undzer ekspres (Our Express).[99] When it hit financial difficulties, the cooperative sold the *LN* to *Haynt* (*Today*) in 1929, and its name was changed to *Hayntike nayes* (*Daily News*).

The Tel Aviv–based *LN* began as a weekly—one of the oldest and most common forms of Yiddish journalism. From issue no. 18 (February 27, 1950), it began to appear twice a week in an eight-page format. From issue no. 45 (June 6, 1950), it was reduced to six pages (following a state-imposed rationing of printing paper).[100] From issue no. 189 (November 2, 1951), the paper appeared three times a week. From issue no. 474 (September 1, 1953), it appeared alternately with another paper by the same owners, titled *Yidishe tsaytung*,[101] with a serialized novel that appeared alternately in each of the papers, cementing their connection. This manipulation helped the paper circumvent a prohibition on publishing a daily Yiddish newspaper in Israel.[102] An ongoing battle against the prohibition ended successfully when, from issue no. 1411 (August 23, 1959), the *LN* began to appear as a daily newspaper.

Looking back (from the year 1992), Tsanin described the establishment of this paper as a civilian-cultural rebellion: he had sought to realize his civil rights to freedom of cultural occupation and freedom of linguistic expression and to expand their boundaries, for "if I have full and declared freedom and full rights,

I have the full right to publish a paper in my own tongue, [a paper] that honors the culture that in Eastern Europe made us a people equal among the other people."[103] He further recounted that even after receiving permission to publish the newspaper once a week, he did not receive the necessary allocation of paper, supposedly because of the "austerity" restrictions. According to Tsanin, he was informed by Yitzhak Gruenbaum (who served as the interior minister in Israel's first government until 1949 and from the 1950s on joined the paper as a regular columnist) that the order not to permit the publication of an independent Yiddish paper in Israel came directly from Ben-Gurion. To expose the discrimination in the rationing of paper, Tsanin began to purchase paper on the "black market": he bought paper surpluses from the Hebrew newspapers, which he claimed received greater allocations of paper than they required. According to Tsanin, he bought the paper at five times the price at which these newspapers bought it from the state. The purchase was done blatantly and as a provocation in the hope of being sued by the minister of rationing and supply, Dov Yosef, and thus forcing the government to admit the cultural discrimination against the Holocaust survivors or else to take an official stand against it. But the minister likely understood Tsanin's intent and ignored the violation. Then Tsanin requested permission to publish the paper twice a week, and the permission was granted (January 18, 1950), after which he appealed again, this time to publish it three times a week. When that was approved (October 29, 1951), Tsanin continued to appeal for permission to publish a daily paper and, according to him, was refused (March 12, 1953). Instead of trying to expose the policy of discrimination (for instance, by appealing to the Supreme Court), Tsanin opted to continue operating from within the "gray zone" of the de facto discrimination, believing that in the given political reality he could use this gray zone to his benefit: he decided to launch a new paper alongside the *LN*, called the *Yidishe tsaytung*, which also appeared three times a week (on the off days of the *LN*).[104] *Yidishe tsaytung* was first published in October 1953,[105] but Tsanin had not fully reconciled himself to this mode of operation. The state's refusal to allow him to publish a daily paper had hurt him deeply: "I could not accept the evil absurdity that in the language of the Nazis, who murdered our people, the Jewish State allows to print two daily papers, while the language of the murdered Jews is cast out."[106]

Tsanin began searching for a clause in the Mandatory Press Ordinance (which continued to be applied in Israel) that would allow him to sue the Ministry of Interior in the Supreme Court for disallowing him to print a daily paper. He found that, according to Mandatory law, a paper that received permission to be published three times a week could be published daily on the condition that it notified the supervising minister—namely, the interior minister. Tsanin notified the minister of his intention to publish the *LN* as a daily paper based on this clause in the Press Ordinance. And indeed, for two months, February and

March 1956, the paper appeared daily. In response, Tsanin was warned that the paper would be shut down, and according to him, the state's attorney general indeed ordered the Tel Aviv police to carry out the threat. Eventually, he agreed to withdraw his demand and go back to publishing his two newspapers alternately, each one thrice a week. From April of that year, the *LN* returned to its regular mode of publication, alternating with the *Yidishe tsaytung*. In the state's tenth year of independence, 1958, Tsanin found out that the then–interior minister, Israel Bar-Yehuda, intended to visit the Jewish community of Buenos Aires for a fundraising campaign. According to his account, he sent Leyb Bayn, the *LN*'s representative in Jerusalem, to threaten the minister that if he did not grant the *LN* permission to appear as a daily, Yiddish newspapers in Buenos Aires would ensure that he received a hostile reception from the city's Jewish community. The minister promised to lend his support and upon his return kept his word, and the permission was granted in 1959.

Whether or not these were indeed the reasons for granting the paper permission to appear as a daily requires further investigation into official state documents, particularly those of the Ministry of Interior—material that is not always accessible. In the Yiddish press, I found reports that in 1960 the Mapai party bought the *LN* along with other newspapers that were published in Israel in languages other than Hebrew (*L'information* [French], *Viata Noastra* [Romanian], *Uj Kelet* [Hungarian], *Neuste Nachrichten* [German], and *Novini Courier* [Polish]).[107] These reports included harsh criticism of Tsanin by his colleagues for having supposedly surrendered his independence for financial gain and for cooperating with the ruling party (it was for this same reason that his partnership with Yisroel Khadash fell apart).[108] However, a survey of the issues published between 1961 and 1967 reveals that the criticism of the establishment that Tsanin expressed in the pages of the paper did not diminish in either quantity or force, and important battles continued to be waged in the pages of the *LN*. One of the most prominent battles revolved around the treatment of the Yiddish press during the Eichmann trial.[109]

The Israeli establishment's attitude toward the *LN* underwent significant changes: from rejection and boycotting throughout the 1950s ("linguistic chauvinism") to purchasing it in 1960 out of a notion of "linguistic utilitarianism." One of the reasons for this shift may have been the need to reach the public of new immigrants who came to Israel in the 1950s and influence it in the lead-up to elections for the tenth Knesset in 1961—the most tense elections in the state's history to that point, due to the Lavon Affair.[110] In this respect, the *LN* was strategically important, because, as I show later, its circulation was significantly greater than that of the other "foreign language" papers. The 1957 *Biyuletin fun alveltlekhn yidishn kultur-kongres* (*Bulletin of the World Congress for Yiddish/Jewish Culture*) reported that 30,000 copies of the *LN* were distributed during the week.[111] The

LN itself reported that in 1955 and 1956, its Rosh HaShone issue was printed in 40,000 copies.[112] In 1960, Yasny wrote (in the *LN*), "The LN . . . is comparable in circulation to the most popular morning paper in Hebrew, and its influence in the broader Jewish world is far greater than that of all the Hebrew-language daily papers in Israel."[113] According to a late testimony by Yitskhok Korn from 1982,[114] in the 1950s the *LN* ran a printing of 15,000–16,000 copies on weekdays and 25,000 copies on weekends, while its actual number of readers was even higher (for comparison, see the circulation of Yiddish papers in other world centers, in App. B). According to Mordechai Naor, data about the circulation of newspapers was a tightly kept secret in Israel in its early years.[115] According to an article that documents a 1952 speech by ʿAzrie'l Carlebach, he gave the following numbers (referring to January 1950): *Maʿariv* ran a printing of 33,000 copies; *Davar*, 25,000; *Haaretz*, 23,500; *Yediot Aḥronot*, 21,000; *Jerusalem Post* (English), 24,000; *Neuste Nachrichten* (German), 11,500; *Uj Kelet* (Hungarian), 6,800; *El Yaom* (Arabic), 6,000; and *Le ekko d'Israël* (French), 1,000. The relation between the circulation of Yiddish papers and that of other foreign-language papers in Israel reflected a continuation (and perhaps the height) of the trend that had prevailed in the DP camps in Germany: "Upon liberation . . . they immediately began publishing newspapers and journals in German, Hungarian, Romanian, Polish et cetera, yet the numbers of these were negligible compared with the many publications published among ʿoley sheyres hapleyte in Yiddish."[116]

Mapai's presence in the pages of the *LN* was conspicuously felt in the run-up to Israel's fifth Knesset elections, held in August 1961 (right after the close of Eichmann's trial and before the verdict was returned). In the course of that summer, Mapai began publishing entire pages in the *LN*.[117] These pages were published under the title *Foroys* (*Forward*) and looked like a paper-within-a-paper: the election propaganda was formatted like journalistic reports, and the names of the writers in these pages received the same graphical treatment that was standard for the bylines of journalists and writers in the *LN*. The pages featured many photographs, unlike the regular pages of the *LN*. Mapai's thin victory in these elections (in contrast to previous elections) can be attributed to the votes of the new immigrants, who were rallied through the foreign-language papers in an intensive, sweeping election campaign. Mapai was of course not the only political party to publish election propaganda in immigrant newspapers, but the scope of its publications in the *LN* was significantly larger than that of any other party.

The comparison to other Yiddish newspapers printed in Israel (almost all of which were party newspapers) reveals that the private (or theoretically private) *LN* was the main arena in which the community of ʿoley sheyres hapleyte in Israel and abroad consolidated itself and organized. The *LN* quickly became the main place that immigrants turned to for help in a wide variety of matters. In 1957, Tsanin formalized the paper's role as advocate for the immigrant public by creating a new unit whose unique role was to provide consultation to immigrants and announcing the sale of advertisements at special discount prices (job search ads, lost relative ads, buying and selling, etc.).[118] The comparison to other Yiddish papers further reveals that the *LN* was the only paper that gave prominent place to lost relative ads and ads for memorial events and other events by landsmanshaft organizations (the hometown societies). Support for these activities was expressed in the *LN* also at the content level, through the personal involvement of the editor and senior staff in reporting, in researching, and in mobilizing the public (I expand on this in chap. 2). This is how the journalist Yitskhok Luden, who worked at the *LN* as a news editor and reporter from 1953, described Tsanin's enterprise: "The greatest achievement of his brave battle was the establishment, editorship and management of *Letste nayes*—not only as a daily newspaper for nearly forty years, but as a platform for the struggle for Yiddish, and as a social guide for hundreds of thousands of *sheyres hapleyte* from that inferno, which helped them become an organ in the body of the Jewish state and preserve their own identity, [preserve] the link to their spiritual roots."[119] Only in 1980 was the *LN*'s contribution to the absorption of the Yiddish-speaking immigration recognized, when Tsanin, its editor, received the Tel Aviv municipal award for Yiddish literature named after Mendele Moykher Sforim.

Like the Yiddish press published before it in the world centers of Yiddish culture, whose target audience was Jewish immigrants,[120] the *LN* also sought to help the process of acculturation in Israel of 'oley sheyres hapleyte. But unlike these other papers, this one was published in Israel, after the Holocaust. Thus, the reservations expressed in the pages of the *LN* over the absorption policy, whether physical or cultural, were suffused with a deep recognition of the importance of the state's existence and strength. Unlike Yiddish immigrant papers published earlier, in pre-state Israel, the *LN* struggled to preserve the identity and culture that the immigrants brought with them to Israel. It did not regard itself as responsible merely for providing the immigrants with temporary help until they became integrated and could read a newspaper in Hebrew; rather, it took upon itself the task of preserving the cultural identity of its consumers, developing it, and battling for the civil rights involved in such an enterprise. These contradictory goals are attributable to the "sheyres hapleyte consciousness" shared by the paper's editor, its writers, and its readers: they saw themselves as the last representatives of a generation and guardians of the last vestiges of a culture. Alongside the cultivation of a particular ethnic identity, the paper also cultivated in its readers a national identity: unlike the papers published in the communities of Eastern European immigrants outside of Israel, whose ability to influence official policy (American, Argentinian, or French) was quite limited, the *LN* perceived itself as a player whose battles for the advancement of Yiddish, both culturally and linguistically, represented not only the Eastern European immigrants but all the immigrants in Israel. Moreover, the *LN* journalists believed their paper to be capable of significantly influencing government institutions and their policies.

This tension between the particular ethnic identity and the collective national identity is clearly visible in the campaigns that the paper supported and sometimes even initiated and led. Beyond reporting and discussing current events in Israel—political, military, economic, social, and cultural—the paper was a platform for many unique battles. According to Rachel Rojanski, Tsanin went from unconditional support for the young state and its policies in the weekly *Ilustrirter vokhnblat* that preceded the *LN*, to battling the dominant cultural trends in Israel.[121] But a study of the issues of the *LN* suggests that Tsanin in fact maintained a certain balance between the battles he waged and his support for the state and its professed principles, including above all the principle of eligibility for Israeli citizenship for every Jew in the world. Tsanin noted on several occasions that after the destruction of the spiritual center in Poland, Israel had become the spiritual center of the Jewish people, and therefore Yiddish culture was obliged to seek and further the state's fortification.[122] In what follows, I describe Tsanin's battles alongside the support he expressed for the state in the pages of the *LN*.[123] We can decipher three main areas of battle, two of which I describe here; the third (the memory of the Holocaust) is described and discussed separately in the next chapter.

- The battle for the advancement of Yiddish culture in Israel: This included the battle to publish the newspaper as a daily and the battles against constant cutbacks and reductions of the Yiddish programming in the Israeli radio service Kol Yisrael, against declaring Yiddish a "foreign language" in Israel, against discriminatory treatment of the Yiddish theater and its actors, against discriminatory treatment of Yiddish writers in the allocation of state awards, against the exclusion of Yiddish journalists and writers from the Hebrew writers and Hebrew journalists associations, against the decree that required the "foreign" (or "non-Hebrew") press in Israel (a category that included the Yiddish press) to reserve 10 percent of every issue for Hebrew content, and against the limited allocation of paper for the printing of Yiddish literature in Israel and the government's refusal to accept funding offered by Yiddish cultural organizations in the United States for the purpose of such publications; other aspects included internal criticism of Yiddish cultural organizations and Yiddish writers in Israel and abroad for their insufficient engagement in the cause of developing Yiddish culture and fighting for its rights, as well as commitment to the cause of building a safehouse for Yiddish culture.
- The battle for the human rights of the entire population of new immigrants: This included campaigns against the alienating attitude toward immigrants at the Sha'ar Ha-'Aliya processing camp and the Haifa port

> and against the workplace discrimination against immigrants over age forty; campaigns for the creation of more jobs for immigrants; raising funds and other resources to support the gifted children of impoverished immigrant families; rallying to help Holocaust survivors who got "stuck" for many years in the absorption camps in Israel; battling against imposing partisan education and religious or antireligious indoctrination in the camps on immigrants from Islamic countries; battling against the indifference of the veteran population to the predicament in the absorption camps and the policies to which they were subjected; raising awareness of the lack of cultural institutions in the camps and recruiting Yiddish artists to perform there; battling against the hopeless bureaucracy of such state institutions as Kupot Holim (the national health care providers) and the hospitals, the public trustee, and 'Amidar (the state-owned housing company); advising immigrants on how to organize to receive public housing; and cautioning against the dire sanitary conditions in immigrant neighborhoods due to low building standards.

These campaigns, then, reflect two fields of consciousness in which the newspaper acted simultaneously: the ethnic-particular field and the broad all-national field (which also included immigrants not of Eastern European origin). In the Israeli cultural climate of the time, these two spheres were in tension with each other.

The paper's critical stance toward various political moves by the government was expressed not only in editorials or opinion columns[124] but also in many satirical sections. Most prominent among them was Tsanin's popular satirical column on current affairs, "Shabesdike shmuesn" (Shabbat conversations).[125] Other regular sections included "Der tel-oviver lets" and "A tel-oviver tip" (on which more in part 2, in the chapter on Tel Aviv) as well as regular columns of social satire and literary humoresque by Sh. Shidlovski, Dovid Eydlman, Gad Zeklikovski Yankev Noyman, Yitskhok Brat, and others.[126] From 1959, all the humorist columns and some of the satirical columns were assembled together in the weekend editions in a special page titled "Laytish gelekhter" ([idiom] A good laugh).

The *LN*'s criticism of the policy that discriminated against Yiddish and its culture in Israel, and the battles Tsanin supported or initiated and led, took place mostly in the pages of the paper. Even when Tsanin was able to recruit partners and supporters from among other Yiddish cultural organizations and his reading public and to hold actual protest events, these were invariably civilized and polite affairs. Tsanin did not aim to start a mass movement, and his protest, despite its typical rhetoric of conflict and resistance, did not evolve into radical action (such as violent demonstrations). The reason for this, as we saw, was the ideological and political partnership that Tsanin, his writers, and his readers maintained with the state institutions. So, for example, alongside the expressions of criticisms and satire, the paper featured many expressions of patriotism, identification with the state, and concern for its stability and strength: the paper rallied to raise funds from readers for the Israel Defense Forces (IDF) defense fund;[127] weekly columns described the vulnerable predicament of Jewish communities abroad in terms of their security and ethnic-religious cohesion and continuously tracked the rates of their immigration to Israel; pacifying texts by the editorial staff were published in response to scathing letters to the editor sent in by embittered immigrants; independence days were marked by the paper festively and expansively, with editorials enumerating the state's achievements in the face of challenges; a special supplement was issued to mark the state's tenth anniversary, listing all of its achievements with no mention of its failures; and a regular section, "Vos shraybt di hebreyishe prese?" (What is the Hebrew press writing?), surveyed the Hebrew press. The paper also featured sections that brought the new-immigrant reader closer to Israel, including columns by Zionist politicos (like Yitzhak Gruenbaum); a section devoted to profiles of Zionist leaders, "Perzenlekhkeytn in yishev" (Figures in the Yishuv); a section on the history and geography of the Land of Israel, "Tsi kenstu dos land?" (Do you know the land?); and a section on applied agriculture, "Grine felder" (Green fields). These columns demonstrate how the *LN*, like every modern daily newspaper, shaped a "national consciousness" through the dimensions of time and space by representing the national calendar and map.

In a private (or mostly private) paper like the *LN*, the advertisements are of paramount financial importance. Among the paper's big advertisers were commercial companies, political parties, and state institutions. The most intriguing were the ads that told the stories of groups established by 'oley sheyres hapleyte of similar professions or health predicaments,[128] and especially the *landsmanshaftn* (I return to these hometown associations in the next chapter). Advertisements for these associations were published extensively in the paper, especially in the first decade of its existence (and of the state's existence).[129] The activities of hometown associations were described in various sections of the paper (news/culture/remembrance) and also discussed in such sections as "Letters to the Editor."

"Letters to the Editor" was one of the paper's central and most vibrant sections. It featured responses to and comments on national events as well as appeals on more personal matters, typically difficulty in navigating the state bureaucracy but also expressions of distress over difficult health or financial conditions or a failed search for relatives. These letters testify to the close relations that are traditional in Yiddish culture between the intelligentsia and the masses. In 1960, one of the paper's prominent opinion journalists, Nosn Bolel, began addressing the issues raised by readers, in his column "In shpigl fun undzere leyeners briv" (In the mirror of our readers' letters). In this column, Bolel analyzed social and national questions and the ways in which the readers related to them.

Readers of the paper could express their views in other sections, too, like "Undzer fraye tribune" (Our open platform), "Shmuesn vegn ongeveytikte zakhn: Redt zikh arop fun harts [hartsn]" (Conversations about painful things: [idiom] Let it out), or sometimes under the title "Ongeveytikte fragn" (Painful questions). Outside of these regular sections, every so often the paper also published various special appeals by readers.[130] The bond between the paper and its readers was also forged in the "Missing Relatives" section, which reported on extraordinary cases in which relatives were united thanks to the newspaper. The paper also conducted polls and surveys among its readers[131] and reported on journalistic tours in the private homes of immigrants, absorption camps, and immigrant neighborhoods throughout the country. Face-to-face meetings between the paper's staff and readers were held as part of the *LN*'s event series "Lebedike tsaytung" (Living paper), mostly in Tel Aviv but also in various immigrant settlements and camps.

The closeness between the paper's editor and its readers, then, was apparent in the intimate and informal tone that characterized the Yiddish press since its inception. Tsanin's aforementioned column "Shabesdike shmuesn" was written in the form of "conversations" with the reader, and even in the paper's medical section this tone prevailed—it was titled "Meditsinishe shmuesn" (Medical conversations). As I described earlier, the paper rallied to help survivors find each other not just through classified ads in the paper (under such titles as "Ver bin ikh?, Ver zaynen mayne eltern?, Ver ken? Ver veys?"—Who am I?, Who are my parents?, Who recognizes? Who knows?) but also through Tsanin's own appeal, not in the pages of the paper, to survivor organizations and personal acquaintances in an attempt to help find missing relatives. Reunifications enabled by his efforts were covered prominently in the paper.

The *LN*'s populist stance and its appeal to the masses of the gradually consolidating Israeli society continued a long-standing tradition in the Yiddish press. This tradition was expressed in the *LN* in regular columns about workers, tradesmen, and craftsmen (Dovid Eydlman, "Hantverker in Yisroel" [Artisans in Israel]; Nosn Bolel, "Arbeter nayes" [Worker's news]) and about people living in the social and economic margins (Eydlman, "Ufgekhapte bildlekh un gasnstsenes in tel-uviv-yafo" [Brief pictures and street scenes in Tel Aviv-Jaffa] and "Der meylekh-evien af di gasn fun tel-uviv-yafo" [idiom: The great poverty in Tel Aviv-Jaffa], and the reportage columns of Y. Namdirf, pen name of the poet Yankev Fridman).

Another prominent trend was the *LN*'s appeal to women. A census held in 1961 reveals that Hebrew literacy among the female 'oley sheyres hapleyte who came in the years 1948–1954 was lower than that of the men of the same immigration:

55.8 percent of these women knew Hebrew, compared with a 94.9 percent literacy in their languages of origin.[132] The history of the Yiddish press suggests that this appeal to women was nothing new: the very first Yiddish weekly, *Kol Mevaser* (*The Heralding Voice*), published in Odesa in 1862–1873 and edited by Alexander Tsederboym, had already appealed to women and even counted women among its writers.[133] The appeal to women was driven by the ideals of enlightenment that prevailed at the time, but the paper's female readers and writers regarded the Yiddish language as important in its own right and refused to replace it with other languages that were perceived as more highbrow, like Russian, German, or Hebrew. However, these women did not develop a gender-based class consciousness. Throughout its history, the Yiddish press was completely male dominated, and the women who participated in it played marginal roles.[134] Women in the Yiddish press wrote mostly for other women.[135]

These traditional attitudes of the Yiddish press toward women did not change significantly in Israel, but historical events uniquely colored the Israeli case: feminine writing played an important role in restoring traditional gender boundaries that had become blurred during the Holocaust, in service of the burgeoning national identity.[136] Throughout the years, the *LN* published serialized novels written by women or whose protagonists were women.[137] Outside the literary realm, the appeal to women focused on their daily lives in Israel. For instance, Tsanin invited his female readers to describe how they managed to run their households under the restrictions of the austerity policy.[138] Three years later, he invited them to report on how they handled daily life in the absorption camps and immigrant housing.[139] One of the popular regular columns was "Far der froy" (For the woman, which later changed its name to "Froy un heym," Woman and home), written by Khave Levkovitsh. In addition to recipes and tips for the housewife, the column profiled legendary female figures of modern secular Jewish culture, female worker's rights leaders, and female fighters during the Holocaust. Readers—mostly women but sometimes also men—wrote in for advice on the difficulties facing families of survivors that were created after the Holocaust, sometimes in a hurried manner. Among the issues that the column addressed were motherhood in the wake of loss (how to raise a family in the absence of fundamental figures such as a mother/grandmother, starting a family at a late age, how to overcome the loss of a previous family), relationship problems (ideological and cultural differences between the couple, division of labor in the marriage when the woman joins the workforce), educational problems (how a mother was to handle raising adolescents when her own coming of age took place during the war, whether Yiddish should be spoken with the children, how to celebrate holidays when there are no memories of home), and more. Other female writers in the *LN* were Sure Lubatkin (reportage), Rokhl Faygnberg (essays), and Rivke Kviatkovski-Pinkhasik, Khaye Elboym-Dorembus, and Rivke Rus (prose).

The fact that the paper was politically unaffiliated and addressed a broad readership made it more eclectic in terms of the cultural attitudes and ideas it expressed. This was reflected, for instance, in the *LN*'s warm attitude toward Jewish tradition. The paper issued special celebratory issues on Jewish holidays, informed its readers on shabbat times and candle-lighting times, and featured a variety of columns with a distinctly traditional bent: about Jewish folklore (for instance, Gavriel Vaysman, "Di yerushe fun yidishn folklor"; Yish Khosid, "Fun altn oytser"; Gad Zaklikovski, "Reb Zalikl"; Reb 'A. Meir [M?], "Minhogim" [customs]), weekly Torah portion (Reb Khayim Karlinski, "Fun undzer eybikn oyster"), Jewish history ("Perzenlekhkeytn in der yidisher geshikhte"), and Jewish current affairs (Leyb Bayn, "Rabeyim un Khsides in Yisroel"—a series of articles about Hasidic dynasties that were revived in Israel). Holidays and special occasions of the Jewish calendar were also noted in other sections of the paper (holiday recipes in the column "For the Woman," family memoirs and literary texts about the holidays in the literary section, etc.). Thus, Jewish tradition was one of the paper's consistent themes. And its writers included several from the religious and Orthodox sectors, like the journalists Shloyme Zalman Shragai and Leyb Bayn and the author Yekhiel Granatshteyn.[140]

This connection to the Jewish past, near and far, was also expressed in the serialized novels published in the *LN*. These works addressed the distant Jewish history[141] and the time frame that began before the Holocaust and continued after it.[142] The paper also published serialized novels about the Holocaust itself (more on which in the next chapter) and translations of Hebrew novels,[143] some by the leading authors of the time (Sholem Asch, Yekhiel Yeshaye Trunk, and Yekhiel Hofer). A few of these works of fiction were published as books by the LN Press.[144] Alongside these canonical novels, from 1957 the paper also began to publish serialized sensation novels, and they too addressed different aspects of contemporary Jewish life.[145] Other novels appeared by writers known for their sensual style, like Isaac Bashevis Singer and Yitskhok Perlov.[146] The latter (like most of the serialized-novel writers) was ignored by the literary journal *DGK* (I return to this later). The appearance of the serialized novels, and especially of the serial sensation novels, in the *LN* symbolizes more than anything else the return to a life of permanence and routine by Yiddish-speaking ʿoley sheyres hapleyte after the war years, since these forms were absent from the Yiddish surviving-remnant press of the DP camps in Germany.[147]

Another example of the openness of the *LN* and its editor to all corners of Jewish culture is their sympathetic attitude toward the poet Uri Zvi Greenberg, whose works (in Yiddish or in Yiddish translation) were ignored by *DGK* throughout the 1950s and 1960s.[148] The *LN*, by contrast, published them extensively, and in general published works of literature by writers identified with the ideological right. Throughout the 1950s, the paper published a Yiddish translation of parts of the novel *Royte teg* (*Red Days*), the memoirs of the former LEHI (Loḥamei Ḥerut Israel) fighter Matityahu (Mattie) Shmuelevitz. All this, despite the fact that the harshest arguments against the revival of Yiddish culture in Israel were voiced in the pages of the right-wing newspaper *Herut*.

In addition to publishing original works of poetry and prose and Yiddish translations of works written in Hebrew, the paper's literary section ("Literatur-teater-kunst") featured reviews of works in Yiddish and in Hebrew and news related to Yiddish and Hebrew literature in Israel and abroad, including reports on visits to Israel by Yiddish authors, on the activities of Yiddish cultural organizations across the world (such as the Association of Yiddish Journalists and Writers), and on the jubilees and death anniversaries of authors. It also published pieces of memoir and folklore, noted new books published in Yiddish, and hosted discussions on such topics as the role of Yiddish literature in Israel. The literary section's first editor was A. Volf Yasny. Meylekh Ravitsh, Yitskhok Paner, and Mordkhe Yofe were among its regular writers. Tsanin himself also contributed to the literary section under the pen name Matsan or Y. Darin. Many Yiddish writers in Israel published their works in this section before publishing them as independent story compilations: Ts. Ayznman, A. Oley, Yosl Birshteyn, Shloyme Berlinski, Shloyme Varzoger, Yitskhok Perlov, Ka- Tsetnik, Shimen Kants, Rivke Kviatkovski-Pinkhasik, Avrom Karpinovitsh, Yishaye Shpigl, and others. Works describing life in Israel by the authors Khaye Elboym-Dorembus, Yekhiel Granatshteyn, and Zvi Magen (Shits) were published, as far as I know, only in the *LN* and never in books or anthologies. The paper held writing competitions and gave literary awards to Yiddish writers in Israel—in response, as I noted earlier, to the state's discrimination against Yiddish writers and journalists in the allocation of awards.[149] In publishing these serialized novels, literary reviews, and original works of literature, the *LN* contributed not only to the development of the literature but also to the livelihood of its writers.[150]

The paper rewarded its journalists financially and cultivated in them a sense of professional prestige. For staff members, the salary from the newspaper was typically their only income—only a handful made extra money editing *Yizker bikher* (memorial books). The German reparation money was tainted in their eyes, and therefore they designated it for "pure" causes such as savings for their children's education or the publishing of Yiddish books (on which more later). Their employment conditions, including their retirement and pension arrangements, were dictated by state laws and protected by the Histadrut ha'Ovdim ha'Ivriim be-Eretz Yisrael (the General Organization of Hebrew Workers in the Land of Israel) and the professional union in which they were members (and which was headed by Tsanin for several years), so that their salary was equal to that of their colleagues in the Hebrew press. As journalists at a successful newspaper with a wide distribution, they enjoyed a venerable status in Israeli society—among colleagues, advertisers, the organizers of Hebrew and Yiddish cultural events, and the public at large. The paper's staff members were also a social circle unto themselves: most of them lived close to each other (in the Yad Eliyahu neighborhood on the outskirts of Tel Aviv), and they came together for family events, holidays, and so on.[151]

The *LN*'s uniqueness in the world of the Yiddish press lay in Tsanin's intimate involvement in all of the paper's affairs and in his centralized style of management. He was the publisher, the editor in chief, a regular columnist, a reporter on culture and literature, and more. This phenomenon had no parallel among the Yiddish newspapers in Israel (most of which were affiliated with a political party and underplayed the role of the editor in chief, who in some cases even remained unnamed) or in the daily press abroad. Shmuel Yankev Yatskan (1836–1874), whom Tsanin regarded as a model, was similarly the publisher and editor in chief of his daily papers, the *Idishes tageblat* (Jewish daily news, Warsaw, 1906–1911) and *Haynt* (Today, Warsaw, 1908–1939), but he had a partner (Noyekh Finkelshteyn), and the papers he established had large editorial boards and many employees, so that his involvement in them was limited (in 1926–1928 he lived not in Warsaw but in Paris, where he founded another daily newspaper). Similarly, Avrom (Abe) Kahan (1860–1951), one of the founders of *Forverts* in New York and its editor (1903–1946),[152] also worked with a large editorial board and staff, and he himself filled only certain roles. The kind of centralization that Tsanin applied in the *LN* was not characteristic of the work culture of modern industrialized society, which is based on a complex and extensive division of labor among experts from various fields.

The tension between the ethnic-particular identity it shaped in its readers and the national identity is one of the *LN*'s main characteristics, as I have said, but unlike contemporaneous Yiddish newspapers outside of Israel, in Israel this tension took on a unique character simply by virtue of the paper's appearance in the nation-state. The efforts it invested in the process of the socialization of 'oley sheyres hapleyte into Israeli society was not accompanied by a fear of losing their Jewish-national identity but was indeed accompanied by the fear of linguistic and cultural assimilation. This fear propelled Tsanin to wage many political battles (which appear to have done the paper only good from a commercial perspective). These battles reflected an attempt to include Yiddish and its culture in the national culture that was taking shape in Israel. The justification for the existence of Yiddish in Israel, as it emerges from Tsanin's efforts in the *LN*, was therefore largely civilian in nature—namely, realizing Israel's democratic character as a pluralistic state in which different cultural sectors enjoy freedom of expression and an equal allocation of the resources designated for the cultivation of education and culture. According to Tsanin, like the Holocaust survivors themselves,

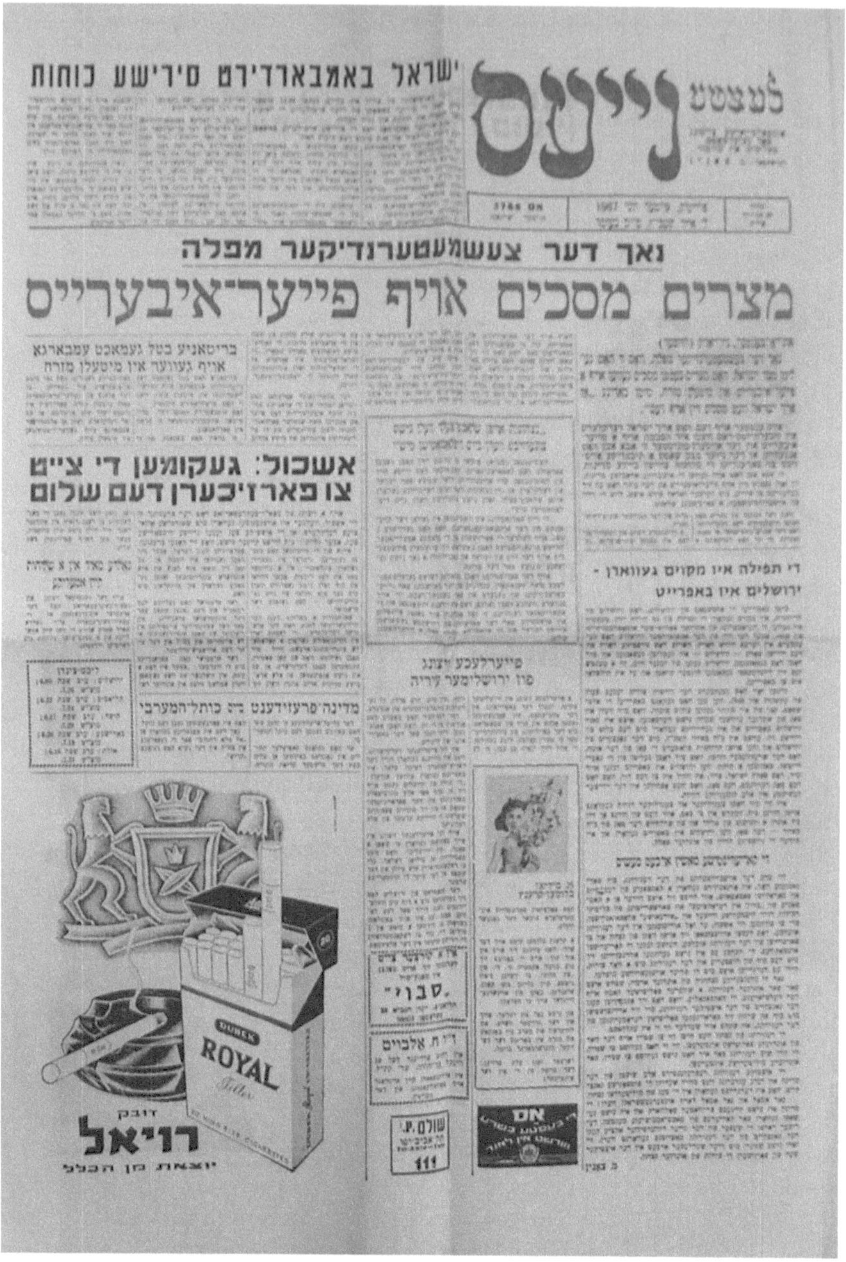
לעצטע נייעס

ישראל באמבארדירט סירישע כוחות

נאך דער צעשמעטערנדיקער מפּלה

מצרים מסכים אויף פייער־איבערייס

בריטאניע בטל געמאכט עמבארגא
אויף געווער אין מיטעלן מזרח

אשכול: געקומען די צייט
צו פארזיכערן דעם שלום

די תפילה אין מקום געווארן -
ירושלים אין באפרייט

פייערלעכע זיצונג
פון ירושלימער קריה

מדינה־פרעזידענט ביים כותל־המערבי

Letste nayes, June 9, 1967. Author's personal archive.

so too Yiddish and its culture needed a "national home," in which they could recover and thereby also strengthen Israel's democratic character.

The Literary Periodical: *Di goldene keyt* and Its Editor Avrom Sutzkever

If *Letste nayes* was targeted at the masses, the literary journal *Di goldene keyt: Fertl- yorshrift far literatur un gezelshaftlekhe problemen* (The golden chain: A quarterly of literature and social problems) belonged to the "high culture" end of the spectrum and targeted the elite of Yiddish readers in Israel and abroad. Centers of modern Yiddish culture considered important were those in which not only daily press but also "thick monthly journals" were published.[153] This type of publication, which Yiddish culture adopted from European cultures (especially Russian), was devoted primarily to cultural fields like literature, theater, philosophical thought, and visual art, as well as to education. These journals, typically monthly or quarterly, dealt with a variety of issues in these fields with as much depth as possible and addressed themselves at the working class so as to further their education. By contrast, *DGK*, as I said, was influenced by the elitist-modernist Yiddish American model and explicitly targeted the literati in Israel and especially abroad.

The first issue of *DGK* appeared in the winter of 1949. Each issue was designed to count two hundred pages.[154] The journal's very title suggests a certain basic duality that lay at its core: it was dedicated both to literature and to social issues. This duality was common among key Yiddish journals in Eastern Europe and North America (of which the most prominent was *Di Tsukunft*). Yet in the case of *DGK*, this coupling of themes appears to have resulted not from the interest of its editor, Sutzkever, in "social problems" but from a need to tread a fine line and placate the journal's financial patron—the General Organization of Hebrew Workers. That *DGK* was funded by the Histadrut was one of the paradoxes that were typical of the phenomenon of Yiddish revival in the young Israeli state. The motivation of the leaders of the Histadrut, especially Yosef Sprinzak, was not to support the development of Yiddish literature in Israel for its own sake; rather, their attitude to Yiddish was instrumental: through it, they sought to cultivate ties with its supporters and donors in the Jewish Diaspora (and especially supporters of the Histadrut in the Po'ale Zion party in America). And indeed, in an internal memo, *DGK* is described as designed for "Yiddish in the diaspora."[155] Unlike Yiddish daily press, an elitist-literary journal in Yiddish was regarded by them not as a threat to the hegemonic culture but as supporting it. Each issue of *DGK* was printed in 1,500 copies.[156] For the sake of comparison, *Moznayim*, the literary journal of the Hebrew Writers Association in Israel, which first appeared in 1929, ran a printing of 2,500 copies.[157] Sutzkever succeeded in using the resources he raised from the Histadrut in such a way that they served the goals of both sides—creating elite culture out of a conscious and explicit hegemonic position of power.[158] *DGK* gradually focused more and more on Yiddish culture and moved away from dealing with social and political problems in Israel. An important step in this direction took place after the death of Avraham Levinson (Lodzh, 1889–Tel Aviv, 1955), director of the culture and education division of the Histadrut, a translator, essayist, and journalist who was fluent in Hebrew, Yiddish, Polish, and Russian and who had been appointed as coeditor of the journal and in effect as a "content supervisor" for the Histadrut.[159] Yet even at the time of his appointment, his health was already failing, and he was unable to participate in all the activities of the editorial staff. After his death, Eli'ezer Pines held the title of deputy editor of the journal from issue no. 23 (1955) to issue no. 114 (1984). The title of editorial secretary was held successively by Noyekh Gris (issues 3–4, 1949), the writer Mendl Man (issues 23–40, 1955–1961), and Meylekh Karpinovitsh (issues 43–74, 1962–1971).[160] The last secretary, whose tenure lies outside the time frame of this study, was Aleksander Shpiglblat (issues 75–141, 1972–1995). As with the *LN* and Tsanin, *DGK*, too, was closely identified with its editor.

The editor of *DGK* placed special emphasis on the journal's tie to Israel and on the importance of the timing in which it was launched. In particular, Sutzkever mentioned on several occasions three fundamental facts: that the journal was published in Israel, that it was "born" together with the state, and that its patron was a national institution central to Israeli society and not a minor private publishing house. As patron of most of the institutions of canonical Hebrew literature, the institutional network of the Histadrut helped shape the general perception of the canonical status of the journal and its self-perception as an all-important generator of national consciousness. This is evident in the journal's self-described vision. At an event marking its two-year anniversary, Sutzkever articulated his belief that the cultural and spiritual revival was an inseparable part of the physical and national revival of the Jewish people in their homeland, since the Holocaust had occurred not merely on the physical plane but also on the cultural-spiritual plane. The Land of Israel he described in national-messianic terms of "the resurrection of the dead" and redemption, which were common in the Hebrew literature of the time, but unlike in this literature, in Sutzkever's description the goal of the state and its land is said to be the revival of Yiddish culture, which was yet another survivor of the Nazi destruction:

> When the "historian of the future" . . . once mentions DGK, he will perhaps find the journal's main importance in the fact that the golden chain was passed through the fire of the Jewish war, in the time of our third revival. . . . This was not mere ambitiousness, mere stubbornness. No, this was my deepest belief, that alongside the revival of the people and its return to the old land, the Yiddish word must also ring out. And the soaring letters, injured, scorched, carried over to us from the pyre in Europe, must find their home here, their reparation. . . . I see the greatest wonder of the land of Israel in the ongoing

> survival of the reality of the resurrection of the dead. Not in the symbolic sense, but in actual fact. It is not in the valley of death of Maydanek that the dead rose up from the grave but in the Jezreel Valley, the valley of life. . . . But the resurrection of the Jewish people in its land cannot and does not wish to amount only to a physical revival, a mere ingathering of the exiles measured and counted in numbers. . . . We must also bring over . . . the quality of the resurrection of the Jewish spirit; the cultural treasures of our great people, which have been scattered to all foreign corners. . . . *May the builders not shun these stones*. In this sacred hour, I wish to say but one short prayer: may these stones not be forgotten. . . . A nation cannot live without a yearning-of-the-soul. In Jerusalem, Jews have put up special tall ladders on their roofs, and they climb them day and night, to glimpse the captive Wailing Wall from afar. We, the writers, must also build our ladders, climb them, and look upon our eternal spirit from on high. . . . DGK, whose name we borrowed from Peretz, does not want merely to boast its name. It wants to be worthy of it.[161]

Thus, Sutzkever set a horizon for the community of Yiddish writers and researchers ("the historian of the future") as well as for the "builders" of the nation (i.e., the state's leaders). Like the idea of "kinus" (gathering) set forth by Ahad Ha'am or Bialik, who sought, each in his own way, to ground Jewish nationality and awaken it through the compilation of canonical Jewish works, Sutzkever returned to this concept of "gathering" while adapting it to the new post-Holocaust national reality. According to this renewed idea, the state was called upon to embrace not only the Holocaust survivors but also their scorched cultural treasures, which, like the survivors themselves, must also "return to life."[162] The reference to Ahad Ha'am and Bialik in this vision also casts its speaker as a new kind of cultural-national "prophet."[163]

Aleksander Shpiglblat (*DGK*'s last editorial secretary) was an active partner in constructing the story of the origin of *DGK* in Israel. Shpiglblat focused on the figure of Sutzkever himself and described him as someone who at the end of World War II had faced a crossroads.[164] According to him, Sutzkever saw no possibility of staying in Europe—not in Moscow, where he was openly embraced, and not in Poland, "where he had neither a continuation nor a beginning."[165] New York was then a popular destination for surviving Yiddish writers (many of them congregated in Paris immediately after the war but regarded it as a transitional station rather than a final destination). Sutzkever could find many advantages in New York, including YIVO (founded in his hometown, Vilna) as well as friends and acquaintances of considerable influence in the Jewish world, most notably the linguist Max Weinreich (who had also lived in Vilna). In 1947, Sutzkever consulted with Weinreich on the option of immigrating to New York, and the latter described the "old age" that had crept up on this center, as expressed in prevalent feelings of despair and resignation, of "making do" with the existing achievements and pretending that that was the best of all possible worlds.[166] In his memoirs, Shpiglblat noted that this letter from Weinreich had convinced

Sutzkever to immigrate to Israel. Like most ʻoley sheyres hapleyte Yiddish writers who came to Israel, Sutzkever was young at the time (he had just turned thirty-four).[167] The fact that his brother lived in Israel also contributed to his decision to go there. Had he wanted, Sutzkever could also have immigrated to Buenos Aires, like his close friend Shmerke Kaczerginski.[168] But in these established centers, he would have had to fight for his place within existing and largely fixed cultural organizations. So Sutzkever chose Israel even though he was aware of the resistance to Yiddish and the difficulty of publishing works in Yiddish there. According to Shpiglblat, "Sutzkever placed the emphasis on 'novelty,' and despite all the reservations, chose Israel."[169]

The novelty for him was dual—both artistic and social-institutional: "He needs to find his place within the great challenge of *ʻoley sheyres hapleyte*, to renew themselves after the catastrophe."[170] On the artistic level, the journal's innovativeness was expressed in Sutzkever's decision to publish it as a quarterly, a format that in the tradition of Yiddish publications was considered highly elitist—referring, of course, to publications for which this format was a deliberate choice by the editors and not the inevitable result of financial pressures.[171] Politically and institutionally, Sutzkever succeeded in harnessing his unique status, and indeed the heroic aura that clung to his figure in the worldwide Yiddish cultural milieu after the Holocaust, to establish the journal and ensure its continued existence.[172] He was the only Jewish poet to be published and gain a certain renown in Moscow while imprisoned in the ghetto (Vilna). His renown later led to a special plane being sent by the Soviets to rescue him from the Naroch forest, where he had fought with the partisans. Sutzkever was also one of the three Jewish witnesses called to testify in the Nuremberg trials, and certainly the most celebrated among them.[173] Thus, Sutzkever came to Israel not as an impoverished refugee but as a visionary Yiddish writer, fully aware of his mission, his status, and his abilities. According to Shpiglblat, Sutzkever was "at the time the only Yiddish writer in the world who had the spiritual and moral clout to create a journal like the DGK, which was undoubtedly a revolution on the Israeli scale."[174] He argued that Sutzkever wanted to create a journal that would be not just a continuation of the Yiddish culture that had been brutally interrupted in Eastern Europe but also new and different from this culture in important ways: a journal whose status no prior Yiddish journals had ever attained or even aspired to attain in the nation-states in which they were published, including Poland. Even in interwar Vilna, which was the symbol of the new and self-renewing Yiddish culture, where important anthologies and compilations were published, no quarterlies of this culture were ever published. The Yiddish writer Avraham Lev (who immigrated to Israel from Vilna in 1932) said of Sutzkever and his enterprise, "When Sutzkever came to Eretz Yisroel . . . he was already famous across the Jewish world. . . . We, the veteran Yiddish writers here in Israel, felt that with Sutzkever's arrival in the country we had not only received another great Yiddish poet, but thanks to him Yiddish gained in prestige and garnered respect in circles that before his arrival had been impossible to reach."[175]

Sutzkever, as I said earlier, understood that in the young Israel a Yiddish journal must not appear on the scene as a marginal and minor project forced to beg for alms for its survival. This was a condition he had set for establishing the journal—that a national institution would sponsor it. This was in contrast to many other figures in the Yiddish cultural scene in Israel who were not in a position to set any such conditions. Another description of the journal's unique and central status in Israel was provided by another veteran advocate of Yiddish culture in Israel, the journalist and editor of *Nayvelt*, Daniel Leybl, a member of Left Poʿale Zion and later of Mapam (he immigrated to Israel in 1924): "DGK has lifted the ban on the Yiddish word printed in Israel. While Yiddish newspapers, books and collections have appeared before it, they have been published by the opposition [of the Yiddish world], and therefore also bore the seal of marginality, lack of acceptance. DGK has removed that seal. It is published by the Histadrut, through the power that is now, more than ever before, the embodiment of Eretz Yisroel, of Israel. And that is no small feat."[176]

Sutzkever, as we saw, emphasized the importance of the fact that the journal had been "born" together with the state. Various aspects of this affinity were apparent in the content of the journal's issues: until 1967, the anniversaries of the state and of the journal were marked together, and it published articles (translated from Hebrew) by leaders and politicians,[177] marked national events,[178] and published Yiddish translations of canonical works of Hebrew literature.[179] Nonetheless, it is evident that the journal's focus was neither on the social and political issues of daily life in Israel nor on Hebrew literature. These themes were present mostly in its early years, after which they receded gradually (and then drastically after 1973). Their appearance in the pages of *DGK* can be explained as a means of pleasing the target audience of the journal's patron, and not as expressing Sutzkever's genuine interest in Hebrew literature and the problems of the budding Israeli society. His negotiations with the Israeli establishment about the status of Yiddish in Israel (which he conducted in his capacity as chairman of the Association of Yiddish Journalists and Writers in Israel and not as editor of the journal)[180] found no echoes in the pages of *DGK*. The journal's main interest was in Yiddish literature and especially the finest achievements of this literature. Sutzkever contended repeatedly that Yiddish literature would be judged by the quality of its works: "In my view, Yiddish literature is, above all else, quality. So it was in the Jewish community in Warsaw and so it was in Vilna, and what remains from those communities, and what remains in terms of literature of the period in Spain, which we now call the golden age—is quality."[181] The quality of the journal was evident also in the linguistic purity that Sutzkever fastidiously maintained (among other things, avoiding the use of words borrowed from German) and in the careful application of YIVO's rules for proper spelling.[182] In this it differs from most of the journals I examined for this study, which were not similarly meticulous in matters of language. *DGK*'s high standard made it a coveted and prestigious platform for Yiddish writers in Israel and across the world. In Israel, writers who had abandoned Yiddish for Hebrew returned to write in Yiddish, and writers who had never before (or hardly ever) written in Yiddish began to write in it because of their desire to participate in the journal.[183]

Alongside its treatment of the various facets of Israeli nationality, the journal also emphasized the global nature of Yiddish and its culture by noting the home city rather than the place of residence of each contributing writer. This convention first started in the monthly *Di Tsukunft*, and it helped establish the journal as the metaphorical meeting place of an "imagined community" whose writers were scattered across many different cities in a transnational world. This was an expression not of antinational sentiments but of the transnational dimension of the community of consumers and creators of Yiddish culture. This aspect in particular was underscored by the column "Kultur Nayes" (Cultural news), which first appeared in issue no. 42 (1962) and which surveyed cultural events not only in Israel but across the world; reported on award receptions, birthdays, deaths, and death anniversaries (*yortsayt*) of writers and other Yiddish cultural figures all over the world; noted visits to Israel by famous Yiddish writers and actors; and published "reception" articles and reports from literary events and parties held in their honor. The Yiddish cultural community in Israel gathered several times a year in Tel Aviv at big literary events. Functioning as a substitute of sorts for the extended family that many of its members had lost, the community came together to celebrate anniversaries, awards, birthdays, private memorials, and collective memorial days.

The works and the writers published in the journal make up the "canon" of modern Yiddish literature, which the editor sought to define and establish. Special issues were devoted to the writers Y. L. Peretz (no. 10, 1951), Dovid Pinski (no. 12, 1952), and Sholem Aleichem (no. 34, 1959), whose works made important contributions to the shaping of the national identity among the consumers of modern Yiddish culture. Conspicuously absent from this act of establishing a canon is the writer regarded as the father of this literature, Mendele Moykher Sforim, who was known for his dissenting attitude toward the national sentiment and the national movement. *DGK* gave extensive coverage to cultural activities that took place in the ghettos and published works written during the Holocaust and in the Soviet Union. A small publishing house established by Sutzkever, also called Di goldene keyt, helped establish the canon of new Yiddish literature written in Israel.[184] This press partnered with the Y. L. Peretz Press to publish the most important and comprehensive anthology ever issued in Yiddish of works of

Yiddish writers murdered in the Soviet Union—*A shpigl af a shteyn* (A mirror on a stone).[185] As Israel became a center of Yiddish book publications, the column "Naye bikher" (New books) began to appear (starting in issue no. 28, 1957), featuring a list of new Yiddish titles published in Israel and abroad, as well as select Hebrew books (the noting of new Hebrew books being based effectively on those books that came into Sutzkever's hands). Yet over time, as I noted, the column turned to survey mostly Yiddish titles and translations of them into Hebrew and other languages. In 1965, the journal raised money from donors to award an annual prize for the best literary works published in it.

Given the journal's elitist character, it is unsurprising to find that it accorded special place to the Yiddish department established at the Hebrew University of Jerusalem.[186] It published speeches delivered at the department's inauguration event in 1951, lectures from conferences hosted by the department, and the words of speakers at an event held by the department in 1963 to mark Sutzkever's fiftieth birthday, attended by the then president, Zalman Shazar. In the column "Forshungen un materyaln tsu der geshikhte fun der yidisher shprakh un literatur" (Studies and material for the history of Yiddish and its literature), which began to appear in issue no. 46 (1963), scholars from the department and from other research institutions published studies and documents. In addition to publishing original works of literature—*DGK*'s aspiration was to publish works of Yiddish writers from across the world, including Yiddish writers who remained in Poland, but in practice most of the original works it published were by writers from Israel—the journal published the correspondences of writers, photocopies of manuscripts, and book reviews.

Another Sutzkever project was the establishment and encouragement of a group of young Yiddish writers, Yung-yisroel (Young-Israel).[187] Sutzkever created this group and was its patron,[188] despite being the same age as its members (or just a few years older than the younger ones among them). The fact that he had come to Israel shortly before them (in 1947) made him someone to whom writers turned when they arrived. The prose writers in this group included Tsvi Ayznman, Yosl Birshteyn, Shloyme Varzoger, and Avrom Karpinovitsh. The poets were Rivke Basman, Moyshe Gurin, Binyomin Hrushovski (Harshav), Moyshe Yungman, Rokhl Fishman, and Avrom Rintsler.

Sutzkever connected these young writers,[189] almost all of whom were 'oley sheyres hapleyte (Birshteyn and Fishman were the only exceptions), encouraged them to write, and published their works in *DGK* from the first issue (1947) until 1953 (after which the writers of the group began to appear in *DGK* independently). Being published in such a prestigious platform was not at all an obvious opportunity for young Yiddish writers in the early 1950s. Their attempts to get published were often met with responses like the following one written by the editor of *Di Tsukunft*, N. B. Minkof, to the group member Tsvi Ayznman after the latter had sent him several works he hoped to publish in the literary monthly: "We are beset by disaster—one by one, important artists of the written word are passing away. This forces us to change almost every issue at the very last minute. The jubilees of older writers also require that we give them the attention they deserve. All this makes our situation difficult. It is especially difficult with respect to stories. Unfortunately, we are unable to publish two stories in each issue, as we had originally planned."[190]

Minkof expressed great interest in the group's activity and even offered to support their own independent journal financially,[191] but he was hard put to find room to publish their works in his own eminent journal. Sutzkever helped the members of the group not only organizationally and financially, in Israel and in the Yiddish centers abroad, but also literarily and linguistically. So, for example, he wrote to Ayznman after agreeing to publish a story that the latter had sent him ("A velt arum broyt un tusker"—A world around bread and sugar, published in issue no. 11), "You need to read more quality prose in Yiddish: Kulbak, Opatoshu, Bergelson, Der Nister. Immerse yourself in the richness and musicality of the Yiddish tongue."[192] This nurturing attitude of an experienced writer toward young Yiddish writers was itself a rarity. The leading Yiddish writers of the time did not live in Israel. The few who came to Israel (Asch, Manger, Pinski, and Shneur) did not live there for long and came in their old age. They did not regard themselves, as Peretz had in his time, as the secular-modern "Rebbes" of a young generation of writers (i.e., as representing the literary establishment). And mostly, they were no longer physically well enough to play this role even if they had wanted to. This is how a member of Yung-yisroel described the feeling among the young writers: "We wander around, as if lost. None of the veteran writers give to us of their experience, of their teaching, which are so important to us."[193] In founding Young-Israel, Sutzkever had become a "literary establishment," whose roles included the nurturing of young literary creation.

Sutzkever was the one who gave the group its name, at its first gathering, in Kibbutz Yagur in October 1951. The name suggests his intention to create a linkage and perhaps even a continuity between these young writers and such literary groups as Di yunge (the Young, New York, 1907 and on), Yung-yidish (Young-Yiddish, Lodzh, 1919 and on), and especially Yung-vilne (Young-Vilna, Vilna, 1929 and on), of which Sutzkever had been a member and which was considered the last important literary group to be established on Polish soil. Young-Israel, then, was created out of Sutzkever's attraction to high culture and hegemonic status and not out of opposition to the dominant Hebrew culture. The members of the group similarly displayed no revolutionary spirit: "I like to drink from quiet springs, the strong current might wash me away," Ayznman said of himself.[194] "I am not an activist of revolutions and I hate revolutions," Yosl Birshteyn claimed.[195] Like the Young-Vilna members, the members of Young-Israel put forth no common platform, whether literary, political, or ideological.[196] But was the option of distancing themselves from social and political battles, which had been available to the group of young writers in pre-Holocaust Vilna, still available to the Yiddish writers in Israel? Criticism of their stance was quick to come: as early as 1952, A. M. Kokhav sought to "shatter the illusion" that Sutzkever had created in his speech at the gathering in Yagur, that a new generation of Yiddish writers had emerged in Israel.[197] The writer argued that this generation had evolved in Poland, and Israel was merely enjoying the fruits. Thus, if Sutzkever was interested in the genuine development of Yiddish writers in Israel in the future, he should fight for the conditions that would make that possible. Three years later, in 1955, the editor of the *LN*'s literary section, Yasny, pondered whether the works of Young-Israel were in fact new and young.[198] His answer was that novelty is not the result of an effort to present a young appearance; rather, its hallmark is the act of disrupting what is old and calcified in the cultural and social life. Yasny compared the young Yiddish writers to those from Tlomackie 13 in Warsaw and argued that the members of Young-Israel were closed off in the world of their own literary works and sheltering under the wings of their "guardian" instead of being active in the writers and journalists association and influencing the general Israeli society. With these words, Yasny posited the Warsaw tradition as a fitting model for a new generation of Israeli Yiddish writers and as an alternative to the Vilna model presented by Sutzkever. These criticisms of Sutzkever for distancing himself from the problems of society and cultural policy in 1950s Israel became more severe and more desperate in 1967 following the drastic drop in Yiddish speakers and consumers of Yiddish culture.[199] Tsanin, for example, wrote this critique:

> The journal is too academic. It is a journal for the intelligentsia, the select few, and does not reach everyone it ought to reach. It needs to come down from the Olympus. Of course it would be good if DGK could afford the luxury of continuing to sustain the same academic level it has thus far sustained. But we are living in a special era: just as every Jew in Israel, uniformed or non-uniformed, is a soldier, so each and every one of us must be a culture-soldier and must remember that the places of Jewish settlement across the world have gone empty over the years and are waiting for someone to nourish them. Thus, we must nourish them mostly with Yiddish. For Yiddish is [not just a language but] a way of life, and in any community you enter you will see that wherever there are Yiddish speakers they are the ones who sustain the life, sustain society, maintain the connection with Israel.[200]

Yung-yisroel was not the only project spearheaded by Sutzkuver that expressed his complex perception of the tension between the continuity of Yiddish culture and its severance from its past. As in the case of other Yiddish journals and newspapers published in Israel, the journal's name itself, *DGK*, also implies a connection with the modern Yiddish culture of Eastern Europe. But this name is especially laden with layers of meaning that were created in each of the versions of the play *Di goldene keyt* (*The Golden Chain*) by Y. L. Peretz, from which the journal takes its name. The play is one of the most well-known and influential works of modern Yiddish culture and has become a prototype of the apocalyptic theme in Yiddish literature.[201] In Sutzkever's works, the play makes repeated appearances: in his book *The Vilna Ghetto*, he wrote that as the literary director of the ghetto theater he chose to include in the program of the first performance a part of the play *The Golden Chain*.[202] The long poem he wrote before leaving Poland after the Holocaust, "Tsu poylin,"[203] ends with an excerpt from the play. In this poem Sutzkever reckons with his own personal and the national relationship with Poland, its culture, and its literature. Its ending suggests a movement toward the Jewish cultural roots and a disengagement from the resources of the foreign culture, which had previously been close to the poet's heart and from which he had now distanced himself permanently.[204] According to Shpiglblat's description,[205] the idea to name the journal after this play came to Sutzkever as he stood over Peretz's grave at the Warsaw Jewish Cemetery, which was his symbolic last stop in Poland. On the tomb where he is buried, that "secular, Jewish monument" known as Ohel Peretz, is etched the sentence from Reb Shloyme's monologue in the play: "Mir shtoltse, shabes-yontevdike-yidn" (We, proud Jews, Jews of Sabbath, festive Jews).[206]

Peretz wrote the play *The Golden Chain* in Yiddish while simultaneously developing an earlier version in Hebrew. In each version, he offered a different ending, one pessimistic and the other optimistic.[207] By adopting the name of the play as the name of his journal, Sutzkever (deliberately or not) effectively adopted the fundamental tension it addresses: between innovation and tradition, between severing the chain and renewing it, between a pessimistic stance and an optimistic stance that identifies the possibility of the chain, the dynasty's continuation.[208] This tension takes on special meaning in the dynamic between the Jewish languages—Hebrew and Yiddish—and all the more so in light of the fact that the Yiddish journal is published in a country whose official language is Hebrew. Niger, the leading Yiddish literary critic in the (free) world of those days, argued in 1949 that Sutzkever chose this name for the journal in order to give the false impression that the attitude toward Yiddish in Israel had changed for the better.[209] Two years later, Niger retracted this position and declared that *DGK*'s appearance was a blessing both for Hebrew literature and for Yiddish literature in Israel.[210] But even in this article, Niger treated the two languages as adversaries and did not anticipate the possibility that they would share a common fate of cultural and linguistic discontinuity.

The tension between these two poles—continuity and severance, the "life" or "death" of Yiddish and its modern culture, the physical aspect of returning

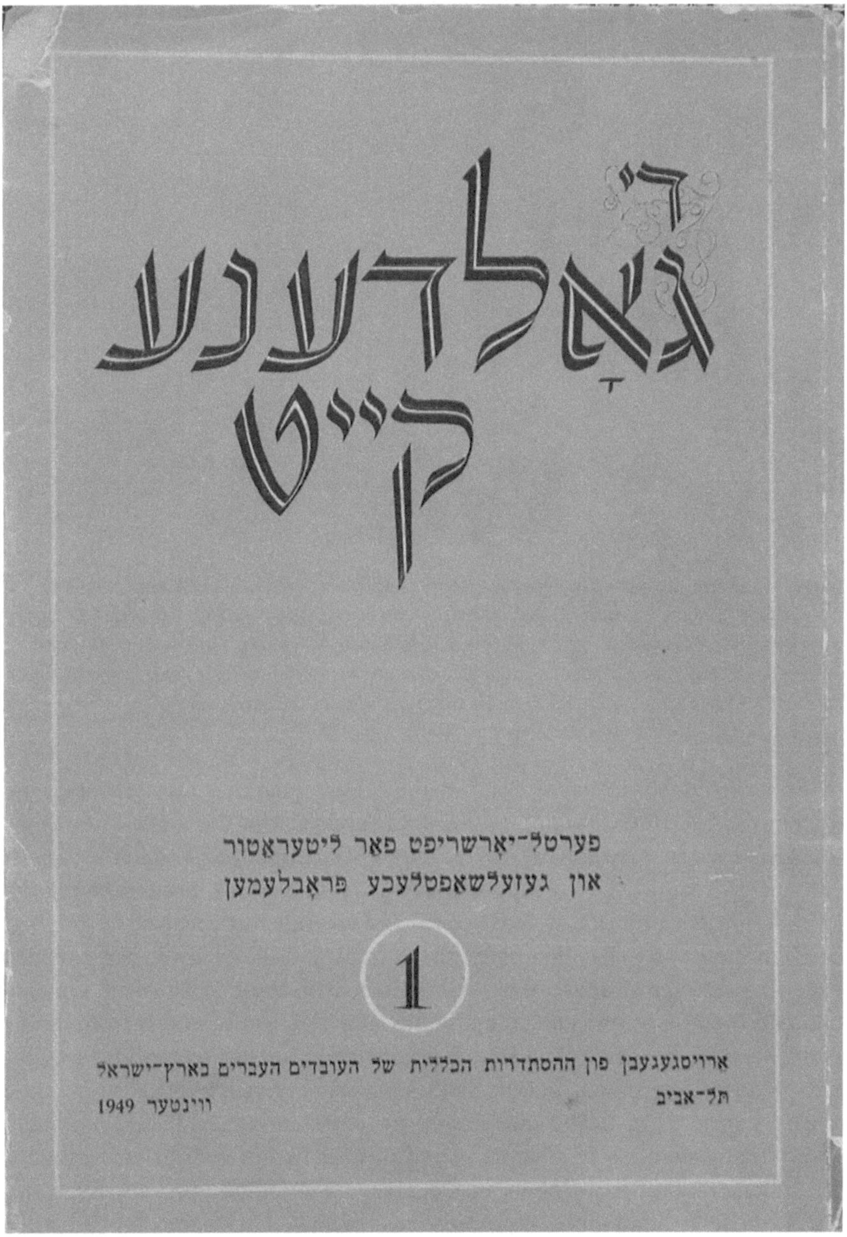

The journal's first issue, Tel Aviv, 1949. Author's personal archive.

Inaugural gathering of the Yung-yisroel group, October 26, 1951, Kibbutz Yagur. *Standing, from the right*: Moyshe Gurin, Tsvi Ayznman, Benjamin Harshav, Avrom Rintsler. *Seated, from the right*: Mendl Man, Avrom Karpinovitsh, Avrom Sutzkever, Yitskhok Paner (guest of the group), Shloyme Varzoger. *Seated behind them*: Peysekh Binetski (another guest), Yosl Birshteyn, Moyshe Yungman. Gnazim Institute, Ayznman Archive, 394.

to life versus life's spiritual aspect, the immortality guaranteed by art versus the present-day social and ideological life—was prevalent in the many discussions that took place in the pages of *DGK*, at the events it organized, and in the various enterprises it launched and supported. In 1964, in a special issue marking the journal's fiftieth anniversary, Sutzkever noted the difficulty involved in standing between these two poles: "Founding the journal, and especially its early annals, were also, in a sense, a war: war with despair, with those in Israel who openly declared the demise of Yiddish and in any case the demise of literature in our mother tongue."[211] *DGK*, therefore, was an attempt not just to continue a tradition of quality literary journals in Yiddish but also to renew it. It did so at a time when the majority of creators and consumers of this culture had been murdered, and a final generation of creators reared in Eastern Europe was struggling to rehabilitate itself after the Holocaust. Sutzkever's ambitiousness, his optimism, and his belief in his ability and power were expressed in his decision to establish and maintain the journal in Israel, as an integral part of its national culture. According to Sutzkever, the raison d'être of Yiddish in Israel was the rehabilitation and cultivation of the avant-garde forces in Jewish high culture, as well as the advancement of modern Jewish culture in general, of which Israeli culture, in his eyes, formed part. But Sutzkever was surely well aware of the signs that suggested the inability of Yiddish to be received as a national language and culture in Israel, and of the rifts that opened up between Jewish culture and Israeli culture. Even though the journal continued to present itself as an inseparable part of the national establishment up until the Six-Day War, it seems that the two categories featured in its title, "literature" and "society," gradually became more and more removed from one another. From the 1960s and on, the journal became increasingly focused on the world of Yiddish literature and its high culture. This world had become a part of the past more than it was part of the present, and it took place mostly in the pages of the journal and not in any given country or society.

The Party Monthly: *Lebns fragn* and Its Editor Y. Artuski [Yisokher Aykhnboym]

Lebns fragn: Sotsialistishe khoydesh-shrift far politik, virtshaft un kultur (Life questions: A socialist monthly for politics, economics, and culture) was launched in 1951.[212] This monthly journal was the mouthpiece of the Bund organization in Israel, which operated under the name Arbeter ring (the Labor Alliance), after the main Jewish workers' organization in the United States. The various ideological institutions and political parties in Israel that produced the Yiddish press (from Herut to the Israeli Communist Party, Maki) did so from "linguistic utilitarianism," as a means to reach a wide readership, typically in the form of weekly or monthly journals.[213] *Lebns fragn* (*LF*) was chosen here to represent the ideological journals (journals of movements or parties) that were published in Yiddish in Israel because of its ideological "linguistic loyalty" to the language and its culture. The members of the Bund saw Yiddish and its culture not just as a means of mass communication but as an end. In this, the *LF* differed from all the ideological press in Israel, including the weeklies *Nayvelt*, published by the Po'ale Zion Left party,[214] and the Communist Party's *Fray-yisroel: Demokratishe vokhnshrift far politik, virtshaft un kultur* (Free-Israel: Democratic weekly on politics, economics, and culture).[215] Even when news about the murder of Yiddish writers in the Soviet Union began to appear in the Yiddish press across the world and in Israel, between the end of 1952 and 1954, no word of protest was published in the pages of *Fray-yisroel* that might have indicated a linguistic loyalty to Yiddish and its culture.

A second reason for choosing the *LF* for this study is the Bund's traditional opposition to Zionism, the ideological position that became its most salient characteristic among the Jewish and Israeli public. This opposition raises the question: Why was this branch of the movement in the Zionist nation-state established in the first place? Studying the pages of the *LF* reveals that the anti-Zionist ideas of the worldwide Bund movement underwent significant changes and allows us to shed light on the ideological variety that characterized the Israeli public, alongside the linguistic variety; it also describes the forces that objected to this variety and ultimately quashed it.

The two movements of Jewish national revival, the Bund and Zionism, were born, as we know, as Jewish responses to the rise and spread of nationalism in Eastern Europe and in response to the economic and social changes that characterized the transition to an industrialized society, changes that severely worsened the material, social, and civil conditions of the nineteenth-century Eastern European Jews.[216] In 1897, the year in which the First Zionist Congress was held in Basel, the Bund's founding convention was held in Vilna (Der algemeyner arbeter-bund fun rusland un poyln [The General Union of Jewish Workers in Russia and Poland]; at the movement's fourth assembly, in May 1901, the name was changed to Der algemeyner yidisher arbeter-bund in lite, poyln un rusland [The General Union of Jewish Workers in Lithuania, Poland, and Russia]).[217] The differences between the solutions that these two movements proposed were immediately evident: whereas Zionism saw the establishment of a nation-state (with Hebrew as its language and culture) as an answer to the discriminatory policy toward Eastern European Jews in economics and civil rights, the Bund proposed a social-economic battle by Jewish workers in the local political arena alongside their non-Jewish comrades.[218] According to Frankel's description, the Bundist idea was shaped as an answer to changing needs and challenges in environments that moved dynamically between the pole of the Jewish-ethnic identity—an identity that was only partial in light of the Bund's rivalry with broad sectors of Jewish society (the religious Jews, the Zionists, and the capitalists)—and the socialist-internationalist pole, from which the Bundists also stood apart because of their basic opposition to identifications based on religion and nationality.[219] Thus, the Bund represented a uniquely blended stance of "ethnic-socialism,"[220] which combines the universal class identity on the one hand with a special sensitivity to the predicament of the Jewish worker on the other. The Bund started out in Russia as an organization that called on a thin stratum of leaders from among the (Russian-speaking) revolutionary intelligentsia to do consciousness-raising work, through education and propaganda, among small groups of workers. But a decisive shift took place in the organization as early as the late nineteenth century. The center of its activity moved to Poland, and the organization began to address itself directly to the proletariat, with a call to organize its members to advance collective demands for improved labor conditions, for the right to strike, and for self-protection. The shift from an elitist movement of individuals to a mass movement was made possible by the adoption of Yiddish and its advanced secular culture as the common ethos.[221] The class consciousness and organized activity were shaped and expressed in the movement's press, worker group activities (*Arbeter-krayzlekh*), women's activities, a network of schools (TSYSHO, mentioned earlier), a youth movement (Tsukunft [Future] and SKIF—Sotsiyalistisher kinder-farband [Socialist Children's Union]), a sports association (Morgnshtern), a health-education institution (Medem-sanatorye), public libraries, and reading rooms, and also through an anthem, a flag, and a culture particular to the movement.[222] Support for the Bund reached its height in Poland in the mid-1930s in the face of a significant deterioration in the financial situation and personal security of Poland's Jews. The Bund's foremost achievement as a political movement occurred when it succeeded in converting its broad support into votes, in the 1938–1939 elections for local councils. It had particular success in the large Jewish communities (Warsaw, Lodzh, Vilna, Lublin, and Bialystok).[223] The Bund not only perceived itself as representing the Jewish public in Poland but in fact did so on the eve of this public's annihilation.

One of the Bund's central and most well-known principles is the idea of *doikayt* (literally, "here-ness"), according to which Jews should focus on bettering the conditions of their lives in the present and in the place in which they presently live—that is, in the independent and multinational Poland, where a democratic regime would guarantee civil equality for the country's ethnic minorities and the freedom to maintain their unique culture alongside the hegemonic national culture. Applying the idea of doikayt in the United States helped many Bund members move from the proletariat to the lower middle class and accordingly to move toward the pole of the religious-ethnic (Jewish) and national (American) identity or join the local socialist parties and forgo their old religious-ethnic identity. The Bund in the United States was thus primarily a social, cultural, and educational organization and not a contender in the political field. The Holocaust, in which were murdered 90 percent of Poland's Jews (among whom the Bund was highly popular), and the founding of Israel determined the future of the organization.

In July 1950, several activists gathered in a carpentry shop in south Tel Aviv and decided to officially launch a Bund branch (Arbeter ring, "workmen's circle") in Israel. This moment was preceded by more than three decades of social and ideological activity in pre-state Israel. The founder of the Bund in Israel was the baker Ben-Zion "Bentsl" Tsalevitsh, and in his memoirs he described his activities before the state's establishment and after it.[224] According to his account, before the establishment of the state his activism consisted in raising class consciousness among the baking workers, organizing them in labor unions, and strengthening their political power. In 1940–1941, he began to devote himself to another mission—disseminating Yiddish literature and press in Israel. Yiddish books and newspapers were sold at a kiosk he opened for this purpose in Tel Aviv. In 1943, after two years of operation, the kiosk was arsoned, and the business moved into his home. The Tsalevitshs' home, on Basel Street (of all places!) in Tel Aviv,[225] became a point of sale for Yiddish books from all over the world, and many packages went out from there to the Bund members and Yiddish writers, actors, and culture activists in the DP camps across Europe and the Soviet Union.

After the establishment of the state, many Bundists began arriving from Poland and the DP camps as part of the mass migration. Their arrival changed the scope of the Bund's operation in Israel, which until then had counted only thirty members. Their decision to launch an official branch in Israel was approved by the organization's organizing committee in New York, and Yisokher Aykhnboym (underground name: Y. Artuski or "khaver [comrade] Oscar"), who had settled in Paris after the war, was sent to Tel Aviv to set up the new center.[226] This approval by the movement did not undo its basic opposition to Israel and Zionism, which was noted officially at the 1947 world congress of the Bund in New York.[227] With Artuski's arrival in Tel Aviv in 1951, the organization grew quickly, and more groups were established across the country (Haifa, Beer-Sheva, Bat Yam, the Krayot, and more). That same year, the Bund held its first nationwide congress in Tel Aviv, where the founding of the Israel branch was officially declared and its mouthpiece, the monthly journal *Lebns fragn*, was launched with Artuski as its editor (he edited the journal until his sudden death in 1971). At the second nationwide congress, held in 1954, there were fifty-two representatives of new groups from across the country. In Tel Aviv the movement founded four professional cooperatives for immigrants (carpentry, printing, weaving, and sewing) and thus enabled immigrants whom the absorbing institutions considered "too old" to work (over forty); it also established a loan fund for immigrants. The organization moved between various small offices in Tel Aviv until settling, on August 24, 1957, in its permanent home, purchased in the center of Tel Aviv, at 48 Kalischer Street, thanks to the support of the friends of the Bund in Israel and abroad.

The arrival in Israel of workers from Eastern Europe in the state's first years and the vigorous activity of the local branch of the Bund with and for this population brought about a change in the attitude of the international Bund toward Israel.[228] At its third world congress, held after the Holocaust, in Montreal in 1955, the movement approved the declaration that precisely because it is an independent Jewish nation-state, Israel stands to play a positive role in the life of world Jewry. The movement continued to oppose the principle of *Kibbutz Galuyot* (the ingathering of the exiles)—that is, the view of Israel as the exclusive "homeland" of all Diaspora Jews—and held that wherever Jews live, including in Israel, there they should fight for a just socialist society, for the modern-secular Jewish individual, and not for "the Jewish place." Nonetheless, some members and leaders of the group still held anti-Zionist views. The reasons that brought about this significant change in less than a decade (the 1947 decision) are clear: the Israeli Arbeter ring (AR) grew at an impressive rate during these years relative to other centers of the movement worldwide. In the United States, as noted earlier, many of the members were no longer of the working class, and their resources were increasingly invested in supporting an aging community and less in educational and cultural activities (in Argentina, Mexico, Australia, and Canada, the Bund's activity was still mostly focused on education). Israel, by contrast, received a big wave of Eastern European immigrants, mostly young, who even before the war had belonged to the working class. Their large number relative to the receiving population made them a social and political force of considerable potential in the political arena. And indeed, the Israeli Bund still saw itself throughout the 1950s as a political organization and sought to become the representative of the organized workers of Eastern European origin.

Its efforts to do so reached a height in 1959, when the Bund ran as a party in the elections to the fourth Knesset, hoping to repeat its political success in Poland on the eve of World War II. The platform of the Israeli Bund party reflected the unique and advanced combination of the traditional Bundist ideology with the new global, Jewish, and Israeli reality. Yiddish and its secular culture featured in it prominently.[229] But the fate of the Bund party was like that of other immigrant parties that ran for election that year (like United Immigrants of North Africa, headed by David Ben Harush, who was one of the leaders of the 1959 Wadi Salib riots in Haifa)—it did not cross the electoral threshold for entering the Knesset.[230] This stinging failure discouraged the activists, and the party disbanded. The electoral result reveals that, like the Jewish voting patterns in the United States, so too in Israel, Bund members, including those most loyal to the movement, tended to vote for the general parties (from Mapai leftward—Mapam and later Ratz and Meretz), a pattern that expressed their identification with Israel and their aspiration to belong to it and not act against it in an institutional or organized way, despite their profound, heightened, and often vocal awareness of its mistakes and sins. According to the testimony of Yitskhok Luden, the *LF*'s second and last editor (1971–2014), the voting for Mapai was driven by fear of the sanctions that were imposed on whoever was exposed as having voted for a party other than the ruling party.[231]

The *LN* was the last secular Yiddish daily to be published in the world. The *LF* was the last publication of the international Bund movement (and also the last Yiddish journal to be published in Israel). Israel thus marks the closing chapter of Yiddish secular journalism. Incidentally, both papers were named after papers published in Poland—in the case of the *LF*, a Bund publication, edited by Vladimir Medem.[232] In the introduction to the first issue, Artuski presented the monthly as the direct spiritual heir of this earlier paper: "This is a new journal in Israel. . . . But it is not new in the annals of the Jewish people. Our paper is the spiritual continuation of the glorious workers' movement in Russia, Lithuania, and Poland which no longer exists, which contributed golden chapters to the book of the struggle for Jewish and human liberation. It is the continuation of the erstwhile *LF* and *Folktsaytung*."[233]

If the *LN* sought to continue the tradition of the daily Yiddish press in Warsaw, which addressed a wide readership, the *LF* sought to continue the Warsaw Bund press, which addressed itself to the Jewish working class and aimed to help it evolve into a conscious and organized class. Unlike in Poland, in Israel the *LF* was published with no state censorship, but not without disruption: on the journal's back cover, the editor in chief was noted as Bentsl Tsalevitsh, even though the de facto editor was Artuski. On the journal's fifteenth anniversary, Artuski explained that Tsalevitsh was declared the official editor to enable the journal's publication.[234] The Israeli Ministry of Interior (which was in charge of press-related licensing) required the editor of a journal to be a certified academic or professional journalist. Artuski met neither requirement: his university studies in Moscow had been cut short after he was accused of holding anticommunist views, and Yiddish journalists were not accepted in those years into the Association of Hebrew Journalists and thus could not enjoy the privileges that attended this official status. As a matter of fact, Tsalevitsh did not meet these requirements either, but he was a veteran resident of Israel and a member of the Workers' Council of the Tel Aviv Municipality. The bureaucratic help that made the journal's publication possible came from an unexpected direction and constituted one more paradox in the long chain of paradoxes that characterized the existence of Yiddish in Israel in general and of the Bund in Israel in particular. It came from Moshe Shapira, the minister of interior, who, despite being affiliated with the Mizraḥi movement, was familiar with the Bund's activity in Eastern Europe and respected it, and was also familiar with Tsalevitsh's social activism; he approved him as the *LF*'s editor and thus enabled the journal's publication.[235] Ironically, just as *DGK*, which advocated Yiddish as a language of culture, was published thanks to the Histadrut, so too the *LF*, which advocated Yiddish as a secular and socialist culture, was published thanks to a member of the Zionist-religious party. After Tsalevitsh's death in 1962, Artuski was officially named editor, until his own death in 1971.

As an immigrants' paper and as a paper of immigrants who had found a home, its position was especially complex: unlike the *LN* and *DGK*, the *LF* was vocally and firmly opposed to a national identity based in religion. In keeping with the tradition of the Bund, which had developed in a multinational environment (in the Russian Empire and later in the independent Poland), in Israel, too, the journal called for a separation of religion from the state and for a strengthening of democratic government and civil rights (primarily the freedom of expression in all languages), to allow for the development "from the bottom up" of a multicultural Israeli identity. The ideological line that Artuski articulated and advanced in the pages of the journal was that the national idea, which he accepted (that is, the existence of a secular-Israeli nation-state), ought to be separated from the principles of Zionism, which he rejected.[236] He argued that Israel's existence should have a socialist rather than capitalist foundation and that its national languages should be Hebrew, Yiddish, and Arabic. Artuski was not only the journal's editor but also one of its prominent writers. The editorials he signed with his familiar pseudonym (Y. Artuski), but he also regularly published opinion pieces and columns under other pen names (including Ben Yankev, Yod-Alef, L. Kestner, Y. Samter, and Y.S.). In its first twenty years, in addition to articles about Israeli daily events in the domains of economics, security affairs, and education, the journal featured articles by writers from all over the world, but mostly from Israel, discussing a variety of historical and current material about the Bund; and the final pages of each issue were a platform for the community of the journal's readers—featuring, among others, the column "Fun organizatsioneln lebn" (From the life of the organizations), which detailed the AR's social and cultural activity, news about visits from abroad by friends of this community, letters to the editor, a "Missing Relatives" section, family announcements (birth, marriages, deaths), and a financial donations section.

Of course, the *LF* also dealt with Yiddish culture: discussions about its status in Israel and abroad, as well as reports on the activities of local and international Yiddish organizations and on international congresses. The journal featured original works of literature—poetry and prose—by Israeli Yiddish writers, both veteran (like Yosef Papiernikov and Avrom Lev) and new (Yitskhok Perlov, Yosef Noyman, Y. D. Mitlpunkt, D. Zakalik, A. M. Fuks, Levi Papiernikov, Gad Zaklikovski, Rivke Kviatkovski-Pinkhasik); memoirs, folklore, and articles about prominent Yiddish writers on the occasion of their birthday or death (Y. L. Peretz, H. Leyvik, Dovid Pinski, Avrom Reyzen); memorial days for Yiddish writers murdered in the Soviet Union; and regular columns (the most prominent were "From My diary in the Kibbutz," by Avrom Lev, and "The Streets of Jaffa," by M. Zehavi [M]). New books in Yiddish published in Israel or abroad were noted in the section "Ongekumene bikher in redaktsiye" (Books that arrived at the editorial desk), art and literature reviews were published regularly (by Gavriel Vaysman, Mordkhe Yofe, Avrom Lev, Meylekh Ravitsh, Yitskhok Paner), data was reported about the publication of Yiddish books worldwide, and the activities of Yiddish cultural organizations (the Association of Yiddish Journalists and Writers in Israel, Friends of YIVO in Israel, and more) were chronicled, alongside criticisms of their activity.

An average issue of the *LF* spanned sixteen pages. Unlike the *LN* and *DGK*, the *LF* published special issues only to mark May 1 and the anniversary of the Warsaw Ghetto Uprising, and not in honor of state-related events (an exception to this rule was the special issue marking the state's tenth anniversary). The monthly also barely touched on Hebrew culture itself and featured almost no content related to Judaism as a religion or tradition, nor any serialized sensation novels (but Perlov's stories, regarded as belonging to a kind of middle genre between sensation novels and high literature, were published frequently in the journal). Throughout the years (and mostly after the Six-Day War), the journal published criticisms of Yiddish writers whose attitude toward Israel was messianic, religious, or based on a sense of the "miraculous." From the second half of the 1960s, there was a drop in the number of original works published in the journal and especially of works about the present Israeli experience.

From its founding in 1951 until the end of the 1960s, several central battles found expression in the pages of the *LF*. The most prominent of these were the battle for including Yiddish as a learning language in the Israeli school system, the battle against the alienation implanted in this system toward the Diaspora and its culture, the battle against the view of Yiddish as a "foreign language" in Israel, and the battle for equal rights for Yiddish journalists and writers (in particular for their right to receive literary awards). Criticism was directed also at the Yiddish-speaking public itself, which on the one hand consumed Yiddish culture intensively in all its forms and levels but on the other hand did not connect the young generation to it. These battles reflect the justification for the existence of Yiddish in Israel as the activists of the Bund in Israel saw it: to them, Yiddish and its culture held political and educational value because of its unique combination of Jewish, secular, and socialist content, a value that for the young generation of Israeli sabras, and for the supernational Jewish society, would constitute a counterweight to the Zionist-nationalist-religious approach on the one hand and the communist-internationalist on the other.

The important battle Artuski waged in the pages of the *LF* concerned a matter of paramount importance in a nation-state—namely, education. As Ernest Gellner has shown, in the nation-state "the monopoly of legitimate education is . . . more important, more central than is the monopoly of legitimate violence."[237] When the language of a minority becomes the language of education of the political center, the cultural characteristics of the minority group change from a difference that holds them back to a difference that contributes to their upward social mobility.[238] In the unique context of maintaining Yiddish in Israel and continuing its maintenance in the world, this reception in the education system determined the image of Yiddish and its prestige in the eyes of the young generation. More than any other organization in Israel, the AR fought to include Yiddish as a learning language in the education system and protested the fact that the only subsidization of independent Yiddish education was offered by "Agudat Yisrael," a hefty subsidy of 85 percent of all expenses but one that was not extended to the secular-liberal Jewish education offered by the AR in the same language to the children of workers (the scope of the latter education was miniscule compared to the ultra-Orthodox Yiddish education in terms of weekly hours of study and the number of pupils).[239] The cultural and political message of this reality was clear, at least to Artuski and his readers: in the opinion of the official

Israel, Yiddish was the language of exile, exile was entirely religious, and its culture was premodern; and the only cultural-political path available to anyone who viewed himself as secular and modern was Zionism and its language—Hebrew.

The battle for Yiddish education of children and adults had already begun in 1950—a year before the Bund was officially established—with the launching of a lending library for Yiddish books in Tel Aviv. In the Bund clubs across Israel, the AR ran various programs of adult education: evening classes on Yiddish language and its culture, Yiddish book clubs (one of the teachers of Yiddish language and literature in Tel Aviv was the writer Yishaye Shpigl), women's groups, and amateur theater groups and choirs. The AR also tried (unsuccessfully) to establish adult education. In the fall of 1955, an afternoon school began to operate in the Bund's Tel Aviv center where Yiddish was taught to children (not only of Eastern European descent). In 1960, a branch of the same school was opened in Beer-Sheva, and in 1963 in Haifa. In the summer break, subsidized day camps in Yiddish (*Kinder kolonyes*, children's colonies) were offered for the children of workers. In 1962, a house was rented in Ramatayim that was named after Artur Zigelboym and became the permanent home for this activity. As was typical of the evolution of this form in Yiddish culture in the interwar years, the AR's educational activity in Israel also yielded children's literature, even if very limited in scope: the *LF* was the only Yiddish publication in Israel that published works of literature by the children who studied in the AR educational institutions or for them by writers of the journal (like Gavriel Vaysman). But the schoolbooks were imported from the United States and Buenos Aires and were not printed in Israel. The scope of the battle that took place over education was limited, since it was funded, like all other AR activities in Israel, by donations from members of the movement in Israel and abroad (a considerable part of the money came directly from the Yidisher arbeter komitet, the Jewish Labor Committee, from New York).

The *LF* did not aim to aid the refugee-immigrants' cultural or ideological-political absorption in their new country and did not allow them to rest in the comfort of the security that the national home was (or was not) prepared to give them. On the contrary, it sought to help preserve their original identity and challenge most of the ideological perceptions that prevailed (and still prevail) in the country, above all the idea that Israel is the nation-state of all the Jews of the world, by virtue of their religion. In this, the journal sought to influence the state's character and expand its linguistic, cultural, and political boundaries while shrinking its geographical borders. But its choice of Yiddish as the language in which these ideas would be communicated necessarily limited its audience and sealed the fate of the political movement whose ideas the journal wanted to disseminate and carry out in practice. Like the *LF*, the Israeli Bund did not succeed in expanding its circles of support from among the working class to

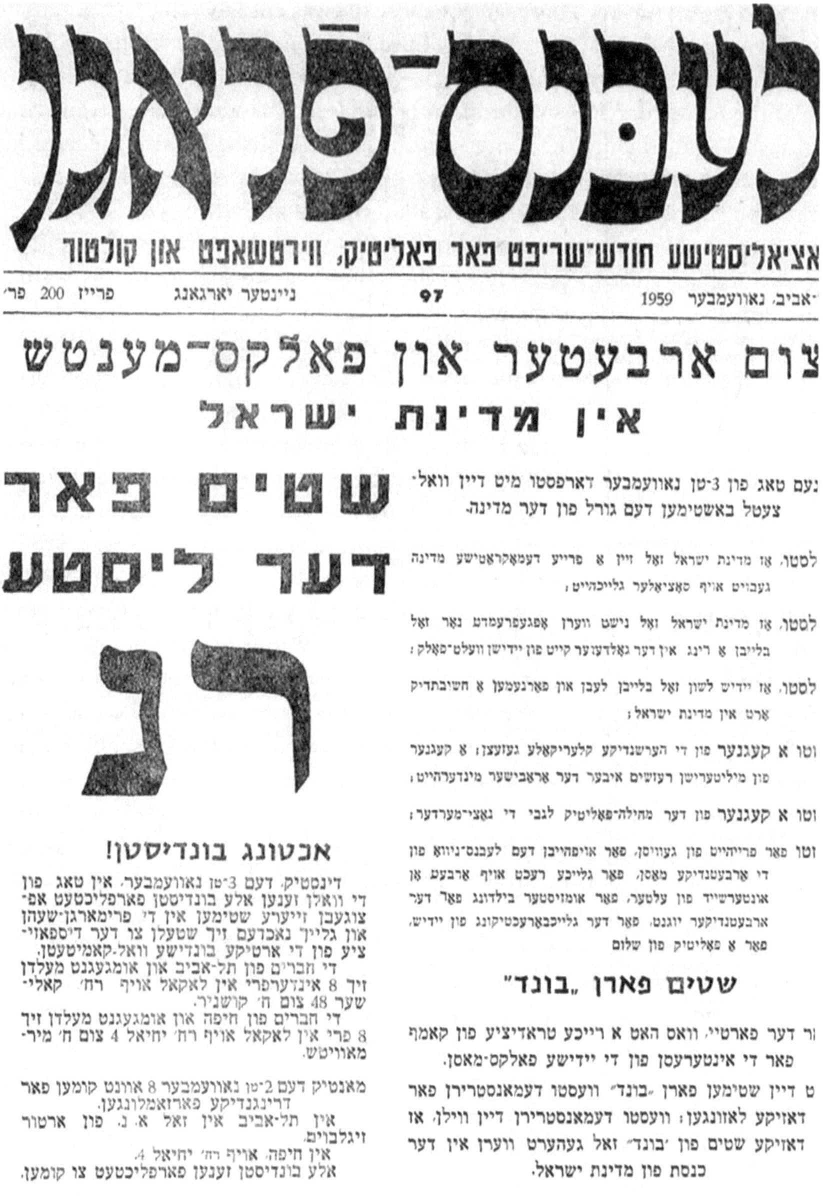

לעבנס-פראגן

אציאליסטישע חודש־שריפט פאר פאליטיק, ווירטשאפט און קולטור

־אביב, נאוועמבער 1959 | 97 | ניינטער יארגאנג | פרייז 200 פר׳

צום ארבעטער און פאלקס־מענטש אין מדינת ישראל

נעם טאג פון 3־טן נאוועמבער דארפסטו מיט דיין וואל־
צעטל באשטימען דעם גורל פון דער מדינה.

לסטו, אז מדינת ישראל זאל זיין א פרייע דעמאקראטישע מדינה
געבויט אויף סאציאלער גלייכהייט;

לסטו, אז מדינת ישראל זאל נישט ווערן אפגעפרעמדט נאר זאל
בלייבן א רינג אין דער גאלדענער קייט פון יידישן וועלט־פאלק;

לסטו, אז יידיש לשון זאל בלייבן לעבן און פארנעמען א חשיבותדיק
ארט אין מדינת ישראל;

וטו א קעגנער פון די הערשנדיקע קלעריקאלע געזעצן; א קעגנער
פון מיליטערישן רעזשים איבער דער אראבישער מינדערהייט;

וטו א קעגנער פון דער מחילה־פאליטיק לגבי די נאצי־מערדער;

וטו פאר פרייהייט פון געוויסן, פאר אויפהייבן דעם לעבנס־ניווא פון
די ארבעטנדיקע מאסן, פאר גלייכע רעכט אויף ארבעט און
אונטערשייד פון עלטער, פאר אומזיסטער בילדונג פאר דער
ארבעטנדיקער יוגנט, פאר דער גלייכבארעכטיקונג פון יידיש,
פאר א פאליטיק פון שלום

שטימט פאר דער ליסטע רנ

אכטונג בונדיסטן!

דינסטיק, דעם 3־טן נאוועמבער, אין טאג פון די וואלן זענען אלע בונדיסטן פארפליכטעט אפ־צוגעבן זייערע שטימען אין די פרימארגן־שעהן און גלייך נאכדעם זיך שטעלן צו דער דיספאזי־ציע פון די ארטיקע בונדישע וואל־קאמיטעטן.

די חברים פון תל־אביב און אומגעגנט מעלדן זיך 8 אינדערפרי אין לאקאל אויף רח׳ קאלי־שער 48 צום ח׳ קרשניר.

די חברים פון חיפה און אומגעגנט מעלדן זיך 8 פרי אין לאקאל אויף רח׳ יחיאל 4 צום ח׳ מיר־מאוויטש.

מאנטיק דעם 2־טן נאוועמבער 8 אוונט קומען פאר דרינגנדיקע פארזאמלונגען.

אין תל־אביב אין זאל א. נ. פון ארטור זיגלבוים.

אין חיפה, אויף רח׳ יחיאל 4.

אלע בונדיסטן זענען פארפליכטעט צו קומען.

שטימט פארן „בונד"

ר דער פארטיי, וואס האט א רייכע טראדיציע פון קאמף
פאר די אינטערעסן פון די יידישע פאלקס־מאסן.

ט דיין שטימען פארן „בונד" וועסטו דעמאנסטרירן פאר
דאזיקע לאזונגען; וועסטו דעמאנסטרירן דיין ווילן, אז
דאזיקע שטים פון „בונד" זאל געהערט ווערן אין דער
כנסת פון מדינת ישראל.

Preparations of the Israeli Bund Party for the Knesset, in the pages of the *LF*, 1959.

The carpenters' cooperative workshop established by the Bund in Tel Aviv. Similar cooperatives were founded for textile and print workers. Arbeter-ring—Beit Sholem Aleichem.

Y. Artuski (*seated in the front row*) with the staff and children of the first and only day camp for workers' children in Israel to be held in Yiddish, 1955. Arbeter-ring—Beit Sholem Aleichem. The organizers saw the day camp as a first step toward establishing an afternoon school for children in Yiddish.

A children's section in the *LF*, July 1, 1961. The *LF* was the only journal in Israel that featured a children's section in Yiddish. It formed part of the broader educational activity for children, which included an afternoon school and day camps.

include local sectors that were not Yiddish speaking, like the Mizrahi Jews and the Arab citizens of Israel, and this despite the deep solidarity that Bund activists expressed (in Yiddish) with the battles of these groups. In choosing Yiddish, then, the *LF* and the Bund in Israel effectively gave up on the masses of workers and relinquished the aspiration to transform them into a politically organized and active class. Their position was therefore neither populist (like Tsanin's) nor elitist (like Sutzkever's), but purist. To whom, for example, were directed the following words, both profound and prophetic, published by Artuski the day after the Six-Day War?

> The logic of occupation creates despair among the occupiers themselves. The longer the occupation lasts, the more severe the Arab uprising may become, the means of suppressing it will necessarily be increasingly violent. . . . The state, whether wittingly or not, will become a military/police camp. Holding on to the [occupied] territories creates a harsh national problem for the state. Demographically, we are already as a matter of fact a bi-national Jewish-Arab state. . . . [But] there is hardly a single Jewish party in Israel, with the exception of small groups, that would support giving the Arabs full political rights so that the state becomes bi-national in the political sense as well. . . . By holding

on to the occupied territories we will solve nothing; we will not attain peace with the Arab countries, nor a peaceful joint existence with the Arabs of Israel; we will become a state of occupiers, and [thus] ipso facto will cease to be a democratic state.[240]

The words point to the ironic similarity between the Bundist ideas in Israel and the Canaanism movement, at least on the question of separating religion from the state and establishing an Israeli citizenship that is distinct and separate from the Jewish (religious or cultural) identity of a portion of its residents. The starting points of these two movements were opposite: the Canaanite native Hebrew identity drew its authority from the local space, whereas the Bundist Jewish-secular identity drew its authority from the Jewish-secular life that existed, even if briefly, in Eastern Europe. The (tragic) fact is that even though they lived and created in the same small space, the people of these two ideological movements appear not to have known each other; and even if they were acquainted, they could not rise above these opposing starting points and unite in a common battle for their common goals.

Public Libraries

A modern Yiddish cultural center is characterized, as I said, not only by periodicals but also by the printing of Yiddish books that have a considerable readership. Public libraries were one of the most important institutions in establishing the modern-Jewish national identity in Eastern Europe, since the cultural and ideological development of the Jewish youth took place mostly in informal educational institutions. Apart from the lending of books, libraries served as places in which to meet and study, and many of them regularly hosted lectures. For many youths, reading and the library activities were a real alternative to their studies that were in many cases interrupted, typically for financial reasons but sometimes also following antisemitic incidents, and thus they were a modern-secular incarnation of the traditional Jewish study hall.[241] With the waves of immigration to the New World, Yiddish libraries were opened in all the cities with sizable immigrant populations: New York, Montreal, Buenos Aires, Paris, and other big and medium cities and towns. The libraries were established both from above, by the municipalities, and from below, by the immigrant organizations, cultural associations (like the AR in New York), or political parties. Hagit Cohen described the public libraries in the United States as "a space in which the drama of immigration unfolded,"[242] because within them clashed the aspirations of assimilation into the hegemonic culture and the sense of loyalty to the culture and language of origin, and within them took root the rift between the immigrant generation and their children. In 1967, two main lending libraries for Yiddish books operated in Tel Aviv—the Y. L. Peretz Library and the Franz Kurski Library—and both had branches across the country. Their reading rooms hosted a variety of cultural activities, including "reading circles," women's groups, and lectures on social and cultural topics. These libraries were established from below, by ʻoley sheyres hapleyte, and were supported by Yiddish cultural organizations outside of Israel. Information about them was never collected by either the municipal or the educational establishment in Israel, making it difficult for the researcher to find. In my own research, it was gathered from reports in the Yiddish press and in other publications in Israel and abroad, as well as from information scattered in memorial books and personal archives. Through these sources I tried to lend an ear to the different and sometimes opposing voices sounded in the Yiddish libraries in Israel, which expressed "the drama of immigration" of ʻoley sheyres hapleyte.

In 1925–1926, the Poʻale Zion Left party opened libraries for Yiddish books across the country, named after Ber Borokhov, as an expression of its support of Yiddish and its culture:[243] in Tel Aviv, Haifa, Jerusalem, Petah Tikva, Rehovot, Ramat Gan, Ness Ziona, Nesher, and more. In the 1930s, there was a rift in the party, and in the second half of the 1940s it merged (as a minority) with the Ahdut Ha-ʻAvoda (labor unity) movement and ceased to exist. The network of libraries it established gradually disintegrated, and its strong branches (like the one in Tel Aviv) became independently run. In 1935–1936, the Tel Aviv branch was given a new name—Y. L. Peretz bibliotek. The Jerusalem branch was named after Leyb Malekh, and the Nesher branch after Shimen Yishibitser.

Until ʻoley sheyres hapleyte immigration began in the late 1940s, the Peretz Library in Tel Aviv had been in gradual decline and nearly closed down. But this immigration dramatically increased the scope of its activity and the size of its readership. The *LN* received many letters from readers complaining about the lack of Yiddish libraries, books, and newspapers in the Maʻabarot,[244] the outlying immigrant settlements, the urban neighborhoods, and even the IDF camps.[245] Several bookstores in Tel Aviv attempted to meet this demand by distributing Yiddish books across the country, alongside independent distributors (one of them was Bentsl Tsalevitsh, from whose home on Basel Street, as I described, Yiddish books were distributed to cities and Kibbutzim, in part through the libraries of the Histadrut and the movements Ha-Kibbutz Ha-Artzi and Ha-Shomer Ha-Tzaʻir). The large number of the immigrants and probably also the knowledge about what they had undergone in the Holocaust lessened the resistance to Yiddish in the Israeli population (though the establishment still stuck to an official policy of resistance to the language and its culture). A letter from November 1950 sent by Yisroel Alster (one of the operators of the Y. L. Peretz Library) to Sutzkever, who was then on a visit to South Africa, reveals how the library attempted to meet the growing demand for Yiddish books, which in those years were scarcely printed in Israel: "The Yiddish readers are growing in numbers here from day to day, and may they continue to do so. Unfortunately, we cannot meet all the requests from readers simply because not enough new Yiddish books are published to meet the demand. In particular, there are no published translations of world literature. . . . Thus, we are left with no choice but to turn to the aid of the Yiddish cultural world."[246]

The demand for translations of world literature testifies to the desire of the masses to become integrated in the modern culture, since translated literature was regarded as a quintessential tool of modernization in its bridging of a linguistic gap. Paradoxically, this desire was an expression of the national identity of the masses and not of a universalist impulse.

Following the many shipments of Yiddish books that arrived from all over the world at the Y. L. Peretz Library, as well as the vigorous activity of its manager—the new immigrant Yoisef Rotnberg—the library was forced to move from its small room on 1 Alenby Street to a bigger home on the same street. Rotnberg, who had grown up in the youth movements of Po'ale Zion Left, saw no contradiction between Yiddish and Zionism (just as Po'ale Zion Left, at the time, had held socialist, Marxist, and Zionist views all at once). On the contrary, he believed that Yiddish makes an important contribution to Zionism and especially to its leftist wing, since it enhances in its speakers the sense of belonging to the Jewish people, its culture, and its state. His advocacy of Yiddish in Israel he perceived as a bridge between Zionism and the Bund, which had many supporters among ʿoley sheyres hapleyte. And thus wrote Rotnberg: "Because we are Zionists, rooted in the land of Israel, we are the ones who paired 'Yiddishkeyt' (in the sense of modern secular Yiddish culture)[247] with the love of Israel. . . . Those who want to exploit Yiddish to put the boot in on Israel . . . are doing something bad, and they are also undermining the battle for Yiddish."[248]

This perception, which regards Yiddish and its culture as compatible with the nationalist-Zionist position, is evident in the substantial financial contributions that Diaspora Jews made toward the establishment of Yiddish cultural institutions in Israel. So, for example, in the new home of the Y. L. Peretz Library, a reading room with a capacity of 150 people was inaugurated thanks to a contribution from New York.[249] The reading room served immigrant-workers and their children, and entrance was free of charge. It was stocked with Yiddish press from all over the world and hosted literary and cultural events, like book launches for prominent Yiddish writers in Israel, memorial events, lectures, and more. This reading hall was especially significant for children and youth, since in their homes they typically did not have the necessary conditions for studying. Apart from Yiddish literature, books in Hebrew and Polish were also lent out. The library's book-cataloging methods were the same as those used in the Jewish libraries in Warsaw. According to the testimony of the Warsaw librarian Batya (Basia) Temqin-Berman,[250] three of the fifty Jewish libraries that operated in Warsaw on the eve of the Holocaust were named after Y. L. Peretz. These libraries were located specifically in neighborhoods in which Jews were a minority, and they were designed to serve the Jewish workers and their families. These were small-scale libraries with no noting system (at least, no such written documentation has been found to date).

In 1953, another branch of the Y. L. Peretz Library was opened in the Ajami neighborhood of Jaffa, designed to serve the newly immigrated Yiddish-speaking residents of Jaffa, Giv'at 'Aliya, Nuzha, and the surrounding area. Throughout the 1960s, the library opened more branches in Beer-Sheva and Netanya.[251] These libraries that sprung up in working-class neighborhoods in Israel were described by Yiddish cultural figures as a direct extension of the cultural life of the Jewish workers in the cities of Eastern Europe:

> When you find yourself in the evening hours in this neighborhood, you are back in some shtetl in the "old home" . . . with the poverty, worries and modest simplicity, with parents exhausted by labor, with radiant Jewish children . . . and indeed, as in the shtetl of yore, with a thirst for culture. Because the workers of the neighborhood yearn for culture, for a book, for a cultural lecture . . . and also for a place in which to meet a cultural audience, to read a paper, converse quietly with a friend, listen to the radio, talk about the news, etc. And perhaps more than the adults, the children of the neighborhood need this kind of place. Their parents are at work all day, and in the small apartments it's not easy to do homework.[252]

The new socioeconomic reality in Israel is described here as an extension of the ("exilic") Jewish reality in Eastern Europe and not, as the Zionist ethos would have it, as a revolutionary alternative to that reality. The similarity is evident in the spatial dimension (the Tel Aviv neighborhood and the Eastern European shtetl), in the challenges (economic hardship), and in the ways of coping with them (enlightenment and education). Immigration to Israel is not described here as a move that changed the economic status of the surviving-remnant 'olim, who for the most part remained workers and small tradesmen and grocers even after immigration. As in Poland, so too in Israel, the responsibility for satisfying the cultural and educational needs is described as lying with the immigrants themselves and not with the state and its institutions. The tone of the description is idyllic and devoid of any anger or complaint—a surprising tone given the revolutionary ethos of the Po'ale Zion Left party. It is also conspicuously lacking a central theme in the "drama of immigration"—namely, the gap between the Yiddish-speaking parents and their children, who speak the language of the state. On the contrary, the Yiddish library appears in this description as a space that is shared by the two generations and that provides both of them with a vital extension of home. Is this a description of an existing reality or of a wish? After all, in the same neighborhood of Jaffa, there were also active branches of the municipal library and libraries established and operated by the Histadrut, which targeted the young generation and aimed to encourage and facilitate its assimilation into the new Hebrew Israeli melting pot. The very creation of this idyllic picture of the Yiddish library as a national and multigenerational space in Israel that amounts to a kind of rebirth of the Jewish shtetl on Israeli soil therefore constitutes an interesting alternative to the prevalent ethos, according to which Israel was the polar opposite of the exile in general and of the Eastern European shtetl in particular.

The need to assimilate into the general population through the Hebrew language and its culture was present and evident also in the various branches of the Y. L. Peretz Library. In 1953, the editor of the *LN*'s literary section, Yasny, reported that the Y. L. Peretz Library held 14,631 books, of which 8,893 were in Yiddish (61 percent).[253] The library performed 22,076 loans of Yiddish books, compared with 9,993 of Hebrew books. In 1957, the number of Yiddish books in the library reached 10,000 according to Yasny.[254] Two years later, in 1959, Michał Weichert reported an almost double number of books (19,569), approximately 60 percent of them Yiddish, 30 percent Hebrew, and 10 percent German (it is interesting that Polish books were not mentioned at all).[255] According to Weichert, the library had 4,698 listed users, of whom 1,855 were especially active (39 percent). On average, the library was attended by 160 readers daily and 4,000 monthly. In 1964, the Y. L. Peretz Library reported having over 20,000 books (a figure that suggests that the growth rate had slowed down), half of them in Yiddish, 7,000 in Hebrew, and the rest in other languages.[256] For the sake of comparison, on the eve of the Holocaust, the three Y. L. Peretz Yiddish libraries in Warsaw held 800, 600, and 450 books. The largest private lending library, Humanita, held 60,000 books.[257] Tel Aviv in 1948 was home to the public library Sha'ar Zion, which in the 1950s and 1960s opened eleven more branches in the city's neighborhoods, especially immigrant neighborhoods. In 1956, the various branches of this library contained 136,000 books, and in 1965, 408,489 books. The library and its branches also held Yiddish books among its various non-Hebrew titles, but their number was not noted. In 1961, the library had 21,940 listed users, which constituted 5.6 percent of the city's residents, and in 1965 it had 32,765 members, 8.2 percent of the city's population.[258]

Another library that operated in Tel Aviv and opened branches in other parts of the country was the Bund Library in Israel, named after the Bundist archivist Franz Kurski (1874–1950).[259] What were the reading patterns of its members? Did they, too, perceive reading in Yiddish as complementing their national (and Zionist) identity? The decision to inaugurate this library was taken, as I said earlier, in 1950, before the AR was officially established in Israel. According to Weichert, the library then held 1,000–1,500 books, which it received from

The Kurski Library at Beit Brit Ha-'Avoda (the AR Home), Kalischer 48, Tel Aviv. In the center is the librarian, comrade Rosman. Arbeter-ring—Beit Sholem Aleichem.

The AR Library in Haifa, inaugurated in December 1954. Arbeter-ring—Beit Sholem Aleichem.

Inauguration of the AR Library in Beer-Sheva, 1957. *Fourth from the right*: Ben-Zion "Bentsl" Tsalevitsh. *Fourth from the left in the same row*: Y. Artuski. Arbeter-ring—Beit Sholem Aleichem.

Yidisher arbeter-komitet (the Jewish Labor Committee) in New York.[260] In 1953, the library moved to an apartment on 25 Aharonson Street, purchased by the New York AR members. In 1957, the AR settled in its permanent home on Kalischer Street, where the library has remained ever since. Throughout the 1950s, it opened branches in Haifa, Petah Tikva, and Beer-Sheva, as well as smaller branches in Nazareth 'Ilit, Tiberias, Herzliya, Netanya, Ramat Ha-Sharon, Bat Yam, Ramla-Lod, Ashkelon, Kfar Yavne, and Kiryat Gat. In addition to Yiddish books, the library and its various branches offered books in Polish, Hebrew, and English. The Kurski Library in Tel Aviv had both a reading room and a special section for children's books, and its reading room was a hub for young and old immigrants, especially from Poland. In 1957, Yasny reported that the Kurski Library held 12,000 books in Yiddish.[261] According to Weichert's report, in 1959 there were more than 15,000 books in the library, 12,000 of them in Yiddish (80 percent) and some 1,500 in Hebrew and Polish.[262] For the sake of comparison, the Bund Library in Warsaw, the Grosser Library, which was the city's largest party-affiliated library, held 20,000 books.[263] The Kurski Library had 560 members. An average of 40–50 readers attended it daily, and approximately 1,300 monthly. In an average month, 1,800–2,000 books were lent out. The Israeli Bund, as we saw earlier, placed special emphasis on education, establishing an afternoon school where Yiddish was taught to children, as well as summer camps. And indeed, the children and young adults section of the Kurski Library contained many schoolbooks sent in from Yiddish schools in New York and Buenos Aires. The interesting piece of data, which most powerfully reflects the identity dilemma and the ideological split of the Bund activists in Israel, is the division of languages of the books in this section: of 1,300 books, 900 were in Hebrew, and only 400 in Yiddish. By comparison, in the children and young adults section of the Warsaw Grosser Library (established in 1931), most of the books were in Polish.[264]

Publishing Houses

In 1955, the Alveltlekher yidisher kultur-kongres (World Congress for Yiddish/Jewish Culture) devoted its gathering in New York to the worldwide state of the Yiddish book, which was in steady decline. The crisis in the Yiddish book market had in fact already begun in the 1930s. It reflected a declining number of buyers of Yiddish literature, but not its de facto number of readers.[265] Yiddish books were printed in small numbers and distributed mainly by the author. The statement published by the congress declared that the fate of the Yiddish book is the fate of Yiddish culture, and thus all advocates of this culture—especially in the United States—must encourage its distribution in the world, especially among ʿoley sheyres hapleyte, and support the establishment of libraries and publishing houses.[266] In Israel in 1967, there were three functioning Yiddish publishing houses: the Y. L. Peretz Press, Ha-Menora, and Yisroel-bukh. According to Khone Shmeruk's estimate, in the 1960s Israel published more Yiddish books than any other country.[267] How did Tel Aviv become the leading world center for the publication of Yiddish books? The data required to establish an answer to this question was hard to come by, since like the Yiddish libraries in Israel, the country's Yiddish publishing houses too were privately owned and did not leave behind ordered archives. I therefore gathered the relevant information from the Yiddish press and other publications in Israel and abroad, from personal archives, and from the unique source that serves the research into the history of publishing—the catalogues.[268]

In 1956, the Tel Aviv Y. L. Peretz Library began to function also as a publishing house of Yiddish books thanks to a joint effort of several world Yiddish centers.[269] From 1945 until the establishment of this press in Tel Aviv, Yiddish books had been printed in New York,[270] Buenos Aires,[271] and Paris.[272] Other Yiddish publishers existed beyond the Iron Curtain, in Poland[273] and Romania.[274] The number of books published by these firms decreased gradually throughout the 1950s.[275] Until the founding of the Y. L. Peretz Press, Yiddish writers in Israel sent their works overseas to be published. Their books were also distributed, discussed, and read all over the world. For example, the works of Man and Perlov were written in Israel in the early 1950s and published by the Kiyum and Yidbukh publishing firms in Buenos Aires. In the early 1960s, the reverse process took place: Yiddish writers from all over the world began sending their manuscripts to Israel to be published and distributed.

The idea to establish the Y. L. Peretz Press was Rotnberg's, the library's manager and a former member of Poʿale Zion Left. In April–July 1959, Rotnberg traveled across the United States and Canada raising funds for the new press. He laid the foundations for its establishment and ran it until his untimely death in 1960.[276] From then until 1963, it was run by Shimen Roznberg (also a former member of Poʿale Zion Left), and after him Abraham Lis held the position. The

Y. L. Peretz Press not only published books but also founded literary awards for Yiddish writers: the first, named after the writer and playwright Dovid Pinski (who immigrated to Israel in his old age and settled in Haifa), was awarded in the year of Israel's tenth anniversary (1958). It also hosted literary events at various venues in Tel Aviv, sometimes with visiting Yiddish writers and journalists from abroad. It published catalogues of its recent titles and a pamphlet advertising its activities—*Yediyes fun Y. L. Peretz farlag* (The Y. L. Peretz press news)—which it distributed in Yiddish centers across the world. The press also invested in newspaper and radio advertisements and even planned to employ sales agents who would sell the books directly in the immigrant neighborhoods (but this plan apparently did not materialize). One of the distribution agreements they signed was with the *LN*, and it stipulated that the paper would buy its subscribers series of three to four books, nine hundred to one thousand pages.[277] Finally, the press made efforts to subscribe members in Israel and abroad who would purchase its books in advance.[278]

On its tenth anniversary, in December 1966, the Y. L. Peretz Press hosted a festive gathering at the Ohel Shem Hall in Tel Aviv, where it announced that it had become the largest Yiddish book publisher in the world.[279] According to the data it made public at the event, the press had published 193 titles in various genres during that decade:[280] prose, 57; poetry, 45; memoirs, 18; Holocaust literature (*khurbn-literatur*), 18; essays, 22; history, 7; travel literature, 6; sociology, 3; opinion journalism, 2; drama, 4; philosophy, 1; aphorisms, 1; album, 1; and anthologies, 5. Of these, 160 were in Yiddish, 25 in Hebrew, 8 in bilingual Yiddish-Hebrew, and 19 were translations from Yiddish to Hebrew and from Hebrew to Yiddish. The total number of authors was 139, of whom 70 were residents of Israel and 69 were from abroad; 14 books were jointly authored.

This data reveals several surprising facts. The first is that, contrary to what I had assumed initially, the number of Yiddish writers from Israel and from abroad was almost equal. In other words, not only Yiddish writers from abroad could afford to publish their books in the Israeli publishing house thanks to the low printing costs (compared to the United States), but also Yiddish writers from Israel participated in this market—most likely with the support of Jewish individuals and organizations from abroad. A second surprising fact concerns the genres published by this press: whether or not the Y. L. Peretz Press applied a strict policy to its selection of manuscripts, it is evident that "belletristic literature" was its preferred medium, with a slight advantage for prose over poetry. This is surprising in light of the common assumption in the broad public and in the study of Yiddish culture that Yiddish literature declined after the Holocaust. The literary expression of this decline is supposedly the writing of memoirs and memorial books (and not belletristic), as well as the focus on Holocaust literature. But apart from a few Yizker bikher,[281] the press published a handful of quality "Holocaust books," which were initiated by the press itself, including the first volume of *Lite* (Lithuania) and Yasny's monograph *Di geshikhte fun yidn in Lodzh in di yorn fun der Daytsher oysrotung* (*History of the Jews in Lodzh in the Years of the German Extermination of the Jews*). In the category of fine literature, prominent titles include *Dos hoyz fun di lialkes* (*House of Dolls*), by Ka- Tzetnik; *Lider fun khurbn*, an anthology of Holocaust poems edited by Kadia Molodowski; nonfiction titles (*Eyrope on kinder* [*Europe without Children*], by Dr. Mark Dvorzhetski); and a very small number of survivor testimonies (for example, *Geven iz a geto* [There once was a ghetto], by Moyshe Pulaver; *In a fremder hoyt* [In a foreign skin], by Simkhe Polakiyevitsh, about life under guise on the "Aryan" side).

The bulk of the Y. L. Peretz Press publications, then, were works of prose, and the vast majority of them were written by living authors, many of them young. Among the prose writers who immigrated to Israel after the Holocaust and whose books were published by this press were Rokhl Oyerbakh, Tsvi Ayznman, Yosl Birshteyn, Avrom Blay, Shloyme Berlinski, Yekhiel Hofer, Shloyme Varzoger, Dovid Zakalik, Malsha Mali, Mendl Man, Levi Papiernikov, K. Tsetnik, Rivke Kviatkovski-Pinkhasik, Avrom Karpinovitsh, Rivke Rus, and Yishaye Shpigl. Their books were reviewed not only in the Yiddish press in Israel and abroad but in the Hebrew press as well. In the journal *Heymish: Zhurnal far literatur kritik un sotsiyale problemen* (Homey: Journal for literary critique and social problems), the editor Moyshe Grosman documented references to Yiddish literature in the Hebrew periodicals in Israel in a special column: "Yidishe shafungen in der hebreisher prese" (Literary works in Yiddish in the Hebrew press). The column clearly demonstrates that the Hebrew press published many reports about modern Yiddish literature and Yiddish culture. Contrary to my initial assumption, I found that the Hebrew press gave attention not only to the works of the definitive writers but also to new works, and even those by writers living in Israel: Sutzkever, Ayznman, Man, and others.

Thus, unlike publishing firms abroad, which published editions of the definitive works of Yiddish literature (and especially Sholem Aleichem and Peretz), the Y. L. Peretz Press focused on later writers, such as Eliezer Shteynbarg, whose book *Mesholim* (*The Jewish Book of Fables*) was published by them. Of the works of the classic authors, the press published little more than a symbolic anthology of poems about Peretz—*Y. L. Peretz in der Yidisher dikhtung* (Y. L. Peretz in Yiddish poetry), edited by Nakhmen Mayzel—which received little attention. A more prominent anthology was the aforementioned *A shpigl af a shteyn* (A mirror on a stone), which compiled works of Yiddish writers murdered in the Soviet Union. The anthology was published in 1964 in collaboration with *DGK* and the Yiddish Studies Department at the Hebrew University of Jerusalem, and it was edited by Shmeruk. It was one of the most important enterprises of the

Y. L. Peretz Press and contributed to its establishment as a prominent and high-quality publishing house.

The press's focus on high culture was also expressed in its choice of nonfiction titles. In 1966, the Y. L. Peretz Press published a collection of works by the Zionist-socialist thinker and political activist Ber Borokhov, *Shprakh-forshung un literatur-geshikhte* (The study of language and history of literature), edited by Nakhmen Mayzel (who had also settled in Israel in his final years). Borokhov developed two areas of thought: one is the national domain, in which he demonstrated that Zionism and socialism could be combined (and he indeed was the leader of the Po'ale Zion movement); and the other is the cultural domain, where, through a profound study of Yiddish and its literature, he found that they do not contradict Zionism but rather bolster the Jewish national consciousness and help establish it. In this context, it is worth noting that the first book published by the Y. L. Peretz Press (1956) was *Bleter fun a lebn* (*The Pages of a Life*)—the memoirs of Ya'akov Zerubavel (1886–1967), one of the leaders of the Po'ale Zion Left party. In 1996, the press published another volume of this book, as well as a Hebrew translation. This choice was not accidental, since the Y. L. Peretz Press was founded by members of this party. Apart from Zerubabvel's memoirs, it also published the memoirs of Nahum Nir-Rafalkes (1884–1968), who was a Knesset member from Mapam and Ahdut Ha-'Avoda-Po'ale Zion, *Ershte yorn* (*First Years*), as well as the memoirs of the major Yiddish writer H. Leyvik, *Af tsarisher katorge* (*In Tsarist Penal Labor*). This combination of memoirs reflects the ideological mixture that guided the press, of Zionism and Yiddish culture, a combination they perceived as one that broadens the political and cultural horizons. In the field of literary criticism, the press published *Mit mayne fartog bikher* (*With My Dawn Journals*), by the important poet and literary critic Yankev Glatshteyn, who also combined diverse and prolific creative work in Yiddish culture with support for Zionist ideas, and *Der mehus fun dikhtung* (The essence of poetry), by the literary critic Y. Rapoport.

Another way in which the Y. L. Peretz Press established its status and expanded its readership was through translations of classic Yiddish works of literature into Hebrew. Prominent among them was N. Ginaton's translation of *Malhut haYehudim* by L. Shapiro.[282] In this domain it competed with the big Hebrew publishing firms in Israel.[283] The works of Yiddish writers from Israel were also translated into Hebrew, but they preferred to publish the translations with firms unassociated with Yiddish culture, especially the large public publishing houses, as part of various series devoted to Yiddish literature,[284] but also with small, private houses.[285] Like the original books, these translations were reviewed both in the Hebrew press and in the Yiddish press printed in Israel.

According to the reports of the Y. L. Peretz Press, the public of consumers of Yiddish books in Israel included Hebrew readers who went back to reading original works in Yiddish after years of not reading in this language.[286] The press appealed to the Ministry of Culture and Education for financial support,[287] and it indeed participated in events organized by the state, like the international book fairs held in Jerusalem and the Hebrew Book Week (beginning in 1963), and it was a member of the Book Publishers Association of Israel (from 1964). However, Israel did not present any Yiddish books at the international book expos in which it participated. From 1966, the Y. L. Peretz Library received modest financial support from the state budget and the Zionist movement (the Jewish Agency).[288] For the managers of the Y. L. Peretz Press, the fact that it was flourishing precisely in Israel was proof that the "linguistic chauvinists" on both sides—Hebrew and Yiddish—were wrong:

"It was both appealing and irritating that in Israel, of all places, a publishing house should emerge that prints Yiddish works in a clean and aesthetic manner, of fine taste, in both content and form. This should have posed a challenge both to those who maliciously deride Yiddish in this country and to all the instigators and bitter opponents of the Jewish state, who hide behind the pretext that the Yiddish word is entirely boycotted here, and who must go on hiding it, like many years ago when the defenders of the language ruled the roost."[289]

Despite the press's success and rapid growth, its writers had to play an active role in raising the necessary resources to publish their books and distribute them to literary critics and readers in Israel and abroad.[290] The common view among scholars of Yiddish is that the Yizker bikher were a central source of funding for the Yiddish literature published by the Yiddish publishing houses, since the decades following the Holocaust saw a significant rise in the overall number of such memorial books published worldwide and Israel became a leading center for their publication, as the numbers in table 1.1 suggest.

And indeed, in 1963 the Y. L. Peretz Press published an ad in its pamphlet inviting hometown associations to submit memorial books for publication. The ad suggests clearly that the press regarded these books as a vital and desirable means for its financial subsistence.[291] Quite possibly, its decision to produce the monograph *Lite* (Lithuania) was a strategic move designed to help the press establish itself as a central player in this field. Yet from the list of Holocaust books published by the Y. L. Peretz Press in this decade (1956–1966), the fact stands out that only two Yizker bikher were printed by the press (Sefer Borshtshev and Sefer Stry). Apparently, the committees that handled the preparation of these manuscripts preferred to take them directly to the printing house without involving a publishing firm and thus to control not only the content but also the production process and pricing. The Yizker bikher, therefore, were ultimately not a source of income for the publishing houses, or even—contrary to the common perception in the study of Yiddish culture—for the vast majority of Yiddish writers (from Israel and abroad). Those of them who edited Yizker bikher did so typically without

Table 1.1 Publication of Yizker bikher in 1946–1970 according to place of publication

Year	Europe	United States	Argentina	Israel	Other (Canada, South Africa, Australia)	Total
1946–1950	6	14	4	8	—	32
1951–1955	1	5	8	23	2	39
1956–1960	1	9	5	51	1	67
1961–1965	—	9	4	78	1	92
1966–1970	—	10	1	105	3	118
Total	8	47	22	265	7	348

Note: This data is based on the New York Public Library's printed catalogue of Yizker bikher, the Jewish Division Dorot, and the National Yiddish Book Center in Amherst, Massachusetts (the data was gathered and processed in 2012–2013). The topic of my postdoctoral research is the Holocaust Yizker bikher. As part of this research, I updated and revised the basic data of the catalogue. A dash indicates that no books were published that year. See Gali Drucker Bar-Am, "'Record and Lament:' Yizker Bikher as History and Literature Conflated," *Yad Vashem Studies* 51, no. 2 (2023): 101–28.

pay, on a voluntary basis, for the sake of memorializing their community. Only a small number of Yiddish journalists served as editors of multiple Yizker bikher, devoted themselves to this field, and gained experience in it. One of the most prominent among them was Dovid Shtokfish (who was associated with Po'ale Zion Left and Mapam, served as the editorial secretary of the journal *Nayvelt*, and edited the party papers *Af der vakh* ['Al Ha-Mishmar, On guard] and *Yisroel shtime* [Kol Israel, The voice of Israel] and the Jewish Agency's publication *Folk un tsion* ['Am Ve-Zion, People and Zion]). Another was Yasny, who was the editor of the literary section of the *LN*.

How, then, did Yiddish writers finance the printing of their books in the absence of support from either state institutions or the hometown associations? As I said earlier, the German reparation money that some of the survivors received was regarded by them as "tainted" and was therefore designated to serve "pure" goals, such as the printing of Yiddish books and the development of Yiddish culture. "Money," wrote the anthropologist Mary Douglas, "is only an extreme and specialized type of ritual."[292] Both money and ritual are external and overt signs of internal states; both link the present with the future and provide a way of measuring worth. The participation of the survivors—the writers as well as the public of readers—in financing the publication and distribution of the books often carried a ritual and value-laden significance that exceeded the basic financial meaning of this act.

Alongside the Y. L. Peretz Press, several smaller publishing houses of Yiddish books were established in Tel Aviv. The private press Ha-Menora (sometimes called "Menorah") was founded in Tel Aviv by Moyshe Zonshayn. It operated for some fifteen years, from 1962 until Zonshayn's death in 1977, and published approximately four hundred titles, including translations (a biography of Ben-Gurion by Robert St. John; *Doctor Zhivago* by Boris Pasternak, which was highly popular among Yiddish readers in Israel), Holocaust literature (*The Diary of Anne Frank*; a second edition of *Togbukh fun Lodzher geto* [Diary from the Lodzh Ghetto] by Shloyme Frank, the first edition of which was published the same year, 1959, in Buenos Aires by the Tsentral-farband fun poylishe yidn in argentine [The Central Association of Polish Jews in Argentina]), and original Yiddish fiction (a collection of stories by Mendl Man, *Dos hoyz tsvishn derner* [*The House among Thorns*]). The publication of original Yiddish literature was in most cases fully funded by the authors. According to its advertisements, the press intended to publish an anthology of Yiddish prose from Y. L. Peretz up to "the latest writers," but the plan was never realized.[293]

Another Yiddish press, Yisroel-bukh, was initiated by Mapam members and established in 1965 with the party's backing. A few facts about its activity can be gleaned from a text written by its editor, the poet and translator Arie Shamri.[294] Shamri was appointed editor of the press by the party's cultural department and served in this role from its founding until his death. According to him, the goal of the press was threefold: first, it sought to publish the finest works of Yiddish literature out of a loyalty to preserving the high quality of this culture in the face of waves of graphomania that in his view prevailed at the time; second, the press aimed to reach the general Israeli public and to present to it the achievements of Yiddish literary creation; and third, it sought to showcase the cultural life in Israel to the Jews of the Diaspora. This latter aim it tried to realize also through Yiddish translations of Hebrew works of literature. Its first enterprise was the anthology *Vortslen* (Roots), in 1966. Following that, the press published books of poetry and prose, memoirs and essays. Shamri describes the press's activity as the initiative of individuals driven by a love of the Yiddish word, a strong tenacity, and the ability to make do with little. After Shamri's death, the press announced a literary award in his name.

Apart from these publishing firms, Tsanin also published books in his paper's press. Khaye Elboym-Dorembus's book *Af der arisher zayt* was published by the LN Press in 1958. As early as 1950, Tsanin established in Tel Aviv the Kleynbibliotek Press (The Small Library), which published softcover "pocket books" of fine Yiddish literature (these small books were popular in the Yiddish cultural centers like Warsaw and New York). It published the works of Israeli Yiddish writers like Tsanin himself, Yosef Papiernikov, Avrom Blay, Yoel Mastboym, Shloyme Berlinski, Yitskhok Paner, Gavriel Vaysman, Moyshe Grosman, and Yitskhok Perlov. These books were sold in kiosks across Tel Aviv. In 1960, Tsanin announced the founding of another press—Yidishe folks-bibliotek (Yiddish People's Library).

Subscribed readers of the *LN* could purchase its books at a special price. The books this press intended to publish ranged from high literature (the poetry of Mordkhe Gebirtig; S. Y. Agnon) to Shund literature (sensation novels, such as *In di negl fun shpionazsh* [*In the Claws of Espionage*], by an author who went by the pen name A. Put), and in between these poles—memoirs (a translation of Devorah Dayan's book *Mit trern un freyd*, *be'Osher uveYagon* [*In Happiness and in Grief*]) and folklore (Y. Rafael, *Fun di kvaln funem khsidishn humor* [*From the Wells of Hasidic Humor*]).

Data regarding the worldwide publication of Yiddish books that was gathered by various elements in the world of Yiddish culture in 1948–1967 demonstrates Israel's rise to the status of a world center for the publication of Yiddish books. In a report published in 1967, Daniel Tsharni noted a modest rise in the number of Yiddish books published in Israel (in private publishing houses, like *DGK*, *LN*, and others).[295] According to him, in 1953, forty-eight Yiddish books were printed in the United States, thirty-four in Argentina (which before the Holocaust was in the fifth or sixth place worldwide), and thirteen in Israel (which before the Holocaust was in the last place worldwide), moving the latter up to the third place worldwide in the publication of Yiddish books (ahead of France, Poland, Mexico, Brazil, and South Africa). The data compiled by the YIVO institute in New York regarding the worldwide publication of Yiddish books in 1960–1961 shows Israel's fast rise as a center for the publication of Yiddish books.[296] In 1963, the phenomenon was given an explanation: "There was a 'mass production' of Yiddish books in Israel and Argentina, where labor was cheaper than in the United States. The United States, however, produced scholarly Yiddish books requiring carful preparatory work, and luxury editions."[297] In that same year, it was reported that Israel had become a center for the printing of Yiddish books:[298] a total of fifty-seven Yiddish books were printed there in 1963, while in the whole of the United States, forty-one Yiddish books were printed, and in Argentina, twenty-four. Similar numbers were reported for 1964.[299] (For the sake of comparison, in each of the years 1951–1955, some nine hundred books and publications in Hebrew were printed in Israel.)[300]

Israel became a world center for the printing of Yiddish books thanks to the support of Yiddish cultural organizations and Jewish communities across the world. In their view, part of the role of "the national home of the Jewish people" was to rehabilitate the Holocaust survivors not only physically but also culturally. They perceived Yiddish and its culture not as elements that undermined the national identity but in fact as having created this identity and as contributing to its solidification.[301]

Israel became a worldwide center for the printing of Yiddish books thanks also to ongoing investments by individuals, simple Holocaust survivors who directed their private and often modest resources toward the printing of Yiddish

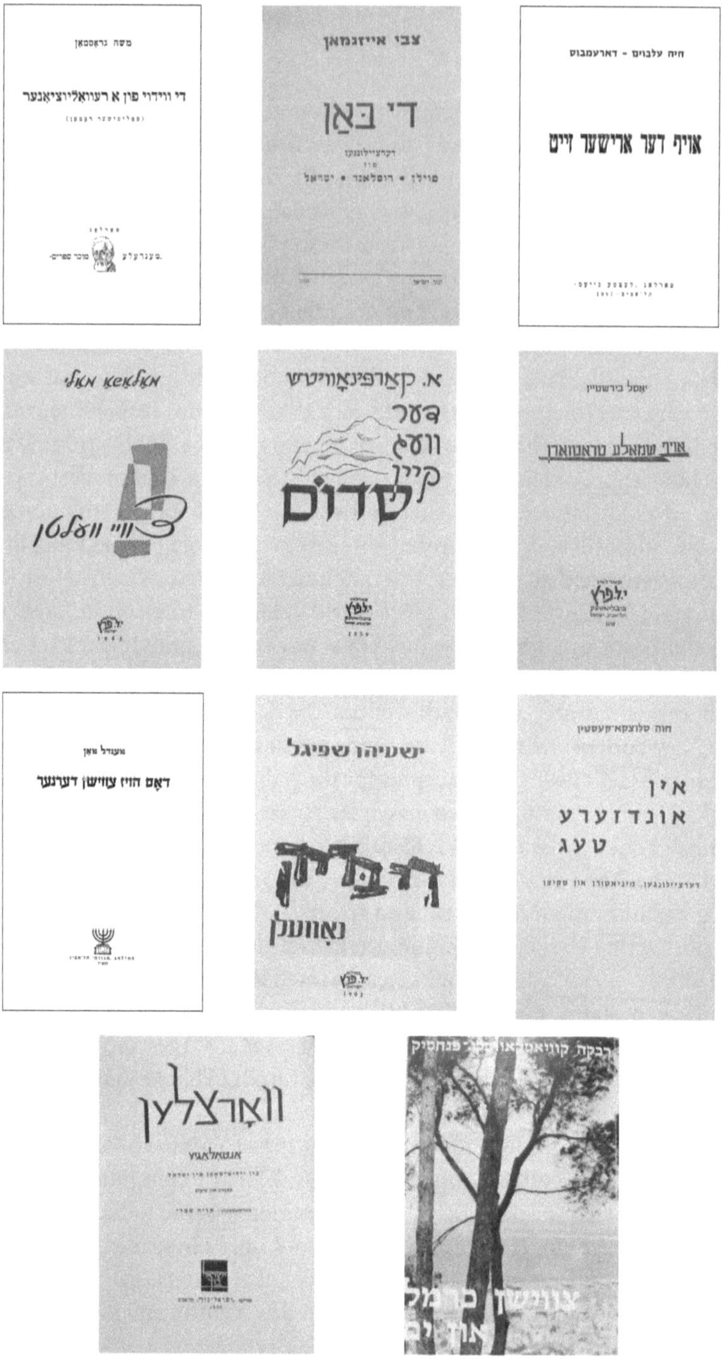

A selection of Yiddish books published in Israel by the large publishing houses (Y. L. Peretz, Menora, and Yisroel-Bukh), collaborative publications (Tsvi Ayznman, Young-Israel Press [Kibbutz Yagur, 1956]; Khaye Elboym-Dorembus, LN Press [Tel Aviv, 1957]), and self-publications (Moyshe Grosman, Mendele Moykher Sforim Press [Tel Aviv, 1955]; Khave Slutska-Kestin, Meir Press [Tel Aviv, 1966]; Rivke Kviatkovski-Pinkhasik, "Aleyn" [Haifa, 1975]).

books. For them, too, the justification for maintaining the Yiddish book in general and its printing in Israel in particular was the bolstering of democracy, freedom of speech, and freedom of cultural and linguistic occupation in Israel. These views received expression in the historic Po'ale Zion party (at least in some of its branches). So it is not surprising that the Y. L. Peretz Press, which was established and managed by members of the party, became the largest and leading publisher of Yiddish books in Israel in its first two decades, and even globally, at least from the early 1960s.

Anthologies

Anthologies, alongside the daily paper and the novel, played a central role in the modern culture, helping consolidate a new, national identity for their readers by shaping and representing dimensions of space and time that are common to the imagined nation community.[302] As in the paper, so too in the anthology, the editing was key. The Greek word *anthologia* means "flower-gathering," and it suggests the artificiality involved in the act of compiling the works and positing them side by side, according to some organizing principle (or several), which combines aesthetic, ideological, and political motivations. The appearance of anthologies in modern culture heralds a change of epochs. In addition to preserving the old and summarizing it, they served in modern Jewish culture as tools for shaping the present by means of canonizing the past—that is, as tools for "inventing tradition" and creating new artistic and social norms in the present and the future.[303] During the period of modern Yiddish culture's consolidation as well as in the time of its disintegration, a rather large number of anthologies appeared within it. The most important among them were edited as acts of commemoration, from a perspective that looks back on a bygone world and out of a desire to create a new culture from its ruins.[304] A prominent example of this is the seminal anthology published in Vilna in 1913 and edited by Niger, *Der pinkes: Yorbukh far der geshikhte fun der yidisher literatur un shprakh, far folklore, kritik un bibliyografye* (*Annals: Yearbook for the History of Yiddish Literature and Language, Folklore, Criticism, and Bibliography*).[305]

Literary anthologies in modern Yiddish culture are typically situated at the intersection of two main areas of interest: the local (anthologies that compile works created in a particular geographic area) and the thematic (anthologies that compile works created on a certain subject). The anthologies that demonstrate this most clearly are those created by the editor Shmuel Rozhanski of Buenos Aires in the series *Musterverk fun der Yidisher literatur* (Masterpieces of Yiddish literature). The preoccupation with these two domains is usually apologetic: the very act of compiling the anthology is designed to "prove" that a particular region in which immigrants settled and established a Yiddish cultural life has yielded and ample and worthy literary crop and has thereby become a significant center of this culture, and similarly that a particular subject (typically a certain country in which Jewish immigrants or refugees have settled) has preoccupied the writers of Yiddish literature in a particular area and period or else across the world and over a long stretch of time. This apologetic motivation created two conflicting principles of editing. On the one hand, editors desired to include as many works as possible so as to demonstrate the existence of a critical mass of literary work in each of these domains and thus to prove its importance. In addition, the guild of Yiddish writers and editors was always a rather small one (despite its broad geographic dispersion), and therefore editors found it hard to withstand the pressures exerted by writers to have their work included in an anthology. On the other hand, editors were motivated by the qualitative standard that underlies the anthology form and defines its nature. Unlike other compilations, the anthology is characterized by the meticulous selection of works.[306] This dilemma, between expansion and selection, became more painful and difficult after the Holocaust. Many important anthologies were edited in the decade that followed the Holocaust out of a desperate effort to convert the unfathomable loss into new life.[307]

Two anthologies were published in 1966 that compiled works of Yiddish literature written in Israel, and they signal the decline of Yiddish culture in Israel: *Vortslen: Antologye fun yidish shafn in Yisroel, poezye un proze* (*Roots: An Anthology of Yiddish Works in Israel, Poetry and Prose*), edited by the abovementioned poet and translator Arie Shamri, a member of Kibbutz ʿEin Shemer, which was affiliated with the Mapam party; and *Mikan uMiqarov: ʾAntologia šel sipurei yidiš beʾEreṣ Yiśraʾel, meRešit haMea weʾAd yameinu* (From here and from near: Yiddish stories in Eretz Yisrael, from the start of the century to the present), Yiddish fiction translated into Hebrew, edited by the journalist and translator Mordechai Halamish (who wrote for ʾAl Ha-Mishmar and was a member of its editorial board alongside his work in the realm of Yiddish literature).

The compilers were not from among ʿoley sheyres hapleyte. Shamri and Halamish represent the generation of Yiddish writers and activists who came to pre-state Israel in the 1920s and 1930s, whose immigration was motivated by Zionism (expressed, among other things, in the choice to Hebraize their names: Rivo became Shamri and Flint, Halamish) but who nonetheless chose to write in Yiddish (and about Yiddish). To this same generation also belong Moshe Bassok and Shimshon Melzer, editors of anthologies of Yiddish poetry in Hebrew translation, published in the late 1950s and early 1960s.[308] Even though in terms of their biographies these editors almost belonged to the generation of Yiddish writers who were Holocaust survivors, they were perceived as "veterans" and enjoyed the special prestige that attends this status in every immigrant society. The arrival of ʿoley sheyres hapleyte offered the "veteran" Yiddish writers a favorable opportunity, since it provided them with a large reading audience, many platforms for the publication of their work, and various earning opportunities in related fields (as editors in the Yiddish press and Yiddish book publishing, as well as editors of Yizker bikher). But with the new opportunities came new challenges: the veterans of Yiddish culture were forced to make themselves relevant to a new public of readers, with whom they did not share such formative experiences as the Holocaust or (on a different scale) the hardships of absorption in a young independent state.

The two anthologies are mostly "local" insofar as they intend to present a large selection of works of prose written in Yiddish in Israel. The aim of both was to demonstrate the centrality of Israel as a hub of Yiddish culture that produced a significant mass of literature. In both anthologies, the works are organized in two main units: the first is of early works written in the period of the Yishuv, mostly by writers who came to Israel as pioneers, and the second is of works written after the establishment of the state by Yiddish writers from among the ʿoley sheyres hapleyte. Despite the similarities, there are also significant differences between the anthologies: one appeared in Yiddish and targeted readers of this language in Israel and abroad; the other appeared in Hebrew and targeted the general public in Israel.

The anthology *Vortslen* included the works of sixty Yiddish writers residing in Israel: forty-two poets (of them, six women) and eighteen prose writers (including one woman—Malsha Mali); over a third of the writers (twenty-five) were Holocaust survivors, and the rest came to Israel before the Holocaust. The image of roots, the word that appears in the anthology's title, is one that took on many layers of meaning since the rise of modern nationalism. Gellner showed that one of the fundamental contrasts that inhere in modern nationalism is between the particular identity and the universal one. Romantic nationalism regarded the bearer of the universal identity as a rootless person who seeks to impose his values on society. This person was typically involved in occupations that require great mobility, like trade or thought. By contrast, the bearer of the particular identity, typically a farmer or soldier, was perceived as a "rooted" person, strongly grounded in the land.[309] The Jews of Europe did not fit this framework since they were considered both "rootless" (because until the modern period they were typically not allowed to own land and thus worked mostly as brokers and traders) and as possessing their own distinct particular identity. The Zionist idea aimed to correct this state of affairs by establishing a Jewish national identity based on ownership of land. The name of the anthology *Roots*, therefore, attests to the wish to put down roots—that is, to establish a particular national identity on the land of a nation-state. The same metaphor played a central role in an anthology published in 1949 with a similar name (though it is unlikely that Shamri was familiar with it)—*The Root and the Bough: The Epic of an Enduring People*, edited by Leo Schwartz, who dedicated it to the surviving-remnant survivors he met during his activities in the DP camps in Germany. The anthology's final chapter is titled "Homecoming in Israel," and it ends with the arrival of the surviving-remnant ʻolim in Israel. From a national-romantic point of view, the Jewish Holocaust survivors are doubly rootless: both because of their Judaism and as refugees who were uprooted from the nation-state in which they lived. Thus, naming an anthology of Yiddish works of literature written in Israel *Roots* implies that the Yiddish language did not prevent the "universal" Jew from becoming a "rooted" Israeli. On the contrary, Shamri saw an option of combining these two elements and thereby enriching the overall cultural creation: "What is unique in Israeli cultural creation is this dual imbibing of a rooted Israeli essence and a global Jewish culture. . . . A global Jewish horizon that is in close contact with a local rootedness—this is the united-dynamic force that underlies Yiddish cultural creation in Israel."[310]

What makes the Yiddish literature written in Israel unique, in his view, is its combination of local and universal qualities. The importance of the value of rootedness is expressed in the order in which he chose to present the writers in the anthology—according to their seniority in Israel.[311] The length of their life in Israel is a fact relevant not just to the historical-biographical realm but also to the aesthetic evaluation of the works, since according to Shamri, the longer a writer lived in Israel, the better he conveyed the atmosphere of the place: "From the very first contact of Yiddish with Eretz Yisrael . . . new words emerged in Yiddish [soaked in] Eretz Yisrael's fragrance of young growth. Later on, many Yiddish poets and writers showed and proved how an occasional visitor sees all faults [expression] . . . and thus enriched the literary creation in Yiddish in all places. But the main achievements in this area belong to those Yiddish writers who tied their fate with the land, and through many years of perseverance soaked up the Israeli essence and became enrooted in it."[312]

Shamri distinguished, then, between the many traveling-writers who wrote about Israel in Yiddish out of a brief encounter with it, and the resident-writers, who wrote on this topic out of their own personal experience gained throughout a long process of life in Israel. This distinction is echoed in the title of the anthology and in the distinction that underlies it between those who are rooted and those who are not. The tension between these two poles—putting down roots versus wandering—is expressed in the story with which Shamri chose to open the anthology, "A talent tsu erets yisroel" (A talent for Eretz Yisrael), by Sholem Asch. The story describes a Jew from Yekaterinoslav, Rabbi Noykh, who arrives in the Jezreel Valley—a symbol of the Labor Settlements Movements—and out of a connection to the land of the valley transforms himself from a merchant into a farmer. R. Noykh is described not as someone who immigrated to Israel because he had become a "new Jew," a pioneer with the appropriate training and ideological and national consciousness, but as a traditional "old" Jew who possesses a "talent" for Eretz Yisrael—in other words, not a skill that can be taught and cultivated. The significant change in fact occurs not in the life of the protagonist but in the lives of his children. The big change in R. Noykh's life is reflected only in his new occupation—in the fact that he becomes a farmer; another novelty the new land holds for him is his encounter with Palestinians (or, as they are called in the story, "the Arab"). But this encounter, too, does not change the protagonist: he regards the Palestinians as his brothers because of their common Semitic origin. The lives of his children, by contrast, are radically different from the life their father led in Eastern Europe: in Palestine/Eretz Yisrael, they grow up on the land and partake in working it instead of devoting themselves to study or running about the market. The narrator of the story is apparently a traveling-visitor, who describes the surprising encounter with the powerful Jew.

This early work was written after Asch's first visit to Israel (1908). Between the world wars, Asch became the most popular writer in the worldwide Yiddish reading public from among the generation of young writers that came after the generation of the great classic writers.[313] Throughout his adult life, Asch moved between Warsaw, New York, and France. In his late years, he came to Israel to settle (but died in London). Like Manger, Asch was a kind of symbol of the wandering universal Jew who came to settle in Israel after many years of traveling. But as in Manger's case, in this case too, the putting down of roots was not so simple: while Asch declared that he had come to Israel to settle[314] and even built a house there,[315] in practice he only visited the country a handful of times, for stays of varying lengths.[316] Moreover, his visits were accompanied by heated controversies stemming from the anger that many in the world of Yiddish culture felt toward his preoccupation with Christianity and Christian themes during the very years of the Holocaust.[317]

And so, Shamri's choice in 1966 to open an anthology entitled *Roots* with a story by a "wandering Jew" like Asch actually demonstrated the complexity of the process of putting down roots. But the gap between the extratextual information about the writer and the content of the story he wrote is the only complexity found in it. In fact, most of the stories selected to portray Israel and life within it are romantic and simplistic in nature. The works deal with such topics as agricultural and social life in the Kibbutzim and natural phenomena (like heat waves, rain, spring, etc.), and they take place, apart from the Kibbutzim, in religious-traditional sites (like Rachel's Tomb) and ancient cities (like Jerusalem and Safed). The anthology includes no works that describe new cities, and above all Tel Aviv. The works that survivor authors wrote about life in Israel present a more complex perspective on the reality they describe, as well as more complex modes of expression. The anthology also included no stories about such loaded topics as the past in Eastern Europe or the years of the Holocaust. It ends with a poem by Aleksander Shpiglblat giving thanks to God ("Danklid"), a choice that gives the whole anthology a conservative and romantic framing. In the introduction Shamri ended his words with a look to the future: "We do not see the present collection as the final word but as one of the barns for the crop of Yiddish literary creation that has grown on our land. We hope that in the subsequent anthologies we will be able to add the works of new writers, who arrived with the waves of 'aliya."[318]

Do these words reflect an optimism about the future of Yiddish in Israel? Shamri expected to discover the next generation of Yiddish writers in the waves of immigration. On the face of it, this is an optimistic statement, which expresses faith in the future of Yiddish in Israel. But for him this renewal is linked to the ongoing immigration to Israel—in other words, the new generation of Yiddish writers will not emerge from among the natives of Israel. Yiddish and its literature will continue to be tied to foreignness and not nativeness. This statement effectively neutralizes the political aspect of the existence of Yiddish in Israel, for which various elements in the Yiddish world fought throughout the first two decades of the state. They fought to change the establishment's view and treatment of Yiddish as a foreign language, to include the language and its literature in the curriculum of the secular education system from kindergarten through high school, and to provide funding for private secular Yiddish education, thereby raising another generation of secular Yiddish speakers who would go on to become writers, journalists, editors, teachers, actors, and directors in Yiddish.

The question of the next generation lies also at the heart of the anthology *Mikan uMiqarov*, which featured works of Yiddish prose in Hebrew translation. As I said, it too was published in 1966. It features sixty-five writers (seven of them women). In his introduction to the anthology, Halamish spelled out its goals:

> The aim of the anthology is to provide the Hebrew readers (and especially the young ones), who do not read Yiddish, with a selection of the prose created in this language in the land (and State) of Israel from the start of our century up to the most recent years. . . . This kind of collection . . . may also fill a certain gap, which was perhaps most felt by the high-school teacher of literature. . . . For there is no doubt that literature that seeks to be the literature of all the people cannot afford to ignore the existence of five-sixths of the people.[319]

The aim of the anthology, then, is to present the treasures of modern secular Yiddish literature to a new reading public. And indeed, it was published with the help of the Vaynfer-Morgenshtern Foundation, and its title page included the statement that "[the foundation] seeks to make accessible to the Hebrew reader literary riches created in Yiddish." As in the case of anthologies of Yiddish works translated into other languages (mostly English), the act of translation was perceived also as an act of rescuing the works from oblivion.[320] Yet translating works of literature from one language into another involves not only aesthetic considerations but also ideological and political ones, certainly in the case of translating Yiddish works into Hebrew in Israel, and especially when the ambitious goal is to introduce Yiddish literature to the first Israeli "Sabra" generations within the state school system. Presenting the works in Hebrew made the task easier but risked obviating the need for the original language. As I show later, Halamish did not skirt this loaded issue but chose first to prepare the groundwork by tackling several obstacles that stood in the way of the acceptance of Yiddish in Israel. The first was, of course, the war of languages or battle of the tongues. He describes this phenomenon as having gone from the world, a thing of the past, and not because it has been resolved but rather because its spokesmen were murdered in the Holocaust. This description of the conflict made it easier for the target audience to receive the works:

> The languages polemic, which went on among our people for two generations and more, is finally about to be forgotten. In any case, no person in his right mind would argue today that our national language in Israel is in any danger from its "enemy"—the Yiddish language. Unfortunately, the end of the battle of tongues came not naturally but by the hand of 'Amalek [the enemy of the Israelites], who ripped out the tongue of masses of Jewish people in Eastern Europe with white-hot pliers, and had 'Amalek been allowed, God forbid, to carry out its scheme, he would then have destroyed and annihilated not only them. . . .
>
> What will be the fate of this language? What and which language is its heir in the existing Diaspora, and who will be charged with carrying forth the great culture that created in it—national and original spiritual assets that many generations cultivated, and just when they were prospering and flowering, they were destroyed?. . . . Our generation, which awakened the Hebrew language and even made it the language of its daily life, is conscious of its responsibility toward the legacy of the generations of the "mother tongue" that it shall not be lost. . . . If indeed we succeed in maintaining and passing on to the next generation the treasures that are in the language of East European Jewry, which for hundreds of years was the very foundation of this people, it is imperative that the nation that sits in its revived state, it, first and foremost, shall fulfill this obligation.[321]

Halamish emphasized the common enemy of speakers of Hebrew and Yiddish alike—the Nazis. The preoccupation with Yiddish in Israel, then, is explained in terms of a moral obligation toward those who are no longer alive, those who were murdered, and as part of the question of the legitimate legacy of Eastern European Jewry, which stems from a sense of obligation and duty—and not necessarily from recognition of the aesthetic value or importance of Yiddish and its culture to contemporary Israeli culture. To prove that the preoccupation with Yiddish does not imply adherence to a Yiddishist ideology, Halamish mentions other generations of Yiddish speakers, who were among the founders of the new Hebrew culture:

> The men and women of the first *'aliyot*, **for the most part**, Hebrew was not their language. . . . Those who rose up as pioneers to make *'aliya* and build the land of Israel—usually the language of their daily dealings was Yiddish . . . Not for reasons of ideology, but simply because they did not speak Hebrew fluently. Moreover, even among the first to take up pen and paper—those writers blessed with creative talent who sought to give literary expression to the moods and atmospheres that prevailed at the time in the small Yishuv . . . among them, too, quite a few chose Yiddish as the language of their literary work; and perhaps they were even a majority.[322]

The question of the importance of Yiddish and its culture to contemporary Hebrew culture was one that concerned Dov Sadan, the first head of the Yiddish Department at the Hebrew University of Jerusalem. In an introduction he wrote for the anthology, Sadan presented the two languages—Hebrew and Yiddish—as one literary and cultural whole. He had already articulated this thesis as early as 1913 in "Eyn literatur in tsvey shprakhn" (One literature in two languages). He too repeated the claim that the war of languages (or battle of the tongues) was over, and he also reinterpreted it: even when it was being waged, it was no more than a minor, passing episode whipped up by interested parties who stood to gain from it and not by those who represented it from among the people or among the writers: "More than the languages battled each other, the battle was waged between factions who used these two languages as a tool of war—with the means eventually becoming an end in itself. And one should not exaggerate the scope of this war—the majority of the general public did not partake in it, since they considered both languages as one in their purpose, now as always, and more importantly: many of the nation's writers did not partake in it, since many of them, and for rather long stretches of time even most of them, were bilingual."[323] Unlike Shamri, who noted at the top of his introductory words (in Yiddish) that the next generation of Yiddish writers would grow out of the immigrants who came in the mass 'aliya and did not address the problem of training a new generation of Yiddish speakers from among the children of the immigrants, Sadan chose to tackle this issue head-on, and in Hebrew, in an anthology targeted primarily at the public of educators in Israel:

> And since this language, including its literature, is an important value in the values of the nation, the question of the bond to the language and its literature is a question of the bond to a piece of the nation's masterpieces, and more than the obligation to think about ways of forging this bond lies with its speakers, the obligation lies with those who are not its speakers, as the former know it and the latter do not know it, and sometimes do not even know of it. And quite a few different paths may lead to this important destination—especially among the Hebrew speakers—of course, the main path is the study and teaching of the language, and the first step that was launched fifteen years ago, by the university in Jerusalem, ought to find its continuation in our high schools.[324]

Sadan makes direct reference here to the need to include the study of Yiddish in high schools (as an elective class), a step that was approved that same year (1966) and applied on a very limited scale: in a single high school (in Kirayt Haim).[325] In keeping with the didactic goal its editors set for the anthology—to present Yiddish literature and its writers to readers unfamiliar with the language and its culture—each story was preceded by a page featuring a picture of the author, biographical information about him or her, and a bibliography of their work. However, the date and place of the first publication of the story selected for the anthology were not given in most cases.

Unlike Shamri, who saw the works as reflecting a (naive) national sentiment, Halamish addressed the criticism that Yiddish literature was not Zionist because its writers did not immigrate to Israel before the Holocaust but only after it. He did not attempt to counter this claim but argued that this disadvantage was in fact an advantage because, as such, Yiddish literature was not committed to any particular theme or mode of writing and thus could express itself on a variety of topics and in various styles: "Regarding Yiddish literature the argument was often heard that for the most part it lacked an ideological compass, and more precisely: a national ideological (i.e., Zionist) tension. . . . This very argument can also imply a positive note from the **literary** perspective: for without the obligation to strive at an ideological goal—the author can be broader in his themes, more profound in the individuation and the authenticity of the styling, and what is lost in the lack of tendentiousness will then be compensated for by an accurate strike at vitality, at the multi-faceted nature of things."[326] This tendency of aiming to separate literature form the political field and from party politics was prevalent in contemporary Hebrew literature from the second half of the 1950s. And indeed, the stories selected for this anthology present a more varied mosaic of life in Israel, and especially in Eretz Yisrael, than the one compiled by Shamri. For example, the section of stories about Eretz Yisrael features four stories about Tel Aviv (in Shamri's anthology there were none on this topic) and even stories about the war of languages or battle of the tongues. Halamish also included in the anthology stories that take place outside of Israel, in the "old home" before the Holocaust or during it in the various diasporas (about twenty out of a total of sixty-five stories). Thus, the stories selected for this anthology paint an almost equal picture of three main realms: the Diaspora, Eretz Yisrael, and Israel. This fact sheds light on the title of the anthology: *Mikan uMiqarov*, "from here and from near"—not only stories written here, in Israel, but also stories from other places, described as "near," emotionally and ideologically, to "here." Yiddish fiction written in Israel is presented, then, within its broad, "exilic" context, which is not perceived as threatening or contemptible as in the concept of the "negation of the Diaspora," an ideological current that in 1966 appeared to be losing force. Thus, like the title of Shamri's anthology, so too that of Halamish suggests a clear attempt to cast Yiddish and its literature as deeply rooted in Israel. But unlike *Roots*, the title *From Here and from Near* implies a broader and more complex perception of the national notion of putting down roots.

An example of the thematic and stylistic complexity that characterizes the stories compiled in *From Here and from Near* is the stories selected to open and close the anthology. The opening story, "BeṢel haḤermon" (In the shadow of the Hermon), was written by Zalman Brokhes, and the closing story is "HaQuqiya" (The cuckoo), by Yishaye Shpigl (which is discussed in chap. 4).[327] "BeṢel haḤermon" takes place during the time of the Ottoman rule in an agricultural colony near Safed that is adjacent to an Arab village. One of the farmers in the colony is distressed when harvest time comes round because the labor force available to him—namely, his family—is small, in part because it is divided: both of his sons are in the United States, and he is left with his wife and two teenage daughters. In this moment of need, he proposes to an Arab youth from the neighboring village to come work for him and in return receive his eldest daughter in marriage. The father does not intend to fulfill his promise, but the two youths end up falling in love, and the daughter even becomes pregnant from her Arab lover. The Jewish father wants to kill his daughter and her lover, and an Arab sheikh rescues them from his hands. The daughter wants to convert her religion to marry her lover, despite knowing full well that she will thereby be banned from her family forever and even among her new family will not be honored. Following the trauma, her father sells his land and moves back to Safed, the old city. This is a bold and complex picture of life in the Land of Israel, made up of layers upon layers of meaning on many levels: emotional, gender and class related, national, environmental, and more. It intimates the dark aspects of the life of a farmer, a man of the land, whose roots run deep into the soil—he is destined to live a traditional and violent life.

Unlike Asch's story that opens *Roots*, here the protagonist is not reborn as a farmer thanks to the land; on the contrary, he himself is responsible for the disintegration of his home and family, a disintegration symbolized by the return to the old Jewish city. The protagonist, who lives as a "new Jew," is destined to revert back to the "old Jew," and this time not because of antisemitism but because of his own seclusionism, not to say racism—he did not keep his word and marry his daughter to the Arab. Unlike in Asch's story, in Brokhes's even the members of the young generation do not become new Jews. Though the daughter does succeed in rising above national and ethnic boundaries and falls in love with the Arab, neither of them chooses to sever all ties from the tribe and from religion and to live as anonymous individuals in a big modern city. The daughter is willing to convert her religion and live in a village, in a tribe that would scorn her for the rest of her life for this choice. It is interesting that Halamish, like Shamri, chose to present the earliest period of Yiddish in Israel in the time of the ʿaliyot, as part of the national revival. Through his choice of Asch's story, Shamri effectively applied new qualities to the image of the old Jew, qualities drawn from familiar and accepted national categories (new Jew versus old Jew, a laborer of the land versus a person without roots). Halamish, by contrast, through his choice of Brokhes's story, points out the fragility of these categories, their dark side, and the painful gap between them and actual life. The Land of Israel is described not as holy but as demanding and destructive. Many different voices are heard both among the Jews and among the Palestinians, which together weave a multicolored picture as opposed to the superficial dichotomy that characterizes the descriptions of "the Jew's" relationship with "the Arab" in the story "A Talent for Eretz Yisrael." It is also interesting to note Halamish's choice to open the anthology with a writer who left Israel after only a few years and who in the world of Yiddish culture was considered a detached outsider.

The fact that two of the three important anthologies of Yiddish fiction, published in Israel in 1948–1967, dealt with the topic of Israel (the third, as I said earlier, is *A shpigl af a shteyn* [A mirror on a stone]) attests to the need of Yiddish cultural agents to present its literature as having been an integral part of the Israeli landscape and of its cultural and national climate. It is to that end that they both shaped the history of Yiddish literature in Israel through the selection of works for the anthology and the order of their appearance. In both anthologies, the earliest period of Yiddish is Eretz Yisrael of the early twentieth century, and among the pioneers rather than in the old Yishuv. It seems that the stories chosen to open each of the anthologies shed significant light on the present of the year in which they were compiled: for Shamri, this past (the period of the Yishuv) is memorialized as in an idyllic and nostalgic postcard; the present—the lives of 'oley sheyres hapleyte in Israel—is presented in its full complexity; and the future is described as dependent on the power of the Zionist institutions to continue bringing immigrants to Israel, since the authors of the future will emerge from among those immigrants. The works chosen to open and close *Roots* seem to enclose the complex and problematic present within an idyllic and comforting framework, lending the anthology the quality of a memory book. This framework attests to the decline that occurred in the vitality of the Yiddish intelligentsia class and the masses of its speakers and consumers, in Israel and abroad. This is in contrast to Halamish's anthology, which clearly demonstrates the vitality of Hebrew culture: the willingness to tackle complex, disturbing, and stimulating messages and the straightforward discussion of difficult and weighty problems involving the incorporation of Yiddish into the educational system in Israel and the question of its future. The works selected for the anthology seem to imply that the future of Yiddish and its literature depends on the willingness of the state institutions to change and recognize their importance to the modern Jewish national culture—and not, as in Shamri's case, on their own unchanging nature. The works with which Halamish chose to open and close the anthology do not calcify the present and cradle its problematic aspects but rather provide it with historical background and a horizon open to the future.

* * *

In 1959, Tel Aviv was indeed the site of a new center of modern Yiddish culture. It had a public—a critical mass of addressees that together formed a community with a common cultural and linguistic identity; it had an "intelligentsia" class, or in more current terminology, a group of cultural leaders that assumed the responsibility and burden of leadership; and it had a network of communication outlets and financial organizations, which allowed the intelligentsia to earn a living and supported its creative production. As we will continue to see in the next chapter, members of this community shared common concepts of the past, present, and future, a sense of identity and desired direction, and a desire to belong to the community.

What Sutzkever saw in his visit to Montreal, which provided the backdrop to his letter to Tsanin, was the predicament of the big, established centers of Yiddish culture in North America. He witnessed their aging and the linguistic and cultural assimilation that dissuaded young generations from participating in this culture. In Israel, by contrast, another generation of Yiddish speakers arrived, relatively young and large both numerically and in terms of its percentage in the population, and they preserved the unique character of their modern culture created in Eastern Europe and also shared deeply unsettling common experiences that influenced their shared will and consent to live together as a nation, in Ernest Renan's phrase. Sutzkever also felt the support that Israel enjoyed in those communities and their extensive willingness to invest in the development of Yiddish culture there, out of a national vision that saw Israel as the place in which modern Jewish identity is shaped. And this identity is shaped through a shared culture.

What Sutzkever did not see—so it seems from his observation—is that the arrival of this further generation in Israel, however determined and influential, and even the money donated by the Jews of the Diaspora were not enough to transform Tel Aviv from a small town to a metropolis on the world map of Yiddish culture, when the latter is situated within the framework of a nation-state. The year 1959 was a high point in the development of this young cultural center, and even a turning point because many projects undertaken by advocates of Yiddish culture in Israel reached fruition in that year: the *LN* officially became a daily paper, the Y. L. Peretz Press established itself as the leading Yiddish publisher in the world, and the local branch of the Bund established a political party that ran in the national elections. Had all the activists of Yiddish culture rallied together to get this party over the electoral threshold, their culture might have made this the year in which Yiddish, as a modern and secular cultural language, was recognized as an important part of Israeli culture. But as we saw, it was not recognized as such, and the year 1959 therefore marks the beginning of its demise. The organizational foundation of this cultural center could not exist solely on donations, without the state's support and recognition of its importance, and it gradually disintegrated. And above all, the masses of Yiddish speakers sought integration into the hegemonic society and its culture and embraced its prevalent ethos (a nationalism that increasingly became religious, messianic, and capitalist). The resounding absence of a new generation of speakers of the language and producers of its culture made *DGK*, which continued to exist until the 1990s, a glowing vestige of a faded culture, which received modest reinforcements from a small number of Yiddish writers who came from Romania and the Soviet Union in the 1960s and 1970s. Among the immigrants who came to Israel from the Soviet Union in the 1990s there were, of course, Yiddish speakers and readers, especially among the older immigrants. But their language of communication was not Yiddish, not even within the family. These immigrants did not need a daily Yiddish paper, and their knowledge of Yiddish was of no help in the process of their absorption. The absence of a young generation of consumers and producers of Yiddish culture caused the entire cultural multi-system to atrophy. Tel Aviv was perhaps more than a small town in terms of the Yiddish cultural enterprises established in it in the first two decades of the state's existence, and more than a periphery on the Yiddishland map, but it did not rise to the level of a metropolis, a cultural center capable of generating new cultural producers whose influence would be recognized beyond the boundaries of Israel. Thus, Yiddish and its culture were rejected by Israel not because they were the last traces of a premodern religious (ultra-Orthodox) culture, for which despondent Holocaust survivors yearned with nostalgia, or because they expressed anti-Zionist Bundist ideas—as their popular image in Hebrew culture would have us believe. The bulk of Yiddish culture in Israel was essentially nationalist, secular, and modern. And precisely for that reason, because it supported Zionism with the aim of expanding it, and because it found a sympathetic ear with the Jews of the Diaspora, Yiddish culture posed a considerable challenge to the Hebrew culture, which Israel had chosen as its only official culture. The results of the Six-Day War bolstered the religious-messianic and capitalist ideas in the dominant society and culture as well as in Yiddish culture.

2

May the Place Comfort You

Memory, Space, and Consolidation of National Identity in the Yiddish Press

1. Memory, Identity, Yiddish

Writing in her diary several months after her arrival in Israel, Rokhl Oyerbakh described her life in Israel as a montage, or a dissolve,[1] between Tel Aviv of the 1950s and prewar Warsaw—the city that had become the quintessential symbol, even the myth, of modern Yiddish culture:[2]

> Have been here in Israel for half a year already, but the emotion, the warming of the heart, and the joy at this have not waned. . . . This emotion [the joy of life in Israel] must be manifest in particular among those who are connected to Yiddish culture, and especially someone like me, who has seen the Jewish masses at their lowest point, in their greatest despair; who knew the bustling Jewish streets of Warsaw—the Jewish dark continent,[3] . . . when the streets throbbed with Jewish life, with a Jewish struggle for existence, with the shouts, the temperament, with all that goes with it. . . . At the end of the war . . . I already knew that only here in Israel would I be able to imagine the dead and the murdered returning to life. And this indeed happened. When I walk the streets of Tel Aviv it is as if I am walking the streets of Warsaw of the past. At every step . . . comrades, relatives, acquaintances, and old friends. . . . Even those whom I had never seen before—appear before me as good, old friends.[4]

The multitudes of Holocaust survivors on the streets of Tel Aviv take the speaker back to the "Warsaw of the past." She characterizes life among these masses as joyful, despite having seen them at their "lowest point" during the war, despite having been witness to the disintegration of the social (and personal) cohesion of her friends in the wake of their extreme distress. Amid the loss and destruction experienced by the Holocaust survivors came also the betrayal by their immediate human environment or milieu—betrayal by family members, neighbors, friends, colleagues, and acquaintances; and the betrayal by the "place" in which they lived and which they had experienced as a familiar (albeit threatening) home—betrayal by non-Jewish neighbors, friends, acquaintances, and colleagues. Her description of the new "place" (Israel) conveys a longing for the healing of the inner ability to read the intentions of the other correctly and to put one's trust in them, to correctly read the place and its threats, and to find in it solace and healing. In this uncharacteristically emotional text (according to accounts by the writer's acquaintances), Oyerbakh testifies to a feeling of joy that is awakened in her, a feeling of intimacy and empathy for other survivors, whom she dubs "acquaintances" and even "friends." She describes the "new place," Israel, as the continuation of the place and time she had inhabited before the war, which was full of meaning for her. Israel and Tel Aviv are described here as a place of comfort and consolation for the lost place, a place where the "dead and the murdered return to life."

In recent years, the concept of place has become the focus of research that studies the ideas and myths in light of which societies create their notions of their environments.[5] In Jewish tradition, the term *place* expresses two conflicting and interchangeable dimensions of experience—material and spiritual. Its direct meaning is concrete, while its borrowed connotation refers to God/the divine or to the existence of the sublime, the abstract, and the pure within the daily earthly realm. These two contradictory and interchangeable aspects are accentuated in the context of mourning. For example, in the familiar condolence "May the Place comfort you among the remnant mourners of Zion," the mourner is offered to convert the pain of the concrete loss (the human "surroundings") into an immersion in the abstract object (the geographical-cultural "environment") and to transform the pain of personal loss into a social and spiritual reward. Melanie Klein describes the human projection of the emotion of love onto new objects, such as spaces or places ("new lands" in her terminology), as an essential stage in healthy emotional development, since the child is driven to weaken his or her attachment to the most important person—namely, his or her mother. Since she provided all of the child's needs and protected him or her, the child perceives her as the source of all good and the source of life. In the unconscious fantasy, she becomes an inseparable part of the child, and thus her death is tantamount to his or her death. When these feelings are very strong, attachment to loved ones can become an unbearable burden.[6] According to Klein, the mother constitutes a primal territory for the baby. In a later developmental stage, she writes, we speak of our country as a "homeland" because it may unconsciously represent our mother, and this allows us to love it with feelings whose nature is borrowed from our attitude toward her. In Klein's picture, a new territory represents a new mother, to replace the real one who was lost.[7] Therefore, the feeling of love awakened in Oyerbakh toward Israel can be understood as a projection of a similar feeling that she feels for her "lost mother" (Warsaw). Obviously, the feeling toward the mother (and toward the secondary territory) is not always a positive one. Indeed, modern Yiddish literature boasts no small number of works expressing a wide range of negative feelings toward these two "territories," from bitter ambivalence to visceral, aggressive hatred. The Holocaust changed the range of emotions and the means for their expression. And indeed, we see in the publications in the daily newspaper *Letste Nayes* (*LN*) that many of the *'oley sheyres hapleyte* saw the establishment of Israel as a consolation, if only a small one, for the loss of the place in which they were born and came of age and which they continued to seek. And so they also began to create anew in the new place, as a kind of solace. For example, survivors from Lublin said, "The few survivors . . . are dispersed to the four corners of the earth. Most of them are in Israel—this, too, is a comfort, even if small. In Lublin a small number of Jews remains, but there is no Jewish life."[8] The commitment to the development and salvation of the secondary territory can therefore be seen as compensation for the inability to save the primary territory, the mother.

In this chapter, I examine how the myths created by the Holocaust survivors in Israel about the destroyed places of their past helped formulate the new national space through practices of memory while nurturing a feeling of national belonging. The past and the memory of it are invaluable resources for communities imagining a shared national identity; belonging to a national community means internalizing common myths about the past, from which behavioral norms in the present and a vision of a longed-for future are derived. Research on collective memory has shown that societies build a unique identity through the retelling of a shared narrative that is presented as their past and through imagining or inventing a common tradition, thereby creating a "collective memory."[9] Sociologist Maurice Holbwachs demonstrated that collective memory, which is distinguished from personal memory and historical memory, is a social concept: communities create practices of memory through whose performance a collective coalesces.[10] Collective memory is an engine of change and renewal in the present. Like the process of editing an anthology, collective memory is created through the selection of contents from the shared tradition and history of the members of the collective, and their interpretation according to the objectives of the present. The intellectual class in modern societies was instrumental not only in driving change but also in dealing with the crises created in its wake. Sociologist Jeffrey Alexander demonstrated how the intellectual class plays a central role in the very definition of an event as traumatic for a society and in contending with the painful process of processing the trauma. This process allows its members to share their pain with one another, to develop empathy for one another, and thus to strengthen the cohesion and resilience of the collective. Successful collective processing of trauma can create a willingness to recognize the human suffering of members of other groups and to take responsibility for it on a personal and collective level.

Scholarship in recent decades has identified the contribution of the Holocaust survivors to the formation of the memory of the Holocaust in Israeli society and culture, in contrast with the past emphasis on the agency of the establishment in this realm.[11] But the intimate connection between the culture and language of the survivors and the top-down institutional paradigms of memory of the Holocaust in Israel have not yet been described or elaborated on in depth; nor have the ways in which paradigms of memory of the Holocaust "from below" influenced the Israeli space. The spatial patterns of memory of the Holocaust that I review here began to be formed on the pages of the Yiddish press. These are not *lieux de mémoire* in the sense described by historian Pierre Nora, whose important studies on the consolidation of French identity focused on the agents of the establishment and the way in which they fashioned this identity "from above."[12] The "realms of memory" described here were created from below by and for ʻoley sheyres hapleyte in Israel. As I have described, the Yiddish press printed in the young Yiddish center in Tel Aviv differed from the press printed in established Yiddish cultural centers around the world: the latter was mostly produced by Jewish émigrés from as early as the end of the nineteenth century and the beginning of the twentieth century; in Israel, by contrast, the vast majority of Yiddish papers began to be published after the Holocaust, and many of its writers and readers were survivors. It is no wonder, then, that the Holocaust was discussed in the Yiddish press in Israel consistently and at length from its inception. A comparative look at the patterns of memory of the Holocaust that coalesced in Israel and those created outside of Israel highlights the uniqueness of the former. The paradigms of memory in Israel were fashioned in light and in service of Israel's struggle to consolidate a national identity, while in other places the formative struggle was primarily that of an ethnic minority to consolidate its ethnic distinctiveness. The studies on patterns of memory of the Holocaust outside of Israel do document discrete patterns of memory that were formed among various ideological streams within the communities, but with no real distinction between those created by "veteran" immigrants and those created by the Holocaust survivors themselves.[13] The focus in this chapter is on the first decade after the establishment of Israel—from the 1948 war to the Eichmann trial. The reason for this periodization is twofold. First, this decade saw the formation of the top-down, state-guided patterns of Holocaust memory, whereas the patterns of memory created by ʻoley sheyres hapleyte developed from below, in their unique language and with their unique content and modes of expression; as such, they constitute a necessary completion of the picture of the memory of the Holocaust in Israel in this period. Second, the Eichmann trial has been perceived in scholarship until recent years as a turning point in attitudes toward the Holocaust survivors by the Israeli establishment and society because the latter were exposed, through the trial, to the survivors' suffering and to manifestations of their heroism in the years of the Holocaust. In my opinion, if indeed the trial was a turning point, this was in large part the result of the ongoing and intensive preoccupation of the survivors with the Holocaust, in their language and in the cultural frameworks they created, throughout the 1950s.

2. “Undzer Akropol” (Our Acropolis): Myth, History, Newspaper

The Holocaust, as a theme and a formative event in the life of the nation, in the lives of Jewish communities and individuals, readers, and writers, appeared regularly in the Yiddish press in Israel. It was described in short stories and serial novels,[14] mentioned in news items on literary works (from around the world) and in reviews of these works, and of course portrayed in various testimonials,[15] documents, diaries, memoirs, folktales, and classified ads searching for lost relatives.[16] The preoccupation with the Holocaust and its memory was not only the purview of professional journalists and intellectuals. The readership itself expressed a strong desire to use the press as a medium for channeling its feelings and thoughts on this formative event, and their desire was met. The letters-to-the-editor section of the *LN*, for example, was much more expansive than similar sections in the Hebrew press of the time. In November 1950, the column “Yizker iber shtet un shtetlekh” (In memory of cities and towns) began to appear (later also under the title “Di fartilikte yidishe kehiles” [The destroyed Jewish communities][17]), featuring descriptions of communities, from various cities and towns, that had been devastated in the Holocaust. These pieces were written by the paper’s readers from Israel and around the world, and not by its professional writers. Some of the texts were chapters from memorial books-in-progress, and some were attempts at organizing new hometown associations.[18]

These columns, written from the “bottom up,” were unique to the *LN*. A random sampling of popular Yiddish daily newspapers in New York, *Forverts* and *Der Tog*, from 1949 to 1951, indicates that those newspapers did not include any such section. Research on the memory of the Holocaust has dealt with the phenomenon of Yizker books (although not exhaustively),[19] but this unique form of Holocaust memory as it appeared in the newspapers has yet to be described and discussed. Unlike Yizker books, the memorial columns appeared regularly and frequently in the *LN*, enabling different groups to give their versions of the community’s memory or of a formative event in its history. The column was published at certain times in the year and thus took part in the cyclical “national calendar” that the newspaper shaped for its readers.

The writing in the readers’ columns varied between historical documentation and mythologization of life in the communities. As in the Yizker books, the period covered by the descriptions in the newspaper spanned some fifty to one hundred years, as the writers based themselves mostly on personal memories. The descriptions generally included a survey of the history of the community aimed at pointing out its uniqueness and its development from a traditional community to modern society. They included descriptions, biographies, and anecdotes from the lives of rabbis and descriptions of the activity and challenges of the community's religious-traditional institutions (from the synagogue to the *beys medresh* [religious study hall] and the *kheyder* [religious primary school] to the *hekdesh* [the community trust]) as well as modern-secular ones (libraries, schools, youth movements, theater groups, newspapers, social aid organizations, hospitals, and more). The communities were generally described as a tapestry of characters woven into the typical social and economic classes and their underlying ideologies. Finally, these columns often included detailed descriptions of the annihilation of the community and its members during the Holocaust. These columns were a fascinating combination of documentary-historical style along with personal mythicization. For example, writers made an evident effort to include precise details, such as dates and names of victims, as well as the identity of the sources of these details. The writing strove to be "historical"—not for intellectual purposes but as a practice of memory of the destroyed community. By contrast, other descriptions by community members were more mythical or attempted to draw ideological conclusions. This was especially true of descriptions of the brave standing of members of the communities in the face of the terrors of the war. For example, in the description of the heroism of one young woman, the daughter of Leyzer Bukhbinder, it is evident that the writer sees her as an embodiment of the traditional ideal of martyrdom in Judaism and seeks by means of the story of her heroism to unite this ideal with the modern national ethos of sacrifice for the continuity of the nation. Also evident is his use of the archetypical image of the "nation as woman" in an attempt to transmute the woman's heroism into a national ethos.[20] Furthermore, the writing of these columns was seen as a ritual practice of the memory of the destroyed community. For example, a column dedicated to the Lublin community ends with this invocation: "May these words serve as the memory of the martyrs of Lublin on the eighth year to their destruction. May their memory be a blessing!"[21] Some of the descriptions ended with a description of the active lives of the survivors in the present and their organization in hometown associations in Israel and the world.[22] In these descriptions, the memories of the past and of the destroyed place are presented as positive forces in the present-day lives of the survivors, and in particular in their consolidation into a national collective.

In 1956–1961, the *LN* published approximately twenty Yizker sections annually. Despite the fact that during these years many significant events related to the Holocaust took place (like the passing of the Holocaust and Heroism Remembrance Day Law in 1959, Eichmann's capture in May 1960, and the beginning of his trial on April 11, 1961), the rate of publication did not change. By contrast, it seems that national events did affect the rate of publication—for instance, in the year of Israel's tenth anniversary, 1958, only nine columns were published. Mordkhe Tsanin, the *LN*'s founder and editor, described this powerful movement "from below" to the New York readers of the *Forverts*: "Now, when we mark the anniversary of the destruction of most of the Jewish cities and towns in Poland by the Germans, I am approached by dozens of new immigrants who bring me essays, memoirs and letters about their cities and towns. They want everything to be printed and to tell the world once again what their towns symbolized and how everything has gone with the wind."[23] Why did this systematic practice of recounting the annals of the destroyed communities and reflecting on their meaning take root in Israel above all other places? What did this intermediate genre, between history and myth, afford its writers? I interpret this practice as part of the communal processes of grieving and part of the communal processing of trauma, which made it possible for the survivors to create new homes. It can be seen as a modern verbal and linguistic variation of the traditional "symbol of destruction" affixed to Jewish homes and of the allusions to *ḥurban haBayit* (the destruction of the Temple; literally, the destruction of the home) in the Jewish liturgical poems, prayers, and customs related to the traditional ritual of starting a new family. As reflected in the poems of Manger and Judah ha-Levi, the process of returning to Zion and to Israel included a stage of grief and processing of trauma. According to Dominick LaCapra, the processing of trauma takes place in language, as an act of working-through and of articulation: "To the extent one works through trauma . . . one is able to distinguish between past and present and to recall in memory that something has happened to one (or one's people) back then while realizing that one is living here and now with openings to the future."[24] As I pointed out (note 19 in the introduction), LaCapra distinguishes between two kinds of emotional pain: absence, whose source is existential, and loss, caused by a concrete separation. Trauma blurs the boundaries between these two types of pain and causes them to be interchanged, while a successful working-through of the trauma makes the distinction between them possible: "When absence is converted into loss, one increases the likelihood of misplaced nostalgia or utopian politics in quest of a new totality or fully unified community. . . . When loss is converted . . . into absence, one faces the impasse of endless melancholy, impossible mourning, . . . any process of working through the past and its historical is foreclosed and permanently aborted."[25] Unlike Klein's approach mentioned earlier, which highlights the advantages for proper psychic development of converting one emotion into another and one place into another, LaCapra underscores the risks involved in these conversions. In his view, the two distinct kinds of pain, absence and loss, need to be processed through different and distinct forms of writing, the historical and the mythical. Claude Lévi-Strauss noted the central difference between myth and history: the myth is a closed and therefore circular storyline, whereas history is a series of linear events whose end is unknown.[26] Were the Yizker columns in the *LN* an expression of the processing of the traumas and losses of the war or an expression of their repression?

The early beginnings of modern Yiddish culture were characterized by considerable creativity in the fields of history and literature alongside a reflecting on their distinct natures.[27] As in every modern culture, so too in Yiddish culture historical writing played an important role in consolidating the national society by shaping its shared consciousness of time, and literary writing played a central role in creating a common ethos for its member citizens. Like every other modern culture, modern Yiddish culture was created by the intelligentsia, even when it displayed distinctly populist tendencies. For instance, we are familiar with Dubnow's and An-sky's call to the masses in the late nineteenth century and early twentieth to transform themselves into "historians" in light of the profound and rapid changes their communities were undergoing as a result of economic, social, and political processes.[28] The echoes of their call continued to be heard after the Holocaust by its survivors. Already in the DP camps in Germany, Yisroel Kaplan, one of the editors of the paper *Undzer veg* (Our way), published a call similar to that of Dubnow and An-sky in his paper.[29] Figures like Rokhl Oyerbakh, Nakhmen Blumental, Mark Dvorzhetski, Yekhiel Yeshaye Trunk, Philip Friedman, and Yosef Kermish documented the Holocaust and produced historical writing about it that grew out of their own close connection to the "people," the survivors themselves. Mark Smith has described this connection as "the Lay-Professional Partnership."[30] This fact alone already casts the history they wrote as an act that lies somewhere between the critical and emotionally removed work of the historian and that of a representative of a community or tribe telling the annals of his family. But the column "In Memory of Cities and Towns" started out as the spontaneous writing of readers of the *LN*.[31] No calls were published by political leaders, opinion leaders, or institutions encouraging the masses to write, and these were not literary works by established authors. This fact further blurs the boundaries between the two types of writing (and increases the risk that attends this blurring). I have already noted that after the Holocaust the gap between the "polo intelligentsia" (half-intelligentsia) and the masses was significantly diminished, and with it also the gap that had gradually opened in the interwar years between the Jewish community created and consolidated in Eastern Europe and the one forged in the United States. These same trends were also evident in Israel of the 1950s, perhaps even in a more pronounced form because of the overall smallness of Israeli society and the large percentage of survivors of Eastern European origin within it, and also because, contrary to the United States, the dominant ethos in Israeli society was still Eastern European socialist in nature.

In the 1950s, the academic discipline of history became established in Israel and was showcased in respected platforms, including in particular the history of the Holocaust. The writing of history from below was regarded by the institutional historians as unprofessional.[32] Only recently has the scholarship found interest and value in this type of writing and recognized a variety of motivations for producing it, emotional as well as social-cultural.[33] Several of these motivations also drove the writers of the *LN*'s Yizker columns for the destroyed communities—the need of the survivors to create a symbolic memorial monument for many relatives and acquaintances from their community and thus to fulfill a moral obligation toward them in an attempt to free themselves of feelings of guilt for having stayed alive and for their inability to prevent the deaths of their loved ones. In this respect, the column gave the survivors of these communities a specific date on which those who did not know the date of their relatives' death could mourn them and a place in which they could contribute to the documentation of their community's annihilation. In addition to its role as a channel for communal grieving, a central impulse for writing the column was educational: it is evident in the texts that their function was not just to transmit information to the next generations about what the Nazis had committed during the war but also and indeed especially to impart to them the worldview, which had nearly been lost, of the members of these destroyed communities. This educational impulse became all the more important in light of the tendency toward alienation from and even negation of the Diaspora that prevailed in the burgeoning Israeli culture and in light of Israeli society's tendency to distance itself from the near Jewish past in Eastern Europe. This tendency was evident, for instance, in the activity of the "Canaanites," which reverberated in broad swaths of the Israeli population and especially among the youth.[34] One harsh and harmful expression of such alienation was the prevalent view that in the years of the Holocaust, the Jews of Eastern Europe were led "like sheep to the slaughter." The survivors of the Holocaust, in Israel and elsewhere, saw this as a painful and dangerous libel. Not only did it tarnish an entire population of victims and survivors, but even more harmfully, it alienated the young generation born in Israel from its past in Eastern Europe. In the new Hebrew culture, the Holocaust was perceived as a source of shame and embarrassment that Zionism and its ultimate outcome—Israel—were supposed to solve. The Holocaust survivors who came to Israel after its establishment were described as weak people who had survived in dubious ways, and they were even perceived as having brought their fate upon themselves to some extent, because they had stayed in exile and had not come to Israel before the war.[35] Their language—Yiddish—was a symbol of exile and drew considerable scorn, especially from the generation of Sabras born in Israel. We find literary descriptions of this negative image in, for instance, the novel that became a symbol of the Sabra generation, *Days of Ziklag*:

> Love of the Jewish people! Who loves it? Do we not flee as if scalded from anything Jewish, and that is our glory and pride. . . . We despise anything that has even the slightest trace of it. From the Jewish history lessons, with all the troubles, to the Jewish foods and groans, anything that has a Diaspora accent, Diaspora customs and Yiddish in general, that joke that is called Yiddish, with

> all of its sounds and inflections, its untanned faces exposing teeth fixed with silver and gold and a thread of saliva of recollections from their old shtetls. And all of their biblical talk and their wisdom, which they brought from their "Tarbut" schools, or from the teachers' seminary in Grodno or from wherever—what are all of these, tell me, compared to, say, scoring a goal from outside the sixteen-meter field with the left foot?[36]

By contrast, in Yiddish culture the Holocaust was called *khurbn* (destruction), its victims were called *kdoyshim* (the sacred ones), its ruins *yidishe kdushe* (Jewish sanctity), and their language became a new *loshn koydesh* (sacred language). The program applied in Israeli schools in the 1950s to enhance Jewish consciousness with the aim of reducing the gap between Hebrew culture and the Diaspora was harshly criticized by advocates of Yiddish culture in Israel, since "the Diaspora," the near past of the Jewish people in Eastern Europe and its spiritual contents, were described in this program as purely religious. The secular and national Yiddish culture was denied (I return to this point later).

The Yizker columns in the *LN*, then, allowed the community of Yiddish speakers to establish a positive "myth of origins" for its readers and their families, which could function as a counternarrative to the negative image that surrounded them in Israeli society,[37] although the tradition and practice of writing about destroyed places was created in Yiddish culture tens and even hundreds of years before the establishment of Israel. These alternative narratives filled the vacuum created by the absence of elderly family members, family photos, and family documents and records. As with every myth of origins in every culture, in these stories of communities and their aftermath the Holocaust survivors in Israel found reinforcement, encouragement, and guidance in coping with the challenges of life in the absence of the older generations and a stable community. These stories allowed them to forge a positive connection to the past, as a source of vitality and creativity. Even the descriptions of the Holocaust focused on manifestations of heroism and resistance (on the cultural and spiritual level as well as the physical) and not on descriptions of helplessness and humiliations. An example of this founding myth is evident in an essay by Nakhmen List (one of the regular writers for the *LN*) about Warsaw, whose title is "Af di khurves fun undzer akropol" (On the ruins of our Acropolis) and from which the title of this subsection is borrowed. He writes,

> In Eastern Europe, where millions of Jews once lived, a unique Jewish culture was created and developed. . . . Warsaw! . . . Your memory is deeply etched in my mind. Behind your walls lies the place that symbolizes the Jewish spirit. . . . Under the influence of the memory of the Acropolis the great French writer Ernest Renan one prayed on its ruins for the pursuit of the perfection of humanity. . . . We stand before our Acropolis and honor . . . the memory of the cultural center that he [the barbaric hater] has destroyed.[38]

With these words the writer alludes to the destruction of Warsaw during World War II and compares its ruins to those of the Acropolis so as to render it a sacred symbol of Israeli national culture. This image (somewhat forced) belongs to the realm of mythical writing insofar as Warsaw before the Holocaust was not in fact attributed with cultural prestige, as Vilna was, for instance. The Jewish culture that developed in Warsaw was a varied mosaic of ideological movements and sociopolitical approaches. But above all, the writer ignores the fact that Jewish culture in Warsaw had already begun to disintegrate before the Holocaust. It is interesting that the writer chose the image of ancient Athens's center of worship and not the image that prevails in Jewish culture and especially in the Talmud, of the destroyed Jewish temple. The historical context in which this passage was written gives this choice special significance—the essay was published on the occasion of the Holocaust Memorial Day in Israel. The Warsaw Ghetto uprising was a central image in the ceremonies marking that day. List sought to expand the myth so that it also encompassed the culture created in Warsaw before the Holocaust. The "lesson of the Holocaust" that he proposed in the myth he created is not a severing of the new national culture from Western culture (symbolized by the Acropolis) after the Holocaust but in fact a view of the culture of the Israeli nation as a product and part of Western culture. Another interesting item that emerges from the myth List created is the image of the ruins as a cultural site that underscores the importance of proximity to the physical remnants of the destroyed site for the growth of a new culture out of these ruins. The literary description of the ruins compensated for the physical distance between Israel and the ruins of the Jewish communities in Eastern Europe.[39]

Thus, the *LN* Yizker columns for the murdered communities gave expression, week after week, to many and changing voices of survivors pursuing the commemoration of their communities. The cyclical manner in which these voices were heard, their language, and the medium that disseminated them consolidated the survivors into a unique, national community of memory. Israel, in this respect, was a unique space. On the one hand, the survivors there participated in a broader process, accentuated and intensified, of building a new life as part of a new society searching for its way: unlike in other places to which Holocaust survivors immigrated, in Israel they were not an ethnic minority forced to fit into an existing society and state; the mourning of the home that had been lost and the processing of the trauma of the war were an inseparable part of the renewal of everyday life in this private and national home, and they were expressed in the Yizker sections published in the *LN*. On the other hand, because the absorbing class of the Israeli population did not always choose to participate in the survivors' processes and rituals of mourning and did not necessarily regard them as part of the new national ethos, the survivors' grieving practices sometimes took on an air of resistance against the prevalent ethos in the hegemonic culture and absorbing society.

3. "*Der ovnt fun bagegenishn*" (An Evening of Meetings): Ceremony, Community, Trauma

"Communities of memory," then, were consolidated through the pages of the Yiddish press in Israel from the first years of its existence. Toward the end of 1950, ads placed by hometown associations (*landsmanshaftn*) began to appear in the *LN* inviting survivors to participate in public events to commemorate the Holocaust. From July 1950 to December 1951, 110 such ads appeared in the paper (in addition to missing relative ads). Most were published in the latter half of each year, from July to December, because many communities were annihilated around the time of the Jewish High Holidays, known in Hebrew as *Yamim nor'aim* (days of awe). Reading through these ads reveals that the communities of memory soon changed from imagined communities that existed in the pages of the newspaper into communities of memory that were active in the actual space. The great demand on the part of survivors in Israel to form such communities of memory was expressed in the large number of ads published in the *LN* and in the atmosphere of "commemorative density" that prevailed in their culture.[40] An expression of this density is found, for instance, in a 1950 letter to the editor by an *LN* reader who complained that "Israel is a little America, at least according to the large number of hometown associations that exist here."[41] Surveying the ads published by hometown associations in 1950–1951 sheds light on the process through which they came into being. At first, individual survivors, who in some cases were representatives of hometown associations outside of Israel, asked survivors from their hometown living in Israel to contact them.[42] Afterward, an ad would be placed in the paper calling on survivors from the town to attend a meeting at which the association would be inaugurated and the desired modes of commemorating the destroyed community would be discussed.[43] These ads were typically signed by *Der tsaytvayliker komitet* (the temporary committee). Later on, ads appeared inviting the survivors to attend memorials and association meetings that were held after the memorials. These ads were signed *Der va'ad* (the committee). In 1961, the Union of Polish Immigrants in Israel reported that it was acting as an umbrella organization for 104 hometown associations, most of which began to operate after the establishment of the state. Though most of these associations commemorated Polish Jewish communities, some associations were established to commemorate communities outside of Poland.

The memorial events held by the associations were typically described in the ads using the traditional Jewish term *hazkore* (memorial ceremony),[44] but also *hazkore-ovnt* (memorial evening), *hazkore farzamlung* (memorial assembly), *ondenkungs-hazkore* (remembrance memorial), *zikorn-tog* (memorial day), *yizker-farzamlung* (remembering assembly), *kines tsu fareybikn di kdoyshim* (gathering to commemorate the martyrs), *asifes-evel* or *troyer-ovnt* (evening mourning event), *troyer-akademie* (memorial assembly), and *troyer-farzamlung* (mourning assembly). Most of these names contain a traditional linguistic element borrowed from the "holy tongue" (Hebrew) and a linguistic element from modern Yiddish. These combinations, which Yiddish allows, exemplify the advantage, noted by Ernest Gellner, of a people with a high, ancient culture on which to draw—an asset of inestimable value in state-building and a definitive factor in attaining a preliminary political sense of ethnicity.[45] Combining traditional elements in the name of the public event makes it possible to create an immediate link to the past and to "invent a tradition" (in Eric Hobsbawm's oxymoronic phrase) for a new community, as well as to contribute to its homogeneity by bridging ideological differences among its members.[46]

These memorial events were usually held on the anniversary of the destruction of the communities, or in the case of larger communities, on the anniversary of the beginning of the destruction or the destruction of the ghetto.[47] The destroyed communities were almost always referred to in the ads as *di umgekumene kdoyshim* (the perished martyrs, or holy ones). In a few interesting cases, they were called *di gefalene* (the fallen) to emphasize that the members of the community were killed while fighting.[48] This wording may reflect the influence of the commemoration of the soldiers who fell in Israel's "War of Independence"—in other words, the influence of the images that were created in Western European national culture and prevailed in that culture in the interwar years.[49] The ads were usually designed like death notices, even though many of them also announced a general assembly of the association where administrative issues were discussed, like the election of an administrative board or the setting up of loan funds for housing, education, social assistance, cultural events, and more. This mixture of the sacred and the secular testifies to the extent to which daily life in the present, with all of its challenges, shaped the memory of the past according to the needs of the society that created it.[50]

After the Holocaust, the hometown associations all over the world directed their resources not only to providing physical aid to survivors but also to the domain of Holocaust commemoration.[51] They had already organized public memorial evenings in the DP camps and all over the world.[52] Even after state-sponsored national memorial days and ceremonies were instituted, the survivors continued to participate in memorial events organized by their associations. From literary descriptions we learn that 'oley sheyres hapleyte often attended several memorial events every year—for instance, one event for the community in which they were born and another for the town to which they moved as adults, or two events for the communities in which each one of the couple was born. The ads published by hometown associations in the *LN* between 1950 and 1951 reveal that the vast majority of these communal events were held in Tel Aviv—and not in Jerusalem, where the Chamber of the Holocaust Museum was built and the national memorial ceremonies were held. The events were held at various venues in the city: Beit Ha-Halutsot on King George Street, Mizrahi on Ahad Ha-ʿAm, Beit Strauss on Balfour Street, Ohel Shem on the same street, Betty Hall on Dizengoff Square, Beit Israel on Dizengoff Street, Beit Yeshayahu on Chlenov Street, and the halls of the Talpiot and Herzliya gymnasiums. More traditionally oriented associations held memorial events in synagogues: Ahavat Zion on Keren Kayemeth Le-Israel Boulevard (now Ben-Gurion Boulevard), Torat Moshe on Judah ha-Levi's Street, and the Central Synagogue in Jaffa.

There are interesting differences between the descriptions of memorial events held in Hebrew in the general society and those held in Yiddish by the survivors. In the public memorial events, "since 1945 the ghetto resistance fighters and the Jewish partisans were central speakers."[53] By contrast, the descriptions of the memorial events held by the survivors emphasize the participation of Yiddish authors from the hometown or renowned cantors from among the ʿoley sheyres hapleyte. This difference attests to the different heroic ethos in each of these sectors: in the hegemonic society, the ethos of the soldier as hero prevailed, whereas the survivors typically adhered to a broader notion of heroism that included cultural activity and manifestations of the human spirit in wartime. The perception of loss was similarly broadened in the survivors' society, so that the culture that was murdered along with its subjects and of course Yiddish, the language of the victims and the survivors, were also accorded a sacred status.

The descriptions of the survivors' memorial events place special emphasis on the communal aspect. The hometown associations that organized these memorial gatherings often charged a participation fee and advertised that all proceeds would go to taking care of the needs of the new immigrants.[54] These meetings were important to the survivors, and they attended them from all across the country. Something of the atmosphere at these events is captured in the following description by the writer Yitskhok Perlov:

> The Beit Ha-Halutsot [hall] was already full. The hall was lighted up and loud. As always before the *hazkores* [memorials], the place was noisy-cheerful. All the "hazkore" events are cheerful. Because an "hazkore" is after all an evening of meetings. An "hazkore" brings together all of the compatriots, and not just [those] from Tel Aviv, with whom one meets from time to time. People come from the most distant cities and towns, from the country's most remote *moshavot* [agricultural colonies] and *Kibbutzim*. Here people meet who have not seen each other for years, or decades, [who] did not even know of each other's existence. Boyhood friends recognize one another, embrace, pat each other joyfully on the shoulder. Girlhood friends, once slender schoolgirls with charming braids, now bulgy ladies with dyed hair and puffed up hairdos, meet with made-up lips, wipe away a tear and immediately start asking and telling

> about the past decades. . . . From the crowded hall rises up a heat, sweaty fumes mixed with perfume, naphthalene moth balls from the Sabbath and holiday suits, and cigarette smoke.[55]

A description of the memorial evenings as social encounters appeared also in the *LN* section of letters to the editor: "The public often comes to the memorials as to a social outing: they chat, they joke, etc.," complained the reader Nosn Sholem, "and this do people who have lost so much and who have actually experienced all the horrors." [56] Another reader (identified by a pseudonym and the name of his town) articulated a profound perspective on the need for this kind of encounter: "The few remaining survivors . . . will gather from all corners of Israel . . . to bear together the pain that words cannot describe." This pain, according to his description, is caused by their feelings of guilt for having stayed alive. The survivors' gatherings brought them relief by replacing their solitary "meetings" with the dead: "Relatives come to you. . . . They come in the midst of the tumult of daily life and in the silence of night. They come—your wife, your children, your brother, your sister, your father, your mother, your friend—they come, they look at you, they talk to you. And you are ashamed of your life and feel that your heart stops beating."[57]

These memorial evenings, then, were an important institution in the lives of the survivors.[58] Mary Douglas has pointed out the importance of ritual to society in general and to modern secular society in particular: "As a social animal, man is a ritual animal. If ritual is suppressed in one form, it crops up in others, more strongly the more intense the social interaction." According to Douglas, social rituals create for a society a framework and a reality that could not exist without them. The values of the society are reflected in them: "Ritual [is an] attempt to create and maintain a particular culture, a particular set of assumptions by which experience is controlled."[59] LaCapra noted the importance of the social ritual to the processing of trauma. According to him, modern societies are characterized by a small number of effective social rituals, which enable social processes of mourning and grief. Working through the trauma as a social process prevents individuals from sinking into endless melancholy grief and is able at least partially to return them to the demands and responsibilities of social life.[60] The shared mourning allows the individual and the group to develop distance from the past, awareness of the new possibilities that the present affords, and an ability to feel empathy for others. The collective mourning enables a joint processing of the feelings of guilt associated with the renewed interest in life, feelings that many of the survivors regarded as a betrayal of their murdered loved ones. The public memorial ceremonies, then, allowed them to shift the identification with the trauma and with those who were murdered from a mode of resistance into a mode of processing, which in turn enables the creation of a new life, supported by the collective identity. Thus, not only individuals but the group as a whole could experience itself as capable of acting in the cultural, social, and political realm.

The communities of memory that were forged in the public ceremonies effectively became a kind of new incarnation of the murdered communities: the survivors of these communities met repeatedly, on the same day every year, and the group consolidated around joint memories and experiences shared before the Holocaust, during it, and after it, in a common language. These gatherings allowed ʻolim of all social classes, who lived in peripheral areas, to come to Tel Aviv and meet friends who shared a similar past and present. In this "support group," they could give and receive support, create a tight network at a time when communication technologies were limited, and through this network receive and give information about the fate of relatives and friends, and help and be helped with the challenges of their present lives, like livelihood and bureaucracy, education, and health. In many cases, these ties served as substitutes for the original families who had perished, and they provided the children born in Israel with "substitute" relatives. Moreover, in these gatherings the communities were able to bridge the present and the past by creating shared positive images of the past, in their shared language, and thus to thwart the attempts of the Nazis and their collaborators to turn them into victims by stripping them and cutting them off of their past, their families, and their culture.

These loyalties to the "*alte heym*" (old home) were very problematic from the point of view of the melting-pot policy. They unified Jews from centers of Jewish culture all over the world and gave them a common object of yearning that was not Zion. "The new Zion," Israel, sought to be "the big home" of the Jews of the world. This was a new home, one that demanded bearing the burden of building and protecting it. By contrast, the yearning for the alte heym was a yearning for everything that had been lost: for the perished loved ones, for the places that existed in the past and the landscapes of Eastern Europe, for the life that had taken place in those landscapes, for the bonds that were created during the war and dissipated thereafter, for the freedom and chaos that the war had enabled, and sometimes for existential losses unrelated to the war, like the loss of childhood and youth. The feelings of guilt for having stayed alive, the pain of longing, and the hardships of the present life created a need for a consoling and empowering image of the Jewish life that had existed "there"—in Eastern Europe and in its quintessential symbol, the shtetl. This was also aided by the growing distance between their present lives and the past. The hardships of life before the war were often dwarfed by the events of the Holocaust. And thus, the destroyed community became the abstract focus of a yearned-for identification, which joined the concrete Israeli identification. Reports published in the *LN* and the *LF* about memorial days organized by the hometown associations suggest that the survivors were aware of the contradiction between their particular ethnic identification and the efforts—including their own—to belong to the new Hebrew national identity. Consider, for example, the following description of a memorial-day ceremony held by the Lodzh hometown association in Tel Aviv in 1953:

> The Ohel Shem hall, with its many passages, was full to the brim, a larger crowd stood in the street. . . . The two thousand Jews . . . who came to honor the memory of their tortured fellow townsmen . . . demonstrate the kind of cultural and social power that lies hidden in the movement of the hometown associations in our country. Official Zionist circles ignored . . . this movement based on the argument that hometown associations cannot exist in Israel, here everyone must all mix together in one cauldron, in which everyone must be cooked together anew.[61]

It is important to know that these "official Zionist circles" sometimes included members of the survivors' hometown associations. This aspect of the complex politics of memory—the conflict between the particular identity and the general identity—was lodged at heart of the survivors' identity. The tension between the multiple identities of these 'oley sheyres hapleyte was expressed in the choice of language in which to conduct the communal memorial service. Some members wished to hold it in Hebrew, the ancient language that held special prestige in the multilingual Jewish culture in Europe and was the language of the nonquotidian. It was also the language of the hegemony of the nation-state, with which most of the survivors identified. However, there were also those who regarded this linguistic choice as an insult to the memory of the destroyed community, whose language and culture was Yiddish, as well as an insult to the members of the new community forged in Israel, who had made a significant effort to come to Tel Aviv and who for the most part were not proficient in Hebrew,[62] and especially not in its Sephardi pronunciation that took hold in Israel.[63] This is how Tsanin described to readers of *Forverts* an incident that took place at a memorial evening in 1950 attended by survivors from Lodzh:

> In Tel Aviv . . . dozens of memorial evenings are currently taking place, organized by the hometown associations. . . . In one such memorial evening for Lodzh . . . someone insisted on speaking only in Hebrew, while the gathered audience demanded that, in order for them to understand what he was saying about their Lodzh, that he speak in Yiddish. . . . They drove the speaker off the stage. And this did not occur because of some kind of protest for Yiddish or against Hebrew. Many of those who attended the event speak Hebrew and cherish Hebrew. But about their own Lodzh they want to hear and understand everything, and that is why they want Yiddish to be used. Because Jewish Lodzh spoke Yiddish, because their parents expressed their joys and sorrows in this pleasant tongue, which to them was sanctified and had become a new *loshn koydesh* [sacred language].[64]

The language is described as a highly significant component both of the myth created by the community of memory about the destroyed community and of the consolidation of this new community in the present.

The hometown associations and Yiddish cultural organizations in Israel did not aim merely to hold these memorial events for the Holocaust; in addition, from the early 1950s, alongside their independent action, they fought for the establishment's recognition of this widespread popular phenomenon, in the form of establishing an official national memorial day for the Holocaust.[65] This was an attempt to expand the boundaries of those substitute "Jewish communities" that were recreated in the gatherings of the hometown associations and to include in their public more segments of the burgeoning Israeli society. Apart from the importance of the institutional recognition of their loss, these organizations hoped that marking a joint memorial day for the whole of Israeli society would help bring its various sectors, some of which held prejudices against the survivors, closer together. The negotiations about receiving reparations from Germany and the possibility of establishing diplomatic relations with it pained many of the survivors and added special weight to their demand that the state fulfill its obligation toward the victims. Even events seemingly unrelated to this struggle, like the Wadi Salib riots (1959), which the press covered extensively at the time, demonstrated to the survivors the need for such a day. The Yiddish press focused on the offensive stereotypes hurled at the survivors, which were a painful demonstration of their unflattering image in the eyes of various parts of the Israeli public.

In the run-up to the ten-year anniversary of the Warsaw Ghetto Uprising, marked in 1953 (the year in which Israel began receiving the reparation money from Germany), writers at the *LN* debated the question of how the uprising should be commemorated and honored.[66] In an editorial marking the anniversary, Tsanin wrote,

> The government of Israel has declared itself the heir of the six million Jews who were murdered, and for their blood has signed a compensation agreement with the heirs of Hitler. But that same government did not even see fit to organize an official Yizker [memorial event] to commemorate the six million Jews that have now already been sold. The Yizker was left [to] parties and groups, each of which made the uprising in the ghetto into an uprising of a party and an uprising of a group. . . . The best sons of the Jewish people must carry forth the uprising for the salvation of the Jewish spirit.[67]

The battle of communities of memory from among the survivors to establish a national memorial day continued throughout the 1950s. It revolved both around the very existence of such a day, a battle that ended successfully, and around its timing, a battle that was unsuccessful. Yiddish cultural organizations in Israel, of all political stripes, were united in their request to hold the main memorial day on April 19,[68] the first day of the Warsaw Ghetto Uprising and a date on which Jews across the world had already been marking the memorial day for the Holocaust—a custom that began spontaneously in Eastern Europe soon after the end of the war. The reason they sought to preserve this date, as opposed to the one that was ultimately chosen, was their desire for solidarity with survivors all over the world.[69] Their wish was that their Israeli national belonging would not exclude them from the general public of survivors. Even after Israel declared in 1959 the observance of a national Holocaust memorial day, or as it was called, the Holocaust and Heroism Remembrance Day, the survivors still felt that Israeli society had not yet learned the proper lesson from the Holocaust—namely, that Israel belongs to the Jewish tradition, as they represented it. They perceived the addition of the word *heroism* to the name of the memorial day as an implied criticism of the victims who supposedly had not behaved "heroically"—that is, had not participated in armed uprisings. In the war there were many different kinds of heroism, they argued, and these were no less important or significant as a legacy deserving of a place in the Israeli ethos. So, for example, this is how Artuski described the passing of the Holocaust and Heroism Remembrance Day Act:

> Ten years late, and under pressure from the masses who survived the suffering of Hitler's destruction, the Knesset finally passed the law that establishes the "Holocaust and Heroism Remembrance Day". . . . Though we are not pleased by the fact that the memorial day was set for the 27th of Nisan and not April 19th—thereby effectively making permanent the split in the marking of the memorial day for the ghettos—we do nonetheless see this law as a positive fact. It is a step forward relative to the silence—and thus inevitably also the desecration—that had thus far prevailed with respect to the destruction and the heroism of the Jews who were murdered. This fact—giving a national character to the memorial days—has important national significance. It also carries educational significance for Israeli youth, who knew nearly nothing except for this legend [that the Jews were led "like sheep to the slaughter"], which was disseminated with the intent of humiliating the Diaspora. . . . The truth is that [this legend] is a "chauvinist" lesson, which leads to horrifying conclusions.[70]

This description raises an interesting fact: the "silence" about the Holocaust was attributed to the Israeli establishment, while the survivors—contrary to the familiar portrayals—actually tried to combat the silence by campaigning for the establishment of a national memorial day for the Holocaust in Israel, which would include sectors of the Israeli population, including the young generation, that knew nothing about their catastrophe.[71] These examples of the tension between the communities of memory and their national identity and hence between them and the national establishment suggest the subversive potential that lay within the Holocaust memorial events organized by the survivors.[72]

An example of the tension that characterized Yiddish culture in Israel, which moved between the particular ethnic identity and the national identity,

A gathering of members of the Novi dvor hometown association, Tel Aviv, 1951. The meeting's agenda included a memorial service for the murdered Jews of Novi dvor, a discussion about building a memorial monument for the community's victims, and updates on the building of a neighborhood for its survivors. Tzvika Palchinsky, the Committee of Jews from Novi-Dvor.

can be found in the Holocaust and Heroism Remembrance Day events held in 1960 and 1961. In 1960, Yad Vashem held a central memorial ceremony for the first time, in Heichal Ha-Tarbut in Tel Aviv. That year was the first time that a two-minute siren was sounded and silence observed throughout the country in memory of the victims, and theaters and cinemas shut down for the first time as a sign of national mourning. The communities of memory from among the Yiddish-speaking ʿoley sheyres hapleyte could count this as another victory in their struggle to make the memorial day inclusive of all the citizens of Israel and recognized by the state institutions. But very soon upon the ceremony, they realized that this was not the achievement they had hoped for, since none of the official speakers at the ceremony was a survivor, the texts were not by survivors, and Yiddish—their language and the language of the victims—was not mentioned. Numerous articles and letters of protest about this situation appeared in the *LN*, even a month after the ceremony.[73]

On the twenty-seventh of Nisan, 1961, the eve of the opening of the Eichmann trial, the survivors won another victory in the process of making the Holocaust memorial day a national day: on that day, an amendment to the Remembrance Day Law was added mandating that shops and places

Memorial ceremony for the Holocaust, Ohel Shem, Tel Aviv, in the early 1960s. Seated in the front row, second from the right, is Sutzkever. Behind him stand the members of the Vilna Choir, established by Vilna immigrants in Israel. Ami Yechieli, the Association of Jews from Vilna.

of entertainment like cafés, restaurants, and so on be closed on that day (in addition to the earlier order to close cinemas and theaters). Despite this step, that year Yiddish cultural organizations decided once again to hold a separate memorial event. All the Yiddish cultural organizations in Israel participated in this gathering (the Association of Yiddish Journalists and Writers in Israel, the Society of Friends of YIVO in Israel, the Kurski Library, the Y. L. Peretz Library), as well as Yiddish writers (including Sutzkever), prominent Yiddish cultural figures (like Tsanin and Artuski), representatives of the hometown associations and Yiddish cultural figures who were members of Yad Vashem (including Rokhl Oyerbakh, Dr. Mark Dvorzhetski, and Nosn Eck), and more. The evening was held at the grand new hall of the Tel Aviv Cinema on Pinsker Street. This time all the speakers were survivors, and the whole evening was conducted in Yiddish. According to reports in the press,[74] the hall, which seats nineteen hundred, was overflowing, and hundreds more people filled the street outside (for the sake of comparison, the memorial ceremony held that same year in Manhattan was attended by some twelve hundred people).[75]

The public Yizker evenings, then, were a highly important forum for the public of Holocaust survivors in Israel. The survivors regarded the preoccupation with the past and with its remembrance as a positive and constructive step that helped them organize themselves as a community of memory and thus enabled them to take successful action toward assimilating the memory of the Holocaust into the culture of the burgeoning state. These ceremonies expressed the multiple and conflicting identities of the survivors: their loyalty to the memory of the Holocaust, to their language and their unique culture, and to the worldwide public of survivors, alongside their aspiration to belong to the nation-state's general society and to its culture.

4. "*A Nashelsk in mitn Hebreyishn Erets-Yisroel!*" (Nashelsk in the Heart of the Hebrew Land of Israel): Memory, Place, Nation

The memory of the destroyed communities, as I said, was highly and consistently present in the daily press as well as in the communal memorial days organized by the survivors. In the pages of the *LN* in the early 1950s, immigrants from these communities in Israel and abroad debated the proper ways for hometown associations to commemorate their communities.[76] Should the commemoration be physical or spiritual? Should they ingrain and fortify a memory of the past or create new experiences in the present that are related to the bygone world?

Many of the survivors were not content merely with a "calcified" memory of the past, through Yizker books or commemorative monuments, and sought practices of memory that they regarded as "live memories," practices that would make the past an integral part of life in the present and in which the heritage, culture, and language would continue to grow and develop. These forms of "living memories" included, as I have mentioned, funding the publication of Yiddish books with the German reparation money and holding annual communal memorial ceremonies. Another form, new and unique, of live memory was the building of the Israeli space. This form of physical commemoration created a concrete physical link between the Jewish life destroyed in Eastern Europe and the present building of the new state and strengthening of its population. This link between the memory of the Holocaust and the Israeli space embodies the ideological position that prevailed among 'oley sheyres hapleyte, according to which the resurrection of the Jewish people was tied inextricably to the building of Israel.[77] So, for example, the hometown associations planted memorial forests and gardens,[78] even though this form of commemoration had not been common in the Jewish culture in Eastern Europe. A form of commemoration that contained a more balanced blend of Yiddish culture and the new national space was the building of housing projects, cultural centers, schools, and kindergartens named after cities and towns that were destroyed in the Holocaust, as memorial sites.[79] Through these housing projects built in Israel, the symbols of family and home—which the hometown associations sought to grant to their members—became a reality. In many ways, this form of commemoration was perceived as a complementary pole to the Yizker books, which in Yiddish culture were called "paper gravestones." This metamorphosis of the "soaring letters" into immigrant neighborhoods in Israel embodies, perhaps more than anything else, the complexity and uniqueness of the modern national identity of the Yiddish-speaking 'oley sheyres hapleyte.

This pattern of commemoration highlights the significant contribution of the hometown associations founded by immigrants, refugees, and new 'olim from the cities and towns of Eastern Europe to the economic, social, cultural, and educational development of the destination countries—through the many philanthropic projects they launched.[80] After the Holocaust, these associations faced ethical and political dilemmas as well as practical questions that sometimes led to considerable crises. What was the meaning of identifying themselves as the residents of a city that had been obliterated or whose original, place-centered communal life had been destroyed? What were the immediate goals of the associations? Should they continue to care for the now-elderly immigrants from their hometowns by building and maintaining senior homes and investing in health insurance and grave plots, or should they rather establish new welfare projects to support the Holocaust survivors? And should the bulk of their capital be invested in welfare or in commemoration? Hanna Kliger conducted a comparative study of the hometown associations in New York, Philadelphia, and Tel Aviv before the Holocaust and after it and showed that these organizations functioned as agents of both tradition and change, since they worked to preserve a collective identity based on place of origin and worked also to help immigrants and refugees become acclimated outside of these places.[81] After the Holocaust, these associations changed from organizations operated by and for immigrants to organizations operated mostly by former immigrants for present-time, recently arriving refugees. These two conflicting tendencies, preserving continuity and creating novel contents, continued to characterize their policies. The nature of the projects they established after the Holocaust changed in light of the radical changes in the historical reality and the subsequent changes in the nature of the associations themselves.

One of the main changes in the policy of the New York hometown associations after the establishment of Israel was a diversion of their resources from the old home in Eastern Europe to the new home in the young Israel.[82] Rebecca Kobrin described this shift in the umbrella organization of Jewish immigrants from Byalistok. In the immediate aftermath of the Holocaust, its members started directing funds toward the reconstruction of the ruins of their city, out of faith in the possibilities that the new Poland held for its Jews; but following various events, and especially the repeated outbreaks of antisemitism that extinguished any possibility of renewing Jewish life there, they decided to stop investing in Byalistok and to redirect their resources toward the building of a "new Byalistok" in Israel. And indeed, from the 1950s and on, the implicit mission that connected the members of this dispersed community was to create spaces—both physical and literary—for the grand heritage of the Jewish community of Byalistok.[83] When this shift occurred, the old home of the Byalistok Jews in the Diaspora—Jewish Byalistok—existed no longer in the city of Byalistok but only in their memory: the city was in ruins, and its dwindled Jewish organizations struggled for their physical survival.[84] The identification of the Jewish immigrants from Byalistok all over the world with the new national home that had been established for the Jewish people involved a painful recognition that the old home would not be resurrected in Eastern Europe and a transferring of their loyalty to its reestablishment on the national soil. This reinstatement of their physical and cultural existence they regarded as a new and unique opportunity, morally, culturally, and economically. This effort was raised by former residents of Byalistok who had already settled in the new home in the United States, Argentina, and Australia and most likely did not intend to live in their old-new city in Israel. But the task of building it channeled the trauma they experienced from the destruction of their hometown into a positive and active joint identity with refugees whom they never met and with a country they did not know.[85] Not only survivors were drawn once again into the Jewish collective by the Holocaust but also those who had emigrated from Eastern Europe before the war and who in its aftermath experienced themselves as the refugees of a destroyed culture.

The building of housing projects in Israel named after Jewish communities from Eastern Europe that were eradicated in the Holocaust is a form commemoration that is unique in history in general and in Jewish history in particular.[86] Apart from the desire of Jewish communities across the world to partake in the building of the nation-state, the young state was also a convenient location for such projects compared with Jewish communities in various cities in the world that did not easily provide vacant lands for the construction of new buildings on a large scale. Communities that wanted to raise new buildings there faced many difficulties related to the attempt to fit into the city's existing ethnic-cultural-religious fabric. Moreover, in Israel, compared to the Jewish communities in America, Argentina, and Australia, the weight of 'oley sheyres hapleyte relative to the size of the general population was the greatest (4:1). Their average age was young (thirty), and they had young families. In the late 1940s and 1950s, the associations in the United States (but not yet in Argentina) invested their money mostly in senior citizen homes, hospitals, and funds for medical insurance.

This pattern of spatial memory—the building of immigrant housing projects and neighborhoods in Israel named after towns destroyed in Eastern Europe—embodies the reversal that the Holocaust and the establishment of Israel created in Jewish memory: from a memory of the ruined cities of Zion in Jewish homes in Eastern Europe, to a memory of the ruined cities of Eastern Europe in homes in Israel. Yet by building the housing projects named after the destroyed communities, Yiddish culture posited a unique and even competing alternative to the monuments and memorial sites that were built by Hebrew Zionist movements across Israel and symbolized the national battle for the land and the legitimacy of possession over it, monuments that the sociologist Oz Almog has called "Zionist sanctuaries."[87] The uniqueness of the Yiddish alternative lies in the essential connection it posited between the near past in Eastern Europe and the Holocaust, and the national present in Israel—unlike the ethos of the "negation of the Diaspora" and the ambivalent attitude toward the Holocaust that prevailed in those years in the hegemonic culture.

The *LN* closely tracked and followed the housing projects built in Israel in memory of destroyed communities for the survivors of those communities, including Nahalat Nashelsk in Kiryat Ono, Kiryat Bialystok in Yahud, Shikun Kosin in Havatselet Ha-Sharon, Shikun Lita (Lithuania) in Ramat Ha-Sharon, Shikun Bukovina in Rishon Le-Zion, Shikun Novi-Dvor in Holon, and more. In advertisements published by the hometown associations, these neighborhoods were called *shtetlekh* (shtetls), and not ironically or cynically. In modern Yiddish culture, the word *shtetl* changed from a neutral diminutive that designates a small city to the name of a unique cultural phenomenon—an Eastern European Jewish town. The frequent use of this name charged the neutral label with mythical meaning. The neighborhoods built in Israel were perceived as the longed-for incarnation of destroyed Jewish towns.

The description in the *LN* of the building of Kiryat Lipcan (Lipcani) in 1951, "Der vidergeburt fun a shtetl" (The rebirth of a town), shows how the Zionist perception that the Jewish individual was "reborn" in Israel was expanded and became the idea that entire Jewish towns could be reborn on its land. The yearning for the destroyed hometown was kindled after several years of life in Israel. Immigrants from the town all over the world united around the building of the new housing project that commemorated it; and thus was born, alongside the yearning for the old destroyed town, a new association, positive and young and fresh:

> A small part of the survivors from Lipcan managed to come to Israel, get through the Cyprus affair, and more or less begin to live a calm and normal life. The force of the "old home" . . . gradually began to blossom among all of them, and they started looking for a way to find each other anew and a way to strengthen their connection to the "old home". . . . To rebuild the town, but this time not in the Siberian wilderness but on the glaring sand dunes of Eretz Yisroel, that would carry the name "Kiryat Lipcan". . . . [To that end] survivors from the old town come together from all corners of the world. A new yearning was thus created, but now it was for something real, something living that only made the town's name bigger in its land—Kiraytt Lipcan.[88]

This new search for a way of consolidating communities of memory and commemorating the past after a period of calm marks an advanced stage in the processing of the trauma: "As the heightened and powerfully affected discourse of trauma disappears, the 'lessons' of the trauma become objectified in monuments. . . . The new collective identity will be rooted in sacred places and structured in ritual routines."[89] The renewed appearance of "exilic" Jewish towns in Israel, like the preoccupation with the past in memorial ceremonies, was perceived as threatening by the general society. Tsanin described this threat in the context of the dedication of the Nashelsk housing complex in 1953—the year in which the ten-year anniversary of the Warsaw Ghetto Uprising was marked, and Israel began receiving the German reparation money—and his words echo the survivors' perception of the Israeli space, a space they actively participated in shaping as the site of a living memory of a destroyed life:

> There are those people here . . . who will frown upon this matter: what is this, they will say, we've just barely been released, just barely escaped the exile, and here they are once again bringing out their exilic names and their exilic cities; here, look, they will say, Nashelsk in the heart of the Hebrew Land of Israel! Let them say and think what they will. The local Yishuv will bless this achievement and will wish that more such cities and towns—Polish, Romanian, and other—be built, right here, in Jewish Israel, and carry forth the Jewish life that was woven with such dynamic force in these towns. . . . [They will wish] that the Nashelsk neighborhood will indeed set an example for other hometown associations. That from their remaining survivors many more such miniature towns will rise up in Israel, and that together they will form a living monument for the great Jewish Yishuv that was annihilated in Poland.[90]

The founders of these neighborhoods and housing projects hoped the survivors' children would grow up in them with a connection to their near past. Passing on the heritage of a city or town to the young generations concerned the hometown associations, since the cultural and spiritual foundation of Israel was based on severing relations with the near past and rejecting the Diaspora, its language and culture. Thus, these neighborhoods often included not only housing but also culture centers, libraries, kindergartens, and archives, in which cultural activities were planned. This is how Yasny described a visit to Kiryat Bialystok with members of the city's US hometown association who were visiting Israel on its thirteenth ("Bar-Mitzva") anniversary, the 1961 Independence Day, which coincided with the height of the Eichmann trial:

> Some 208 houses stand there, and in them some one thousand people. A new generation is already growing up here. . . . A generation that no longer knows the language of the tortured Jews of Bialystok. But the older generation . . . tries in every way to give the town the mark of the old town of weavers. The streets carry names of important Bialystok Jews. . . . Ghetto fighters were also commemorated. . . . The Bialystok hometown association in the United States has also provided for the spiritual life of the residents. A community center was built, with a library containing four thousand books, in Hebrew and

> Yiddish, including the works of the great Yiddish writers. . . . The kindergarten commemorates the daughter of the Alpert family, a heroine who fell in the War of Independence.[91]

As this description, too, suggests, the survivors in Israel and beyond it saw no contradiction in commemorating the fallen soldiers of the wars of Israel by building Yiddish cultural institutions in Israel. Did these housing complexes fulfill their designation as carriers of the memory and legacy of a destroyed community? What contents were etched in the memories of the children who grew up in these neighborhoods?[92] One testimony is provided in the memoirs of Shai Pilpel, who grew up in Shikun Lita in Ramat Ha-Sharon:

> Not many people know that in Ramat Ha-Sharon there was actually a Lithuanian reserve. In the early nineteen fifties, the organization of Lithuanian immigrants in the United States helped with mortgage guarantees for families of Lithuanian origin. And so it was that in Ramat Ha-Sharon, a place that was then (1951–1952) the end of the world, "Shikun Lita" was established. . . . In this way a kind of "little Lithuania" was created, with representatives from all over the country: Vilna, Kovno, Telz, mazheyk, Kelm, and more and more. If we want to describe what it means to be a "Litvak" [Lithuanian Jew], we need only to look at the generation that grew up in this place. Well, what is it to be a Litvak: first, it is to grow up in Lithuanian Yiddish, to hear this language all the time, with all of its expressions and colorfulness. . . . The spoken language in Shikun Lita was Yiddish. We, the youth, already spoke Hebrew, but all the—! was in Yiddish. Many of my friends spoke only Yiddish with their parents. It goes without saying that Kol Israel [Israel's public radio service] was heard in Yiddish. . . . But above all, being a Litvak meant growing up into all the problematic issues of the survivors, of a world that existed and was destroyed violently and cruelly; effectively, growing up without a past. The parents did not share with us what they had been through. No one was ever released of what he had been through. . . . In retrospect, I think the wall that they put up around themselves was intended to keep us, the next generation, sane. . . . We knew nothing about whole families, with uncles and aunts and cousins etc. There were fragments: a brother here, a cousin there. . . . Obviously, none of us had a grandfather or grandmother. In a housing complex of eighty families there were only one grandfather and one grandmother. Being a Litvak meant that there were conversations that you, as a child, were not part of. There were questions you would not ask and answers you would not receive. Not even questions about memorial candles that would be lit every once in a while, Kadish spoken with no explanation. The geography changed too, turning into a collection of camps and ghettos. When they say, the one from Telz or Shavel, they mean the Telz Ghetto or the Shavel Ghetto. The seventh day of [the Jewish month of] Cheshvan was a well-known date and the main street of Shikun Lita was named after it; for those who don't know, that is the day of the big actzia [violent deportation] in Kovno. . . . Don't get me wrong. Being a kid in Shikun Lita was not sad or depressing. On the contrary—it was a fun

The cornerstone ceremony of the Kdoshey Novi dvor neighborhood in Ḥolon, April 23, 1954. Its building was enabled by funds raised by the Central Committee of Jews from Novi dvor in New York, which united immigrants from this community in the United States, Argentina, France, Canada, and Israel. Tzvika Palchinsky, the Committee of Jews from Novi-Dvor.

> childhood with family, neighbors and friends. The shared past, or perhaps its absence, created a closeness of people and neighbors that is not found today.[93]

This testimony clearly suggests the link between language, culture, and the shaping of communities of memory. The memory of the Holocaust was passed on to the second generation mostly through "communicative memory"[94] (stories, customs) that was created in the daily life between the generations. This form of memory has special importance in Israel, where Yiddish and its culture were not studied in the school system. Pilpel's testimony opens by noting the importance of language to the consolidation of the unique culture of the community of memory. The generational gap, too, was marked through linguistic identity: the language of the adults was Yiddish, while the language of the young generation was Hebrew. This was already characteristic of Jewish immigrant families in many places in the world prior to the Holocaust, but the family described here was not just a family of immigrants or refugees; its members were also "new 'olim" who had chosen to live in Israel after the destruction of Jewish Eastern Europe. This context gave added significance to the linguistic choice that every immigrant faced. The linguistic rebellion that was common among second-generation immigrants was typically charged with equal amounts of shame and guilt for supposedly "betraying" the parents, their language and culture, and the burden of memory that they carried. Pilpel's testimony makes no mention of passing on the memory of the past through the rich modern Yiddish culture that existed in Lithuania before the Holocaust. This absence went along with the negative image of Yiddish in the hegemonic culture. But life in this unique setting nonetheless ingrained the language in the young generation, or at least ingrained symbolic traces of it in layers that even the finest works of literature most likely cannot reach. Without knowledge of the language and its treasures, Yiddish culture, even for some of the second generation, had already become a lost civilization.

5. "*A Tsavoe fun a farbrent loshn*" (A Last Will of a Burnt Language): Capital and Memory

The memorial columns in the papers, the community memorial events, and the housing complexes built by 'oley sheyres hapleyte in Israel were not aimed merely at commemorating the past. They expressed an aspiration to distill from the past values and contents that would enable and enrich the lives of survivors and emigrants. Literary scholar Aleida Assmann discusses two forms of memory and disremembering: active and passive. According to Assmann, passive memory preserves the past as a past; this kind of memory functions like forgetting insofar as it renders the past irrelevant to the present and future.[95] The first issue of *DGK* (in the midst of the "War of Independence") featured a short piece in bolded font that was essentially the mission statement of the new literary journal, even though it was untitled and unsigned:

> Our enemy did not aspire to destroy only the Jews and turn them into soap, but also their language and their golden chain. But the language survived the enemy. And the chain, through ghettos, forests, and uprisings, continued underground, wounded, tortured, soaked with the dying tears of those who fortified it, sanctified by *Kidesh ha-Shem* [the martyrdom; literally, sanctification of the Name] of our closest kin—and it fastened its links more forcefully, ploughed in the depths through the destroyed cities and shined like a sparkle—in the land of many-generations-old Jewish yearning, to which the remnant of the nation now flows.[96]

Not only the physical existence of the Jews of Europe was targeted by the Nazis, argues the writer of this passage, but also their culture and language. The language here is tantamount to a central symbol in Yiddish culture, "the golden chain," a symbol that functions as a metonymy for the culture in which it was created. The golden chain symbolizes both the reservoir of cultural knowledge that Eastern European Jewry created and accumulated over some one thousand years and from which it drew its unique identity, a "cultural memory" in the terms of archeologist Jan Assmann, and the mode of revival of the culture that it symbolizes: contact between generations that allows for an intergenerational transference of language and culture in the course of daily life through communicative memory. This valuable load of cultural memory and communicative memory that ʻoley sheyres hapleyte brought with them, and which had the power to transform a group of individuals who shared a common ethnic origin into a national society, was what made them fit for the description "the remnant of the nation." Like Manger's poem with which I opened the book, this passage, too, revisits the idea that ʻoley sheyres hapleyte, Israel's new citizens, were its raison d'être and the source of its importance. In this passage, Sutzkever—who later revealed himself to be its author—describes Yiddish culture as one that has been sanctified with the blood of the victims of the Holocaust. This is a new sanctity, a kind of modern secular theology, which dictates new commandments, obeyance of which gives the national collective in Israel its moral validity—a modern incarnation of the phrase "who has sanctified us with His commandments." Yet after the Holocaust the source of these commandments (and the reason for their existence) is not divine but human.[97] The moral obligation imposed on the survivors, then, is to rebuild the cultural golden chain and its language.

This moral obligation reappears and is spelled out in another text published (and this time signed) by Sutzkever, thirty years later, in *DGK*'s one hundredth issue: "There is also, in the beginning of the DGK, issue number one, a very brief anonymous text. . . . Let us now reveal that it was written by my own hand and heart, but it is unsigned, not even with initials, because this was only a few years after our third destruction, and it seemed to me that the text is not only mine: it is a *sheyme*[98] that was found, a last will of a burnt language."[99] The anonymous passage in *DGK*'s first issue, then, was written as the last will of a burnt language, not as a work of literature. The author is described here as functioning as a medium for the "burnt language," not as someone who used the language for his own needs. And indeed, the sense of moral obligation toward Yiddish and its culture, because they too were targeted by the Nazis, was very prevalent in the sources created by the survivors. Funding the publication of Yiddish books was one memory practice that developed from below and gave the survivors a sense that they were legitimizing the German reparation money, which some of them perceived as contaminated. Supporting organizations that preserved, cultivated, and developed Yiddish and its culture carried similar significance for the survivors. As I have described, Yiddish cultural organizations in Israel aimed to sustain their culture and continue to develop it, and they did so out of a national sentiment and the belief that their culture represented a vital contribution to the development of the general Israeli culture, and not out of a desire to undermine it. The establishment accepted their existence with half-hearted tolerance. But as we saw in the case of the official Holocaust memorial ceremony, the clash was unavoidable, and not only with the establishment. Yiddish speakers were themselves divided on the fundamental questions—namely, what their obligation was toward Yiddish and its culture, and what they hoped to achieve through the ongoing preoccupation with Yiddish and its culture.

The volume of Yiddish cultural activity in Israel was large, as I said, thanks to the financial support of communities across the world and in Israel. Yiddish cultural organizations began to grow and expand, and they initiated the establishment of cultural and educational institutions through which they sought to integrate themselves into the Israeli space and the Israeli ethos. In 1955, the Association of Yiddish Journalists and Writers in Israel began raising funds to build a physical home for an international center of Yiddish culture, in which the association itself would be housed after having operated for many years out of a basement on 25 Dov Hoz Street in Tel Aviv.[100] These efforts bore fruit only in 1970, after many delays (including the Six-Day War), when the association inaugurated Beit Leyvik in Tel Aviv.[101] The members of the association at that time included Tsanin, Sutzkever, Artuski, Moyshe Gros-Tsimerman, Mordechai Halamish, Yosef Papyiernikov, Avrom Karpinovitsh, Eliyezer Rubinshteyn, Yitskhok Brat, and the painter Mula Ben Khaim. In addition to being the permanent home of the association, Beit Leyvik held an auditorium, library, reading room, and archive.

Paradoxically, though in a way that undoubtedly reflects its existence in Israel, even the Bund movement raised projects of "living memory" that bound together the building of the nation-state with Yiddish cultural education. The world Bund movement commemorated its heroes who were murdered in the Holocaust, in an attempt to broaden, in Israel and elsewhere, the boundaries of ideas about heroism and which heroes deserved to be commemorated. In 1955, the *LF* announced the opening of a children's library named after Hinde Vaser, a sixteen-year-old girl murdered in the Warsaw Ghetto, within the Franz Kurski Library.[102] One year prior, in 1954, the AR began battling for the commemoration of Artur Zyglboim through the naming of a street in Tel Aviv after him.[103] The AR sought to change the name of the street in which the organization was situated, Kalischer, to Zyglboim's name. The battle lasted nearly a decade, and in the meantime the AR commemorated him by giving his name to the performance hall it opened in the AR home on Kalischer in 1957. In 1963, the battle ended in partial victory when the *LF* reported on a ceremony for the naming of a street after Zyglboim, although not the street where the Bund stood but rather a street in the working-class immigrant neighborhood of Kiryat Shalom.[104] The children's house established by the AR in Ramatayim was also a focal point of living memory of the Jewish-Bundist culture in Poland.[105] This house, which at first hosted summer camps for the children of workers and in 1966 began to offer year-round activities for children, was also named after Zyglboim. Donations from centers all over the world enabled the establishment of a library in the house[106] and the building of a second floor.[107]

DKG operated out of buildings of the Histadrut. Sutzkever did not aim to erect a special building that would house Yiddish-related cultural encounters, not even for those that the journal hosted at least once a year and were attended by large audiences from all over the country. These events were held in various rented halls in Tel Aviv, like Beit Ha-Halutsot on King George Street. As early as 1951, Sutzkever expressed his concern that the practices of "spatial memory" would replace the more important cultural-spiritual essence that he sought to revive. In his view, the only worthy practice for maintaining in the Israeli space a living memory of the destroyed Jewish life in Eastern Europe was to develop the culture that this life had created:

> The Jewish spirit does not like decorations. There cannot be a street named [after] Peretz if we do not shelter in his "Folktales"; cannot be a street named [after] Yehoyesh—if people do not enjoy the works of Yehoyesh; cannot be a Vilna street—unless we live and breathe the sanctity of Yerusholayim-deLita [literally, the Jerusalem of Lithuania; a term used to describe the Jewish community of Vilna]; there is no sense in the names Yad Mordechai and Anilevitsh Monument, if those who live there, and have erected it, are not illuminated by the light of the fire pillar of the Warsaw Ghetto uprising.[108]

With these words, Sutzkever points out the two contradictory measures of memory, the physical and the metaphysical. The questions he reflects on are whether Israel intends to commemorate Yiddish and its culture, whether it acknowledges its rich legacy, and perhaps the most fundamental question: What type of "Judaism" should Israel adopt, and why?

Throughout the 1950s, the Israeli public was preoccupied with the question of what the nature of Jewish culture should be in light of the Holocaust and the establishment of Israel. Two basic moves took place in Israel in those years: the first, as noted, was the "Jewish consciousness" program applied in the state school system in the second half of the 1950s; and the second was the constitutional, religious, and political "who is a Jew" debate, a part of the Law of Return legislation, especially from 1958 (when the ministers from Mafdal, the National Religious Party, resigned from the government over disagreements concerning this definition). Advocates of Yiddish culture repeatedly warned that the education system in Israel was creating a distorted image of Jewish life in "exile"—for example,

> What is the solution to this situation [the Sabra youth's alienation toward the Diaspora]? Zionism cannot provide a solution here since . . . Zionist education . . . has lost its "connection to Yiddishkeyt." Nor does the belated "Jewish consciousness," twisted by religious notions, provide a solution. What is required here . . . is a return to the Jewish source, not the source of the bible and of the faith of Moses, but that of the universality of the Jewish people, as a secular

> people, that built and established its national existence for generations, even without its own territory, on the basis of a secular Jewish culture. [What is required is] to bring back the Israeli youth to this language and culture, to instill in it the consciousness that in addition to Hebrew and the Laws of Moses the Jews in the world have created unique national movements and unique Jewish cultural values that transformed the Jewish people from a religious group into a trans-territorial modern secular nation. Only in this manner can there once again exist a spiritual and linguistic bond between Israeli youth and the Jewish people.[109]

Instead of affirming the Israeli national identity as part of the long continuum of modern Jewish identities, the education system in Israel created a misrepresentation, as if the modern and secular Israel whose language was Hebrew were the negating opposite of a Yiddish-speaking religious-Orthodox "Diaspora." Yiddish advocates warned repeatedly that the "Toda'a Yehudit" (Jewish Consciousness) program was teaching Israeli youth that the Jewish culture destroyed in Eastern Europe was solely religious-Orthodox; that it was teaching them that the Diaspora and its culture in Israel were irrelevant to the new present in Israel and thus that it was only because of the manner in which they passed from the world (the injustice of the Holocaust) that the Diaspora and its culture should not be ignored or forgotten; and finally that it was teaching them that because of the Holocaust, Israel had to sever the ties to its near past and rely only on its physical strength.

On the eve of the Eichmann trial, the state decided to fund 85 percent of the private Orthodox education in Yiddish (in Kiryat Sanz in Netanya and in the Bobov and Vizhnitz Hasidic communities, in addition to the schools of Agudat Yisrael) and to give no support to the Yiddish cultural organizations established by Holocaust survivors—for whose sake Israel was receiving the reparations in the first place.[110] The future of the Yiddish community cultural centers, with their various activities and particularly the afterschool curricula for children (since the teaching of Yiddish in state schools was not approved), depended on the private support of survivors from Israel and especially from other countries.

The news of Eichmann's capture and of the intention to try him in Israel caused great excitement among the Holocaust survivors.[111] Their hope was that at the trial, through the witnesses that would be called to testify, they would be able to present the breadth of their cultural loss. Surprisingly, Sutzkever, who had been very active in the cultural life of the Vilna Ghetto and risked his life to save Jewish cultural treasures from the YIVO and Strashun libraries, and who had also been one of the only Jewish witnesses called to testify at the Nuremberg Trials, was not called to testify at the Eichmann trial. Rokhl Oyerbakh, who was in charge of testimony collection at Yad Vashem, was called to testify about life in the Warsaw Ghetto and about its destruction. For many weeks she worked on composing her testimony, which she titled "What Was Jewish Warsaw and

How Was It Destroyed."[112] She focused on the cultural and spiritual life that had existed in the city because she felt that this could be her unique contribution as a journalist, essayist, author, literary editor, and cultural activist, and as someone who had worked alongside Emanuel Ringelblum on the "Oyneg Shabes" archive. The goals of her testimony were

> A. To show the activity and positivity and organizational skill of the Jews of Warsaw and of all of Poland in their struggle for their lives and their humanity in the face of humiliation and annihilation. . . . B. To emphasize the scientific, literary, and artistic creation and the bitter fate of hundreds of noted people who lived in the Warsaw Ghetto. . . . C. To highlight the phenomenology of unique phenomena and psychosocial processes that developed in the society of the besieged city. . . . D. To praise the figure of a great historian and activist of the Warsaw Ghetto, Emanuel Ringelblum, as someone who symbolizes the eternal values of the Jewish people.[113]

Even before the ceremonial opening of the trial, the survivors began to suspect that this was not the trial they had hoped for. On the eve of the opening, various figures in the world of Yiddish culture got word that the state was planning to provide journalists covering the trial with translations of the court proceedings into German, English, French, and Spanish, but not Yiddish—which in those years was considered a foreign language in Israel. The fact that the proceedings would be translated into several languages and primarily German but not into the language of most of the victims and the survivors in Israel and abroad shocked the readers of the *LN* (and readers of the Yiddish press throughout the world). Yiddish cultural organizations in Israel and across the world rallied to try and prevent the injustice. The whole affair became increasingly convoluted and triggered a profound self-examination and reckoning among the writers of the *LN*. To whom, they wondered, was the Jewish trial in Jerusalem directed, if the many immediate victims of the crimes under consideration—the survivors in Israel and in the Diaspora, who were not proficient in Hebrew—were excluded from it? "For whom are they preparing this spectacle?" asked Tsanin in his weekly column, and he answered, "Not for the people. . . . The Jewish people in the world, those whose interest in this trial is the greatest . . . will be able to follow all the details about it from the German, English or French [press] but not from the Yiddish press."[114] In the course of the trial itself it became clear that this was not a mere technical exclusion: the deliberations focused on the physical annihilation and not on cultural loss. In a report by Oyerbakh to her superior at Yad Vashem, she wrote about the "injury" her testimony had caused her, one that pained her "severely" and from which she would not recover "easily and quickly." According to Oyerbakh, her testimony was postponed several times, and the time allotted her was gradually reduced. Eventually, she was given half an hour, and her testimony was scheduled for the afternoon, after the testimonies of Zivia Lubetkin and Antek Zuckerman:

> I thought that after the description of the facts by Antek-Zivia my words would take the form of some kind of ideational synthesis and that it [the testimony] would also offer *a special added component about the spiritual and mental heroism and about the annihilation of intellectuals*. . . . I thought this day was devoted entirely to the Warsaw Ghetto, that I could speak for an hour to an hour-and-a-half. I could not by any means have guessed that I would not be allowed to speak at all, because "everything" is already known about Warsaw. . . . That after twenty years of documentation and research of the events and phenomena that are the subject and content of this trial, I would not be given the minimal possibility to express a single idea, to recount a fact or a phenomenon. When in fact I had to tell about things that are not at all "irrelevant," that relate directly to the annihilation of the Jewish people—to the annihilation of intellectuals and cultural treasures—and that, too, is part of biological annihilation and no less important and no less takes revenge on us than the physical annihilation.[115]

Sutzkever, who only rarely responded to current affairs in the pages of *DGK*, made an exception and published a short text signed with his initials, as though it were his testimony:

> The trial in Jerusalem is the first great *Mitsve* that the State has already performed in honor of its own *Bar-Mitsve*. . . . The trial in Jerusalem has raised with terrifying clarity all of our experiences on our deaths from the years of the destruction. Now the Sabras, too, are being immersed in the white-hot lava and inhaling the souls of the murdered people. . . . However, it must be said that, regretfully, one important testimony is missing in the trial: the Yiddish language, which is sacred to us, and in the name of whose burnt lips this statement of claim is heard in court.[116]

The "burnt language" features here as the raison d'être of the prosecution. In Sutzkever's view, which many of the survivors shared, the trial had a cultural dimension that preceded any other aspect, such as the bureaucratic or the physical. Eichmann had to be tried first and foremost for the eradication of a culture. And the remedy for this kind of crime had also to take place first in the cultural dimension. Sutzkever's expectation and that of many survivors in Israel was that the "trial in Jerusalem" would represent their notion that fulfilling "the last will of a burnt language" was the moral mission and reason for the establishment of the "national home"; that by virtue of fulfilling this, Israel would be able to become "the place" in which "those who were killed and murdered were resurrected."

* * *

In this chapter, I surveyed four practices of Holocaust memory that ʻoley sheyres hapleyte performed in Israel in the first decade after its establishment. These practices of memory were created from below, as a need felt by the survivors in response to the growth of new life. These practices developed and took shape in the pages of the Yiddish press. Around these practices developed "communities

The street-naming ceremony in honor of Artur Zyglboim, Kiryat Shalom, Tel Aviv, 1963. Luden family album.

of memory" that were mostly national in nature: they regarded the building of the collective home as an answer to the destruction of the old home and as a dignified and fitting memory practice. The new national place and the Israeli space were regarded as consolation and compensation for those places and spaces that had betrayed them, expelled them from their midst, and made them refugees and displaced persons. Yet the language of memory highlighted the gaps that had opened between the survivors and the hegemonic culture with respect to the image of the Diaspora and the proper place of the past in the life of the present. The practices of Holocaust memory reflected the multiple and conflicting loyalties of both the survivors and the state institutions.

The Eichmann trial changed the attitude of Israeli society toward the Holocaust, its memory, and its survivors. But this change was the summation of a process and not its inception. The struggle to assimilate the memory of the Holocaust into Israeli society clearly began from below, from among the survivors themselves. The hegemonic culture in Israel embraced only a small part of the broad ethos of Holocaust memory articulated by the survivors. Those components that were rejected shed light on the hegemonic culture—and no less on the rejected culture.

Part II

The Israeli Experience in Yiddish Prose, 1948–1967

3

The Nostalgic Paradox of Yiddish Prose

1. Looking Back, Looking Forward: Holocaust, Memory, and the Promised Land

On the occasion of one of the gatherings of the Yung-yisroel group, held regularly in Kibbutz Yagur in the first half of the 1950s, the writer Tsvi Ayznman reflected on the challenges he faced as a young Yiddish writer after the Holocaust. He compared his predicament to that of earlier groups of young writers in the field of Yiddish literature—Di yunge (the Young, New York, from 1907 and on) and Yung-vilne (Young-Vilna, Vilna, 1929 and on). He felt that their creative activity had shaped Yiddish literature, that thanks to it this literature took its first steps, but that by the time he and his fellow writers in the Yung-yisroel group had started writing, on the eve of World War II or during the war, Yiddish literature in all of its centers was past its prime, in some cases calcified for several years and in others actively declining: "When we came to literature, we found the Yiddish poem at the height of its shine, distilled and refined, and no less so was the word of prose. On the one hand, our situation is easier: we have prepared everything in advance for you, says the literature. Taste, take as much as you wish, and learn. But on the other hand, our situation is much more difficult. Young people must come with a new word."[1] What "new word" could Ayznman and the writers of his generation contribute to the "modern tradition" of the literature to which they belonged and that they wished to carry forth and develop? What new word (if any) did the readers of Yiddish literature seek after the Holocaust? It is evident that the challenge Ayznman pondered, to "renew" the declining Yiddish literature, was both social and personal: "This is my wish and this is my prayer and creed. That we be strong, that we create, create . . . so that Yiddish literature will not be ashamed of us. Amen."[2]

Like any modern literature, Yiddish literature dealt extensively with the challenges of modernity: the inevitable disintegration of the traditional home, family, and community, the challenges of secularization, urbanization and the modern economy, mass migrations, national movements, and the spread of conflicting ideologies. Yiddish literature expressed these tensions and the traumas they left in their wake through a distinctive "backward glance," a somewhat nostalgic yearning for the old traditional world that was abandoned, but with a painful recognition that returning to it was no longer possible (or, in many cases, desirable). This is a central characteristic of Yiddish literature, and it both stems from and is enhanced by the declining status of Yiddish as an everyday language. Any writer who refused to join the modern project by writing for the masses about their new and exciting modern identity in their newly acquired national language, and chose instead to recount his own personal lament for the world that was lost and to do so in the language of the self-secluding community from which he hailed, inevitably confronted this theme. In stark contrast to Yiddish literature, modern Hebrew literature harnessed itself from the start to the task of breaking with the near past. Like every literature that sought to be national, it drew on ancient myths that supposedly grounded the national sentiment, but this ancient and imagined past merely allowed it to sever itself more easily from the near and immediate and from its spoken language. Thus, Hebrew literature was modern by virtue of joining the project of the Enlightenment and the national excitement of the peoples of Europe. By contrast, Yiddish literature became modern by virtue of confronting the forces of modernity, with ironic optimism and a hopeful belief in its ability to explore and learn, evolve and progress despite modernity—and in this lay its uniqueness. It therefore sought to contain and express the conflicts that Hebrew literature, in its infatuation with the new, sought to repress. Modern Yiddish literature, then, embodied the loaded encounter of old and new from the position of a critique of the old, on the one hand, but a refusal to disengage from it on the other.

The destruction of Jewish Eastern Europe presented modern Yiddish writers with a new and nearly impossible challenge. It is one thing to face a critical dilemma vis-à-vis the old-world institutions that surround you, and another to face the same dilemma when you are surrounded by the ruins of these institutions and when among these ruins lie the bodies of your beloveds and acquaintances. The criticism seems to lose its sting, and the literature that aims to shed light on this conflict seems to lose its point. How can a prose that feeds on conflict with the past continue to preserve itself when the conflict no longer exists? And how can it honor its own belonging to this past without becoming a mere nostalgic lament? It appears that the range of emotions was reduced, and so was the range of the modes of expression that a post-Holocaust Yiddish writer could use. This new predicament is described here as the "Lot's wife dilemma": it denotes the inability to ignore the past on the one hand and the past's petrifying effect on the other. A modern Yiddish writer after the Holocaust expressed the desire to "redeem" the world that was lost as well as the "I" of the author who identified with it, alongside an awareness, more or less conscious, of the futility of this wish, and sometimes even of the grandiose nature of this sentiment.

The theme of looking back appears in Walter Benjamin's famous image of modern history in the form of a "new angel" (Angelus Novus), as it appears in the painting by Paul Klee.[3] The similarities between this image and the image of Lot's wife proposed here as a simile for modern Yiddish literature are the backward glance toward the ruins of the past and the inability to redeem it or be redeemed by it. The differences between these images are also interesting: Benjamin's image seeks to represent the challenge of (modern) history, whereas the image offered here seeks to represent the challenge of modern literature; history in Benjamin's image is embodied in the figure of the angel hovering above the reality that he seeks to explore and describe—he does not partake in the traumatic experiences he explores—whereas Lot's wife (Yiddish literature) stands right in the midst of reality and is both the traumatic subject and its object of narration, partaking in the drama of the destruction she seeks to express. In this chapter, I describe the challenges that Yiddish literature faced in light of the *longue durée* of its existence; I describe how the encounter with Israel allowed the writers of Yiddish who faced this dilemma to find a creative solution. We will see how and why the "Israel-theme" enabled a development of the unique theme of Yiddish fiction and how it allowed its writers after the Holocaust to process the trauma they had experienced without becoming submerged in it.

2. Yiddish Prose after Bergelson's *When All Is Said and Done*

The first important modern novel in Yiddish literature, *Nokh alemen* (*When All Is Said and Done*), by Dovid Bergelson, was published in Vilna in 1913, on the eve of World War I (the same year that Sutzkever was born).[4] It describes the annulment of the wedding engagement of the novel's protagonist, Mirl, the only daughter of the town's formerly wealthy man, Reb Gdalye Hurvits, to Velvl Burnes, the son of one of the town's newly rich families, following her father's financial downfall (and that of the town's landowner whose business the father ran for many years), the loss of the dowry money deposited with the father, and the subsequent financial dispute that breaks out between the two families. The novel portrays the decline of Mirl and Velvl, young people in their late twenties who remain unmarried, and alongside them the decline of their generation, "students" who left their town for the big city, acquired a profession, but returned to the town defeated and emotionally blunted, culturally and morally no longer fitting into either world. Nothing carries meaning for them—not their financial situation (still described as reasonable); not their present life, for all the familial and social ties it includes, or the ideology and artistic ideas teeming in their culture; and not their future. The novel ends with the preparations for Mirl's wedding with another young man from a wealthy city family, a move that is supposed to save Mirl and her father from financial ruin. Mirl faces her wedding with deep emotional emptiness: with no love, joy, excitement, or hope, nor even with a sense of obligation and a functional satisfaction from fulfilling it. The wedding, a central theme in traditional Jewish literature, is described as an act devoid of all meaning, whether personal or collective. The protagonist does not rebel against the tradition, and upholding it gives her neither pleasure nor meaning.

"The disintegration of the Jewish family," observed Avraham Novershtern, "was in these years [the first decades of the twentieth century] one of the most prevalent and popular themes in the world of Yiddish literature in all of its manifestations. . . . Oftentimes it became integrated with the literary shaping of those familiar sociological and historical processes of the move from the town to the city or immigration to the United States."[5] The disintegration of the family and of the communal institutions that it represented in Yiddish culture are what made the novel a more coherent and common form in this culture and allowed it to fit into the European tradition of the novel, since the modern novel focused at the time on the theme of disintegration. The pioneers of the Jewish modern novel, Mendele Moykher Sforim and Sholem Aleichem, created it as an oxymoronic form of a "loveless novel," a "romance without romance": unlike in the classic European novel, it did not revolve around romantic love, the beating hearts of young individuals did not conquer social and traditional institutions or transform their values, and the heroism of these individuals was not tested by their willingness to die for their naive ideals. Bergelson belonged to the second generation of writers in Yiddish literature (alongside Sholem Asch, Moyshe Kulbak, Der Nister [Pinkhes Kahanovitsh], Lamed Shapiro, Yosef Opatoshu, I. J. Singer, Bashevis Singer, and more). In his novel, the generation of the parents in the two families, the one that is declining (Hurvits) and the one that is ascending (Burnes), are still described as possessing a certain ability to act in the world, much like their descriptions in the works of Mendele and Sholem Aleichem. But this time their control over the young generation is gradually dissolving. Emotional emptiness and absent-mindedness are the central characteristics of the young generation, traits that function as expressions of an inner resistance—rather passive but frighteningly effective—against parental control.

Together with Asch, Bergelson was highly popular among the young generation, especially those of refined taste. He also enjoyed critical acclaim. *Nokh alemen* symbolizes the entry of the young and renewing generation of writers into Yiddish literature, and yet the dominant feeling it evokes is of a dead end. Unlike, for instance, the ridicule in the works of Mendele Moykher Sforim, who sharply criticized the shtetl-minded Jewish society (and especially its wealthy members) and the hopes it pinned on the move from the shtetl (a symbol of familial and communal intimacy) to the big city (a symbol of integration into the general society and modern culture),[6] Bergelson's novel lacks any social or political criticism and contains no echoes of the revolutionary spirit and political activity that filled the cities and towns of Eastern Europe on the eve of its writing (1905–1907). In the Jewish society of Eastern Europe, women were regarded as "agents of modernity" thanks to their access to general education, which was not perceived as threatening their traditional roles. In Sholem Aleichem's early novels, the challenge facing the young woman upon her marriage is to overcome the mental and cultural gaps that have opened up between herself and her groom, who remains tied to his mother's apron, and to gain an education and agree to assume her traditional role in the family and the community. The "city" needs to adapt itself to the dimensions of the "shtetl," to fit into its traditional institutions and become part of it. And indeed, the young brides are described as a metonymy for the shtetl. The spatial analogy drawn in *Nokh alemen* is more complex. Mirl represents the big city in many respects—her alienation, her disintegrating family, and the annulment of her engagement to Velvl, who is described as homey and provincial ("Der heymisher kleynshtetldiker shidekh")[7]—in other words, as familiar and close. In contrast to Mirl, Velvl and his extensive nouveau riche family represent the small town, which is described in the novel as economically and socially vibrant. But the protagonists' emotional barrenness voids their main features of any real content, since the home, family, and shtetl community are not characterized by intimacy, interest, and concern among the family members or friends but by an absence of meaning, by loneliness, alienation, and suffocation. The big city provides temporary relief from all that, but there too, emptiness and boredom soon rear their head again. Even the natural landscapes that unfold between these two spaces, the village or even the farm, fail to rouse the characters from their emotional numbness and, if not rescue them from their deep depression, then at least comfort them. Unlike the descriptions of nature in the works of Mendele and Sholem Aleichem (and Bialik), for these characters nature is not a liminal space that allows them to break out of the shtetl and the mindset shaped within it. Unlike Benjamin III or Stempenyu, the characters in *Nokh alemen* seemingly refuse to be symbols of a space (either the shtetl or the modern city) or else perhaps collapse under the weight of this task. In this work, it is rather the space that functions as a metonymy for their inner world.

In this novel, Mirl is revealed only gradually as a heroine. Her centrality is not suggested in the work's title, and the novel opens with a description of the secondary character (Velvl), his actions and impressions, rather than hers. Mirl is shaped through the consciousness of secondary characters, who are preoccupied with topics that to her are unimportant: the financial and social activity of Mirl herself and of her family and that of their acquaintances in the shtetl, the village, and the city. This "diagonal" technique for character development is one of the important innovations Bergelson introduced in this work, and it underscores its theme—the void in the lives of his characters. Even though Mirl is the novel's heroine, most of the content described in it is not focused on her, not described through her eyes, and not important to her. The novel revolves, then, around characters that are inconsequential from the point of view of its heroine, that are emotionless, and especially loveless, characters that concern themselves with pointless activities, in spaces that are all alike insofar as they have little to no impact on the characters, and in a language that does not succeed in evoking any emotion, expressing any emotion, or even creating communication. In contrast to Sholem Aleichem's chatty characters, who take pleasure in the interaction (even imaginary) that Yiddish enabled and sometimes even in the act itself of playing with the language, the characters in the novel before us barely talk to one another. The interaction between them, when it does take place, is shaped in the third-person voice, which voids the Yiddish of the intimacy that is associated with it. And in many cases the characters' speech is reduced to no more than groans and sighs. Berglson performs here, in Yiddish, a nihilistic abolishment not only of the basic tenets of the Yiddish culture of the time but also of the language that creates and carries them.

This disheartening negation of all meaning and hope in all the areas of Jewish life in the city as well as in the shtetl was achieved by virtue of the contrast between the (superb) literary descriptions of decay, and reality. When this work was published, Jewish life in Eastern Europe was intensely alive and bustling. The challenge Bergelson and his colleagues faced in the aftermath of the two world wars was that the contrast that nourished their work, between a lively everyday reality and literary descriptions of impending decay, had disappeared: the protagonists, the theme, and the setting of their drama had all faded into oblivion.

3. The Enduring Memory of Y. L. Peretz in Post–World War II Yiddish Culture

In 1908, in one of his articles, Y. L. Peretz described the building that functioned as the center of the largest Jewish community in Eastern Europe, the Warsaw community, as a metaphor for the future of this community:

> It is possible that some years from now, the house on Grzybowska Street, number 26/28, will be a mound of ruins, not a single piece of the building will remain, demons and wild goats shall dance there and frolic in the ash and scatter it over seven days to all corners of the world. . . . Elsewhere, a grand building will stand tall . . . a large smoke-chimney rising up from it, as from the biggest factory, and from its windows large torches of fire will burst out and up, as from a furnace, while above the chimney will swirl a thick and fatty smoke of human flesh, bones, marrow and blood, like over an altar—a crematorium, in which the dead will be burned.[8]

Peretz's essay was about a disagreement in the Jewish community over issues concerning circumcision and burial, a disagreement that reflected the tension between traditional Jewish identities and modern ones. Peretz sought to caution that the controversy could threaten the common home unless the rival parties regained their composure, and this at a time in which the Jewish home was endangered not only from within the community but also from its environment:

the community existed in a hostile environment and therefore could not afford internal divisions.

Andreas Huyssen has proposed the ruin as the paradoxical metaphor that underlies modernity in all of its manifestations. Despite the purportedly forward-looking gaze of modernity, it was the forces of entropy that characterized it most. In his view, the ruin not only underscores the inevitable fate of any and every magnificent present but also functions as an architectural (that is, spatial) embodiment of the rapid and unstoppable effect of time.[9] When reality itself picks up speed under our feet, control over processes of disintegration is lost. The ruin then becomes a quintessential embodiment of our inner world. Peretz, like many contemporaneous Yiddish writers, described the Jewish shtetl as such a ruin, as a ruin in the making.[10] Like others of his time, he identified the lament for ruins as a traditional Jewish theme, which captures something of the essence of Judaism. But more than others, Peretz sought to develop the character of the modern Jewish literary creation around the theme of proud steadfastness in the face of this ruin, as a constant heroic battle against this disintegration (in the sense described in the Haggadah—"In every generation they rise up to destroy us, yet nevertheless, we are here" ["*Mir zaynen do*"]). In many cases, this is the steadfastness of the individual in the face of the dismalness to which he is doomed by virtue of the circumstances of his life in Eastern Europe, as a member of an economically and civilly disadvantaged minority in the modern age. But it is also a steadfastness of the Jewish community as a whole, since Peretz sought to draw links between the ongoing erosion of the status of the community and the possibility of an original and self-renewing Jewish artistic creation emerging from this community. Thus, his work deals directly with death, and the notion of destruction follows it throughout, like a shadow, a vital and inevitable companion. His work indeed drew on death and destruction—Peretz earned a living as a clerk at the Warsaw *Khevre kedishe* (burial society), and this work undoubtedly influenced and expressed his view of death as ever-present. Death and destruction are not just the typical lot of Peretz's protagonists; they are the inherent features of the domestic and communal space in which his characters live and act. His macabre surrealist play *Bay nakht afn altn mark* (At night at the old marketplace)—a work published only a few years (1907–1910) before Bergelson's *Nokh alemen* (1913)—is a distinctive example. In the face of this disintegrating space and in contrast with it, the actions of the protagonists take on meaning and actuality. In this way, Peretz found moral beauty in places where his contemporaries least expected to find it: in the extreme poverty of the *khosid* (A hasidic devotee), in the meager abode of the simple tradesman, in their modest perseverance in the face of the injuries of their fate in the new world. Paradoxically, he saw them as embodying in their perseverance the ideal that ought to guide the modern Jewish writer. It is no wonder, therefore, that Peretz's work was perceived as a moral directive for the cultural and ideological movements that rejected territory-based national identity and instead followed the idea of *doikayt* (here-ness)—namely, to persevere with a distinct Jewish existence in foreign cultural environments, which are often hostile and in any case environments in which the Jews are a negligible minority. He emphasized the need to be proud of this steadfastness by virtue of being *Shabes-yontefdike-yidn* (Jews of *Shabat* and *yom ṭov* [the term for Jewish holidays])—that is, by virtue of their ability to transform the hardships they faced because of their ethnic origin and to creatively develop their culture, which drew on the familiar traditional content, on the shared "cultural memory," as well as on the hegemonic cultures among which they lived.

As a romantic novelist whose main interest was the meaning of the life of the individual in the face of the material and moral disintegration of his traditional environment, Peretz tended to intensify the impact of the troubles due to which he offered his readers guidance. And as a passionate ideologist pained by the troubles of the community whose problems he sought to solve, he tended to exaggerate the loss of way for which he offered its members guidance. Even his unique style contributed significantly to the constant influence and almost prophetic status of his work, since Peretz often tended to achieve his literary goals through a very literal understanding of worn metaphors. This technique transforms them into symbols, into allegory, which in turn gives them a timeless, surreal power. If, for example, the Talmud says that "a poor person is like a dead person" but few take the saying at face value, Peretz, who seeks to jolt his readers and move them to act, intensifies the description of the suffering of the poor and depicts them as truly dead. Thus, the readers get a rather nightmarish and Kafkaesque image of a town of living-dead inhabitants (*Di toyte shtot* [*The City of the Dead*], 1895–1900). This allegory would later be easy to read as a chillingly laconic prophecy when reality surpassed even the imagination of the romantic novelist, who lets his apocalyptic imagination run wild here by means of a somewhat technical—but deliberately so—interpretation of a metaphor.

Already in his lifetime, Peretz was described as a "secular Admor" thanks to his literary preoccupation with enhancing and improving the moral standing of his audience vis-à-vis the challenges of Jewish existence in Poland and thanks to his social activism to promote the values he preached. From this perspective, the cliché about the three great prose writers of Yiddish culture being like a grandfather (Mendele), a father (Peretz), and a grandson (Sholem Aleichem) seems surprisingly accurate as a psychological observation. Of course, this cliché does not intend to order them chronologically—they lived and wrote during the same years more or less (and died one after the other with gaps of one year). Rather, it captures, in my view, a fundamental observation: the grandfather, father, and grandson symbolize three typical responses to the basic problem that preoccupied Yiddish literature in those days—namely, the waning of the traditional Jewish way of life in Eastern Europe and the need for Jews to reorient themselves in the face of the changes brought on by modernity. Within this theme is mixed together the moral-ideological-political dilemma regarding the question of what makes the nontraditional Jew Jewish, with the unique kind of pain involved in observing one's disintegrating community with a sober eye. The archetypal grandfather, Mendele, represents (like every typical grandfather) an unimposing respectability and a moral critique that despite its validity remains somewhat distant—Mendele's work largely leaves the solution to the flaws it exposes to future generations. He contents himself with affecting derisive alienation toward the forlorn state of the next generation. By contrast, the grandson, Sholem Aleichem, symbolizes a kind of irresistible magic, which connects us to feelings of identification with the pain, an identification that softens the pain and makes it containable, without underestimating its gravity but also without resolving it as such or even directly discussing any such resolution. In contrast to both grandfather and grandson, the father, Peretz, symbolizes the spirit of seriously and gravely assuming responsibility for leadership. He is the only one among them who seeks to provide for his community, in all senses.

Peretz's centennial year, 1952, was declared by the World Congress for Yiddish/Jewish Culture as the "Y. L. Peretz year." That year saw many hundreds of literary, theatrical, and educational events in his honor held across the world, spanning (nearly) the whole spectrum of the political landscape, from the Bundists to the Zionists. In a book he published in honor of the event, the important literary critic Shmuel Niger noted that, like Reb Nakhmen Bratslaver, the "secular Admor" Peretz also became a "living rabbi" after his death even more so than he was in his life.[11] Niger's observation relates primarily to the tumultuous period between the world wars in which Peretz's legacy was memorialized not only through the publication of all of his works, of collections of the works, and of special issues of leading journals devoted to his work but also through giving his name to Yiddish writer associations, libraries, cultural centers, theaters, schools, orphanages, and streets in various cities across the world. Niger further noted that even during the years of the Holocaust itself, in the ghettos and throughout Europe, Peretz's writings continued to be a most important educational source as well as a source of encouragement for the establishment of educational, cultural, and communal organizations. He enjoyed a similar status in the cultural activity that took place in the DP camps in Germany.[12] It was taken as a given that he deserved a central place in the projects that memorialized Yiddish culture in Poland in general and Warsaw in particular—for instance, in the 175-volume series *Dos poylishe yidntum* (Polish Jewry), published in Buenos Aires beginning in 1946 and edited by Marek Turkow; in the six volumes of *Poyln* (Poland), the memoirs of Y. Y. Trunk, published in New York in 1944–1951; in the three volumes of *Di geshikhte fun yidn in varshe* (The history of the Jews in Warsaw), by

Yankev Shatzky, published in New York in 1947–1953; and in the leading Yiddish literary journal *Di goldene keyt*, named after Peretz's famous play.

Thus, Peretz's work received a special place and status after the Holocaust, above and beyond its place as the work of a canonical writer of the first rank, mostly because of the unique way in which the content, style, and overall character of his work fit the needs of an audience he could not have known and events that no one could have predicted. Peretz's uniqueness among Yiddish writers and readers after the Holocaust lies in what was perceived as his spiritual legacy: to persist in creating a Jewish culture that is at once both traditional and frequently self-renewing, and especially one that looks toward the future, despite and even because of the processes of disintegration of its old world. Indeed, the culture requires this disintegration as a self-preserving motivation. Thus, at the most difficult times, Peretz's work suited the emotional and social needs of Holocaust survivors and the rest of the producers and consumers of Yiddish culture after the Holocaust. It suited them even more than the works of more popular and elegant writers, like Sholem Aleichem, whose work is essentially a heartrending and ironic description of said disintegration, and certainly more than the work of such subtle writers as Bergelson, who did not seek to chart a path for others and whose work observes the lyrical nuances of the disintegration and waning with refined sophistication.

The Holocaust was a realization of Peretz's worst nightmares and indeed surpassed them immeasurably. Reality itself eroded the force of his metaphors and their liveliness, and thus, his prophecy lost something of its innovative and invigorating spirit. Yet the establishment of Israel was regarded by many Holocaust survivors as a kind of apocalyptic miracle, an end-of-the-days resurrection of the dead, which the typical Peretz stock of images and way of putting things suited well. As Sutzkever wrote in 1951, on the two-year anniversary of the journal *Di goldene keyt*,[13] the journal's cultural activity was effectively an attempt to rearticulate Peretz's legacy—contra his original "here-ness" position—as part of the unique Zionist narrative of the worldwide community of survivors and grievers.

Peretz's work earned its special status because, more than anyone else, he sought to unify his readers around the idea of transforming suffering into a motivating force. But this was also the source of its weakness, since in its reliance on ruins as a motivating tool it was sustained and nourished by fixating its gaze on them, as in the case of Lot's wife. How, then, would the Holocaust survivors be able to preserve this backward gaze without becoming petrified in the later stages of communal grief, stages in which they wished to reclaim daily life? How could Yiddish writers continue to draw inspiration and consolation from Peretz's work after the Holocaust—that is, continue to identify with the ruin while building their new home and without allowing it to become a new ruin?

4. The Waning of the Shtetl-to-Metropolis Theme

In 1948, a thick anthology (over a thousand pages long) was published in New York featuring a compilation of works of Hebrew literature (in Hebrew, Yiddish, and Aramaic) from all periods, whose topic is manifestations of *Kidesh Ha-Shem* (sanctification of the Name).[14] The works appear in the anthology in reverse chronological order (from the Holocaust all the way back to ancient history) and in geographical order: they are arranged according to the places in which the manifestations of *Kidesh Ha-Shem* took place. The message conveyed by this editorial choice is clear: not only "in every generation" do they rise up to destroy us but also in every place. This radicalized reiteration of the traditional message by none other than one of the founders of Yiddish culture, Shmuel Niger, attests to the deep conservativeness, both creative and political, that gripped Yiddish culture after the Holocaust. And indeed, the comparison between this anthology and the first modern anthology of this culture, *Der pinkes: Yorbukh far der geshikhte fun der yidisher literatur un shprakh, far folklore, kritik un bibliyografye* (Annals: Yearbook for the history of Yiddish literature and language, folklore, criticism, and bibliography), which he himself edited in 1913, encapsulates rather fully the evolution of this short-lived culture both conceptually and spatially—from the shtetl (the premodern traditional culture) to the big world (modern, liberal, universal culture) and "back into the ghetto slamming the door shut," in the words of Yankev Glatshteyn in his "prophetic" Peretzian poem "A gute nakht, velt" ("Good Night, World," 1938; i.e., back to the religious ethnic identity). Glatshteyn's poem was written in New York and published there on the eve of the Holocaust; it thus demonstrates that conservativism had begun to wash over Yiddish culture before the Holocaust, in tandem with the deepening social and economic crises of the 1930s. If before the Holocaust the shtetl was distinct from the big city in Eastern Europe, after the Holocaust this distinction collapsed under the consoling wings of the myth. Yiddish writers stood at a personal and creative crossroads after the Holocaust. This is how the writer and editor Arie Shamri expressed this feeling: "Yiddish literature after the Holocaust was left without a shtetl and without a world. The path that Yiddish literature travelled in the twentieth century is the path from the shtetl to the world. Yiddish literature dreamed: here, here, we are about to merge into the grand panorama—the world. But it turned out that the shtetl was gone and the world had slapped us in our face."[15] The shtetl, the big city, and especially the movement between them were the main themes of modern Yiddish literature and evocative images within it. The enormous movement of the masses that took place between the end of the nineteenth century and the 1920s, in which roughly a third of the Jews of Eastern Europe left it (mainly for the United States[16] but also for Canada, the countries of South America, South Africa, Australia, and pre-state Israel), posed a special challenge for modern Yiddish literature: several of its writers experienced and represented this movement as a crisis and others as an opportunity. The scholar of Yiddish literature Mikhail Krutikov identified three main modes of representation of the experience of immigration: the romantic-sentimental mode, oriented toward the past; the realistic mode, oriented to the present; and the modernist mode, oriented to the future.[17] These three modes describe three types of literary responses to the crisis of immigration that had appeared in dozens of works of literature up until the Holocaust and thus were largely exhausted in Yiddish literature. I describe them here in more detail to illustrate the challenge of renewing Yiddish literature, on which Ayznman reflected in the quote at the beginning of this chapter.

The first mode of representation, the romantic-sentimental, is the one that looks back to the past. Immigration is depicted in it as a disaster for the protagonist and for the traditional community from which he hails. The sentimentality of this approach is expressed in its emphasis on the tragic aspects involved in the loss of the traditional values and communal support following immigration. The advantages of immigration are denied, as are the internal changes that had already taken place in the communities in Eastern Europe prior to the immigration and which had triggered the disintegration of the traditional life. These works focus on a traditional past, embodied in the image of the Eastern-European shtetl and its protagonists. Both of these are described in a rather ideal manner. The protagonist (like its metonymic parallel, the shtetl) is unable to put down roots in the new land, and the present life dooms him to complete destruction, capitulation to his new circumstances, and death. Immigration is perceived in these works as one more in a series of catastrophes that have befallen the Jewish people.

The second mode of representation, the present-oriented realistic mode, draws on the tradition of European social realism (from the middle to the end of the nineteenth century). The Jewish immigration is perceived in it as an historical event occurring within the context of a general process of social change. The works focus on a single protagonist, on his or her struggle for survival and success, and on the significant change this individual undergoes in light of the new circumstances. Optimism is one of the traits of this mode of representation, and thus the outcome of the protagonist's battle for survival is typically marriage and not death. The work's ending confirms the new order despite its shortcomings and challenges. The traditional Jewish lifestyle and Jewish ethics are presented as the protagonist's point of departure and are not ascribed absolute supreme value. Their loss therefore does not doom the protagonist to destruction but rather causes him or her to undergo a fundamental change, and this change is the work's main subject. However, the process that the protagonist undergoes strengthens his or her recognition of the relative value of the old traditional world and its moral values. The protagonist's actions in the face of the various difficulties and challenges of the new reality drive the plot. Thus, this mode of representation emphasizes the agency of the individual and not the stagnation and impotence of the traditional community, as in the first mode.

The third mode of representation is the future-oriented modernist one. Immigration is described here as a force that is of central importance to the spiritual and physical revival of the Jewish people. Works that employ this mode focus on innovations in the Jewish experience, but ones that are not necessarily revolutionary in nature—that is, that emerge not from a rejection of the past or disengagement from it. Even though there is no room in the destination country for the traditional way of life and its values as embodied in the shtetl, still, according to this approach, it is possible and appropriate to embrace some of the features of this old life—primarily its language, Yiddish—as part of the new lifestyle in order to preserve the ethnic character of the Eastern European Jewish public. According to Krutikov, the writers who created this type of representation were attuned to the physical aspects of the new environment and imbued it with spiritual meanings. They drew inspiration from the modernist European aesthetic, from Jewish messianic metaphysics, and from Hasidism, as well as from certain aspects of the ideology and ethics of Russian populism (Narodism). The future is shaped as a spiritual renewal, sometimes as the result of a utopian social lifestyle, in which productive work, and especially working the land, is cast as an ideal (the "ideal chronotope," in Mikhail Bakhtin's words).[18] This mode of representation contrasts with the sentimental idealization of the past in the Jewish shtetl, as well as with the capitalist urbanization and industrialization of the present. These literary works avoided narrative structures with a closed ending, like a wedding or a death, and instead offered an open and inconclusive ending.

The spectrum of attitudes toward the two significant "places" in the drama of immigration, the starting point and the destination—from romantic nostalgia, through realism, all the way to utopic enthusiasm—had already been nearly exhausted by the time of the Holocaust, as I said. The destruction of Eastern Europe also dramatically changed the spatial perception of Yiddish culture, which now saw itself as a "periphery with no center." How, then, was it to describe Jewish life after the Holocaust? In 1913, Niger argued that the "diaspora novel" was the most faithful and fitting representation of Jewish life in the twentieth century:

> Modern Yiddish literature is not and cannot be a literature of one region or one country, just as it is not and can no longer be the literature of one ethnic group. . . . The "diaspora novel" should take place not in a particular place, a particular country, but throughout the Jewish diaspora, in all corners of the world. Its protagonists should be not the poor or rich Jew, not the religious or clever Jew, educated or ignorant; not the Jew from the city or from the shtetl; not the Russian or Galician or American Jew; its protagonist is the Jew in general, *the wandering Jew*, the Jew in the world, the Jew for whom God's land is both a home and the stake [at which he is burned], the Jew whose name is

> "Ahasver" [the wandering Jew]. . . . This "Ahasver-novel" must be the form, the most exalted form, of our modern national epos.[19]

This paradoxical ideal, which posits the diasporic aspect as the core of the new Jewish literature (and identity), became increasingly hard to realize after World War I and in the crises that the Jews experienced between the wars, both in Eastern Europe and in the United States. Until the Holocaust, Yiddish fiction, which was focused on a "local" subject matter (namely, on new places of settlement outside Eastern Europe, including agricultural settlements mostly in North and South America—"regional literature," in Bakhtin's terms),[20] was not particularly popular among Yiddish critics and readers across the world and remained marginal. This is because many of the Yiddish writers (and readers) did not regard these new places of settlement and daily life within them as worthy subjects that deserved to be the focus of a literary creation. So long as it existed, the "old home" and the emigration from it were the preferred theme in this literature.[21] The local literature had a distinctly romantic style. Its protagonists, the laborers, were typically distinguished by their physical-sensual quality, and they moved between enthusiastic hope and an apocalyptic-messianic sense of finality and doom. The modernist works, whose treatment of this theme was more complex in terms of style and content, did not have a big readership.

Until the establishment of the state, the topic of "Eretz Yisrael" formed part of the local literature in the worldwide Yiddish literature.[22] This literature was full of glorifying romantic, mythical-messianic, and sentimental descriptions of encounters with ancient cities (Jerusalem, Safed, Tiberias)—a phenomenon described in the critical literature as the *Tsien motiv* (Zion motif)—as well as descriptions of the lives of the pioneers in a style of naive realism (these were termed the *Erets-yisroel-motiv*, "Eretz Yisrael motif"). Shmuel Rozhanski pointed out the difficulty that attended this literary preoccupation with the theme of Zion/Eretz Yisrael: namely, that even secular writers who objected to the territory-based national revival—Y. L. Peretz foremost among them—created sentimental and romantic-messianic descriptions of it (for instance, in his work *Dray matones* [*The Three Gifts*], where the whole of Eretz Yisrael is encapsulated in a small bag of dirt worthy of being redeemed in return for a human life, according to the simple and prevalent interpretation of this image).[23]

Throughout the 1940s, as word reached the Jewish communities in the free world about the scale of the catastrophe in Eastern Europe, modern Yiddish literature increasingly expressed a plunge into deep mourning, which was reflected in conservative choices of content (a focus on the past), form (nostalgia), and ideology (a return to religious narratives and traditional themes as the common content of the new Jewish collective).[24] In 1946, Niger described the Jews of America (himself included) as "survivors" and the "surviving remnant" of a process of cultural assimilation, which he called a "spiritual destruction."[25] Therefore, he argued, it was incumbent on these "survivors" to acknowledge their obligation and the mission entrusted to them to retreat from their national (American) identity to their ethnic identity and create a "continuation" of their culture. The literary critic Shiye Rapoport, a Holocaust survivor who settled in Melbourne, described this same tendency, in 1948, in a more subtle way: "Just as in the past the Jew ran from himself toward the world, so now he has begun to run from the world into himself."[26]

5. The Israel-Theme and Its Contribution to the Rejuvenation of Literature

The life of the present in the young state of Israel, with its processes of setting up home and establishing oneself, was a new time in the life of the Holocaust survivors, which replaced a decade-long period of horrors during which they had experienced extensive loss and the destruction of their homes, their families, their communities, and their world as they knew it. They had experienced loss and violence in all of their forms, as well as betrayal and a loss of faith in the goodness of human beings, in the goodness of the world, and in their ability to influence their fate. The traumatized person, Dominick LaCapra argued, is determined to repeat the past compulsively, with no ability to exist in the present as an individual and as part of a society or to identify the unique challenges and opportunities that the present offers.[27] And yet, upon their arrival in Israel, many Yiddish writers began to describe in their works the daily life in these new spaces and the challenges they faced in the process of building their personal and communal home within the burgeoning national society. The critics of Yiddish literature, in Israel and the rest of the world, received this new focus on what they called "*Yisroel-tematik*" (the Israel-theme) with great enthusiasm. For instance, this is how the editor Shmuel Rozhanski estimated the contribution of this theme to the contemporary Yiddish world literature:

> Thanks to the establishment of the Jewish state the Yiddish word was spared from pushing itself into *a ghetto of lamentation-literature* and seeing nothing other than the horrible past and the catastrophe. . . . From all directions, new impulses began to sparkle, new aspirations, a fortified passion to live and to create. . . . The Israel-theme is a real God-given gift for post WWII Yiddish literature. . . . In immersing himself in the Israeli reality, precisely in the years of sorrow and pain, [the writer created] a new world, new horizons, new hopes, a fresh courage, fresh forces. Yiddish literature became younger through the Israel-theme.[28]

The establishment of Israel, then, transformed daily life within it from a "local" and largely exhausted topic to a powerful drama that Yiddish readers across the world followed intently, and it thus contributed to their renewed consolidation as a community. It is no wonder, therefore, that the literary establishment encouraged writing on this theme. Like the New York–based literary journal *Di Tsukunft*, *Letste nayes* also announced a literary prize for the best short story and reportage that dealt with the Israel-theme and whose protagonists were *'oley sheyres hapleyte*, the goal being to support writers who chose to write on this topic and to encourage more writers to address it.[29] In the terminology of the anthropologist Zali Gurevitch, the drama stems from the tension between the mythical place and time (the "big time" and "big place") and daily life in the private sphere (the "small time" and "small place"). The Israel-theme is a crossroads (chronotope) of a defined time and place: it describes the encounter of 'oley sheyres hapleyte with Israel—its human, geographic, and environmental landscapes and their daily life within it. Yet in many works of literature, this theme functioned as a stable and positive base from which the writers were able to travel back to the past and even to revisit traumas without becoming submerged in them and without turning their work into a lamentation.

For example, the vast majority of the young Yiddish writers chose to structure their first books, published after their arrival in Israel, as "travel diaries," whose stations (in space and time) are metonyms for the life of the protagonist narrator (the "path of life" chronotope) and for the important points of development in this life: an opening section featuring stories of childhood in Poland, a middle section with stories from the war years (typically in the Soviet Union), and a concluding section of stories that describe the new life in Israel (for instance, *Vint un vortslen* [Wind and roots], by Yishaye Shpigl, 1955, or *Di Ban: Dertseylungen fun poyln, rusland, yisroel* [The railroad: Stories from Poland, Russia, Israel], by Tsvi Ayznman, 1956). But many others depicted a reverse journey, beginning with the present time in Israel and from there going back to the period of the war and ending with their childhood in Poland (for instance, *In eygenem land* [In one's own land], by Yitskhok Perlov, 1952; *Bilder un dertseylungen* [Images and stories], by Shloyme Berlinski, 1958; *In der nayer heym* [In the new home], by Levi Papiernikov, 1960). In both these structures, the Israel-theme functions as the culmination of the "path of life" chronotope—a central chronotope in modern European literature.[30] The first (chronological) structure paints a teleological picture—characteristic of pilgrimage accounts—in which the past in Eastern Europe leads to the journey's destination (and thus its culmination), the present life in Israel, which retrospectively casts its sanctity back on the entire journey with all of its trials and pitfalls. The latter structure casts the Israel-theme as a kind of anchor that allows the author to travel, safely and with a sense of value, from the stable present back to the past in Eastern Europe with its terrors and disasters.

The Israel-theme, then, gave its creators (and its readers) a stable foothold, a new model of action, of heroes and heroism, as opposed to those formed on the eve of the Holocaust, during it, and after it. It also provided its creators with a new mission. This is how Sutzkever described this new mission in 1954:

> Lonely and imbittered are some of the Yiddish writers in Israel. Vilna, Warsaw, Lodzh are a cloud that darkens our bright homes. We are mourners, and so we will remain. Mourners with joyful children. We are afraid of the mirror. Our dream is a temple of skeletons. But the eyes of all Yiddish writers are turned to us and to our creation. . . . All of Y. L. Peretz's life and literary creation amounted to one single cry: to be a tortured Jew is a privilege. But may Peretz forgive me: to be a freed Jew, a Jew from the Jewish state, is an even greater privilege!. . . . Here in our country we must create a new literary style [*nusah/nusekh*]: an Israel style. Just as there was a Poland style. . . . We are not step-citizens and we are not step-writers, our word in Yiddish is our most sacred possession. . . . We, Yiddish writers, seek "to renew the Land [of Israel]" . . . from here, from the holy land on which we live. We seek "to renew the Land" in a language that is paired with Hebrew. In the language of Sholem Aleichem we bid the people: Sholem Aleichem![31]

The mission of Yiddish writers in Israel, according to Sutzkever, was "to renew the Land" for readers of Yiddish, not only in Israel but all over the world. It is not the moon that ought to be "sanctified" (as in the name of the series of prayers recited to bless the new moon—*Kidush Levana / Kidesh Levone*, sanctification of the moon), since the darkness that prevailed on the face of the earth during World War II originated from within it, from a dimming of the light that emanated from it, and not from an absence of the moon. Therefore, renewing the light must also take place from within the land itself. Art is an expression of the renewal of the light, and especially literature that describes the life being created in Israel, in Yiddish, the language of the culture that was devastated. The very act of creating this literature allows the readers of Yiddish in Israel and beyond to renew their faith in life, in the ability to act, and in goodness. This is the new practice of the "renewal/sanctification of the Land." Here Sutzkever expands the "Israel-theme" into an "Israeli style." This is a secular modern paraphrase on the two styles of religious practice (*nusahim*, denoting the exact text of a prayer service used by a particular community) that were upheld in exile: nusah Ashkenaz and nusah Sefard. Yet "nusah Israel" is not a direct incarnation of these religious styles but rather of "nusah Poyln/Polin," which is, of course, distinct from nusah Ashkenaz. Nusah Israel is to be a unique modern-literary expression of life in Israel, just as modern Yiddish literature was an expression of the unique character of the life that existed in Poland.

The task of "renewing the Land," then, invites renewal of the literature, as Ayznman reflected. Sutzkever, in the previously quoted passage, proposed significant innovations: writing the works of literature and reading them as a new incarnation of the traditional Blessing of the Moon, transcending tradition (embodied by Peretz) in the context of the appropriate motivating force for life and artistic creation after the Holocaust, and defining the social responsibility of the Yiddish writer and his status as a modern incarnation of a cantor, who plays a central role in the religious ritual. The Yiddish writer's work, then, ought to stem from engagement with the place about which he or she writes, from participating in the collective effort to build a new life, and not from abstaining from these activities or ignoring them by retreating (or collapsing) into the "I" (which was the stance of the "In-zikh" poets in New York between the world wars), as if the writer "lives on the moon" and from this safe haven "renews/sanctifies" the Land. And indeed, in an article published in *Di Tsukunft*, Mendl Man argued that because the Yiddish writers had experienced in their flesh "tremendous" historical events—the Holocaust and the ʿaliya to Israel—their works captured the new Israel, Israel of the mass ʿaliya: "The blank page in Israeli literature can only be filled by a Yiddish writer. He comes from within, together with the first residents from Jaffa, Yazur, Ramla and Lod. And this sounds perhaps like a paradox: the *new* Israel can be found in Yiddish literature."[32]

The paradox Man refers to lies in the fact that the literature that depicts the new national experience, the Israeli experience, was written not in the country's official national language but rather in its denied historical language, which was presented as outdated. It is interesting to compare this portrayal with a statement made around the same time by the canonical Hebrew writer Moshe Shamir, in response to the demand by literary critics that young Hebrew writers describe the mass migration in their work: "A work of prose, and especially in the expansive and compelling form of the novel, is made possible only by close, continuous, and organic contact with the social reality. To those who ask where is the story about the maʿabara, we therefore say: this story will be written by the youngster who grows up in the maʿabara and who is now learning for the first time how to write his name."[33]

If we ignore the patronizing attitude embodied in the image of "the youngster . . . learning for the first time how to write his name," what Shamir expresses is a recognition of the limitations, both creative and ethical, of the native-born Hebrew writer in tackling the Israel-theme. For natives cannot and ought not put themselves in the place of refugees, immigrants, or Holocaust survivors. This limitation applied also to Yiddish writers who came to Israel before the establishment of the state. When they tried to write about the Israel-theme, in an attempt to connect with the new audience of readers, their attempts met with piercing criticism.[34]

"In a certain sense we are past the big time, past the historical moment, and the big time today is a yearning for the civilization of the present, for an Israeli style," argued Gurevitch. Yet, "the Israeli present is one that resists the present, resists the everyday. . . . As a cultural essence, the present is never sealed. . . . It contains a certain agitation and excitement or a certain festivity. . . . And there is therefore no time to really complete the work, to get to the fine details, to stay in the details."[35] These details, for which, according to Gurevitch, Israeli culture has no time, are the daily lives in the various spaces where 'oley sheyres hapleyte arrived; they become the contents of the Israel-theme in Yiddish fiction. This theme therefore completes a portrait of Israel that Israeli culture could not produce. Michel de Certeau regarded the "innumerable practices of everyday life" as the way in which the space was "performed," one that does not necessarily obey the order that society dictates through its mechanisms of power and surveillance.[36] According to him, an examination of these varied practices of daily life, performed by many "users," "from below," reveals a wide range of "opposing meanings" to the single hegemonic meaning imposed by society on the individuals within it.

The Israel-theme described daily life in a range of spaces, voices, and styles: from realism through "magical realism" to surrealism. The treatment of biblical themes was common mostly among the older Yiddish writers who came to Israel, including Sholem Asch, who wrote the novels *Moyshe* (*Moses*) and *Der novi* (*The Prophet*), and Dovid Pinski, who in the same years wrote the plays *Moyshe un di kušit* (Moses and the Negress), *Shoel hameylekh* (King Saul), and *Shimshen un Dlile* (Samson and Delilah). These themes, as well as romantic, mystical-messianic, and apolitical representations, were perceived by Yiddish writers of the younger generation as a shirking of the responsibility imposed on them by the times in which they lived, toward their contemporaries: "Because the mission is difficult, painful, and God did not give strength to bear it, just as he did not give to [the prophet] Jonah Ben Amittai, one escapes to Tarshish; escapes the living, suffering generation itself in favor of the dust of generations from the distant past."[37] This unease on the part of writers of the young generation about mystical-messianic or apocalyptic descriptions was common mostly throughout the 1950s. The Suez Crisis (1956), and much more so the Six-Day War, brought on a flood of writing in this vein, but after 1967, very few voices protesting against it were heard. This resistance echoes the debate that took place during the second 'aliya between proponents of the "genre" style of representation of life in pre-state Israel in fiction, with its ideological, romantic, and ideal approach, and those of the "anti-genre" representation of this life, focused on the inner life of the tormented individual and his or her life qua individual.[38] Of this polemic Avner Holzman has said that "in truth, the battle between the 'genre' dimension and the 'non-genre' dimension took place within the soul and the writing of each one of the writers more than between two rival groups of writers."[39] This holds true also of the similar dilemma that gripped Yiddish writers with respect to the Israel-theme.

* * *

In this chapter, I presented some of the challenges that Yiddish writers faced in Israel after the Holocaust in their efforts to create "a new word." The traumas of the Holocaust were central to these challenges. They were a new form of what I termed here the "Lot's wife dilemma." Like every modern literature, Yiddish literature moved fervently between nostalgia and realism, utopian idyll and dystopic nihilism, enthusiasm and depression, and it expressed both optimism and pessimism regarding the inevitable embrace of the new world. Yiddish literature dealt extensively with this range of approaches and references even before the Holocaust. However, World War II radically changed the reality in which Yiddish writers lived, and along with it the literary references to this reality. The multiplicity and variety that had characterized these references before the war were reduced and darkened in its aftermath. A new outlet was discovered for this literature after the establishment of Israel, especially in prose. Yiddish literature began increasingly to turn its attention to the Israel-theme—that is, to the encounter of ʻoley sheyres hapleyte with the young state and their daily life within it. In these works, a new style crystallized—unique ways of characterizing and shaping that distinguished the Israel-theme from Yiddish literature's long-standing preoccupation with Eretz Yisrael and the act of ʻaliya to Zion. The Israel-theme was a rather "Huyssenian" solution to the problem of literary writing after the Holocaust in the sense that instead of focusing on descriptions of the destruction, instead of evoking the past and becoming submerged in it, the writers allowed it to emerge subtly through descriptions and contents that were supposedly antithetical to it: the new life bustling in the various spaces to which they came, as well as the excitement and disappointment from the encounter with the locals (veterans, sabras, immigrants from the various diasporas, Palestinians) and from their attempts to fit into the space and into the society. For the Yiddish writers the Israel-theme summoned new challenges, which the writers of Hebrew had faced before them, upon their own encounter with the Land of Israel. Foremost among these challenges was the question of how to describe daily life in the Israeli present after the waning of the "big historical events," with all of this new life's human variety, which was expressed in a mosaic of cultures, languages, occupations, and lifestyles. Examining the Yiddish literature written in Israel from a literary point of view, and from the perspective of the literary history, allows us to see beyond the long and heavy shadow cast on it by the Holocaust, and beyond the loaded ideological debates that accompanied its existence in Israel about the "life," "decline," or "death" of this rich and complex literature.

4

Israeli Spaces in Yiddish Prose

1. Preliminary Terminology: Space, Place, and Home

At the high point of the novel *Dzshebelye* (Jebelye) by Yitskhok Perlov (a detailed reading of which follows), the protagonist reencounters his former wife, from whom he separated in Warsaw on the eve of the Nazi invasion when he fled to the Soviet Union with their two children. Since that separation, each of them has suffered various trials and torments. Meeting again, in Tel Aviv's Meir Park, they try to bridge the years and their traumas, and even contemplate the possibility of reestablishing their family and reerecting their home. "Everyone is healing their wounds and everyone is rebuilding their homes,"[1] the woman argues. And the protagonist ruminates, "Shall we perhaps try again and build our home?"[2] However, he is gripped by the fear that the attempt to reconstruct what once existed will end in travesty: "A parody about a human family life . . . about domestic happiness . . . Yes, nothing but a parody!"[3]

This passage illustrates the central tension that characterizes the "Israel-theme" in Yiddish fiction written in Israel after the Holocaust. Like any modern literature, it was suffused with an awareness of the inability to return to the past and to the "old home"—to life as it was lived in traditional society, within a close-knit family and community. And yet, this fiction drew its impetus and its inspiration from the backward glance at the past and its structures. The Holocaust exacerbated the gap—temporal, moral, and the gap of consciousness—that had opened between the present and the past. The fundamental question that this fiction raised, and which is echoed also in the quoted passage, is whether it is possible to "step into the same river twice." Not only had the time that elapsed changed the heroes and heroines as well as the notions of home and community, but the traumas of war and refugeehood had demonstrated just how fragile human beings, their homes, and their communities truly are. The experience of this fragility is like a taste of the tree of knowledge, after which there is no more holding on to a naive notion of the paradise embodied by a stable and harmonious home, family, and community. And yet, "everyone is rebuilding their destroyed homes," as Perlov's heroine argued: between 1939 and 1943, some thirty million Europeans were uprooted or exiled from their homes, and between 1943 and 1948, approximately twenty million refugees and displaced persons were on the move, seeking a place of rest and refuge where they could rebuild their homes. In Yiddish, as in English, the word *heym* (home) denotes the private one and by extension also the communal, national home (*heymland*, homeland). Unlike the Yiddish word for "house" (*hoyz*), *heym* underscores the intimate aspect and therefore also the sense of security that goes along with being in a geopolitically, socially, and culturally familiar landscape, a social and emotional econiche.

The Israel-theme in Yiddish literature after the Holocaust, therefore, rises from the inescapable yet unfulfillable desire for a new home, private as well as communal. It is strewn with descriptions of a particular time and place, while expressing the trauma of losing the normal senses of time and place—the inability to belong once again to a space, to turn it into a home, an econiche, and to realize a sense of sovereignty over a land.[4] The tension between these opposing layers lies at the heart of these works.

In the passage quoted earlier, Perlov's characters describe the failure to relive the past as parodical. Among the Yiddish writers in Israel, there was a prevalent sense that models of writing and modes of reference that characterized Yiddish fiction in the past were no longer usable. They felt the need for a new theme and new modes of addressing it. The new "place" and its contrast with the old home became a major literary theme. The basic models that were available to Yiddish writers as places in which to set their plots—the shtetl and the big city—had lost their relevance in the post-Holocaust reality, and there was now a need for a new literary place and a new literary style (*nusah*) to describe it. The new style was needed also for descriptions of the protagonists, since "in Israel, not only was a new regime established but a new people was created,"[5] as Dvora Hacohen argued in her assessment of the influence of the big ʿaliya on Israel. And indeed, the encounters between various survivors of communities, between refugees from all over the world, were not some sort of incarnation of the Eastern European Jewish shtetl, as was still the case during the mass migration from the shtetl. And therefore these encounters could not be described with the same literary tools.

In this chapter, I present and discuss select examples of literary works in a variety of forms (from the novel, the novella, the short story, and the vignette to the journalistic feuilleton) that deal with the Israel-theme—that is, with the encounters of ʿoley sheyres hapleyte with several sites that were typical of Israel of the 1950s and 1960s: depopulated Palestinian villages and towns, the maʿabara, the immigrant housing project, the Kibbutz, and Tel Aviv. The first three sites are historical stages in the absorption of ʿoley sheyres hapleyte in Israel;[6] the latter two are symbols of the new Jewish nationality and its culture. The Kibbutz was not a common place of settlement among ʿoley sheyres hapleyte since it accentuated their loneliness. The only exceptions to this were the few Kibbutzim that were established by ʿoley sheyres hapleyte, where their loneliness as refugees could find some consolation within the group. But because of the Kibbutz's central place in the ethos of Israeli society, I chose works that describe it from the point of view of Yiddish writers; and Tel Aviv, more than any other city in Israel, is mentioned in most of the works that deal with the Israel-theme. Cities were a common theme in modern Yiddish literature, and thus my analysis examines Tel Aviv against the backdrop of this tradition.

Naturally, not all the works that have been written on the Israel-theme can be presented and discussed here, and my reading of the works that are discussed cannot pretend to exhaust all the layers of meaning that are embedded in them. The reading focuses on the following questions: How do these works describe the tension between mythical perceptions of the place and the experience of daily life within it (the "big place" versus the "small place" as well as the mythical and cyclical "big time" versus the prosaic and linear "small time")? How do they create the experience of "being at home" in the national home—the experience of ownership of the home and the land as well as the rights and obligations that this generates? How do they represent the encounter with members of the "imagined national community" and with the "national other"? How do they represent the violence involved in realizing this ownership of the place? How do they represent the encounter with the national language? Finally, did Yiddish prose indeed succeed in creating new modes of reference and description for the places of the new space?

The challenges of the act of renewing are explored here in relation to the tradition of modern Yiddish fiction as well as to contemporaneous Hebrew fiction, with which this literature shared not only a geographic and social space but also a new cultural field—namely, Israeli literature: "The debate about the traditional boundaries of the canon helps us identify both the boundaries of the Israeli identity represented by those literary works and the canonization processes themselves."[7] Yiddish fiction written in Israel on the Israel-theme was located in the margins of the familiar canon in the field of Israeli literature. The unique perspective afforded by this location exposes new and sometimes surprising facets of this theme.

2. Depopulated Palestinian Dwelling Places

The refugees from the Holocaust who came to Israel in the first decade after its establishment were the outlying ripples of an enormous movement of tens of millions of refugees who washed over Europe after World War II, and after which the European space became nationally and ethnically more homogenous (in contrast to the more multinational and multiethnic reality that prevailed there between the world wars). The survivors of some five thousand Jewish settlements that were destroyed in Eastern Europe were housed in some four hundred depopulated Palestinian villages and towns—that is to say, places of dwelling whose original residents had fled or were forced to leave by the fighting. Placing them in these villages and towns was done not as an organized state policy but as part of the chaotic arrangements of the emergent state. The ʻolim were forced to take care of various aspects of their absorption on their own. And indeed, three out of every four ʻolim withstood this "self-absorption."[8] Settlement in recently depopulated areas was common among ʻoley sheyres hapleyte of the first wave of the mass ʻaliya (1948 to the end of 1949). It began in cities (or specific quarters within them)[9] and later spread to rural settlements.[10]

It is an interesting fact that in Yiddish literature, of all the types of settlement in Israel, this type—the settlement in recently depopulated villages and neighborhoods—despite being characterized by disorganization and a sense of lack of stability derived from the nature of the places in which the ʻolim were housed, became the topic not only of short stories but even of two novels. It is typically assumed that novel writing, more than the writing of any other literary form, requires stability and security—both existential and financial. But Yiddish prose about the settlement in Maʻabarot, Kibbutzim, immigrant housing projects, or big cities was written mostly in its short forms (short stories, feuilletons, images, impressions, etc.), whereas the two novels—*Dzshebelye* (1955) and *In a farvorloztn dorf* (In a deserted village, 1954)—deal with the immigrants' arrival in the depopulated Palestinian villages and neighborhoods and their settlement there. The works were published only a few years after their authors' arrival in Israel.

The authors, Perlov and Mendl Man, shared similar biographies: when World War II broke out, they both fled to the Soviet Union; when Europe was liberated, they both returned as repatriates to Poland and from there moved to DP camps; and upon arrival in Israel, they were both sent to live in places that resembled those about which they wrote—Perlov in the Jebelya neighborhood (now Givʻat ʻAliya) of Jaffa, and Man in Yazur (Azur).[11] Thus, their work is based on their personal experiences. Both were regarded by the leading literary critics as "promising" writers. Perlov was considered a popular writer whose work appealed to the broad worldwide Yiddish readership (and he was indeed widely known), whereas Man was considered a writer for the elite, one whose readers were more refined and sophisticated.

A. Jaffa

Dzshebelye is a family novel that encompasses three generations of a single family and tells the story of its disintegration and rehabilitation after the Holocaust. It was published by Yidbukh (Buenos Aires) in 1955, but like many other Yiddish novels, before its publication as a book it was serialized in the New York daily *Forverts* (the *Forward*) under the title *Tsu a nayem lebn* (Toward a new life).[12]

The novel recounts the tale of Zekharye Karlsbakh, the first resident to settle in this Jaffa neighborhood after its occupation.[13] Until World War II, the protagonist, a printer by trade, lived with his wife and two sons in Warsaw. When war broke out, he escaped with his sons to the Soviet Union, leaving behind his wife (Perl-Libe). When the war ended, the father and sons returned to Poland and from there continued to the Heidenheim DP camp in Germany. There, the protagonist learns of his wife's fate: she was sent to a concentration camp, was liberated, and then traveled to Munich and finally Israel. But in Munich she was remarried to an old acquaintance who eventually became the Beitar Youth Movement's envoy to the DP camps. Karlsbakh contacts his wife, and thanks to her Israeli citizenship, their sons (now sixteen and eighteen) are granted ʻaliya permits and move to Israel. Only one and a half years later, Karlsbakh succeeds in making his own way to Israel, but no one comes to welcome him when he arrives. Two days later, late at night, his elder son (ʻAzriel) comes to see him. It turns out that the son was serving in the army and fighting in the 1948 War but has been given a special leave of several hours to accompany his father to a house in the very neighborhood that his own unit has just conquered on the outskirts of Jaffa. Karlsbakh discovers that his younger son (Leybush) was also enlisted shortly after arriving in Israel, because he was considered a "lone soldier," with no immediate family. Thus he comes to understand that Leybush's mother, who in the meantime took a new Israeli name (Pnina Gafni), did not take her younger son under her wing, and now this son is lying in the hospital recovering from a leg injury.

Israel in the novel is not described mythically, as a "big place" (either religiously or nationally) that has the power to redeem the "small place," the private home. The Karlsbakh family is not united simply by virtue of arriving in Israel and living in it; on the contrary, its disintegration continues in Israel, with almost no possibility of rehabilitation—ʻAzriel falls in the battle against the Egyptian-held police fort of Iraq-Suwaydan,[14] Leybush has difficulty recovering from his injury, and the father, Zekharye, wallows in complicated bureaucratic procedures in an attempt to clear through customs the shipping containers that hold the printing machines he purchased in Germany with his meager savings, in the meantime leaving him with no source of income. In addition, Jebelya becomes increasingly crowded, and his home is taken over by greedy, "stout" men from among ʻoley sheyres hapleyte who envy the house he was given and threaten to banish him from it.

When he arrives in Jebelya, the protagonist is described as "Robinson Crusoe" (an image that recurs several times throughout the novel)—the lone and lonely survivor of a shipwreck who wakes to find himself on a strange island. Zali Gurevitch has proposed reading Defoe's *Robinson Crusoe* (1917) as a work in which the entire world capsizes and becomes an island, a nonplace, with the novel describing the ways in which it is transformed into a place: "Robinson Crusoe is the story of a place, of the making of a place. From the moment he arrives on the island, he works on the place—builds a house, takes refuge from the savagery of the island that threatens to devour him (whether an animal or a human being)—and on creating agriculture and small industry and even religion. In other words, Robinson creates a world—a home-world, a home in the world."[15] Like Crusoe, Karlsbakh too is described as trying to create "a home-world, a home in the world." Throughout the novel's plot, like Crusoe he defends himself against "savage" elements that threaten the home he is trying to build. Of course, in Karlsbakh's world the "savagery" (like its opposites, "culture" and "home") is defined altogether differently than in Defoe's novel. The savage threats are no longer traditional, prenational elements that the national culture (English-Christian-imperialist culture) is supposed to domesticate and subjugate. Now, the "savage" elements are distinctly modern—they are the vicious and violent human tendencies that erupted and culminated in World War II: the war uprooted people from their homes and placed them in the forests or in foreign homes; uprooted moral sensitivities, compassion, and justice and made them impervious to the suffering of others. It recreated a space in which the strong dominate, dismantled the old structures (like family and community) and the values that had guided them, and left in its wake pain and trauma that most likely cannot be healed. This "savagery" is expressed also within the protagonist's own family, in the differences and rifts that have opened up between himself and his son. For example, 'Azriel expresses a patronizing attitude toward the "abandoned property" that was "left behind" by the neighborhood's previous residents, a tone that perplexes and saddens his father, who is far more sensitive to the universal nature of the tragedy of forced banishment from one's native land and home.

Curiously, this foreignness of the new place in which Karlsbakh finds himself is represented in this novel, and in many other works of fiction on the Israel-theme, by animals: the howling of jackals at dusk recurs as a symbol of the horrors that revisited the survivors in the nights, when memories of the war, repressed during the daytime, resurface.[16] The pets "left behind" by the fleeing Palestinian families embody the eerie absent-presence of the previous tenants. In the novel before us, the protagonist's new house in Jebelya is "invaded" from the moment he arrives by a black cat that apparently belonged to the family that lived there before him. The recurring need to deal with this pet serves as a constant reminder that he is the one invading a home that is not his own.

The foreignness of the place where Karlsbakh arrived is expressed also in the way in which the community that gradually formed there is represented. Jebelya did not become anything like a typical Eastern European "Jewish town," even though it did gradually fill up with 'oley sheyres hapleyte, to the point that two and even three families were forced to share a single home.[17] The concentration of 'oley sheyres hapleyte in one place was typically described in the Israel-theme as a blessing: it enabled people to glean information about loved ones who were lost in the war[18] and sometimes even to locate them and be reunited.[19] As I described earlier, stories of moving reunifications of this kind were given prominent place in the Yiddish press.[20] Because of its high concentration of Eastern European Jews, Jaffa was often described as an "authentic" and intimate Jewish place whose atmosphere, especially on shabbat and holidays, was somewhat reminiscent of "the old home"—in contrast to Tel Aviv, where the atmosphere was new and unfamiliar.[21] However, in this novel, Perlov chose to highlight the negative aspects of the immigrants' tight concentration in Jebelya, like a kind of renewed echo of the critical and sarcastic tone that Mendele Moykher Sforim took in his works toward the overcrowded Jewish communities in the Pale of Settlement region of the Russian Empire. The physical density in Jaffa even had tragic effects. One of the many real-life events that are included in the novel is a historical incident in which a four-story building collapsed on its many inhabitants, after the immigrants, in the general desperation for a home and shelter, either were not warned by the authorities or did not heed their warnings that the building was not safe for living.[22] The tension between neighbors in Jebelya escalated to the point of violence and even murder. This is how Karlsbakh describes the neighborhood's residents: "Jebelya with the mixed multitude, the ingathering of the exiles, the broken, uprooted, hopelessly wounded men and women of the surviving remnant, whose nerves are frayed and whom even a sanatorium could not help."[23] Despite the protagonist's critical attitude toward the neighborhood's residents, the novel allows them to express their voice in a series of monologues by marginal characters that are unique and rare in the landscape of Israeli and Jewish literature. For instance, Yoikhenen, a Bundist shoemaker, voices harsh criticism of the Jewish Agency's absorption policy:

> And on top of everything else, the Jewish Agency made another big mistake in isolating the 'olim. If they had dispersed us across the whole country, among the veteran residents, we would have fit in faster in the local atmosphere. . . . People with urban professions should have been sent to a city. The rest should have been settled on the land, with productive agricultural work. . . . But as things are—we're living here like in an UNRWA camp in Germany. . . . Living still with the mentality of the camp, with the conflicts of the camp, with the suspicions of the camp and with a spirit of refugeehood, of those who have not yet reached a safe shore. . . . Working for the time being, getting by for the time being, and trading for the time being . . . Everything for the time being. Not becoming citizens and not getting used to the thought that we will stay here forever.[24]

Perlov also gives voice, in a reference that was rare in the contemporary Yiddish literature, to a group of women he calls *Lots tekhter* (Lot's daughters). These are concentration-camp survivors who were boycotted by other survivors, first in the DP camps in Germany and later also in Israel, because they had been sexually promiscuous with German men. The novel allows these women to deliver to society their "statement of defense":

> Sin?—If wanton hatred is not a sin, why should wanton love be a sin? And the god who calmly observed the disgrace of the beating of naked women, the disgrace of the gas chambers and the crematoriums—let him now deign to observe the disgrace of the liberated women of the concentration camps who no longer know what "sin" is. . . . Oh, morality? . . . —Morality has gone up in flames in the flames of the furnaces, along with fathers and mothers, brothers and sisters. Along with teachers and instructors, with the rabbis and the Admors—along with all the righteous people, the educators and the leaders. There is no more morality after such a sweeping downfall.[25]

One of the new forms of expression that modernity created, a form that both shaped and represented the national society, was the novel. Mikhail Bakhtin saw multivocality as a central ploy characteristic of the novel, one that communicates the various points of view—social, ideological, generational, professional—that were created by modernity. He described the capitalist economy and the socialist and communist responses to it, as well as immigration, depth psychology, and so on, as forces collapsing into and onto themselves in a centripetal fashion.[26] "Multivocality," he argued, represents modernity's confident poise, since a variety of speakers using diverse modes of speech, expressing conflicting narratives, reflecting a variety of sociopsychological layers of meaning, may seem to undermine the homogenous, univocal, unilingual national image. In other words, modernity allows fragility by virtue of its strength.

Similarly, if we inspect the "family novel," we find that it often deals extensively with those destructive forces of home-seeking that modernity accelerated in a centripetal fashion, such as displacement and alienation. In the novel before us, prostitution and crime have a space of their own, an urban area, somewhere between Jaffa and Tel Aviv, populated by a multitude of newly arriving refugees and emigrants: "The 'big area' in Jaffa is the famous place of the underworld of the worst variety. As part of the uncontrolled mass 'aliya, criminals came from all over the world, and there, in Jaffa's 'big area,' their stock market takes place. It is there that the traders of stolen goods, thieves, robbers and whores find their hiding places."[27] The "big area" is a known motif in Yiddish fiction symbolizing the liminal possibilities of its characters' quest for a home—it echoes the genre of Jewish underworld stories, which tends toward a social-realist style. It is a site of cultural fragments and material ruins in which traces of the violence of the war have been preserved.[28] In Perlov's novel, it is a space where one can still encounter vestiges of the last stages of the 1948 Arab-Israeli War and, at the same time, remnants of an Eastern European Jewish ghetto during the Holocaust. In the passage quoted earlier, this curious brotherhood of fates is manifested in the interesting use of the word *malines* (hiding places), which originated in the Polish and Yiddish "thieves slang," but whose later use during the Holocaust denoted places where Jews hid from the Nazis.[29] The "big area," then, is described as a place populated by ghostly characters that did not find the strength to transition from the horrors of the war to daily life in its wake. The novel represents this space as a force that threatens to undermine the protagonist's attempt to rehabilitate his home and family.

Another liminal space featured in the novel is Café "Gan-Tamar" (literally, the date-palm garden), located in Jaffa's fenced-in Arab quarter.[30] Unlike the "big area," this space has a positive role: it is there that the protagonist receives information that helps him reestablish himself professionally. Despite the café's Hebrew name, the owner is a Palestinian, as are the waiters, the musicians, and the singers. The clientele is mixed—Muslims and Jews. In Jewish culture (and in Yiddish literature), the date palm is one of the quintessential symbols of Zion.[31] The environment of the café is described through the eyes of the protagonist as homelike and familiar, because he was first acquainted with it in Uzbekistan, where he ended up as a refugee during the war years. The fact that the novel's resolution stage, which is related to the protagonist's professional rehabilitation, begins in a Palestinian Jewish coffeehouse that echoes his past as a refugee is important and meaningful. Perlov, as I have noted, was among the few Yiddish writers who published regularly in the Bundist monthly journal *Lebns fragn*, and one of the tenets of the Bundist movement was economic- and class-based solidarity with the Palestinians of Israel.

Karlsbakh's profession, printing, has special significance in modern culture. Mikhail Krutikov, in his discussion of a different literary protagonist with the same profession, explained that printing was considered one of the most advanced and prestigious modern professions, because it was a vehicle of the enlightenment movement.[32] And indeed, unlike Bergelson's protagonist, Karlsbakh succeeds in overcoming the obstacles and bureaucratic procedures the state sets before him, and he opens a printing house (in Tel Aviv, not in Jebelya). His first orders at the printing house are a newspaper and a novel, which are given a rather realist, concrete characterization: "The first and biggest job is a weekly, which is soon supposed to become a daily. The second job is a novel of some four hundred pages. The latter was ordered by a big and popular Tel Aviv publisher."[33] Work, then, is described in the novel as vital to the individual's rehabilitation, and his return to life is manifested by his return to the "game" of economic and social mobility. As the owner of an independent business, Karlsbakh is no longer at the mercy of the employment office bureaucrats, who, in the reality of Israel of those days that included severe unemployment, regarded all men over forty as "old" and unfit for work.[34] This is not merely a personal or financial achievement: the protagonist's profession makes him an agent, whose personal rehabilitation embodies the recovery possibilities of the community. Similarly, destructive forces operate on both levels. So, for example, Perlov narrates in the novel the healing influence of a play staged by the Goldfaden Theatre for an audience of 'oley sheyres hapleyte in an abandoned orchard on the outskirts of Jebelya. This joint gathering of families of survivors is described as a day of celebration, a communal ritual. Yet the play is stopped by a police raid; the actors, Holocaust survivors, are arrested; and the fears and terrors of the past once again break into the comforting present.[35]

The challenge that drives the plot of *Dzshebelye* is Karlsbakh's attempt to rehabilitate his family and rebuild his home in that foreign place, Israel, in which he wound up. Early on in the novel, the plot takes a dramatic turn when ʻAzriel, the son, dies in the 1948 "War of Independence." To evaluate the significance of this event, it is helpful to compare *Dzshebelye* to a prominent work of Hebrew literature of the same period: *Hu halak̲ baŚadot* (He walked through the fields, 1947), by Moshe Shamir, which describes the birth of the "new Israeli" and which attained a place of honor in the literary and cultural canon of the young Israeli society.[36]

The two works, *Hu halak̲ baŚadot* and *Dzshebelye*, contain similar textual elements: a son who dies in battle (Uri/ʻAzriel) and leaves behind a pregnant partner who is not married to him (Mika/Ilana), a Holocaust survivor with no other family who lives on a Kibbutz. In both novels, the relations between the parents of the fallen son are tense. The son's death constitutes a kind of offering up of a sacrifice (a modern-national variation on the myth of the *ʻakeda*, the binding of Isaac),[37] in "return" for which not only is the national home conquered but the parents are reconciled and rebuild the private, "small home." In both novels, Tel Aviv is described as the opposite pole of the settlement of the land (the Kibbutz/Jebelya), which is represented by the fallen son. Throughout both novels, the parents deliberate between the two spatial options. In Shamir's novel, Rutke, Uri's mother, escapes with him to Tel Aviv in an attempt to spare him the fate of a victim, which awaits him if he stays in the Kibbutz; and the father, Willy, brings them back. In *Dzshebelye*, Zekharye Karlsbakh decides to move to Tel Aviv and leave the house left to him by his son. The fathers in both novels (Willy/Zekharye) are described as men of action, and the descriptions of their emotions are typically external and delivered to the reader by the omniscient narrator.

But there are also interesting differences between *Hu halak̲ baŚadot* and *Dzshebelye*, and these reflect the differences between the cultures in which they were produced. First, *Hu halak̲ baŚadot* takes place primarily in a Kibbutz, and *Dzshebelye* in a poor, depopulated Palestinian urban quarter. We can view this as an attempt to create a new mythical space, the habitat of the new Israeli hero, ʻole sheyres hapleyte, a Yiddish-speaking Eastern European Jew. If Shamir's work is a bildungsroman that describes the transition of its Sabra protagonist from an Israeli childhood to an Israeli adulthood, Perlov's work is a bildungsroman that describes the process in which a refugee immigrant evolves from a newly arrived resident in the young Israel into a veteran citizen. This process begins with

Zekharye rebelling against the myth that prevailed in the young Israeli society that it is "only thanks to the audacity of the Sabras that the country was built" and posits an alternative version in the form of a "countermemory": "Several times and in several different places Zekharye had already heard that saying, that it is only thanks to the audacity of the Sabras that this country was built. And each time, it pierced his heart: What do you mean? Only the Sabras? And what about the thousands of youngsters, survivors of ghettos and camps, of the partisans, bunkers, and of Soviet deportations, who came here and here laid their head?. . . . These youngsters from Europe have indeed had a different upbringing, had respect for their parents. . . . But their blood was spilled here!"[38] Unlike *Hu halak̠ baŚadot*, *Dzshebelye*'s main protagonist is not the "Isaac," the son ('Azriel), but the "Abraham," the father (Zekharye). Shamir's novel focuses mainly on the son (Uri) and presents a coming-of-age story that revolves around an oedipal drama. This significant difference sheds light on the audience at which each of these works was targeted: whereas the Hebrew novel was aimed at the young generation, the Yiddish one was aimed at the interim generation, to which most of the readers of Yiddish belonged. But perhaps more importantly, in *Dzshebelye*, the "heroism" of the hero stems precisely from his authority as an adult who is in his prime and who fulfills his responsibility as a father, as a breadwinner and family man. By contrast, in Shamir's novel, the "heroism" of the hero, Uri, stems from his courage and his willingness to sacrifice himself for the sake of building the country, but not from how he functions on the private domestic front, where he does not assume responsibility for his actions. Israeli Yiddish literature, then, offers a different model of masculinity and of the father-son relationship. The essence of masculinity, on this model, lies in the father's active, daily, and exhausting responsibility for the integrity of the family unit. Similarly, the integrity of the nuclear family—not sacrificing one's life—is described as the essence of fulfilling the national project.

In *Hu halak̠ baŚadot*, the emotional bond between the father and his son is expressed paradoxically in a stoic or even spartan distance between them, as befits fighters who are partaking in the building of the national home, the father as a corporal in the British army and the son in his work on the Kibbutz and as a fighter with the Palmach. The devastating war experiences of the Jews in Europe strengthen in both of them the belief in the necessity of the national home and in the justification of the toll of victims required to achieve this goal. Indeed, the novel contains almost no discussion of the treatment of the "national other," and the violent consequences that attend the effort to secure ownership of the place are described only as they affect the Jewish victim. The nature of the relationship between the father and the son is expressed in the language they use in their dialogues—a formal register of Hebrew that lacks any traces of intimacy. In *Dzshebelye*, by contrast, the father and son are described as having an intimate bond, alongside deep disagreements, especially about the attitude toward the national other and the property it left behind. The obvious background is the devastating war experiences they themselves endured in the Holocaust with rest of the Jews of Europe. Their closeness makes it possible for them to discuss these disagreements, in an informal register that is conversational in tone. For example, referring to the fact that the remaining Arab population in Jaffa is assembled in one particular area surrounded by barbed wire, ʻAzriel calls this area the "Arab ghetto" and justifies its existence by arguing that it represents the safest solution for both populations; when his father balks at this description, ʻAzriel responds with more than a hint of ridicule of his survivor father:

—Here, beyond the barbed wire, is the Arab ghetto.
—What do you mean, "Arab ghetto"?
—You're used only to Jewish ghettos? Huh, father?[39]

Expressions of this kind trigger arguments between the father and his son. The son argues that the Palestinians are the ones who are responsible for their misfortune since they started the war by attacking Jewish settlements. He notes that the Arab population of Israel had "left" of its own will to the surrounding countries. The father counters that the Jews of Israel ought to treat their enemies with extraordinary mercy because they are the chosen people: "Esau must be distinguished from ʻAmalek" (a name reserved for describing the Nazis and the Communist Soviets). Even if occupying the Land of Israel is a necessity, argued the father, the taking over of "abandoned" private property left behind by fleeing Arab refugees is a sin.[40] The son points out that the private property of the immigrants from Europe, Yemen, Iraq, Syria, and Lebanon was also plundered and that his father should not take upon himself so much moral responsibility. In *Hu halaḵ baŚadot*, the conflict between the "big home" and the "national other" is not discussed in the realm of the "small home"—in the dialogue between the father and his son. By contrast, in *Dzshebelye*, the small home is described as a reflection of the big home, like a small-scale model of it. Moreover, even ʻAzriel's death and his memory do not drive the conflict out of the small home. The argument continues even after his death: the protagonist, Zekharye, decides to leave Jaffa and the "abandoned" home chosen and given to him by his son and moves to Tel Aviv. Despite the grief, the protagonist holds fast to his belief that legitimate ownership of a house is achieved by labor: "Things that are received as gifts . . . for free . . . are not real! What does not dry out your brain, what you do not apply yourself to with blood and sweat, that thing does not belong to you! From that thing you will have no pleasure."[41] Another difference between the two works is evident in the respective ways in which they characterize the Jewish victim. In *Hu halaḵ baŚadot*, the mother, Rutke, tried, as mentioned earlier, to save her son from his fate as a victim; in *Dzshebelye*, the father, Zekharye, tried to save his son from a similar fate when he left Warsaw and fled eastward at the start of the war. But while the fate of both sons is similarly sealed—they are both sacrificed in the process of the building of the new home—their fates are treated differently. Uri's fate is shaped in the novel as inevitable, just as the process of his coming-of-age and maturing is inevitable. This process involves an emotional identification with his father and an internalization of the father's ideological ethos. 'Azriel's fate, by contrast, although heroic and tragic, is entirely coincidental: his parents never encouraged him to put ideology above the human aspiration of self-preservation.

Another important difference between the two works is the attitude of the two fathers to the private home: for Willy Kahana, building the national home comes at the expense of the private home, which is therefore inevitably broken; for Zekharye Karlsbakh, the building of the national home begins with the reestablishment and rehabilitation of the private home—it stems from it by definition. Even though before the war Zekharye did not consider coming to Israel, and after it, he came only because his sons (and former wife) were living there, the Jewish public and the environment in which he was raised played an important part in his life. And indeed, the long-awaited meeting between the protagonist and his wife takes place on the memorial eve for their destroyed community. Under the wings of the memory of their community, they begin to cope with the impact of the events that separated them and thus to rebuild their home.

Moreover, Azriel's orphan is raised in a united and healthy, rehabilitated family. The novel therefore ends with redemption: Zekharye remarries his former wife, and together they move into a new apartment, in Tel Aviv, purchased with their own hard-earned money. They own a thriving printing house. Azriel's younger brother recovers from his injury and becomes a musician. He gains success and marries his brother's widow. The couple moves into a new public housing apartment on the outskirts of the city and raises the son of the dead brother, who is named after him. By contrast, *Hu halak̲ baŚadot* has an open ending that does not provide answers to such questions as, Does Mika remarry? If so, does her new husband raise her son as his own? Do Uri's parents function as grandparents? Does the grandson grow up in a family that is more stable than the one in which Uri was raised? And is the memory of the dead father present in his life?

The closed, redemptive, and optimistic ending of *Dzshebelye* may be taken to demonstrate the novel's conservatism relative to the open and ambiguous ending of *Hu halak̲ baŚadot*. In fact, it demonstrates the essential difference between the "horizons of expectations" of typical readers of these two works (to use Jauss's apt term). Like *Hu halak̲ baŚadot*, *Dzshebelye* is a realistic depiction of life, checkered with references to real events, places, and phenomena. But a whole set of other characteristics make this work innovative for its time in the realm of Israeli literature: positing the father as a hero; the place that shapes him and the place where he resides; the model of heroism that he represents; the values he holds;

the novel's representation of the "national other" and of the price of the violence involved in ownership of the home, both private and national; the special empathy for the victim; and the attitude toward the national public and its definition. All these make it a unique work that offers an original perspective. It even gives us a portrait of Jaffa that no Hebrew work of the time could offer. Descriptions of Jaffa as a place of poverty and filth are familiar in the new Jewish fiction from its beginning.[42] But whereas this poverty was typically described as stemming from the city's "Eastern" character, in Perlov's novel Jaffa's poverty is attributed not to the "Eastern European" features of its population but to the Holocaust inflicted on this population by Nazi Germany and to the "DP camp culture" the residents brought with them from Germany. Nor does fulfilling the "Western" and modern Zionist utopia redeem Jaffa of its illnesses, as in the more prevalent image.

Dzshebelye is a new kind of work also in the landscape of Yiddish literature. It is clearly not an "immigration novel" by Krutikov's standards (see chap. 3), since its protagonists are refugees. The novel does not focus on descriptions of a traditional past or dwell on an ideal and stereotypical shtetl. It is present-oriented and realistic. It focuses on an individual protagonist's struggle to survive and make do, a struggle that emphasizes the individual as the stage of events. The protagonist in *Dzshebelye* does not undergo a fundamental transformation in the course of which he recognizes the value of the old and traditional world that he left behind. On the contrary, the protagonist succeeds in imposing the moral values he held since before the war on the new world and thus makes the new world a "home." The representation of the trauma of displacement here is therefore different from that of immigration and refugeehood novels in modern Yiddish literature. And the representation of the process of building the private home in the new national home receives a new meaning, not possible before the Holocaust.

And yet, *Dzshebelye* is not an altogether new kind of work either. The movement that takes place in the novel, from the small town (Jebelye) to the big city (Tel Aviv), is a traditional movement in modern Yiddish literature. Like the shtetl, Jaffa is described as a place of economic, cultural, and human deprivation that the protagonist would do well to escape for a more advanced society and place of residence. At the same time, the long form of the novel made it possible to document the population of Jebelye, like that of the shtetl, in a detailed manner by giving voice to the types of discourse of marginal characters within this population; and in this respect the novel is a kind of late incarnation of the ambiguous attitude expressed in the works of highbrow Yiddish authors toward the inhabitants of the Jewish shtetls.[43] This attitude is expressed in Perlov's choice to name the novel after this miserable, poverty-stricken place, *Dzshebelye*—instead of the work's original title, *Tsu a nayem lebn*—and the choice to portray the protagonist's leaving of this place as a victory. In his preface to the novel, Perlov described his own connection to the place:

> Who are they, the residents of Jebelye? They are Jews form different countries, survivors from all world-catastrophes. People in rehabilitation from pogroms and slaughters, ghettos, concentration camps, prisons and deportations. People from the forests of the partisans and from the "Aryan side". . . . All of my heroes are displaced, travelling, wandering. Nearly all of them are either just coming from somewhere or getting ready to go. . . . And yet I got close to small towns, to communities, to ethnic groups, I lived among them and befriended them. These were, however, towns on the run, wandering towns, travelling and sailing cities and towns. . . . And because my uprooted Jews tried to put down roots in Jebelye, and because the wandering communities pitched their tents here—Jebelye became close to my heart, Jebelye came to be a part of me.[44]

Like many Yiddish writers before him, Perlov wrote about the Jewish towns and their communities retrospectively, after leaving them and living as a modern individual in a modern metropolis. When he wrote *Dzshebelye*, such communities had already ceased to exist. The unique historical and social conditions that made them "communities" had ceased to exist. Their members were already busy building new lives, in a national home. Jebelye, then, became close to the author's heart precisely because it was a "nonplace": the moment the communities of "wandering Jews" arrived in their new home, they realized that by settling there they had already lost their former identities.

B. The Depopulated Village

Mendl Man, as I noted, was one of the prominent and promising writers of Yiddish literature after the Holocaust. In the years 1945–1947, he published two books of poetry,[45] and after his arrival in Israel in 1948 he began writing short stories. His novel *In a farvorloztn dorf* (In a deserted village, 1954) was the first long work of literature he wrote and the first that deals entirely with life in Israel[46]—in the second half of the 1950s and the early 1960s, he wrote more novels, whose subject was the Holocaust years.[47] His status as a canonical writer is demonstrated by the fact that the Hebrew translation of his *BiḴfar naṭuš* was published in the prominent press Hakibbutz Hameuchad, a year before its publication in Yiddish.[48]

The novel *In a farvorloztn dorf* tells the story of Moyne, a Holocaust survivor who was uprooted from his native village in Poland by the war, and describes his attempts to put down roots in postindependence Israel, in an "abandoned village" named Giv'at HaMisgad (Mosque Hill) where he was sent along with many other 'oley sheyres hapleyte upon arriving in Israel. It echoes Sholem Asch's 1904 work *A Shtetl.* Both works interplay with the literary form that Bakhtin would have called "a regional novel" or, better, "a provincial novel"—that is to say, a work that portrays the idyllic progress of a parochial agricultural family, describing its progress by centering mostly on its handling of its material challenges.[49] These forms deal with the everyday experience, with the basic realia of life (love, birth, marriage, labor, eating and drinking, the various stages of life), which then become quasi metaphorical. For the realia imply a correlation between human life and the life of nature: both are described using the same semantic fields. A special role is accorded to the cyclical recurrence of the process of life. In the idyll and in the regional novel, a special bond is shaped between time and space—the "idyllic chronotope":

> An organic fastening-down, a grafting of life and its events to a place, to a familiar territory with all its nooks and crannies, its familiar . . . valleys, fields . . . and one's own home. Idyllic life and its events are inseparable from this concrete, spatial corner of the world where the fathers and grandfathers lived and where one's children and their children will live. . . . The unity of place brings together and even fuses . . . the life of the various generations. . . . This blurring of all the temporal boundaries . . . also contributes in an essential way to the creation of the cyclic rhythmicalness of time so characteristic of the idyll.[50]

These remarks not only help us portray the general literary type with which *In a farvorloztn dorf* interplays but also help accentuate its uniqueness. Its main characters have been uprooted from their embracing econiche, and so their lives express the rift between human fate and idyllic nature. The plot opens with a description of Moyne as the Biblical first man banished from the Garden of Eden to a piece of land that he must work to make a living. In his first nights in his new home, his sleep is disturbed: he is shaken by nightmares about a dead field, with prickly cactus (sabra) bushes closing in on him from all sides, their thorns stinging his body and preventing him from escaping the "valley of death."[51] The landscape to which Moyne wakes up is described as foreign and uncanny, withering and sad. The reason for this foreignness and alienation unfolds gradually before the reader: unlike Adam, Moyne was not created ex nihilo. He carries a past, and a weighty one at that. He is a refugee who was forced by the war to abandon his village in Poland, and he is also a refugee who finds his new home in Israel by virtue of another's refugeehood. Moyne had hoped to start his life anew in the recently established Israel; he sought to be a "first man" in a promised land, a Garden of Eden. But his past prevents this, and not only his own past but also that of the place where he arrived—the village in which he has settled. Thus, this is a broken idyll, which seeks once again to return to being an idyll. Is such a return possible?

The novel's plot is driven by Moyne's attempt to overpower his past and put down roots. On the surface, this plot is typical both of stories of ʻaliya and of immigration stories in general. But as I show later, the form of the novel and the author's unique point of view complicate this seemingly simple plot. The struggle to put down roots in Israel not only is descried in the novel's plot but also appears in its structure: the novel has twelve chapters, which are divided into those that take place "here," in the abandoned Palestinian village and in Tel Aviv in the present time, and those that take place "there"—in the Jewish village Kokhar (the protagonist's native village, which he was forced to leave because of the war), in Warsaw (the big city to which the protagonist's father moved when the former was a child, leaving him and his mother behind in the village, in the home of his maternal grandfather), and in other places in Eastern Europe where the central characters found themselves during the war years. The novel consists of movements (that are typical of modern literature) between these spaces and times, which intensify the dramatic tension between them and function as an illustration of the content delivered in the novel's plot. Thus, the shifts between the different planes and times from one chapter to the next construct the process of reading the novel: the first chapter takes place "here" and the second one "there"; after this exposition, in which the protagonists and the main planes and tensions are introduced, a balance is achieved, and tension begins to build around the question of which plane will dominate; in the third chapter, an entanglement begins, and it takes place "here," as does the fourth chapter; but the fifth and sixth chapters take place "there." Balance is again achieved between the planes, and thus the tension is intensified; the seventh chapter takes place "here," as does most of the eighth chapter, and the tension continues to build; the ninth and tenth chapters take place "here," and in them the entanglement reaches its height. The reader wonders how the plot will end—with a tie? Or with a conclusive determination in favor of one of the planes? And if so, which one? Chapter 11 also takes place "here," and in it begins to unfold the resolution; the reader's tension is released when it emerges that chapter 12 also takes place "here," thereby completing the resolution with a determination in favor of the "here" plane. Between the planes "here" and "there," then, extends a clear analogy, since both are characterized by a similar tension between the village (Kokhar/Mosque Hill) and the city (Warsaw/Tel Aviv). The central question that emerges from the battle between the planes and the times is, Will Moyne succeed in staying "here," in the abandoned Palestinian village (the local parallel and extension of Kokhar), or will he leave it, like his father before, to go "there," to the city of Tel Aviv (the parallel and extension of Warsaw)? The analogy between the two distinct places, the village and the city, creates another analogy—between the past in exile and the present in Israel. This interesting analogy is typical of the Yiddish literature written in Israel: even though the war indeed destroyed the protagonist's village and carried him far away, leaving him stripped of all his previous contexts, he discovers that the present in Israel is not a new beginning that is opposed to his past in Eastern Europe but rather one that is an extension of this past. Thus, the tension between village and city that torments the protagonist is not described as a new ideological-political question but as a modern psychological and cultural battle. Moyne deliberates between the model represented by his father (who left the village for Warsaw) and the model represented by his grandfather (the farmer from Kokhar), who stayed on his land and with whom Moyne was raised.

The story is built and developed, then, on an analogy between two "abandoned" villages, the Jewish Polish and the Palestinian, with the image of the Garden of Eden hovering above them. Just as in modern literature the terms *home*, *nation*, and *nation-state* contain their opposites (ruin, exile, foreignness), so the image of the Garden of Eden contains its opposite—namely, the expulsion from it and the yearning for a place or situation that has been lost: "The story of the Garden of 'Eden is the story of the creation of an unreachable space. Adam and Eve were placed inside it and then expelled from it. Ever since then humanity is on the 'outside' yearning to re-enter."[52] The biblical Garden of Eden is said to be from *Kedem*, and one of the meanings of this term is "the distant past." The Garden of Eden, then, is always situated in the distant past. Perhaps it was created in retrospect? In the novel before us, the Garden of Eden is a metaphor for the protagonist's dwelling (in Israel and in Poland) and for his nuclear family. As we know from the plot, it is also from the latter that Moyne was expelled, when his father decided to leave him and his mother behind in the village and go to the city. In fact, the protagonist was expelled twice from the Garden of Eden: as a child his family fell apart, and as a young man war uprooted him from his village. During the war years, he snuck back to his village (Kokhar) only to discover that other people were now living in his house and return was not possible. This parallel between the village, the family, and the Garden of Eden raises an ethical question: is one man's Garden of Eden necessarily another's "abandoned" village? At the level of the plot, it raises the question, Will the protagonist succeed in returning to the Garden of Eden—that is, will he succeed in rebuilding a home and family of his own in the (abandoned) village?

The omniscient narrator, in a moment of modernist awareness of his own status, puts this question to the protagonist: "And you, son of man? Cannot you too cling to the land, in the great valley that can bear fruit in abundance?"[53] The verb *Aynklamern* means to put yourself in one group with something or someone in a tight and fastened way (to bracket/to cling). The address to "you, son of man" echoes Ezekiel's prophecy (12:3): "As for you, son of man, prepare for yourself an exile's baggage." Here God instructs the protagonist, this time through the narrator, to become unified with the land and thus provides a kind of late reparation for the curse of banishment to exile. The narrator thus proposes to the protagonist to become one with the land—that is, to cancel all the barriers between them and thus to end their relations of "foreignness." And indeed, in one of the novel's first images, the protagonist is described as having fallen asleep on the land in the field, the drops of dew that fall on his body and on the land seemingly joining them together. The question "Cannot you too cling to the land?" stays open, as I have said, throughout all the novel's chapters, and it not only shapes the novel's plot and structure but also accumulates further layers throughout the novel and becomes more complex: does this "clinging" to the land indeed transform Moyne into the biblical man ("you too")? Does his clinging to the land indeed end the relations of foreignness between them? Is ending this relationship of foreignness appropriate?

The plot's entanglement begins in the third chapter through a series of encounters. One of these is an encounter between the new residents of Mosque Hill, the Jewish refugees, and one of the village's original residents, a Palestinian refugee seeking to return to his home.[54] At first, his presence in the village is not considered a dramatic event because he looks like all the other refugees who populate the place. Only after his identity is revealed are the Jewish residents torn between feelings of compassion toward him, stemming from their own experience of refugeehood, and shock over the prospect that they may once again be forced to be uprooted:

> News spread throughout the streets that there was an Arab in the village. People gathered at the water trough. . . . An Arab . . . An Arab . . . One waved his hand and said: What is upon you people, have you never before seen the shape of a man? He is like all men, a woman added. Why has he come? "Why" has nothing to do with this. Is he not allowed? Of course he is allowed, but . . . maybe—suggested someone—he used to live in this alley and his longings to have another look got the better of him. . . . Leave the man alone, go away, said a brown-eyed woman . . . The woman was overcome with sadness. Here she stands in the middle of the market on a Sunday, just like this old man, propped up against a wall . . . a crowd around her. Hey, Ludzshe, a Jewish woman! No Bratok, you are wrong, a one of us. One of us! A Polish woman? Scolding glances from the crowd pierce her body, tearing her apart with their demand for an answer. . . . One moment, and she's lost. . . . She leapt up from her place, her almond eyes filled with fury, with hatred. . . . She shoved her Aryan papers in their eyes. . . . What are you doing here people? Let him sit, let him be. . . . She went and brought bread from her home. Take, grandpa, take it, she pleaded. . . . These residents of the alley shook their head in sadness and thought: Is it possible that I live under his roof? And they comforted themselves and said: I did not drive him away, nobody drove him away, they left of their own will. And one man said: what if a Jew came to one of their villages? The speaker waited for a concurring response, but all remained silent. And there was one who looked upon the Arab with suspicion and fury . . . His eyes, his hands, his broad frame seemed to say to the people: stop your gazing and your nonsense. He must be expelled, the old fox, let him get the hell out of here, the stranger with the kaffiyeh.[55]

The passage expresses two main voices: one is a deep identification with the Palestinian refugee, and the other is a resistance to this identification. The resistance to the Jewish refugees' identification stems from shock at the possibility that they might have to be uprooted again, and for that reason they regard the Palestinian as a threat. He poses not only a concrete threat to their right to the place in which they currently live but also a metaphysical threat to the very possibility of putting down roots without expelling another. On the one hand, their suffering is too great to contain the suffering of the Palestinian refugee; on the other hand, more than anyone else, they, refugees from the worst of all wars, understand his predicament—whether or not they want to, they are his brothers in refugeehood. Melanie Klein has pointed out the need for gestures of reparation toward the object of our love—that is, our parents, toward whom we feel guilt—because the feeling of love is invariably accompanied by aggressive feelings.[56] According to her, in order to become mature adults—that is, to become parents ourselves—we have to live alongside our parents at a safe distance from them that will enable the reparation and a conversion of the guilt into friendly cooperation. When the feeling toward the concrete objects is too strong and overwhelming, the distance from them is achieved by shifting the emotion from the concrete object onto a partially similar object. The partial similarity enables the safe distance from the concrete objects. For the survivors of the Holocaust, who were uprooted from the space in which they lived and were filled after the war with a burning urge to become part of the new space, the "other" had a central contribution. The gesture of offering bread to the Palestinian refugee and calling him by an endearing name (*altitshker*) is a Kleinian shifting, an attempt by the survivor to create a reparation toward the person who saved her life in Poland when she tried to get back home and was exposed. It is precisely the Palestinian's accentuated otherness that allows the survivors to carry out the reparation needed in order to create a new life on the ruins of the lives that preceded the wars. And indeed, the text makes a clear effort to emphasize the Palestinian's otherness and not to obscure it: the village remains "Mosque Hill" and is not given a Hebrew name; the belongings and pets of the previous tenants remain in the village, in the life and home of the protagonist, and through them he reconstructs the daily lives of their previous owners; and through their crops, which are now in his hands, he tries to learn new farming techniques in a climate, land, and vegetation that are foreign to him. This is how the narrator sums up the sad encounter between the Jewish refugees and the Palestinian refugee, a meeting loaded with equal measures of compassion and shame and with the heavy load of the limited ability to contain the pain of the other: "The Jews from the alley returned to their homes with a great sadness in their heart, an anxiety that stirred up silent memories, both passive and active. A wheel has spun, the wheel of human-destiny, it whirled at a dizzying speed: a home intact, then homelessness, destruction, foreign land, distances, ships on seas, and once again an intact home. Now they felt for this first time that this is not the fate of Jews alone but the fate of human beings in general, of nations, of the whole world."[57] Thanks to the direct encounter between the Jewish and Palestinian refugees, the Holocaust survivors in the novel experience what Dominick LaCapra has called "empathic unsettlement"—that is, the ability to put themselves in the place of the other and at the same time to recognize his otherness.[58] In this case, the "empathic unsettlement" affords them a kind of catharsis that was unprecedented in those days: Holocaust survivors who so soon after the war relinquish the position of the archetype of the victim and perhaps even share the possibility of partial responsibility for an injustice caused because of them to someone else. For if we are all victims in our turn, we also all partake in injustice and thus become brothers in a dizzyingly complex reality.

The theme of the return of the refugees (Jewish and Palestinian) to their towns and villages and the face-to-face encounters between them is not unique to the novel *In a farvorloztn dorf*; it appears repeatedly in the Yiddish fiction written in Israel. For instance, in a feuilleton by Y. Perlshteyn, "A briv fun a mistanen" (A letter from an infiltrator), describing a Palestinian "infiltrator" (that is to say, a refugee who risks his life by returning to his home, newly inhabited by foreigners) who recounts his "visit" to Israel (including a brief visit to the Knesset) while protesting the injustice of being tagged an infiltrator in his homeland. The infiltrator is gifted with finely honed powers of discernment and a juicy, lively Yiddish, which together create in the reader a sense of concrete presence and even evoke empathy toward him.[59] This presence stands out against the backdrop of the Hebrew literature of the time, in which the Arab almost invariably remained distant, "beyond the border" both geographically and emotionally. A fairly well-known example of this typical gaze appears in Hanoch Bartov's *Šeš knafaim le'Eḥad* (*Each Had Six Wings*, 1954), where the Palestinian, in the eyes of the ʻolim, is a hostile and distant character who exists beyond the physical and emotional border and does not cross it.[60] A more empathic gaze is found in S. Yizhar, in works like the short story "HaŠavuy" (The prisoner [of war]) and the novella *Ḥirbet Ḥizʻeh* (the name of the fictional Arab village where the story is set) (1949).[61] But there too, the meeting is not between two refugees but between a soldier and his enemy.

In fact, the Arab refugee's return to his village does not occur only once in the novel *In a farvorloztn dorf* but happens again and again in different forms. Like in *Dzshebelye*, here too the domestic pet appears as a disturbing textual element. As early as the third chapter, a yellow dog who lives in the village makes an appearance. Through his consciousness, the daily life of the Palestinian residents prior to leaving the village is described, as are their subsequent hardships. This modernist reversal of roles between human consciousness and the consciousness of the animal expresses a critique of the human condition after World War II: in the very fact that this war broke out, and certainly in its course and aftermath, man demonstrated that he had descended below the level of an animal. Therefore, an animal was fit not only to serve as a protagonist in a novel but indeed to function within it as an active and formative consciousness.

Daily life in the village before the 1948 War is described in the novel in detail through the consciousness of the yellow dog as well as by the narrator. So, for instance, this is how the novel offers descriptions of the water basin in the center of the village and the life that surrounded it—the livelihood, food, tools, customs, and even prayer:

> Not far from the old mosque-walls, with hyssop growing out of their stones and wild plants poking out of their crevices, there is a curved alcove with a marble base. The basin is concave like a water trough. From the stone-wall dangles the tip of an iron-pipe. This base served as a water basin, in which weary passers-by, wandering from village to village, would quench their thirst. Salama's donkeys parked here, they spread out on the rocky ground surrounding the path, to rest in the cool shade of the tall mosque-walls. The women came here from the clay-streets, from the abandoned mountain that lies between the Arab cemetery and the mosque walls, bringing heaps of colored cloth and with washboards scrubbing the dark-colored kerchiefs and trousers in the marble basin, which was filled with water. The streams of water that flowed from the trough, mixed with soap bubbles from the laundry, were licked by packs of thirsty dogs, who were afraid to approach the stone of the trough. Old pickers of sycamore figs and sabra would lay down their baskets here, a weave of palm fronds and poplar branches, and doze off from fatigue.[62]

These intricate descriptions have a role in shaping the plot and in building the dramatic tension around the question of whether Moyne will succeed in setting up his new home in the "abandoned" Palestinian village, on the painful earlier layers of life that existed there. These two layers of life are symbolized by two very different trees that meet surprisingly on the same piece of land: the palm tree (mentioned also in *Dzshebelye*, as we saw) and the poplar tree. They are described as having stood there facing one another for many years along the path that leads to Mosque Hill, their roots becoming fully entwined. The palm (specifically, the date) is, as I noted, a symbol of the Land of Israel as part of the Middle Eastern space, and the poplar is a symbol of the forests of Eastern Europe. Both trees are described in *In a farvorloztn dorf* as a symbol of old, premodern and therefore also prenational traditions, which existed and prospered in pre-state Israel,[63] until they were uprooted by a tractor—a modern symbol of technological progress—that came to prepare the ground for a tent camp for the masses of new immigrants. The arrival of these 'olim symbolizes in the novel the destruction of the old, idyllic world.

It is interesting to compare these descriptions of daily life in pre-state Israel and in the village before it was abandoned, to the thoughts of Rakefet, the Sabra protagonist of the novel *Each Had Six Wings*, about the settlement of 'oley sheyres hapleyte in an "abandoned" Palestinian neighborhood. The 'olim are described with a distinct tone of alienated remoteness, almost as if they were people who knew nothing at all about war or refugeehood: "The people already live here. Other people who do not know and do not remember. The wound of war is already healing here and peace can begin to be heard, as if nothing ever happened. They do not know that there were other days and other people. . . . Nor do they care that war took place here, and what it caused. They live here, these types of people, strange beings, a mixed multitude that was sown across the neighborhood."[64] A similar concern appears earlier, in *Ḥirbet Ḥiz'eh*: "Long live the Hebrew Ḥirbet Ḥiz'eh! Who would have imagined that there once was a Ḥirbet Ḥiz'eh, which we have cleansed and then took possession of. The people who would live in this village, wouldn't the walls cry out in their ears?"[65] Moyne and the rest of the residents of Mosque Hill know all too well what war is and what changes "it caused." For unlike Rakefet and the soldiers who conquered Ḥirbet Ḥiz'eh, they experienced war of an altogether different scope; thus, they cannot feel the "murmur of peace" even when the tumult of war has died down and cannot pretend that "nothing ever happened." In their ears, the "crying out" of the walls becomes mixed up with the rest of the experiences of the war that uprooted them from their village in the first place.

Thanks to his otherness, the Palestinian and his village are closer to the novel's protagonist even than those who are like him, such as the representatives of the Israeli establishment and the country's veteran residents. In Man's novel, the new residents of Mosque Hill arrived there on their own initiative and discovered that not only does the village have no electricity and not only are its houses destroyed, but even the motors that pump water from the wells were dismantled before their arrival. A similar situation appears in *Each Had Six Wings*.[66] There, the 'olim are described as passive and helpless; they do not arrive at their new neighborhood on their own but are brought there by a "veteran" Israeli driver; they are perplexed by the broken well until an official from the absorption authorities comes and fixes it. In Man's text, the picture is reversed: Moyne himself fixes the broken well pump in his field with considerable effort and racing about;[67] when he finally gets it to work, representatives of the "Custodian of the Absentees' Property" show up and confiscate it, because they have sold the pumps by the pound to iron traders in southern Tel Aviv. This is an interesting role reversal between the veteran Israeli and the immigrant: Moyne, the 'ole sheyres hapleyte, is a farmer and indeed the grandson of a Jewish farmer from Poland. As such, he does not need the veteran Israeli to teach him how to "fix" himself and become a "new Jew" through a connection to the land that supposedly occurs in Israel for the first time. Ironically, the representatives of the establishment, who brought the immigrants to the village in the first place so that they would become land workers, are the ones who actually deal in trade and get in the way of the new immigrant seeking to work in farming. Moyne battles the officials, despite their obvious advantages: they drive a truck, and he drives a horse and cart; they have command of the language, and he speaks it crudely. But despite all that, he wins back the pump. Another meeting with the veterans has the air of a conflict—this time with tractor drivers who have come to flatten the ground near Moyne's field, for the building of a new settlement for immigrants. As they work, they uproot the old local vegetation (orchards, sabra hedgerows, an ancient sycamore tree, a date palm, a poplar, a sycamore) and erase an ancient "camel trail." In Moyne's eyes, the tractor drivers are representatives not of any particular group (the group of veterans) but rather of a distant and vague bureaucracy: "epes an amt" (one of the offices).[68] The surveyors who come to mark out the land appear to him like "etlekhe fremde mentshn" (some strangers).[69] From them Moyne learns that the plans do not include the gardens and fields of the residents of Mosque Hill: "You do not exist in the plan."[70] Thus, not only does Moyne show diligence and a high tolerance to endure hard physical labor; he also expresses a recognition of his own worth and an ability to stand up to an aggressive establishment.

To qualify what I have just described, except for these two encounters, the novel hardly discusses the "veterans" or the absorbing establishment at all but rather focuses on the lives of the survivors themselves. This fact is very important, because it is a line that characterizes the Yiddish ʿoley sheyres hapleyte literature and stands in contrast to the descriptions of the Sabra writers (or those who came to Israel as children and were like Sabras) who describe such encounters. It is extremely rare to find in the works of Yiddish writers manifestations of feelings of inferiority vis-à-vis the veterans or the Sabras, of the sort that appear in the novel *ʾAnašim ʾaḥerim hem* (They are different people), by Yehudit Hendel. This novel is known for its attempt to focus on the point of view of the survivors, but its very title already surprisingly reflects the point of view of the Sabras and is not focused on the immigrant survivors. The gaze of the ʿolim is described as turned entirely on the Sabras, as if their whole inner world consisted in nothing but an admiring observation of the native Israeli. For example, this is how Hendel shapes a dialogue that verbalizes the gaze of two (Yiddish-speaking) ʿoley sheyres hapleyte watching the Sabras:

> "They are young". . . . "They are young and healthy, huh? And handsome". . . . "And natives of this country, damn it." "Natives, that's all." "Like blooming trees they are handsome, huh Leyzer," "Like blooming trees, that's all". . . . "And I, blast you, Leyzer, I'm a broken vessel—good luck trying to glue it back together, huh?" "Yeah, good luck gluing it." "A broken vessel, foolishness!" "Are you jealous, Ruven?" "I am jealous, foolishness." "That's all, foolishness!". . . . "Good they are, good," Šefṭel blurted without wanting to. . . . Then he said: "They are different people, Leyzer, they are simple and natural". . . . "Perhaps you would like us to be that way too—do you?" Šefṭel continued to walk, his head bowed. "I know, Leyzer," he said to the gray of the sidewalk, "I know". . . .

> "Sure, sure, unpleasant people we are," and he chuckled . . . "Sure, sure, we are unpleasant people."[71]

On the linguistic level, this dialogue between the two survivors takes place in a substandard, broken language, even though it is apparently conducted in Yiddish—the survivors' mother tongue. Here the narrator projects his pride as a "Sabra" onto the "other," from whom he is alienated. However, when this other speaks in his own language, in the works written in Yiddish in Israel, the picture is different and far more complex: the gaze is typically of parents upon their Sabra children, and it expresses appreciation for the latter's fighting in Israel's wars,[72] alongside criticism and a sarcastic satire regarding the Sabras' delusions of grandeur and provinciality.[73] In addition, deep concern is expressed for the future of Jewish culture because of the education that young Sabras receive, an education that creates foreignness and alienation between them and their cultural roots.[74] The best of this literature was written in a subtle and complex figurative language, and Man's writing is a distinct example of this form.

Another aspect of Moyne's struggle to cling to the place is embodied in the novel in his indecision between two women. One is his old-time lover Yolana, a famous singer from Warsaw whose father was elected to the Polish parliament at the inevitable cost of estranging himself from his Judaism and even distancing his family from it. Following the Holocaust, Yolana rekindles her relationship to Judaism and performs in the DP camps. With the massive waves of immigration, she comes to Israel and performs in Tel Aviv. The other woman is Moyne's new lover, Ḥamra, a Jew of Yemeni origin with whom he fell in love after meeting her at the "housemaids market" in Tel Aviv and learning that her mother is a farmer and an herbal healer. Moyne and Yolana's love evolved over a short period during the war. Through its reconstruction, the reader becomes acquainted with Moyne's past and with his war experiences. Moyne searched for Yolana incessantly and dreamed of the day when they would be reunited, partly because she is one of the only remaining witnesses to his past. But at the same time, doubts begin to creep into his mind about their true compatibility and their ability to build a home together and share not just a detached and dramatic common past in wartime but also a present life of prosaic labor. Yolana is too similar to certain aspects of the protagonist's mother, who died in tragic circumstances. It is no wonder, therefore, that Moyne ultimately chooses Ḥamra as his partner, and they marry. They do not even have a common language—he speaks Yiddish and she Arabic, but language is not required for them to build their new home. They share a love of working the land, of nature, of quiet. To Moyne these values are a distillation of the home, family, and culture that he lost, and his and Ḥamra's joint devotion to them is a gesture of memory and a corrective measure to his guilt for having stayed alive, a corrective that makes building the new home possible. Man may have gotten slightly carried away with his idyllic descriptions of his protagonists, who are a kind of Adam and Eve of the Israeli ingathering of the exiles. The text clearly betrays his somewhat stereotypical enthusiasm over the fact that for the first time in modern Jewish history there was a "mixing together" of the various ethnic groups within the Jewish people. This enthusiasm goes hand in hand with his search for a new beginning. The protagonist's old love does not fit this kind of new beginning because of his and Yolana's shared past, because of her urban nature, and perhaps even because of her "Westernness." One of the prevalent arguments made by scholars is that the attitude of immigrants from Eastern Europe toward the immigrants from Yemen was "Orientalist"—in other words, the Eastern European immigrants defined themselves as Western and advanced by dismissing and excluding the ethnic other.[75] Yet the relationship portrayed in the novel *In a farvorloztn dorf* complicates this perception: the immigrants from Yemen are presented as the objects of passion, and the Jews of Eastern Europe are depicted as disillusioned after the Holocaust about the charms and promises of "Western" culture (in its Western European version).

At the end of the novel, Ḥamra gives birth to a son. This ending, in which two new immigrants settle in the land of their forefathers, come together, and bring the fruit of their love into the world—a new Sabra—is a motif that appeared also in the Israeli literature written in Hebrew. *Each Had Six Wings*, for example, ends with a girl being born to a pair of ʻolim (Holocaust survivors from Eastern Europe). This choice allows the author to downplay the conflict between the new Israeli and his religious tradition, from which he is estranged or in any case wants to appear to be estranged. In *Each Had Six Wings*, the Jewish shtetl is reborn on the Land of Israel, alongside the birth of the baby girl: a synagogue and a *Beit Midrash* (Jewish school) are established in the neighborhood for the survivor-immigrants, who stand out with their exilic-Jewish features, with their names and garb, and they become "one big ethnic group," harmonious and idyllic.[76] By contrast, in the novel written in Yiddish, the stereotypical Jewish shtetl is not recreated in Mosque Hill. Except the circumcision ceremony for the newborn boy, no religious Jewish practice is mentioned anywhere in the novel (including in Ḥamra's family). The few idyllic representations of the Jewish shtetl written in Yiddish literature are the result of a nostalgic look at a past that was gradually disappearing before the eyes of the writers. But Man's look at the past (like Perlov's) was not nostalgic, and the same is true of his look at the present. From his very first days in Mosque Hill, Moyne settled in a distant part of the village, on the margins, and avoided mixing with the crowd: "He did not know the people of Mosque Hill and they did not know him."[77] The residents of the village he describes first as "*mentshn*" (people) and "*nay-gekumene memtshn*" (newly arrived people) and then as "*di mentshn fun metshet-bergl*" (the people of Mosque Hill).[78] In other words, Man used the broadest term (*people* and not *Jews*), an expression that embodied and intensified his loneliness. When he begins to get to know individuals within the group, Moyne describes them by their communities of origin, not their national affiliations (Polish, Hungarian, etc.): "The Ḥosid from Munkatsh,"[79] "A tailor from Bevzin," "A Vohlyn fair-goer."[80] The ethnic belonging or shared past of the residents of Mosque Hill does not function as a glue that makes them into a homogeneous and harmonious community, as described in *Each Had Six Wings*. At the same time, Man was not critical and sarcastic toward the ethos of the Jewish shtetl as Perlov was in *Dzshebelye*. The only thing that enables a minimal connection between the residents of Mosque Hill is their common language (Yiddish), but even this common ground is typified by the multiplicity of differences within it: the characters are known by their different dialects of Yiddish. Hebrew, too, and especially the Sephardi one that was absorbed in Israel, as opposed to the one they knew—"*Loshn koydesh*" with the Ashkenazi accent—was perceived in their eyes as a foreign and divisive language.

In his passion for the land, Moyne is different from the residents of Mosque Hill, most of whom earn their living as salaried employees in Tel Aviv. His name, too, Moyne, is not among the very common Jewish names,[81] unlike the protagonists of *Each Had Six Wings*, who have typical Jewish names. Overall, Moyne is an extraordinary protagonist in modern Jewish history in general and in its literature in particular—a farmer whose grandfather had already lived as a farmer on the lands of Eastern Europe. Moyne's own passion for the land did not cause him to sever links with his forefathers and their tradition, as in the case of those who came to pre-state Israel as pioneers, but on the contrary—to connect to them.[82]

Modern Yiddish literature was created in the big cities. The common way of life among the Jews of Eastern Europe, in the shtetl, was urban in character. Throughout the modern era, there were Jews who lived in villages (especially in Galicia), but the agricultural way of life was perceived as "marginal" in Yiddish culture, since in the villages there were almost no communal institutions that enabled the religious way of life. Sholem Aleichem's character Tevye der milkhiker (Tevye the Dairyman) is the quintessential example of a Jewish "rural" type: his ruralness is that which renders him a defective *Talmed khokhem* (Torah scholar). New ideas that influenced the Jewish communities in Eastern Europe (like the romantic and nationalist ideas of the return to nature philosophy) created new types of settlement, like Sochochin (where Man lived as a child) and similar villages in the United States (as described in the works of Itskhok Raboy), Argentina (described in the prose of Mordkhe Alperson and others), and pre-state Israel (described by many writers). Several of the Yiddish writers described village life in a positive and complex manner in terms of the Jew-nature relationship. A prominent example of this is one of the canonical works of modern Yiddish literature, the long poem "Raysin" (White Russia, 1921), by Moyshe Kulbak.[83] The presumed influence of this work on Man is palpable: like the speaker in the poem, Moyne too is the grandson of a farmer; like him, Moyne calls all the trees and plants around him by their accurate names and thus shows a mastery of the culture and of nature; he too enjoys the abundances he produces from nature; in Kulbak's poem, the passionate and sensual connection of Uncle Avrom and Nastasia is channeled into marriage and family life and thus becomes more noble, and similarly Moyne's connection to Ḥamra is explained through the pleasure they both draw from nature and from working the land, and their passion is channeled into marriage and family life; and just as the non-Jewish Nastasia joined the family, Man describes non-Jewish women who married Jewish men to save them during the war. And despite the horrors of the war, Moyne too succeeds in connecting with nature in a direct and sensual way. Man did not describe the Israeli landscape through a religious or ideological lens, in a utopian or messianic manner, or even through biblical symbolism, as Itzik Manger proposed in 1954.[84] Like Kulbak, Man describes nature naturalistically and even impressionistically,[85] based on lived experience in it and a perception of it through the senses, on observing the variety that exists within it and the changes that time effects on it (light and shade, both as states of mind and as worldviews). The similarities between these two works underscore their differences: the big family Kulbak describes—grandfather and grandmother with sixteen children—is absent from Man's novel. Moyne stands out in his loneliness, like the first man. His parents were divorced, as noted earlier, and siblings, aunts, and uncles, if he had any, are not mentioned. Even after his marriage, Moyne is described as a lonely man, who did not become "able-bodied," the father of a big tribe. Unlike Kulbak, Man focuses on the life of the grandson (Moyne) and through it sheds light also on aspects of the lives of his parents and grandparents. In Kulbak, unlike in Man, the descriptions of nature are idyllic. The Vilia and Neman rivers, for example, are described positively as a source of income (by day) and wonderful enchantment (by night), whereas in Man the wadi is described as a dark and terrifying place, where cruel and criminal activity takes place (the slaughter of donkeys to sell their meat on the black market during the austerity years). The wadi is described as a threatening place filled with howling jackals, thieves, and infiltrators. Man tends more than Kulbak to explore the soul of his characters, their nightmares, their dilemmas, their loneliness. His characters are not typical "types"; rather, he is drawn to extraordinary characters. The unique relationship that Man proposes in the novel between man and the place and the various others it contains (nature, animals, and the national, ethnic, "immigratory," and gender other) and his way of reducing the distance between them to the point of merging makes it impossible to repress their destructive potential and to avoid confronting it head-on. The novel's ending is only partly positive—the birth of the son happens simultaneously with the murder of Midre, a resident of the village. The murder is a seed of disaster buried in the fertile soil of the village.

The two novels discussed in this section, Perlov's *Dzshebelye* and Man's *In a farvorloztn dorf*, present complicated but rather successful attempts at settlement in Israel by 'oley sheyres hapleyte. The Israel-theme continued to appear in works by these authors throughout the 1950s. It is interesting that these two writers actually did not themselves succeed in putting down roots in Israel. Perlov left Israel in 1961 and settled in New York. Man left Israel at the end of that same year and settled in Paris. They both continued to maintain close contacts with their colleagues in Israel.[86] Man even continued to write about the Israel-theme and publish in Israel after his departure.[87] But the main contribution of these two writers to developing this theme in Yiddish literature was made during the decade that they lived in Israel.

3. The Ma'abara

The daily life of 'oley sheyres hapleyte in the Ma'abarot—the refugee absorption camps and neighborhoods—were the subject of some of the works these immigrants wrote in Yiddish, which began to be published by the early 1950s. Beyond their aesthetic value, these stories also have historical, cultural, and social value: they help correct a common impression that the only residents of the Ma'abarot were 'olim from Islamic countries. This mistaken representation played a part in creating the social and ethnic rift in Israeli society between the "Western" absorbers and the "Eastern"/"Mizraḥi" absorbed. One of the early and fascinating descriptions of such a reality appears in Shimon Ballas's novel *HaMa'abara* (written in Arabic in 1955 and published in Hebrew in 1964), in which he described the difficulties of the Mizraḥi immigrants, who waited in vain for a modicum of help and empathy from the "veterans"—arrogant Ashkenazim (who represent the majority of the officials from the absorbing institutions). Ironically, in this work Ballas consistently refers to the absorbing establishment by the name "Yiddish."[88] In "'Oriya," the ma'abara described in the novel, there are no immigrants from Eastern Europe, even though in 1951 one of every five residents of the transit camps was a Holocaust survivor. The experiences of the latter, which were described in works by Yiddish writers, thus allow us to reexamine the image of the ma'abara as a "Mizrahi" space and also complicate the dichotomy between the "Ashkenazi" absorbers and "Mizrahi" absorbed. These works describe residents of the Ma'abarot who are Jews from Eastern Europe and who were similarly not embraced by the veteran hegemony, despite the fact that they came from Eastern Europe and for the most part spoke Yiddish, or at least understood it. Focusing here on the experiences of 'oley sheyres hapleyte in the Ma'abarot is not an attempt to undermine or question the fact of the suffering of the immigrants from Islamic countries in this loaded site or to diminish the responsibility of the absorbing establishment for this suffering. Rather, the aim of this focus is to create a new understanding of the ma'abara as it was perceived by its tenants and to extract it from the common institutional perception that artificially created within it two groups (Mizrahi Jews and Ashkenazi Jews) that could be pitted against each other. Recognizing the suffering of all the residents of the Ma'abarot while respecting the differences between them is a first step toward processing the trauma.

Settlement in the Ma'abarot was the second stage in the absorption of 'oley sheyres hapleyte in Israel.[89] The Ma'abarot were built beginning in 1950 to provide the 'olim with temporary housing and organize their absorption. Their original goal was to integrate the 'olim into the workforce: "The idea of the Ma'abara amounted to a minor revolution and a turning point in the absorption of the 'aliya, since it involved an attempt to integrate gradually some one hundred thousand 'olim into the workforce by gradually ceasing to provide the free services."[90] The stay of most 'oley sheyres hapleyte in the Ma'abarot was relatively short for several reasons. First, many of them had lived as displaced persons in camps of different sorts from as far back as the early 1940s and thus had gained experience of almost a decade in conducting themselves vis-à-vis organizations and aid groups. Second, in the Eastern European Jewish culture, many and varied institutions of mutual aid were established from as far back as the late nineteenth century, including the hometown associations (*landsmanshaftn*), whose members were scattered all over the world. These associations, alongside professional and ideological-political associations, both local and transnational, provided financial support for the absorption of survivor-'olim and gave them loans for housing, for professional training or starting a business, and so on. The financial dependence of 'oley sheyres hapleyte on the absorbing establishment was therefore quite minimal even before the state began receiving the reparations from Germany for them. Third, 'oley sheyres hapleyte, as I have noted, had small and young families, as well as an education or professional training and experience, and these helped their relatively rapid integration into the workforce. Nonetheless, with all of this, even in the latter half of the 1950s there were still 'oley sheyres hapleyte in the Ma'abarot. These were mostly old, sick, or disabled people, who did not have the physical and mental strength to start a new life in Israel.[91]

The ma'abara embodies the intermediate zone between the destruction of the old home and the building of the new one, between the life of refugeehood and the life of permanence. The very nature of the ma'abara as a place of transit (its name derives from the Hebrew word for passage, *Ma'avar*) invites a literary description of it in light of the chronotope of the threshold, whose meaning, according to Bakhtin, is associated with the "breaking point in life, the moment of crisis, the decision that changes a life (or the indecisiveness that fails to change a life, the fear to step over the threshold)."[92] In places that symbolize this chronotope, like the corridor, staircase, and street, "events take place determining entire human lives—crises, falls, resurrections, rebirths, revelations, decisions."[93] The motif of the encounter is common in this chronotope as an event that accelerates the change that is naturally waiting to occur. In the short stories and novellas written about it in Yiddish, the ma'abara is shaped as a place in which a decade of displacement, detachment, refugeehood, and life in various kinds of camps is supposed to come to a close by finding work and permanent housing. This sense of an impending end to the period of life in camps gradually dismantled the temporary communities that were created and solidified in the camps. Yishaye Shpigl described this process thus:

> He was satisfied now, Mushkat, that he had withdrawn himself from the people of the barracks, from the constant quarreling and hostile glances that gleamed in their Jewish eyes. So long as these people were together on a ship far out at sea, they were united by a kind of warm thread of Jewish joint-destiny. Perhaps because of the foreign sea, filled with danger, because of the green abyss that pulled the ship toward it with the full force of its deep-water whirlpools? Or perhaps because of those evil lands from over there, the death-space of hell, which still burned in the frightened, diffused pupils of their eyes? But as soon as the people set foot on the new land—the warm thread of Jewish joint-destiny was severed, as if by evil magic. Mushkat thought to himself: do people first have to be led over the abyss in order for the good light of joint-destiny, which gives comfort and hope to the destitute, to rise up in them?[94]

In the 1950s, the Orthodox writer Yekhiel Granatshteyn published in the *LN* dozens of short stories about the lives of 'oley sheyres hapleyte in various different places in Israel: in neighborhoods of Tel Aviv, in depopulated Palestinian villages, in housing projects, and in Kibbutzim. Several of them, published in 1952–1953, were about the lives of Holocaust survivors in the Ma'abarot. The fact that Granatshteyn was religious made him exceptional and even one-of-a-kind in the landscape of Yiddish literature in Israel, since nearly everyone, as we have seen, was secular. This surely contributed to his marginal status in the world of Yiddish literature; despite the fact that he played an important role in the rehabilitation of the Orthodox-Ashkenazi culture in Israel,[95] his works about daily life in Israel were barely discussed by critics of Yiddish literature in Israel and abroad. As far as I know, he chose not to translate the stories about the lives of 'oley sheyres hapleyte in Israel into Hebrew and not to compile them in the books he published, in either Yiddish or Hebrew. His works are discussed here, in this book, precisely because of his unique point of view.

The protagonists in Granatshteyn's ma'abara stories are survivors who suffered unbearable losses in the Holocaust. In the course of trying to fit into the new and hopeful life in Israel, they realize, tragically, that the losses they have suffered are too great and that they have not the strength to start over, to realize the new opportunities that reality in the young state offers, and to accept the changes that this reality entails. So, for example, the protagonist of the story "In blekhenem baydl fun der ma'abara" (In a small tin shack in the ma'abara)[96] lost his wife and nine children in the Holocaust. The protagonist of the story "Zayn ershte freyd" (His first joy) lost his wife and three children in Auschwitz. Life in the ma'abara among families with many children causes him pain, daily. The workfare jobs he takes allow him to escape the company of the families that surround him in the ma'abara: "During the day, he works. In the early weeks he went to [work in] construction. [It is] hard work for his years, and maybe not so much for his years as for his past . . . But he actually wanted it. In general, he felt himself to be different from the others after coming out of Auschwitz. People had started a new family life—he had not. People sought out help from charitable institutions—he did not."[97] Even those survivors who were fortunate enough to come to Israel with a young family discovered in the course of daily life there that it was not necessarily a home that allowed them to build a new life. The sense of lack and loss that was ingrained in them during the war and in the years that followed had made survival a way of life, and it is this that ultimately defeated them: out of a strong urge to cling to life, they rushed to remarry and start new families but discovered that the burden of providing for their new families prevented them from fulfilling what was in fact their most simple and basic need after arriving on a safe shore: to recover and heal. So, for example, the protagonist of the story "Sakh-hakl fun a tog: Fun dem togbikhl fun an arbetlozn" (Summary of a day: From the diary of an unemployed man) is unable to find work—not even workfare jobs—and provide for his young family. He is also unable to admit his helplessness openly to his family. He flees the ma'abara to Rothschild Boulevard in Tel Aviv and spends the night there sleeping on one of the benches: "I will return to them, I will tell them the truth, how unhappy I am. That I, the Father, cannot provide them with bread. But in the meantime I will rest, find a bench, sleep through the night. I'm so tired. The feet fold under me and the heart carries such a heavy weight. And the ma'abara is so far, so far."[98] The reader understands, then, that the protagonist did not become homeless but rather gave external expression to a deep sense of "absence of home" that he had been carrying for a long time.

A common motif in stories about the ma'abara, as I have said, is that of encounters that reflect a dramatic change in the lives of the protagonists or else accelerate this change or help it take place. These encounters are of two kinds. The first is meetings with 'olim from other exiles, usually from Islamic countries. Israel was the first place in the modern world in which different Jewish ethnic groups began to mix with each other on a large scale (in the Diaspora they made a point of keeping their lives separate even when they lived in the same cities). The other kind is meetings with acquaintances from the past. A story that describes a meeting of the first kind is "A khasene in a ma'abara" (A wedding in the ma'abara).[99] The protagonist, Khaim Raykhnberg, and his two parents are the only survivors of a big and widespread religious family from Poland that was murdered in the Holocaust. In the ma'abara, Khaim meets Shoshana, a young woman from a family that came from Yemen, falls in love with her, and asks to marry her. This encounter with Shoshana's extensive and fully intact family and with the community in which the family continued to live, even in the ma'abara, drives home to Khaim's parents the social aspect of their loss: they have lost not only family members but also the society in which they had had a place of honor. When they came to Israel, they hoped that their society would also be rehabilitated, and so too their status within it. But the encounter with the burgeoning Israeli society makes clear to them the extent of their social decline: in this society they do not and will not have any status or pedigree. The father tries to explain this change to his son: "Here, in the bookcase, hidden in a briefcase, lies the genealogy-letter [of our family], which is passed down from generation to generation, from father to child, from father to child. . . . God forbid, there is no flaw in the family. What will be of this now? Should I tear up the letter? Burn the inheritance? There are no in-laws for me here [who are] of our customs, of our countries?"[100] The protagonist's father was a wealthy and renowned iron merchant in Warsaw before the war, an esteemed and influential figure in the city's Jewish community. At the time, he hoped to marry his son to the daughter of one of the city's rich and respected families. The parents' later objection to their son's marriage to his beloved, Shoshana, stems not from contempt for her ethnic origin but from a loyalty to the victims, to the society that once exited, to its customs, its values, and its culture. To them, the wedding their son wants represents a betrayal of the role they took upon themselves as survivors, the role of "memory guardians" for a bygone community. Their loyalty to this role allows them once again to reflect their high standing in the destroyed community. For them, marrying their son in accordance with customs that are foreign to them (as they indeed eventually do) amounts to a painful admission of the end of their tradition, and with it the collapse of their social status. Their son, in his desire for life, tries to distill the values that are shared by his own family and the family of his fiancée, an approach that we encountered earlier employed by Moyne, Man's protagonist. Here, Khaim leans on religion as a powerful content that can bring the families together and also, he hopes, console his parents for their loss. He asks them, testily, "And Shoshana is not Jewish? . . . And is Raykhnberg a better family, a better name, than Mizrahi?" But it is actually the Orthodox father who is unable to find consolation in this. His loyalty to the victims and to the world that existed before the war is stronger: "Of course they are Jews, good Jews, conscientious, cherished, but my heart is cut within me. It is so hard to accept, not because I do not want to give in, but because the Landaus and the Volmans are before my eyes . . . I do not want to forget them . . . These were flawless families . . . And now a marriage in the ma'abara, a foreign world."[101] The son urges his parents to accept the difficult fact that these families were murdered and the world that once was no longer exists, hoping to bring them to accept the changed reality, to change with it, and thus to allow themselves to live within it: "After all, they are no more. . . . Something did happen, after all. . . . Have you forgotten that we entered the Biernatski bunker twenty people and came out only three? . . . And everything that happened after that counts for nothing? Jews from all over the world are coming now to the Land of Israel, a land that they have longed for—a new Jewish world."[102]

Khaim's parents had hoped that the Jewish world that was destroyed in Eastern Europe would be resurrected in Israel. That hope was dashed. Could other hopes take its place? Granatshteyn in this story avoids looking with critical eyes at the lives of the Jews who were annihilated in Eastern Europe (for example, he avoids addressing the phenomenon of Jews who left the religion and Jewish culture prior to the Holocaust). His nostalgic attitude toward the Jewish life that was eradicated in Eastern Europe also idealized the present life in Israel, the "ingathering of the exiles." Perhaps he sought in this way to provide some consolation to himself and to his readers.

Meetings of the second kind, with acquaintances from the past, happened at the government-sponsored workfare jobs to which the residents of the ma'abara were assigned.[103] These jobs involved hard physical labor (like tilling the orchards and clearing rocks in preparation for the paving of roads) and were carried out in difficult conditions (usually in extreme heat) by people unaccustomed to physical labor (such as tailors, merchants, or poets). Surprisingly, this work is described in the stories in a positive light and not as a source of frustration and hardship. The trips to work as well as the haphazard and disorganized nature of these jobs afforded the survivors unexpected encounters, usually pleasing, with acquaintances from the past. These helped the 'olim get news about the fate of shared acquaintances from the war years and before, and sometimes also ideas about how to better their lives in Israel.

Unlike these chance meetings with acquaintances from the war years, which were usually gladdening and sometimes even useful, the meetings initiated deliberately were typically a source of disappointment. The survivors living in the Ma'abarot hoped to find distant relatives, friends, and acquaintances in Israel. Sometimes they sought them out and initiated meetings with them in the hope that these familiar people would help them build their lives. But most times the meeting was disappointing. For example, in the humoresque "Mizug galuyot" (Integration of exiles),[104] the speaker, who lives in a ma'abara, describes an encounter with an old-time acquaintance who has already been living in Tel Aviv for a full twenty years. The speaker tells him, sparingly, about some of his difficult experiences during the war, but the acquaintance is more interested in the question of how the speaker managed to survive the war—a loaded question that insinuates that those who survived did so in devious ways. After that, the acquaintance asks him how much money he brought with him to Israel, because "there, in Germany, everyone made millions." He then apologizes, ironically of course, for not being able to invite the survivor and his wife to live with him and his family in their spacious Tel Aviv apartment, and then he gallantly drives the speaker, in his elegant car, to the central bus station. On the way there, he reprimands the speaker: "We built a country for you! [What more do you want?] That we settle you here in hotels and give you vacations?" Finally, the acquaintance advises the speaker to move with his family to the Negev.

Another representation of this kind of encounter, but in a very different style, is found in the novella "Di kukavke" (The cuckoo), by Yishaye Shpigl. Its protagonist (Zvi Mushkat) was able to find two distant relatives in Israel (second cousins), the only surviving relatives from his entire family, murdered in the Holocaust. The protagonist hopes to find in them a warm home and supportive family. His family name echoes Bashevis Singer's famous novel *Di familiye mushkat* (*The Family Mushkat*, published as a book in 1950), which describes three generations of an affluent Jewish family in Warsaw from the beginning of the twentieth century to the Holocaust. Even though this family fell apart before the Holocaust, it is possible that the memory of its fortitude, the potential it embodied and the hope that it would manage to rise up after the Holocaust accompanied Shpigl's readers in their encounter with his hero. To his disappointment, Zvi Mushkat discovers that his relatives' home is run-down and crumbling, conspicuous in its foreignness among the new buildings that surround it. On his way there, he comes upon silent traces of war, and these remind him of the war from which he has emerged. This is how the protagonist feels when he walks into the apartment of his relatives:

> From the moment Mushkat crossed the threshold of this apartment he was struck with such sadness that he felt ashamed to raise his eyes from the floor. This is not at all how he imagined everything while walking over here. He believed that he would meet his relatives here in a proper home, family, children, and everyone enjoying all the good things after so many years of living in the country. It seemed that everything he saw was nothing but a bad nightmare. . . . But it's just not possible, that both of them, Mina and Lena, are not at all in this country but far away on some enclosed island, an island of death. He came here, Mushkat, to find himself a corner in the foreign Jewish city, and what he sees now . . . reminds him of the Jewish homes in Poland, rooms full of despair and generation-long poverty.[105]

The protagonist discovers that the grief over the destruction of Jewish Poland and the guilt for having been far away when the war raged on and having stayed alive when their entire family was murdered have destroyed the souls of his relatives. Not only are they unable to help him get out of the ma'abara and make a life for himself in Israel, but he, the survivor and new immigrant, has to help them cling to life and engage with their environment. Their life in Israel, like their life in Poland, is described in this passage as a life lived on an island, isolated and alienated from their environment, stricken by poverty and despair. The ma'abara, too, is an island of this sort, but the fact that the relatives have been living in this state for many years gives the isolated physical space a mental and emotional dimension that is not necessarily tied to the physical one: if it is possible to live in Tel Aviv as if on an island, maybe it is possible to live in a ma'abara as if it were Tel Aviv? And indeed, in this novel, the way out of the isolated life is made possible by the emotional dimension and not the spatial dimension of the "big home": namely, by the ability of two individuals to overcome the traumas of the past and fall in love.

A similar outlet, but dramatic (and even rather melodramatic), is found in the story "Neqome" (Vengeance), by Perlov.[106] In a chance meeting at the Tel Aviv central bus station between two former residents of the same town, the protagonist learns that the daughter of a wealthy man from his hometown, who had been a member of the Judenrat during the war, has survived and is living in a ma'abara on the outskirts of the city. This news awakens in him a powerful rage, which causes him to change his plans at once and embark on an arduous journey on several buses to take revenge on the daughter for her father's deeds. This takes place in days of heavy rains that have caused flooding in the Ma'abarot (as occurred in the difficult winter of 1951). When the protagonist arrives in the daughter's ma'abara, he sees emergency services rushing in and trying to rescue residents but realizes that some of them have drowned, including the only son of Khinke, the daughter of the Judenrat man. In her anguish and despair, she tries to drown herself and join him. Neighbors, who are from her hometown, prevent her from doing so, and the protagonist finds himself joining the efforts to rescue her. The hometown residents urge him to take her into his home as a guest, since she has no one left in the world. At first, the inability to carry out his revenge amplifies his rage, but the sight of her deep suffering and loneliness gradually causes the rage to subside and make room for more gentle emotions like compassion and ultimately even empathy.

During his long trip to the ma'abara, the protagonist tries to explain to himself (and to the readers) why he has embarked on it. Why did this unbridled rage rise up in him? His life had seemed to him peaceful and whole: he had a lucrative job and was about to be married (to a Yemenite woman). And yet, here a chance meeting had caused him to experience an explosion of powerful emotions, and these in turn drove him to take extreme action that appears, on the face of it, to have shattered or at least undermined the order he had already achieved in his life. But this journey can actually be read as an attempt to establish order and stability in his life. The protagonist's state of being, on the cusp of establishing a home of his own (or on the cusp of failing to do so), triggered a resurfacing of the traumas related to his family of origin and its status in the community, traumas that now demand exploration and processing. The relative serenity of his life in the present allows him to reopen the wounds of the past and cope with them. Khinke appears in the ma'abara—in other words, in a liminal space between exile and the new Israeli society. The ma'abara is described as full of mud—that is to say, "contaminated." Khinke's appearance in Israel threatens to make the new state "impure," in the sense defined by Mary Douglas—namely, to make it matter that is out of its proper place: Khinke and the values she represents "properly" belong in exile. And indeed, when she first arrives in the protagonist's apartment, he suggests that she shower, and then he himself showers, to ensure that he does not "catch" her filth. In *Purity and Danger*, Douglas argues that a group defines its boundaries by articulating oppositions that underlie its identity.[107] One of the most basic oppositions is that between purity and impurity. The laws of purity are an attempt to impose order on impurity, which represents an anomaly and disorder. Implementing them expresses an aspiration to establish political and social unity and to create a single, unified, and pure civilian body. The ma'abara is described in this novel in a new light, as a melting pot in which the survivor-'olim were supposed to shed those qualities and contents that the absorbing society deemed impure, and this often occurred through the offering up of a sacrifice that transformed the impurity into purity and made the immigrants fit to leave the intermediate zone and join the new developing society without threatening its self-perception as pure. The ma'abara, then, was described as a site of rebirth, in which the new immigrant completes one cycle of life as an exilic Jew and then, forgoing various aspects of his past identity, begins a new cycle, the life of a nation-state citizen.

Reality in most of the ma'abara stories discussed here is shaped in a naturalistic realism. In general, writing realist prose poses a special challenge for the victims of trauma, and the success of such prose is to a large extent a sign of the successful working through of the trauma. LaCapra, as I noted in the introduction, highlighted this point: trauma is a case of a painful memory getting a hold of the present and thus the narrative of one's self. The inner narrative thus becomes circular. An example of this inability to enfold a linear narrative is found in Tsvi Ayznman's short story "A mayse vegn nisim fun har-ṭuv, vegn a varshever hoyf un vegn a shpil-foygl" (A tale about Nissim from Har-Ṭuv, a Warsaw courtyard, and a songbird).[108] The story is a lament for the death of Yiddish literature. It is exceptional not only in its somewhat paradoxical content, since the death of Yiddish literature is told to us in Yiddish by a fertile writer, but also in its surrealist style, which breaks with the common patterns of its time and place. The speaker in the story (who is also the protagonist) tells of a strange experience that lies somewhere between dream and reality: the bray of a donkey wakes him from his sleep. He is surprised to discover that he is in

Warsaw, in a room overlooking a typical inner courtyard. Heavy snow is falling, but the speaker notices a figure standing in the snowy courtyard—Nissim, a Yemenite Jewish worker from the "Har-Tuv" Maʿabara, with his donkey at his side. The speaker wonders about the presence of a Yemenite workman in the Warsaw courtyard, and asks him, "What are you doing in a Warsaw courtyard?! . . . I will meet you again at another time, in another place! . . . Too early is our meeting."[109] He is in fact waiting for "a different Jew"—a used-clothes trader who regularly made the rounds of the Warsaw courtyards with his merchandise. This other Jew had once asked to buy something from the protagonist, not clothes but rather the protagonist's "songbird"—in other words, the symbol of creativity in Yiddish culture, the *Goldene pave* (Golden Peacock). The protagonist refuses to sell it, of course. The other Jew eventually acquiesces and asks only for a single feather from the tail of that most precious bird. The speaker agrees to give him that, but only when they next meet. That meeting, however, does not take place. The other Jew vanishes—a symbol of the annihilation of Poland's Jewry in the war. The speaker, then, is steeped in feelings of guilt and regret for having at one point seen his culture as suffocating and perhaps not doing enough to revive it. And here he is now, a lone survivor of his culture, and with the death of his readers, his creativity, which he has guarded so carefully, will thereby also die. The cheerful chatter of the Yemenite man, about the new life in Israel, his growing family, and the urgent business of earning a living, draws the protagonist back to the present moment and to reality. But this reality highlights the contrast between the Yemenite workman and the Polish salesman who is no longer alive, between the Israeli experience and the memory of the Warsaw experience that no longer exists. The more the Yemenite talks about his life in Israel, the more keenly aware the protagonist-speaker becomes of his own loneliness there, of the fact that he is a writer without readers, a man without a future. Toward the end of the story, the Yemenite workman disappears along with his donkey. But his disappearance does not, of course, return the speaker to his past and does not bring back to life the lost salesman (i.e., his readers). Though the speaker does find himself in Warsaw, in the same room overlooking the same courtyard in which he met the Jewish merchant, the courtyard is empty. This is a state of half-sleep of someone who is unable to free himself of the petrifying past. And indeed, in the final lines of the story, the speaker is covered by the falling snow, turns white, and disappears. The character of the Yemenite, then, is the one that drives the plot and thus creates the story, precisely because his presence is a narrative and structural detail that is out of place. The present, represented by the Yemenite character, awakened the protagonist and drove him to try, over and over again, to reinstate the proper order by returning the characters to their time and place. The circumstance of the past rubbing up against the present is what created the story. And thus, for Ayznman too, the

Israel-theme becomes a sophisticated way of returning to the past without sinking into utter destruction.

This story (and several others I have discussed here) suggests that of all the immigrants of the mass ʿaliya, many ʿoley sheyres hapleyte writers identified mostly with Jews of Yemenite origin. My own sense is that this identification has to do with the fact that many of them came to Israel in the same years and lived in the same residences. In addition, the outer appearance of the traditional Yemenite Jews was reminiscent of typical descriptions of the Jews of Eastern Europe: the black eyes, the sidelocks, the kippah. Yiddish fiction also shows that this identification gradually faded when the ʿolim moved to permanent neighborhoods and villages, where they settled separately.[110]

4. The Shikun

The third and in a sense final stage in the absorption of ʿoley sheyres hapleyte in Israel was their settlement in public housing projects built specifically for the immigrants and known as *Shikun ʿolim*. Building them took time and required planning. These new housing projects were the site of many of the stories written in Yiddish in Israel from the mid-1950s to the end of the 1960s. The projects were located in the new "development towns" and on the margins of the big cities.

In Yiddish fiction, these new housing projects were described as suffused with the fresh air of a new beginning. In many of the stories, they are architectural metaphors for the return to a normative family life and social life. To a large extent, the prosaic and minor everyday life that took place in the Shikun was the opposite of the turbulent and dramatic, temporary and nightmarish spaces in which the immigrants had lived during the war and in its aftermath: the ghettos, the labor camps and extermination camps, the DP camps, the detainee camps for the illegal Jewish immigration of ʿAliya Bet (*Haʿapala*), the immigrant camps, and the Maʿabarot. Life in the immigrant housing projects had contrasting and complementary effects on ʿoley sheyres hapleyte: on the one hand, it aroused a need for separation and individuation from the many neighbors, all of whom shared the same socioeconomic status (of a new immigrant), and on the other hand, the crowded living quarters, the distance from urban centers, and their social-cultural isolation drove the residents of these complexes to become intimate communities. Life in these communities exposed the social norms, both new and old, that prevailed in them, as well as the means of control and surveillance through which these norms were implemented and ingrained.

According to Moshe Lissak, very little data was gathered about the settlement of immigrants in these neighborhoods along the city margins,[111] and the few studies that do exist on the subject do not focus on immigrants from Eastern Europe. Lissak notes that the development towns, made up largely of public housing for immigrants, were populated with immigrants from the big waves of 'aliya who were sent there immediately upon their arrival in Israel in accordance with the changing circumstances at the time of each of the waves.[112] This dispersion policy created, at least initially, different types of development towns, which differed from one another in their levels of population homogeneity: some towns had a majority of immigrants from a single country, while others were populated by immigrants of various origins.[113] The makeup of these towns changed frequently due to the immigrants' mobility. The first to leave were those who had high professional and educational skills, whose chances of being absorbed in the suburbs of the big cities were better. 'Oley sheyres hapleyte, as I described earlier, were not financially dependent on the absorbing institutions because they had access to independent aid organizations.

The life of routine that the Shikun 'olim represented was emphasized in Yiddish prose through descriptions of the Shikun as a place in which lives resembled one another, a place of small identical apartments and even identical furniture, supplied to the 'olim by the Jewish Agency. The daily routines of the residents also appear similar—a life of family and work: in most cases, the men are described as setting out to work in the morning, returning in the early evening, and tending to gardens; throughout most of the day, it was the women and children who populated the Shikun. Against the backdrop of this flattening uniformity, differences between the various 'olim who lived in the Shikun stood out, and so did anyone who deviated from the governing norms—for example, children who because of the war had not been circumcised; non-Jewish women married to Jewish men; solitary survivors; and lone women, whether widows, childless women, or women artists.

And indeed, the stories about the immigrant housing projects feature many women, as protagonists and even as writers. Until the start of the twentieth century, Yiddish literature not only was written by men but also revolved mostly around them (though the hidden readership was mostly female). Women appeared as secondary characters who were supported by a dominant male protagonist. The appearance of women as protagonists in fiction, and especially in novels, was a sign of the literature's renewal.[114] Women started to participate in Yiddish cultural life as writers only in the second decade of the twentieth century. The vast majority of them were poets, so that the female prose writers were in a position of "double marginality."[115] Nearly all the promising female prose writers from among the 'oley sheyres hapleyte came to Israel after the Holocaust. The Israel-theme in almost all of them revolves around life in the Shikun 'olim. To draw out the unique features of their voice, I compare it here to the voice of their male colleagues who came to Israel and wrote Yiddish prose. A central issue that runs through this reading is the question of how the female protagonist was shaped in their works.

The move to the Shikun apartment—from the ma'abara or from depopulated Palestinian houses—involved a lot of work and effort on the part of the family members, sometimes including the teenage children. Male writers tended to dwell on this effort more than female writers. The move was portrayed as accompanied by a deep fear that it would fail and the family would have to move back to the place from which it had hoped to move up. The desire for social mobility was perceived partly as a source of fear, a dangerous hubris. So, for example, the protagonist of Levi Papyiernikov's story "Getsele" is described as an industrious man who succeeds through his hard work as a simple laborer in moving his family out of the ma'abara and into a new housing project.[116] After the move, he continues to work, cultivates a garden, and even makes optimistic plans for the future: he will send his son to the "Technion" (the Israel Institute of Technology) to be trained as an engineer. But then he falls ill, and his family's situation gradually deteriorates. His final wish is that his children will be simple laborers like him.

The financial worries that attended the desire for social mobility lie at the core of the stories written by the teacher and writer Khave Slutska-Kestin in her book *In undzere teg* (In our days), which is devoted to the Israel-theme.[117] As someone who was closely affiliated with communist circles, her position in the world of Yiddish literature in Israel was very marginal. Her story "Vi in yene gasn" (Like in those streets) describes a group of girls role-playing and, through the game, expressing their hopes for the future: Mazal refuses to be a housemaid, and Miriam wants to be a "lady," though one who does not herself earn money but is married to a "gentleman." The name of the story attests to the similarity between the exile and Israel in terms of the hopes of the poor (who are not only of Eastern European origin) for social mobility, and also in terms of the lack and even poverty in the new country. The child Shula, the protagonist of the story of the same name, is overjoyed when new, blue blinds are installed in her porch, which will allow her and her sister to sleep there. She knows that this is thanks to her mother, who works three times a week as a laundress. The mother's work enables not only an improvement of their physical conditions but also a cultural-spiritual improvement (since their apartment is distinguished from the rest by the blue color, which in modern culture symbolizes artistic creation). Unlike this description, which presents the mother's work in a positive light, in another story, Nurit, the protagonist, is described as a lonely "latchkey child," an only child who misses her mother who works long hours outside the home, and her father who "fell in one of the wars"—it is unclear which one and where, whether in Israel or in the Holocaust, a feature that underscores the child's point of view, in which the historical and national circumstances of the father's death are inconsequential. These portraits of children are, on the one hand, a traditional theme of women (as opposed to Papyiernikov, whose protagonists are grown men fighting for social and economic mobility in a world of grownups), but on the other hand this theme expresses the author's unique gender position: her ideological and political position as well as her education and professional training. Slutska-Kestin held a master's degree in education from the University of Warsaw and taught at the Yiddish TSYSHO schools in Warsaw and Biala Podlaska. Even during the years of the Holocaust, she worked as a teacher, in various areas in the Soviet Union, to which she escaped. After liberation she returned to Poland and worked as a teacher, school director, and instructor in training courses for Jewish teachers. It is interesting to note that the Yiddish prose she wrote in Israel was written about the Sabra children but was not aimed at them as an audience. Her stories are not "children's literature" (or literature for children). Works written from the point of view of children, like those by Slutska-Kestin, are extremely rare in the Yiddish prose written in Israel.

The tensions that characterize the descriptions of the lives of 'oley sheyres hapleyte in the immigrant housing—between the uniformity of the buildings and the variegation of their residents, between the residents' need to belong to a collective and their need to be distinguished from it, between their desire to start a new life and their loyalty to the life that was lost—appear repeatedly in many of the works. For instance, Granatshteyn, who lived in a Shikun 'olim in the Tel Aviv neighborhood of Bitzaron, wrote in one of his stories, "Low, whitewashed houses, identical like drops of water in the sea. And in them, people from all countries, languages from everywhere and various manners. Nonetheless, there is a partnership among the people. . . . They are linked by the term '*ole hadash*' [newcomer]. . . . linked by shared complaints and arguments. . . . So strangely shaped are the housing-boxes of the Shikun. So transparent and controllable is life here. . . . So close and intimate, so open, that there is almost nothing left to gossip about."[118] The uniformity of the Shikun triggered in some of its residents an urge to emphasize their own uniqueness. "The deepest problems of modern life flow from the attempt of the individual to maintain the independence and individuality of his existence against the sovereign powers of society, against . . . the external culture and technique of life," argued Georg Simmel.[119] And indeed, this rebellion against the planned and uniform space of the Shikun 'olim is the subject of the feuilleton "Di revulutsye in di 'Amidar-Shikun" (The revolution in the 'Amidar housing projects):

> It started with small "actions," with a kind of passive resistance, which was a silent protest against the "equality-dictatorship" and a manifestation of individual "difference": when, for example, someone installed a red deck on the porch, a second installed a green one; when one of them painted his blinds brown, the neighbor across the street painted them—green; when a resident of the first floor planted flowers in his garden, the neighbor from the basement [apartment] planted—onions. . . . The first step toward the "uprising" was taken and stimulated further, bolder measures. . . . The local council protests loudly, holds trials, threatens to tear down all the buildings, but who listens to them! The more trials, the more the neighborhood changes. All traces of the artistic style of its former appearance have been erased. The 'Amidar town

> is becoming more and more home-like, more Jewish. . . . It is the people who have won![120]

This feuilleton (and especially its final sentence) emphasizes (to the point of grotesque) the competitive atmosphere that prevailed between the different residents of the Shikun and between them and the local council. This competition is described in combative terms (resistance, uprising, victory). The descriptions of the battle between the tenants and the council employ literary conventions that were prevalent in Jewish literature, both Hebrew and Yiddish: the tenants make the "'Amidar town," which represents the Jewish nation-state, "more Jewish" and therefore more familiar and homelike. This tension is created through the use of old enlightenment-era conventions that were used to describe the Jewish shtetl in Eastern Europe as a dilapidated and aesthetically unruly space that needed to be brought under control. In this feuilleton, the Israeli local council is assigned this role of imposing order. The description of the housing tenants as a "people" clashing with the state institution echoes literary conventions from the periods of the 1905 and 1917 revolutions.

The battle to ensure distinctiveness and control of the small space of the Shikun apartment was expressed not only in the use of colors to distinguish one apartment from the rest, or in the styling of gardens, but also in a motif that recurred in several of the Shikun stories—the radio.[121] In these descriptions, various different styles of sounds, in a variety of languages, waft up from every porch (especially in the summer evenings) and express the uniqueness of the tenants. These sounds came from far away, bringing the distant places into attendance in the local space and sometimes symbolizing the yearning for these places. It is perhaps surprising that the radio appeared more frequently in these stories as a marker of cultural difference than did the various odors of cooking that also rose up in the air.

In contrast to these attempts to express uniqueness, those who for various reasons already inevitably stood out as different against the backdrop of the uniformity of the Shikun actually had to undergo a kind of "conversion" to soften their difference and thus to be accepted into the society of the "small home" (the Shikun) and by extension also the "big home" (Israeli society). Such were the Christian women who married Jewish men during the Holocaust (thereby saving the men's lives). In the story "Farshpetike blumen" (Late flowers), by Avrom Karpinovitsh, a Christian woman who is the protagonist's wife leaves him after realizing that she will not be able to abandon the tradition of her own (Christian) culture and live without any alternative (Jewish) tradition. Her partner believed that if they both became entirely secular, they would be able to overcome their cultural differences; but the experiment failed. In Yitskhok Brat's story "Kalmems tfile" (Kalmen's prayer),[122] the protagonist tries to expose his wife (and savior) to the religious life.[123] He wants to go with her and with their children to the synagogue of their Shikun in Holon on the eve of Yom Kippur, and the story describes his concerns about how she will be received there. Unlike in these two stories, in Yishaye Shpigl's story "A fremde" (A foreigner) the main character is a woman (Maria). She wants to understand why the Jews she has met in Israel, in supposedly secular places like the ma'abara and later the Shikun apartment, are so different from the ones she knew in her native Poland, and why they are so hostile toward her. She hopes that her soon-to-be-born child will be treated more kindly.[124] Theresa, the protagonist of another story by Shpigl, "Keter yisroel" (Crown of Israel),[125] wins the respect of her neighbors when she donates silver utensils from the church of her village in Poland, which was abandoned during the Holocaust, to the new synagogue established by several tenants of the Shikun. She decided to make the donation after finding out that her husband, who had been fighting in the 1956 "Sinai War" (the Suez Crisis), was injured slightly and would soon be returning to their home. In response to the donation, the synagogue manager's initial fear of impurity is eventually replaced with an appreciation of the heroism of both Theresa and her husband. The silver utensils become a crown for the Torah scroll, and the protagonist is embraced by the society. Common to all these descriptions is the tension between the supposedly secular character of Israel as a nation-state (which in its first years of existence granted citizenship to anyone who declared themselves Jewish, as part of the "Law of Return") and its de facto religious-ethnic nature. The road to accepting these women into the society of the Shikun passed through the synagogue and through their own willingness to get closer to religion. Stories that dealt with this subject reflect the progressiveness of Yiddish literature in the landscape of Israeli literature insofar as these stories identified and discussed the tension that existed in the country between religion and nationality; but on the other hand, in the choice of these writers to describe only women as the "religious other," the stories reflect the conservativeness of Yiddish literature, insofar as they based themselves on a model that is familiar from the tradition of Jewish literature (Ruth) and did not develop it further.

Children were also sometimes described as foreigners who needed to undergo a transformation before they were accepted into society. This was the case with uncircumcised children, for example. These children, who were uncircumcised not out of principle and choice but because they were born during the Holocaust or on the journey to Israel in conditions that made it impossible to perform the ceremony, had to undergo the circumcision at a later age in order to belong fully to the society.[126] Another category of children who stood out included those whose parents insisted on teaching them Yiddish in the home (in addition to the Hebrew they learned outside the home, in schools) so that they would not lose the connection to their past and their tradition.[127] These children internalized and maintained a sharp separation between the domestic sphere, which was identified with Yiddish and its culture, and the public sphere, dominated by Hebrew and its culture. The attitude of the Hebrew culture toward Yiddish and the children's desire to fit into the dominant culture often caused this split in their lives to be loaded with feelings of shame and guilt. The children of survivors were often described as being doubly foreign: not only in the eyes of society, who saw them as foreign because they were "new 'olim," but also in the eyes of their parents, who saw them as "Sabras" and therefore culturally foreign. Rokhl Oyerbakh described this foreignness in her story "Dos viglid" (The lullaby).[128] It tells of a couple who live with their small children in a Shikun symbolically named Ramat Chaim (Hebrew for "standard of living"). During a visit in their home, the narrator notices difficult, deep currents coursing beneath the surface of the new home. The father lost his daughter, an exceptionally gifted musician who is described as a "wunderkind," in the Holocaust and has turned the new house in Israel into a museum for this child.[129] In the young mother, the narrator senses a hopefulness mixed with a deep tension: will their joint children be as talented as the murdered daughter? To their "Sabra" son, the parents gave the hard name Kami, short for Nekemia, from the Hebrew word for "revenge." The questions that the story addresses are, Will the children who grow up in Israel manage to develop culturally like the children who grew up "there," in Eastern Europe, and were murdered in the Holocaust? Will their parents succeed in loving them for who they are, without having to justify the love by their resemblance to the murdered children? This juxtaposition of the murdered children and the new children is harsh and even shocking for the reader, since the typical descriptions of the survivors cast the new families as compensation and consolation for those that were lost. It is interesting that the thwarting of these expectations is performed with conventional literary tools: this story is the only one among the stories by female writers that uses the narrative form that is considered typical of the female voice in modern Yiddish fiction—namely, first-person singular.

Single Holocaust survivors who did not succeed in creating new families also stood out in the landscape of the Shikun. How was this difference represented from the two descriptive angles, the masculine and the feminine? In his story "Aleyn" (Alone), Granatshteyn described a lonely man who meets a young woman in Israel and hopes to start a new family with her, but she leaves him and the country.[130] He travels to the post office in Tel Aviv to send the letters he has written her in a desperate attempt to bring her back to him so that his neighbors will not sense his difference. The main feeling described in the story is the shame triggered by the intimate proximity among neighbors that crowded Shikun life imposes—shame about his loneliness and about his hope to build a new family despite his advanced age. The feeling of shame appears to have replaced another feeling—pain for the loss of his family during the Holocaust. Khaye Elboym-Dorembus's story "Der pomidor" (The tomato) also describes the relations between neighbors in ambivalent terms: an innocent visit by a neighbor who offers her a fresh tomato becomes a painful ordeal in which she is reminded in precise detail of her husband and young daughter who were murdered in the Holocaust.[131] Unlike the description in Granatshteyn's story, here the loneliness and sense of difference triggered by the excessive proximity of the neighbors and their intrusion into the private space are described as a source not of shame but of pain.

The new immigrant neighborhoods were a symbol, as I said, of the new families created in Israel by the survivors and especially by the young generation. We saw, for example, that in the novel *Dzshebelye*, the young couple (Leybish and Ilana), who met in Israel and married there, move to a Shikun ʻolim and there raise the next generation of their young family. This is indeed a new generation, with new values, which their parents do not always understand and accept. For example, the speaker in the story "Di farshterte simkhe" (The disrupted joy) describes the joy he felt when his daughter (who was given the symbolic name Brokhe, Hebrew for "blessing") married a decent and serious young man.[132] This joy was mixed with wonder at the ambition of the young couple: immediately after the wedding, they moved into a spacious Shikun apartment equipped with what the parents judged as unnecessary luxuries—new furniture and even a transistor radio. The speaker notes that this is not how people behaved in "the old home," where marrying one's children involved many years of saving, and their furniture too was accumulated over years. After the wedding it is revealed that the young couple bought their comfort with loans, whose repayment forces both of them to work from dawn to dusk. Yet despite this effort, they want this standard of living in order to meet the norms of their generation. Such is their drive that the daughter even chooses to have an abortion to be able to work the number of hours necessary to make their loan payments. This act pains her parents deeply, since through it they come to acknowledge not only the shifting of values that has raised a barrier between them and the young generation but also their inability to influence it. It is interesting that the discussion of so sensitive an issue as abortion, and especially in the families of Holocaust survivors, appeared in a work written by a man and not in works written by women.

Another kind of foreignness represented in the works of fiction is embodied by women-artists. This foreignness, too, is a "double foreignness," since artists were perceived in modern Jewish culture as people of the margins, and female artists all the more so. One such character is Louisa Bitner, the protagonist of Rivke Kviatkovski-Pinkhasik's story "Zamd" (Sand).[133] The protagonist is a Vienna-born Jew who came to Israel from Shanghai, where she had ended up during the war years. She is a middle-aged woman, a renowned piano teacher who even in Shanghai succeeded in maintaining a high-bourgeois standard of living. She was the first tenant in the Shikun and thus by default became a pioneer of sorts. She brought with her a lot of furniture, some of it rather grandiose: boxes of books in English and German, framed pictures, and a piano. To the protagonist, and with her, to the readers, it is not clear why she chose to come to Israel in the first place. Indeed, Israel is described through her eyes as a crude and threatening environment. She does not understand how she will manage in such a place, where music is considered a luxury and everyone seems to be preoccupied with financial concerns. Her initial encounter with the country caused her deep discomfort and a sense that she did not fit the place: the vast expanses of sand struck her as an emotional and cultural desert. She felt a strong repulsion for the clerk at the immigrant-processing camp and for the taxi driver who brought her to her new apartment in the Shikun. Then she recalled that this feeling was familiar to her, from her childhood; at the time, it was directed toward the simple Jewish girls who came to Vienna as refugees from Galicia and spoke Yiddish.

The plot's central conflict, then, is between the Jews of Central and Western Europe and those of Eastern Europe, which the former call "Ostjuden," the Jews of the East. This image of the German-speaking Jews as arrogant and condescending and unattached to Judaism and the Jewish state was prevalent in the Zionist establishment in pre- and post-state Israel, if only because the vast majority of the members of this establishment were of Eastern European origin.[134] Modern Yiddish culture had particular sensitivities toward the German culture and toward those who embraced it: the discovery of enlightenment through German texts had convinced many Yiddish speakers that their language was nothing but an inferior "jargon" and that their unique culture, which had begun to develop in Germany in the thirteenth century, was inferior to the German culture. The image of German-speaking Jews in Yiddish literature was fundamentally negative, casting them as people who have lost their national and historical roots. How will Kviatkovski-Pinkhasik treat this cultural-social complex in her story? Will she accept the framework as it was assumed by her readers or rebel against it? Will she shape her heroine as a symbol (of the Western European Jews), or will she dare to buck this convention and present her as a private character?

As the protagonist draws nearer to the Shikun, and especially upon entering her new apartment—the first home she has ever owned since leaving the home of her parents—she is flooded with forgotten childhood memories. She feels like someone who has reached the end of her journey and can contemplate the path she traveled and process her experiences. She suddenly recalls two men who in her eyes embody the two poles of her self-loathing complex: her father, the simple Jew from whom she had sought to alienate herself as a child, and the headmaster of the Christian secondary school she had hoped to attend but from which she was rejected for her Judaism. Her mother had hoped to make of her a "true Viennese," a bourgeois of impeccable education and cultural manners. Music, therefore, was not intended for her personal expression but on the contrary—it was part of the process of her meticulous grooming. This process caused her to become estranged from her father and even to despise her roots and be ashamed of them. Even though her Christian girlfriends assured her that she had indeed become a "true Viennese" and did not in the least resemble a Jew, the headmaster sought to block her social path and brought her mother up against her actual identity. He advised her to enroll her daughter in a Jewish gymnasium, which he said would better serve her training, not only professionally but also socially:

> The merciful Mrs. Bitner, I would gladly see your daughter at my gymnasium. . . . However, I still cannot understand . . . why are you doing this? Your husband is a merchant, would it not be right that your daughter go to school with the children of Jewish merchants. Let her be among her people. An equal among equals. Marry, like you, a merchant or a clerk, and like you be a housewife. You do not have to expel your daughter from your class, from your people. . . . She will then find no place for herself in life, will not start a family, will be left alone, rootless.[135]

This prediction by the professor—who ultimately relented and admitted the girl into his school—was completely fulfilled: the protagonist's dreams of social and cultural assimilation vanished in the mist of war, and she did not marry and did not start her own family. In her modest home in the Shikun, after she has returned to a simple existence, it comes to her that until the moment she arrived in Israel she had been living in the desert, an emotional desert of someone seeking an identity that is not her own, an emotional desert of someone who has spent her entire life scorning her class and her ethnic origin, of someone who has always tried to prove that she was better than her past and her people and wanted to belong to a society that wanted nothing to do with her. War and exile brought her back into the bosom of the collective from which she tried so hard to distinguish herself: "She is no longer the 'little princess,' as she was called for many years. Now, like all those who have been swept up by storms, she is seeking shelter in a calm shore. She is tired and lonely like all those who come here every day by ship from all corners of the globe."[136] The story ends with the protagonist playing her piano. This time she is not playing for money or to secure her social status, but neither is she playing purely for the sake of art: the sounds she produces (*The Moonlight Sonata* by Beethoven, a composer who became one of the towering symbols of German culture) are intended as a delicate response to the howling of jackals that envelopes her. By covering up the foreign environment with familiar sounds, she quells her loneliness and her fears of the unfamiliar place. This loneliness causes her to wish for the arrival of her new neighbors in the Shikun, a reincarnation of those Jewish Galician girls who so repelled her in the past. In her new home and new predicament, she writes a letter to her brother in London after many years of not doing so.

The author's views, then, are reflected clearly in the plot: only in Israel can the protagonist go back to being a "homeowner," "a proprietor." The return to Israel is described as a return to her people and to her family, but first and foremost as the end of a process of self-alienation—that is, as self-acceptance. She dared to confront her past and her origins. This process became doubly meaningful when the story was published on the eve of the opening of the Eichmann trial, and published in Yiddish, for an audience of Yiddish readers, a language that symbolizes, perhaps above all else, the survivors of the Holocaust and their rejected and shameful Jewish identity. As I noted earlier, many ʿoley sheyres hapleyte believed, at least in the first period of their life in Israel, that the establishment of Israel would allow the Jews to stand tall not only because of the way in which the people of the world would look upon them but mostly because of the way in which they would value themselves, through an acceptance of the full spectrum of their identity. To their great disappointment, however, they discovered that the loathing and shame that many Israelis felt toward their past was very often channeled and manifested against the Eastern European culture and against its language—Yiddish. Even the Eichmann trial, which had succeeded in transforming the attitude of Israeli society toward the Holocaust survivors, did not change its attitude toward the culture and the language of the victims.[137]

The Shikun is described in the novella as a kind of small-scale allegory for the young Jewish state. It suggests that in the Shikun in particular and in Israel in general, German-speaking Jews do not have the option (or the luxury) of continuing to run from their Jewish identity, and that they must accept Eastern European Jews as real people, including their culture and language (after having scorned them for years), and especially the denied and rejected parts of their identity and self-esteem. Thus, in this work the author confirmed rather than undermined or questioned the two existing poles: she posited the Eastern European Jewish culture against the German one. The Shikun she described as a symbol of the Jewish state and not as a particular place. In this respect, the protagonist, too, is described as a symbol of Western European Judaism and its integration into the Jewish state. And indeed, from a feminist point of view the author tells a tale of failure despite the fact that the novella is about self-esteem and self-acceptance: the mother of the protagonist tried to train her daughter for a life of financial independence in a Christian male world, but the price the daughter paid for this training was estrangement from her Jewish father and a loss of the possibility of marrying and having a family of her own. In Shanghai she managed to achieve the professional and personal goals that her mother had set her. But it was precisely then that she decided to uproot herself and move to "her father's country," a place that is economically, socially, and culturally poor. On this reading, it is actually the mother that the daughter rebels against and not her forefathers, since it is the mother who had set for her these (cultural and financial) goals and it is the mother who was the driving force behind her training. By returning from the world of the Christian headmaster to the world of the Jewish father, the protagonist makes the opposite journey to the one her mother traveled. Both of these worlds, represented by these two significant men, continued to be the only two options that reflected the boundaries of her world. Louisa Bitner is supposedly shaped as a woman who challenged the prevailing values of the Shikun (and of the young Israeli society)—family and making do with little; but in fact she emerges as a character who internalized the social ethos and the national ethos and did not rebel against them.

It is interesting to compare this protagonist to another "Shikun protagonist," Khane (Khantshe) in the novella "Der forhang" (The curtain), by the female writer Malasha Mali.[138] Khane is a survivor who came to Israel with her husband (Itzik). They live in a Shikun with their two small children, and both of them work. "Khane" is a stereotypical name of a Jewish woman. At first glance, the reader "suspects" that he is facing another protagonist who is in fact a symbol, like Louisa Bitner, and this time a symbol of Polish Jewry. But it soon becomes clear that the central motif is that of rebellion. On the face of it, this is an idyllic frame story about the absorption and rehabilitation of a family of survivors that is successful from the national point of view. But as the plot unfolds, it emerges that the protagonist is a painter who has been unable to paint since her arrival in Israel. This troubles her, since even in Siberia, where she passed the war years, she was able to paint.

The structure of the plot is complicated and difficult to reconstruct, as the narrator allows herself broad digressions from the linear structure, which undermine the reader's sense of orientation in space and in time. So, for example, the plot begins in the protagonist's childhood, while the omniscient narrator moves without warning between details of the portrayed reality and the protagonist's thoughts and dreams, thereby destabilizing the boundaries between them. Even as a child, Khane rebelled against the contrast between the categories of adults and children. She also noticed the manipulations her mother performed on her, and she resisted them. She was angered when her mother sent her to bed while the other children played together and while her mother invited a friend over and plunged with her into a long exchange of whispered secrets. In her frustration, Khane immersed herself in drawing, and by the way discovered that the most effective rebellion against her mother lay in not needing her, in renouncing her. But this renouncing involved a great deal of anxiety, and Khane expressed her frustration at these stormy and conflicting emotions by setting one of the curtains in their house on fire. In this way she hoped to regain the attention of her mother, which was turned on a neighbor, and to prove to her young friend (later her husband), Itzik, that "little girls can do things that he would not even dream of."[139] Over the years, as they grow up together, a healthy competition exists between them: he continues to pursue his own studies so as not to lag behind Khane, who is sent to secondary school in Warsaw and then to study art in France. The protagonist, then, is shaped as an opinionated and ambitious woman who defies and rebels against conventions of gender and culture. This rebelliousness is also expressed in the way in which the plot unfolds in space and time.

In the middle of the novella, the reader learns that Khane's cousin, who lives abroad and is her only surviving relative, will visit her in the Shikun. Khane receives this news with mixed feelings. She has been very pleased with her new life, but it has also been a source of pain because she has had no one to whom to present this life. For many years, she has been deprived of family contact. Since arriving in her Shikun apartment—a permanent home after the long years of wanderings—she has felt, for the first time, the decline of her creative power, expressed in her inability to draw. Her husband suggested that she try to draw their apartment and their yard, but these did not provoke her creative passion. Now she is worried that her cousin will ask her about her art, and she is ashamed by this show of incompetence. This is how the protagonist describes the Shikun when she imagines how it will appear in the eyes of her guest:

> Thus, for the uninitiated eye of a visitor it is almost impossible to distinguish and make sense of such a monotonous environment, which is called: Shikun. The houses all seem to have been made of one mold, all of them have open staircases and their shutters are colored a light brown. In addition, all the buildings here are nearly new, whitewashed and standing next to one another like soldiers on a parade. . . . Even in the gardens that surround every house here—there is as yet no point to look for a unique style: for now, everything is "like the neighbors."[140]

The important meeting in this work is not with the cousin but with her true self. The protagonist projects onto her relative her anxiety over her own fear of becoming, like the Shikun apartments, unexceptional. When the cousin arrives, Khane wants to quench her thirst for family contact, not to let the present time limit their preoccupation with the past, and not to go to sleep but to continue talking and recounting. But the guest refuses, and her husband concurs with him. They make a bed for themselves, and Khane is sent to sleep next to her children. For a moment, she feels the same powerful urge to set fire to a curtain and thus regain their attention and demonstrate her boldness. But this time her concern for her children forces her to restrain her emotions, and in an attempt to calm herself, she steps out into the garden. There, the outdoor air carries distant and foreign smells of the fields of Poland, which evoke in her a mix of love, fear, and jealousy. Filled with these emotions, she walks over to the "porch" that has been closed off and turned into her studio and sits down facing the easel. She finds herself painting the curtain she set aflame as a child, and painting her mother and her neighbor. Thus, she converts into art the frustration and grief, passion and yearning, that resurfaced due to the cousin's visit after having been forgotten for many years, and in doing so she succeeds in "burning down the curtain" that had concealed from her those subjects she could not face and that prevented her from painting.

The protagonists of the two stories described here, Khane and Louisa Bitner, are both artistically creative women who stand out against the backdrop of the uniform environment in which they live—the Shikun. Both are preoccupied with the tension between individual uniqueness and what counts as being "normal." Yet they are shaped in entirely different ways. Khane appears to resemble many other women (survivors who live in the Shikun with their families), but she dares to rebel against the uniformity that the Shikun underscores or even imposes on her and to go back to the easel. Her strong emotions contrast with the rationalism and utilitarianism involved in the planning and building of the Shikun. Louisa, by contrast, travels the opposite path: from an exceptional woman—a musician with no family of her own who enjoys a high economic and cultural standard of living—she is eventually revealed to be a metonymy for the Shikun; like it, she too has become "just like everyone else." When Khane landed in her permanent home, she was confronted with her own helplessness, whereas Louisa came to realize her power as a homeowner. The narrative techniques are also entirely different: "Zamd" adheres to the realistic structure and confirms it, while "Der forhang" undercuts the narrative framework and the linearity of the story's temporal axis. In the latter, the narrator does not impose order on the events and their chronology but rather stays with the protagonist's consciousness and follows the stream of her thoughts, dreams, fears, and passions. It is worth noting that even Mali's protagonist is, after all, traditional: Sholem Aleichem had already shaped female protagonists whose defining tension was between passion and duty (for instance, Rokhele in *Stempenyu*, 1888).[141] Like them, Mali's protagonist chooses duty: she does not disrupt the domestic or national peace for the sake of devoting herself to her art. Art is part of her normative life and not a destruction of it, and she is portrayed as a traditional woman.

This story by Mali was awarded the World Congress for Jewish Culture prize for the best story published in *DGK* in 1952 (alongside a story by Mendl Man). She was considered an original and promising female voice, and perhaps the most interesting among the young female prose writers in Israel. She was a member of the Yung-yisroel group (or at least participated in one of their publications).[142] The Yiddish world's foremost literary critic, Shmuel Niger, discussed her work. He identified in her writing influences of Sholem Aleichem (the character of "Motl Peysi dem khazn's" [Motl Peysi the cantor's son] is reflected in the character of the child Khane) and of the early Bergelson (the surrealist tones) and argued that no less important than these influences is the fact that her voice remained unique and her style impressionistic.[143] But despite this recognition, Mali wrote and published little. A collection of her stories was published more than a decade after the first version of "Der forhang" was published. After her book was published, she seemed to vanish from the world of Yiddish culture, and the book was never translated into Hebrew.

Sadly, Mali's fate as a writer is not different from that of other female writers mentioned earlier, who received even less recognition. Oyerbakh's work on the Israel-theme was valued by the Yiddish literary establishment, but she focused more on her work on Holocaust-related issues at Yad Vashem and devoted very little time to writing literature. After her book about the Israel-theme was published (and not translated into Hebrew), she did not continue to write on this subject. Like Oyerbakh, Kviatkovski-Pinkhasik also focused on the theme of the Holocaust in the books she published.[144] Her stories about the lives of ʻoley sheyres hapleyte in Israel were published in the press and in the leading periodicals and anthologies published in Israel in Yiddish, and they were published together, in a collection, only in 1975. Despite the fact that her works appeared in the press, she remained marginal, as attested by the fact that the collection of her stories on the Israel-theme was published by a private press and was not translated into Hebrew. Elboym-Dorembus also wrote mostly about the Holocaust.[145] Her few stories on the Israel-theme were published in the Yiddish press but were not compiled or translated into Hebrew. In the 1970s, she left Israel and settled in the United States. Slutska-Kestin's stories on the Israel-theme appeared in the radical Yiddish press published in Israel (*Arbeter tribune*, *Kol Ha-Am*, *Fray yisroel*). Her membership in Maki, the Israeli Communist Party, may have contributed to her marginal status even among the women writers: her work is not included in the canonical anthologies and is hardly discussed in the criticism. Her stories were collected, as I said, in a book published by a private publishing firm, and it, too, was not translated into Hebrew.

The marginality of female Yiddish writers in Israel, then, was mostly quantitative and not the result of exclusion by the establishment, since the Yiddish literary establishment in most cases supported and encouraged them. Yiddish literary criticism in Israel and abroad (which was written by men) did not discuss their work collectively, and they themselves did not refer in their work to other female writers or to the works of other female writers as a source of inspiration or as partners-in-status. Most of the stories by women are about the new domestic sphere that was created in the Shikun ʻolim (and not in the depopulated village, the maʻabara, the Kibbutz, or Tel Aviv). In their writing, the (female) protagonists are still identified with the domestic sphere, with home and family. Within this patriarchal picture, certain overtones of class are discernible: these protagonists needed "a home of their own"—not a temporary apartment, a house that belonged to someone else in the near past, or a home whose ownership they would have to share with others (as in the case of the Kibbutz, to which I return later). This new home was itself a central hero in their works. They did not turn it into a simplistic reincarnation of the "old home" but rather highlighted the new and complex human situations its residents faced, situations that were the result of the Holocaust and the establishment of Israel. Nonetheless, most of the female writers showed conservative tendencies, whether in theme or in style. And thus, beginning in the late 1960s, when in Hebrew literature the female voice was establishing itself, in Yiddish literature this voice gradually fell silent.

5. The Kibbutz

In the national culture of Israel in its first two decades, the Kibbutz was a symbol of the new revolutionary society and new Jew that Zionism sought to bring about. The basic tenets of this revolutionary society were socialist justice and modern, secular nationalism. Its novelty was incapsulated in the idea of the "negation of exile"—the rejection of Judaism as a religion, including the old communal structure, economy, culture, and language that were shaped in Eastern Europe. The sociologist Oz Almog has shown that, like the national ideology, the Kibbutz ideology also had characteristics of a "secular religion": orientation toward a future utopia (a social heaven on earth); the mystification and glorification of leaders; a perception of itself as a chosen and exemplary society that is realizing an ancient vision and enjoys divine providence; an articulation of social ideas in metaphysical and theological terms; an understanding of reality in absolute terms; total identification with an ideology (sometimes to the point of fanaticism), a willingness to make extreme sacrifices for the sake of realizing it, and a condemnation of those who steer from it; and an institutionalization of the national ideas by inserting them into every area of private and social life through taboos, cyclical ritual, symbols, bureaucratic systems, and educational institutions.[146] As a place, the Kibbutz embodied the national ideal: it was established and functioned as an "advance military post," which realized and practiced the collective values and ideals. As such, it was a small-scale and radicalized model of the "big home" and "big time," which was present also in the most private and intimate space (like the family bedroom) and defined it. In other words, despite being typically located in the geographical periphery, its inhabitants experienced themselves as the hegemonic center of ideological and cultural activity. In the range of years discussed in this book, the Kibbutz, as an idea, a practice, and an expression of national policy, underwent significant changes. One of its moments of crisis came right after the success of the revolution—namely, with the conclusion of the 1948 "War of Independence." Like the Zionist movement itself, the Kibbutz changed its nature and had to redefine its goals. For example, according to Lissak, the Labor Settlement Movement (ha-hityashvut ha-ovedet) opened itself up to the general population with almost no political or professional selection processes.[147] This move deeply influenced the character of the Kibbutz societies.

'Oley sheyres hapleyte who came to live in the Kibbutzim were typically children and teens who came to Israel with Youth 'Aliya. Adult 'oley sheyres hapleyte typically tried to avoid the difficult experience of attempting to get integrated in a Kibbutz. Some founded Kibbutzim as a group of survivors, but this of course, is not the same case.[148] Still, I discuss the Kibbutz because of the unique interpretation that was given in Yiddish literature to this highly influential symbol of the Zionist ethos in the young Israeli culture. In contrast to the common perception, here too there was a gap between the official policy of the Zionist institutions toward Yiddish and its application on the ground: Yiddish was heard in the Kibbutzim both before and after the establishment of the state, and its culture lived and was created in them. Several of the prominent Yiddish writers and cultural figures (and especially the young ones) lived on Kibbutzim (at least during the 1950s).[149] Even the meetings of Yung-yisroel, the group of young Yiddish writers, were held in a Kibbutz (Yagur). This had special importance in the eyes of the Yiddish cultural figures in Israel and abroad because they saw their acceptance by the Kibbutz as a symbol of their acceptance by the whole of Israeli society.[150]

Krutikov described the future-oriented modernist interpretation of the experience of immigration in Yiddish fiction as a spiritual renewal, which arises from a utopian social way of life. He described immigration as a force of crucial importance in the spiritual and physical renewal of the Jewish people. The innovations in the Jewish experience are emphasized in this representation, but not necessarily in a revolutionary way (i.e., by rejecting the past and disengaging from it). Productive work, and especially working the land, is presented in it in an idyllic manner, with attention to the physical aspects of the new environment that has been loaded with spiritual meanings. This mode of representation shows signs of the influence of the European modernist aesthetic, Jewish messianic metaphysics (Hasidism), and certain aspects of the ideology and ethics of Russian populism. As we will see later, it does not characterize the prose written by sheyres hapleyte writers about the Kibbutz. This fiction focuses on describing the "morning after" the realization of the utopia and describes the Kibbutz as a "small place" in which "*kleyne mentshelekh mit kleyne hasoges*" (little people with little aspirations), as in the title of Sholem Aleichem's famous 1901 novel, struggle for their existence—and in this it preceded Hebrew fiction by several years. The sheyres hapleyte writers' cultural heritage included a whole host of literary treatments of the gap between the grandiose human pretension and its small and sometimes failed realization. This treatment was shaped in a wide variety of styles: from critical sarcasm through comic melancholy and dry naturalism to sentimental tragedy.

The Kibbutz Movement's attitude toward ʻoley sheyres hapleyte was complex. It "vacillated between the existential need for people, and an anxious concern for the movement's human character in light of the 'human material' that came from the DP camps in Europe."[151] For their part, many among the ʻoley sheyres hapleyte and the advocates and creators of Yiddish culture did not see the Kibbutz as an attractive place to live: the experiences of the Holocaust, disappointment with the way in which the communist utopia was realized in the Soviet Union before it, their harsh experiences there during the war years as prisoners and refugees, the persecution of Yiddish writers from the late 1940s culminating in their murder in August 1952—all of these led many ʻoley sheyres hapleyte to a profound disillusionment both with religious ideas and with utopist ideologies and the practices developed to realize them. Another reason ʻoley sheyres hapleyte did not want to live on a Kibbutz had to do with the fact that they were fed up with communal living, which for them was associated with their lives during the war and its aftermath. Tsanin described these reservations in detail in one of his early columns in *Forverts*—"A briv fun yisroel" (A letter from Israel, 1949):

> So I ask the Jew why he does not go live in a Kibbutz. . . . The Jew shakes his head: "Here on my own piece of land I am willing to plow the land with my nose, even if I will have less than I have now. And to the Kibbutz I will not go. I've had enough of communal living in the camps and later in the DP camps in Germany, and here, too, when I came to the country, I sat in a camp for half a year. I've had enough of collective life". . . . I say to the Jew: "Well, you may be able to live a [Jewish] life here, but your two sons must go to a Kibbutz, they will not have to worry about selling the produce, they will live in a collective and be more productive than in your [vegetable] garden." The Jew makes a dismissive gesture with his hand [expression]: "Leave my children alone, they will not be kolkhozniks. They had enough kolkhozes in Russia." "We have come"—he says—"to the land of Israel to become healthy people and this can be done when one lives a private life, as a private citizen. Here . . . we will clear our head of the soot [that has built up in it] from all the difficult experiences [expression]". . . . Everywhere you hear the same words: to work for yourself, forget the hard experiences and become normal people, without the big ideas, which they no longer trust.[152]

Did Tsanin tailor this advocacy of private property and objection to a collective lifestyle specifically to the paper's readers in the United States? A description of ʻole sheyres hapleyte's encounter with the Kibbutz appears also in Perlov's novel *Dzshebelye*: "The first impression the Kibbutz made on Zekharye shortly after passing through the gate was: An UNWRA camp in Germany . . . The wooden shacks with the verandas, the trees and climbing plants, the flowerbeds, the paths, and on all of them—the neatness, made such an impression on him. Even the big dining hall looked to him like the camp kitchen."[153]

The physical resemblance to the camps along with an aversion to communal living led the novel's protagonist to disapprove of the Kibbutz. Another reason for 'oley sheyres hapleyte's aversion to the Kibbutz way of life was the agriculture that underlay it, since up until War World I the vast majority of Eastern European Jews had lived a commerce-based urban life in small towns.[154] Their communities provided a Jewish education for the children and a Jewish framework (religious, and in a later period cultural and varied) for the young members and families. This aversion to the agricultural life was expressed, for instance, in Tsanin's column from which I quoted earlier, whose subtitle read, "A new kind of '*yishuvniks*,' their reasons for not wanting to join groups—interesting conversations with Jewish villagers from the vicinity of Lod." *Yishuvnik* is a name given to Jews who lived in villages in Eastern Europe and thus metaphorically describes the simple, crude, uneducated Jew—in other words, one of low cultural capital. The same reason is mentioned in Perlov's novel, too: the thing that brings the protagonist of *Dzshebelye* to take his grandson out of the Kibbutz is its pigsty. His disgust with the pigs stems not only from reasons of religion and Kashrut but also from the dubious status of agriculture as a profession among Polish Jews: "Zekharye wrinkled [his nose] even more and thought, no! The Kibbutz is not for Azriyel! What will become of him here? A young farmer! Pigs he will feed here! Azriyel Karlsbakh will feed pigs! No, not under any circumstances! As soon as he settles in, he is taking him away from here!"[155]

It is interesting to compare these literary reactions by 'olim (to the idea of sending their offspring to the Kibbutz) to literary reactions to the same idea as described in Hebrew fiction. *Each Had Six Wings* ends with the father's admission that Rakefet (his son Menashe's Sabra teacher) was right when she decided to send him to live on a Kibbutz, since only there was he able to rid himself of his weak characteristics as a son of exile—his fragile and clumsy physique, his pale complexion, his stuttering, and his nonnative language, Yiddish—as well as of the traditional Jewish labors, which he replaced with the work of the land:

> This Menashe, as he is . . . grew up in forests, in dens. . . . And now I too understand that, indeed, she had his best interests in mind. He, the fool, is jumping with joy . . . there are beasts there, and poultry, and all kinds of machines. So be it. After all, what is it that we wanted—to put him to hard physical labor? To torture him? We wanted him to have something of his own . . . Just take a look at this shoemaking shop and you will understand by yourself that we are not in a rush to make rich. . . . I visited him there several weeks ago. My intention was to pull him by the ears and bring him back. And when I arrived, I did not have the courage. . . . Indeed, it is a big and rich village. In our places, I admit, there were no such villages. And this Menashe, he is like a nail with no head: once he has been fixed in place, there is no force in the world that will pull him out of there. . . . I now believe that the teacher was right to decide as she decided. Let him sit on the land, let him sit.[156]

The immigrant father and son are described, then, as passive and as people who do not know what is good for them, in contrast to the active and "right" character of the Sabra teacher. In the descriptions of 'oley sheyres hapleyte in Yiddish fiction there is, of course, no trace of these characteristics. Their reservation is expressed through the shaping of protagonists who live on the Kibbutz and who do not become "well-built" like Menashe but rather remain lonely and detached and have a hard time fitting into Kibbutz society. Such is the case, for example, of Lipa shvayger (Lipa the silent), the protagonist of Eliezer Rubinshteyn's story "Zayn ershter tants" (His first dance).[157] The detachment of this protagonist is particularly interesting, first because of the literary association of the protagonist's name, which echoes one of the most familiar and influential models of the modern Jewish identity, created by Y. L. Peretz in the character of Bontshe shvayg (Bontshe the Silent, 1894). This is a character of a simple Jew, one of no possessions and no voice, poor and exploited, whose greatness stems from his ability to bear the hardships and injustices of life in humbleness, without bitterness or complaint. Bontshe is the anonymous "lonely man" in the crowd, whose life (and its commemoration after his death) was not driven by passion for power, fame, and fortune. The small reward he asked for in the heavenly tribunal, after a life of making do with very little, conceding, and suffering, was a warm roll with fresh butter, the "small" aspiration (*hasoge* in Sholem Aleichem's sense) of a soul that had already ceased to exist in the physical dimension but whose aspirations nevertheless remained physical. Thus, his soul did not know itself and was unaware of its full possibilities. Is this how Yiddish fiction imagined the character of the Kibbutznik? Lipa shvayger is one of the first portraits of the new Kibbutznik to be published in the Yiddish press in Israel. The Kibbutz described in "Zayn ershter tants" is not one of the veteran Kibbutzim established by pioneers but a new Kibbutz established by camp survivors after the founding of the state. Yet even here the description is of the gap between the egalitarian society in theory and the stratified and alienated society in practice: among the founders of the Kibbutz are a small number of survivors who passed the war years as refugees and enlisted in the Soviet army, and the two types of war experiences created in the Kibbutz two distinct classes—survivors of the concentration camps, identifiable by the number tattooed on their arm, belonged to the high class, while the refugees from the Soviet Union (who were a minority) belonged to the low class. The latter were regarded (and often regarded themselves) as having no right to complain about what they had undergone in the war; they were expected to keep silent and indeed feel ashamed of the "comfort" they enjoyed in those years:

> Those who came from Russia were regarded as happy people, who had been spared by the war, who are unaware of the suffering and horrors people experienced at the hands of the Germans. Those from Auschwitz and other camps, those with numbers on their hands, were the "privileged". . . . They used to sit

> in evenings and tell of their experiences, of their battles with death. . . . At first, the "Russians" hardly spoke. They just used to listen. They did not dare to tell about what they went through and what seemed to them like child's play compared to what "those" had gone through. "When we were in Russia," one of them once said, "we thought that when we came home after the war we would have what to tell for many years to come. Little did we know that there would be no one to tell to, that all our loved ones would no longer be living. Now we are ashamed to speak; now is the time to be silent and listen to what they are telling—the young men and women with the numbers on their hands."[158]

This story sheds light on some of the roots of the silence-of-the-survivors myth: the different classes within the group of survivors caused some of them—those who fled east, to the Soviet Union—to remain silent about their wartime experiences. Even though they, too, had been orphaned by the war, both personally (the loss of loved ones) and socially-culturally (the loss of the world they had known), they were considered as having suffered less and thus as unentitled to speak up. It is interesting that the group of refugees (as opposed to camp survivors) was a majority in the general population of survivors, and yet their status was regarded as lower because their war experiences were regarded as easier.

The protagonist of the story, then, who belongs to the group of camp survivors, has a hard time fitting into the society of his Kibbutz despite the fact that everyone in it is a survivor. He is described as someone who fulfills all of his duties to society, in his capacity as director of cultural activities. Thus, he is the very person who shapes the collective ceremonies of the Kibbutz and thus consolidates its society, but he himself does not participate in these ceremonies. For this, the society imposes sanctions on him: he is reprimanded and asked to explain his behavior. In response, he offers that his orphanhood has left him with no joy of life and with deep feelings of guilt for having stayed alive:

> I will never rejoice again. I'm happy to see them cheerful, radiant and lively, but this is not for me. . . . Who knows if I will ever be capable of this again. It's hard to return to life with its pleasures, seeing . . . what has become of our closest and dearest. I admire them—they have suffered so much and yet have so much zest for life, as if they wanted to make up for all the [lost] time. . . . People say it is a privilege that we stayed alive and we need to be thankful for this every minute; I do not think so. For me it is . . . such a punishment, staying alive, a torture. Understand! Living, eating and drinking, going to sleep and sewing yourself a new garment, reading a book and looking at the blue sky and at the flourishing earth and knowing that they will not do this . . . this is a punishment. This is not a privilege. Staying alive is the punishment for—staying alive.[159]

The writer's political and ideological stance is evident in the ending he gave the story: the protagonist succeeds in overcoming his grief only at the Independence Day celebrations in Tel Aviv. There, among the anonymous dancing masses, he is able to bring himself to join a circle of Hora dancing. According to Almog, the traditional Hora folk dance was "one of the prominent manifestations of the cult of the pioneer group and of the religious fire that was ignited within it, [and it symbolized] the individual's submergence in the group circle and his assimilation into the united Hasidic group."[160] The protagonist joining the circle of dancers is the resolution point of the entire story. The author chose to make this resolution happen in Tel Aviv and not in the Kibbutz, on a national holiday in the company of the "imagined community" and not within the everyday life of the small social circle of active ideologues.

The protagonist agrees to join the circle of dancers on a day that he regards as "holy," but he does not regard everyday life on the Kibbutz as such. The attitude of the Kibbutz Movement toward Tel Aviv was ambivalent from the start: on the one hand, this was the first Hebrew city, and on the other hand, it represented bourgeois life and was cast as the polar opposite of the Kibbutz life of *hagshama* (a concept that roughly translates as fulfillment and was used to denote the active practice of Zionist ideology in one's life). In the story before us, the city is described as a form of settlement that is no less worthy from the national point of view than the Kibbutz.

A more extreme model of detachment from the place and time appears in Ayznman's story "Mentshelekh" (Little-people).[161] Like Lipa the Silent, the protagonist of Ayznman's story, Avigdor, is a solitary survivor who did not start a family. He too sits at Kibbutz meetings feeling disengaged and introverted. But Avigdor does not even take upon himself any jobs or duties in the Kibbutz society and indeed stops attending the meetings. The Kibbutz on which he lives is portrayed very abstractly, with almost no descriptions of the environment or of daily life. Avigdor prefers to spend his time alone in the fields (they too are not described in concrete terms); there, he feels free to surrender himself to his thoughts and imaginations without the constant shame and guilt that accompany them (these include erotic hallucinations about women, as well as memories involving his mother). Another place in which he spends time in solitude is his room, where he likes to carve figures of people on small pieces of wood. Invariably, these figures bear worried or angry expressions. He tries in vain to vary them or at least to understand them. One evening, Avigdor receives an invitation to a memorial evening for his town that was destroyed in the war. It is the first time he has been invited to these memorial events, because he has not kept in touch with the people from his hometown who now live in the city. This protagonist, then, is detached from both social worlds: the one he came to and the one he came from. The invitation awakens in him the realization that he belongs to the world of the past and that his carved figures are not abstract images but the replicas of people he once knew:

> The invitation stirred many thoughts and memories in Avigdor. It suddenly became clear to him that he was still attached to a world he had long since

> renounced. At this late night hour, Avigdor felt more strongly than he had felt at other times his attachment to this vanished world, and as his gaze fell on the shelf, he shuddered: in all his little people, the little people he carved for many years, he recognized familiar faces. He could even call some of them by name. It took so many years, took the arrival of that piece of paper with those lines, for him to open his eyes to the fact that his little people are completely his own and he recognizes them.[162]

This realization changes not only his view of himself but also the people he carved: their expressions become cheerful, and their limbs, which had seemed to him caricatural, now become harmonious. Unlike Rubinshteyn's story, this story ends with the protagonist sinking into the company of his figures and thoroughly enjoying this shame-free immersion.

Avigdor's imagination is shaped as more highly developed than that of Lipa the Silent: he does not need to leave the Kibbutz and travel to the city in order to undergo a transformation that will enable him to assimilate into the new world in which he finds himself. He requires no more than the symbolic representation of the city—in the form of the invitation to the memorial evening—to bring about a change in his personality. This change is opposite in nature to the one that Lipa the Silent undergoes: both men are driven by the feeling of shame over their inability to fit into the Kibbutz society and the new present, but whereas Lipa overcomes this feeling, if only for a single day, Avigdor gives up the desire to fit into the society of the Kibbutz and devotes himself, wholeheartedly and with no inhibition, to the fantasies that fill his soul, including above all his repressed yearning for the world of the past: for his mother, his hometown, and the characters that populated it. This is why Ayznman's hero remains an antihero. "The man is lonesome, lonely," wrote Moshe Bassok to Ayznman after reading this story; "does the togetherness of the Kibbutz really provide no purchase, no door to redemption, to being saved?"[163]

Had the plot of Ayznman's story not been situated in an Israeli Kibbutz of the 1950s, its subject—the yearning for the past and for the life that was destroyed in the shtetl—would probably not have succeeded in creating such a subtle and complex aesthetic and emotional effect. The context in which the events unfold, the Kibbutz, contrasts with the content of the story: the Kibbutz was associated with youth and with the public domain, with a collective gaze fixed on the future, and with a transformation of private passions into a drive for society's collective self-realization, whereas the protagonist of "Mentshelekh" is the opposite of all these things—his name is the name of an old man who is not a Sabra, and his gaze is fixed on the past, which is the object of his passions. The latter remain in his own private domain and are not assimilated into any collective, or even into the urban space of the survivors from his own hometown. The protagonist of "Mentshelekh," then, remains a separate, detached, marginal individual. These qualities and the tension generated by the contrast between the protagonist's character and his environment are the factors that create the story's complexity. The story's title echoes the titles of two canonical stories of modern Yiddish literature: "Dos kleyne mentshele" (The little man, 1864), by Mendele Moykher Sforim, and Sholem Aleichem's abovementioned work *Kleyne mentshelekh mit kleyne hasoges* (1901). In choosing the title "Mentshelekh," Ayznman associated himself with a tradition marked by a critical attitude toward the shtetl, like Mendele's, or at least an ambivalent one, like Sholem Aleichem's. Ayznman also applied this approach to the Kibbutz: the protagonist feels alienation from the Kibbutz society, but at the same time the Kibbutz gives him a private space, a "small home," in which his artistic creation takes place, and his immersion in it releases him of his inhibitions. Ayznman testified that the same was true of himself: "Only here, in the domestic silence of my own four walls, did I feel that somewhere inside me a train was still traveling, its engine racing and the wheels sounding the turmoil and terror of those days. I tried to redeem those . . . gray people—passengers who are still in motion, still dragging themselves, and like me, have not yet found a station."[164] So, writing about present life in the Kibbutz, as part of the Israel-theme, enabled Ayznman to deal with the past without becoming submerged in it. The tension and sometimes the clash between the environment in which the story takes place and its content, given the readers' associations with this environment and this content, yielded a complex work that introduced something fresh into the landscape of Yiddish literature of the time. An early example of this innovation appeared in Ayznman's story "Arum beys-hamedresh" (Around the beit-midrash).[165] It revolved around a question that was almost not discussed (even and maybe especially not in Hebrew literature): What was the life of old people on a Kibbutz like? The answer to this question involved descriptions of a space and way of life that were atypical of—even antithetical to—the common literary descriptions of the Kibbutz: the story depicted an old-age home and especially the beit-midrash (the place of Torah study) set up within it for its elderly residents, who were not from the generation of pioneers who had built the Kibbutz but rather were the parents of the Holocaust survivors, the refugees from the Soviet Union. It is possible that this aspect of life on the Kibbutz and indeed of life in Israel was never discussed in Hebrew literature.

Ayznman's stories about the Kibbutz are notable not only for their expansion of the thematic range—through their shaping of the protagonists and the cultural and temporal spaces in which they act—but also for their formal aspects. The prose he wrote, like the prose written in Hebrew in those years, sought to free itself of "the bonds of realism," as Gershon Shaked put it—that is, to distance itself from the pole of realistic description and social criticism articulated by an omniscient and authoritative narrator or in the first-person plural. In his stories, Ayznman moved closer to the pole of the impressionist-poetic description articulated from within the boundaries of the first-person singular consciousness.[166]

When the first Yiddish novel about the Kibbutz was published in Israel, a small corpus of works that addressed this subject as part of the Israel-theme had already accumulated, mostly short stories. The novel *Af shmole trotuarn* (On narrow sidewalks) was the first long work of Yosl Birshteyn, who had started out as a poet and turned to prose after moving to Israel from Australia in 1950.[167] Although he lost his family and cultural home in the war, Birshteyn was not himself a Holocaust survivor but a refugee—he left Eastern Europe for Australia in 1936—and in this he differs from the other writers of his generation in Israel. The story describes a group of "small" characters in Kibbutz Yilon, from winter (before Purim) to "the end of summer" (after Sukkot). The time in which the plot takes place is not a festive "big time" but an everyday prosaic "small time," which happens "after the holidays" and beyond them (the novel includes no descriptions of Passover, Rosh Ha-Shana, or Yom Kippur). The Kibbutz as a place is also described as a prosaic small setting. The novel's opening scene takes place in the entrance to the dining hall, not in the hall itself, and in the fourth watch of night, just before daybreak. In addition to this, the work portrays many "liminal moments": the Kibbutz is on the verge of entering the fourth decade of its existence, and its protagonists are on the verge of middle age. These descriptions of the Kibbutz as a liminal place (like the ma'abara) are surprising, since it is supposed to be a symbol of the connection to the country and its land and of the setting down of roots.

The main difference in the shaping of the Kibbutz between this novel and the works of Rubinshteyn and Ayznman lies in the fact that Birshteyn's protagonists, like the author, are not Holocaust survivors. The novel's protagonists—Ze'ev, Asia, Menuha, and several supporting characters—came to pre-state Israel from Eastern Europe as young Zionists before the war and founded the Kibbutz. Two other protagonists probably came after the establishment of the state (Lotti, who was born in Germany and moved to the Kibbutz apparently on the eve of the Holocaust, and Daniel, a native of "an English-speaking country"). The novel does mention survivors: Efraim and Mashele Zilberman, who came with Efraim's son from a previous marriage (Fayvl), and Golde, described briefly at the end of the novel as someone who showed an ungrateful attitude toward the Kibbutz and left it "slamming the door behind her." But the novel is told not from their point of view but from the point of view of the characters who are the veteran-founders of the Kibbutz (or from the point of view of 'olim who are not survivors and not from Eastern Europe, like Lotti and Daniel). Even when the omniscient narrator follows the consciousness of the survivors, it retains the values of the veterans, and through this lens, the survivors are judged as miserable and pitiable people who do not suit Kibbutz life, do not belong to it, and will not stay in it.[168] This judgment is especially conspicuous in light of the veterans' attitude toward Lotti and Daniel, who as I said are not survivors from Eastern Europe and who do no physical labor but rather belong to the intelligentsia: Lotti is an English teacher, and Daniel is a writer who had to stop his brief work as a shepherd after being shot, apparently by infiltrators, and thereafter devotes himself to writing. But this kind of difference did not prevent the group of founders from seeing Lotti and Daniel as fit to assimilate into the Kibbutz society, in contrast to the Eastern European Holocaust survivors. When Udi (the son of Ze'ev and Menuha) learns that his mother has started socializing with the Zilberman family (and especially with Fayvl) and has even started speaking Yiddish with them, he is ashamed and keeps a distance from her, because he hates the language: "She made new friends who were not to his liking. Zilberman, Mashele and Fayvl sit there every evening and make noise. They speak Yiddish, a language that is incomprehensible to him and which he hates. He wondered what common interest his mother has with them. . . . He was ashamed of his mother for befriending these people and saw it as an insult. . . . He regards himself as deprived and carries a deep hatred."[169] This attitude of the veteran members of the Kibbutz, and especially the young Sabras, toward the new immigrant-survivors is characteristic of the Hebrew fiction written about the Kibbutz (for example, Shamir's *Hu halaḵ baŚadot* and Hendel's *'Anašim 'aḥerim hem*, mentioned earlier).

Another common characteristic of the Kibbutz in Hebrew fiction and in *Af shmole trotuarn* is that almost all the nuclear families are broken and alienated following the couple's betrayal of one another. In Birshteyn's novel, there is a "love triangle," or more accurately a three-way relationship (since love is hardly described as part of it) between Ze'ev and Lotti, who is married to Daniel. Ze'ev's two previous wives (Asia and Menuha) also live in the Kibbutz, as do the children and the elderly parents of this threesome. Alongside the disintegration of the nuclear families, the novel describes a close family life with the broader circles of these families, between the protagonists and their parents and between the grandchildren and grandparents:

> Now Yilon was no longer a children's game, a whim of young men and women looking for a life filled with romance. Yilon was full of mothers and fathers, grandfathers and grandmothers. A seriousness had settled on their eyelids and the burden of life weighed down their shoulders. These were people whose eyes more than once betrayed despair and bitterness and in whom emptiness and sadness sometimes crept into a hidden corner of their soul. Now they no longer danced every evening after work, and no longer sang as they walked out to the field with shiny sickles over their shoulders.[170]

This is an expression of a central theme in Yiddish fiction—the Jewish family and its annals. This combination of the two opposite portrayals of family life on the Kibbutz yielded a unique picture of it: life on the Kibbutz according to

Birshteyn did not spell separation from the extended family; this is in contrast to the descriptions that prevailed in Hebrew fiction, where the grandparents are not alive, and in contrast to the perception that prevailed in the Yiddish-speaking public in Israel about Kibbutz life.[171] Moreover, the founders in the novel maintain a constant and warm connection to their past in Eastern Europe and are not alienated from it. For example, Ze'ev tells his Sabra son about the Passover customs his family kept in his hometown, which were passed on to him by his grandfather. Another Kibbutz member (Hasia) likes to tell Udi about the life that had existed in the home of his grandfather and grandmother. Udi's grandmother lives on the Kibbutz, but she has not become a "Kibbutznik": she is described as someone who covers her hair with a wig and shows her grandson how she performs the *Mitzve* of *Hafrashat Chala* (separating the challah bread). It is also noted that there was a beit-midrash for the grandfathers and grandmothers in the Kibbutz, where they not only prayed but also were served kosher food. By describing the past in Eastern Europe in purely religious terms, the novel confirms the myth of the "negation of exile," which posited a dichotomy between the past in Eastern Europe (which was identified with religion and with Yiddish) and present life in Israel (which was supposedly secular and conducted in Hebrew). Yet on the other hand, the Sabra is described in the novel not as someone who is raised to believe that he is a "new man" born "of the sea" but rather as someone raised with an awareness of the fact that he is one more link in his family chain and an awareness of his family's life in Eastern Europe. The description of this life is not idyllic or romantic (Udi's grandfather left his grandmother and refused to grant her a divorce; his great-grandmother is described as resembling a man). The link to the past, to exile, and to Yiddish is presented in the novel not as a professed ideological position but as part of the everyday life of the protagonists. Even when Birshteyn is called on to explain his own connection to the past, he does so not in ideological or political terms but in naturalistic-psychological terms: "One cannot escape one's own past. . . . I can destroy my past and leave it like a felled tree, but fresh roots will sprout from the same trunk, and the tree will be a tree again. . . . Not only do I carry my father's life in me, but I feel that, despite all the new worlds that I've absorbed into myself, with every day I am turning more and more into my father."[172]

Kibbutz life, then, was described not as the opposite of life in exile but as its continuation in a new incarnation of sorts, since this new life is not identical to life in the shtetls of Eastern Europe. Those who left the shtetl before the war and their children only recall that place in their memories and imagine it stereotypically. The physical and ideological world in which they live is no longer that same world.

Birshteyn's focus on quotidian life in the Kibbutz and on the private, small lives of his protagonists, which are far removed from big ideas, echoes a tendency that became increasingly common in descriptions of the Kibbutz in the Hebrew prose of those years. For instance, Yigal Mossinson's novel *Derek̠ gever* (A man's way) features a character of a writer who is writing a book about the Kibbutz. One of the protagonists reproaches him for mythologizing their lives:

> You're making our lives into some strange and unrealistic idyll, a place where passionate speeches are delivered and everyone goes on missions for the sake of the people and Zionism and volunteers with fanfare to join the Brigade and the Palmach. In other words, heroics. And yet you know that this is not the full picture. Me you can't fool. You know this is not the full truth. Listen, listen, don't stop and don't shake your hand. I believe that you don't want to lie—but you're afraid, Nahum, like me, just like me, of coming up face to face with reality and with the society in which you live, just like me. Perhaps you may tell me, please, why are you idealizing our life in the Kibbutz?[173]

It is interesting to compare this claim with a conversation in *Af shmole trotuarn* between one of the protagonists and Daniel, the writer, who, like the writer in *Derek̠ gever*, is also busy writing a book about his Kibbutz:

> "You have permission to describe me as I am. But do not adorn me. Write the whole truth and do not cover up anything. And have no fear of what the readers will say. Listen only to your own heart. . . . And do not depict me as a hero. . . . There are no longer any heroes in the Kibbutz, just ordinary people with their weaknesses and their various qualities, good and evil. And there's a lot of evil here. In me too. . . . If you plan to describe Yilon as a paradise populated by angels . . . it will not do. When I read about a Kibbutznik who is always thinking only about the Kibbutz, about ideals, about country and socialism, and all he ever has in mind is the fight for a better tomorrow, as described in the propaganda, I throw this book away." "And do you think that ʻAqiva is not the real Kibbutznik,?" asked Daniel. "No," replied Katriel. "Not ʻAqiva but me and people like me, those who work day after day, for years . . . and never have time to raise their heads, to go on missions, to deal with politics and ideologies; we who do the manual labor and not those at the helm are the real Kibbutzniks. We are the Kibbutz." "And do you not appreciate the ideal, Katri'el?" . . . "It has become a habit to me. Habit is the strongest ideology."[174]

The tendency of giving a realistic description of life on the Kibbutz, without hiding the protagonists' faults, their limitations, or their simple quotidian lives far removed from big ideas and from the needs of the nation, increasingly grew and developed in the Hebrew literature in Israel in the 1950s. The Yiddish criticism that reviewed this novel in Israel was apparently unaware of this trend and saw it as an original and innovative stance of the young Birshteyn.[175] But in fact, the novel's originality and innovativeness lie in the sophisticated and innovative literary models that were available to Birshteyn and on which he drew in applying the realistic description to the personal, private lives of his protagonists in the Kibbutz. This helped him resist the temptation to make the lives of his protagonists once again into an allegory for the big home, for the Israeli society of his day. And indeed, the novel makes no mention of the dramatic events that took place during those years in Israel and in the Kibbutzim. Unlike Ayznman, whose story "Mentshelekh" separates the individual and society (both urban and Kibbutz society), Birshteyn separates Kibbutz society from the general national collective. The consequence of this separation is disturbing and even threatening, for if the Kibbutz as the cradle of the avant-garde forces of the new Jewish nation has ceased to exist as such, what force will fill its place?

Describing the social aspect of the Kibbutz as separate from the national one was markedly novel against the backdrop of the Hebrew literature of the time. The plot of *Derek̠ gever*, for example, is driven by the tension between the individual and society. This tension is represented through current events that shook the Yishuv and the young state and indeed through their dramatization (and even melodramatization). The tension between the two poles created an effect of an externalized rebellion against the political, cultural, and Kibbutz establishments. Two other important novels that dealt with the Kibbutz and tried to focus on the life of the individual are *Ḥedwa we'Ani uFarašat qoroteynu ba'Ir tel-'aviv* (1953; published in English as *Hedva and I*, 1957), by Aharon Meged, and *Maqom 'aḥer* (1966; published in English as *Elsewhere, Perhaps*, 1985), by Amos Oz, who belonged already to a different generation of writers. Both authors succeeded only partially in this mission: *Hedva and I* indeed described a world of "small people" but did not manage to keep them in the Kibbutz (or to keep itself in the realm of drama, veering instead toward the realm of comedy). The Kibbutz, according to this novel, is not a place for small people; only the big city, Tel Aviv, suits them (and only the form of comedy). In *Elsewhere, Perhaps*, Oz also tried to tell the story of "flesh and blood human beings . . . who know pain and suffering, ugliness and nausea. But mercy and joy and brotherhood are also not foreign to them."[176] Yet his protagonists cannot help but concern themselves with weighty subjects, like relations with the Palestinians, the Zionist revolution, and its victims. His main protagonists, and primarily Reuven Harish, are of a "high" origin (German) rather than a "low" one (Eastern European), and in general, members of the Kibbutz are shaped in the novel through contrast with the other—that is, as the opposites of the "simple people" (the Tiberias fishermen). The high status and sophistication of the Kibbutz members is shaped through many textual details and above all the name of their Kibbutz—*Metzudat Ram* (literally, the high fortress). Yilon, by contrast, is a name that has no meaning, high or low. The few dramatic events that occur in the novel, like Menuha and Fayvl's wedding and Fayvl's suicide, are described in a reserved tone that seems to want to take the edge off the drama. This attempt to undermine any dramatic potential is expressed also in the novel's structure and in the shaping of its plot:

more than the common structure of the traditional epos, which unfolds according to the rules of the dramatic genre (conflict that reaches a climax and leads to resolution), the structure of *Af shmole trotuarn* fits what Shaked called "a story of characters" or "a social story."[177] The effect of this story on the reader is not created through the plot, since very little happens in it, and the events that take place have very little influence on the psychological or existential development of the characters. What, then, is the effect that Birshteyn created on his reader, and how did he create it? A clue is offered in these words that he wrote in 1956, two years before the book's publication: "Some writers build the story's tension on plot. The plot ends—the tension ends. This is certainly also a way, but it seems to me that when the tension is built upon the relation between the image and the form, the tension remains in the experience of the reader for a longer time after he has finished [reading] the story."[178]

Thus, like Ayznman's technique, Birshteyn built the tension in his story not on the plot but on the tension between the place in which it occurs (the Kibbutz) and the "image" that takes place in it—the nature of the characters that populate it and their lives. One of the prime examples of tension that is a product of this relation between image and form is writing a novel whose theme is the Kibbutz but that lacks all drama. This contrasts with the expectation of the (Yiddish and Hebrew) reader, who was accustomed to seeing the Kibbutz and its members as an "advance military post" in a constant war: war over the country's borders and its land, war in the Jewish and the human history and psychology, war with the challenges of the local and world economy and the social issues that it raises, war with the Mediterranean climate, and more. And here this novel indeed takes place on a Kibbutz and in its public arena (twenty-two of the book's twenty-six chapters take place in the communal dining hall and other communal sites in the Kibbutz), yet it is concerned not with the big issues but with the private, small, and indeed petty lives of its protagonists. The "narrow sidewalks" of the title are not just a metaphor for the crowded nature of Kibbutz society; they are also a site where the balance of power between those who walk in it is tested time and again: the weak step down from the narrow sidewalks onto the lawn, while the strong stay on them.

Unlike the populist and superficial perceptions of the Kibbutz that cast it as a space that is opposed to that of the ma'abara, in Birshteyn's Kibbutz novel the protagonists never actually succeed in extricating themselves from the liminal area in which they first settled and undergoing a change of identity. The novel's ending also takes place in an in-between zone: it ends on the night after the Sukkot harvest celebration—in other words, after the period of the holidays and on the verge of the new year. The novel's protagonists have undergone no significant development in their character or identity. Their surprising qualities—namely, that they grow old, that they are family people who bear the burden of providing for their families, and that they are connected to their past in Eastern Europe—are what made this complex literary representation of the Kibbutz attractive and indeed disturbing to Ayznman's and Birshteyn's readers, since they paint a picture of the demise of the Kibbutz as the ideological standard-bearer and the national spirit of the new Israeli society. As it approached its middle age, the Kibbutz did not experience an ideological renewal but only a waning of spiritual passion. Birshteyn left the Kibbutz in 1960. Ayznman, by contrast, chose to live his whole life in the framework of the Kibbutz and saw it as his home. The Kibbutz continued to appear in their later works as well, but no other novel devoted entirely to the subject of the Kibbutz appeared in the realm of Yiddish fiction.[179]

6. Tel Aviv

Modernity was created in the big cities of Europe, and big cities are therefore the symbol of modernity.[180] And indeed, modern Yiddish culture was created mostly in big cities in Eastern Europe and the United States. Cities provided the masses that flocked to them from the periphery with many new and varied work opportunities; the masses were those who churned the wheels of the economy and culture in the cities. Abundance and surplus, foreignness and alienation are the characteristics of the urban society: on the one hand, the masses who fill the city create a diverse human mosaic, but on the other hand, the individual's stay in the city is usually temporary, his life there is expensive, and his time is typically devoted to work. The fast turnover of city residents makes it hard to establish close and intimate relationships between residents and between them and their environment. The inevitable routine of rubbing up against masses of strangers in the city streets or on its public transportation underscores the sense of foreignness and alienation that stands between the city's residents. The crowdedness of city life emphasizes the separations between its rich and poor populations. The distance between them is maintained and indeed deepened through their employer-employee relations. The city is the place of the imagined national community, the opposite of the intimate traditional community.

Unlike in the European culture and literature, where the common opposite of the city was the village[181] (and by extension, the "old world"—religion, community, and the ideal and traditional family life), in modern Yiddish culture and literature the Eastern European Jewish town replaced the village as the opposite of the big city. But here the picture is far more complex since even the shtetl had a somewhat urban character, as Jews were generally not allowed to be farmers and so existed within the shtetl as somewhat urban agents, as merchants and craftsmen.[182] Odesa, Warsaw, and Lodzh were, however, relatively new places of dwelling for Jews, and they offered a very different setting. Becoming integrated into these cities, economically and socially, meant forgoing or canceling one's separate Jewish identity. These historical-political circumstances led to a curious reality in which, despite the fact that the Jews of Eastern Europe were an urban class economically, and even though they pioneered the immigration to the Eastern European cities and were among the founders of the industry in these cities, their development was halted by antisemitic policies, as was their full integration into society.[183] Their existence in these cities therefore remained largely communal, and indeed they were so described by Yiddish writers of the period. It was a synthesis of a modern culture facing modern challenges and yet having at its disposal a premodern set of communal tools to handle them.[184] How was the tension between the national identity and the particular identity expressed in the literary image of Tel Aviv? Was the big city still a source of inspiration for the Yiddish writers to produce a "new word"?

Earlier we saw Tel Aviv as a center of Yiddish culture, and here I present its literary image in the work of ʻoley sheyres hapleyte. In the Hebrew literature (in the period of the Yishuv and in Israel), the attitude toward Tel Aviv was ambivalent.[185] On the one hand, the city was a symbol of the new and modernist Jewish culture, while on the other hand, the Zionist movement sought to connect the "new Jew" to the land, as representing the opposite of the old Jewish life in Eastern Europe, whose nature was urban. So, for example, in *Hu halaḵ baŚadot*, Tel Aviv was identified with Yiddish culture (whose representative is the painter Yosl Brumberg)—that is, with the "uprooted" and "disconnected" avant-garde-bohemian pole of modernism, as opposed to the "rooted" national, physical pole represented by the Kibbutz.[186] In Yiddish culture, the fact that Tel Aviv was the first city in the modern world to be established as a Jewish city (and not an agricultural colony) made it a symbol of the Zionist identity.[187] The sheyres hapleyte ʻaliya, as noted earlier, was largely "an urban ʻaliya, whose life revolved around the city. . . . For the most part, this ʻaliya continued the work patterns that had characterized it in its countries of origin."[188] These immigrants were noted by their education and professional training, especially in the areas of crafts and industry, administration and professional bureaucracy, and free professions.[189]

In many of the works, Tel Aviv is not the only site where the plot takes place; rather, it features as a horizon in relation to some other site: in Perlov's *Dzshebelye* it is the opposite of Jaffa, which did not become "Jewish" even after it was occupied. Zekharye Karlsbakh, the protagonist, aspires to settle in Tel Aviv, and his move there marks the culmination of the process of his professional, emotional, and familial rehabilitation; in Man's *In a farvorloztn dorf*, Tel Aviv is the traditional opposite of the village as a financial, administrative, and cultural center, analogous to the contrast that existed in Poland between Warsaw and the village of Kokhar; and in Granatshteyn's maʻabara stories, Tel Aviv (and especially Rothschild Boulevard) is described as a place to which the lost and detached protagonists escape, a place that can contain their foreignness and their despair because in it they are anonymous. In the lives of the women and the children of the immigrant housing projects, the city was barely present, except as a place to which one goes (and mostly the men go) to earn a living. In Rubinshteyn's and Ayznman's Kibbutz stories, Tel Aviv appears as the opposite of the intimate Kibbutz life because of the mass cultural events that take place in it; in Birshteyn's *Af shmole trotuarn*, the city is the object of fantasies of escape (that are not realized) from the claustrophobic Kibbutz life.

The modernity that developed in Europe's big cities (and to a large extent also created them) also gave birth to the form of the novel, and especially the urban novel. It is therefore surprising to discover that the 'oley sheyres hapleyte writers hardly wrote any novels about post-state Tel Aviv. While Hebrew Israeli fiction did gradually move closer to the urban theme beginning in the late 1950s (for instance, in Meged's abovementioned *Hedva and I*), post-Holocaust Yiddish fiction gradually retreated from this theme. Perhaps this retreat was an expression of the disappointment from the big promises that modernity had held for Yiddish writers, the same modernity from which Yankev Glatshteyn had wanted, as early as the eve of the Holocaust, to turn back "slamming the door shut" into the comfort of the traditional and imagined ethnic-religious "ghetto." The 'oley sheyres hapleyte writers wrote about Tel Aviv mostly in the short forms of prose: short stories, novellas, and feuilletons, which were printed in press publications (another modern form) that were distinctly grounded in the urban environment in which they were created.

The only Yiddish novel I found that appeared as a book and whose plot takes place entirely in Tel Aviv is *Flora ingber: A hoyz in tel oviv* (Flora Ingber: A house in Tel Aviv).[190] This is a very mediocre work, which suffers from many problems of content and form, but it powerfully illustrates the difficulties Yiddish writers faced in their attempts to describe Tel Aviv as the setting of an urban novel in Israel of the 1950s and 1960s. The source of inspiration for *Flora ingber* was apparently one of the canonical urban works of modern Yiddish literature—Sholem Asch's trilogy *Dray shtet* (*Three Cities*, 1929–1931), whose plot takes place in St. Petersburg, Warsaw, and Moscow on the eve of and during the 1917 revolution.[191] In this time and this space, the main contrasts that characterized the big city in the urban novel—wealth versus poverty, the private domestic sphere versus the tumultuous and threatening outer sphere, tradition versus innovation—reached a dramatic high point. Perlov tried to shape the protagonist, Flora Ingber, as the later Israeli equivalent of Zakhary Mirkin, the trilogy's protagonist. Like him, Flora is described as a bohemian type whose life is complicated by becoming involved in an unusual family setting that quickly falls apart: in the trilogy, Mirkin falls in love with the mother of his young fiancée, leading him to call off his wedding to her, and eventually it is his father who marries her; similarly, Ingber marries the father of her lover. But Zakhary Mirkin was a lawyer, the son of a prominent, wealthy, and successful lawyer in St. Petersburg. They belonged to the decadent high-bourgeois class and could enjoy all the pleasures of the big city, the conventional as well as the more eccentric ones. How could Perlov create a parallel character in Tel Aviv of the 1950s? It did not have the size or the intensity that characterized the urban landscape in the big cities of Europe and the United States; their wealth or social, economic, and cultural tradition; or the time during which were amassed the money and the tradition that made these cities the site of the modern novel. Tel Aviv as a theme also lacked the sense of revulsion and alienation of the writers toward the city and the decadence that characterizes people who have accumulated money, power, and control in inverse proportion to their emotional wisdom and moral integrity. Of course, Yiddish writers did feel difficulty, foreignness, and sometimes even alienation toward life in the new Israel, which Tel Aviv symbolized, but their recognition of the importance of statehood and their joy in this achievement were stronger than these feelings. And of course, Tel Aviv did have various mechanisms of power and a social stratum of high bourgeoisie with its own unique characteristics, but writers like Perlov did not know these circles from direct experience. If certain Yiddish writers did succeed in finding a place within the mechanisms of power, they did not describe them in their work, whether because they lacked the courage to expose the corruption or because they hoped to benefit from it.

To create a bourgeois heroine, Perlov had to distance her from the workers' circles, and indeed he described her as having been a Revisionist before the establishment of the state. But she still has neither the wealth nor the tradition that characterized the Russian high bourgeoisie, to which Mirkin-the-father aspired to belong. By contrast, his son, after moving to Warsaw, rediscovers his national belonging, his family, and his identity in their new worker-revolutionary version. All Flora Ingber can do in Tel Aviv is rediscover her conservatism, which is embodied in the value of family. To start a family, she abandons the petit-bourgeois hedonistic life of the city in favor of an idyllic life of agriculture in the country. Perlov could not describe a sharp change in the life of his protagonist that would resemble the shift that came with Mirkin's move from the high-bourgeois life in St. Petersburg to the life of a penniless teacher in Warsaw, and he had to rely on the traditional literary contrast between the city and the country (though he does not even give a convincing description of the unique country life in Israel).

The protagonist's failure to maintain a home and a family in the city is a traditional difficulty of the urban novel.[192] But Yiddish writers had unique problems in attempting to create an urban novel after the Holocaust in the new nation-state: as Holocaust survivors who had lived as refugees for many years, they had experienced a dissolution of the two spheres, the private and the social, and aspired to restore the boundary between them. They had also experienced the destruction of modern culture, in its European and its Jewish versions, and had lost faith in both. This led to a withdrawal into the local national culture and to a strong focus on rebuilding home and family. The relative homogeneity of the residents of Tel Aviv, alongside its modest size, buildings, and economy, the lack of industry, and the technologically backward transportation system—all these made the writing of the urban novel difficult but enabled short works of prose that described Tel Aviv on the unique model of the (small and medium) Eastern European Jewish town. Thus, the novel *Flora Ingber* illustrates a double failure: a failure to shape Tel Aviv as a modern big city and the failure of Yiddish fiction to tackle within the form of the novel the theme of the city in the national space and to shape a new heroine that would represent life in this city. To a large extent, this was an inevitable failure for its time, since in the 1950s and early 1960s, the Yiddish writer lacked a deep sense of despair and alienation toward the depicted present as well as a social environment that had turned its back on him and let him down, one whose wealth was accumulated in an inverse relation to its values and whose hypocrisy was second only to its greed and lust for power, and thus he could not create a modern urban novel. In present-day Tel Aviv, it would seem that conditions are ripe for the writing of such a novel, if only it held any Yiddish writers or readers.

Another reason for the novel's failure is the disillusionment of its readers with revolutionary ideologies, whether because these failed to deliver on their promises (like communism or the Bundist Jewish socialism) or because they succeeded (like Zionism in general and its socialist strains in particular). Criticism of the state and even revolutionary ideas were at the core of the Yiddish urban novel, but it was hard for the writers to continue with this line after the Holocaust and in Israel. And as Irving Howe explained, "Political fiction has not flourished in the relative stability of the Western countries during the decades after the Second World War. Neither conservative statis nor social democratic moderation . . . are able to inspire first-rate novels dealing with political themes."[193] An example of this is found in the novel *Di vide fun a revolutsiyoner: A politisher roman* (Confessions of a revolutionary: A political novel). Its protagonist (Hersh-mekhl) is a communist revolutionary who was disillusioned during the Holocaust years and became a staunch opponent of communism and an ardent supporter of the Jewish national idea. Tel Aviv is described in this novel with the familiar means of the urban novel (the speaker roams the city, and the urban topography is described in detail, noting names of streets and institutions), but the city does not exist as an independent theme in the novel. Its influence is drawn primarily from contrasting it to another space—the ma'abara: "When Hersh-mekhl first came to Tel Aviv—came from the Beer Ya'akov camp—his breath, it seems, stopped for a while, ceased from admiration and from pleasure, and also—from resentment. Beer Ya'akov camp and Tel Aviv are two opposite and hostile worlds. A stark and screaming contrast."[194] The contrast between the city and the ma'abara appears to awaken in the protagonist his revolutionary rage at the injustice of the state's handling of the ma'abara. Yet when he comes to Tel Aviv, and even more so when he encounters the frustrating party and state bureaucracies, the protagonist seems to lose his ideological sting, and he focuses on justifying the status quo and does not try to improve it through criticism:

> When he goes to Tel Aviv, he goes only to the party headquarters. A limited stretch of road from the Central Station to that alley near Allenby. Sometimes he also has to be on 'Aliya Street, where the offices of the Immigration Department of the Jewish Agency are located. Here he needs to get the first financial support. . . . He must stand and sit for long hours in line and wait. . . . But Hersh-mekhl is content. He always looks with two pairs of eyes—the historical, and the current, and all those small, temporary twists and turns of the present reality do not lessen and do not disguise the great, historical reality. Even all the other pains—whether necessary or unnecessary, do not disrupt his sense of historical happiness. Happiness in a lofty sense, which only people like Hersh-mekhl and his kind can feel. Hundreds of generations of Jews yearned for this moment, and there is compensation for the crying blood of the slain and the strangled—a country of our own, a language of our own, without fear, without a national inferiority complex.[195]

Hersh-mekhl's heroism during the Holocaust, his courage, and his dedication to the Jewish national project give him no special credit when he stands before state officials asking for work. Eventually, he finds work as a gravedigger thanks to his own connections, without waiting for any dubious favors from the "Employment Office" or from the party of which he was a member, both of which let him down (and indeed he eventually leaves the party). After his disillusionment with the communist ideas, the old revolutionary fervor is replaced by a national-social conservatism with a focus on his own personal survival and a withdrawal from tackling social issues. Still, the protagonist does not reach a point of nihilism and a breakdown of identity. His national identity remains stable despite the disappointments. From the point of view of the former revolutionary and ideologue, Tel Aviv is portrayed as a promising city that fails to deliver on its promise.

A similar experience is described in the short story "Der onheyb" (The beginning), by Perlov.[196] Binyomin was a prominent Zionist activist in his city before the Holocaust. When he reaches Israel at a late age, he is certain he will be given a respectable position on the strength of his long and dedicated work for the party. But that is not the case: he is forced to travel back and forth to various offices in Tel Aviv, to plead his case before indifferent clerks who do not recognize the importance of his contribution and even lecture him that there is dignity in all work and that even the country's leaders started out as simple laborers. The friends with whom he came to Israel and who had not been involved in any public activity before the war find work and settle long before him. Finally, he manages to get a job, like Hersh-mekhl, through personal connections—as a garbage collector. To demonstrate his insult and his resistance to this humiliation, he comes to work wearing the same suit he used to wear during his Zionist activity before the war, a suit that he insisted on carrying with him throughout the war years, believing that he would need it once he arrived in Israel and resumed his public activity. In both these stories, the success of finding work is in fact a failure and indeed a deep insult to the protagonists, but it is no less a failure of the new state, which managed with shameful speed to grow an indifferent and corrupt bureaucratic system. In this sense, Tel Aviv, the big city, operates on connections and personal ties, so that in fact it is a small town.

A similar description of Tel Aviv as an alienated and even cruel labor market is found in Avrom Karpinovitsh's sentimental story "Di mame vet nokh spondzhe makhn" (Mummy will yet be able to do her floor-washing).[197] The story won first prize at the literary competition held by the *LN* in 1954 for the best story on the Israel-theme. Its protagonist is a child (Shloymele), and the story is told from his point of view. This point is significant, since modern Yiddish literature (certainly after the Holocaust) targeted an audience of the interim generation, not young readers and certainly not children. Thus, most of its protagonists were middle-aged men and women, unlike the contemporaneous Hebrew literature, whose protagonists were mostly young. The story describes the protagonist and his mother, who live in Petah-Tikva. The story's sentimental aspect is grounded in the mother-child axis and in the child's keen awareness of their unstable financial situation.

The story opens with a dramatic turn for the worse in the mother and son's already difficult predicament. One morning, the mother falls ill and asks her son to go to the "lady" who employs her as a housemaid and inform her that she will be absent from work; otherwise, the lady will hire someone else in her place. Shloymele's concern for his mother's health and for their financial situation is mixed with a big disappointment, since he was supposed to go on a school trip that very morning. He forgoes the trip and heads out to fulfill his mother's request. The wealthy lady from Frishman Street not only does not show consideration for the vulnerable predicament of the mother and her son but indeed shuts the door in his face after announcing with great demonstrativeness that she will promptly go to the "housemaids market" on Sheynkin Street and bring back another maid.[198] Shloymele's mother had been avoiding that market because there were maids of Yemeni origin and they had called her "Shiknaz, Yidesh."

As a result, Shloymele decides to take a job, at an earlier age than normal, as a popsicle vendor at a movie theater, to make up for the lost income. On his way there, he roams the city streets as a stranger among strangers and thus is exposed to the diverse and polarized human mosaic of the city population. He comes to be aware of his mother's foreignness among women of other ethnic backgrounds (like the women at the Sheynkin market) and other social classes (like the lady from Frishman Street). His own foreignness among the children of the neighborhood also drove him to the city: he loves to play the piano. Out of a wish to protect his hands, his mother does not allow him to sell sabra fruit, like the other children, despite the relatively good profits to be made in this work. She hopes that the job in the movie theater will help develop his talent: there is an old piano there, on which he has been given permission to practice between screenings. In modern culture, the city is shaped as a place that attracts the talented and exceptional or unusual people. But when Shloymele arrives at his new job, the older workers start abusing him and eventually injure his hands. To himself he explains their behavior as resulting from his inferiority—his young age and his low social-economic status: his mother is a mere housemaid, his shoes are worn out, and they live in a poor neighborhood. But the reader understands what the protagonist could not fathom: his coworkers attacked him because of the sense of inferiority they themselves feel in his presence—his situation can still improve, whereas their chances of attaining a different profession and achieving upward mobility are very low. At the end of the story, Shloymele comforts himself with the hope that his mother will get well, return to work in full force, and buy him a piano, and he will be able to devote himself to music.[199] Tel Aviv, then, is not described in the story as a cultural center with concert halls, music schools, and music teachers, a place that attracts the talented but poor individual from the periphery and in which he can evolve and find his luck. Rather, this individual, the immigrant child, is described as someone who is submerged in a frustrating reality of poverty, alienation, and even violence that only gets worse in the city. This description of poverty-stricken children and women of Eastern European origin is an important corrective to an impression that took hold in the literature and scholarship according to which only immigrants of Mizrahi origin suffered this fate.[200]

Unlike New York, the city to which Yiddish fiction's most famous child-protagonist—Motl Peysi the cantor's son, Sholem Aleichem's protagonist (1907–1916)—immigrated, Tel Aviv is not described as providing the working child with either entertainment or pleasures: the movie theater is his place of work, not a place where he goes to enjoy his day off, and in this story there is no buying of food or drink like the ice cream, soda, and chewing gum that enthralled Motl in Manhattan. In Tel Aviv, the protagonist is not exposed to the "wonders" of that place and time, like the escalators, elevators, and subway that Motl discovers in Manhattan. The times in which these two protagonists "lived" also affected their different fates. Motl came to New York before World War I, and the author's view of the future that awaited the Jews is expressed in the shaping of Motl's family: despite the death of the father, the extended and still-expanding family successfully pulls through the crisis of immigrations. By contrast, Shloymele came to

Israel after the Holocaust, and the author's view of the future of the Jewish people is similarly reflected in the shaping of the protagonist's family, only this family falls apart almost entirely and loses nearly all of its friends. The fate of the most nuclear family unit, the mother and son, is also cast in doubt in light of the mother's illness. In this case, no distant relatives, Jewish community, or Jewish institutions rush to the aid of the nuclear family. The protagonist of Karpinovitsh's story lives in an altogether new environment, geographically, socially, and culturally, with no familiar safety net, whether familial or communal. In this story (and in the two previous works I discussed), the qualities that make Tel Aviv a big city are the alienation and cruelty of its labor market and the complexity and indifference of its bureaucratic mechanisms, but not the horizon of economic, cultural, and educational possibilities it offers its residents.

Many of the descriptions of Tel Aviv appeared in the pages of the Yiddish press, in satirical feuilletons, vignettes, and short sketches. It is no wonder, then, that the modes in which they were shaped were mostly realist and concerned with social challenges. Some of the descriptions had impressionist overtones: the place and the time were described through the writer's own unique angle of observation. One of the subjects that attracted writers was the city's craftsmen. Crafts, as noted earlier, was one of the two main occupations of shtetl Jews (alongside trade). As industrialization grew, many of the craftsmen became laborers (in small- and medium-scale industry), clerks, and, to a lesser degree, free professionals (in Eastern Europe only a single-digit percentage).[201] In the Israeli Hebrew culture of the time, the craftsmen represented the "exilic professions" and as such had little to no prestige. Prestige was assigned to the urban blue-collar laborer on the one hand and to the tradesman and clerk on the other hand, for these roles had a distinct place in the grand national project of establishing a new nation-state.[202] For example, in the novel *Hedva and I*, the novel's protagonists, the young "Sabras" Hedva and Shlomik, leave the Kibbutz for the city. Hedva and her parents urge Shlomik to get a clerical job at one of the government bureaus, while he himself yearns to return to the Kibbutz. On one of his roaming walks of the streets, he sees writing on a wall: "Let us live our small lives on this earth!" This writing troubles him and makes him wonder, "Who is not letting its writer live freely?" Is he himself not free to choose his profession and thus his role in the nation-state foundation project as he pleases?[203] But Yiddish fiction was actually drawn, as we have seen, to describing the lives of the "small people" living their "small lives." In his sketch "'Arie, der yunger shuster af rehow bazel" ('Arie, the young shoemaker from Bazel Street), Y. Burshteyn described a conversation with a young Sabra who chose a traditional Jewish craft and thus one that was atypical of the "new Jews"—shoemaking. The writer's position in this encounter is articulated right at the outset: "Why are we witnessing a remarkable phenomenon, not only among bourgeois circles, snobs, and ostentatious intellectuals, but also in the ranks of organized labor, the attitude toward crafts and especially toward specific Jewish professions, like shoemaking and tailoring, is to this day indifference? Why did the followers of A. D. Gordon sanctify work and discount craft?"[204] These questions reflect the stance of "synthetic Yiddishism" as a literary mode that seeks to combine cultural and national progress with tradition. The young Sabra seeks—in a way that was characteristic of his generation—to avoid touching on these big questions but does admit to Burshteyn that his peers are ashamed of their professions. The fault for this predicament lies, in his view, with the parents, but the challenge of coping with it falls to the young generation: "The parents, and especially the mothers, who brought the exile here and instilled the 'aristocratic feelings' in their children, are to blame. But it depends on the character and, above all, on the spiritual development of the young man. If he is a khevre-man [an outgoing, social type]—Arie assures me—he can even be a shoemaker and still successful in the business and 'the girls go crazy for him.'"[205] "Exile," in the eyes of the Sabra, is embodied not in the traditional profession but rather in the vulgar urge for social mobility, which among the Jews of Eastern Europe is expressed primarily in the United States. Burshteyn describes the shoemaker as a unique kind of Sabra: though he chose a "typically Jewish" profession, this did not undermine his "Sabra" qualities—his avoidance of the big questions, his negative perception of exile and of the immigrants who came from it, his adherence to the ideal of the "khevre-man." One of the reasons for this is that the choice of profession was motivated partly by a rebellion against the generation of the parents, a rebellion that is an integral part of the Sabra culture.

Unlike in the case of the Sabra, an immigrant's choice to be a craftsman does harm his social status. In his satirical column, titled "Ufgekhapte bildlekh fun tel-oviver rabinat" (Captured images from the Tel Aviv rabbinate), Dovid Eydlman described the case of a woman seeking to divorce her husband because she was ashamed of his profession: "If Kive Roshpil of the Hadar Yosef neighborhood in Tel Aviv had not been a shoemaker, but a merchant or someone who deals in more noble things, then Feyge-beyle his little wife would not have asked Kive for a divorce."[206] The woman is the one who asks for this divorce. Like Hedva, Shlomik's wife, Feyge-beyle wants to climb the social ladder (and thus becomes the object of parody). But unlike Hedva, she is not a native Israeli but a newcomer and therefore cannot afford to have a husband—himself a recent immigrant from Eastern Europe—who works as a shoemaker. Both of these representations display an evident tension between the description of Tel Aviv as a small, preindustrial town and its description as a big city in terms of the transformation it enables through choice of profession: the "Sabra" becomes an incarnation of the traditional Jew, while the new immigrant becomes (or seeks to become) a "veteran" by pursuing a prestigious profession.

This tension between describing Tel Aviv as a small town and describing it as a big city also appeared in Eydlman's columns targeting the petty thieves and colorful types he observed in the courthouse and on the streets. The court is one of the symbols of the nation-state's autonomy and power. Eydlman's columns focused on the subjects and not the court officials—the various colorful types and their small, everyday problems. His columns are a kind of early version of what we might today describe as a local-paper style of writing, which describes the anonymous and alienated urban community as a small and intimate one. His columns were written as satire, with a distinctly humoristic and parodic tone.[207] In the 1950s and 1960s, satirical writing was common in the Hebrew press as well, in the form of the feuilleton (for example, in the writing of Amos Kenan and Efraim Kishon). In the realm of Hebrew writing, the feuilletonic essay preceded literature "in recognizing that most of the models had been eroded, and what was left for the satirist was to tackle them."[208] Hegemonic Hebrew culture experienced everyday life in postindependence Israel partly as an identity crisis and a loss of way. One of the expressions of this was "the return of the repressed": a satirical description of the Sabra as an exilic Jew. Eydlman's columns featured all of those eroded models that the satire in Hebrew referenced—the mythical character of the naive and idealist Sabra, which had become a caricature; truths that were voided of meaning and became empty slogans; the bureaucracy and corruption that spread throughout the young establishment—as a welcome and healthy return to the modest everyday life of the small people. Thus, the satire in his columns was not as bitter and stinging as in the Hebrew writing but rather more forgiving and humoristic. The Tel Aviv that Hebrew satire shaped as a strange and foreign place was shaped in the Yiddish satire as a familiar and amusing place.

Capitalism created a new form of poverty, and indeed, beggars and homeless people are an integral part of the image of the modern city. They also appeared in the descriptions of Tel Aviv. Eydlman wrote a separate column devoted to this issue, which was printed in the *LN* in the 1950s and titled "Der meylekh-evyen af di gasn fun tel-oviv-yafo" ([expression] Portraits of paupers on the streets of Tel Aviv-Jaffa). Yoysef Noyman, too, in his column "A tel-oviver tip" (A Tel Aviv type) in the same paper, offered portraits of poor people and sometimes also of idlers who came to beg for alms in the city. Y. Namdirf (the pen name of Yankev Fridman) sought in one of his columns to understand the phenomenon of "the homeless," and to that end, he struck up a conversation with a homeless man he encountered in the Sheynkin park.[209] In talking, they discovered that they had both grown up in the same place (Czernowitz) and even passed the war years in the same place (Transnistria). To his surprise, the narrator discovered that it was precisely during the war years that his interlocutor had felt most at ease in Jewish society, as an equal among equals: everyone lived in tents and was unable to work for a living. But when he arrived in Israel, he began once again to feel his foreignness: everyone started chasing work, money, and status, whereas he had detested working ever since childhood. The narrator was struck by the homeless man's honesty and high level of self-awareness. He realized that this man was not like the unemployed types he would regularly meet on Rothschild Boulevard, who wanted with all their might to work, but no work was found for them. They protested against the dire state of employment in the country, whereas his interlocutor was "unemployed out of principle," someone who wanted freedom and was willing to pay its price—not starting a family. This radical difference can exist, and persist in existing, only in a big city.

These homeless people are the most extreme form of the "detached" type of individual whom the national movements sought to "redeem" by connecting them to the nation and to their land. And perhaps even more than this, the homeless attracted interest because of their position as marginal figures, who have the power to implicitly undermine the picture of normative society. The poor people who flooded the streets of Tel Aviv were a troubling disturbance to the realization of the national vision of a state that takes care of its citizens and nurtures them, and especially the weakest among them (partly with the reparation payments from Germany). This was pointed out, for example, by one of the *LN* writers in his column: "With the establishment of the state, it seemed certain . . . that this would no longer happen, that Jewish begging [*Shnoreray*][210] would no longer return. . . . We used to justify it and blame everything on the exile. I would like to ask: who is to blame today, here in Israel, for this disease spreading?"[211]

A special type of beggar was described by Shloyme Berlinski in his story "Gasn shpiler" (Street musicians). His protagonists are two older musicians who play on the streets for money. One is a klezmer musician who plays traditional Jewish wedding tunes from Eastern Europe while begging for alms. This beggar reminds the residents of the city that the young Tel Aviv, so joyful and quick to start a new life, is the continuation of the cities of Eastern Europe, and reminds them also of the tragic way in which these cities were obliterated:

> They are scattered over various places in Tel Aviv, in all places where the streets are packed; at the bus stops, where people line up to get on the buses; by the cafés and entertainment venues. You see them everywhere, the street players. One plays the violin. He always plays wedding tunes from the former Jewish towns in Poland. In the old home he was probably a klezmer. . . . Donations drop. The Jewish towns in Poland are no more, the weddings of yore have disappeared, but the old klezmer continues to play the Jewish wedding, without a bride and groom, without in-laws . . . Take a look around—you're on a Tel Aviv street. But in the heart he has awakened something, the old klezmer.[212]

The other musician is a Jew from one of the Islamic countries, and he too plays folk music with an instrument that is unique to the culture from which he hails—the santur. His music reminds the passersby that Tel Aviv is an inseparable part of the "East" and reminds them also of the share of suffering of the Jews of the East. The donations showered on the two musicians by the passersby are an expression not only of their pity but also of the desire of some of them to redeem, with money, their moral duty to the past and to its memory, for which the two musicians function as living monuments in their bodies and their music. This picture, of the two "Eastern" Jews—Eastern Europe and Middle Eastern—who are Easternizing Tel Aviv with their sounds, each with the unique content he pours into this Easternness, complicates the supposedly stable identity dictated from above of Tel Aviv as a Western city that denies its Easternness.[213]

Yiddish fiction not only described Tel Aviv as a place of "Eastern" Jewish character but also expressed unease about its Westernization. In the vignette "Peysekhdike reportazhn" (Passover reports), by Tsvi Magen, the narrator describes a chance meeting with an acquaintance from past years who is living in the United States and has come to Tel Aviv as a tourist a few days before the Passover holiday. The narrator asks him about his impression of the city, and the tourist expresses disappointment that one does not sense in Tel Aviv the kind of preholiday bustle and excitement he recalls feeling in his childhood town in Lithuania: "For some reason Passover is not felt here. One does not see the unique Jewish commotion of the Jewish towns of Eastern Europe before Passover. Is this Naomi?—Is this what a one-hundred percent Jewish city looks like before Passover? With the smooth paved roads of the streets of Tel Aviv, with the flower-decorated facades, with the rushing limousines? This is all very beautiful in a Jewish country, thinks the American tourist with a warm Jewish heart. But where is the Jewish pre-Passover [atmosphere] that is so ingrained in the heart of every Jew born in Europe?"[214]

The Jewish American tourist had imagined Tel Aviv to be a kind of Jewish enclave in which the special atmosphere of his childhood town in Eastern Europe continued to prevail and perhaps even was enhanced, because, unlike the town, Tel Aviv was known as a city established by and for Jews. The narrator explains to him that the residents of Tel Aviv sought to create a new Jewish way of being to suit their needs and vision rather than replicating the old way. To appease the tourist, the narrator takes him on a tour of a place in which the atmosphere he sought is indeed present—Jaffa. And there, of all places, among the narrow, winding alleys and the former Palestinian houses, where Jews from various diasporas live together in conditions of crowding and poverty, the tourist finds what he is looking for. Tel Aviv itself is described in this vignette as an affluent and well-ordered Western city, like a small-scale version of an American city, and thus as disappointing.

Encounters with tourists and guests from abroad are characteristic of the fiction about Tel Aviv. Meetings between family members are a metonymy for the character of the city insofar as they deal with the tension between intimate closeness and foreignness. The existence of various kinds of hotels attests to the size of the city and to its economic status. The miniature "Tsvey brider" (Two brothers) by Granatshteyn tells of two brothers (Menakhem and Yisroelik) who are the sole survivors of their family.[215] Menakhem (or, as he was called in his hometown, Mendl khane-ester-rokhls) fled to the United States years before the Holocaust to avoid military enlistment. He settled in Miami Beach, Florida, and became a businessman. He changed his name to "Men Barns." His brother Yisroelik stayed in Eastern Europe, endured all the terrors of the war, and came to Israel. The two brothers kept in touch during their years apart and especially since learning that they were the only survivors from their family. When Menakhem finally comes to Israel for a visit, Yisroelik is deeply disappointed. His brother looks and behaves like a nouveau-riche, loud and materialistic. Yisroelik, by contrast, looks to Menakhem like a pauper and a beggar. Yisroelik drives Menakhem to the lavish Tel Aviv hotel in which he is staying, and then he prefers to go back to his home in the immigrant camp and to the fantasy he had nurtured about his brother. In this story, Tel Aviv is a place in which the difficult and complicated economic and human reality came crashing down on the dreams of a family reunion. This painful gap between the expectation for intimacy and the reality of alienation is one of the features of Tel Aviv as a city that is on the one hand small and Jewish and on the other hand big and alienated.

The large number of ʻoley sheyres hapleyte who came to Israel during those years and the small size of the country made Tel Aviv the site of surprising meetings between people who had known each other during and after the Holocaust. So, for example, on the Tel Aviv beach, the narrator of "Er vart af zey" (He waits for them) by Eliezer Rubinshteyn comes across a man he has met several times in the past:[216] in the Soviet Union, in the DP camp in Germany, and in Paris. This man wanted to come to Israel because he was sure that all the Jews he had left behind when he fled eastward at the start of World War II were now living there. He comes regularly to the beach, orders two cups of coffee, and waits for them. On Rothschild Boulevard, the narrator of "Far vos iz zi avek?" (Why did she leave?) comes across an acquaintance whom he met in Italy when they waited together for the ship that brought illegal immigrants (*Maʻapilim*) to Israel and with whom he parted ways at the Shaʻar Ha-ʻAliya processing camp.[217] In Gan Ha-ʻAtzmaut, the narrator of "Dos oysgeloshene lebn" (The extinguished life) meets a mother and daughter;[218] the mother he knew before the war, and now he learns that the Nazis abused her daughter. At his new office, the narrator of "A mame" (A mother), a young accountant, identifies the woman who dispenses the tea as the sister of his first love, from the town he left for the big city before the war.[219]

Some of the meetings continued in coffeehouses in Tel Aviv. These are described as "Middle Eastern" sites, very different from the cafés of the cities of

Central and Western Europe.[220] Like the movie theater, mentioned earlier, the café is not purely a place of entertainment; it is also often frequented for the sake of work and livelihood: the unemployed go there to learn about potential jobs, and merchants go to meet middlemen and fellow merchants. The café is a kind of "market" and sometimes even a "stock exchange." Sitting in a café is often described in negative terms: a scene of shady traders and profiteers, or of youngsters who have fallen into bad ways.[221] Unlike the Hebrew writers, who created small bohemian groups that gathered regularly in Tel Aviv cafés, the Yiddish writers met in the cultural clubs, reading rooms, and staff rooms of the various cultural institutions they established, or in the adjacent kiosks and cafeterias. Most Yiddish writers and Yiddish cultural activists were family-oriented people who hosted colleagues in their homes, introduced their families to each other, and held house parties despite the typically modest size of their apartments.

In addition to the experience of sitting in cafés for leisure and entertainment, another quintessentially urban experience missing from the descriptions of Tel Aviv in Yiddish fiction is that of roaming the streets for the purpose of shopping or window shopping. In Eastern Europe, no real bourgeois class had developed. The protagonists of the Yiddish fiction written in Israel were typically *Yidn fun a gants yor* (simple people) from the working class, the merchants or low-level clerks. Thus, their main means of transportation was buses, which they used for travel into the city and within it. It is hard to see these bus rides as an Israeli incarnation of Benjaminian flânerie—one of the central symbols of the modern urban experience[222]—since the essence of this flânerie was reminiscing about the personal past of the writer, whose knowledge of the city was intimate, like that of a native. The bus-riding experience described in Yiddish literature was based on a crowded and sweaty encounter with new residents. These encounters yielded surprising reunions with relatives and acquaintances not seen since the Holocaust,[223] as well as various conversations and discussions—for instance, about the status of Yiddish in Israel,[224] or simply small talk with other Jews, a chance to vent frustration by complaining (a traditional theme in modern Yiddish literature, associated particularly with Sholem Aleichem's "Ayznban geshikhte" ["Railroad Stories"]).[225] The conduct of Jews on the bus also made a fine subject for satire.[226]

Overall, it is very rare to find in Yiddish literature representations of a life of high culture in Tel Aviv, like concerts, art exhibits, cinema, or even mass cultural happenings (like the Purim carnival), sports and entertainment events, or commercial events (like fairs or exhibitions). The cultural events that appeared repeatedly in several works were mass national events like the Independence Day celebrations and the IDF parades. The fact that these prominent national events took place in Tel Aviv bolstered the city's image as a symbol of the young state. Their literary descriptions stress the tension between the individual (the grieving and therefore foreign Holocaust survivor) and the (national, celebrating) masses. This tension appears, for instance, in two of Granatshteyn's stories. The first, "Ven dos folk fayert" (When the people celebrate), describes the masses celebrating between Mugrabi Square and the beach. The many streetlights are described as staving off the darkness of night, and despite all this bright light, the narrator's gaze is drawn, of all things, to a blind man groping his way through the crowd and being swept along with it toward the beach. There, he stops and appears to be staring at the horizon and crying with exhilaration. It is evident that the blind man expresses the emotions of the narrator, who feels himself to be separate from the celebrating masses because of his private grief, yet he too is out on the streets, exhilarated and eager to participate in the collective joy: "This is the fifth year that it is so. Every year, on this day, the same wonder. Maybe, maybe in the future it will be normal."[227]

The story "Khvalyendike likht" (Wavy light)[228] also takes place on the eve of Independence Day. The streets are filled with many lights and many families walking along the beach toward Tel Aviv to celebrate in its streets. The protagonists, two Holocaust survivors who live in Jaffa, have stayed home, in their dark and quiet shared room. They lost wives and other relatives in the Holocaust and joined the partisans to avenge their loss. The light and the singing fill the streets, brightening the dark sea and infiltrating the protagonists' room. This has an opposite effect on each of the men: in one, it awakens the desire to converse, to join the masses, to go to Mugrabi Square and celebrate with them; in his friend, by contrast, it stirs painful memories, yearnings, feelings of guilt for having failed to prevent the deaths of his beloveds, and a fear of seeing in the faces of the women in the crowd the face of his dead wife, to remind him that he is grieving and forbidden from rejoicing. To this his friend replies that, of all days, on this day they are allowed to be joyous and maybe even obliged to be joyous, because this joy is not a private but a national one, a collective joy for all Jews, the living and the dead (in accordance with the Jewish tradition in Eastern Europe that regarded the dead as part of the community).

In the Yiddish fiction written in Israel, then, Tel Aviv is described through the familiar modern contrast between the small town and the city. Perhaps surprisingly, it is described more as a town than as a metropolis: it is characterized by an intimate and nationally and religiously homogenous community, adherence to a unified national identity, traditional and fixed professions, and a lack of high-culture institutions. Given that 'oley sheyres hapleyte were expecting a modern city, one might have thought that their descriptions of Tel Aviv would be tinged by a certain disappointment, but no such disappointment is directly expressed in them. Alongside these descriptions, the stories also include certain descriptions that fit the characterization of major cities—most prominently, portraits of the masses flowing into Tel Aviv, the diversity of these masses in terms of ethnicity and class, and the existence of a bustling labor market and of national and commercial institutions. It is possible that these contrasts are in fact an accurate reflection of Tel Aviv of those days, and it is also possible that they reflect a compromise between the immigrants' expectations and the reality they discovered. Tel Aviv, then, emerges as a small but mixed workers' city that combines East and West, and also as a Jewish (exilic) and distinctly Israeli city. As such, it is a breath of fresh air on the map of the "Yiddishland" cities. Conspicuously lacking are descriptions of teeming urban might: noisy technology, mass media, vibrant intellectual activity, and an exciting international culture. In the realm of Israeli literature, the Yiddish fiction about Tel Aviv expands the contemporaneous descriptions of the city found in Hebrew literature: its protagonists are simple people of modest ambitions who have known deep pain and suffering and are somewhat naive in their belief in the simplicity of the national "collective" they have joined.

Tel Aviv as a space in the Israel-theme began to wane gradually from the mid-1960s. In the 1980s, a different urban space gained prominence in works of Yiddish literature—Jerusalem. The theme of these works was no longer the new national present and the hope of the masses to establish themselves within it, but the author's elegiac disengagement from the world, whose fractures are still reflected in his withdrawn inner world.

* * *

This chapter dealt with the literary representations of 'oley sheyres hapleyte's encounter with the Israeli experience in sites that were typical of the period. Each of the spaces reflected different aspects and different practices involved in the building of the "destroyed home," both personal and national. Building the destroyed home necessarily entailed facing different facets of the immigrants' loss. The Israel-theme is a fascinating expansion of the immigration theme that was typical of Yiddish literature from the late nineteenth century and throughout the twentieth, and also an expansion of its main subject: the ways in which the Eastern European Jewish family coped with the inevitable disintegration of its old world. The literary focus on the new present allowed the writers to contend with their traumatic past without repressing it but also without wallowing in it and becoming submerged. Because they came equipped with a rich and varied literary heritage, and because they were mature observers who had gained their experience in another place and in different circumstances, they were not blindly carried away by a romantic ideological utopianism. Instead, the national place and time were enriched in their works with a heightened awareness of their temporary and fragile nature. Whereas Hebrew Israeli literature swerved between enthusiasm over the establishment of Israel and the bitter cynicism of disillusionment with the dream, Yiddish Israeli literature presented a cautious, secular perspective, of those whose bitter and complex experience prevented them from yielding to these extreme emotions. The Yiddish writers did allow themselves to be moved and excited by Israel's historic success, but they did not repress or hide its cost. In particular, they showed awareness of and even empathy (rare at the time) for the "other"—whether the otherness was national, ethnic, class-related, or gender-related. This empathy grew out of the trauma they experienced—the traumas of the Holocaust, displacement, and immigration—and it attests to their processing of these traumas and not to a capitulation to them. Alongside all of this, it seems that the unprecedented extent of their loss in the Holocaust gave them back something of the modern national audacity, a fierceness devoid of cynicism and decadence, and something of the unapologetic conservatism of those who have seen the evil at the far end of nihilism and no longer find it banal, romantic, or symbolic. Also evident in their work is a renewed (traditional) loyalty to the values of the old world that was destroyed, a loyalty that writers and readers who did not share with them such a harsh fate might identify as anachronistic, or in any case as regressive in relation to writers who came before them. For example, the predominant style of the stories I analyzed here is naturalistic realism. Surrealism and symbolism are less common. The latter styles gained prominence only later and are characteristic of the next stage of Yiddish literature in Israel.

The uniqueness of the point of view of 'oley sheyres hapleyte Yiddish writers stands out in comparison to that of the writers who wrote in Hebrew in the 1950s (Bartov, Hendel, Yizhar, Meged, Shamir). The latter were roughly the same age as the Yiddish writers or a few years younger, but their formative years, personally and culturally, took place in the young state of Israel. Even and perhaps especially those of them who were born in Eastern Europe sought to embrace Hebrew culture devoutly and even to become "natives," thereby denying to a large extent the experience of refugeehood and immigration. When the new generation of prose writers (like Oz and A. B. Yehoshua) began to write about these experiences, starting in the latter half of the 1960s, Yiddish writers had already produced an eminent corpus of rich and complex literary works on these themes. Yiddish writers from among the 'oley sheyres hapleyte need to be distinguished also from the survivor-writers who came to Israel as children (like Uri Orlev, Aharon Apelfeld, Ben-Zion Tomer, Shamai Golan, and Itamar Ya'oz-Kest), who began to write about their past after a formative period of coming-of-age in Israel and wrote in Hebrew. The Yiddish writers came to Israel as mature, formed, and experienced individuals, and they experienced the new reality as such. Their works were written as early as the first years after their arrival and in their own language. One final group of writers (Balas, Kishon, Shlomo Kalo, and others) comprises those who wrote in Israel in the 1950s in languages other than Hebrew or Yiddish (Arabic, Hungarian, and Bulgarian, respectively). The extent to which their output resembles that of 'oley sheyres hapleyte will remain an open question here. Was, for example, their writing in these languages a form of "linguistic loyalty"? Was it sheer pragmatism or immigrant inflexibility? Did they abandon writing in these languages after mastering Hebrew because they had mastered it, or did this express a deeper change in their worldview? These questions are outside the scope of my study.

Many of the writers in Hebrew during this period were interested in the refugees from Eastern Europe and expressed this interest in their work. For example, Haim Hazaz, Lea Goldberg, and Nathan Alterman expressed genuine excitement over the enormous potential contribution of the Jewish war refugees to the burgeoning state, as they imagined it. They even called on the Hebrew writers to "go to the people," to spend time in the Ma'abarot, among the 'olim, and to convey the historical enormity of the moment: a secular ingathering of the exiles, as close as possible to the secular days of the Messiah. But herein lies the paradox in which they were trapped: they sought to be a voice for the refugees. Anyone who sees a refugee as raw material for the lofty ideals that excite his imagination is not listening to him, to his pains and his needs. We give voice to those who are mute. On this note, Yizhar's words in 1958 are accurate: "For the most part, they are mute toward us, and we, for the most part, are deaf to them."[229] This, I believe, is the sad source of the myth of the "silence of survivors"—the absence of attentive listening. "Israel," as the street saying went, "wanted the 'aliya, but the Israelis didn't want the 'olim." In other words, the state needed the masses, their manpower, but cared little about them as individuals, about their personal motives, difficulties, and needs. To listen to the refugees in their own voices and their languages requires giving their voices and their languages a space and means of existence.

The Israel-theme in Yiddish fiction gradually faded over the course of the 1960s. The reason for this may be that Israel was no longer a novelty for the 'olim turned veterans. The anthology compiled by Shmuel Rozhanski and published on the eve of the Yom Kippur War, *In dem eygenem land: 25 yor yisroel in der yidisher poezye un proze* (In our own country: 25 years of Israel in Yiddish poetry and prose), is to a large extent a summary of the Israel-theme. Its evident goal is to provide its readers with a broad panorama of a theme that had reached a point of maturity and largely exhausted itself. By the time of the anthology's publication, the exhilaration and enthusiasm of the early works was most likely already read as an anachronism.

From the late 1960s and on, daily life in Yiddish gradually died out in Israel, and along with it declined the Yiddish cultural life in Israel. In the 1970s, they showed signs of vitality again, but only limited, following the 'aliya of Jews from the Soviet Union. This 'aliya included Yiddish writers (like Hirsh Osherovitsh, Rokhl Boymvol, Meir Kharats, Ziyame Telesin, Meir Yelin, Y. Lerner, Motl Saktsier, Eliezer Podriatshik, Yoysef Kerler, and Eli Shekhtman). The scope of their influence on Yiddish cultural life in Israel was limited relative to the period discussed here. The number of ʿolim from the Soviet Union in those years was significantly smaller than the mass immigrations of the 1950s, and even more so their percentage in the absorbing population, which in the 1970s was already institutionally organized and established in its cultural outlook. Thus, their potential to influence Israel's cultural character was small to begin with. Moreover, the Yiddish writers who came to Israel from the Soviet Union were already in midlife. They came to an existing environment, institutionally and culturally. They could try to fit into it, but they could not reinvent it. Generationally speaking, most of these writers were born in the same years as the ʿoley sheyres hapleyte writers, but they were shaped by different life experiences. Their literary taste was also shaped in different realities: access to the Yiddish literature produced in the West in general and in Israel in particular was very limited in the Soviet Union, leaving these writers largely isolated. They focused mostly on Jerusalem, and their work symbolizes, to a large extent, the decline of Yiddish culture in Israel.

Conclusion

The End of Yiddish Culture and the Invention of an Israeli Jewish Identity

Bist nit fargangen. Dayn pustkeyt is ful.
Ful mitn folk vi mayn oyg mit der mamen.

You have not vanished. Your emptiness is brimful
Brimful of your people, as my mother fills my eye.
Avrom Sutzkever, "Yidishe gas" ("The Jewish Street")[1]

On summer evenings in my childhood neighborhood, Ramat Eliyahu, in the 1970s, neighbors used to bolt out of their steaming apartments and head down to the street to sit in the open air. The benches and low stone fences on Hilel Tsaitlin Street, Sholem Asch Street, Zalman Shneur Street, and Mordekhe Anilevitsh Street filled with grandmothers and grandfathers and carried the wonderful tune of their animated, lively chatter. Yiddish newspapers, journals, and books were passed from hand to hand, from door to door. The speech and actions of these people expressed a sense of common fate, solidarity, and mutual support; these stood above the political, cultural, and personal disagreements between them and united them as an "affective community." Yiddish culture was thus a valuable asset to them: through it, they transformed the new and foreign place to which they had come into a home; through it, they mourned their beloved who were murdered, mourned everything that was left in the past. The Israeli space and those who populated it were foreign to them, but this foreignness actually helped them in their processes of grieving; and the distance from the ruins of their old home helped them understand and digest what had happened there. Yet the price of assimilating into the Israeli space was the somewhat "Stockholmian" renunciation of their otherness and thus of their language, culture, and organizational uniqueness. Israel sought to expropriate from them the collective sentiment and to appropriate for itself exclusive control over shaping it. It expropriated their memorial day and memorialized their culture in street names that soon became devoid of any meaning to the new generations born in those very streets. After the Six-Day War (1967), after the occupation of Jerusalem and the cities of the West Bank, a new style of Judaism, as well as Yiddish and Yiddishkeyt, was increasingly used to establish a new common identity for the Israeli Jews, one that gradually replaced even the Sabra Israeli identity and obviously also excluded non-Jews from the cultural and geographical space. The exclusivity that Israel claimed for itself even in managing and charting the relationship with the Diaspora Jews obliterated the role of Yiddish speakers as those who had managed these ties until then, naturally and as a matter of course, by virtue of their common past and common language. And so, as the generation of ʿoley sheyres hapleyte grew older, its members increasingly retreated into an individual existence, alienated and isolated. Secular modern Yiddish, as a practice of an affective community, establishing its character from below, faded. Here and there a handful of institutions, private as well as public, whose cultural goals lay elsewhere, profited from advancing programs that seemed to intersect with its agenda. But educational programs directed from above do not tend to successfully cultivate the intimate and immediate sense of shared identity so crucial for the existence of a vital cohesive community. These programs often served other, more capitalistic ends. The modern secular Yiddish community ceased to exist.

A little over a decade ago, before writing this book, I presented my hopes for this study to experts and colleagues as well as to less professional lovers of literature and culture. The uniformity of their initial response astounded me: nearly all of them were dumbfounded by the very suggestion that writers from among the ʿoley sheyres hapleyte had created prose in Israel, let alone prose that was worth revisiting. This piqued my curiosity. "Maybe a small amount of fine poetry in Yiddish was written here," many of them conceded after a while, "but the prose written in Yiddish in Israel after the Holocaust (and for the most part also outside Israel) was of low, memoir-like quality and holds little scholarly interest." Then would begin a fascinating process of "negotiation" between my interlocutors and me, which reflected their own internal negotiation with their repressed past and their cultural and moral stance toward their repression. I would name several of the prominent Yiddish writers who wrote in Israel at that time, some of them well known and esteemed. Many of my interlocutors were of course familiar with them. How does recognizing this fact sit with their denial that any Yiddish prose worth studying was written here? I would ask. Alongside these names I would also mention the fact—which my interlocutors fully accepted and indeed took for granted—that the Yiddish prose written before World War II is still recognized today as one of the groundbreaking heights of Jewish literature. Is it possible, I asked, that this entire tradition of innovative artistic creativity should fall silent and vanish all at once? At this, my interlocutors would pause, since they do acknowledge the avant-garde nature of some of the high points of Yiddish literature between the world wars. Why indeed had they assumed that after the Holocaust this literature had all at once become a collection of nostalgic memories written through the force of inertia by refugees who lacked artistic refinement? To me, what was interesting and important in these conversations was that nearly all my interlocutors both acknowledged and canceled, in the same breath, the possibility and the value of the work I wanted to study, and both of these pronouncements were made very decisively, with a sense of certainty. Finally, when they had softened a bit, they would admit with a shrug the existence of a body of work that deserves to be studied. Then the only question left open was about the extent of the innovativeness of the prose I wished to study—and this is a question that will to some extent always remain open given the absence of a consensus regarding the criteria for literary innovation, as Borges and others have shown. These kinds of conversations, and especially the fact that, over time, I was able to predict how they would unfold and almost reproduce them in advance like a flow chart, are what gave me the structure for the book you have just read. I realized I had to focus first on correcting the misconceptions that enabled the loaded ambivalence my interlocutors expressed, and that this would be achieved through comprehensive and thorough research. Only then could I portray in detail the richness of the literary findings that would be revealed to those who agreed to recognize their existence.

Yiddish writers from among the ʻoley sheyres hapleyte were part of a large group that changed the demographic face of the young Israel. Their writings in Israel are of a scope and creative wealth that contradicts the myth about their silence. What silenced their voice is largely the public's acceptance of this myth. In other words, the only way to reconcile the contradiction is by appreciating the role that their new country assigned to their voice, and especially to their silence. When the ʻoley sheyres hapleyte finally integrated, they themselves accepted their assigned social role, the myth of their silence. ʻOley sheyres hapleyte writers created literature in Israel in a variety of forms and registers and shared with their readers complex feelings of detachment and refugeehood alongside the joy of returning to the homeland, of irreparable grief alongside efforts to put down new roots, and of national pride accompanied by a painful awareness of its emotional and cultural price. They described daily life in their new country and the experiences of its "ordinary people." These ordinary people and their experiences significantly expand the gallery of characters and plots that were created in the Hebrew literature of the time, and in this lies the innovation and contribution of the works of ʻoley sheyres hapleyte writers to the cultural history of Israel. Particularly evident in their works is empathy, rare in those days, for the suffering of the other, whoever he or she may be, empathy that in part reflects the traumas they themselves experienced but also their success (partial, like any success) in processing it. This prose, and especially the novels, expressed the many voices, varied and sometimes conflicting, that made up the new national society, from the unique point of view of those who had only just joined it.

In addition, the work of ‘oley sheyres hapleyte writers in Israel in the 1950s and 1960s forged a link between the millions of members of the imagined community of the former Eastern European Jewry who were now dispersed across the world. By giving expression to contents and experiences that were more than just a repeated treading through a common past, it gave these members a tool to strengthen and consolidate their communal feelings. The role of the Israel-theme is prominent in these works, as a subject that enables the writers and their readers to expand familiar schemes from their past literary tradition with the help of a new space and new time, in the description of their lives in the independent Jewish state. In this way, new life was cast into familiar molds. And in this way, survivors were able to process painful traumas through descriptions of their experiences in the present, to draw constructive lessons from the paralyzing memories of the past to an active future, and sometimes even to draw optimism regarding their future. The work of ‘oley sheyres hapleyte writers largely seals what was the central topic of modern Yiddish literature from its inception: the irrevocable disintegration of the old Jewish world. But it also embodies one of the fascinating opening chapters in the story of the new Israeli literature.

The Holocaust is of course a watershed event in Jewish history, and it obviously forever changed the lives of those who survived it and of everyone who was born Jewish (in any of the many senses of that term) or Israeli after it. Its effect is necessarily also felt in the culture that Jews (and others) created after it. But, as my study suggests, contrary to the common belief, Yiddish and its culture did not cease to exist in the Holocaust, along with the many millions of its speakers, consumers, and creators. The Holocaust, it appears, did not stop the survivors from feeling that their creative contribution had essential added value for Israel's emerging cultural fabric. They sought to develop this contribution through organized cultural and institutional activity, which was significant in scope and is to a large extent denied because it is significant. Especially prominent is their contribution in challenging the exclusivity of the Sabras' rights to the sentiment of secular Israeli nationalism and in positing alongside this sentiment, without canceling it, the possibility of a secular Jewish Israeliness that does not nervously shake off its rich Jewish past and its limitations and does not rush to reinvent this past as an imagined return to values that never existed, in the manner of the architects of the Ben-Gurion-style Sabra Israeli ethos. Thus, it appears that the myth of the silence of the survivors is partly an expression of the fact that the veteran population in Israel felt threatened by a difficult challenge in the cultural space in which it developed. The "linguistic loyalty" to Yiddish among many ‘oley sheyres hapleyte, their choice of Yiddish as a language of culture, literature, and memory, was not an expression of the wish to distinguish themselves from Israel and its culture; on the contrary, it allowed them to establish their new national identity while at the same time developing the predominant national identity and making it more malleable and elastic.

"The slogan 'One people, one country, one language' is nationalist and harmful," wrote Y. Artuski in 1957, "and it is also anti-democratic in essence. It cannot be applied in a democratic way."[2] These words in my view express above all the challenge posed to the young Israel by the 'oley sheyres hapleyte. The latter saw themselves as representatives with equal rights in the new national space in whose building they participated and as carrying the historical and national responsibility to enrich this space in their image, which was in many cases bilingual or even multilingual. As I have described, the Israeli establishment in the 1950s was not sympathetic to these aspirations. Unlike other centers of Yiddish culture in the world, the center in Tel Aviv was forced to deal with legislation that circumscribed its activity and even more so with unofficial quiet regulations that expressed the state institutions' sense of threat from this linguistic pluralism: Israel was the only place in the free world after World War II in which a daily newspaper in Yiddish could not be published. This continued until there was a downturn in the influence of 'oley sheyres hapleyte as a group with dominant cultural characteristics and uniting institutions, some of them with a distinct cultural agenda. Though Israel did participate, and still participates, in funding Orthodox educational institutions in Yiddish, it has adamantly refused to help fund secular educational institutions of modern Yiddish culture. In its first few decades, the state also opposed the teaching of Yiddish as a foreign language in state schools.

The fact that a diverse, multilingual, and fascinating cultural reality can exist in an immigration country that is in its infancy is unsurprising. What remains open and intriguing is the question of whether such a country can persist in its multilingual and multicultural character over time without breaking down into various ethnic-linguistic elements. The possibility of such cultural-linguistic wealth coexisting with a national uniformity undoubtedly requires a special kind of maturity on the part of both the citizens and the establishment. And this is doubly true in times of crises. Yet the scholars and lovers of culture ought to allow themselves to acknowledge the complexity of a reality that nation-states naturally want to simplify. It is the job of culture to illuminate what is possible and what is ideal, and not just to anchor in myth what *is*. In Western countries, there have been signs of recognition that they are multilingual cultural spaces. In the United States, for instance, a fascinating anthology of multilingual literature written in the American space was published two decades ago.[3] The anthology exposes the vital role of multiculturalism and multilingualism as foundational

New immigrant housing in Mitzpe Ramon, 1960. Photograph by Micha Bar-Am (Bar-Am Archive).

features of American culture. The wealth that comes with mass immigration, so the anthology suggests, is not a problem that the absorbing establishment needs to solve through socialization in light of a given ideology but an opportunity for cultural growth. This wealth is a blessing to anyone willing and able to contain it.

Israel was marked from its inception by a repressed multiculturalism and indeed a repressed multinationalism. The reasons for this are many and exceed the boundaries of the discussion that concern me in this book. But it is the task of scholars and lovers of culture to acknowledge this wealth and explore the value it brings to both the "absorbing" and the "absorbed" cultures. It is well known that the meeting with the Yiddish language enriched spoken Hebrew in Israel, and some argue that it indeed helped shape the latter's character.[4] It is less known that Yiddish literature also grew and developed as a result of the meeting with Israel (as I have tried to show in this book), as did the Yiddish language itself: Hebrew words began to replace words of Slavic or German origin in Yiddish descriptions of the Israeli reality.[5] Recognizing this kind of wealth is possible only when we rid ourselves of the misconceptions that Yiddish and its culture ceased to exist after the Holocaust, that in Israel there existed (and exists) a secular culture only in Hebrew, and that in the Israeli space no culture worthy of attention and discussion is created unless it is in Hebrew. A comparative study of Israeli literature of all kinds, which would explore the range of voices and literatures that exist there side by side, influenced by and influencing one another, each in the language of its speakers, holds fascinating possibilities. After all, as Manger implies in the poem I discussed at the opening of this book, Israel is not just the piece of land on which it exists but also the rich spectrum of cultures created within it and inspired by it.

Ramat Gan,
Tisha be-Av, 2023

Appendix A

Biographical Details of Yiddish Writers and Journalists in Israel

Writers and journalists who have entries in *Leksikon fun der nayer yidisher literatur* (*The Lexicon of Modern Yiddish Literature*) appear here with only their date and place of birth, date of ʿaliya, and date of death.

The *Lexicon* is one of the important historical sources on modern Yiddish literature, but it does have several limitations. First, not all writers discussed in this book are included in it. Some writers refused to participate in it because it was funded by the German reparation payments, and others were excluded because they were not considered prominent enough. Second, the entries were based on information provided by the writers and journalists themselves, and thus they sometimes suffer from inaccuracies. Third, the work on this lexicon began in 1951, and the first volume appeared in 1956, so that the information provided in it has not been updated in many decades. For example, many of the late entries lack the place and year of death. These details are added below from other sources, along with references to those sources. One of the tasks that Berl Cohen, author of *Leksikon fun yidish-shraybers* (*The Lexicon of Yiddish Writers*), took upon himself was to fill in the information missing in the *Leksikon fun der nayer yidisher literatur*, and indeed that is where a large part of the missing information is found. Information about Israeli Yiddish writers also appears in the anthology *Mikan uMiqarov: ʾAntologia šel sipurei yidiš heʾEreṣ Yiśraʾel, meRešit haMea weʾAd yameinu* (*From Here and from Near: Yiddish Stories in ʾEreṣ Yiśraʾel, from the Start of the Century to the Present*), edited by Mordechai Halamish, and in his book *Yidiš be Yiśraʾel: ʿAl sofrim, mešorerim, amanim* [Yiddish in Israel: On writers, poets, artists] (Tel Aviv: Aked, 1990).

The other sources are abbreviated as follows: Cohen = Berl Cohen, *Mikan* = *Mikan uMiqarov*. Wherever not stated otherwise, the place of birth is Poland.

Editors

Aykhnboym Yisokher [Y. Artuski / khaver [comrade] Oscar]: Born in 1903 in Warsaw. Was orphaned at the height of World War I. Lived in a convent from ages twelve to fifteen. Began his ideological path as a communist and moved to socialist Marxism. Studied political economy at Moscow University. Sought and found his way back to the Jewish people: he joined the Bundist youth organization Tsukunft and became one of the prominent essayists in the Bundist press there. When World War II broke out, he sought to escape to the Soviet Union but returned to Warsaw. From there he wanted to escape to Vilna but following a tip from an informer was arrested at the Soviet border. Thanks to the underground names he used, his communist and Bundist past was not discovered; he was jailed for nine months. After his release from prison, he was sent to a labor camp. In late 1949, he was freed (as part of the Sikorski-Mayski Agreement) and migrated to Tashkent and Teheran. His wife and daughter, who had stayed in

Warsaw, were murdered. In 1943, he arrived in Tel Aviv, but after a while he left for Paris to continue his work for the Bund. In 1950, he was sent by the Bund's Coordinating Committee to Israel to strengthen the newly established center in Tel Aviv. Artuski founded the monthly *Lebns fragn*, the mouthpiece of the Bund movement, and edited it from its inception until his death in 1971. Sources: Meylekh Ravitsh, *Mayn leksikon 3: Yidishe un hebreyishe shraybers in medines Yisroel* [My lexicon vol. 3: Yiddish and Hebrew writers in Israel] (Montreal: A komitet, 1958), 62–63; *Yid, mentsh, sotsialist: Y. Artuski undenk-bukh* [Jew, human being, socialist: Memory-book for Y. Artuski] (Tel Aviv: Lebns fragn farlag, 1976).

Grosman Moyshe: Koriv, 1904–Tel Aviv, 1961. 'Aliya: 1950 to Ramat 'Amidar, Ramat Gan, and from there moved to Ramat Aviv.

Zonshayn Moyshe: Warsaw, 1902–Tel Aviv, 1977.

Khadash Yisroel: Vilna, 1912–Tel Aviv, 1972. 'Aliya: 1936. Additional source: Roznboym Mikhl, *Ondenk-bukh fun Yisroel Khadash: Grinder un redaktor fun "Yidishe Tsaytung"* [Memorial book for Yisroel Khadash: Founder and editor of *Yidishe tsaytun*] (Tel Aviv: Nay Lebn, 1973).

Halamish [Flint] Mordechai: Góra Kalwaria (Ger), 1911–Tel Aviv, 1989. 'Aliya: 1935 to Ramat Yohanan. Additional source: Mordechai Halamish, "Mordechai Halamish-Flint," in *Yidiš be Yiśra'el: 'Al sofrim, mešorerim, 'amanim* [Yiddish in Israel: On writers, poets, artists] (Tel Aviv: Aked, 1990), 399.

Sutzkever Avrom: Smorgon, 1913–Tel Aviv, 2010. 'Aliya: 1947. Settled in Yad Eliyahu and from there moved to the center of Tel Aviv. Won dozens of literary awards, including the Israel Prize for Yiddish Literature (1985).

Tsanin Mordekhe: Sokolov, 1906–Tel Aviv, 2009. 'Aliya: 1942 to Tel Aviv. Received the Itzik Manger Award for a Literary Work in Yiddish (1973) and the Mendele Moykher Sforim Award for Yiddish Writers (1983).

Shtokfish Dovid: Lublin, 1912–Petah Tikva, 2008. 'Aliya: 1948 to Tel Aviv.

Shamri [Riba] Arie: Kalushin, 1907–Ein Shemer, 1978. 'Aliya: 1929 to Kibbutz Hashomer Ha-Tsair in Hadera. Additional source: Arie Shamri, "Bio-bibliografishe shtrikhn" [Bio-bibliographical characteristics], in *Aynzamlung: eseyen, ophandlungen, redes* [Collection: essays, treatises, speeches] (Tel Aviv: Yisroel-bukh 1982), 1–6.

Yiddish Cultural Activists

Rotnberg Yosef: Lodzh, 1914–Tel Aviv, 1960. 'Aliya: 1949.

Journalists

Yasny [Tsiperman] Avrom Volf: Zhelekhov, 1893–Tel Aviv, 1968. In his youth, moved to Lodzh, where he was a textile laborer and active in the Bund. When the war broke out, he escaped to Bialystok, was arrested, and was sent to a Soviet labor camp. Returned as a repatriate to Poland in 1946 and there learned that in the Lodzh Ghetto his wife, two children, parents, and sister had been murdered. Moved to Israel in 1949 (to Yad Eliyahu). Was identified with the Socialist Zionism circles. Source: Cohen.

Levkovitsh Khave: Skiernivitz, 1919–?

Luden Yitskhok [Ben-Uris; Esterman]: Warsaw, 1922–Giv'atayim, 2017. Made 'aliya in 1948 to Yad Eliyahu and later moved to Giv'atayim. Won the Mendele Moykher Sforim Award for Yiddish Writers (2010).

Kants Shimen: Shanlinda (Czechoslovakia), 1914–Tel Aviv, 1990. ʻAliya: 1957 to Tel Aviv. Additional source: *Mikan*.

Translator

Rubinshteyn Eliezer: Sokolov, 1917–?. ʻAliya: 1949. Received the Itzik Manger Award for a Literary Work in Yiddish (1973).

Prose Writers

Avni (Shteynmats) Shmaye: Strimtere (Romania), 1923–2003(?). Studied at the Vizhnits Yeshiva in Oradea. During the war years, was sent to do forced labor in the forests of the Carpathians. In 1940 was arrested on charges of "communist subversion." In 1941 was sent to a labor camp. In 1944 returned to Bucharest, joined the underground of the pioneer Zionist youth, and was one of the leaders of "HeHalutz" (the pioneer) movement in Romania. Was arrested for his Zionist activity. In 1954 was sentenced to seven more years in prison but was released in 1954. Until he received his ʻaliya permit, worked at a religious elementary school (Talmud Tora) in Bucharest. Made ʻaliya in 1960. Source: *Mikan*.

Oyerbakh Rokhl: Lanovits (Eastern Galicia), 1903–Tel Aviv, 1976. Studied in a Polish high school and at the Lwów University. Began her literary and journalistic path in 1927 in Lwów. In this year, she was one of the founders of the literary journal *Tsushtayer* (Contribution), which she edited until 1931. From 1933, lived in Warsaw. During World War II, lived in the Warsaw Ghetto, where she was active culturally, among other things in the archive Oyneg Shabes. In 1943, moved to the "Aryan" side. Made ʻaliya in 1950. Founded and directed the Department for the Collection of Witness Testimony at Yad Vashem. Source: *Mikan*.

Eydlman Dovid: Ginivishov, 1909–Tel Aviv, 1989. As a child, received a traditional education (*kheyder*). Spent his youth in Lublin. During World War II, escaped to the Soviet Union. After liberation, lived in DP camps in Germany. Made ʻaliya in 1950 to Jaffa. From there moved to Yad Eliyahu and then to the center of Tel Aviv. Additional source: Edna Nahshon, June 29, 2012.

Ayznman Tsvi: Warsaw, 1920–Kibbutz Alonim, 2015. ʻAliya: 1949 to Kibbutz Yagur, and from there moved to Kibbutz Alonim.

Elboym-Dorembus Khaye: Born in Stok to a religious family. Studied in public school there, and at age thirteen moved to Zhelekhov. There she met the writer A. M. Vaysnberg and under his influence began to write and publish. She graduated from the Likova high school for girls, where she later worked as a teacher. She married in Plotzk. When World War II broke out, she fled to Warsaw and lived there in the ghetto until the uprising. Her daughter, mother, and other relatives were murdered in the ghetto. Moved to the "Aryan" side, where she lived until the liberation. Came to Israel in 1947, to Kiryat Motzkin. From there she moved to Kibbutz Eilon and later settled in Tel Aviv. She died in Boston in 1998. Sources: *Mikan*; Ruth Meron, April 1, 2019.

Berlinski Shloyme: Keltz, 1900–Tel Aviv, 1959. Was raised in a religious home in poor neighborhoods in Lodzh and Warsaw. His first story was published in 1922. Published in the Yiddish press in Warsaw and published three books up until World War II. When the war broke out, fled east, and from 1941 stayed in the Soviet Union. In 1946, returned to Poland and continued to the DP camps in Germany. Made ʻaliya in 1948. Source: *Mikan*.

Granatshteyin Yekhiel: Lublin, 1913–Bnei Brak, 2008. ʻAliya: 1950 to the Bitzaron neighborhood of Tel Aviv and from there to Bnei Brak. Additional source: Dr. Michal Shaul, September 6, 2011.

Zakalik, Dovid: Likova, 1905–?. ʻAliya: 1949 to Tel Aviv.

Mali Malasha: Lodzh, 1913–?. ʻAliya: 1950 to the Givʻat Rambam neighborhood of Givʻatayim.

Man Mendl: Plonsk, 1916–Paris, 1975. ʻAliya: 1948 to Yazur and from there to Tel Aviv. In 1962 settled in Paris. Additional sources: *Mikan*; Cohen.

Slutska-Kestin Khave: Warsaw, 1900–Tel Aviv, 1972. Made ʻaliya in 1950 to Tel Aviv. Additional source: Cohen.

Panner Yitskhok: Dobromil (Galicia), 1893–Ramat Gan, 1979. His childhood and youth were spent in Kimpolung, southern Bukovina. Studied in a *kheyder* and also acquired a general education. Lived in New York between the ages of fourteen and eighteen, and in 1912 returned to Eastern Europe, to Tshernovits. Made ʻaliya in 1949 to Bat Yam. Sources: *Mikan*; Cohen.

Papiernikov Levi: Warsaw, 1900–Haifa, 1985. ʻAliya: 1947 to Haifa. Additional source: Cohen.

Friedman Yaakov [Y. Namdirf]: Melnitza, 1910–Tel Aviv, 1972. ʻAliya: 1949 from Cyprus to Beit Dagan and later to Ramat Aviv.

Perlov Yitskhok: Podlyashe, 1911–New York, 1980. ʻAliya: 1949 to Jebelye (Givʻat ʻAliya) and from there to Tel Aviv. In 1961 left for New York. Additional source: Cohen.

Kviatkovski-Pinkhasik Rivke: Lodzh, 1920–?. ʻAliya: 1949 to Kiryat Motzkin.

Karpinovitsh Avrom: Vilna, 1913–Tel Aviv, 2004. Made ʻaliya in 1945 to Givʻat Rambam in Givʻatayim and from there moved to Tel Aviv. Won the Mendele Moykher Sforim Award for Yiddish Writers (1976), the Itzik Manger Award for a Literary Work in Yiddish (1981), and the Prime Minister's Prize for Yiddish Literature (1988).

Shpigl Yishaye: Lodzh, 1906–Tel Aviv, 1990. Made ʻaliya in 1951 to Givʻatayim. Won literary prizes in the world of Yiddish culture. In Israel, won the Itzik Manger Award for a Literary Work in Yiddish (1972). Additional source: Yechiel Szeintuch, *Yišayahu Špigl: Proza sipurit miGeṭo Lodzh* [Yišayahu Špigl: Yiddish narrative prose from the Lodzh Ghetto] (Jerusalem: Magnes, 1995).

Appendix B

Global Centers of Yiddish Culture, 1948–1967[1]

The following data is based on the bibliographic guide composed by Joseph Fraenkel for the World Jewish Congress.[2] It is taken from two editions of the guide: 1953 and 1967 (of a total of five published editions), because these years are the closest to the time frame discussed here (1948–1967). The point of presenting this data is to sketch a map of the worldwide centers of Yiddish in the given period. As I said in chapter 1, the first measure of the size of a given center of Yiddish culture is the presence (or absence) of daily press: the number of newspapers published there, their political affiliation (or nonaffiliation), and the number of distributed copies. This press attests to the scope of the demand for daily media in this language within the community of its speakers. The second measure is the overall number of periodicals in a given center, since these attest to the readers' devotion to their unique culture.

Fraenkel's survey is limited both in terms of the variety of the data and in terms of its credibility. One of the disadvantages of his research is that it includes no reference to the size of the Jewish communities in which the surveyed press is published. Nonetheless, this is one of the only sources available to us, and it is important to make the most of it. Errors found in his data (in the names of publications, their founding year, the frequency of their publication, etc.) have been corrected here and have also been compared to other sources on the topic, if available. The numbers given in the "Total" rows in the tables include these corrections.

In what follows, I have included only the secular and national-religious publications from Fraenkel's study and only those that appeared exclusively in Yiddish (in other words, I excluded bi- or trilingual publications and publications by Orthodox communities). The system of notation was changed in the 1960s to include different details (like the names of the editors and the year of foundation). This information is added here in parentheses to the information from 1953. Among the information added in the later edition is data on distribution. This data needs to be treated with particular skepticism, since Fraenkel does not say where it is from, and it is likely that he relied on numbers provided by the publications themselves. The names of the publications appear here as they appeared in the actual publication, and not in accordance with the YIVO guidelines for transliteration.

Centers of Yiddish culture in the world according to daily press

City	1953	1967
New York	*Forverts* (Liberal-socialist, founded in 1897)	*Forverts* Editor: H. Rogoff Distribution: 80,000
	Der morgn zshurnal (Founded in 1901; in 1953 was unified with *Der tog*)	*Der Tog-morgn zshurnal* Editor: L. Fogelman Distribution: 60,000
	Der tog (Zionist, founded in 1914)	—
	Morgn frayhayt (Communist, founded in 1922)	*Morgn frayhayt* Editor: Novik Distribution: 8,000
Total	**4**	**3** Distribution: 205,000*
Buenos Aires	*Di yidishe tsaytung* (Founded in 1914)	*Di yidishe tsaytung* Editor: M. Stoler
	Di prese (Founded in 1918)	*Di prese* Editor: Y. Yansovitsh
Total	**2**	**2** Distribution: ?
Montevideo (Uruguay)	*Folksblat* (Zionist, founded in 1931)	—
	Undzer fraynt (Progressive, founded in 1935)	*Undzer fraynt* Distribution: 1,500
Total	**2**	**1** Distribution: 1,500
Montreal	*Keneder odler* (Independent, founded in 1907)	Ceased to appear as a daily and began to appear three times a week (see below)
Toronto	*Der yidisher zshurnal* (Independent, founded in 1911)	*Der yidisher zshurnal*
Total Canada	**2**	**1**
Paris	*Naye prese* (Communist, founded in 1934)	*Naye prese* Editor: G. Kenig
	Undzer shtime (Bund, founded in 1935)	*Undzer shtime* Editor: B. Gutman
	Undzer vort (Po'ale Zion, founded in 1945)	*Undzer vort* Editor: L. Dumenkevitsh
Total	**3**	**3** Distribution: ?

(*continued*)

(Continued)

City	1953	1967
Tel Aviv	*Letste nayes* (Independent, founded in 1949, editor M. Tsanin, distribution 16,000, on weekends—30,000)	*Letste nayes*
Total	**1**	**1**
Worldwide Total	**14**	**11**

*According to the data provided by Izik Ramba, in 1967 the daily Yiddish newspapers in New York, *Forverts* and *Tog-morgn zshurnal*, were distributed altogether in some 200,000 copies, but this figure appears to be highly exaggerated for that year. *Morgn frayhayt* was printed in approximately 5,000 copies. Izik Ramba, "'Orot uŞlalim baYomonim beYidiš be'Arşot haBrit" [Lights and shadows in the Yiddish daily press in the United States], *Qorot ha'Etonayi'm haYehudiyim: Buleṭin šel haLiška ha'Olamit šel ha'Etona'im haYehudiim beYerušalaim* [The annals of Jewish journalists: Bulletin of the World Federation of Jewish Journalists in Jerusalem] 12 (1967): 5–7.

Centers of Yiddish culture in the world according to periodicals

City	1953	1967
New York	**Weeklies**: *Der amerikaner; Yidisher kemfer* **Biweeklies**: *Der veker; Fraye arbeter shtime; Undzer veg* **Monthlies**: *Der mizrakhi-veg; Dos vort bibliyotek; Dos yidishe folk; New yorker vokhnblat; Faktn un meynungen; Folk un velt; Kinder-zshurnal; Kinder-tsaytung; Kultur un dertsiyung; Afn shvel; Undzer tsayt; Yidishe kultur; Yungvarg;*† *Di tsukunft* **Quarterlies:** *Undzer shtime; Yidishe shprakh* **Yearlies**: *Yivo-bleter*	**Weekly**: *Yidisher kemfer* **Monthlies**: *Folk un velt; Fraye arbeter shtime; Undzer veg; Undzer tsayt; Der veker; Yidishe kultur; Pedagogisher biyuletin; Di tsukunft* **Bimonthlies**: *Fraynd; Kinder-zshurnal; Kinder-tsaytung; Kultur un dertsiyung; Der mizrakhi-veg; Afn shvel; Dos yidishe shul-lebn** **Quarterlies**: *Undzer eygn vinkl; Yidishe shprakh; Yugntruf; Zamlungen; Zayn* **Irregular**: *Der seminarist; Zshelekhover biyuletin*
Total	**22**	**23** While there is a slight increase in the number of publications, there is a marked decrease in their frequency.

(continued)

(*Continued*)

City	1953	1967
Los Angeles	**Bimonthly**: *Literarishe heftn*	**Quarterly**: *Kheshbn*
Total	1	1
Cleveland	**Weekly**: *Di yidishe velt*	
Total	1	0
Total US	24	24
Paris	**Weeklies**: *Arbeter vort*; *Tsionistishe shtime*; *Undzer veg* **Biweekly**: *Tsionistishe bleter* **Monthlies**: *Kunst un visnshaft*; *Der veg*;§ *Folksgezunt*; *Frayland*; *Fraye horizontn*; *Kiyem*	**Weekly**: *Undzer veg* **Monthlies**: *Arbeter vort*; *Frayer gedank*; *Di naye shtime*;‡ *Parizer shpilkes*; *Undzer kiyem*; *Folksgezunt* **Quarterly**: *Parizer tsaytshrift* **Irregular**: *Tsionistishe shtime*; *Der shtriker fabrikant*
Total	10	10
Tel Aviv	**Three times a week**: *Dos vort*; *Haynt*;¦ *Yidishe tsaytung* **Weeklies**: *Bleter far oylim*; *Nayvelt*; *Fray yisroel*; *Ilustrirter vokhnblat*; *Moment* (Herut) **Biweekly**: *Folk un tsiyen* **Monthly**: *Yisroel* (Poʿale Zion); *Lebns fragn* (Bund) **Quarterly**: *Di goldene keyt*	**Weeklies**: *Folksblat*; *Fray yisroel*; *Ilustrirte veltvokh*; *Der veg* (Communist); *Yidishe tsaytung*; *Yisroel shtime* (Mapam) **Biweekly**: *Zamlung* **Monthlies**: *Folk un tsiyen*; *Lebns fragn* **Quarterly**: *Di goldene keyt* **Yearly**: *Haifa*
Total	12	11
Mexico City	**Three times a week**: *Der veg*; *Di shtime* **Weekly**: *Frayvelt* **Monthly**: *Foroys* **Irregular**: *Dos vort*; *Kultur lebn*; *Mizrakhi-Lebn*	**Three times a week**: *Der veg* **Twice a week**: *Di shtime*
Total	7	2
Buenos Aires	**Weekly**: *Di naye tsayt*; *Bleter* **Monthlies**: *Di yidishe Velt*; *Argentiner magazin*; *Dos fraye vort*; *Undzer vort*; *Undzer gedank*; *Der shpigl* **Quarterlies**: *Davke*; *Shriftn* **Irregular**: *Argentiner beymelekh*; *Farn folks gezunt*	**Monthlies**: *Argentiner magazin*; *Der shpigl*; *Dos fraye vort*; *Yediyes*; *Undzer gedank*; *Undzer vort*; *Di yidishe velt* **Quarterlies**: *Davke*; *Shriftn* **Irregular**: *Argentiner yivo-shriftn*; *Landsmanshaftn* **Yearly**: *Arkhiv fun prese oysshnitn*
Total	12	12

(*continued*)

(*Continued*)

City	1953	1967
Johannesburg	**Weekly**: *Afrikanishe yidishe tsaytung* **Monthly**: *Dorem afrike*	**Weekly**: *Afrikanishe yidishe tsaytung* **Monthly**: *Dorem afrike* **Quarterly**: *Yontef-bleter* **Yearly**: *Rosh hashone yorbukh*
Total	**2**	**4**
Warsaw[#]	**Three times a week**: *Folks-shtime* **Quarterly**: *Bleter far geshikhte*	**Three times a week**: *Folks-shtime* **Yearly**: *Bleter far geshikhte*
Total	**2**	**2**
London	**Weekly**: *Yidishe shtime* **Monthly**: *Loshn un lebn*	**Irregular**: *Yidishe shtime* **Monthly**: *Loshn un lebn*
Total	**2**	**2**
Munich	**Biweekly**: *Naye yidishe tsaytung*	**Weekly**: *Naye yidishe tsaytung*
Total	**1**	**1**
Bucharest	**Weekly**: *Yikuf-bleter***	—
Total	**1**	**0**
Toronto	**Three times a week**: *Kaneder-nayes* **Weekly**: *Vokhnblat*	**(Bi)weekly**: *Vokhnblat*
Total	**2**	**1**
Montreal	—	**Three times a week**: *Keneder-odler*
Total	**0**	**1**
Total Canada	**2**	**2**
Melbourne	**Weekly**: *Di oystralishe yidishe nayes*; *Di yidishe post*	**Weekly**: *Di oystralishe yidishe post* **Quarterly**: *Der lamdsman*; *Undzer gedank*
Total	**2**	**3**
Montevideo (Uruguay)	**Weekly**: *Der moment*	**Weekly**: *Der moment*
Total	**1**	**1**
Santiago (Chile)	**Weekly**: *Dos yidishe vort*	—
Total	**1**	**0**
Havana (Cuba)	**Weekly**: *Havaner lebn*	—
Total	**1**	**0**
Rio de Janeiro (Brazil)	—	**Weeklies**: *(Braziliyaner) Yidishe tsaytung*; *Yidishe prese*
Total	**0**	**2**
Sao Paolo (Brazil)	—	**Biweekly**: *Der nayer moment*
Total	**0**	**1**

(*continued*)

(Continued)

City	1953	1967
Birobidzhan	—	**Three times a week**: *Birobidzhaner shtern*
Total	0	1
Moscow	—	**Monthly**: *Sovetish heymland*
Total	0	1
Worldwide Total	80	79

*This publication is not mentioned in these years in the Israeli National Library's unified catalogue of publications.

†This publication is not mentioned in these years in the Israeli National Library's unified catalogue of publications.

‡This publication does not appear in the Israeli National Library's unified catalogue of publications.

§This publication does not appear in the Israeli National Library's unified catalogue of publications.

|This publication does not appear in the Israeli National Library's unified catalogue of publications.

#On Yiddish press in the Soviet Union and Poland, see also Mordechai Altshuler, *Yahadut brit haMo'eṣot ba'Aspaqlaria šel 'etonut yidiš bePolin: Bibliografia, 1945–1970* [Soviet Jewry in the mirror of the Yiddish press in Poland: Bibliography, 1945–1970] (Jerusalem: Hebrew University of Jerusalem, 1975), 11–17.

**This publication does not appear under this name in the Israeli National Library's unified catalogue of publications. A publication titled *Yikuf bleter far di kindersvegn* appears in the catalogue and is described as printed in Bucharest, probably in the years 1950–1952.

Notes

Introduction

1. The visit was arranged by the state committee that oversaw the ten-year celebrations, the World Jewish Congress, and the Y. L. Peretz Library. See the advertisement in *Davar*, May 23, 1958, 10; the invitation sent to I. Manger by Dr. Leo Bernshtein, head of the Israeli administration of the World Jewish Congress, the National Library of Israel, I. Manger Archive, 4:628/4°.1357. On the Y. L. Peretz Library, see chap. 1.

2. Avrom Sutzkever, "A vort tsum poet" [A word to the poet], *DGK* 31 (1958): 14. Sutzkever delivered these words when he spoke at the poet's festive reception at the Ohel Shem Hall in Tel Aviv. For a report on the event, see "Itzik Manger—yontef fun yidisher poezye in yisroel" [Itzik Manger—a festival of Yiddish poetry in Israel], *LN*, May 30, 1958, 6. According to this report, twelve hundred people attended the event. I return to this event later.

3. Moyshe Grosman, "Borekh habo Itzik Manger!" [Welcome, Itzik Manger!], *Heymish* 24 (1958): 1.

4. "In 1958 Manger visited Israel for the first time, as a guest of the 'ten-year anniversary' committee. In preparation for this trip, Manger wrote . . . : 'For years I wandered in foreign lands, now I shall wander at home.'" Leyb Vaserman, "Manger, Itzik," in *Leksikon fun der nayer yidisher literatur* [The lexicon of modern Yiddish literature], ed. Shmuel Niger and Yankev Shatski (New York: Alveltlekhn yidishn kultur-kongres, 1956–1981), 5:438.

5. On the back side of a draft of the song in the Manger archive of the National Library of Israel appears the following note: "Written by Manger, August 17, 1952." 2:418/4°.1357. For the poem's publication in the daily Yiddish press in New York, see Itzik Manger, "K'hob zikh yorn gevalgert" [For years I wandered], *Der tog*, September 19, 1952, newspaper clipping with no page number, the National Library, Manger Archive, 8:162/4°.1357.

6. Both of these authors visited Israel before the establishment of the state: Opatoshu in 1934 and Leyvik in 1937.

7. See advertisement: "Qabalat panim beḤasut wa'ad haKavod šel sar haḤinuḵ weHatarbut mar Zalman 'Aran weŠel yošev roš haSoḵnut haYehudit mar Zalman Šazar" [Reception sponsored by the honors committee of the Minister of Education and Culture Mr. Zalman Aran and of the Chairman of the Jewish Agency Mr. Zalman Shazar], *Davar*, May 23, 1958, 10.

8. See the list of participants in the advertisement, "Kaboles ponim Itzik Manger" [Reception Itzik Manger], *LN*, May 23, 1958, 8; and in the *LN*'s report on the event, "Itzik Manger—yontef," 6 (see n. 2).

9. K. Shabtai [Shabtai Keshev Klugman], "Itzik Manger 'al 'aṣmo we'Al širato" [Itzik Manger on himself and his poetry], *Davar*, June 3, 1958, 3.

10. Anonymous, "Itzik Manger oreaḥ 'itona'ey Tel Aviv" [Itzik Manger guest of Tel Aviv journalists], *Davar*, June 21, 1958, 6.

11. Anonymous, "Itzik Manger—ba'Areṣ" [Itzik Manger—in Israel], *Davar*, May 14, 1958, 6; Shabtai, "Sefer bišvil haNaśi" [A book for the president], *Ma'ariv*, May 14, 1958, 2; Shraga Har-Gil, "Itzik Manger," *Davar*, May 23, 1958, 22–25; Rivka Katsenelson, "Širati hi—siyum: Siḥa 'im Itzik Manger" [My poetry is an ending: A conversation with Itzik Manger], *Ma'ariv*,

May 30, 1958, 15; Mordechai Sever, "Širato šel Itzik Manger" [Itzik Manger's poetry], *Masa*, May 30, 1958, A-B; B. Kalman, "Itzik Manger," *HaTzofe*, June 6, 1958, clipping with no page number, the National Library, Manger Archive, 8:4339/4°.1357.

12. On images of the Holocaust survivors in the eyes of the Israeli Yišuv (the body of Jewish residents of pre-state Israel), Israeli establishment, and Israeli cultural elite, and on the different attitudes toward them, see Dina Porat, *Israeli Society, the Holocaust and Its Survivors* (London: Vallentine Mitchell, 2008), 337–50.

13. For all quotes from Manger's poem, see "Kh'hob zikh yorn gevalgert," in *Lid un balade* [Poem and ballad] (Tel Aviv: Y. L. Peretz, 1976), 486–87. The English translation is by Leonard Wolf, "For Years I Wallowed," in *The World According to Itzik: Selected Poetry and Prose* (New Haven, CT: Yale University Press, 2002), 106. Here and in the body of the text, I use my own translation for the phrase "k'hob zikh yorn gevalgert"—"for years I wandered"—and not the published translation, "for years I wallowed."

14. For other readings of Manger's "For Years I Wandered" alongside ha-Levi's "Zion, Won't You Ask," see Naomi Brenner, "Itzik in Israel: Itzik Manger's Yiddish in Hebrew Translation," *Prooftexts* 28 (2008): 73; Zvi Jagendorf, "Got fun Avrom: Itzik Manger and 'Avot Yešurun Look Homewards," in *Insiders and Outsiders: Dilemmas of East European Jewry*, ed. Richard Cohen, Jonathan Frankel, and Stefani Hofman (Oxford: Littman Library of Jewish Civilization, 2010), 34.

15. So writes, for example, Israel Levin about Judah ha-Levi's canonical work: "This is the most famous 'Zion song' in the entire history of the Hebrew language. It was added to the Tisha be-Av lamentations nusaḥ Ashkenaz, and a great many people lamented with it the destruction of their ancient homeland. . . . Its influence on Jewish culture is profound and continuous, more so perhaps than any other single poem. This poem is at once a traditional hymn for Zion and an emotional personal expression of the poet." Israel Levin, "Libi baMizraḥ" [My heart is in the East], in *Yehuda haLewi: Poems*, ed. Yisrael Levin (Tel Aviv: Tel Aviv University Press, 2007 [1125–1141]), 256. On the Yiddish translations of the poem, see Hayyim Schirmann, "Targumei Ṣion halo tiš'ali leYehuda haLewi: Rešima bibliografit" [The translations of Judah ha-Levi's "Zion, Won't You Ask": A bibliography], *Qiryat Sefer* 15 (1939): 360–67. Schirmann lists six Yiddish translations of "Zion, Won't You Ask." The most famous is H. N. Bialik's translation (number forty-four on the list), but he also notes other interesting translations, like those of Moris Roznfeld and Y. Y. Shvarts. The list should be updated to include, among other items, Arn Tseytlin's translation of "Zion, Won't You Ask," in *Lider fun hurbn un lider fun gloybn* [Poems of the Holocaust and poems of faith], vol. 2 (New York: Bergen Belsen Memorial Press, 1970), 349–51.

16. For all quotes from ha-Levi's song, see Judah ha-Levi, "Zion, Won't You Ask," *Poems from the Diwan*, trans. Gabriel Levin (London: Anvil Press Poetry, 2002), 100–102.

17. Ha-Levi: "I walked in your groves and fields and lingered / in Gilead, astonished at the range beyond." Manger: "I'll stand and gape at the blue Kinneret"; "Musing, I'll stand before your great desert."

18. "Dust" is the literal meaning of the Yiddish word *shtoyb*, and it echoes the labeling in Israel of the surviving-remnant immigrants as *'avaq 'adam* ("human dust"). The choice to render it in Hebrew as *'afar* ("earth," "dirt") retains the allusion to ha-Levi's poem ("I'd . . . favor your dust"). This choice appeared also in the translations of Moshe Bassok (1963), Binyamin Tene (1968), and Yaakov Shabtai (1992). For a comparison of these translations, see Benny Mer, "Kh'hob zikh yorn gevalgert: Maqor weTargum" [For Years I Wandered: Original and translation], *Davke* 3 (2006): 56–57.

19. Historian Dominick LaCapra distinguished between two kinds of emotional pain: "absence," whose source is existential and which characterizes the life of every human being (it is caused, for instance, by the separation from the mother, entry into language, etc.), and "loss," caused by a concrete separation from close individuals, communities, or cultures as the result of an exceptional historical event. Trauma blurs the boundaries between these two types of pain, while a successful working through of the trauma makes the distinction between them possible. In language, the blurring of boundaries is articulated through nostalgic, utopian, or melancholic terms. Dominick LaCapra, *Writing History, Writing Trauma* (Baltimore: Johns Hopkins University Press, 2014), 46.

20. Manger's poem was similarly interpreted by the Yiddish poet and author Alexander Shpiglblat. See Shpiglblat, *Pinot kḥulot: Itzik Manger—ḥaim, šir uBalada* [Blue corners: Itzik Manger—life, poem and ballad], trans. Yehuda Gur-Arie (Jerusalem: Carmel, 2009), 105.

21. Galit Hasan-Rokem, "Contemporary Perspectives of Tradition: Moving On with the *Wandering Jew*," in *Konstellationen Über Geschichte, Erfahrung und Erkenntnis* [Constellations about history, experience and knowledge], ed. Nicolas Berg et al. (Göttingen: Vandenhoeck and Ruprecht, 2011), 314, 316.

22. Galit Hasan-Rokem, "Contemporary Perspectives of Tradition," 312, 326–27; see also Galit Hasan-Rokem, "HaQrav bein Liviatan weHaYehudi haNoded: Ra'ayion haMedina šel Qarl Šmidṭ weHaFolqlor haEropi" [The battle between Leviathan and the wandering Jew: Carl Schmitt's idea of the state and European folklore], in *Folqlor we'Idiologia* [Folklore and ideology], ed. Haya Bar-Itzhak (Haifa: Pardes, 2014), 91–92.

23. Max Weinreich, "Yidish un ashkenaz: Der forshobiyekt un der tsugang" [Yiddish and Ashkenaz: The object of study and the approach], in *Geshikhte fun der yidisher shprakh* [History of Yiddish language] (New York: YIVO, 1973), 1:3–47.

24. On the development of modern Yiddish culture and its characteristics, see Avraham Novershtern, "Ṣmiḥatan šel sifrut weTarbut yidiš haModerniot" [The rise of modern Yiddish literature and culture], in *Toldot yehudei Rusia* [The history of the Jews of Russia], ed. Ilya Luria (Jerusalem: Zalman Shazar, 2012), 2:333–63.

25. Israel Gutman, "Še'erit haPleṭa: Be'ayiot weHavharot" [The surviving remnant: Problems and clarifications], in *Še'erit haPleṭa, 1944–1948: HaŠiqum weHama'vaq haPoliṭi* [The surviving remnant, 1944–1948: The rehabilitation and political struggle], ed. Israel Gutman et al. (Jerusalem: Yad Vashem, 1990), 461–79. Gutman noted that most of the Jews from Western European countries and Hungary returned to their homelands after the war. By contrast, Jews from Eastern Europe, Poland, and the Baltic countries became displaced (465). On the broadening and limiting meanings of the term *surviving remnant*, see Ze'ev Mankowitz, *Life between Memory and Hope: The Survivors of the Holocaust in Occupied Germany* (Cambridge: Cambridge University Press, 2002), 1–10; Dan Michmann, "On the Definition of Še'erit haPleṭa," in *Holocaust Historiography: A Jewish Perspective—Conceptualizations, Terminology, Approaches, and Fundamental Issues* (London: Vallentine Mitchell, 2003), 329–32.

26. Gutman, "Še'erit haPleṭa," 462.

27. For a summary of this move, see Mankowitz, *Life between Memory and Hope*, 11–23.

28. Hagit Lavsky, *New Beginnings: Holocaust Survivors in Bergen-Belsen and the British Zone in Germany, 1945–1950* (Detroit: Wayne State University Press, 2002), 222.

29. Mankowitz, *Life between Memory and Hope*, 6–7.

30. Hasia R. Diner, *We Remember with Reverence and Love: American Jews and the Myth of Silence after the Holocaust, 1945–1962* (New York: New York University Press, 2009).

31. Ella Avital-Florsheim, "Hanṣaḥa be'Emṣaut te'ud viYeṣira: Ha'Yiton *undzer shtime* miMaḥane ha'Aqira Bergen Belsen, 1945–1947" [Memorialization through documentation and creative production: The paper *undzer shtime* [our voice] from the DP camp Bergen-Belsen, 1945–1947] (Master's thesis, Hebrew University, Jerusalem, 2003), 13–14; see also Ella Florsheim, *Tarbut yidiś beMaḥanot ha'Aqurim* [Yiddish culture in the DP camps] (Jerusalem: Zalman Shazar and Yad Vashem, 2020).

32. See Guy Miron, "Legašer 'al pnei tehom- ḥeqer haŠo'a mul ḥeqer toldot Yiśra'el" [Bridging the divide: Holocaust versus Jewish history research—problems and challenges], *Yad Vashem Studies* 38, no. 2 (2011): 129–60.

33. Dalia Ofer pointed out the variety of identities that lie within supposedly homogenous phenomena and groups (such as "'aliya Bet" or the "ha'apala" [ascension]) and the importance of distinguishing between the various and sometimes contradictory identity components of their members. Dalia Ofer, *Escaping the Holocaust: Illegal Immigration to the Land of Israel, 1939–1944* (New York: Oxford University Press, 1990). On the differences between the terms *immigrant* and *refugee* and on the importance of distinguishing between them in the case of *'oley sheyres hapleyta*, see Gali Drucker Bar-Am, "BeQolam uVisfatam: Yiśra'el biRe'i siporet yidiš šeNiḵteva beYiśra'el biYedey oley šeerit haPleṭa" [In their voice and in their language: Israel through the prism of Yiddish fiction written in Israel by members of Še'erit haPleṭa], in *Yiśra'el be'Eyney niṣoley hašoa' weŚordea* [Israel in the eyes of the survivors of the Holocaust], ed. Dalia Ofer (Jerusalem: Yad Vashem, 2015), 353–81.

34. Gila Menahem and Efraim Ya'ar, "Mehagrim, pliṭim weNiṣolim beYiśra'el: HaDor haRišon weHašeni" [Immigrants, refugees, and survivors in Israel: The first and second generation," in *Bein 'Olim leWatiqim: Yiśra'el ba'Aliya haGdola, 1948–1953* [Between new immigrants and old-timers: Israel in the great wave of immigration, 1948–1953], ed. Dalia Ofer (Jerusalem: Yad Ben-Zvi, 1996), 191–209.

35. Dan Laor, "Bein meṣiut leḤazon: 'Al hištaqfuta šel ha'Aliya haHamonit baRoman haYiśra'eli" [Between reality and vision: Reflections of the massive immigration in the Israeli novel], in *'Olim uMa'abarot, 1948–1952*, ed. Mordechai Naor ['Olim and Ma'abarot, 1948–1952] (Jerusalem: Yad Ben-Zvi, 1986), 217; Dalia Ofer, "Watiqim we'Olim ba'Aliya haGdola" [Old-timers and new immigrants in the great wave of immigration], in Ofer, *Bein 'Olim leWatiqim*, 7–8.

36. Dan Laor, "Ha'Aliya haHamonit keToḵen uKeNośe baSifrut ha'Ivrit"[The mass immigration as content and subject in Hebrew literature in the first years of statehood], *HaZiyonut* 14 (1989): 174–75; Avner Holzman, *'Ahavot Ṣion: panim baSifrut ha'Ivrit haḤadaša* [Loves of Zion: Studies in modern Hebrew literature] (Jerusalem: Carmel, 2006), 361.

37. According to Moshe Lissak, the "melting pot" policy, also known as the "guardianship strategy," sought to bring about "a disengagement from all the unique elements of ethnic traditions and the creation of a cultural system . . . governed by a single dominant element, the Western European Ashkenazi culture, however it is defined." Moshe Lissak, *Ha'Aliya haGdola biŠnot haḤamišim: Kišlono šel kur haHituḵ* [The mass immigration of the 1950s: The failure of the melting pot] (Jerusalem: Bialik Institute, 1999), 68. He argues that in the second half of the 1950s this absorption strategy began to change and was replaced by a "pluralist principle" according to which "the cultural assets of the absorbing population was carefully preserved, but a certain degree of self-definition on the part of the immigrants was legitimized . . . At the same time, even within this limited understanding, it was agreed by all that the goal, ultimately, is to gradually change the immigrants" (72).

38. Max Weinreich, "Kriteries far periodizirn di geshikhte fun yidish" [Criteria for the periodization of Yiddish], in *Geshikhte fun der yidisher shprakh*, 1:383–97.

39. Benedict Anderson, *Imagined Communities: Reflections on the Origin and Spread of Nationalism* (London: Verso, 1991), 24–25.

40. LaCapra, *Writing History, Writing Trauma*, 46.

41. On Holocaust survivors from the Orthodox religious sector in Israel, see, for example, Michal Shaul, *Holocaust Memory in Ultra-Orthodox Society in Israel* (Bloomington: Indiana University Press, 2020).

42. On the national space and its construction as a "place" and even as the "great place," see Zali Gurevitch and Gideon Aran, "'Al haMaqom: Antropologya yiśra'elit" [On the place: Israeli anthropology], in *'Al haMaqom* [On the place], by Zali *Gurevitch* (Tel Aviv: Am-Oved, 2007), 8–9.

43. Eli Lederhendler, *Jewish Responses to Modernity: New Voices in America and East Europe* (New York: New York University Press, 1994).

44. On the evolution of the notion of "denial of exile" before the establishment of the state and after it, see Anita Shapira, *Yehudim, ṣionim uMa šeBeynehem* [Jews, Zionists, and in-between] (Tel Aviv: Am-Oved, 2007), 63–110.

45. Lederhendler, *Jewish Responses to Modernity*, 9–22.

46. Itamar Even-Zohar, "HaSifrut ha'Ivrit haYiśra'elit: Model hisṭori" [Israeli Hebrew literature: A historical model], *HaSifrut* 4 (1973): 430.

47. Gilles Deleuze and Felix Guattari launched the use of the terms *minor literature* and *major literature*. See Deleuze and Guattari, *Kafka: Toward a Minor Literature* (Minneapolis: University of Minnesota Press, 1986), 16–27.

48. On these "turns" in the humanities, see Guy Miron, "Lašon, tarbut uMerḥav: Etgerei haHistoryografia haYehudit be'Edan haTafniyot" [Language, culture and space: The challenges of Jewish historiography in the age of the "turns"], *Zion* 76 (2011): 63–94.

49. The debate about the status of Yiddish in pre-state Israel, known as "the war of languages" or "the battle of tongues," took place in the years 1918–1924. See Arie Leyb Pilovski, *Tsvishn yo un neyn: Yidish un yidishe literatur in erets- yisroel, 1907–1948* [Between yes and no: Yiddish and its literature in mandate Palestine, 1907–1948] (Tel Aviv: Y. L. Peretz, 1986). Pilovski makes the important observation that "the 'war of language' (or 'battle of tongues') was waged not between Zionists and anti-Zionists (for instance, Communists or Bundists), but rather within the Zionist camp" (359).

50. Gershon Shaked, *HaSiporet ha'Ivrit, 1880–1980* [Hebrew fiction, 1880–1980], vol. 4 (Tel Aviv: Hakibbutz Hameuchad, 1993), 173–85.

51. This, despite the fact that in Israel literary works were written by new immigrants in languages other than Hebrew besides Yiddish, like Hungarian (Ephraim Kishon, *Ha'Ole haYored leḤayenu*, 1952), Bulgarian (*Kuḵim beYafo*, 1954), and Arabic (Shimon Balas, *HaMa'abara*, 1955). For more, see Laor, "Bein meṣiut leḤazon," 212–17; Laor, "Ha'Aliya haHamonit keToḵen uKeNośe," 171–73; Holzman, *'Ahavot Ṣion*, 361.

52. Werner Sollors and Mark Shell showed how, for years, studies of American literature took for granted and indeed encouraged the false assumption that this literature was a homogeneous space of unilingual readers and writers (i.e., exclusively English speakers). This false assumption, they argued, not only distorted the picture of the literary creation in the American space but also limited and flattened the questions posed about it. Their studies inspired me to pursue a similar examination of the Israeli literary space. Mark Shell and Werner Sollors (eds.), *The Multilingual Anthology of American Literature* (New York: New York University Press, 2000).

53. For an example of a fruitful expansion of the principle for selecting works, see Liora R. Halperin's comparative study of the Yishuv's attitude toward English, Arabic, and

Yiddish. The basic premise of her study is that the nature of the space of pre-state Israel was multilingual. Halperin, *Babel in Zion: Jews, Nationalism and Language Diversity in Palestine, 1920–1948* (New Haven, CT: Yale University Press, 2015).

54. Dovid-hersh Roskes, "Di shrayber grupe yung-yisroel" [The writers group Young-Israel], *Yugntruf* 28–29 (1973): 7–12; 33 (1975): 7–8; 34 (1976): 4–7; David Roskies, *A Bridge of Longing: The Lost Art of Yiddish Storytelling* (Cambridge, MA: Harvard University Press, 1995), 307–46; Avraham Novershtern, *'Avraham Sutzkever biMl'ot lo šiv'im* [Avraham Sutzkever on his seventieth birthday] (Jerusalem: Beit haSfarim haLe'umi ṿeHaUniversiṭa'i, 1984) [in Hebrew and Yiddish]; Avraham Novershtern, *Avrom Sutzkever: Bibliografie* [Avrom Sutzkever: Bibliography] (Tel Aviv: Yisroel-bukh, 1976); Avraham Novershtern, "The Multicolored Patchwork on the Coat of a Prince," *Modern Hebrew Literature* 8–9 (1992): 56–59.

55. Pilovski, *Tsvishn yo un neyn*; Yael Chaver, *Ma šeḤayavim liškoaḥ: Yidiš baYešuv heḤadaš* [That which must be forgotten: Yiddish in the new Yishuv] (Jerusalem: Yad Ben-Zvi, 2005).

56. Joshua A. Fishman and Dovid E. Fishman, "Yiddish in Israel: The Press, Radio, Theater and Book Publishing," *Yiddish* 1, no. 2 (1973): 4–23; Avraham Novershtern, "Between Town and Gown: The Institutionalization of Yiddish at Israeli Universities," in *Yiddish in the Contemporary World: Papers of the First Mendel Friedman International Conference on Yiddish*, ed. Genady Estraikh and Mikhail Krutikov (Oxford: Legenda, 1999), 1–20; Rachel Rojanski, "HaOmnam śafa zara weṢoremet'? LiŠe'elat yaḥaso šel Ben-Gurion leYidiś leAḥar haŠoa' [Indeed a "foreign and grating language"? On the question of Ben-Gurion's relationship to Yiddish after the Holocaust], *Iyunim Bitkumat Israel* 15 (2005): 463–82; Rachel Rojanski, "The Status of Yiddish in Israel, 1948–1958: An Overview," in *Yiddish after the Holocaust*, ed. Joseph Sherman (Oxford: Boulevard Books, 2004), 46–59; Rachel Rojanski, "The Final Chapter in the Struggle for Cultural Autonomy: Palestine, Israel and Yiddish Writers in the Diaspora, 1946–1951," *Journal of Modern Jewish Studies* 6 (2007): 185–204; Rachel Rojanski, "HaTarbut šelanu hi' haMedina šelanu: Meqoma šel medinat yiśra'el baDiyun 'al 'aṭid haYidiš 'aḥrei haŠoa'" [Our culture is our state: The place of Israel in the debate over the future of Yiddish after the Holocaust], *Zmanim* 113 (2011), 68–77; Diego Rotman, *HaBima keVayt 'ar'i: HaTe'aṭron šel Džigan weŠumaḵer, 1927–1980* [The stage as a temporary home: On Dzhigan and Shumakher's theater, 1927–1980] (Jerusalem: Magnes, 2017).

1. Tel Aviv after the Holocaust

1. Avrom Sutzkever, *A. Sutzkever: Selected Poetry and Prose*, trans. Barbara Harshav and Benjamin Harshav (Berkeley: University of California Press, 1991), 3.

2. Letter from Sutzkever to Tsanin, Montreal, April 15, 1959, Gnazim Institute, Tsanin Archive 504–2558/15. A recording of the reception held for Sutzkever on his arrival in Montreal has been made available online by the Yiddish Book Center's Frances Brandt Online Yiddish Audio Library, accessed March 29, 2024, https://archive.org/details/AbrahamSutzkeverReceptionPart1april17th1959.

3. On the centers of Yiddish culture in New York, Warsaw, and Moscow in the 1920s, see Avraham Novershtern, *Kan gar ha'Am haYehudi: Sifrut yidiš beArṣot haBrit* [Here dwells the Jewish people: A century of American Yiddish literature] (Jerusalem: Magnes, 2015), especially 46–76; Mikhail Krutikov, "Yiddish Literature: Yiddish Literature after 1800," in *YIVO Encyclopedia of Jews in Eastern Europe*, ed. Gershon David Hundert (New Haven,

CT: Yale University Press, 2008), 2:2065–84; Nathan Cohen, *Sefer sofer we'Iton: Merqaz haTarbut haYehudit beWarša, 1918–1942* [Books, writers and newspapers: The Jewish culture center in Warsaw, 1918–1942] (Jerusalem: Magnes, 2003), 115–25.

4. For the most well-known articulation of this phenomenon, see Georg Simmel, "The Metropolis and Mental Life" (1903), in *Georg Simmel: On Individuality and Social Forms*, ed. Donald Levine (Chicago: Chicago University Press, 1971), 324–39.

5. Ernest Gellner, *Language and Solitude: Wittgenstein, Malinowski and the Habsburg Dilemma* (Cambridge: Cambridge University Press, 1998), 24. On the "traditional guise" and its expressions in the work of the "father" of modern Yiddish literature, Mendele Moykher Sforim, see Dan Miron, *A Traveler Disguised: The Rise of Modern Yiddish Fiction in the Nineteenth Century* (Syracuse: Syracuse University Press, 1996).

6. For descriptions of Jewish cultural centers in Warsaw, Moscow, and Kiev from the end of the nineteenth century to World War II, see Khone Shmeruk, "Qawim leToldot haMerqaz šel sifrut yidiš beWarša" [A brief history of the center of Yiddish literature in Warsaw], in *Beyn štey milḥemot 'olam: Praqim beḤayei haTarbut šel yehudei polin liLšonoteyhem* (Between two world wars: Chapters in the cultural life of Jews in Poland in their languages), ed. Khone Shmeruk and Shmuel Werses (Jerusalem: Magnes, 1997), 157–68; N. Cohen, *Sefer sofer we'Iton*; Scott Ury, *Barricades and Banners: The Revolution of 1905 and the Transformation of Warsaw Jewry* (Stanford, CA: Stanford University Press, 2012); Kenneth Moss, *Jewish Renaissance in the Russian Revolution* (Cambridge, MA: Harvard University Press, 2009); Gennady Estraikh, *In Harness: Yiddish Writers' Romance with Communism—Judaic Traditions in Literature, Music, and Art* (Syracuse: Syracuse University Press, 2005), 37–64.

7. On the contribution of cultural institutions to the crystallization of modern Jewish identities, see Jeffrey Veidlinger, *Jewish Public Culture in the Late Russian Empire* (Bloomington: Indiana University Press, 2009).

8. Bal-Makhshoves, "Dray shtetlekh" [Three towns], in *Geklibene verk* [Collected works] (New York: Tsiko, 1953), 270.

9. On the relation between the centers of Hebrew culture in Eastern Europe before the rise of Tel Aviv as the leading center, see Dan Miron, *Bodedim beMo'adam: LiDmuta šel haRepubliqa haSifrutit ha'Ivrit biTḥilat haMea' haEsrim* [When loners come together: A portrait of Hebrew literature at the turn of the twentieth century] (Tel Aviv: Am-Oved, 1987), 331–81.

10. The strongest dilemma was between the centers in Moscow and Warsaw, on the one hand, and that in New York on the other. See Dovid Bergelson, "Dray tsentren" [Three centers], *In shpan* 1 (1926): 84–96.

11. Avraham Novershtern, *Qesem haDimdumim: Epoqalipsa uMešiḥiut beSifrut Yidiš* [The lure of twilight: Apocalypse and messianism in Yiddish literature] (Jerusalem: Magnes, 2003).

12. For a critique of the "diasporic nationalism" view, see Gali Drucker Bar-Am, "Review of *Jewish People, Yiddish Nation: Noah Prylucki and the Folkists in Poland* by Kalman Weiser," *Studies in Contemporary Jewry* 27 (2015): 296–97.

13. Kalman Weiser, *Jewish People, Yiddish Nation: Noah Prylucki and the Folkists in Poland* (Toronto: University of Toronto Press, 2011); J. M. Karlip, *The Tragedy of a Generation: The Rise and Fall of Jewish Nationalism in Eastern Europe* (Cambridge, MA: Harvard University Press, 2013).

14. Novershtern, *Kan gar ha'Am haYehudi.*

15. Eli Lederhendler, *New York Jews and the Decline of Urban Ethnicity, 1950–1970* (Syracuse: Syracuse University Press, 2001), 1–12.

16. The image of the ghetto appeared in the works of leading Yiddish writers in the United States in the 1930s; the most well known among them is Yankev Glatshteyn. Gali Drucker Bar-Am, "The Anthological Affect: Memory and Place in Early Post WWII Yiddish Culture," in *Memory, Lament and Endurance in Early Post WWII Yiddish Culture: Yiddish after 1945*, ed. Marion Aptroot (Amsterdam: Menasseh ben Israel Institute, 2018), 18.

17. With the outbreak of World War II, Zelig Kalmanovitsh, a philologist and founding member of YIVO (Yidisher visnshaftlekher institut, Yiddish Scientific Institute) in Vilna, proposed transferring the center's activity to New York. His proposal was opposed by leading Yiddish culture activists, who were wary of the impact that this kind of symbolic act—a transferring of the institution that perceived itself as the highest expression of Yiddish culture from its centers in Eastern Europe to a realm regarded as peripheral—would have on the creators of Yiddish culture. See K. Weiser, "The Jewel in the Yiddish Crown: Who Will Occupy the Chair in Yiddish at the University of Vilnius?," *Polin: Studies in Polish Jewry* 24 (2012): 240.

18. Simon Dubnow, *Divrey yemei 'am olam: Toldot 'am Yiśra'el miYemei qedem 'ad haYom haZe* [History of the eternal nation: The annals of the Jewish people from antiquity to this day] (Tel Aviv: Dvir, 1958), 1:7.

19. Yankev Leshtshinski, "HaBehala miSviv leYidiš" [The frenzy around Yiddish-speaking], *Gesher* 1 (1960): 114.

20. Shmuel Rozhanski, "In keyn land redt men nit azoyfil yidish vi in yisroel" [In no country is Yiddish spoken as much as in Israel], *Biyuletin fun alveltlekhn yidishn kultur-kongres* [Bulletin of the World Congress for Yiddish/Jewish Culture] 11 (1957): 5.

21. Leo Kenig, "Vidergeburt fun folk un shprakh" [Rebirth of the people and their language], *Di tsukunft* 60, no. 9 (1955): 399.

22. Moyshe Gros-Tsimerman, "Yisroels-yidish" [Israeli-Yiddish], in *Intimer videranand: Eseyen* [Intimate contradiction: Essays] (Tel Aviv: Y. L. Peretz, 1964), 318.

23. David Sha'ari, "Yiḥuda šel še'erit haPleṭa" [The uniqueness of the surviving remnant], in *Briḥim šel štiqa: Še'erit haPleṭa we'Ereṣ Yiśra'el* [Bonds of silence: The surviving remnants and mandatory Palestine], ed. Yoel Rappel, *Mesua* 28 (2000): 30. Between May 15, 1948, and the end of 1953, Israel received between 309,567 'olim (according to Dvora Hacohen, *'Olim biSe'ara: Ha'Aliya haGdola uQliṭata beYiśra'el, 1948–1953* [Immigrants in turmoil: The great wave of immigration to Israel and its absorption, 1948–1953] [Jerusalem: Yad Ben-Zvi, 1994], 323–24 and 373,852 'olim (according to Dalia Ofer, "Niṣolim qe'Olim: HaMiqre šel 'aṣurey qafrisin" [Holocaust survivors as immigrants: The case of Israel and the Cyprus detainees], in Rappel, *Briḥim šel štiqa*, 225). By comparison, from Western Europe, 25,503 immigrants came to Israel during those years (the origin of most Jewish immigrants who arrived from Germany in that period was probably Poland). From the whole of Asia arrived 243,836 immigrants, and from Africa, 107,867. The internal breakdown among the immigrants from Eastern Europe was 122,712 from Romania, 104,208 from Poland, 13,986 from Hungary, and 8,126 from Russia. Hacohen, *'Olim biSe'ara*, 6.

24. Israel Gutman, "HaŠoa' weRišuma beToldot 'am yiśra'el" [The Holocaust and its significance in the history of the Jewish people], in *Sugiot beḤeqer haŠoa': Biqoret veTruma* [Issues in Holocaust scholarship: Critique and contribution], ed. Israel Gutman (Jerusalem: Zalman Shazar, 2008), 21.

25. Sha'ari, "Yiḥuda šel še'erit haPleṭa," 30; Ze'ev Mankowitz, *Life between Memory and Hope: The Survivors of the Holocaust in Occupied Germany* (Cambridge: Cambridge University Press, 2002), 21–22. According to Hanna Yablonka ("Ṣayarim niṣoley šoa' beYiśra'el: Hebet

nosaf laŠtiqa šelo hayta" [Holocaust survivor painters in Israel: Another aspect of the silence that never was], in *HaŠoa': Historya weZikaron* [The Holocaust: History and memory], ed. Shmuel Almog et al. [Jerusalem: Yad Vashem, 2002], 207), 70,000 people from among the 'oley sheyres hapleyte immigrated to Israel in 1945–1947, 280,000 in 1948–1951, and a further 100,000 in the second half of the 1950s. See also Hanna Yablonka, *Survivors of the Holocaust: Israel after the War*, trans. Ora Cummings (London: Palgrave Macmillan, 1999), 4.

26. By comparison, 82,000 is the estimated number of immigrants in the fourth 'aliya, in the mid-1920s, and their estimated number in the fifth 'aliya of the early 1930s is approximately 217,000. Hacohen, *'Olim biSe'ara*, 6.

27. Yablonka, *Survivors of the Holocaust*, 9.

28. Sha'ari, "Yiḥuda šel še'erit haPleṭa," 30.

29. Sha'ari, "Yiḥuda šel še'erit haPleṭa," 37. Sha'ari (*Survivors of the Holocaust*, 9–10) estimates that 125,394 'oley sheyres hapleyte from Poland came to Israel in 1946–1956. Yablonka notes the difficulty involved in quantifying the countries of origin of 'oley sheyres hapleyte because it is unclear from the sources whether the documentation was done according to the immigrant's country of origin or the country from which he or she came to Israel. She argues that most of the immigrants listed as "German Jews" were originally from Poland or Lithuania.

30. In a Polish government population census from the end of 1931, 80 percent of Jews gave Yiddish as their mother tongue (8 percent Hebrew and 12 percent Polish). Of course, this data must be qualified: the extent of the Jewish population's cooperation with the Polish government is questionable, and the data cannot be assumed to be an accurate reflection of the actual use. So, for example, those who declared daily use of Hebrew likely did so for ideological reasons and in actuality used Yiddish in their day-to-day lives. See Nathan Cohen, "Sifriot yehudiot weQor'eyhen bePolin beyn štey milḥamot ha'Olam" [Jewish libraries and their readers between the two world wars], *Zion* 67 (2002): 166.

31. Roberto Baki, "Tḥiyat haLašon ha'Ivrit be'Aspaqlariya sṭaṭisṭit" [Revival of the Hebrew language in a statistical view], *Leshonenu* 21, no. 1 (1958): 10. Baki argues that "the great variety of the cultures and tongues brought to Israel by the immigrants from their countries of origin [might have] constituted a serious impediment to the cultural life and life in general in Israel, had the Hebrew language not been revived as a common language for all" (1). His work is one of the only studies I was able to find on the topic of the immigrants' languages of origin. Baki even examined the use of each one of the "foreign" languages separately and did not treat them as a single entity. His analysis is grounded in many different sources, including the 1948 population census, data collected among new immigrants in Jerusalem in 1948, a survey of immigrants who came to Israel in 1948–1949 and were questioned with the help of UNESCO in 1950–1951, and data collected for a manpower survey in 1954.

32. Baki, "Tḥiyat haLašon ha'Ivrit," 12.

33. Baki, "Tḥiyat haLašon ha'Ivrit," 32.

34. Baki, "Tḥiyat haLašon ha'Ivrit," 37.

35. Gutman, "HaŠoa' weRišuma," 20.

36. Hagit Lavsky, *New Beginnings: Holocaust Survivors in Bergen-Belsen and the British Zone in Germany, 1945–1950* (Detroit: Wayne State University Press, 2002), 222.

37. Benjamin Harshav, *The Polyphony of Jewish Culture* (Stanford: Stanford University Press, 2007), 29.

38. Most 'oley sheyres hapleyte were between the ages of fifteen and fifty-nine. In 1946–1948, approximately 62 percent of them were aged fifteen to twenty-nine. This trend

continued in 1948–1949, but more moderately. The sheyres hapleyte immigration was marked by a particularly low number of unmarried men and women. In its early days, it counted more men than women. In 1950–1954, the number of women surpassed that of men. Yablonka, *Survivors of the Holocaust*, 11.

39. ʻOley sheyres hapleyte families had three times more children under the age of four than the veteran Jewish families. On more characteristics of ʻoley sheyres hapleyte families, see Yablonka, *Survivors of the Holocaust*, 10–13.

40. Yablonka, *Survivors of the Holocaust*, 13; Ada Schein, "Bne beytḵa beQarov: Še'erit haPleṭa baHityašvut haMošavit, 1944–1955" [Build your home soon: The surviving remnant in the Moshavim settlements, 1944–1955], in *"WeYašavtem beṭaḥ": Niṣoley haŠoa' baHityašvut haʻOvedet, 1945–1955* ["Dwell in safety": Holocaust survivors in the labor settlement, 1945–1955], ed. Shlomo Bar-Gil and Ada Schein (Jerusalem: Yad Vashem, 2010), 152.

41. According to Yablonka, "the *ʻoley sheyres hapleyte* were absorbed in Israel whether on their own or with the support of special organizations that they themselves established." Hanna Yablonka, "Qliṭat niṣoley haŠoa' biMdinat Yiśra'el: Hebeṭim ḥadašim" [The absorption of Holocaust survivors in Israel: New aspects], *ʻIyunim biTqumat Yiśra'el* [Studies in Israeli and Modern Jewish Society] no. 7 (1997): 285.

42. Moshe Lissak, *HaʻAliya haGdola biŠnot haḤamišim: Kišlono šel kur haHituḵ* [The mass immigration of the 1950s: The failure of the melting pot] (Jerusalem: Mosad Bialik, 1999), 1.

43. Lissak, *HaʻAliya haGdola biŠnot haḤamišim*, 3.

44. Lissak, *HaʻAliya haGdola biŠnot haḤamišim*, 6.

45. Gila Menahem and Efraim Yaʻar, "Mehagrim, pliṭim weNiṣolim beYiśra'el: HaDor haRišon weHašeni" [Immigrants, refugees, and survivors in Israel: The first and second generation], in *Bein ʻOlim leWatiqim: Yiśra'el baʻAliya haGdola, 1948–1953* [Between new immigrants and old-timers: Israel in the great wave of immigration, 1948–1953], ed. Dalia Ofer (Jerusalem: Yad Ben-Zvi, 1996), 191–209.

46. Menahem and Yaʻar, "Mehagrim, pliṭim weNiṣolim beYiśra'el," 196–209.

47. Yablonka, *Survivors of the Holocaust*, 11.

48. Shimon Herman, "Ḥaqirot baPsiḵologya haḤevratit šel bḥirat haLašon beYiśra'el" [Studies in the social psychology of language choice in Israel], in *ʻOlim beYiśra'el: Miqra'a* [Newcomers to Israel: A reader], ed. Moshe Lissak et al. (Jerusalem: Academon, 1969), 419–36.

49. Lissak, *HaʻAliya haGdola biŠnot haḤamišim*, 1.

50. Eli Lederhendler, *Jewish Responses to Modernity: New Voices in America and East Europe* (New York: New York University Press, 1994), 20.

51. Ben-Gurion to Tsanin, April 1, 1963, SA/43/GL/ 22/11888, State Archive, Jerusalem.

52. Memo from Yael Vered (secretary of the Prime Minister's Office), undated, SA/43/G/ 7/5551, State Archive, Jerusalem.

53. Memo from Sh. K [M] to the prime minister, undated, SA/43/G/ 7/5551, State Archive, Jerusalem.

54. For biographical information on Yiddish journalists and authors mentioned in the book, see Appendix A.

55. Arye Leyb Pilovski, whose work surveyed the attitudes toward Yiddish in Palestine/ Eretz Yisrael during the 1930s and 1940s, claimed that the 1940s were the most violent years toward Yiddish (and not the 1920s, when the "war of languages"/"battle of the tongues" was waged]. Arye Leyb Pilovski, *Tsvishn yo un neyn: Yidish un yidishe literatur in erets- yisroel, 1907–1948* [Between yes and no: Yiddish and its literature in mandate-Palestine, 1907–1948] (Tel Aviv: Y. L. Peretz, 1986), 245. He surveyed the responses in the Yiddish press in the

United States to the predicament of Yiddish in Israel and mentioned a questionnaire on this issue that was given out to Yiddish writers across the world (230).

56. On Oyerbakh's activities and writing, see Carrie Friedman Cohen, "Rokhl Oyerbakh: Rašey praqim leḤeqer ḥayea weYeṣirata" [Rokhl Oyerbakh: Outline of her life and work], *Huliyot* 9 (2005): 297–304; Boaz Cohen, "Rachel Auerbuch, Yad Vashem and Israeli Holocaust Memory," *Polin: Studies in Polish Jewry* 20 (2007): 121–97.

57. Rokhl Oyerbakh, "Tsvishn Yidn," [Among Jews], Yad Vashem Archive, Rokhl Oyerbakh Collection, P-16/69.

58. Shmuel Niger (Tsharni), "Di yidishe inteligents un ire naye ufgabn" [The Yiddish intelligentsia and its new tasks], *Di tsukunft* 50, no. 3 (1945): 141–43.

59. On the definitions of this term and its evolution, see Martin Malia, "What Is the Intelligentsia?," in *The Russian Intelligentsia*, ed. Richard Pipes (New York: Columbia University Press, 1961), 1–18; Richard Pipes, "The Historical Evolution of the Russian Intelligentsia," in Pipes, *Russian Intelligentsia*, 47–62; Ela Bauer, "The Ideological Roots of the Polish Jewish Intelligentsia," *Polin: Studies in Polish Jewry* 24 (2012): 95–109.

60. Jonathan Frankel, *Prophecy and Politics: Socialism, Nationalism, and the Russian Jews, 1862–1917* (New York: Cambridge University Press, 1981), 2.

61. Eli Lederhendler, "Classless: On the Social Status of Jews in Russia and Eastern Europe in the Late Nineteenth Century," *Comparative Studies in Society and History* 50 (2008): 514–15.

62. On Ber Borokhov, Nokhem Shtif, and Shmuel Niger and the process of specialization they underwent and that Yiddish high culture underwent through them, see Barry Trachtenberg, *The Revolutionary Roots of Modern Yiddish, 1903–1917* (Syracuse: Syracuse University Press, 2008).

63. Frankel, *Prophecy and Politics*, 173.

64. Frankel, *Prophecy and Politics*, 103.

65. Frankel, *Prophecy and Politics*, 128.

66. On the YIVO Institute, see Cecile Esther Kuznitz, *YIVO and the Making of Modern Jewish Culture* (New York: Cambridge University Press, 2014). On the Folkspartey (or the Jewish People's Party, or the folkist party), see Weiser, *Jewish People, Yiddish Nation.*

67. Novershtern, *Kan gar ha'Am haYehudi*, 54.

68. Novershtern, *Kan gar ha'Am haYehudi*, 96.

69. On the palpable shift in Niger's work as an editor after the Holocaust, from elitist cosmopolitanism to nationalism, see Drucker Bar-Am, "Anthological Affect," 7–27.

70. Yaron Baleslav, "He'Aśor haRišon leHitpatḥut śḵunot Tel Aviv šeMe'ever laYarqon 1947–1958" [The first decade of development of the neighborhoods of Tel Aviv beyond the Yarqon stream], *'Eyunim Bitkumat Israel* 23 (2013): 252–53.

71. 'Ido Bassok and Avraham Novershtern, "Ma'rḵot haḤinuḵ liYehudei Polin beyn štey milḥemot ha'Olem" [The education systems for Polish Jews between world wars], in *'Alilot ne'urim: Oṭobiyografiot šel bnei ne'urim miPolin bein štey milḥemot ha'Olem* [Tales of youth: Autobiographies of youth from Poland between the two world wars], ed. Avraham Novershtern (Jerusalem: Zalman Shazar, 2011), 731.

72. The independent Polish state barely subsidized Jewish schools, and they were defined as "private." The government policy was grossly paradoxical: "It aspired to Polishize the Jews, but without fully integrating them into the country's social, cultural and economic fabric" (Bassok and Novershtern, "Ma'rḵot haḤinuḵ liYehudei Polin," 734). This policy was evident, for instance, in the composition of the elementary school teachers: in the Jewish elemen-

tary schools, Jewish teachers made up 24.2% of all teachers, compared with only 1.3% in the general schools (750). This demonstrates the unique features, as discussed earlier, of the East European intelligentsia.

73. On the Jewish education in Poland in the interwar years, see Bassok and Novershtern, "Ma'rḵot haḤinuḵ liYehudei Polin," 731–64.

74. On the various Jewish youth movements, see Ido Bassok, "Tnu'ot haNo'ar haYehudiyot bePolin beyn štey milḥemot ha'Olem" [Jewish youth movements in Poland between the two world wars], in Novershtern, *'Alilot ne'urim*, 769–92.

75. A distinct example from among the intelligentsia of 'oley sheyres hapleyte who came to Israel is Sutzkever, who studied at the Jewish Polish gymnasium Herzeliya (but did not graduate) and then was an auditor at Vilnius University. According to his testimony, when he began writing poetry at age fourteen, he was not aware of the existence of Yiddish literature. Avraham Novershtern, *'Avraham Sutzkever biMl'ot lo šiv'im* [Avrom Sutzkever on his seventieth birthday] (Jerusalem: Beit haSfarim haLeumi veHaUniversiṭa'i, 1984), 9.

76. On Yiddish culture in the ghettos, see N. Cohen, *Sefer sofer we'Iton*, 304–14.

77. For a description of Sutzkever's activity in the Vilna Ghetto, see Avrom Sutzkever, *Vilner geto: 1941–1944* (Paris: Farband fun di vilner in frankraykh, 1946); Novershtern, *'Avraham Sutzkever biMl'ot lo šiv'im*, 32–49. For a description of Oyerbakh's activity in the Warsaw Ghetto, see her book *BeḤuṣot Warša: 1939–1943* [On the streets of Warsaw], trans. Mordechai Halamish (Tel Aviv: Am-Oved, 1954). On Shpigl's writing in the Lodzh Ghetto, see Yechiel Szeintuch, *Yišayahu Špigl: Proza sipurit miGeṭo Lodž* [Yišayahu Špigl: Yiddish narrative prose from Lodzh Ghetto] (Jerusalem: Magnes, 1995).

78. Expressions of the "return" to Yiddish culture after the Holocaust are found, for example, in Yoisef Rotnberg, *Fun Varshe biz shankhay: Notitsn fun a polit* [From Warsaw to Shanghai: Notes of a refugee] (Mexico: Shloyme Mendelson fond bay der gezelshaft far kultur un hilf, 1948), 234–40; Mendl Man, *In a farvorloztn dorf* [In a deserted village] (Buenos Aires: Kiem, 1954), 155–56; Rivke Kviatkovski-Pinkhasik, *Našim me'Aḥorey haGader* [Women behind the fence], trans. K. Shabtai (Tel Aviv: Y. L. Peretz, 1961), 149–53, 196–98.

79. Interview with Rivke Kviatkovski-Pinkhasik, March 7, 1971, by Yechiel Szeintuch, Oral History Collection, the Avraham Harman Institute of Contemporary Jewry, the Hebrew University of Jerusalem, tape no. 1769 A6 (87).

80. On Yiddish in the DP camps, Lavsky noted that "the most common language in which these [cultural] activities were held was Yiddish" (*New Beginnings*, 157). On Yiddish culture in the DP camps, see Ella Florsheim, *Tarbut yidiś beMaḥanot ha'Aqurim* [Yiddish culture in the DP camps] (Jerusalem: Zalman Shazar and Yad Vashem, 2020).

81. YIVO Archive, Y. L. Peretz Shrayber-Fareyn Kolektsiye (Y. L. Peretz Yiddish Writers' Union Records), RG 701/459 (emphasis in original).

82. Ben-Tsion Hayvel, "Literatur, teater un kunst bay der sheyres-hapleyte: Yerlekher iberblik" [Literature, theater and art of the surviving remnants: Yearly review], *Undzer veg* 129 (1947): 3–4.

83. Oyerbakh, "Tsvishn Yidn."

84. Niger, "Di yidishe inteligents un ire naye ufgabn," 141–43: "Di same ershte funktsye fun der yidisher inteligents vet itst muzn zayn—tsu zayn . . . [un] onheybn boyen fun dos nay dos yidishe kultur-lebn, di yidishe institutsiyes, dos heyst di yidishe shul, di yidishe prese, di yidishe farlagn, dos yidishe teater un azoy vayter."

85. On these newspapers and journals, see Pilovski, *Tsvishn yo un neyn*, 14–15, 192, 216–20, 252. Pilovski emphasizes the modest scope of Yiddish literature in Palestine/Eretz Yisrael until 1948.

86. A. Volf Yasny, "Yisroel—der nayster yidish literatue-tsenter" [Israel—the newest Yiddish-literature center] *LN*, November 6, 1953, 5; Leyb Shpizman, "Khalutsim far yidish" [Pioneers for Yiddish], *Biyuletin fun alveltlekhn yidishn kultur-kongres* 16 (1958): 3; Yonas Turkov, "Fun funkn—a flam" [From sparks—a flame], *Folksblat* 2 (1958): 5; Mordkhe Yofe, "Tsen yor yidish-literatur un kultur in yisroel" [Ten years [of] Yiddish literature and culture in Israel], *Jewish Book Annual* 19 (1958–59): 23; "Der matsev fun yidishn farlag-vezn" [The situation of Yiddish publishing houses], *Yediyes fun Y. L. Peretz farlag* [News from Y. L. Peretz Press] 1 (1964): 16; Mordkhe Tsanin, "Fayerung lekoved zekhtsik bend 'di goldene keyt'" [Celebrating sixty volumes of DGK], *DGK* 62/63 (1968): 336; Yitskhok Luden, "Der dernerveg fun yidish in yisroel" [The "thorns way" of Yiddish in Israel], in *In geyeg nokh momentn: Aktuele publitsistik fun hayntike un fun nekhtike teg* [In pursuit of the moment: Actual publications of todays and of yesterday] (Tel Aviv: Leyvik, 2009), 1:456.

87. Khone Shmeruk, "Yiddish," in *The Hebrew Encyclopedia*, 19, ed. Yeshayahu Leibowitz (Tel Aviv: Encyclopedia Publishing Company, 1968), 809.

88. Dov Schidorsky, *Gwilim nisrafim ve'Otiyot porḥot: Toldoteyhem šel osfey sfarim we-Sifriyot be'Ereṣ yiśra'el weNisyonot leHaṣalat śrideyhem le'Aḥar haŠo'a* [Burning scrolls and flying letters: The history of book collections and libraries in mandatory Palestine and the efforts to save their remnants after the Holocaust] (Jerusalem: Magnes, 2008), 75.

89. "Jerusalem became a center of academic thought, revolving mostly around The Hebrew University, whereas Tel Aviv had the largest concentration of artists and performers in the fields of literature, theatre, music and visual arts. Tel Aviv was where most of the important works in these fields were created, it had a vibrant literary and artistic life, and was home to a significant portion of the consumers of Hebrew culture in Israel and the Jewish world." Ya'akov Shavit and Gid'on Biger, *HaHisṭoria šel Tel Aviv* [The history of Tel Aviv] (Tel Aviv: Ramot, 2007), 2:235. On the establishment of the Hebrew cultural center in Israel in general and in Tel Aviv in particular, see Itamar Even Zohar, "HaṢmiḥa weHaHitgabšut šel tarbut 'ivrit meqomit be'Ereṣ Yiśra'el, 1882–1948" [The growth and establishment of local Hebrew culture in mandatory Palestine, 1882–1948], *Katedra* 16 (1980): 165–206; Zohar Shavit, *HaḤaim hasifrutiyim be'Ereṣ Yiśra'el, 1910–1933* [The literary life in mandatory Palestine, 1910–1933] (Tel Aviv: Hakibbutz Hameuchad, 1982). On Tel Aviv as a myth, see Ma'oz Azaryahu, *Tel Aviv ha'Ir ha'Amitit: Mitografiya hisṭorit* [Tel Aviv the real city: A historical mythography] (Be'er Sheva: Ben Gurion University Press, 2005), 27–118.

90. Peretz's story, "Tsvishn tsvey berg" ("Between Two Mountains"), appeared in Yiddish in 1900 as part of the series *Khsidish* and in Hebrew in 1901.

91. Khone Shmeruk, *HaQri'a leNavi': Meḥqerey historia weSifrut* [The calling for a prophet: Studies of history and literature] (Jerusalem: Zalman Shazar, 1999), 156; N. Cohen, *Sefer sofer ve'Iton*, 1–4.

92. Khone Shmeruk, "Ivrit-yidiš-polanit: Tarbut Yehudit tlat-lešonit" [Hebrew-Yiddish-Polish: Tri-lingual Jewish culture], in Shmeruk and Werses, *Beyn štey milḥemot 'olam*, 14–18.

93. Shmeruk, "Qawim leToldot haMerkaz šel sifrut yidiš beWarša," 165.

94. On the role of the press in creating a national identity, see Benedict Anderson, *Imagined Communities: Reflections on the Origin and Spread of Nationalism* (London: Verso, 1991).

95. On these tensions in Yiddish culture, see Novershtern, *Kan gar ha'Am haYehudi*, 111.

96. In 1971, attempts were made to publish a Haredi daily paper in New York, but they were unsuccessful.

97. The *LN*'s first issue was preceded by sixty-three issues of the weekly *Ilustrirter vokhnblat* (*Illustrated Weekly*).

98. On Tsanin and the *LN*, see Meylekh Ravitsh, *Mayn leksikon 3: Yidishe un hebreyishe shraybers in medines Yisroel* [My lexicon vol. 3: Yiddish and Hebrew writers in Israel] (Montreal: A komitet, 1958), 350–53.

99. On the Warsaw *LN*, see N. Cohen, *Sefer sofer we'Iton*, 97, 101. Daily papers in Yiddish tended to take as their name a translation of the title of a prominent paper in the local language—for instance, *Di tsayt* in London and *Di prese* in Argentina. It is possible that Tsanin also chose the title *LN* as a translation of the Hebrew paper *Yedi'ot Ahronot*. In the years 1948–1953, this Hebrew paper struggled financially and was less prominent than *Ma'ariv* and *Ha'aretz* or the party-affiliated papers *Davar* and *'Al Ha-Mishmar*. Tasanin's choice in his memoir to refer to *Yidishe tsaytung* by the name *Hayntike nayes* also attests to his intention to memorialize the Warsaw-based *LN* and to cast his paper as a direct continuation of it.

100. According to Tsanin, this reduction applied only to the Yiddish press and not to papers in other "foreign" languages. See, for example, Mordkhe Tsanin, "Vemen iz itst neytik der kamf kegn yidish" [Who needs now the battle against Yiddish?], *LN*, May 26, 1950, 3; M"Ts [Mordkhe Tsanin], "Far vos zeks zaytn letste nayes?" [Why six pages to *Letste nayes?*], *LN*, June 9, 1950, 3; M"Ts [Mordkhe Tsanin], "Hefkeyres kegn di Letste nayes" [Wantonness against *Letste nayes*], *LN*, June 30, 1950, 1; Farband fun vokhnshriftn un periyodishe oysgabn in Yisroel (Association of Weeklies and Periodicals in Israel), "Tsu undzere leyener" [To our readers], *LN*, February 23, 1951, 1; M"Ts [Mordkhe Tsanin], "Sine un tsvies" [Hatred and hypocrisy], *LN*, October 9, 1952, 2; Luden, *In geyeg*, 427.

101. The solution of publishing a Yiddish paper under different names was common in Poland, especially among the Bund papers. See Mordkhe Tsanin, "Der ufgang un untergang fun der yidisher prese in poyln [The rise and fall of Yiddish press in Poland], *Kesher* 6 (1989): 112–15. Moyshe Grosman, editor of the literary journal *Heymish* (1956–1962), appears also to have used this solution when he encountered difficulties in his attempt to publish another Yiddish literary journal in Israel. Thus, in its first year of publication, the new journal appeared under the names *Naye-heymish*, *Yisroel heymish*, *Yidish-heymish*, *Kultur-heymish*, *Nitsokhn-heymish* (*Home Victory*, referring to the 1956 Suez Crisis), and *Literarish-heymish*.

102. This prohibition was reported in the Yiddish press in Israel and elsewhere, as well as in the accounts of various figures in the world of Yiddish culture—for instance, Yitskhok Korn, *Dos gerangl far yidish: Eseyen* [The struggle for Yiddish: Essays] (Tel Aviv: Veltrat far yidish un yidisher kultur, 1982), 192. The State Archive holds a file titled "The Status of Yiddish in Israel" (23/55/חת/מ“א), but when I asked to look at it on my visit to the archive, I was told by the staff that it was classified "indefinitely secret" and therefore was not accessible to researchers. Following a second appeal to the archive (April 12, 2012), I was informed (May 12, 2012) that the contents of the file had been moved and were now in file 5551/7/ג. But when I looked through that file, it contained only two photocopies of handwritten drafts, with no indication of the author's name or the date. The file held no copies of the correspondences or other documents from the original file I had asked to review. A further appeal to receive the file (June 25, 2014) yielded a denial that the file was closed indefinitely (June 29, 2014) as well as a scan (July 14, 2014) of what the archive claimed to be the only document in the file: a handwritten memo on the subject of "The status of Yiddish in Israel following a proposal to legislate a law for the administration of the Hebrew language."

103. Mordkhe Tsanin, *Zumershney: Noveln, eseyen, reportazhn* [Summer-snow: Novellas, essays, reports] (Tel Aviv: H. Leyvik, 1992), 175.

104. In his description of this event, Tsanin changed the name of the new paper he established, calling it *Heyntike nayes*, like the second name of the Warsaw-based *LN*, and not

Yidishe tsaytung, as the paper was effectively titled in its own publicity. For example, an advertisement from August 7, 1953, on page 1, read, "Di yidishe tsaytung vet, vi LN, dershaynen unter der redaktsye fun M. Tsanin, in di teg ven di LN dershaynt nisht" ("The *Yiddishe Tsaytung* will be published, like *LN*, under the editorship of M. Tsanin, in the days when *LN* is not published"). This change of name was due apparently to a conflict that arose between Tsanin and Yisroel Khadash over Mapai's purchase of the paper, a conflict that caused a rift between the two men. The choice of the name *Hayntike nayes* attests to Tsanin's wish to establish a link to the Warsaw paper and more broadly to the tradition of Yiddish press in Poland.

105. All "editorial messages" that appeared in the *LN* until the establishment of *Yidishe tsaytung* were signed simply "*LN*"—for example, "Bekorev heybt on LN tsu dershaynen tsvey mol in der vokh" [Soon *LN* will be published twice a week], *LN*, January 27, 1951, 1. After its establishment, editorial messages were signed by both papers—for example, "The editorial staff and workers of *Letste nayes*, *Yidishe tsaytung*, the workers of haKarmel Press: We express our condolences to Mr. Matsliah Zeytuni on the passing of his brother," *LN*, October 5, 1953, 1.

106. Tsanin, *Zumershney*, 177. Tsanin was referring to the two daily papers in German, *Yediʿot Hadashot* and *Yediʿot Ha-Yom*, which were allowed to be published in Israel in those days despite the fact that only 3.2 percent of the immigrants between 1948 and 1954 (10,842 people) were born in Germany and Austria, versus 32 percent of immigrants who were born in Poland (106,414 people). Lissak, *HaʿAliya haGdola biŠnot haḤamišim*, 8.

107. On December 30, 1960, an advertisement in the name of all these papers appeared on the first page of the *LN*, containing a message to the public about an increase in the price of the paper. The flourishing of newspapers in languages other than Hebrew and the identification of their potential for propaganda purposes were noted by the scholar of communications Yechiel Limor, "ʿItonut, radio veṬeleviziya" [Press, radio and television], in *The Hebrew Encyclopedia*, vol. 6, ed. Benzion Netanyahu (Tel Aviv: Encyclopedia Publishing Company, 1970),1011: "In the first years after the state's establishment there was a blossoming in the media, and especially in the foreign language press. These newspapers served the new immigrants, who had not mastered the Hebrew language, and at the same time were a valuable tool, which aided the processes of the immigrants' social and political integration and absorption into the new society. Various parties, and above all Map'ai, quickly discovered the importance of these papers as tools of socialization, and published newspapers in foreign languages, targeted at the new population." See also Yechiel Limor and Dan Caspi, "Ṣmiḥat haʿitonut haLoʿzit uDeiḥata" [The rise and the fall of the foreign-language press], in *HaMetavḵim: ʿEmṣaey haTiqšoret beYiśraʾel, 1948–1990* [The mediators: Mass media in Israel, 1948–1990], ed. Yechiel Limor and Dan Caspi (Tel Aviv: Am-Oved, 1992), 49–51.

108. "A nayes nit letste nayes" [News about *LN*], *Heymish* 50 (1960): 122; "Oykh di letste nayes" [*LN* too], *LF* 105 (1960): 9.

109. See also Gali Drucker Bar-Am, "The Holy Tongue and the Tongue of the Martyrs: The Eichmann Trial as Reflected in *Letste Nayes*," *Dapim: Studies on the Holocaust* 28, no. 1 (2014): 17–37.

110. For more on these elections, see Yechiam Weitz, "ʾAvi ʿavot haQonṣenzus: Lewi ʿEškol, haʾIš weZmano" [The grandfather of the consensus: The life and times of Levi Eshkol], in *HeʿAśor haŠeni: 1958–1968* [The second decade: 1958–1968], ed. Zvi Zameret and Hanna Yablonka (Jerusalem: Yad Ben Zvi, 2000), 171–77.

111. Yankev Pat, "Yidishe un hebreyshe shrayber in medinas Yisroel" [Yiddish and Hebrew writers in Israel], *Biyuletin fun alveltlekhn yidishn kultur-kongres* 13 (1957): 6.

112. "Rosh hashono numer" [New year's issue], *LN*, August 23, 1954, 4; *LN*, July 30, 1955, 1.

113. A. Volf Yasny, "Rand bamerkungen tsu der for-konferents fun di yidishe zshurnalistn" [Side remarks for the preliminary conference of Yiddish journalists], *LN*, December 30, 1960, 6.

114. Korn, *Dos gerangl far yidish*, 193.

115. Mordechai Naor, "Ha'Itonut biŠnot haḤamišim" [The press in the fifties], in *He'Aśor haRišon: 1948–1958* [The first decade: 1948–1958], ed. Zvi Zameret and Hanna Yablonka (Jerusalem: Yad Ben-Zvi 1998), 219–20.

116. Tsemah Tsamriyon, *Ha'Itonut šel Še'erit-haPleṭa beGermanya keVitui leBa'ayoteha* [The surviving remnants' press as an expression of its problems] (Tel Aviv: Irgun Sheerit-Hapleta me-ha-Ezor ha-Briti Bergen-Belzen beYisrael, 1970), 64.

117. See, for example, "Foroys: Far zikherheyt, demokratiye un ufboy, dos vort fun mifleget po'ale Eretz Yisrael" [Forward: For security, democracy and construction, the word of the workers-party in mandatory Palestine], *LN*, July 12, 1961, unpaginated.

118. "Naye Olim!" [Newcomers!], *LN*, April 26, 1957, 1.

119. Luden, *In geyeg*, 327–28.

120. The description of this dual role of the Yiddish press in America belongs to Samuel Margoshes: "Characteristic of the dialectic of Jewish history is the fact that, for all its dedication to Americanization, the impact of the Yiddish press was ultimately felt in the direction of the shaping of Jewish life on American soil. Hand in hand with the role of Americanization proceeded the role of furthering the creation of Jewish institutions and consolidating a Jewish way of life in America." Shmuel Margoshes, "Tafqida šel ha'Itonut haYidit" [The role of the Yiddish press], *Korot Ha'itonaim Hayehudim* [The annals of Jewish journalists] 6 (1964): 13.

121. Rachel Rojanski, "Meruṣa meHaSṭen šela" [Happy with her sten gun], *Davka* 3 (2007): 44.

122. For instance, Mordkhe Tsanin, "Di yidishe literatur un medinas-yisroel" [Yiddish literature and Israel], *DGK* 66 (1969): 30–36.

123. Tsanin "exploited" the transnational nature of Yiddish culture for the benefit of the new immigrants and Yiddish in Israel by addressing these themes in his regular column in the New York Jewish daily *Forverts* (*Forward*), for which he served as the reporter in Israel. See, for example, "Yidn in Yisroel laydn fun mangl in kleyder," *Forverts*, February 21, 1952, 2; "Vos men darf visn baym shikn shpayz-peklekh keyn Yisroel" [What one has to know while sending food packages to Israel], *Forverts*, 4, undated clipping, the Gnazim Institute, Tsanin Archive, 504.

124. Among the writers from Israel were Ruven Rubinshteyn, Nosn Bolel, Ovadye Feld, Meyer Khosin [M], Yitskhok Luden, and Nakhmen List. Rubinshteyn had edited several daily newspapers in Yiddish before the Holocaust, most notably *Di Idishe Shtime* (*The Jewish/Yiddish Voice*). He played an important role in the surviving remnant Yiddish press in Germany and especially in the *Undzer Veg*. Nosn Bolel also participated in that paper. See Tsamriyon, *Ha'Itonut šel Še'erit-haPleṭa*, 86, 88–90.

125. Some of these columns were compiled in a book: Mordkhe Tsanin, *Shabesdike Shmuesn* [Shabbat conversations] (Tel Aviv: Letste Nayes, 1957).

126. The vast majority of these writers had been active in the press of the DP camps and appear in the survey by Hayvel, "Literatur, teater un kunst bay der sheyres-hapleyte," 3–4.

127. "Leyener fun LN bashtayern zikh far dem geverfond" [*LN* readers donate for the IDF weapons fund], *LN*, October 24, 1955, 1; October 26, 1955, 1.

128. Surviving remnant organizations that advertised in the *LN* included, for instance, Farband fun partizaner geto-kemfer un untergrunt-kemfer (Organization of Partisan-Ghetto-Fighters

and Underground-Fighters), Farband fun invalid fun der milkhome kegn di natsis (Organization of Invalids of the War against the Nazis), Land-farband fun gevezene katsetler (Land Organization of Concentration Camp Survivors), and Farband fun bafrayte zelner fun khuts-laarets vos hobn gekemft kegn der natsisher armey un ire farbindete (Organization of Former Soldiers from Abroad Who Fought against the Nazi Army and Its Collaborators). On ʻoley sheyres hapleyte's organizing in Israel, see Yablonka, "Qliṭat niṣoley haŠoa' biMdinat Yiśra'el," 285–99.

129. Immigrants of Polish Origin in Israel was an umbrella organization of over one hundred hometown associations, established by immigrants from cities and towns that existed in Poland before the war. See Liber Lush, *Landsmanshaftn in Yisroel: Spetsyele oysgabe tsum velt-ḳongres fun poylishe yidn* [Hometown associations in Israel: Special publication to world-congress of Jews from Poland] (Tel Aviv: Hitachadut ʻolei Polin be-Yisrael, 1961).

130. For example, the letter by survivors with lung disease: "Di lungen-kranke olim fodern an entfern!" [The lung-sick ʻolim demand an answer!], *LN*, November 24, 1950, 1.

131. For example, "Mir vendn zikh tsu undzere khosheve leyener . . ." [We address our respected readers], *LN*, June 10, 1951, 1.

132. Ofer, "Niṣolim qeʻOlim," 244.

133. Shmuel Werses, "Qol haIša baŠvuon beYidiš ʻQol mevaser'" [The woman's voice in the Yiddish weekly "Herald Voice"], *Huliyot* 4 (1997): 53–82.

134. Avraham Novershtern, "HaQolot weHaMaqhela: Širat našim beYidiš beyn štey milḥemot haʻOlam" [The voices and the choir: Women's poetry in Yiddish between two world wars], *Biqoret uParšanut* 40 (2008): 61–145.

135. Nurit Orhan pointed out the stages of development of women's writing in the Russian Yiddish press (1881–1914) and showed that one of the main themes in their writing was the disillusionment with the idea of the traditional family. Nurit Orhan, *Yoṣ'ot me'Arbaʻʻamot: Našim kotvot baEmperiya haRusit* [Staking a claim: Women writing in the Yiddish press in Tsarist Russia] (Jerusalem: Zalman Shazar, 2013). On the women's section in the New York daily *Forverts*, see Maxine Schwartz Seller, "Defining Socialist Womanhood: The Women's Page of the *Jewish Daily Forward* in 1919," *American Jewish History* 76, no. 4 (1987): 416–38.

136. Gali Drucker Bar-Am, "'Normal People in a Land of Their Own': On Gender and Nationalism in Khaye Elboym-Dorembus's *Af der Arisher Zayt*," *Nashim: A Journal of Jewish Women's Studies and Gender Issues* 27 (2014): 62–74.

137. For example, Tsila Bat David [M], "Mirele" (1949); Sara Hamer-Dzshaklin, "Mayn mames Kholem" [My moms' dream] (1950); Mordekhe Tsanin, "Reb Tankhum un zayne fir tekhter [Reb Tankhum and his four daughters] (1950); Yoel Mastboym, "Yerusholaymer tekhter" [Daughters of Jerusalem] (1950); M. Zand [M?], "Dem Rebins tokhter: A lebn fun shturem un tshuve" [The rabbi's daughter: A life of storm and repentance] (1953); Zalmen Rabinovitsh, "In shturem: Roman fun yidishn lebn in ratn-farband" [In storm: A novel of Jewish life in the USSR] (1954); Yitskhok Perlov, "Flora ingber" (1956); A. Sandler [Mordkhe Tsanin], "Di yidishe tokhter un hans shtraus" [The Jewish daughter and Hans Shtraus] (1960); and more.

138. Mordkhe Tsanin, "Eyn tog inem lebn fun a froy in Yisroel" [A day in the life of a woman in Israel], *LN*, December 30, 1949, 4; *LN*, January 6, 1950, 3; Mordkhe Tsanin, "Hinershe bunkers in tel-oviv" [Bunkers of hen in Tel Aviv], *LN*, March 3, 1950, 3.

139. "Undzere leyenerins shraybn: Di froy in der maʻabara un maḥane" [Our female-readers write: The woman in the transit-camps], *LN*, August 29, 1952, 5.

140. Alongside his essayist writing in the Orthodox press, Granatshteyn published short stories in the *LN* about the lives of ʻoley sheyres hapleyte in the absorption camps. For more on Granatshteyn and his stories, see chapter 4.

141. For instance, A. Itamar [Yankev Khorgin], "Yerusholayim in flamen: Historisher roman" [Jerusalem in flames: A historical novel] (1949)—a translation of a novel published in Hebrew in 1936; Shimen Roznberg, "Der yidisher kenig bay der volge: Historisher roman fun der tsayt ven di Kuzarim hobn ongenumen dem yidishn gloybn un gegrindet a yidishe melukhe baym kaspishn yam" [The Jewish king at the Volga river: A historical novel of the time in which the Kuzarim accepted Jewish faith and established a Jewish kingdom in the Caspian Sea] (1955); Dovid Flinker, "In meshiyekh's fustrit: Historisher roman" [In the redeemer's footsteps: A historical novel] (1961).

142. For example, Yekhiel Yeshaye Trunk, "Ikh khap banditn" [I catch bandits] (1950); A. Sandler [Tsanin], "Profesor Shapiro: Roman fun yidishn lebn in poyln far un in der tsveyter velt-milkhome" [Professor Shapiro: A novel of Jewish life in Poland before and during WWII] (1950); Sh. Ram [M], "Yidn forn aheym: A dertseylung vegn 'aliya fun di vos zaynen geven biz 1939 poylishe birger" [Jews travel homeward: A story about the 'aliya of those who were Polish citizens until 1939] (1950); Yoel Mastboym, "Afn layter: Tsvishn lodzh un varshe" [On the ladder: Between Lodzh and Warsaw] (1953); Yekhiel Hofer, "Mayne varshever heyf: A roman fun varshever lebn fun far der tsveyter velt-milkhome" [My Warsaw courtyards: Novel of life in Warsaw before WWII] (1954); Shloyme Berlinski, "Di nezire" [The nun] (1955); B. Demblin, "Tsu a nay lebn" [Toward a new life] (1958). Some of the works were later published as books.

143. For example, Sh. Y. Agnon, "A poshete mayse" ("A Simple Story"), translated by Eliezer Rubinshteyn (1959). This translation was published in 1958 as a book by the New York–based Kval Press, with an introduction by Arn Tseytlin, an essay by Dov Sadan on Agnon's work in Yiddish, and illustrations by Yosl Bergner.

144. For example, Sholem Asch, *Der Novi* [The prophet] (1956).

145. For example: Y. Din [M], "In shotn fun toyt: Emese pasirung vos klingt vi a shpanendiker roman" [Under the shadow of death: A true event that sounds like a thriller] (1957) and "Ver bin ich? Vey-geshrey fun a yidish kind vos iz durkh kristn geratevet gevorn fun natsishn gehenem, nokh dem vi zayne eltern zenen umgekumen in maydanek" [Who am I? A cry of pain of a Jewish child who was saved from the Nazi hell by Christians, after his parents were executed in Maydanek] (1957); Sh. Y. Dorfzon [Harndorf Shmuel-Yankev], "Sensatsiyonele un shpanande[!] geshikhte fun a yidish meydl vos hot likvidirt di daytsh shpiyonazh-nets in kayir beys der tsveyter velt-milkhome" [A sensational and suspenseful story about a Jewish girl who wiped out a German espionage network in Cairo during World War II] (1958); Sh. Vislits, "Der man fun tsvey froyen: Roman fun oysergeveyntlekhe iberlebung fun a nayem oyle fun poyln, libe un flikht vos zenen shtarker fun toyt—der gerangl mit tsvey veltn" [The man of two women: A novel about the outstanding experiences of a new immigrant from Poland, a love and duty that are stronger than death—the battle with two worlds] (1958). On sensation novels in the Yiddish press in Poland before the war, see N. Cohen, *Sefer sofer we'Iton*, 105–14; on sensation novels in *Forverts*, see Ellen Kellman, "Der groyser kundes un di shund-romanen in dem altn Forverts" [The big mischief and the sensation novels in the old *Forverts*], *Di Tsukunft* 111 (2008): 10–19.

146. For example, Yitskhok Perlov, "Nekome" [Revenge] (1952); Y. Bashevis, "Der hoyf" [The court] (1956); Yitskhok Perlov, "Flora Ingber" (1956).

147. Tsamriyon, *Ha'Itonut šel Še'erit-haPleṭa*, 165–67.

148. Three of Uri Zvi Greenberg's poems appeared in *DGK* beginning in 1976.

149. "Literatur-premye fun LN-YTS: Di redaktsye . . . hot bashtimt tsvey premyes far der bester dertseylung un bestn reportazh af Yisroel-tematik" [A literary grant from LN-YTS: The editorial

board has declared two grants for the best story and best reportage on the Israeli theme], *LN*, August 20, 1954, 1.

150. For example, in 1955 the writer Shloyme Berlinski received 200 Israeli pounds for the publication of his serialized novel "The Nun." *LN* contract with S. Berlinski, October 17, 1955, Gnazim Institute, Tsanin Archive, 504–2520/15. Hebrew writers also earned money from publishing in the paper: in 1958 S. Y. Agnon received 30 Israeli pounds for an introduction he wrote to a novella he published in the *LN* (*A poshete mayse*). Letter from Tsanin to Agnon, Gnazim Institute, Tsanin Archive, December 2, 1957, 504–2689/15.

151. For this information I thank the journalist and editor Yitskhok Luden (interviewed on December 7, 2009) and Dr. Edna Nahshon, daughter of the writer and journalist Dovid Eydlman (interviewed on June 29, 2012).

152. On Abe Kahan, see Ehud Manor, "Abe Kahan keMetaqen ʻolam: ʻEiyun beDarko haPoliṭit waHaʻEtonait šel ʻoreḵ haForverts" [Abe Kahan as a "perfecter of the world": a study of the political and journalistic vision and activities of the editor of *Forverts*], *Kesher* 32 (2002): 64–74.

153. On this type of publication, see Yehuda Slutsky, *Ha'Etonut haYehudit-rusit baMea' haTšaʻ-ʻesre* [The Jewish-Russian press in the nineteenth century] (Jerusalem: Mosad Bialik, 1975), 284–85; Moss, *Jewish Renaissance*, 77.

154. Letter from *DGK* to Yekhil De-Nur, August 31, 1948, Gnazim Institute, De-Nur Archive, 523—9743/7.

155. Memo from the financial department of the Zionist General Council to Avrom Levinson and Avrom Sutzkever, August 5, 1948, the National Library of Israel, Sutzkever Archive 4°.1565, the General Organization of Hebrew Workers in Israel folder. This note also stipulates that the funds for establishing the journal (2,600 Lira Eretz-Yisraelit) are allocated for one year only and that the editors should not hire permanent employees. On the argument in the General Council between linguistic pragmatism and pluralism in the debate about the publication of *DGK*, see Yablonka, *Survivors of the Holocaust*, 264.

156. On the size of the print run, see "DGK iz aroys" [*DGK* is published], *Biyuletin fun alveltlekhn yidishn kultur-kongres* 32 (1950), 14; letter from Yankev Sharfshteyn (*DGK* financial manager) to Mrs. Hermona Grau (the Department of Culture in the Ministry of Education), March 9, 1992, the National Library of Israel, Sutzkever Archive, 4°.1565, *Di Goldene Keyt* folder.

157. Josef Fraenkel, ed., *The Jewish Press of the World* (London: Cultural Department of the World Jewish Congress, 1961), 44.

158. Novershtern (*'Avraham Sutzkever biMl'ot lo šivʻim*, 78) quotes a correspondence between Sutzkever and Niger that illustrates the difficulty of maintaining the delicate balance between the demands of the Yiddish world and those of the Histadrut. The conflict between these two sets of demands was especially pronounced in the journal's early years.

159. On Levinson's activity, see "Nishto mer Avrom Levinson" [Avrom Levinson is no more], *DGK* 22 (1955): 3–4; Noyekh Gris, "Dos ershte yor DGK: Zikhroynes fun a gevezenem redaktsye-sekretar" [The first year of *DGK*: Memories of a former editorial-secretary], *DGK* 71 (1970): 170–78.

160. A letter circulated by *DGK* among Yiddish writers soon after its foundation urging them to send in materials for publication was signed by Nosn Ek as editorial secretary. Letter from the *DGK* editorial board to Yekhil De-Nur, August 31, 1948, Gnazim Institute, De-Nur Archive, 523–9743/7.

161. Avrom Sutzkever, "Tsvey yor di goldene keyt" [Two years of *DGK*], *DGK* 9 (1951): 214–15 (emphasis in original).

162. The image of Yiddish culture as "soaring letters," which, after the liberation, like the survivors themselves, had undergone a process of "resurrection of the dead," had already appeared earlier, in the surviving remnant press in Germany. See Tsamriyon, *Ha'Itonut šel Še'erit-haPleṭa*, 66, 87.

163. On further aspects of Sutzkever's national "rythm of largeness" in the epic poem "*Gaystike erd*" ("Spiritual Soil"), see Gali Drucker Bar-Am, "Gaystike erd by Avrom Sutzkever: Between Personal Mythology and National Ideology," *Journal of Jewish Studies* 67, no. 1 (2016): 157–81.

164. Aleksander Shpiglblat, "'DGK' un ir melukhishe maymed" [*DGK* and its national status], *Yidishe Kultur* 1 (1990): 38–43.

165. Shpiglblat, "'DGK' un ir melukhishe maymed," 38.

166. Avrom Sutzkever, "Briv fun Max Weinreich tsu Avrom Sutzkever (1/30/1947)" [Letter from Max Weinreich to Avrom Sutzkever [1/30/1947]], *DGK* 95–96 (1978): 174–77. On Weinreich's influence on Sutzkever, see Novershtern, *'Avraham Sutzkever biMl'ot lo šiv'im*, 9–10.

167. Aleksander Shpiglblat, *Durkh fareykherte shayblekh* [Through a smoked glass panel] (Tel Aviv: H. Leyvik, 2007), 245–46.

168. According to Esther Rozhanski, her father, Shmuel Rozhanski, the Yiddish teacher, theater critic, author, and editor, invited Sutzkever and Kaczerginski to immigrate to Buenos Aires, despite the restrictions imposed at the time by the government of Argentina on the absorption of Holocaust survivors. Kaczerginski accepted his invitation only in 1950 and lived in Buenos Aires for a short time until his untimely death in a plane crash in 1954.

169. Shpiglblat, *Durkh fareykherte shayblekh*, 39.

170. Shpiglblat, *Durkh fareykherte shayblekh*, 39.

171. Yiddish publications that appeared as quarterlies (Fertlyor-shriftn) or every three months (Dray-Khadoshim zshurnaln) until the year of *DGK*'s publication include (in chronological order): *Yidish teater* (Yiddish theater, Warsaw, 1927), *Tsushtayer* (Contribution, Lemberg, 1929–1931), *Bodn* (Ground, New York, 1934–1937), *Visnshaft un revolutsye* (Science and revolution, Kiev, 1934–1936), *Studyo* (Studio, New York, 1934–1935), *Heftn* (Notebooks, Montreal-Detroit, 1936–1937), *Fun noentn over* (From the near past, Warsaw, 1937–1938), *Yidishe shriftn* (Yiddish writing, New York, 1941–1958), *Gedank un lebn* (Thought and life, New York, 1943–1948), *Svive* (Surroundings, New York, 1943–1974, initially published as a bimonthly), *Getseltn* (Tents, New York, 1945–1949), and *Davke* (Spite, Buenos Aires, 1949–1981). Most of these journals, except for the last few, were published for only short periods. For this information I thank Eliezer Niborski at the A. I. Lerner Index to Yiddish Periodicals, the Hebrew University of Jerusalem, and Beth Shalom Aleichem.

172. Novershtern, *'Avraham Sutzkever biMl'ot lo šiv'im*, 69.

173. On the participation of Jews in the Nuremberg trials, and in particular on Sutzkever and his testimony, see Laura Jockusch, "Justice at Nuremberg? Jewish Responses to Nazi War Crime Trials in Allied Occupied Germany," *Jewish Social Studies* 19, no. 1 (2012): 107–47. A segment of his testimony at the Nuremberg trials can be watched online (with English voice-over translation): https://www.youtube.com/watch?v=rY4GnquFCmE.

174. Shpiglblat, *Durkh fareykherte shayblekh*, 40.

175. Avraham Lev, "Avrom Sutzkever: A bintl dermonungen tsu zayn yubileum" [Avrom Sutzkever: A bundle of memories for his jubilee], *LF* 143–44 (1963): 15.

176. Daniel Leybl, "Di goldene keyt," *Neyevelt*, February 11, 1949, 4.

177. The most prominent among them were Yigal Allon, Levi Eshkol, David Ben-Gurion, Izhak Ben-Zvi, Meir Weisgal, Yitzhak Tabenkin, Yigael Yadin, Bracha Habas, Berl Locker, Pinhas Lavon, Mordechai Namir, Zalman Shazar, Yosef Sprinzak, and Moshe Sharet.

178. For example, the death of President Chaim Weizmann, the Suez Crisis, the state's ten-year anniversary, the Eichmann trial, the inauguration of the Knesset building, the death of Izhak Ben-Zvi, and the appointment of Zalman Shazar as president of Israel.

179. For example, stories by Sh. Y. Agnon, Gershon Shofman, 'Asher Barash, Moshe Shamir, S. Yizhar, Amos Oz, Nathan Shacham, and Yehoshua Bar-Yosef; poems by Avraham Shlonsky, Lea Goldberg, Nathan Alterman, and Haim Gouri; and poems and songs from *Sefer haPalmaḥ* (*The Palmach Book*). Issue no. 6 (1950) and issue no. 64 (1968) also featured translations of young Hebrew poetry, and issue no. 59 (1967) included a translation of a short story by Amalia Kahana-Carmon. But works by young writers were published infrequently relative to the canonical works. In addition to the works of Hebrew literature, *DGK* published several articles (usually translated) on Hebrew literature: an article by Lea Goldberg on Shlonsky's poetry and on Alterman's "HaṬur haŠvi'I" ("The Seventh Column"), a review of Yigal Mossinson's "Be'Arvot haNegev" ("In the Negev Plains"), Meir Mohar on Shofman, Yitzhak Twersky on directions in modern Hebrew prose, Menahem Kapeliuk on new Arabic literature and its problems, Meir Yofe on Hebrew literature in Israel, Avraham Kariv on "HaSofer, ha'Am weHaMedina" ("The Author, the People, and the State"), Yofe on Berkovitch and Alterman, Gitl Meisel on Shamir, Moshe Braslavski on the Kibbutz in Hebrew prose, and Sh. Shalom on "HaŠira ha'Ivrit le'an?" ("What Does the Future Hold for Hebrew Poetry?").

180. See, for example, the appeal by Yidisher literatn un zshurnalistn-fareyn in yisroel (The Association of Yiddish Journalists and Writers in Israel [TO]), headed by Sutzkever, to the Israeli government and Knesset members from June 1954 demanding to remove Yiddish from the list of foreign languages, before the Knesset debates proposed legislation concerning restrictions on foreign-language press in Israel. Gnazim Institute, Ayznman Archive, 394. Sutzkever rallied Yiddish organizations across the world to support this appeal: "Kultur kongres shikt telegrame keyn yisroel untershtitsndik di foderung fun yidishn literatn un zshurnalistn-fareyn tsu der kneset un tsu der regirung" [Culture Congress sends a telegram to Israel in support of the demands of the Association of Yiddish Journalists and Writers in Israel from the Knesset and the government], *Biyuletin fun alveltlekhn yidishn kultur kongres* 1 (1954): 3–4.

181. Avrom Sutzkever, "Fayerung lekoved 50 bend DGK" [Celebration honoring fifty volumes of *DGK*], *DGK* 51 (1965): 340.

182. Sutzkever's correspondence with Weinreich reveals how disturbed he was by the fact that there were no machines in Israel capable of printing diacritics. Weinreich sent him the necessary technological means from the US, and as of issue no. 40 (1961), *DGK* appeared with all the requisite marks. Sutzkever, "Briv fun Max Weinreich," 174–77. On *DGK*'s strict linguistic practices, see Novershtern, *'Avraham Sutzkever biMl'ot lo šiv'im*, 78–79.

183. Novershtern, *'Avraham Sutzkever biMl'ot lo šiv'im*, 77.

184. In this press were published Mendl Man's book *Ufgevakhte erd* (*Awakened Earth*, 1953), as well as Sutzkever's books *In fayer vogn* (*In the Chariot of Fire*, 1952), *Ode tsu der toyb* (*Ode to the Dove*, 1955), and *Firkantike oysies un moftim* (*Square Letters and Magical Signs*, 1968). For an appeal by the writer Yishaye Shpigl to publish with this press, see letter from Yishaye Shpigl, Hadar Yosef, September 9, 1954, the National Library of Israel, Sutzkever Archive 4°.1565, Yishaye Shpigl folder. In a later period described in this book, the press published Avrom Karpinovitsh's *Af vilner gasn* (*On the Streets of Vilne*, 1981) and Alekander Shpiglblat's *Papirene zeglen* (*Paper Sails*, 1973) and *Volknbremen* (*Cloudy Brows*, 1989).

185. On this undertaking, see Sutzkever, "Fayerung lekoved 50 bend DGK," 234.

186. On the founding of the Yiddish Department at the Hebrew University of Jerusalem and on *DGK*'s relation with it, see Avraham Novershtern, "Between Town and Gown: The

Institutionalization of Yiddish at Israeli Universities," in *Yiddish in the Contemporary World*, ed. Gennady Estraikh and Mikhail Krutikov (Oxford: Legenda, 1999), 1–20.

187. On the circumstances that led to the establishment of Young-Israel and on its activity, see Dovid-hersh Roskes, "Di shrayber-grupe yung-yisroel" [The writers group Young-Israel], *Yugntruf* 28–29 (1973), 7–12; 33 (1975), 7–8; 34 (1976), 4–7; Gali Drucker Bar-Am, "Sifrut yiśra'elit, sifrut Yehudit: HaMenifesṭim šel ḥavurat "liqra't" veŠel ḥavurat yung-yisroel" [Israeli literature, Jewish literature: The manifesto of the Liqrat group and the Young-Israel group] (seminar paper submitted as part of the MA studies program, Tel Aviv, 2007).

188. In 1951, Mendl Man estimated that publication of an independent journal by the Young-Israel group would cost approximately 600 Israeli lira, before the cost of paper (which was especially high due to the austerity policy). Letter to Tsvi Ayznman, Gnazim Institute, Ayznman Archive 394–5449/13.

189. See letters from Man to Ayznman from the following dates: February 2, 1950 (394–5438/13); August 20, 1950 (394–5442/13); October 9, 1951 (394–5446/13). Gnazim Institute, Ayznman Archive, 394.

190. Minkoff to Ayznman, February 10, 1954, Gnazim Institute, Ayznman Archive (394–5270/13). For more letters between the two men, see September 23, 1951 (394–5264/13); November 1, 1951 (394–5265/13); December 29, 1951 (394–5266/13); May 29, 1952 (394–5267/13); August 18, 1952 (394–5268/13); December 28, 1953 (394–5269/13); November 19, 1954 (394–5271/13); January 5, 1955 (394–5272/13).

191. See his letter of December 8, 1953, in which he offers to help with funding and with paper (because it was rationed in Israel at the time) for the publication of a Young-Israel journal (394–5429/13), as well as a letter from December 28, 1953 (394–5269/13), in which he repeats this offer. Gnazim Institute, Ayznman Archive, 394.

192. Letter from Sutzkever, Tel Aviv, to Tsvi Ayznman, Kibbutz Yagur, November 3, 1951, Gnazim Institute, Ayznman Archive, 394.

193. Letter from Karpinovitsh of Giv'at Rambam to Tsvi Ayznman at Kibbutz Yagur, September 1, 1951 Gnazim Institute, Ayznman Archive, 394.

194. Quoted in a letter from Dov Noy of Tel Aviv to Tsvi Ayznman in Yagur, March 27, 1951, Gnazim Institute, Ayznman Archive, 394.

195. Letter from Birstein of Kibbutz Gvat to Tsvi Ayznman in Yagur, May 19, 1959, Gnazim Institute, Ayznman Archive, 394.

196. On Sutzkever and Young-Vilna, see Novershtern, *'Avraham Sutzkever biMl'ot lo šiv'im*, 11–15; Avraham Novershtern, "Sifrut uPolitiqa biYeṣirata šel qvuṣat 'yung-vilne'" [Literature and politics and in work of the Young-vilne group], in Shmeruk and Werses, *Beyn štey milḥemot 'olam*, 169–81.

197. M. A. Kokhav [Mordekhe-Arye Shtern], "Tsi hobn mir take a literarishn nokhvuks?" [Do we indeed have a new literary growth?], *LF* no. 1 (1952): 12.

198. A. Volf Yasny, "Yung-yisroel zogt zayn Yidish vort" [Young-Israel says its Yiddish word], *LN*, February 4, 1955, 5.

199. Moss (*Jewish Renaissance*, 157) noted that the tension between the view of high culture as an end in itself that serves the intelligence and its perception as serving the masses reached its height in Russia in the decade before the 1917 revolution. Thus, criticism of the kind directed at *DGK* had already been voiced in the early years of the twentieth century against the pioneering literary journal published in Vilna in 1908, *Literarishe monatsshriftn* (*Literary Monthly*) (whose editors included Niger). But the historical context in which this criticism was leveled at *DGK*—following the Holocaust and the annihilation of millions of speakers of

the language and creators and consumers of its culture—gave it a more pronounced aspect of urgency and tragedy.

200. Tsanin, "Fayerung lekoved zekhtsik bend," 336.

201. Novershtern, *Qesem haDimdumim*, 34–36.

202. Sutzkever, *Vilner geto*, 101.

203. On the poem, its ties to the play *The Golden Chain*, and their influence on the founding of the journal of the same name in Israel, see J. D. Cammy, "Visions and Redemption: Abraham Sutzkever's Poems of Zion(ism)," in *Yiddish after the Holocaust*, ed. Josef Sherman (Oxford: Boulevard Books, 2004), 240–43.

204. Novershtern, *'Avraham Sutzkever biMl'ot lo šiv'im*, 68.

205. Shpiglblat, "'DGK' un ir melukhishe maymed," 39; Novershtern, *'Avraham Sutzkever biMl'ot lo šiv'im*, 38.

206. Novershtern, *'Avraham Sutzkever biMl'ot lo šiv'im*, 37. On the circumstances that led to the building of this monument, see N. Cohen, *Sefer sofer ve'Iton*, 32–38.

207. The play's first version, in Hebrew, titled Ḥurban Beit Ṣadiq ("Destruction of a Hasidic Dynasty"), was written in 1903. In 1906 a second version was written, this time in Yiddish, *Der nisoyen* (The attempt). In 1907 Peretz wrote another version of the play, in Yiddish, called *Di Goldene Keyt* (*The Golden Chain*; this incarnation of the play received three more versions). The changes in the play's name reflect the changes that occurred in Peretz's attitude to the question of the continuity of the Hasidic dynasty and the question of its quality (personal and religious) at the time of the waning of the traditional Jewish world: The name of the original play in Hebrew is negative and pessimistic (destruction). By contrast, the names of the play in Yiddish express a more positive and maybe even optimistic attitude ("The Attempt," "The Golden Chain"). See Shmeruk, *HaQri'a leNavi'*, 344.

208. Following the Yiddish literary critic Max Erik, Shmeruk proposed to read the versions not linearly but simultaneously, as different aspects of a single work. Novershtern also suggested reading the play in light of the fundamental tension it contains between destruction and redemption, and not as an attempt to resolve this tension. Novershtern, *'Avraham Sutzkever biMl'ot lo šiv'im*, 39.

209. Shmuel Niger, "Di goldene keyt," *Di tsukunft* 54 (1949): 310–14. One possible reason for this criticism of *DGK* is found in Novershtern (*'Avraham Sutzkever biMl'ot lo šiv'im*, 39). He describes a letter from Sutzkever to Niger in which Sutzkever apologizes for having to shorten an article by Niger that appeared in *DGK*'s first issue so as to maintain the delicate balance between the Yiddishist approach, with which Niger was associated, and the Hebrew-Zionist approach of the Histadrut.

210. Shmuel Niger, "Tsvey yor Di goldene keyt," newspaper clipping from an unknown source, YIVO Archive, Niger Collection, RG 360/1781.

211. Avrom Sutzkever, "Tsum fuftsikstn numer" [For the fiftieth volume], *DGK* 50 (1964): 4.

212. Issues of the journal are accessible at the National Library's Historical Jewish Press website. The site also includes a description of the journal's history and content: see Gali Drucker Bar-Am and Yitskhok Luden, "Lebns Fragen: An Introduction," National Library Newspaper Collection, accessed March 29, 2024, http://web.nli.org.il/sites/JPress/Hebrew/Pages/Lebens-Fragen.aspx. On the challenges of the Bund in Israel, see Gali Drucker Bar-Am, "The Bund in Israel: Searching for Jewish Working Class Secular Brotherhood in Zion," in *"Real" Spaces versus "Displaced" Time? Bundist Legacy after the Second World War*, ed. Vincento Pinto (Leiden: Brill, 2018), 56–69.

213. For example, the Federation of Anarchists published *Problemen* (Problems, a Hebrew-Yiddish bilingual quarterly, 1959–1964); the Communist Party published *Eynikeyt* (Unity, 1948) and *Fray-yisroel* (Free Israel, 1948–1977), and after the split Raqaḥ published *Der veg* (The way, 1965–1996); Mapam published *Af der vakh* (On the watch, a translation of its Hebrew newspaper Al Ha-Mishmar, 1954–1956) and *Yisroel shtime* (The voice of Israel, 1957–1997); Ahdut ha-Avoda published *Folksblat* (People's paper, 1958–1968, as a continuation of Po'ale Zion's *Nayvelt*); Mapai published *Yisroel tog-ayn tog-oys* (Every day Israel, 1957–1959); Agudat Israel, *Der veg* (The way, 1951); and the Union of Revisionist Zionists, *Der moment* (The moment, 1959). The Histadrut published *Biyuletin* (Information, 1957); the Jewish Agency for Israel published *Di vokh in yisroel* (The week in Israel, 1947–1948), *Folk un Tsion* (People and Zion, 1948–1993), and *Prese biyuletin* (Press information page, 1952–1953); the Ministry of Defense published *Zamlung* (Collection, 1949–1957); and Keren Ha-Yesod UIA (United Israel Appeal) published *Bletlekh* (Pages, 1956–1974).

214. The weekly *Nayvelt* (which from 1949 was published twice and even thrice a week) did put into practice the ideology of Po'ale Zion, which supported Yiddish at the time of the party's founding, and even featured an excellent literary section that published the works of leading Yiddish writers even before they came to Israel (like Sutzkever, Ayznman, Man, and others), but its pages never echoed the battles that various individuals and institutions in the world of Yiddish culture in Israel (and globally) waged for state recognition of the importance of Yiddish and its culture and for the equal allocation of resources to develop them and integrate them into the Israeli education system and cultural world.

215. The front page of *Frei-Yisroel*'s first issue detailed its goals. Yiddish and its culture were not mentioned. Anonymous, "Far a fray yisroel" [For a free Israel], *Fray-yisroel*, July 15, 1948, 1. On its second anniversary, the weekly's founders explicitly (but anonymously) noted that the reason they chose to publish it in Yiddish was their wish to reach a wide readership, and not any "linguistic loyalty" to the language and its culture: "In the summer of 1948 . . . it was decided . . . to publish a weekly in Yiddish. . . . The reasons for that were many: broad layers of the veteran population still lived in the language of their old home, and the masses of new immigrants flowing into the country certainly did not yet have any other options for communication but Yiddish." "Kultur farn folk" [Culture for the people], *Fray-yisroel*, July 19, 1950, 4–5.

216. Lederhendler, "Classless," 509–34.

217. Kh. Sh. Kazhdan, "Der bund biz dem finftn tsuzamenfor" [The Bund up to the fifth convention], in *Di geshikhte fun bund*, ed. Gregor Aronson et al., vol. 1 (New York: Undzer tsayt, 1960), 119, 176.

218. On the differences between the two movements, and also on the similarities, see Yosef Gorny, *Converging Alternatives: The Bund and the Zionist Labor Movement, 1897–1985*, trans. Naftali Greenwood (New York: State University of New York Press, 2005).

219. Frankel, *Prophecy and Politics*, 171–257.

220. Yo'av Peled, *Class and Ethnicity in the Pale: The Political Economy of Jewish Workers' Nationalism in Late Imperial Russia* (New York: St. Martin's, 1989).

221. David E. Fishman has noted the interesting fact that the movement's identification with Yiddish—which came to be the Bund's main marker—developed gradually. D. E. Fishman, *The Rise of Modern Yiddish Culture* (Pittsburgh: University of Pittsburgh Press, 2005), viii.

222. On the culture of the Bund movement and on these organizations, see Daniel Blatman, "HaBund: Mitos haMahapeḵa we'Avodat haYomyom" [The Bund: The myth of

revolution and the work of the everyday], in *Qiyum waŠever: Yehudei polin leDoroteihem* [Exitance and rupture: The Jews of Poland over the generations], vol. 2, ed. Israel Bartal and Israel Gutman (Jerusalem: Zalman Shazar, 2001), 521–28; Jack Jacobs, *Bundist Counterculture in Interwar Poland* (Syracuse: Syracuse University Press, 2009).

223. Daniel Blatman, *For Our Freedom and Yours: The Jewish Labor Bund in Poland, 1939–1949*, trans. Naftali Greenwood (London: Vallentine, Mitchell, 2003), 37–39.

224. Bentsl Tsalevitsh, "Mayne 35 yor in yisroel: Mayne ranglenishn far yidish un far bundizm" [My 35 years in Israel: My battles for Yiddish and for Bundism], *LF* (1957): 14–17.

225. See Luden, *In geyeg*, 361–65.

226. M. Grin, "Isokher Aykhnboym: Biyografishe shtrikhn" [Issachar Eichenbaum: Biographical lines], in *Yid, mentsh, sotsialist: Y. Artuski ondenk-bukh* [Jew, human being, socialist: Memory-book for Y. Artuski] (Tel Aviv: Lebns fragn farlag, 1976), 123. Artuski first came to Tel Aviv as a refugee from Teheran, in a circuitous route, as early as 1943, but after the war he left for Paris.

227. David Slucki, *The International Jewish Labor Bund after 1945: Toward a Global History* (New Brunswick, NJ: Rutgers University Press, 2012), 179. The movement's opposition to supporting the establishment of Israel had several grounds, among them the argument that founding it would cause an all-out war in the Middle East, and therefore not only would it not guarantee the existence of the Jewish people in the Diaspora; it would in fact pose an existential threat to the Jews living in Israel. Other reasons for this opposition were the movement's commitment to socialist ideas and to Yiddish and its culture, ideas that were rejected by the burgeoning Israeli establishment.

228. Slucki, *International Jewish Labor Bund*, 202–5.

229. The platform of the Israeli Bund party included (inter alia) equal rights for all citizens regardless of race, religion, nationality, ethnicity, and language; ending martial law over Arab settlements; separating religion and state and enacting secular civil laws; abolishing censorship of press (both Hebrew and Yiddish); according Yiddish and its culture equal support to that of Hebrew culture; and incorporating the study of Yiddish and its literature into the education system. Y. Artuski, "Val-platform fun bund: Vos vil der bund in yisroel?" [The Bund's election platform: What does the Bund want in Israel?], *LF* 95 (1959): 2.

230. On the results of the 1959 elections, see *LN*, November 6, 1959, 1.

231. Gali Drucker Bar-Am, "Zayn a bundist in Yisroel: An interviyu mitn redaktor," [Being a Bundist in Israel: An interview with the editor], *LF* 735–36 (2014): 39–41.

232. *Lebns fragn* was first published as a Bundist weekly in Russia in 1912. It was shut down by police and then appeared again in Warsaw in 1916. In 1918 it became a daily. On Bund press in Poland, see Pinkhes Shvarts, "Folkstsaytung" [People's newspaper], in *Fun noentn over* [From the near past] (New York: Alveltlekhn yidishn kultur kongres, 1956), 2:303–439; Tsanin, "Der ufgang un untergang fun der yidisher prese in poyln"; Nathan Cohen, "'Itonut yomit yehudit bePolin" [Daily Jewish press in Poland], in Bartal and Gutman, *Qiyum waŠever*, 313.

233. Y. Artuski, "In an akhrayesfuler tsayt" [In a time filled with responsibility], *LF* 1 (1951): 1.

234. Yisokher Aykhnboym, "Undzer basheydener yubiley: 15 yor bundishe organizatsye un lebns-fragn in Yisroel [Our modest jubilee: 15 years for the Bund organization and *LF* in Israel], *LF* 173 (1966): 5.

235. Aykhnboym, "Undzer basheydener yubiley."

236. On Artuski's ideological positions, see Y. Artuski, "Tsvantsik yor lebns-fragn" [Twenty years for *LF*], *LF* 230–31 (1971): 4; Ravitsh, *Mayn leksikon*, 62–63.

237. Ernest Gellner, *Nations and Nationalism* (Ithaca, NY: Cornell University Press, 1983), 34.

238. Gellner, *Nations and Nationalism*, 63–64.

239. Yod-Alef [Y. Artuski], "Rekht far yidish in shul?" [The right for Yiddish in school?], *LF* 104 (1960): 11; M. Grin, "Tsen yor yidishe nokhmitog-shul in tel-oviv" [Ten years for the afternoon-school in Tel Aviv], *LF* 162–63 (1966): 12. To get a sense of the differences between the Haredi and secular Yiddish educational systems, Fishman and Fishman give the following numbers: five thousand pupils attended Haredi schools in 1962/1963, compared with one hundred pupils at the AR schools in Tel Aviv and Beer-Sheva (probably in the early 1970s). Joshua A. Fishman and Dovid E. Fishman, "Yiddish in Israel: The Press, Radio, Theater and Book Publishing," *Yiddish* 1, no. 2 (1973): 14.

240. Y. Artuski, "Der nitsokhn on sholem" [Victory without peace], *LF* 188–89 (1967): 4.

241. On the importance of libraries in the transition of Jewish communities in Eastern Europe from religious institutions to institutions of modern secular culture, see N. Cohen, *Sefer sofer we'Iton*, 163–88; David Shavit, *Hunger for the Printed Word: Books and Libraries in the Jewish Ghettos of Nazi-Occupied Europe* (Jefferson, NC: McFarland, 1997), 3–39; Veidlinger, *Jewish Public Culture*, 24–66. On the central importance of libraries to the Jewish youth in Poland in the interwar years, see Ido Bassok, "Mapping Reading Culture in Interwar Poland: Secular Literature as a New Marker of Ethnic Belonging among Jewish Youth," *Simon Dubnow Institute Yearbook* 9 (2010): 15–36.

242. Hagit Cohen, *Nifla'ot ba'Olam heḤadaš: Sfarim weQori'm be'Arṣot haBrit, 1890–1940* [Wonders of the New World: Books and readers in Yiddish in the United States, 1890–1940] (Ra'anana: Open University Press, 2016), 251–93.

243. See Michał Weichert, "Yidish-bibliyotekn in tel-oviv" [Yiddish libraries in Tel Aviv], *LN*, September 25, 1959, 6; [The editors], *Yoisef Rotnberg: Tsu zayn ershter yortsayt* [Yoisef Rotnberg: For the first anniversary of his death] (Tel-Aviv: Y. L. Peretz, 1961).

244. For example, "Briv fun leyener" [A reader's letter], *LN*, January 6, 1950, 4; February 5, 1951, 2; September 7, 1951, 2; August 1, 1952, 6. Tsanin addressed the cultural-spiritual aspect of the absorption of the Eastern European Jews: Mordkhe [Tsanin], "Di 'aliya un der kultur-krizis" [The 'aliya and the culture crisis], *LN*, July 13, 1951, 3; Michał Weichert, "Der gaystiker qliṭa-protses" [The intellectual absorption process], *LN*, December 19, 1958, 3.

245. The long and fruitful writing career of the Yiddish journalist Yitskhok Luden began with a letter he published in the *LN* as a soldier. In the letter, which he addressed to the then prime minister, Ben-Gurion, he protested the fact that those who were responsible for cultural activities at the military base in which he served refused to order Yiddish newspapers for the reading room, while press in other foreign languages, and especially German, was ordered. Yitskhok Luden, "In vemens nomen? A por fragn tsum premiyer-minister ben guriyon" [[In whose name? Questions for Prime-Minister Ben-Gurion], *LN* December 1, 1950, 3. It should be noted that in 1948–1949, the IDF published a Yiddish "information bulletin" for immigrant soldiers called *Inderheym: Informatsye biyuletin far ḥayalim 'olim* (At home: Information bulletin for immigrant soldiers). On the IDF as a framework for social and cultural absorption in the years of the mass immigration, see Lissak, *Ha'Aliya haGdola biŠnot haḤamišim*, 83–84.

246. Letter from Yisroel Alster to Sutzkever, the National Library of Israel, Sutzkever Archive (4°.1565), the Y. L. Peretz Library folder. On the library's call for books from Jews all over the world, see also "Di Y.L. Peretz-bibliyotek in tel oviv hot farefentlekht a ruf" [The Y. L. Peretz Library in Tel Aviv published a public call], *Biyuletin fun alveltlekhn yidishn kultur-kongres* 40–41 (1951): 21.

247. "Yiddishkeyt" in the sense of secular and modern Yiddish culture, "doikayt" (hereness), and "khavershaft" (camaraderie) were the three main tenets of the international Bundist culture and of the socialization between its members. See F. Wolff, "Revolutionary Identity and Migration: The Commemorative Transnationalism of Bundist Culture," *East European Jewish Affairs* 43, no. 3 (2013): 314–31.

248. [The editors], *Yoisef Rotnberg*, 108. For more on Rotnberg and his activity, see [The editors], *Shimen Roznberg gedenkbukh* [Shimon Rozenberg memorial book] (Tel Aviv: Y. L. Peretz, 1966), 233–37; Gali Drucker Bar-Am, "Tsvey Yoisef Rotnberg" [Two Yoisef Rotnberg], *LF* 701–2 (2011): 19.

249. "Derefenung fun leyen-zal bay der peretz-bibliyotek" [Opening of a reading-hall in Peretz library], *LN* May 3, 1960, 3; "Leyen-zal" [Reading-hall], *Yediyes fun Y. L. Peretz farlag* [News of Y. L. Peretz Press] 1 (1963): 6.

250. Batya Temqin-Berman, "Sifriyot yehudiot beWarša" [Jewish libraries in Warsaw], *Yad La-Kore* 3–4 (1953): 145–56. Temqin-Berman passed the war years on the "Aryan" side of Warsaw, immigrated to Israel in 1950, and died in Tel Aviv in 1953. On her life, see Batya Temqin-Berman, *Ir beTok̲ ir* [City within a city], trans. Uri Orlev (Tel Aviv: Am-Oved, 2008).

251. For a description of the library's inauguration, see Rokhl Tukhman, "Leyenes briv: An ovnt fun peretz-bibliyotek in natanya" [Readers' letters: An evening of the Peretz Library in Natania], *LN*, November 23, 1960, 3.

252. Nosn Bolel, "Azoy vi in der amoliker heym: Derefenung fun a bibliyotek in šk̲unat nuzha" [Like in the old home: Opening of a library in the Nuzha neighborhood], *LN*, October 20, 1960, 3.

253. Yasny, "Yisroel—der nayster yidish literatur-tsenter," 7.

254. A. Volf Yasny, "Yidish-sektor in der yosroel-kultur" [Yiddish sector in Israeli-culture], *LN*, May 5, 1957, 6.

255. Weichert, "Yidish-bibliyotekn in tel oviv," 6.

256. "Di bibliyotek" [The library], *Yedies fun Y.L. Peretz farlag* 1 (1964): 5.

257. Temqin-Berman, "Sifriyot yehudiot beWarša," 146–48.

258. Snunit Shoham, "Sifria beLev 'Ir," [A library in the heart of the city], in *'Ir waSefer: Sifriyat ša'ar ṣion-beit 'ari'ela* [City and book: The Sha'ar Zion-Beit Ariela Library], ed. Ora Ahimeir (Jerusalem: Keter, 1987), 80–95.

259. Franz Kurski was the underground name of Shmuel Kahan (1874–1950), opinion journalist and one of the founding fathers of the Bund. The Bund Library in Warsaw is named after Grosser and was managed by Herman Kruk. It was the largest movement-affiliated library in Poland, and in addition to lending books, it had a reading and study room and hosted lectures, conferences, and classes and group activities for workers. Blatman, "HaBund," 525.

260. Weichert, "Yidish-bibliyotekn in tel oviv."

261. Yasny, "Yidish-sektor in der yosroel-kultur."

262. Weichert, "Yidish-bibliyotekn in tel oviv."

263. Temqin-Berman, "Sifriyot yehudiot beWarša," 146–48.

264. N. Cohen, *Sefer sofer we'Iton*, 175.

265. N. Cohen, *Sefer sofer we'Iton*, 204–15.

266. "Dekleratsiye fun der konferents farn yidishn bukh" [Declaration of the conference for the Yiddish book], *Biyuletin fun alveltlekhn yidishn kultur-kongres* 4 (1955): 12–13.

267. Shmeruk, "Yiddish," 809.

268. On this source, and for an extensive survey of the history and practice of the study of publishing houses, see Moti Neiger, *Moṣi'im la'Or kiMetavk̲ei tarbut: Hisṭoria tarbutit šel*

mea' šnot mol"ut 'ivrit beYiśra'el, 1910–2010 [Publishers as cultural mediators: A cultural history of 100 years of Hebrew publishing, 1910–2010] (Jerusalem: Man, 2017).

269. Moyshe Grosman, "Farlag Y.L. Peretz-bibliyotek in Yisroel" [The Y. L. Peretz Press in Israel], *Heymish* 18 (1957): 19; "10 yor Y.L. Peretz farlag" [10 years Y. L. Peretz Press], *Yediyes fun Y. L. Peretz farlag* 6 (1966): 3.

270. By the publishing houses (alphabetically) Arbeter Ring, CYCO (pronounced "Tsiko," Tsentrale yidishe kultur-organizatsye, Central Yiddish Cultural Organization), Der Kval, Matones (Gifts), YIVO, and Ykuf (Yidisher kultur farband, Yiddish Culture Association).

271. By the publishing houses (alphabetically) Alveltlekher yidisher kultur-kongres—argentiner opteyl (World Congress for Yiddish/Jewish Culture—Argentinian Branch), Dos poylishe yidntum (Polish Jewry), Kiyum (Existence), Yidbukh (a combination of "Jew" and/or the prefix of "Yiddish" with "book"), and Ykuf.

272. By the publishing houses (alphabetically) Di goldene pave (The Golden Peacock) and Farlag baym kultur kongres—eyropeisher opteyl (Yiddish Culture Association Press—European Branch).

273. By the publishing houses (alphabetically) Yidish-bukh (Yiddish Book) and Yidisher historisher institute (Yiddish Historical Institute).

274. The publishing house Melukhe-farlag far literatur (State Press for Literature).

275. On this decline in Paris, see "Di yidishe literarishe produktsye in pariz" [The Yiddish literary production in Paris], *Almanakh pariz* [Paris almanac] (1960): 251–57.

276. See Yekhiel Hofer, "Yoisef Rotnberg: Tsu zayn azoy fritsaytikn toyt" [Yoisef Rotnberg: For his so-too-early death], *Di Tsukunft* 65, no. 6–7 (1960): 292; [The editors], *Yoisef Rotnberg*; "Tsen yor Y.L. Peretz-farlag" [Ten years for Y. L. Peretz Press], *Yediyes fun Y. L. Peretz farlag* 6 (1966): 3; Korn, *Dos gerangl far yidish*, 186–88.

277. "Farshpreytung fun undzere oysgabes" [The distribution of our editions], *Yediyes fun Y. L. Peretz farlag* (1964): 3.

278. "Abonentn-aktsye farn Y.L. Peretz-farlag" [Members campaign for the Y. L. Peretz Press], *Yediyes fun Y. L. Peretz farlag* (1964): 7.

279. "Tsen yoriker yubiley funem farlag Y.L. Peretz gefayert in ohek shem" [Ten-year jubilee for the Y. L. Peretz Press celebrated in 'Ohel Šem], *LN*, December 12, 1966, 5; *LF* 179–80 (December 1966): 17.

280. "In Y.L. Peretz-farlag zenen dershinen biz itst 193 bikher" [In Y. L. Peretz Press 193 books published to date], *Yediyes fun Y. L. Peretz farlag* 6 (1966): 13. The source lists only 190 books.

281. For an extensive study of Yizker bikher as "history from below" and as literature, see Gali Drucker Bar-Am, "'Record and Lament': Yizker Bikher as History and Literature Conflated," *Yad Vashem Studies* 51, no. 2 (2023): 101–28.

282. "Undzere hebreyishe un yidish-hebreyishe bikher" [Our Hebrew and Yiddish-Hebrew books], *Yediyes fun Y. L. Peretz farlag* 6 (1966): 12.

283. On Rokhl Faygnberg's efforts in 1945 to create a series of Hebrew translations of classic works of Yiddish literature, see Rokhl Faygnberg, "Berl Katsenelson der grinder fun Am-Oved" [Berl Katznelson the founder of Am-Oved], *LN*, March 8, 1957, 5; Rokhl Faygnberg, "Der plan fun Berl Katsenelson aroysgebn in hebreyish di yidishe literatur" [Ber Katznelson's plan to publish Yiddish literature in Hebrew], *LN*, March 29, 1957, 5. The *Sifriyat Yalqut* book series included translated works by Asch, Opatoshu, and Pinski. At *Sifriyat Bilaik*, Dov Sadan edited a series of Hebrew translations of classic works of Yiddish literature (including H. Leyvik's *Ḥeziyonei ge'ula* [*Plays of Redemption*]). See Novershtern, "Between Town

and Gown," 16. At Sifriyat Po'alim, Shlonsky translated and published Manger's *Dmuiot qrovot* (*Close Images*) and H. Leyvik's "Balada 'al beit ḥolim beDenver" ("A Ballad of Denver Sanatorium"). On Shlonsky's attitude toward Yiddish after the Holocaust, see Hagit Halperin, *HaMa'esṭro: Ḥayav viYeṣirato šel 'Avraham Šlonsqi* [The maestro: The life and work of Avraham Shlonsky] (Tel Aviv: Sifriyat Po'alim, 2011), 305. In the 1960s, Sifriyat Po'alim began collaborating with the Vaynfer-Morgenshtern Foundation, established by Joseph Morgenstern of Hollywood with the aim of making seminal works of Yiddish literature available to the Hebrew reader. The foundation supported the publication of Nakhmen Mayzel, *Y. L. Peretz uVnei doro* (Y. L. Peretz and his generation); Khaim Zhitlovski, *Ktavim* (Writings); Peretz Markish, *Dor holeḵ veDor ba'* (One generation passes and another arrives); Y. Trunk, *Polin* (Poland); Dovid Berglson, *Ktavim*; Der Nister, *Ktavim*; Ruven Branin, *Ktavim nivḥarim* (Selected writings); Zisho Vaynfer, *Širim uPo'emot* (Poems and long poems); and Mordechai Halamish, ed., *Mikan uMiqarov: Antologia šel siporei yidiš be'Ereṣ Yiśra'el miRešit haMe'a we'Ad yanenu* (From Here and from near: An anthology of Yiddish stories in Eretz Yisrael from the turn of the century to our days). On the Hebrew translations of Yiddish works published in the large publishing houses in 1939–1947, see Ruven Levi, "Di bikher produktsye in yisroel" [Book production in Israel], *DGK* 1 (1949): 239–40.

284. From the 1950s and on, it was primarily Hakibbutz Hameuchad that published works by young Yiddish writers, like Ayznman, Man, and Shpigl.

285. For example, Moyshe Grosman's book *Ha'Areṣ ha'Agadit haKšufa* (The enchanted legendary land) was published by the Tversqi Press in 1951. His book *Widuio šel mahapḵan: Roman poliṭi* (Confessions of a revolutionary: A political novel) was published by this press in 1957. Yosl Birshteyn's *Bemidraḵot ṣarot: Roman meḤayei ha-Kibbutz* (On narrow sidewalks: A novel of life in the Kibbutz) was published by HaMatmid Press in 1959.

286. "Y. L. Peretz farlag: A brik tsvishn yidish un hebreyish" [Y. L. Peretz Press: A bridge between Yiddish and Hebrew], *Yediyes fun Y. L. Peretz farlag* (1963): 5.

287. "Der matsev fun yidishn farlags-vezn: Memorandum fun Y.L. Peretz farlag tsum bildungs un kultur-ministeriyum" [The predicament of Yiddish publishing houses: A memorandum from the Y. L. Peretz Press to the Ministry of Education and Culture], *Yediyes fun Y. L. Peretz farlag* (1963): 15.

288. "Subsidiyes un fondn" [Subsidies and funds], *Yediyes fun Y. L. Peretz farlag* 6 (1966): 4.

289. "Tsen yor Y.L. Peretz farlag," *Yediyes fun Y. L. Peretz farlag* 6 (1966): 3.

290. See, for example, Tsvi Ayznman's appeal to Tsiko-farlag un bikher-tsentrale (CYCO Press and Distribution) regarding fundraising for the publication of his book *Mazoles* with the Y. L. Peretz Press, dated December 23, 1964; letter from Ayznman to the Y. L. Peretz Press in which he reports on his efforts to raise funds, December 31, 1964; the press's reply, dated January 6, 1965, in which details of the process of publication are spelled out. Gnazim Institute, Ayznman Archive, 394.

291. "Y. L. Peretz farlag git aroys yizker-bikher un monografiyes fun kehiles" [Y. L. Peretz Press publishes memorial books and monographs on communities], *Yediyes fun Y. L. Peretz farlag* (1963): 13.

292. Mary Douglas, *Purity and Danger: An Analysis of Concepts of Pollution and Taboo* (London: Routledge, 1966), 70.

293. "Farlag ha-Menora" [Ha-Menora], *Heymish* 50 (1960): 138.

294. Arie Shamri, "Mi un uftu farn yidishn vort: 5 yor farlag 'yisroel-bukh'" [Toil and accomplishment for the Yiddish word: Five years for the "Israel-book" press], in *Aynzamlung* [Anthology] (Tel Aviv: Yisroel-bukh, 1982), 44–48.

295. Daniel Tsharni, "Vegn yidish in Yisroel un in der gorer velt" [On Yiddish in Israel and in the whole world], *LN*, February 26, 1954, 5. The report first appeared in the New York paper *Tog-morgn zshurnal*, December 26, 1953. See also Dina Abramovitsh, "Dos yidishe bukh in amerike" [The Yiddish book in America], *Jewish Book Annual* 12 (1953–54): 139–40.

296. Dina Abramovitsh, "Dos yidishe bukh in amerike," *Jewish Book Annual* 19 (1961–62): 169–71. This year was the last in which YIVO published statistical information about the global printing of Yiddish books. From 1963, the institute published only a list of the Yiddish books it received.

297. Dina Abramovitsh, "Dos yidishe bukh in amerike," *Jewish Book Annual* 19 (1962–63): 180.

298. Avrom Goldberg, "156 yidishe bikher zenen dershinen in 1963" [156 books in Yiddish were published in 1963], *LF* 157 (1965): 12.

299. Avrom Goldberg, "141 yidishe bikher un broshurn zenen dershinen in 1964" [141 books and brochures in Yiddish were published in 1964], *LF* 168 (1965): 14.

300. Gedalia Elkoshi, "Yevul sifrutenu biŠnat taši"a" [The yield of our literature in the Hebrew year taši"a [1950–1951], *Taw šin yod bet: Šnaton davar* [1951–1952: The Davar annual publication] (Tel Aviv: Davar, 1951), 374–75; "Yevul haSifrut beTašat tšṭ"w" [The literary yield of 1954–1955], in *Sefer haŠana šel ha'Etona'im tšṭ"z*" [The 1955–1956 journalists' yearbook] (Tel Aviv: Agudat ha-'Etonaim, 1956), 179.

301. J. Fishman and Fishman, "Yiddish in Israel," 11.

302. Anderson, *Imagined Communities*.

303. David Stern, "An Introduction," in *The Anthology in Jewish Literature*, ed. David Stern (Oxford: Oxford University Press, 2004), 3–14. On the Hebrew anthologies edited in the time of the Yishuv as tools for the dissemination of Hebrew culture and the consolidation of the image of Eretz Yisrael as a new national space, see Israel Bartal, *Qozaq uBedwi* [Cossack and Bedouin] (Tel Aviv: Am-Oved, 2007), 109–21.

304. For example, Moyshe Basin, "Antologye find hundert yor yidishe poeziye" (Anthology of five hundred years of Yiddish poetry, 1917); Zisho Landoy, "Di yidishe dikhtung in amerike biz yor 1919 ("Yiddish Poetry in America until 1919"); Basin, "Amerikaner yidishe poezye" (American Yiddish poetry, 1940); Pinye Kats et al., "Antologye fun der yidisher literatur in argentine" (Anthology of Yiddish literature in Argentina, 1944); Y. Y. Trunk and Arn Tseytlin, "Antologye fun der yidisher proze in poyln" (Anthology of Yiddish prose in Poland, 1946); Nakhmen Mayzel, "Amerike in yidishn vort" (America in the Yiddish word, 1955); and Meylekh Ravitsh, "Dos amolike yidishe varshe" (Jewish/Yiddish Warsaw of yesterday, 1966). For a bibliography of the poetry anthologies published in Yiddish, see Nakhmen Mayzel, *Tsurikblikn un perspektivn* [Retrospectives and perspectives] (Tel Aviv: Y. L. Peretz, 1962), 354–96. On Basin's anthologies, see Avraham Novershtern, "Yiddish Poetry in a New Context," *Prooftexts* 8, no. 3 (1988): 356–57.

305. On this anthology and its influence on anthologies edited after the Holocaust, see Drucker Bar-Am, "Anthological Affect," 7–27.

306. In 1962 and 1967, the Yidisher shrayber un zshurnalistn-fareyn in yisroel (Association of Yiddish Journalists and Writers in Israel) published two almanacs featuring works by members of the association. Here I discuss only anthologies and not almanacs, which featured current works and whose editors did not intend to provide the readers with an anthological picture.

307. For more, see Drucker Bar-Am, "Anthological Affect."

308. Shimshon Melzer, *'Al neharot: Tiš'a maḥzorei šira miSifrut yidiš* [By the rivers: An anthology of Yiddish poetry] (Jerusalem: Mosad Bialik, 1956); Moshe Bassok, *Mivḥar širei*

yidiš leMin Y. L. Peretz we'Ad yamenu [A selection of Yiddish poems from Y. L. Peretz to the present] (Merhavia: Hakibbutz Hameuchad, 1963). An early anthology of Yiddish poems in Hebrew translation, *Bein sa'ar leSa'ar: MiSifrut yidiš baTfuṣot* (Between storms: A selection of Yiddish literature from the Diaspora), was edited by Dov Ber Malkin and published in 1944. Since the present book is concerned with prose and not poetry, these anthologies are not discussed here.

309. Gellner, *Language and Solitude*, 19.

310. Arie Shamri, "Araynfir" [Introduction], in *Vortslen: Antologye fun yidish-shafn in yisroel*, ed. Arie Shamri (Tel Aviv: Yisroel-bukh, 1966), 7.

311. Shamri, "Araynfir," 8: "In determining the order of the table of contents we took into consideration a unique Israeli principle: seniority, according to the time of immigration [to Israel] and the first contact with the country."

312. Shamri, "Araynfir," 5–6.

313. See N. Cohen, *Sefer sofer we'Iton*, 183.

314. "'Ikh vil zayn mitn folk yisroel' derklert Sholem Asch unkumendik keyn lod" ["I want to be with the people of Israel," declared Sholem Asch upon arriving in Lod], *LN*, February 1, 1956, 1.

315. "Sholem Aschs hoyz—far 'iriyat bat-yam" [Sholem Asch's house—for Bat-Yam municipality], *LN*, December 25, 1957, 1.

316. "Sholem Asch kumt keyn yisroel" [Sholem Asch is coming to Israel], *LN*, June 11, 1951, 3; "Sholem Asch gekumen in land" [Sholem Asch has arrived in the land], *LN*, April 25, 1952, 1; "Sholem Asch in yisroel" [Sholem Asch is in Israel], *LN*, October 6, 1954, 1.

317. Mordkhe Tsanin, "Sholem Aschs bazukh in yisroel: Der kalter kaboles-ponim bay der shif" [Sholem Asch's visit in Israel: The cold reception by the ship], *Forverts*, May 17, 1952, Gnazim Institute, Tsanin Collection 504; Mordkhe Tsanin, "Sholem Asch: A shmues mitn mayster fun der yidisher literatur, an araynfir tsu der parshe Asch" [Sholem Asch: A conversation with the master of Yiddish literature, an introduction to the Asch affair], *LN*, November 12, 1954, 4. The debate continued to unfold in the pages of the *LN* as well as in other Yiddish papers in Israel.

318. Shamri, "Araynfir," 9.

319. Mordechai Halamish, ed., *Mikan uMiqarov: Antologia šel siporei yidiš be'Ereṣ Yiśra'el miRešit haMe'a we'Ad yanenu* [From here and from near: An anthology of Yiddish stories in Eretz Yisrael from the turn of the century to our days] (Tel Aviv: Sifriyat Po'alim, 1966), 7–15.

320. Jeffrey Shandler, "Anthologizing the Vernacular: Collections of Yiddish Literature in English Translation," in Stern, *Anthology in Jewish Literature*, 304–23.

321. Halamish, *Mikan uMiqarov*, 7.

322. Halamish, *Mikan uMiqarov*, 7 (emphasis in original).

323. Dov Sadan, introduction to Halamish, *Mikan uMiqarov*, 13–14.

324. Sadan, introduction, 14–15.

325. See Yechiel Szeintuch, "Yidish limed in yiroelisher mitlshul-dertsiyung" [Yiddish learning in middle-school education in Israel], *DGK* 91 (1976): 51–60. My own late grandmother, Sara Khashke-Novodvorski, taught Yiddish at this high school from the late 1960s.

326. Halamish, *Mikan uMiqarov*, 7–8 (emphasis in original).

327. This story is from Brokhes's first collection of stories, which bears the same title as the story—*Untern shotn fun khermon* (*In the Shadow of the Hermon*, New York, 1918). On the writer and his works, see Yael Chaver, *Ma šeḤayavim liškoaḥ: Yidiš baYešuv heḤadaš* [That which must be forgotten: Yiddish in the new Yishuv] (Jerusalem: Yad Ben-Zvi, 2005), 75–113.

2. May the Place Comfort You

1. These two devices, taken from the realms of print and film editing, respectively, indicate the transition between two images, characterized by the effect created from the projection of two images on top of one another.

2. On the place of Warsaw in modern Yiddish culture and literature, see Khone Shmeruk, "Qawim leToldot haMerkaz šel sifrut yidiš beWarša" [Aspects of the history of Warsaw as a Yiddish literary center], in *Beyn štey milḥemot ʻolam: Praqim beḤayei haTarbut šel yehudei polin liLšonoteyhem* [Between two world wars: Chapters in the cultural life of Jews in Poland in their languages], ed. Khone Shmeruk and Shmuel Werses (Jerusalem: Magnes, 1997), 157–68; Shmuel Rozhanski, "Di role fun varshe in der yidisher litertur" [The role of Warsaw in Yiddish literature], in *Musterverk fun der yidisher literatur* [Masterpieces of Yiddish literature], vol. 80, ed. Shmuel Rozhanski (Buenos Aires: Instituto Científico Judío IWO, 1979), 5–18.

3. Oyerbakh's reference to Warsaw of independent Poland as "the Jewish dark continent" refers to the Pale of Settlement where Jews were permitted to live in Czarist Russia (although Warsaw and Congressional Poland were not formally within the Pale of Settlement). On the comparison of the Jewish Pale of Settlement to a "dark continent," see Nathaniel Deutsch, *The Jewish Dark Continent: Life and Death in the Russian Pale of Settlement* (Cambridge, MA.: Harvard University Press, 2011), 1–15.

4. Rokhl Oyerbakh, "Tsvishn Yidn" [Among Jews], Yad Vashem Archive, Rokhl Oyerbakh Collection, P-16/69.

5. For an analysis of the terms *place* and *memory*, see Zali Gurevitch, *ʻAl haMaqom* [On the place] (Tel Aviv: Am-Oved, 2007), 22–73; Barbara E. Mann, *Space and Place in Jewish Studies* (New Brunswick, NJ: Rutgers University Press, 2012), 11–25.

6. Melanie Klein, "Love, Guilt and Reparation," in *Love, Guilt, and Reparation: And Other Works, 1921–1945* (London: Virago, 1988).

7. Klein, "Love, Guilt, and Reparation."

8. Yankev Raykhnshteyn, "Lezeykher di kdoyshey-lublin" [In memory of the martyrs of Lublin], *LN*, November 30, 1951, 4.

9. Many studies have been written on the subject of collective memory over the past two decades. Of these I mention Yael Zerubavel, *Recovered Roots: Collective Memory and the Making of Israeli National Tradition* (Chicago: University of Chicago Press, 1995); Nira Feldman, "Lama we'Eiḫ ḥevra zoḵeret" [Why and how a community remembers], in *Liqro' qirot: Mismaḵ tarbuti ḥazuti* [Reading walls: A visual cultural document], ed. Ziona Shimshi and Dalit Lahav (Ra'anana: Even Hoshen, 2007), 12–14; J. K. Olick, Vered Vinitzky-Seroussi, and Daniel Levy, "Introduction," in *The Collective Memory Reader*, ed. J. K. Olick, Vered Vinitzky-Seroussi, and Daniel Levy (Oxford: Oxford University Press, 2011), 3–62.

10. Maurice Halbwachs, *On Collective Memory*, trans. L. A. Coser (Chicago: University of Chicago Press, 1992). For a critical analysis of Halbwachs's term, see Olick, Vinitzy-Seroussy, and Levi, "Introduction," 16–22.

11. A pioneering study in the field is by Hanna Yablonka, "Ma lizkor weKeiṣad? Niṣolei haŠoa we'Eiṣuv yedi'ata" [What to remember and how? Survivors of the Holocaust and the shaping of its memory], in *ʻIdan haṢionut* [The age of Zionism], ed. Anita Shapira et al. (Jerusalem: Zalman Shazar, 2000), 297–316.

12. Pierre Nora, *Realms of Memory: Rethinking the French Past*, trans. Arthur Goldhammer (New York: Columbia University Press, 1996–98).

13. On patterns of memory of the Holocaust among Jewish communities in the world, see, for example, Hasia R. Diner, *We Remember with Reverence and Love: American Jews and the Myth of Silence after the Holocaust, 1945–1962* (New York: New York University Press, 2009); Annette Wieviorka, "Un lieu de mémoire et d'histoire: Le Mémorial du martyr juif inconnu," *Renue de l'université de Bruxelles* 1–2 (1987): 107–32; Simon Perego, "Les commémorations de la destruction des Juifs d'Europe au Mémorial du martyr juif inconnu du milieu des années cinquante à la fin des années soixante," *Revue d'histoire de la Shoah* 193 (2010): 471–507; Milena Chinski, "Memorias en plural: Los judíos de Buenos Aires ante el Holocausto, 1945–1955" (PhD diss., Universidad Nacional de General Sarmiento, 2017).

14. The publication of Holocaust-themed serial novels in the daily press, presented not in a fine-literary form, is a unique phenomenon in the Yiddish press. For example, beginning on July 14, 1961, and continuing throughout the summer months between the end of the Eichmann trial and the handing down of the verdict, Ka-Tzetnik's book *Piepel*, described as a "chronicle," was published in serial form; and the memories of Khaye Elboym-Dorembus, *Af der Arisher Zayt* (On the Aryan side), were printed in installations from the end of 1954 until 1956 and were also published in book form by the *Letste nayes* press (Tel Aviv, 1957). On this novel, see Gali Drucker Bar-Am, "'Normal People in a Land of Their Own': On Gender and Nationalism in Khaye Elboym-Dorembus's *Af der Arisher Zayt*," *Nashim: A Journal of Jewish Women's Studies and Gender Issues* 27 (2014): 62–74.

15. For example, on the anniversary of the Warsaw Ghetto uprising in 1954, the *LN* published Bundist Marek Edelman's version of the uprising. Marek Edelman, "Azoy hobn mir gekemft kegn di daytshn" [How we fought the Germans], *LN*, April 19, 1954, 3.

16. On holidays, historical essays were published in the articles section, short stories and memories from the old home in the literary section. In the festive Passover issues in 1956 and 1957, the *LN* offered its readers an addition to the Haggadah—a "Yizker" page written by the Jewish American writer and historian Rufus Learsi. See Rufus Learsi, "Yizker-blat tsu der alter hagode" [Memorial page for the old Haggadah], *LN*, March 26, 1956, 2; Rufus Learsi, "Yizker blat tsu der alter hagode," *LN*, April 15, 1957, 8. On Learsi's work in the field of Holocaust memory, see Diner, *We Remember*, 18–21, 64, 401, n. 124.

17. Toward the end of the 1950s, the title of this column was changed to "Tsun ondenk fun fartilikte yidishe kehiles" (In memory of the destroyed Jewish communities), and it appeared under this name throughout the 1960s.

18. The Association of Polish Immigrants in Israel was established in 1952 following the Fourth 'Aliya and the arrival of many new immigrants from that country. It included about ten associations from specific towns, including Kroke (1925), Tshenstokhov (1925), Pintshev (1920s), Lomzhe (1930), Shedlitz (1933), Zhelekhov (1934), Stry (1934), Lublin (early 1930s), Khelm (early 1930s, was closed and reopened after the establishment of the state), and Mezritsh (1937). For the sake of comparison, see Hannah Kliger's survey of two thousand Jewish hometown associations in New York in 1939: *Jewish Hometown Associations and Family Circles in New York* (Bloomington: Indiana University Press, 1992), viii. In 1961, the Association of Polish Immigrants in Israel reported that it was an umbrella organization for 104 hometown associations. More than one-third of these 104 associations reported that they had been established after the discovery of the fate of the communities in the Holocaust and up to the establishment of Israel. These included 'Irgun yoṣ'ei Warša and Byalistok [in Israel from] 1940, Oshpitsin (1940), Pultosk (1941), Kovel (1941), Rovne (1941), Novi dvor (1942), Betshotsh (1942), Zhidlovetza (1942), Hantzevitsh (1943), Lantzut (1943), Libivne (1943), Stolin (1943), Ivia (1944), Brisk (1944), Tomashov (1944), Lida (1944), Steibtz (1944), Pabianitz (1944), Pshemishl

(1944), Kosov (1944), Rozhishtsh (1944), Ostrov-Mazovyetsk (1945), Baranovitsh (1945), Podlyashe (1945), Zamoshtsh (1945), Lintshits (1945), Mlave (1945), Smorgon (1945), Plotsk (1945), Prushkov (1945), Horodok (1946), Levertov (1946), Mordy (1946), Stashev (1946), Klodava (1946), and Rave (1946). See Liber Lush, *Landsmanshaftn in Yisroel: Spetsyele oysgabe tsum velt-ḳongres fun poylishe yidn* [Hometown associations in Israel: Special publication to world-congress of Jews from Poland] (Tel Aviv: Hitahadut ʻolei Polin Be-Israʻel, 1961), 33–206. On the activities of the hometown associations in Israel after the Holocaust, see Dovid Shtokfish, "Landsmanshaftn in yisroel" [Hometown associations in Israel], *Argentiner Yivo-shriftn* 15 (1989): 56–64.

19. The main sources on the Yizker books are the anthology *From a Ruined Garden: The Memorial Books of Polish Jewry*, edited by Jack Kugelmass and Jonathan Boyarin (Bloomington: Indiana University Press, 1998), and the collection of essays *Memorial Books of Eastern European Jewry: Essays on the History and Meaning of Yizker Volumes*, edited by Rosemary Horowitz (Jefferson, NC: McFarland, 2011). See also Gali Drucker Bar-Am, "'Record and Lament': Yizker Bikher as History and Literature Conflated," *Yad Vashem Studies* 51, no. 2 (2023): 101–128.

20. For example, the description of Layser Buchbinder's daughter of Bilgoray, who succeeded in getting out of the ghetto and smuggling food into it for her daughter but was caught and shot. Moyshe Taytlboym, "Naynter yortsayt fun der yidisher kehile in bilgoray" [Ninth anniversary of the [destruction of] the Jewish community in Bilgoray], *LN*, November 16, 1951, 3. On the contribution of female characters to the formation of national identity, see George L. Mosse, *Nationalism and Sexuality: Middle-Class Morality and Sexual Norms in Modern Europe* (Madison: University of Wisconsin Press, 1985), 90–113.

21. Yankev Rikhnshteyn, "Lublin: Di ʻir wa'Em beYiśra'el" [Lublin: The Ir wa'Em [important city, literally "city and mother"] in Israel], *LN*, November 3, 1950, 4.

22. Yankev Susokh, "Vegn shtetl zdunske-volye" [On the town Zdunske-Volye], *LN*, December 1, 1950, 3; Y.P., "Khurbn zhelekhov" [The destruction of Zhelekhov], *LN*, November 6, 1951, 2.

23. Mordkhe Tsanin, "Geratevete yidn in yisroel gefinen zeyere payniker fun di lagern" [Jewish survivors in Israel find their torturers from the camps], *Forverts*, November 19, 1950, newspaper clipping with no page number, Gnazim Institute, Tsanin collection, 504.

24. Dominick LaCapra, *Writing History, Writing Trauma* (Baltimore: Johns Hopkins University Press, 2014), 22.

25. Dominick LaCapra, "Trauma, Absence, Loss," *Critical Inquiry* 25 (1999): 698.

26. Claude Lévi-Strauss, *Myth and Meaning* (London: Routledge, 1978), 15–18.

27. Max Weinreich, *Shturemvint: Bilder fun der yidisher geshikhte in zibtsntn yorhundert* [Strom wind: Images from Jewish history in the seventeenth century] (Vilne: Tamar, 1927); Max Erik, *Di geshikhte fun der yidisher literatur fun di eltste tsaytn biz der haskole-tkufe* [History of Yiddish literature: From earliest times to the Haskalah period] (Varshe: Kultur-Lige, 1928), 373–91.

28. See Laura Jockusch, *Collect and Record! Jewish Holocaust Documentation in Early Postwar Europe* (Oxford: Oxford University Press, 2012), 18–45.

29. Ada Schein, "'Everyone Can Hold a Pen': The Documentation Project in the DP Camps in Germany," in *Holocaust Historiography in Context: Emergence, Challenges, Polemics and Achievements*, ed. David Bankier and Dan Michmann (Jerusalem: Yad Vashem and Berghahn, 2008), 106–8.

30. M. L. Smith, "No Silence in Yiddish: Popular and Scholarly Writing about the Holocaust in the Early Postwar Years," in *After the Holocaust: Challenging the Myth of Silence*, ed. David Cesarani and Eric J. Sundquist (London: Routledge, 2012), 55–66.

31. For example, Yankev Lever, "Der umkum fun a yidisher kehile: Tsum akhtn yortsayt fun khurbn tshenstokhov" [The destruction of a Jewish community: On the occasion of the eighth anniversary of the destruction of Tshenstokhov], *LN*, September 22, 1950, 6; Moyshe Goldlist, "Di yidishe shtot khmelnik: A bintl zikhroynes tsum akhtn yortsayt nokh khmelniker kdoyshim" [The Jewish city of Khmelnik: A bundle of memories on the occasion of the eighth annual memorial day for Khmelnik martyrs], *LN*, October 6, 1950, 4.

32. On the tension between "popular" and "professional" historians of the Holocaust at Yad Vashem, see Bo'az Cohen, *HaDorot haBai'm—eiḵeḵa yed'u? Leidato weHitpatḥuto šel ḥeqer haŠoa' haYiśra'eli* [The next generations—how will they know? The birth and evolution of Israeli Holocaust studies] (Jerusalem: Yad Vashem, 2010).

33. See, for example, Kugelmass and Boyarin, *From a Ruined Garden*, 1–43.

34. On the Sabra's image of the Holocaust survivor, see Gershon Shaked, "Bein haKotel uVein meṣada: HaŠoa' weHatoda'a ha'Aṣmit šel haḤevra haYiśra'elit" [Between the Wailing Wall and Masada: The Holocaust and Israeli society's self-awareness], in *Tmurot yesod ba'Am haYehudi be'Eqvot haŠoa'* [Major changes within the Jewish people in the wake of the Holocaust], ed. Israel Gutman (Jerusalem: Yad Vashem, 1996), 511–23.

35. On the image of the Diaspora in the Hebrew culture of the Yišuv, the concept of the negation of the Diaspora, and the attitude toward the Holocaust and its survivors in Israel of the 1950s, see Yechiam Weitz, "'Eṣuv ziḵron haŠoa' baḤevra haYiśra'elit biŠnot haḤamišim [The shaping of Holocaust memory in Israeli society in the 1950s], in Gutman, *Tmurot yesod ba'Am haYehudi*, 473–93; Roni Stauber, *HaLeqaḥ laDor: Šoa' uGvura baMaḥšava haṢiburit ba'Areṣ biŠnot haḤamišim* [The lesson for this generation: Holocaust and heroism in Israeli public discourse in the 1950s] (Jerusalem: Yad Ben-Zvi, 2000), 1–33.

36. S. Yizhar, *Yemei Ṣiqlag* [Days of Ziklag] (Tel Aviv: Am-Oved, 1958), 1:374. This familiar description is joined by a recollection by Ariel Hirshfeld, *Rešimot 'al maqom* [Local notes] (Tel Aviv: Am-Oved, 2000), 75, about his childhood in the small immigrant town of Pardes Hanna: "All the truly fascinating things were discussed there [in the author's hideout with his boyhood friends] (including the question of whether Yiddish is an actual language or a kind of garbled speech and distortions forced upon the Holocaust survivors because of the Nazi tortures)."

37. On the meaning of the term *countermemory*, see Zerubavel, *Recovered Roots*, 10–11.

38. Nakhmen List, "Af di khurves fun undzer akropol" [On the ruins of our Acropolis], *LN*, April 22, 1960, 6.

39. The need for some kind of closeness to the destroyed communities in Eastern Europe was of course expressed in Yiddish culture in Israel not only in the press. For example, an exhibit of Yizker books was held in April 1961 (on the eve of the opening of the Eichmann trial), at the Ginza Museum of Jewish Art in the heart of Tel Aviv (Bialik Street). The exhibit was accompanied by a catalogue in Hebrew and Yiddish. It was organized by survivors who were members of Friends of YIVO in Israel and by the Kurski and Y. L. Peretz libraries. It was probably inspired by a large exhibition held by YIVO in New York in 1959, titled "Dos yidishe shtetl in mizrekh-eyrope fun 1900 biz 1939" (The Jewish shtetl in Eastern Europe from 1900 to 1939). The exhibit in Israel was more modest, but according to Dr. Yoseph Kermish and Rokhl Oyerbakh, who wrote the introduction to the catalogue, the Tel Aviv exhibit had a national and not just ethnic character.

40. On the notion of "commemorative density," see Zerubavel, *Recovered Roots*, 8–9: "Commemorative density thus indicates the importance that the society attributes to different periods in its past: while some periods enjoy multiple commemorations, others attract

little attention, or fall into oblivion. . . . The high commemorative density attributed to certain events not only serves to emphasize their historical significance. It may also elevate them beyond their immediate historical context into symbolic texts that serve as paradigms for understanding other developments in the group's experience."

41. "Ongeveytikte fragn: Landsmanshaftn" [Painful questions: Hometown associations], *LN*, June 16, 1950, 3.

42. For example, "Shavler landslayt: der komitet fun shavler lansdlayt in yohanesburg . . . bet zeyer ale shavler landslayt velkhe gefinen zikh in yisroel, zikh registrirn . . . af dem adres: max grin, Holon, shikun chadash, rachel st. 248" (Fellow natives of Shavli: the committee for immigrants from Shavli in Johannesburg strongly requests all former residents of the town who are living in Israel to register at the address: Max Green, Holon, shikun chadash, 248 Rachel Street). *LN*, July 14, 1950, 5.

43. For example, "Akhtung ostrover bay lublin! Donershtik . . . kumt for in yafo, ajami . . . in der voynung fun yitskhok goldshteyn a tsuzamentref fun ale ostrover landslayt mit der bateylikung fun undzer landsman khayim kahan fun amerike . . . der tsaytvayliker komitet" (Attention former residents of Ostrava near Lublin! On Thursday . . . a meeting will be held . . . in Ajami in Jaffa . . . in the apartment of Yitskhok Goldshteyn, of all immigrants from Ostrava with the participation of our own fellow Ostraver khayim kahan of America. . . . The temporary committee). *LN*, May 4, 1951, 1.

44. The YIVO guidelines dictate that in Yiddish (unlike in Hebrew), the spelling *hazkore* (which originates in Hebrew) is to be used; therefore, in this book the word appears in this form. But it should be noted that both in the Yiddish press and in Yiddish literature the word almost always appeared as *azkara* (a spelling whose origin is Aramaic). According to Weinreich, both forms, the Hebrew (*hazkara*) and the Aramaic (*azkara*), are valid in Yiddish. Max Weinreich, "Yidish in gerem yidishe leshoynes: Ashkenaz in gerem yidishe eydes" [Yiddish within the framework of Jewish languages: Ashkenaz within the framework of Jewish groups], in *Geshikhte fun der yidisher shprakh* [History of the Yiddish language] (New York: YIVO, 1973), 1:75.

45. Ernest Gellner, *Nations and Nationalism* (Ithaca, NY: Cornell University Press, 1983).

46. Eric Hobsbawm, "Introduction: Inventing Traditions," in *The Invention of Tradition*, ed. Eric Hobsbawm and Terence Ranger (Cambridge: Cambridge University Press, 1983), 1–14.

47. For example, "Groyser lodzher ovnt . . . tsum ondenk fun der ershter masn-shkhite fun yidn in lodzh" [A big Lodzh evening . . . in memory of the first mass-slaughter of the Lodzh Jews], *LN*, June 30, 1950, 6.

48. For example, "Hazkore fun di krasnabroder gefalene durkh di natsis mit zeyere mithelfer" [Hazkara for the people of Krasnobrod who fell at the hands of the Nazis and their helpers], *LN*, October 20, 1950, 4. In Yiddish, as in Hebrew, the euphemism *gefalene* (fallen) designates those who died in battle. The first ad quoted here is somewhat paradoxical insofar as it suggests that the town's residents "fell" at the hands of the Nazis—in other words, they are described as fighters on the one hand and victims on the other.

49. It is interesting to compare the Israeli case to the French one. As Simon Perego showed, the memorial ceremony for the "unknown Jewish victim" was shaped by the existing model in the French national cultural arsenal—namely, the memorial ceremonies "for the unknown soldier," which were held beginning after World War I. See Perego, "Les commémorations de la destruction des Juifs d'Europe," 477. On the European culture of commemoration, see also George L. Mosse, *Fallen Soldiers: Reshaping the Memory of the World Wars* (Oxford: Oxford University Press, 1990).

50. According to Halbwachs, even when we reconstruct the past, our imagination is still affected by the present social environment (*On Collective Memory*, 49).

51. Kugelmass and Boyarin, *From a Ruined Garden*, 6–7.

52. On memorial days organized by the AR in the DP camps, see Mankoviş, *Bein zikaron leTiqwa*, 220–28.

53. Dalia Ofer, "Ma we'Ad kama lizkor meHaŠoa': Zik̲ron haŠoa' biMdinat Yiśra'el ba'Aśor haRišon leQiuma" [What and how much to remember of the Holocaust: Commemorating the Holocaust during the first decade of Israel], in *Aṣmaut: 50 haŠanin haRišonot* [Independence: The first 50 years], ed. Anita Shapira (Jerusalem: Zalman Shazar, 1998), 185.

54. For example, an ad for a memorial evening organized by the Lodzh hometown association, *LN*, June 30, 1950, 6: "Di gantse hakhnose iz bashtimt far naye 'olim" [All proceeds go to new 'olim].

55. Yitskhok Perlov, *Dzhebeliya* [Jebelye] (Buenos Aires: Yidbukh, 1955), 282.

56. Nosn Sholem, "Leyeners briv: Nisht azoy darfn oyszen di hazkores tsum ondenk fun di kdoyshim" [Readers' letters: This is not what the memorials for the martyrs are supposed to look like], *LN*, October 19, 1960, 3.

57. A. Panievezher [M], "20 yor nokhn umkum fun litvishn yidntum" [20 years after the destruction of the Jewish community of Lithuania], *LN*, November 12, 1961, 3.

58. On the advantages of preserving the initial, homogeneous communities within the mass 'aliya and on the limitations of these frameworks, see Moshe Lissak, "'Ereṣ Yiśra'el haRišona' we'Ereṣ Yiśra'el haŠnia': Tahalik̲im mu'aṣim šel qiṭuv ḥevrati-tarbuti biŠnot haḤamišim" [The "first Israel" and the "second Israel": Accelerated processes of social-cultural polarization in the 1950s], in *Bein 'Olim leWatiqim: Yiśra'el ba'Aliya haGdola, 1948–1953* [Between new immigrants and old-timers: Israel in the great wave of immigration, 1948–1953], ed. Dalia Ofer (Jerusalem: Yad Ben-Zvi, 1996), 8–12.

59. Mary Douglas, *Purity and Danger: An Analysis of Concepts of Pollution and Taboo* (London: Routledge, 1966), 63.

60. LaCapra, *Writing History*.

61. An Onveznder [M], "2000 perzon af di hazkore far di fartilikte lodzher yidn" [2,000 people at the memorial for the annihilated Lodzh Jews], *LN*, October 12, 1953, 2.

62. For example: a letter to the editor published in the *LN* on December 23, 1951, complains that the Petrikov hometown association held a memorial evening in Hebrew despite the fact that, according to the writer, 80 percent of the new 'olim did not understand it; a letter to the editor from October 1, 1959, protests the choice of the Mezeritsh hometown association to conduct the memorial evening exclusively in Hebrew, arguing both that among the participants were new 'olim who did not understand the language and that the language of the destroyed Jewish community was Yiddish.

63. On the reasons for and circumstances of the adoption of the Sephardi pronunciation, see Binyamin Haršav, *Lašon biYemei mahapek̲a: HaMahapek̲a haYehudit haModernit weTḥiyat haLašon ha'Ivrit* [Language in revolutionary times: The modern Jewish revolution and the revival of the Hebrew language] (Jerusalem: Carmel, 2008), 168–85.

64. Tsanin, "Geratevete yidn in yisroel."

65. On the role of surviving remnant organizations in the legislation of the Holocaust Memorial Day Act, see Yablonka, "Ma lizkor weKeiṣad?," 303; on the processes within the Israeli political establishment that led to the setting of this memorial day, see Ofer, "Ma we'Ad kama lizkor meHaŠoa," 171–93; Stauber, *HaLeqaḥ laDor*, 48–60.

66. For example, Meylekh Ravitsh, "Erev dem tsentn yortog fun varshever ufshtand" [Tenth memorial evening for the Warsaw uprising], *LN*, November 14, 1952, 3.

67. "10ter yortog nokhn geto-ufshtang [Tenth memorial day for the ghetto-uprising] (editorial), *LN*, April 17, 1953, 1. For a protest against the government's pattern of ignoring the survivors' mass "sorrow gatherings," see "Di fartilikye yidishe kehiles" [The annihilated Jewish communities] (editorial), *LN*, October 26, 1951, 3.

68. Leftist circles also marked April 19 with memorial services from 1944 and until the establishment of Israel's National Holocaust Memorial Day. So did national institutions on the eve of the establishment of Israel—for instance, the Jewish National Council. See Ofer, "Ma we'Ad kama lizkor meHaŠoa'," 176; Stauber, *HaLeqaḥ laDor*, 48–50, 55–57.

69. For example: A. Sored [M], "Der regirungs-proyekt tsu fareybikn dem khurbn" [The governmental project for commemoration of the destruction], *LN*, February 20, 1952, 2. On the public battle of survivors' organizations to make the remembrance day a national commemorative event, from national, educational, and political considerations, see Stauber, *HaLeqaḥ laDor*, 142–45.

70. Y. Artuski, "Di lektsiye fun yidishn khurbn" [The lesson of the Jewish destruction], *LF* 92 (1959): 4–5.

71. The ruling party Mapai and Ben-Gurion at its head did not regard the Holocaust as part of the desired ethos for the burgeoning Hebrew culture in Israel, especially in the first half of the 1950s. See Stauber, *HaLeqaḥ laDor*, 64–70.

72. "The preoccupation with the past is . . . less about a paradise lost than skeletons in the closet. The past threatens to penetrate the contemporary social and political scene, to change the hegemonic narrative, to encourage new voices, to demand justice and recognition." Vered Vinitzky-Seroussi, "Commemorating a Difficult Past: Yitzhak Rabin's Memorials," *American Sociological Review* 67, no. 1 (2002): 30.

73. For example, "Leyener briv" [Readers' letters], *LN*, April 27, 1960, 3; "Leyener briv," *LN*, May 5, 1960, 3; "Leyener briv," *LN*, May 9, 1960, 3; "Leyener briv," *LN*, May 19, 1960, 3; "Leyener briv," *LN*, May 24, 1960, 3.

74. For example, "Ayindruksfuler gedenk-ovnt in yidish" [Memorial evening filled with impressions, in Yiddish], *LN*, April 13, 1961, 1; Khave L-tsh [Levkovitsh], "Impozante akademiye fun umkum un gvure" [Impressive ceremony for the Holocaust and the heroism], *LN*, April 16, 1961, 3.

75. "1200 gekumen tsu yizker-farzamlung fun kultur-kongres" [1,200 came to the remembering-assembly of the Culture-Congress], *Biyuletin fun alveltlekhn yidishn kultur-kongres* 22 (1961): 7–8.

76. For example, Yankev Leshtshinski, "A gaystiker denkmol far di khorev gevorene yidishe kehiles in eyrope" [A spiritual monument for the destroyed Jewish communities in Europe], *LN*, July 13, 1951, 3; Gedaliye Fraytog, "A denkmol far khoreve kehiles" [A monument for destroyed communities], *LN*, August 3, 1951, 2.

77. Israel Gutman, "HaŠoa' weRišuma beToldot 'am yiśra'el" [The Holocaust and its aftermath in the history of the people of Israel], in *Sugiot beḤeqer haŠoa': Biqoret weTruma* [Issues in Holocaust scholarship: Critique and contribution], ed. Israel Gutman (Jerusalem: Zalman Shazar, 2008), 20.

78. On this way of commemorating the survivors, see, for example, Doron Bar, "Le'an nifne beYom haŠoa'? 'Ya'ar haQdošim' weHaHitlabṭut beŠe'elat hanṣaḥat haŠoa'" [Where shall we turn on the Holocaust remembrance day? The "Forest of the Martyrs" and the ambivalence regarding the question of Holocaust commemoration], *Catedra* 140 (2011): 103–30.

79. This book, as I have said, is about secular Yiddish culture and not the Yiddish-speaking parts of the Orthodox and ultra-Orthodox world. In recent years, much has been written

on the religious institutions established to commemorate the Holocaust (the building of synagogues, the writing of Torah books, the establishment of religious educational institutions). See, for example, Michal Shaul, *Holocaust Memory in Ultra-Orthodox Society in Israel* (Bloomington: Indiana University Press, 2020).

80. According to Rebbecca Kobrin (*Jewish Bialystok and Its Diaspora* [Bloomington: Indiana University Press, 2010], 173), in 1919–1939, hometown associations worldwide raised a total of approximately $100 million, which they invested in Jewish life in Eastern Europe. The worldwide association of Jews from Byalistok alone raised more than $9 million in that period, which they invested in helping the residents of Byalistok in their battle with poverty and hunger (133). In 1950 alone, members of the association raised $107,000 for the building of a "Byalistok Housing" in Israel (230).

81. "These immigrant organizations continue to function as bodies that carry both the cultural continuity and change in the land of new settlement." Kliger, *Jewish Hometown Associations*, 119.

82. Kliger, *Jewish Hometown Associations*, 122–23.

83. Kliger, *Jewish Hometown Associations*, 208.

84. According to Kobrin (*Jewish Bialystok*, 210–13), in 1938, 107,000 Jews lived in Byalistok. In 1944, there were 114 Jews in the city. Poles had taken up the place of the masses of murdered Jews.

85. On this form of "imagined identity," see Benedict Anderson, *Imagined Communities: Reflections on the Origin and Spread of Nationalism* (London: Verso, 1991), 187–206.

86. In Jerusalem in the late nineteenth century, neighborhoods like Batei Warsha (Warsaw Homes; 1884) and Batei Ungarin (Ungarin Homes; 1891) were built as part of the city's expansion beyond the walls. These neighborhoods were named after the Jewish communities that donated the funds for their construction (Warsaw) or after the place of origin of their founders (Hungary). At the time of their construction, the European communities still existed, so the neighborhoods were not built to preserve their memory. After the Holocaust, Hasidic housing was built in Jerusalem that was typically named after the town of origin of the Hasidic dynasty (such as the neighborhoods Kirayt Belz in Jerusalem and Kiryat Sanz in Jerusalem and Netanya; an exception to this rule is perhaps Kirayt Matersdorf in Jerusalem, established in 1959 and named after the Hungarian city of the same name—now part of Austria—which had a large Jewish community). The Hasidic housing complexes were built in Israel several years after the secular ones began to be constructed (at least according to the advertisements published in the *LN*). In the United States (specifically in the Bronx borough of New York City), two housing projects were built between the world wars by immigrants from Eastern Europe, but they were not named after Jewish communities: the Internatsiyonaler arbeter-ordn (the Yiddish Department of the International Workers of the World [IWW]) built projects designed for Jewish workers of Eastern European origin—the "Amalgamated Houses" (Amalgamated Clothing Workers of America); and so also were constructed the *Sholem Aleykhem hayzer* (Sholem Aleichem houses), which were identified with secular Yiddishist Judaism. These two projects were not built to commemorate Jewish communities destroyed in the Holocaust, and their residents were chosen not according to their community of origin in Eastern Europe but according to their class and positions in the United States.

87. Oz Almog, *The Sabra: The Creation of the New Jew*, trans. Haim Watzman (Berkeley: University of California Press, 2000), 38.

88. Y. Flek [M], "Der vidergeburt fun a shtetl" [The rebirth of a town], *LN*, September 14, 1951, 3–4.

89. J. C. Alexander, "Toward a Theory of Cultural Trauma," in *Cultural Trauma and Collective Identity*, ed. J. C. Alexander et al. (Berkeley: University of California Press, 2004), 28.
90. Mordkhe Tsanin, "Shikun 'olei Nashelsk" [The housing section of immigrants from Nashelsk], *LN*, March 24, 1953, 2.
91. A. Volf Yasny, "A Byalistoker shtetl af yisroel erd" [A Bialystok-like town on Israeli land], *LN*, May 10, 1961, 3.
92. On intergenerational transference, see Marianne Hirsch, "The Generation of Postmemory," *Poetics Today* 29 (2008): 103–28.
93. Shai Pilpel, "Liṭa' lo reḥoqa miPo" [Lithuania is not far from here], on Jewishgen website, accessed March 30, 2024 https://kehilalinks.jewishgen.org/mazeikiai/Lipnitzky2.doc.html.
94. Jan Assmann, *Moses the Egyptian: The Memory of Egypt in Western Monotheism* (Cambridge, MA: Harvard University Press, 1997), 9–17.
95. Aleida Assmann, "Communicative and Cultural Memory," in *Cultural Memory Studies: An International and Interdisciplinary Handbook*, ed. Astrid Erll and Ansgar Nunning (Berlin: Walter de Gruyter, 2008), 97–106.
96. [Sutzkever], "Nit nor di yidn" [Not only the Jews], *DGK* 1 (1949): 9.
97. This moral view of loyalty to Yiddish as a duty to fulfill a testament appeared as early as 1946: "Now after the destruction in Europe, it is on us especially that a sacred duty is imposed to protect and keep the great testament of Jewish history . . . We now have one big Jewish tradition . . . [and] two Jewish languages: *Loshn hakodesh* (the holy language, or language of holiness; an appellation attributed to the Hebrew language), the holy language of the prophets; and *Loshn hakdoyshim* (the language of the holy people), the Yiddish of the parents, the language of the holy people." Avrom Menes, "Yidish folk, yidish loshn, yidish gloybn" [Jewish people, Yiddish language, Jewish belief], *Di Tsukunft* 51 (1946): 426. The contrast between Lešon haQodeš and Lešon haQdošim is attributed to Israel's first president, Chaim Weizmann, who told journalists at the Twenty-Second Zionist Congress (held in Basel in 1946), "Hebrew is Lešon haQodeš, but Yiddish is Lešon haQdošim!" Refael Bashan, *Siḥot ḥulin šel Waiṣman* [Weizmann's casual conversations] (Jerusalem: Mosad Bialik, 1963), 12.
98. *Sheyme* (derived from the Hebrew word *shem* [name]) is a popular name for a worn-out stray page of a Jewish holy book. These pages are typically collected and stored in a special storage place (*geniza*) in the synagogue because they contain the name of God.
99. Avrom Sutzkever, "A por verter vegn unheyb" [A few words on beginning], *DGK* 100 (1979): 3.
100. Mordkhe Tsanin, "A heym far yidisher kultur" [A home for Yiddish culture], *LN*, January 21, 1955, 3.
101. See, for example, "Dos Leyvik-hoyz in tel oviv" [Leyvik-House in Tel Aviv], *Ha'Etona'i haYehudi: 'Egud 'olami šel 'etona'im yehudim* 1–2 (1970): 17.
102. "Kinder bibliyotek in nomen fun hinde vaser bay der frants kurski-bibliyotek" [Children's library named after Hinde Vaser in the Frants Kurski Library], *LF* 50 (1955): 15.
103. "Comrade Arthur" was the underground name of Shmuel Mordkhe Ziglboym (1895–1943), a member of the Bund's central committee and its representative in the Polish government in exile in London. After failing in his diplomatic efforts to raise world public opinion against the annihilation of the Jews, he committed suicide, in the hope that this act would draw public attention to the suffering of the Jews in occupied Europe. See J. S. Hertz, ed., *Ziglboym Bukh* (New York: Undzer Tsayt, 1947); Daniel Blatman, *For Our Freedom and*

Yours: The Jewish Labor Bund in Poland, 1939–1949, trans. Naftali Greenwood (London: Vallentine, Mitchell, 2003), 135–51.

104. "Derefnt di gas in nomen fun Artur ziglboym" [The street named after Artur Zyglboim is inaugurated], *LF* 138–39 (1963): 10.

105. "Farn kinder-hoyz in ramataim: Khaver zalmen vayland shenkt 1000 dolar tsu fareybikn dem nomen fun zayn umgekumener froy fradl" [For the children's-house in Ramataim: Comrade Zalmen Vayland donated 1,000 dollars toward the commemoration of his murdered wife, Fradl], *LF* 138–39 (1963): 13.

106. "A bibliyotek in nomen fun moyshe bloshteyn in kinder-hoyz in ramataim" [A library named after Moyshe Bloshteyn in the children's-house in Ramataim], *LF* 174–75 (1966): 5.

107. Moyshe Grin, "Undzer kinder-kolonye" [Our children's colony], *LF* 176–77 (1966): 19.

108. Avrom Sutzkever, "Tsvei yor di goldene keyt" [Two years of *DGK*], *DGK* 9 (1951): 215.

109. Y. Artuski, "Toda'a Yehudit tsi heymland gefil? Oder umvegn fun der yisroelsher yugnt" [Jewish consciousness or nationalism? Or the roundabout ways of the Israeli youth], *LF* 79 (1958): 7.

110. Mordkhe Tsanin, "Yidish un yidishkeyt" [Yiddish and Yiddishkeyt], *LN*, May 9, 1961, 1; Yod-Alef [Y. Artuski], "Rekht far Yiddish in shul" [The right for Yiddish in school?], *LF* 104 (1960): 11.

111. For a description of the trial and its image in Yiddish Israeli press, see Gali Drucker Bar-Am, "The Holy Tongue and the Tongue of the Martyrs: The Eichmann Trial as Reflected in *Letste Nayes*," *Dapim: Studies on the Holocaust* 28, no. 1 (2014): 17–37.

112. Rokhl Oyerbakh, "Me haita we'Eiḵ neḥreva warša haYehudit: Meo'ra'ot weḤawaiot 1939–1943, taqṣir haToḵen šel 'eduti haMuṣa'at beMišpaṭ 'aiḵman" [What was Jewish Warsaw and how was it destroyed? Events and experiences 1939–1943, a summary of the content of my prepared testimony for the Eichmann trial], Yad Vashem Archive, Rokhl Oyerbakh collection, P-16/41.

113. Rokhl Oyerbakh, "Me haita we'Eiḵ neḥreva," document no. 85.

114. Mordkhe Tsanin, "Nisht keyn yom-tovdike shmuesn" [Conversations of an unhappy day], *LN*, April 6, 1961, 2.

115. Rokhl Oyerbakh, report, Yad Vashem, Rokhl Oyerbakh collection, P-16/41, document no. 49 (emphasis in original).

116. A. S. [Avrom Sutzkever], "Der mishpet in yerusholoim" [The trial in Jerusalem], *DGK* 40 (1961): 5.

3. The Nostalgic Paradox of Yiddish Prose

1. Tsvi Ayznman, "Ikh un yung-yisroel," manuscript, Gnazim Institute 394.

2. Ayznman, "Ikh un yung-yisroel."

3. Walter Benjamin, "On the Concept of History," in *Illuminations*, ed. Hannah Arendt, trans. Harry Zohn (New York: Schocken, 2007), 257–58.

4. Avraham Novershtern, "Aspeqṭim mivniyim baProza šel dawid bergelson meRešita we'Ad 'midat haDin'" [Structural aspects in Dovid Bergelson's prose from its beginnings to *Midat haDin*] (PhD diss., Hebrew University of Jerusalem, 1981).

5. Avraham Novershtern, *Kan gar ha'Am haYehudi: Sifrut yidiš beArṣot haBrit* [Here dwells the Jewish people: A century of American Yiddish literature] (Jerusalem: Magnes, 2015), 328.

6. Gali Drucker Bar-Am, "Mas'a bein 'masoes': Diyun haŝwa'ati biŠloš girsa'ot 'masa'ot binyamin haŠliši' me'et mendele moykher sforim" [Traveling through *The Travels*: A comparative study of three versions of *The Travels of Benjamin III* by Mendele Moykher Sforim], *Jerusalem Studies in Hebrew Literature* 14 (2011): 93–124.

7. Dovid Bergelson, *Verk* [Works], vol. 5, *Nokh alemen* [When All Is Said and Done] (Berlin: Vostok, 1922), 7.

8. Y. L. Peretz, "Vegn mile-skandal" [On the scandal of circumcision], in *Ale verk* [Complete works] (New York: CYCO, 1947), 108–9; See also Y. L. Peretz, "'Al 'odot ša'aruriyat haMila" [On the scandal of circumcision], trans. from Yiddish into Hebrew by Shimshon Melzer, Project Ben-Yehuda, accessed March 30, 2024, http://benyehuda.org/perets/pina43.html.

9. Andreas Huyssen, "Nostalgia for Ruins," *Grey Room* 23 (2006): 9.

10. Avraham Novershtern, "Meḥolat haMawet" [Dance of death], *Huliyot* 1 (1993): 93–123.

11. Shmuel Niger, *Yitskhok leybush Peretz: Tsu zayn hundertn geboyrntog, 1852–1952* [Yitskhok Leybush Peretz: For his hundredth birthday] (New York: CYCO, 1952), 534.

12. Ella Florsheim, *Tarbut yidiś beMaḥanot ha'Aqurim* [Yiddish culture in the DP camps] (Jerusalem: Zalman Shazar and Yad Vashem, 2020), 122.

13. Avrom Sutzkever, "Tsvey yor di goldene keyt" [Two years of *DGK*], *DGK* 9 (1951): 214–15.

14. On this anthology and its comparison to Niger's first anthology, see Gali Drucker Bar-Am, "The Anthological Affect: Memory and Place in Early Post WWII Yiddish Culture," in *Memory, Lament and Endurance in Early Post WWII Yiddish Culture: Yiddish after 1945*, ed. Marion Aptroot (Amsterdam: Menasseh ben Israel Institute, 2018), 7–27.

15. Arie Shamri, "Fayerung lekoved zekhtsik bend 'di goldene keyt'" [Celebrating sixty volumes of *DGK*], *DGK* 62/63 (1968): 338–39.

16. Eli Lederhendler, "Classless: On the Social Status of Jews in Russia and Eastern Europe in the Late Nineteenth Century," *Comparative Studies in Society and History* 50, no. 2 (2008): 514–15.

17. Mikhail Krutikov, *Yiddish Fiction and the Crisis of Modernity, 1905–1914* (Stanford: Stanford University Press, 2001), 120–22.

18. Mikhail M. Bakhtin, "Forms of Time and Chronotope in the Novel," in *The Dialogic Imagination: Four Essays*, ed. Michael Holquist, trans. Caryl Emerson and Michael Holquist (Austin: University of Texas Press, 1981), 224–36.

19. Shmuel Niger, *Dertseylers un romanistn* [Story writers and novelists] (New York: CYCO 1946), 525–26 (emphasis in original). For the original essay, see Shmuel Niger, "Briv vegn der nayer yidisher literatur" [Letter on the new Yiddish literature], *Di yudishe velt* 12 (1913): 50–59. The essay was compiled in Niger's book *Shmuesn vegn bikher* [Conversations on books] (New York: Yidish farlag, 1922), 162–82. The quoted passage appears there on pp. 163–64.

20. Bakhtin, "Forms of Time and Chronotope," 226.

21. See Shmuel Rozhanski, *Dos yidishe gedrukte vort un teater in argentine* [The Yiddish printed word and theater in Argentina] (Buenos Aires: A gezelshaftlekher komitet fun yoyvl bukh, 1941), 64–72, 137–38.

22. On Eretz Yisrael as a theme in Yiddish literature, see Mordkhe Yofe, *Erets-yisroel in der yidisher literatur: Antologye* [Eretz Yisrael in Yiddish literature: Anthology] (Tel Aviv: Y. L. Peretz, 1961), 7–23.

23. Shmuel Rozhanski, "Yisroel un yidishe literatur" [Israel and Yiddish literature] (lecture at the Jewish Public Library in Montreal, February 3, 1974). Accessed at the Yiddish Book Center's *Frances Brandt Online Yiddish Audio Library*: https://archive.org/details/ybc-fbr-374_4373 (accessed March 30, 2024).

24. Freud defined mourning, melancholy, and profound mourning in these words: "Mourning is regularly the reaction to the loss of a loved person, or to the loss of some abstraction which has taken the place of one, such as one's country, liberty, an ideal, and so on. . . . The distinguishing mental features of melancholia are a . . . cessation of interest in the outside world, loss of the capacity to love, inhibition of all activity, and a lowering of the self-regarding feeling. . . . Profound mourning, the reaction to the loss of someone who is loved, contains the same painful frame of mind, the same loss of interest in the outside world . . . the same loss of capacity to adopt any new object of love (which would mean replacing him), and the same turning away from any activity that is not connected with thoughts of him." Sigmund Freud, "Mourning and Melancholia" (1917), in *The Standard Edition of the Complete Psychological Works of Sigmund Freud*, vol. 14 (1914–16), *On the History of the Psycho-Analytic Movement, Papers on Metapsychology and Other Works*, trans. and ed. James Strachey, Anna Freud, et al. (London: Hogarth and the Institute of Psycho-Analysis, 1964), 243–44.

25. Shmuel Niger, "Sheyres hapleyte," newspaper clipping from an unidentified source, dated February 16, 1946, YIVO Archive, Niger Collection, RG 360/2153.

26. Shiye Rapoport, "Di shlikhes fun der yidisher literatur" [The mission of Yiddish literature], *Di Tsukunft* 53, no. 7 (1948): 484.

27. Dominick LaCapra, *Writing History, Writing Trauma* (Baltimore: Johns Hopkins University Press, 2014), 44, 49.

28. Shmuel Rozhanski, "Medinas yisroel in der yidisher literatur" [Israel in Yiddish literature], in *Yidishe literatur-yidish lebn: Shraybers, bashraybers un vizyonern in unzer literatur-geshikhte* [Yiddish literature-Jewish/Yiddish life: Writers, describers, and visionaries in our literature-history] (Buenos Aires: A grupe fraynd fun der literatur gezelshaft baym IWO, 1973), 616–19 (emphasis in original).

29. "Literatur-premye fun LN-YT: Di redaktsye . . . hot bashtimt tsvey premyes far der bester dertseylung un bestn reportazh af yisroel-tematik" [Literary Prize by LN-YT: The paper declared two prizes for best story and best reportage on the Israel-theme], *LN*, August 20, 1954, 1.

30. Bakhtin, "Forms of Time and Chronotope," 26.

31. Avrom Sutzkever, "Yisroel, der yidisher shrayber un di yidishe velt" [Israel, the Yiddish writer and the Jewish world], *DGK* 19 (1954): 222–24.

32. Mendl Man, "Der yidisher shrayber in yisroel" [The Yiddish writer in Israel], *Di Tsukunft* 64 (1959): 287 (emphasis in original).

33. Moshe Shamir, "HaRoman weHaBiqoret ʻal haRoman" [The novel and its critique], *Masa'*, August 27, 1953, quoted in Avner Holzman, *'Ahavot Ṣion: Panim baSifrut haʻIvrit haḤadaša* [Loves of Zion: Studies in modern Hebrew literature] (Jerusalem: Carmel, 2006), 363–64.

34. A. Volf Yasny, "Yidish kinstlerishe proze af yisroel-tematik" [Yiddish artistic prose on the Israel-theme], *Yisroel-shriftn* 1 (1954): 63–78.

35. Zali Gurevitch, *ʻAl haMaqom* [On the place] (Tel Aviv: Am-Oved, 2007), 84, 86.

36. Michel de Certeau, *The Practices of Everyday Life*, trans. Steven Rendall (Berkeley: University of California Press, 1984): "These 'ways of operating' constitute innumerable prac-

tices by means of which users reappropriate the space organized by techniques of sociocultural production" (xxii).

37. Yitskhok Perlov, "Der shrayber antloyft fun zayn dor" [The writer escapes his generation], *LF* 18–19 (1952): 14.

38. Yosef Haim Brenner, "HaŽaner ha'Ereṣ-yiśra'eli we'Avizarehu" [The Eretz-Israeli genre and its accoutrements], in *Kol kitvei Y. H. Brenner* [Complete works of Y. H. Brenner], vol. 8 (Tel Aviv: Shtibl, 1937), 164. And see Gershon Shaked, *HaSiporet ha'Ivrit, 1880–1980* [Hebrew fiction, 1880–1980], vol. 2 (Tel Aviv: Hakibbutz Hameuchad, 1983), 17–154; Nurit Govrin, *Brenner: 'Oved 'eṣot uMore dereḵ* [Brenner: "Nonplussed" and mentor] (Tel Aviv: Misrad Ha-Bitahon, 1991), 179–200.

39. Holzman, *'Ahavot Ṣion*, 178.

4. Israeli Spaces in Yiddish Prose

1. Yitskhok Perlov, *Dzshebelye* (Buenos Aires: Yidbukh, 1955), 290.

2. Perlov, *Dzshebelye*, 294.

3. Perlov, *Dzshebelye*, 295.

4. Zali Gurevitch, *'Al haMaqom* [On the place] (Tel Aviv: Am-Oved, 2007), 8–9, 40.

5. Dvora Hacohen, *'Olim biSe'ara: Ha'Aliya haGdola uQliṭata beYiśra'el, 1948–1953* [Immigrants in turmoil: I great wave of immigration to Israel and its absorption, 1948–1953] (Jerusalem: Yad Ben-Zvi, 1994), 1.

6. Hanna Yablonka, *Survivors of the Holocaust: Israel after the War*, trans. Ora Cummings (London: Palgrave Macmillan, 1999), 9–17.

7. Hannan Hever, *HaSipur weHaLe'om: Qri'ot biqortiyot beQ'anon haSiporet ha'Ivrit* [Narrative and the nation: Critical readings in the canon of Hebrew fiction] (Tel Aviv: Resling, 2007), 176.

8. Yablonka, *Survivors of the Holocaust*, 18–19.

9. On the settlement of 'oley sheyres hapleyte in depopulated Palestinian villages and towns (including Jaffa), see Yablonka, *Survivors of the Holocaust*, 18–32. According to Moshe Lissak, 36 percent of all the 'olim who came between May 15, 1948, and December 1949, a total of 124,000 people, were placed in these houses. Moshe Lissak, *Ha'Aliya haGdola biŠnot haḤamišim: Kišlono šel kur haHituḵ* [The mass immigration of the 1950s: The failure of the melting pot] (Jerusalem: Mosad Bialik, 1999), 24.

10. According to Ada Schein, approximately 10 percent of the 'oley sheyres hapleyte 'olim who were absorbed in rural settlements (including depopulated Arab villages that became moshavim) did not go there independently but were directed by the state's absorption system and the Moshavim Movement. Ada Schein, "Bne beytḵa beQarov: Še'erit haPleṭa baHityašvut haMošavit, 1944–1955" [Build your home soon: The surviving remnant in the Moshavim settlements, 1944–1955], in *"WeYašavtem beṭaḥ": Niṣoley haŠoa' baHityašvut ha'Ovedet, 1945–1955* ["Dwell in safety": Holocaust survivors in the labor settlement, 1945–1955], ed. Shlomo Bar-Gil and Ada Schein (Jerusalem: Yad Vashem, 2010), 152.

11. According to Benny Morris, Yazur fell to the Hagana without battle in late April 1948 as part of "Operation Ḥameṣ." Morris, *The Birth of the Palestinian Refugee Problem, 1947–1949* (Cambridge: Cambridge University Press, 1987), 100. On the Palestinian refugees from the point of view of a Palestinian scholar, see Adel Manna, *Nakba and Survival: The Story of*

the Palestinians Who Remained in Haifa and the Galilee, 1948–1956 (Oakland: University of California Press), 2022.

12. The editor of *Forverts*, Hilel Rogof, contacted Perlov while the latter was still in a DP camp in Germany and encouraged him to continue writing. Perlov began his literary path before the war, with poetry, but toward the end of his stay in the DP camps he turned to prose, and his stories appeared in the pages of *Forverts*. After moving to Israel, he published his stories in the *LN* and the *LF*.

13. On the occupation of Jaffa, see Morris, *Birth of the Palestinian Refugee Problem*, 95–101.

14. The Iraq-Suwaydan police fort was occupied in the 1948 War on November 9, 1948, by the Eighth Brigade, commanded by Yitzhak Sadeh. In the novel, there is indeed a character named Major-General Sadeh, or "the old man."

15. Gurevitch, *'Al haMaqom*, 135.

16. The theme of howling jackals appeared in Yiddish literature from the early 1950s in dozens of stories, feuilletons, and journalism pieces. The theme was central in several works, including Yitskhok Perlov, "Shakaln" [Jackals], in *Matilda lebt* [Matilda lives] (Buenos Aires: Farband fun brisk de-lite un umgegnt in argentine, 1954), 103–12; Mendl Man, "Der alter shakal" [The old Jackal], in *Kerner in midber: Dertseylungen* [Grains in the desert: Stories] (Paris: Undzer Kiyem, 1965), 25–29; Yitskhok Paner, "Dos geveyn in der nakht" [The howl at night], in *Zun un shotn: Yisroel-motivn* [Sun and shadows: Israeli motifs] (Tel Aviv: Y. L. Peretz, 1964), 71–74; Rokhl Oyerbakh, "Es vakst a nayer yishev: Shakaln in der nakht" [A new settlement grows: Jackals at night], in *In land yisroel: Reportazshn, eseyn, dertseylungen* [In the Land of Israel: Reportages, essays, stories] (Tel Aviv: Y. L. Peretz, 1964), 128–29. In Hebrew literature, this theme received prominent expression only in 1965 (but with an entirely different meaning than the one it received in Yiddish literature) in the collection of short stories *Be'Arṣot haTan* (*Where the Jackals Howl*), by Amos Oz.

17. According to Lissak (*Ha'Aliya haGdola*, 24), between September 1 and April 1, 1949, thirty thousand 'olim were housed in Jaffa, and they were joined by thousands of discharged soldiers and especially "Gahal" soldiers (an acronym of the Hebrew term *Giyus ḥuṣ la'areṣ*, literally "overseas recruitment"; these were recent 'oley sheyres hapleyte recruited to the IDF as reinforcement during the 1948 War).

18. For example, Anonymous, "Soydes fun yafo" [Secrets of Jaffa], *LN*, April 5, 1954, 4.

19. For example, Levi Papiernikov, "Di shpil fun goyrl" [The game of fate], *LF* 77 (1958): 11.

20. For example, "Dramatishe bagegenish tsvishn tsvey shvester in yafo: Hobn gevoynt in eyn šḵuna bemeshekh yorn un nisht gevust eyne fun der anderer" [A dramatic meeting between two sisters in Jaffa: Lived in the same neighborhood for years and did not know of one another], *LN*, July 27, 1955, 4.

21. Tsvi Magen, "Peysekhdike reportazhn" [Passover reports], *LN*, April 5, 1953, 2. Ya'akov Shavit and Gid'on Biger quote the military governor of Jaffa, who argued in late 1948 that "Yiddish is the second language of Jaffa. There is no meeting, notice, lecture or any kind of advertisement that is not also done in Yiddish." Shavit and Biger, *HaHisṭoria šel Tel 'Aviv: MiŠḵunot le'Ir, 1909–1936* [The history of Tel Aviv: From neighborhoods to a city, 1909–1936] (Tel Aviv: Ramot, 2011), 244.

22. Perlov, "Shakaln," 201. On the disaster, see, for example, Mordkhe Tsanin, "Unter di khurves fun yafo ligt undzer gevisn!" [Under the ruins of Jaffa lies our conscience!], *LN*, April 21, 1950, 1.

23. Perlov, "Shakaln," 137.

24. Perlov, "Shakaln," 381.

25. Perlov, "Shakaln," 77. For an analysis of this passage, see Gali Drucker Bar-Am, "Revenge and Reconciliation: Early Israeli Literature and the Dilemma of Jewish Collaborators with the Nazis," in *Jewish Honor Courts: Revenge, Retribution and Reconciliation in Europe and Israel after the Holocaust*, ed. Laura Jockusch and Gabriel N. Finder (Detroit: Wayne State University Press, 2015), 279–302.

26. Mikhail M. Bakhtin, "Discourse in the Novel," in *The Dialogic Imagination: Four Essays*, ed. Michael Holquist, trans. Caryl Emerson and Michael Holquist (Austin: University of Texas Press, 1981), 290–95.

27. Perlov, *Dzshebelye*, 322.

28. Other works that describe the "big area" include Yoysef Noyman, "Yafoer kasba" [Jaffa's casbah], *LN*, May 14, 1954, 6; Yishaye Shpigl, "Di yerushe" [The inheritance], in *Di brik: Noveln* [The bridge: Stories] (Tel Aviv: Y. L. Peretz, 1963), 293–327; Avrom Karpinovitsh, "Ganovim" [Thieves], in *Der veg keyn sdom* [The road to Sodom] (Tel Aviv: Y. L. Peretz, 1959), 35–48; Shloyme Varzoger, "Zina," in *Mikan uMiqarov: Antologia šel siporei yidiš be'Ereṣ Yiśra'el miRešit haMe'a we'Ad yanenu* [From here and from near: An anthology of Yiddish stories in Eretz Yisrael from the turn of the century to our days], ed. Mordechai Halamish (Tel Aviv: Sifriyat Po'alim, 1966), 516–23; Shmaye Avni [Shteynmats], "A khezhbn" [An account], in *Almanakh fun di Yidishe shrayber in Yisroel* [Almanac of Yiddish writers in Israel]. (Tel Aviv: Fareyn fun yidishe shrayber un zshurnalistn in yisroel, 1967), 281–86.

29. On the meaning of this word during the Holocaust and on its sources, see Nakhmen Blumental, *Verter un vertlekh fun der khurbn-tkufe* [Words and sayings from the Holocaust era] (Tel Aviv: Y. L. Peretz, 1981), 175–76.

30. Gan-Tamar was in fact the name of a popular Jaffa coffee house, and the neighborhood was named after it. See Shavit and Biger, *HaHisṭoria šel Tel 'Aviv*, 248.

31. On the date as a symbol in Israeli culture, see Ori Berzak, "Nawad Šorši: Tmurot beNof haDqalim beMerḥavei 'Ereṣ Yiśra'el beMahalaḵ haMe'a haEśrim" [A rooted nomad: Changes in the landscape of palm trees in the Land of Israel during the twentieth century] (MA thesis, Haifa University, 2003).

32. The other protagonist is Froyke Tsherkis in Bergelson's novella *In a fargrebter shtot* (In a backwoods town), 1914. See Mikhail Krutikov, *Yiddish Fiction and the Crisis of Modernity, 1905–1914* (Stanford: Stanford University Press, 2001), 47.

33. Perlov, *Dzshebelye*, 348.

34. Unemployment was one of the main reasons for the phenomenon of 'oley sheyres hapleyte leaving Israel in the 1950s. Yablonka, *Survivors of the Holocaust*, 16. See, for example, Mordkhe Tsanin, "Kibets-golyes mit diskriminatsye: Ofener briv tsum premier-minister [An ingathering of exiles with discrimination: An open letter to the prime minister], *LN*, July 14, 1950, 3.

35. As I noted in chapter 1, Yiddish cultural organizations (whose activity was not banned) carried out a wide variety of volunteer cultural activities in the depopulated Palestinian settlements and in the Ma'abarot: artists and writers gave performances and readings, libraries and reading rooms were established, and more.

36. On Moshe Shamir and his novel *Hu halaḵ baŚadot* [He walked through the fields] (Merhavia: Sifriyat haPo'alim, 1947), see Avner Holzman, *'Ahavot Ṣion: Panim baSifrut ha'Ivrit haḤadaša* [Loves of Zion: Studies in modern Hebrew literature] (Jerusalem: Carmel, 2006), 320–21.

37. The American literary scholar Werner Sollors called this theme the home-making myth. According to his reading, the motif of the son's death at war in American literature written by immigrants constitutes a "gift" in return for a unity with the dominant culture of the national society. Werner Sollors, *Ethnic Modernism* (Cambridge, MA: Harvard University Press, 2008), 44–45.

38. Perlov, *Dzshebelye*, 243.

39. Perlov, *Dzshebelye*, 21.

40. Perlov, *Dzshebelye*, 41–44. The aversion and necessity involved in using the private property left behind by the Palestinians in Jaffa is expressed in other literary works that dealt with the settlement in Jaffa. For example, Tzvi Ayznman, "A hoyf in yafo" [A courtyard in Jaffa], in *Mazoles* [Zodiac signs] (Tel Aviv: Y. L. Peretz, 1965), 9–19. The novella appeared in the second issue published by the Yung-yisroel group (1957), 44–49, and was first published in *Nayvelt* under the title "A hoyz in yafo" (A house in Jaffa) on June 6, 1952.

41. Perlov, *Dzshebelye*, 152.

42. For a Yiddish translation of Theodor Herzl's *Altneuland* (*The Old New Land*), see *Altnaylend*, trans. Isidor [Yisroel] Eliashev [Bal-Makhshoves] (Warsaw: Hatsfire, 1902). Other, later descriptions of Jaffa are found in the works of Yosef Haim Brenner, Agnon, Nisim Aloni, and many others.

43. Dan Miron, *Bein Ḥazon le'Emet: Niṣanei haRoman ha'Ivri veHa'Idi baMe'a haTš'a 'eśre* [From romance to the novel: Studies in the emergence of the Hebrew and Yiddish novel in the nineteenth century] (Jerusalem: Mosad Bialik, 1979), 186.

44. Perlov, *Dzshebelye*, 8–9.

45. Mendl Man, *Di shtilkeyt mont: Lider un baladn* [The stillness calls: Poems and ballads] (Lodzh: Borokhov-farlag, 1945); Mendl Man, *Yerushe: Lider* [Inheritance: Poems] (Regnsburg: Yidishe zester, 1947).

46. Mendl Man, *In a farvorloztn dorf* [In a deserted village] (Buenos Aires: Kiem, 1954). The novel was first developed from short stories that contained the kernels of its theme and plot: Mendl Man, *In a kfar naṭuš* [In a deserted village], *DGK* 8 (1951): 140–52; Mendl Man, *Afn metshet-bergl* [On Mosque Hill], *DGK* 12 (1952): 97–110. These stories appeared in Man's first collection of stories, published by *Di Goldene Keyt* press: Mendl Man, *Oyfgevakhte erd* [Awakened earth] (Tel Aviv: Di goldene keyt, 1953). In this collection, the story *In a kfar naṭuš* became *In a farvorloztn dorf*, and another story was included that is an early version of the novel: "Tsufusns fun di harei-yehuda" (At the foot of the Judea mountains) (154–74). These stories were published in Hebrew by Am-Oved as part of the educational series Ha-Sifriya Ha-Menukedet La-'Ole Ve-La-'Am (The vowelized library for the immigrant and for the people): Mendl Man, *Adam ba-Ohel* [A man in a tent], trans. Ya'akov Eliav (Tel Aviv: Am-Oved, 1953).

47. Mendl Man, *Bay di toyern fun moskve* [At the gates of Moscow] (New York, 1956); *Bay der vaysl* [On the Vistula] (New York, 1960). These novels were planned to appear as a trilogy and did indeed appear in a renewed edition under the title *Di milkhome-trilogye* (War trilogy), in Paris, 1965.

48. Mendl Man, *BiḴfar naṭuš: Sipur* [In an abandoned village: A story], translated into Hebrew from a manuscript by E. D. Shapir (Tel Aviv: Hakibbutz Hameuchad, 1953).

49. Mikhail M. Bakhtin, "Forms of Time and Chronotope in the Novel," in *Dialogic Imagination*, 229.

50. Bakhtin, "Forms of Time and Chronotope," 225.

51. The motif of the threatening cactus recurs in Man's works—for example, "Dos hoyz tsvishn derner" (The house among thorns), which appears in the short story collection *Di gas fun bliendike mandlen* [The street of blooming almonds] (Buenos Aires: Kiem, 1958). It describes a couple living in an "abandoned village" nearly identical to "Mosque Hill"; but unlike the novel, the novella ends with the heroine's insanity and the disintegration of the couple's shared home. Thus, the name of the novella ironically echoes the phrase "As a lily among thorns" (Song of Solomon 2:2).

52. Gurevitch, *'Al haMaqom*, 150.

53. Man, *In a farvorloztn dorf*, 11.

54. Encounters between Jewish and Arab refugees in the literature under discussion were typically not encounters of equal-sized groups but rather of a group of Jewish refugees with a single or small number of Palestinian "infiltrators." This balance of power played an important role in shaping the meeting, including its tragic aspects, its characteristic dynamics, and its ending and aftermath.

55. Man, *In a farvorloztn dorf*, 66–67. One of the important differences between this passage in the original Yiddish and in the Hebrew translation is that, in the original, the reflections about the Palestinians are placed in the mouths of individuals ("One of the residents of the alley shook his head in sadness and thought"; "And the other comforted himself and said"), whereas in the Hebrew translation they are presented as collective reflections, like a kind of shared imagination ("These residents of the alley shook their head in sadness and thought"; "And they comforted themselves and said: I did not drive him away"). This collective characterization nullifies the emphasis placed in the original version on the variety of opinions as well as on the loneliness of the individuals who contemplate these thoughts. As I demonstrate in what follows, this "collectivization" of the 'olim is typical of the descriptions of them in Hebrew literature, written by those who were observing them from the outside.

56. Melanie Klein, "Love, Guilt and Reparation," in *Love, Guilt, and Reparation: And Other Works, 1921–1945* (London: Virago, 1988).

57. Man, *In a farvorloztn dorf*, 67.

58. Dominick LaCapra, *Writing History, Writing Trauma* (Baltimore: Johns Hopkins University Press, 2014), 41.

59. Yankev Perlshteyn, "A briv fun a mistanen" [A letter from an infiltrator], *LN*, May 7, 1954, 7. See also Yitskhok Brat, "A shmues mit a mistanen" [A conversation with an infiltrator], *LN*, September 2, 1955, 6. On the powerful presence of the Palestinian residents in the Yishuv in the eyes of the new residents, see Dovid Eydlman, "Dos shtetele yazur" [The townlet of Yazur], *LN*, February 1, 1953, 2. In the story "Sheikh Munis" (notable for its low quality) by Yoysef Shtshavinski, the narrator reports on a question that prevailed among the new residents of the village—which is expressed in the auditory similarity between the name of the village and the Yiddish expression for the customary Purim basket (*Shalekh mones*)—about whether the exchanges of refugees, Arab and Jewish, had already reached their end or whether they would continue, and include the return of the sheikh to his village. Yoysef Shtshavinski, "Sheikh munis," in *Unter eyn dakh* [Under one roof] (Tel Aviv: Measef Yisroel, 1964), 184–93.

60. Hanoch Bartov, *Šeš knafaim le'Eḥad* [Each had six wings] (Merhavia: Sifriyat Ha-Po'alim, 1954), 24–25: "And where do we sit now, do you know? Right under the blade of the Arab's knife. . . . Indeed it is a miracle that I did not return in a coffin. Here I am walking and looking for a grocery store, and their faces peer out at me, three blocks from here. Sitting and waiting for a moment fit for slaughter. Without so much as a greeting they would murder us. . . . It is a miracle that a soldier happened upon me and warned me."

61. S. Yizhar, *Ḥirbet Ḥiz'eh*, trans. Nicholas de Lange and Yaacob Dweck (Jerusalem: Ibis, 2008); S. Yizhar, "HaŠavuy" [The prisoner], in *'Arba'ah Sipurim* [Four stories] (Tel Aviv: Hakibbutz Hameucḥad, 1959), 11–138.

62. Man, *In a farvorloztn dorf*, 64–65.

63. This motif of two trees and their mutual relationship has a long tradition in world literature. The symbol of the two trees, the local and the Eastern European, whose roots are interwoven in the soil of Israel, recurred several times in Man's work (though its meaning changed slightly, depending on context). Compare, for example, "The modern Israeli-Yiddish novella has deep roots in Israel. It is one ongoing poem in Yiddish that continues from those sad prayers of our fathers and our mothers, from those first yearnings for those 'white birch trees' [a theme from Dovid Eynhorn's famous poem "Beriozkele"] to the two trees, the poplar and the palm tree, which grown side by side at the edge of the orchard, a symbol of the old home and the new Israel, their roots braided together." Mendl Man, "Der yidisher shrayber in yisroel" [The Yiddish author], *Di Tsukunft* (1959): 286.

64. Bartov, *Šeš knafaim le'Eḥad*, 34.

65. Yizhar, *Ḥirbet Ḥiz'eh*, 109.

66. Bartov, *Šeš knafaim le'Eḥad*, 11–27.

67. Complaints by 'olim who lived in depopulated Arab Palestinian villages about the authorities' deficient treatment of the problem of the missing water pumps appeared every now and then in the *LN*'s letters-to-the-editor section. For example, "The story happened in a certain Arab village, now populated by 'olim. In the past there was water in the village. But when the Palestinians fled, they buried the motors of the well pipes . . . We found out that only now, after the long summer months in which they unnecessarily tortured the residents of an entire village with thirst, the relevant authority decided on a budget for the few tens of [Palestinian] pounds needed to dig and retrieve the motor." "Shmuesn vegn ongeveytokte zakhn: Vaser un hefkeyres" [Conversations about painful things: Water and lawlessness], *LN*, November 17, 1949, 3. See also "Tog-fragn: Oylim hobn geboyt un zey makhn khorev" [Questions of the day: 'Olim built and they destroy], *LN*, February 3, 1953, 2.

68. Man, *In a farvorloztn dorf*, 123.

69. Man, *In a farvorloztn dorf*, 123.

70. Man, *In a farvorloztn dorf*, 124.

71. Yehudit Hendel, *'Anašim 'aḥerim hem* [They are different people] (Merhavia: Sifriyat Ha-Po'alim, 1950), 52–58.

72. For example, Rivke Kviatkovski-pinkhasik, "Ilan kunt aheym" (1968), in *Tsvishn karmel un yam* [Between Carmel and the sea] (Haifa: Aleyn, 1975), 314–20.

73. For example, in the satirical columns by Yoysef Noyman that were published in the 1950s and 1960s in the *LN* under the title "Tel-oviver tip" (Tel Aviv types).

74. For example, Yitskhok Perlov, "Ben-amile geyt shoyn in gan-yeladim" [Ben-'Amile already goes to kindergarten], in *In eygenem land* [In a country of our own] (Buenos Aires: Yidbukh, 1952), 77–98.

75. See, for example, Aziza Khazzoom, *Shifting Ethnic Boundaries and Inequality in Israel: Or, How the Polish Peddler Became a German Intellectual* (Stanford: Stanford University Press, 2008), 123: "What stands out is the similarity between the German Jewish orientalization of the Ostjuden in Europe and the Ostjudisch orientalization of the Mizrahim in Israel less than a generation later. In orientalizing the Mizrahim, the Ostjuden simply took the arsenal of images and symbols that had been used to exclude them, and applied them wholesale

and nearly unchanged to the Mizrahim. They thus presented themselves as the westerners that they had, up until that point, never been."

76. Bartov, *Šeš knafaim le'Eḥad*, 315.

77. Man, *In a farvorloztn dorf*, 15–16.

78. Man, *In a farvorloztn dorf*, 7–8, 254.

79. Man, *In a farvorloztn dorf*, 16.

80. Man, *In a farvorloztn dorf*, 17.

81. In Yiddish the name "Moyne" echoes names like Monish and Mane as well as the author's name, Man, Mendl—all of which are associated with the name Menakhem.

82. Man, *In a farvorloztn dorf*, 10: "The village of his grandfather and great-grandfather, the dam, the pasture, the meadow—all of these began to rise up in the depths of the soul and be reflected through the pupils of the eyes . . . Here awakens in him a longing of generations for earth."

83. Moyshe Kulbak, "Raysn" [White Russia], in *Geklibene verk* [Complete works] (New York: CYCO, 1953), 183–200.

84. Itzik Manger, "Der Litvak un di landshaft" [The Litvak and the landscape], *Di Tsukunft* 59 (1954): 116–17. The article was also printed in his book *Shriftn in proze* (Tel Aviv: Y. L. Peretz, 1980), 185–89.

85. On the meanings of this term in literary description, see Avner Holzman, "LiŠe'elat haŠimuš baMunaḥ 'impresionizm beMaḥševet haSifrut" [On the question of the use of the term "impressionism" in literary thought], in *Mel'eḵet maḥševet tḥiyat ha'Uma: HaSifrut ha'Ivrit leNoḵaḥ ha'Omanut haPlasṭit* [Aesthetics and national revival: Hebrew literature in light of the visual arts] (Haifa: Zmora-Bitan and Haifa University Press, 1999), 280–94.

86. See, for example, the correspondence between Perlov and Tsanin (Gnazim Institute, Tsanin Archive, 504) or the correspondence between Man and Sutzkever (the National Library, Sutzkever Archive 4°.1565, Man Folder). These letters contain no negative or bitter expressions toward Israel, of the sort that might explain their decision to leave.

87. Man, *Kerner in midber*; Mendl Man, *Fun golan biz sharem a-sheikh* [From the Golan to Sharm El-Sheikh] (Tel Aviv: Y. L. Peretz, 1973).

88. See, for example, Shimon Balas, *HaMa'abara* [The ma'abara (emigrant and refugee absorption camp)] (Tel Aviv: Am-Oved, 1964), 16, 31, 59–60, 100, 102, 121. This paradox was articulated by Pilovski: "The political and cultural elite in Israel, which acted, out of a conscious ideology, to drive out Yiddish as a language of culture in Israel, was itself identified with the Yiddish language. Yiddish became the immediate object at which were directed feelings of discrimination on the part of non-'Aškenazi Jews toward this elite." Arye Leyb Pilovski, "Yidiš weSifruta be'Ereṣ Yiśra'el, 1907–1948" [Yiddish and its literature in Eretz Israel, 1907–1948] (PhD diss., the Hebrew University, 1980), 195.

89. In 1949–1950 came the second wave of 'oley sheyres hapleyte, which comprised half of the total number of 'olim. Many of them were absorbed in the Ma'abarot. After 1951, the percentage of 'oley sheyres hapleyte dropped to 28 percent of all the 'olim (a percentage that was maintained until the second half of the 1950s, when another wave of 'olim from communist Eastern Europe arrived). In 1951, the immigrants from Eastern Europe constituted approximately 20 percent of the quarter-million residents of the Ma'abarot. Hacohen, *'Olim biSe'ara*, 177–219, 298–301. Hacohen divides the immigrants into "the 'olim from Europe" and "the 'olim from Asia and Africa." As other studies mentioned earlier clarify, the vast majority of the "Europe" 'olim are of Eastern European origin.

90. Lissak, *Ha'Aliya haGdola*, 26.

91. For an example of this, see an essay published by Tsanin about a group of camp survivors from Poland who because of their physical, mental, and financial predicament were unable to leave the ma'abara: Mordkhe Tsanin, "Talpiyot" [Talpiyot [the name of a ma'abara in Jerusalem]], *LN*, November 2, 1952, 2; "Leyener briv: 'Olim fun ma'aberet talpiyot danken di LN" ['Olim from the Talpiyot ma'abara thank the *LN*], *LN*, December 2, 1952, 2.

92. Bakhtin, "Forms of Time and Chronotope," 175.

93. Bakhtin, "Forms of Time and Chronotope," 176.

94. Yishaye Shpigl, "Di kukavke" [The cuckoo], in *Di brik*.

95. Michal Shaul, *Holocaust Memory in Ultra-Orthodox Society in Israel* (Bloomington: Indiana University Press, 2020).

96. Yekhiel Granatshteyn, "In blekhenem baydl fun der ma'abara" [In a small tin shack in the ma'abara], *LN*, September 19, 1952, 5.

97. Yekhiel Granatshteyn, "Zayn ershte freyd" [His first joy], *LN*, June 20, 1952, 5.

98. Yekhiel Granatshteyn, "Sakh-hakl fun a tog: Fun dem togbikhl fun an arbetslozn" [Summary of a day: From the diary of an unemployed man], *LN*, October 9, 1953, 3.

99. Yekhiel Granatshteyn, "A khasene in a ma'abara" [A wedding in the ma'abara], *LN*, August 8, 1952, 3.

100. Granatshteyn, "A khasene in a ma'abara," *LN*, August 8, 1952, 3.

101. Granatshteyn, "A khasene in a ma'abara," *LN*, August 8, 1952, 3.

102. Granatshteyn, "A khasene in a ma'abara," *LN*, August 15, 1952, 4.

103. For example, Yekhiel Granatshteyn, "A bagegenish af dereḵ petaḥ-tiqwa" [A meeting on Derekh Petah Tikva], *LN*, September 26, 1956, 5; Y. Namdirf [Yankev Fridman], "A dkhak-arbeter" [A lowly worker], *LN*, September 1, 1959, 3; Levi Papiernikov, "A nayer veg-arbeter" [A new road-worker], in *In der nayer heym: Dertseylungen* [In the new home: Stories] (Tel Aviv: Y. L. Peretz, 1960), 38–43; Shpigl, *Di brik*, 328–46.

104. Y. Akh [M], "Mizeg-goleyes" [An integration of exiles], *LN*, December 3, 1954, 7.

105. Shpigl, "Di kukavke," 139–40.

106. Yitskhok Perlov, "Nekome" [Vengeance], in *Matilda lebt*, 92–102. The story was first published in the *LN* in three parts: February 20, 1953, 3; February 27, 1953, 5; March 6, 1953, 4. For a detailed analysis of this work, see Drucker Bar-Am, "Revenge and Reconciliation," 279–302.

107. Mary Douglas, *Purity and Danger: An Analysis of Concepts of Pollution and Taboo* (London: Routledge, 1966).

108. Tzvi Ayznman, "A mayse vegn nisim fun har-ṭuv, vegn a varshever hoyf un vegn a shpil-foygl" [A tale about Nissim from Har- Ṭuv, a Warsaw courtyard, and a songbird], in *Di ban: Dertseylungen fun poyln, rusland, yisroel* [The railroad: Stories from Poland, Russia, Israel] (Yagur: Yung-yisroel, 1956), 119–22. For the first version of the story, see Tzvi Ayznman, "Dray mayses" [Three tales], *Yung-yisroel* 2 (1956): 14–16.

109. Ayznman, "A mayse vegn nisim fun har-ṭuv, vegn a varshever hoyf un vegn a shpil-foygl," 119.

110. Lissak notes that "the combination of a physical, cultural, and social separation between the different groups, which gave the stratified structure in the nineteen fifties a character of ethnic stratification, also explains the low rate of inter-group marriages in the given period . . . approximately 9%." According to him, the most common mixed marriages were between Iraqi women (and not Yemenite women, as it would appear from Yiddish fiction) and men of Eastern European origin. Moshe Lissak, "Ereṣ Yiśra'el haRišona weEreṣ Yiśra'el haŠniya: Tahaliḵim mua'ṣim šel qiṭuv ḥevrati-tarbuti biŠnot haḤamišim" [The "first

Israel" and the "second Israel": Accelerated processes of social-cultural polarization in the nineteen fifties], in *Bein 'Olim leWatiqim: Yiśra'el ba'Aliya haGdola, 1948–1953* [Between new immigrants and old-timers: Israel in the great wave of immigration, 1948–1953], ed. Dalia Ofer (Jerusalem: Yad Ben-Zvi, 1996), 6.

111. Lissak, *Ha'Aliya haGdola*, 91. One of the only studies about the immigrant neighborhoods is a study about the Musrara neighborhood in Jerusalem in 1951–1952. Like many other immigrant neighborhoods, Musrara became a troubled neighborhood, and in the 1970s it even came to symbolize such neighborhoods because of the activities of some of its residents, the activists of the Black Panthers.

112. Lissak, *Ha'Aliya haGdola*, 39. Some researchers dispute this claim and argue that the population of 'olim was assigned to the various development towns in accordance with a deliberate discriminating policy that was based on their countries of origin. See, for example, Aziza Khazzoom, "Did the Israeli State Engineer Segregation? On the Placement of Jewish Immigrants in Development Towns in the 1950s," *Social Forces* 84, no. 1 (2005): 115–34.

113. According to the data for 1961, the percentage of immigrants from Poland and Russia in the development towns was approximately 40 percent of their percentage in the veteran cities, and the percentage of immigrants from Romania was approximately equal to their percentage in the veteran cities (compared with immigrants from Germany and Austria, whose percentage was approximately 25 percent, and the percentage of immigrants from North Africa, which was 2.5 times greater than their percentage in the veteran cities). Lissak did not consider the highly problematic nature of determining the category of "country of origin" with respect to the 'olim from Europe. See the discussion in the introduction about determining the language of the 'olim according to the category of "country of origin."

114. Krutikov, *Yiddish Fiction and the Crisis of Modernity*, 64.

115. On the claim that poetry was the main artistic channel of expression of women in Yiddish between the two world wars and on possible reasons for this, see Avraham Novershtern, "HaQolot weHaMaqhela: Širat našim beYidiš beyn štey milḥemot ha'Olam" [The voices and the choir: Women's poetry in Yiddish between two world wars], *Bikoret Uparshanut* 40 (2008): 88–89.

116. Levi Papiernikov, "Getsele," in *In der nayer heym*, 34–37. The story first appeared under this name in the *LF* 46–47 (1955): 15.

117. Khave Slutska-Kestin, "Kinder" [Children], in *In undzere teg* [In our days] (Tel Aviv: Meir, 1966), 333–74.

118. Yekhiel Granatshteyn, "Azoy lebn mir in Shikun" [Living in the public housing], *LN*, September 30, 1953, 3.

119. Georg Simmel, "The Metropolis and Mental Life," in *Georg Simmel: On Individuality and Social Forms*, ed. Donald Levine (Chicago: Chicago University Press, 1971 [1903]), 324.

120. Y. Avash [M], "Di revulutsiye in di 'Amidar Shikunim" [The revolution in the Amidar public housing projects], *LN*, January 9, 1953, 4.

121. As a central theme, the radio appeared in Shimen Kants's story "Shhunot vos darfn shtern undzer ru" [Neighborhoods that ought to disturb our peace of mind], *LN*, August 12, 1960, 4.

122. Avrom Karpinovitsh, "Farshpetike blumen" [Late flowers], in *Der veg keyn sdom*, 121–27.

123. Yitskhok Brat, "Kalmens tfile" [Kalman's prayer], in *Musterverk fun der yidisher literatur* [Masterpieces of Yiddish literature], vol. 55, ed. Shmuel Rozhanski (Buenos Aires: Instituto Científico Judío IWO, 1973), 149–57.

124. Yishaye Shpigl, "Fremde" [Foreign], in *Di brik*, 52–63.

125. Yishaye Shpigl, "Keter yisroel" [Crown of Israel], in *Di brik*, 195–212. An earlier version of the story was printed under the same name in the *LN*, September 14, 1958, 6. The story in its final version was printed in *DGK* 40 (1961): 56–66.

126. For example, Yitskhok Perlov, "BeDamaiḵ ḥayi" [Live in spite of your blood], in *In eygenem land*, 115–27. On the children who came to Israel uncircumcised, see Mordkhe Tsanin, "A sakh nit gemelte kinder ongekumen keyn yisroel" [Many uncircumcised children arrived in Israel], *Forverts*, November 19, 1949, unpaginated paper clipping, Gnazim Institute, Tsanin Archive, 504; Sh. Kiriyati [M], "Shray nisht, bist dokh shoyn a yid" [Don't scream, you are already a Jew], *LN*, May 10, 1954, 3.

127. For example, Perlov, "Ben-amile geyt shoyn in gan-yeladim."

128. Rokhl Oyerbakh, "Dos viglid" [The lullaby], in *In land yisroel*, 371–82.

129. A description of this girl appeared in Oyerbakh's book *BeḤuṣot warša, 1939–1943* (Across Warsaw, 1939–1943), under the title "Yosima" (Yosima [a girl's name]) (Tel Aviv: Am-Oved, 1953), 177–84.

130. Yekhiel Granatshteyn, "Aleyn" [Alone], *LN*, September 9, 1955, 5.

131. Khaye Elboym-Dorembus, "Der pomidor" [The tomato], *LN*, October 23, 1953, 4.

132. Eliezer Olei, "Di farshterte simkhe" [The disrupted joy], in *Di shtub: Noveln* [The home: Novellas] (Tel Aviv: Eygns, 1959), 148–54. The story was first printed under this title in the *LN*, January 24, 1958, 5.

133. Rivke Kviatkovski-Pinkhasik, "Zamd" [Sand], in *Tsvishn karmel un yam*, 90–100. The story was first published under this title in the *LN*, March 31, 1961, 5.

134. See, for example, Yoav Gelbar, *Moledet Ḥadaša: 'Aliyat yehudei merkaz 'eropa uQliṭatam, 1933–1948* [A new homeland: The 'aliya and absorption of the Jews of central Europe, 1933–1948] (Jerusalem: Yad Ben-Zvi, 1990), 222–33; Guy Miron, *Mi"Šam" le"Kan" beGuf rišon: Ziḵronoteyhem šel ioṣey germania beYiśra'el* [From "there" to "here" in the first person: The memories of Jews of German origin in Israel] (Jerusalem: Magnes, 2004), 29–30, 132–35.

135. Kviatkovski-Pinkhasik, "Zamd," 95.

136. Kviatkovski-Pinkhasik, "Zamd," 97.

137. Gali Drucker Bar-Am, "The Holy Tongue and the Tongue of the Martyrs: The Eichmann Trial as Reflected in *Letste Nayes*," *Dapim: Studies on the Holocaust* 28, no. 1 (2014): 17–37.

138. Malasha Mali, "Der forhang" [The curtain], in *Tsvey veltn* [Two worlds] (Tel Aviv: Y. L. Peretz, 1965), 105–61. The first version of the novella appeared in *DGK* 11 (1952): 81–111.

139. Mali, "Der forhang," 112.

140. Mali, "Der forhang," 148–49.

141. On this tension, see Krutikov, *Yiddish Fiction and the Crisis of Modernity*, 164.

142. Malasha Mali, "In leyter-brand fun gezangen" [The rise of the ignitable poetry], *Yung-yisroel* 1 (1954): 23–26. This work, with which Mali chose to present herself to the public in Israel, is a long poem in which she describes a reading in the poems of the group's patron, Sutzkever.

143. Shmuel Niger, "Premirte dertseylungen" [Award-winning stories], *Der tog-morgn zshurnal*, August 30, 1953, unpaginated newspaper clipping, YIVO Archive, Niger Collection, RG 360/1869.

144. Rivke Kviatkovski-Pinkhasik, *Fun lager in lager* [From camp to camp] (Buenos Aires: Tsentral farband fun poylishe yidn in argentine in buenos-ayres, 1950).

145. From the end of 1954 until 1956, Elboym-Dorembus's book of memoirs from the Holocaust years, *Af der arisher zayt* (On the Aryan side), was published in installments, and it was

compiled and published under the same title by the LN Press in January 1958. For an analysis of this work, see Gali Drucker Bar-Am, "'Normal People in a Land of Their Own': On Gender and Nationalism in Khaye Elboym-Dorembus's *Af der Arisher Zayt*," *Nashim: A Journal of Jewish Women's Studies and Gender Issues* 27 (2014): 62–74.

146. Oz Almog, *The Sabra: The Creation of the New Jew*, trans. Haim Watzman (Berkeley: University of California Press, 2000), 18–22.

147. Lissak, *Ha'Aliya haGdola*, 34.

148. According to the data in Yablonka (*Survivors of the Holocaust*, 155–56), between May 1948 and August 1949, 3,637 'olim were absorbed in Kibbutzim of Hakibbutz Hameuchad (the United Kibbutz Movement); 1,547 were absorbed between May 1948 and July 1949 in Kibbutzim of the Kibbutz Artzi (Nationwide Kibbutz Movement); Hever Hakvutzot ve-ha-Kibbutzim (The Union of the Groups and Kibbutzim) absorbed 1,157 'olim in 1948; and Hakibbutz ha-Dati (the Religious Kibbutz Movement) absorbed 435 'olim (no time frame was given).

149. For example, among the veteran Yiddish writers were the poet and editor Arie Shamri (Ein Shemer), the poet Avrom Lev (Giv'at Ha-Shlosha), and the translator and editor Moshe Bassok (Ashdot Ya'akov). Among the young writers, 'oley sheyres hapleyte, were the prose writers Ayznman (Yagur and later Alonim) and Birshteyn (Gvat) and the poets Rivka Basman (Ha-Ma'apil) and Rukhl Fishman (Beit Alfa) (the latter was born in the United States and grew up there until she moved to Israel).

150. See the words of acknowledgment to the Kibbutz in the literary group's first issue: "Heartfelt wishes to Kibbutz Yagur, where the group's first public appearance was held. Kibbutz Yagur has always been a symbol of friendly attitudes toward every literary phenomenon." *Yung-yisroel* 1 (1954): 37.

151. Yablonka, *Survivors of the Holocaust*, 165–66.

152. Mordkhe Tsanin, "Naye imigrantn in di derfer un kolonyes fun yisroel: A nayer tip yishuvnikes—far vos zey viln nisht arayntretn in di kvutsot? Interesante geshprekhn mit yidishe dorfslayt arum Lod" [New immigrants in the villages and settlements in Israel: A new type of *yishuvniks*—why do they not want to join the groups? Interesting conversations with Jewish villagers from around Lod], *Forverts*, October 9, 1949, unpaginated newspaper clipping, Gnazim Institute, Tsanin Archive, 504.

153. Perlov, *Dzshebelye*, 136.

154. According to Yankev Leshtshinski, in the countries of Eastern Europe in the nineteenth century, 98 percent of agriculture was in non-Jewish hands, while more than 95 percent of commerce in the towns was run by Jews. Yankev Leshtshinski, *HaPzura haYehudit* [The Jewish Diaspora], trans. Moshe Horovitz (Jerusalem: Ha-Mahlaka le-Hinuch u-le-Tarbut ba-Gola shel ha-Histadrut ha-Zionit ha-'Olamit, 1961), 23.

155. Perlov, *Dzshebelye*, 143.

156. Bartov, *Šeš knafaim le'Eḥad*, 95–96.

157. Eliezer Rubinshteyn, "Zayn ershter tants" [His first dance], *LN*, August 3, 1951, 4; August 6, 1951, 2; August 13, 1951, 2.

158. Rubinshteyn, "Zayn ershter tants," 4.

159. Rubinshteyn, "Zayn ershter tants," 2.

160. Almog, *Sabra*, 233–35.

161. Tzvi Ayznman, "Mentshelekh" [Little-people], *LN*, September 28, 1958, 4. An adapted version of the story was compiled in his book *Mazoles*, 43–47.

162. Ayznman, "Mentshelekh," 46–47.

163. Letter from Bassok (Ashdot Ya'akov) to Ayznman (Yagur), July 6, 1956, Gnazim Institute, Ayznman Collection, 394–5203.

164. Draft of a letter from Ayznman (Yagur) to the committee of the Tsvi Kesl award (Mexico) in response to the announcement that he received the award, January 2, 1956, Gnazim Institute, Ayznman Archive, 394–4/370167. See also: "In Yagur I stopped stammering with rhymes and started walking on two healthy prose legs," Ayznman's words at an evening honoring his reception of the Kesl Award for his book *Di ban*, Kibbutz Yagur, undated (probably 1956), Gnazim Institute, Ayznman Archive, 394.

165. Tzvi Ayznman, "Arum beys-haMedresh" [Around the Beit-Midrash], *DGK* 13 (1952): 221–25. The story appeared in his book *Di ban*, 143–49.

166. Robert Alter called this style "Magic Realism" and argued that it entered Israeli fiction only in 1968 in the novel *'Ayen 'Erek: 'Ahava* (*See Under: Love*) by David Grossman. Robert Alter, "Magic Realism in the Israeli Novel," in *The Boom in Contemporary Israeli Fiction*, ed. Alan Mintz (Hanover, NH: Brandeis University Press, 1997), 17. Thus, Ayznman's writing (and that of Yishaye Shpigl, especially in his works "Di kukavke" and "Di brik" mentioned earlier) in the 1950s and 1960s was among the harbingers of this style in the Israeli space.

167. Yosl Birshteyn, *Af shmole trotuarn* [On narrow sidewalks] (Tel Aviv: Y. L. Peretz, 1958). Parts of the novel appeared in journals in Israel in the 1950s: "Der pastekh khonon" [The shepherd Hanan], *DGK* 13 (1952): 195–202; "Der toyt fun an altn oks" [Death of the old ox], *DGK* 18 (1954): 129–32; "Onitses" [Leg warmers], *Heymish* 1 (1956): 11; "Baym akern in der nakht" [At the night plowing], *DGK* 28 (1957): 81–85; "Nakht" [Night], *Yung-yisroel* 3 (1957): 3–22; "Baginen" [Dawn], *Heymish* 22–23 (1958): 11; "'Svet regenen" [It's going to rain], *Heymish* 26–27 (1958): 9–10. On Birshteyn and *Af shmole trotuarn*, see Avraham Novershtern, "The Multicolored Patchwork on the Coat of a Prince," *Modern Hebrew Literature* 8–9 (1992): 56–59.

168. For example, this is what Ze'ev thinks about Mashele: "This woman will stay a housemaid always and everywhere." Birshteyn, *Af shmole trotuarn*, 109. And this is what his son, Udi, a teenage Sabra, thinks about the 'olim: "In Udi's eyes, Zilberman and Fayvl were inferior creatures. They were among the new immigrants who shelter in the Kibbutz like poor people in a foreign city, appearing and disappearing, and there is nothing one can discuss with them as equals." *Af shmole trotuarn*, 64.

169. Birshteyn, *Af shmole trotuarn*, 161.

170. Birshteyn, *Af shmole trotuarn*, 68.

171. See, for example, the *LN* column "Froy un heym" (Woman and home), by Khave Levkovitsh, where she describes Kibbutz life as problematic in terms of the relationship it enables with the extended family. Khave Levkovitsh, "Problemen fun familye-lebn in Kibbutz" [Problems of family-life in a Kibbutz], *LN*, December 6, 1957, 6; Khave Levkovitsh, "A mishpokhe-drame in Kibbutz" [A family-drama in a Kibbutz], *LN*, December 30, 1960, 6.

172. Yosl Birshteyn, "A yidisher shrayber in Kibbutz" [A Yiddish writer in a Kibbutz], *DGK* 11 (1952): 165–66.

173. Yigal Mossinson, *Derek Gever* [A man's way] (Tel Aviv: Tberski, 1953), 7.

174. Birshteyn, *Af shmole trotuarn*, 264–66.

175. For example, Yitskhok Paner, "Der Kibbutz on shminke" [The Kibbutz with no makeup], *DGK* 31 (1958): 228–30; A. Volf Yasny, "Ershtling verk fun a yungn mekhaber" [The first work of a young author], *LN*, July 4, 1958, 5.

176. Amos Oz, *Elsewhere, Perhaps*, trans. from the Hebrew by Nicholas de Lange in collaboration with the author (New York: Harcourt Brace Jovanovich, 1973).

177. Gershon Shaked, *HaSiporet ha'Ivrit, 1880–1980* [Hebrew fiction, 1880–1980], vol. 4 (Tel Aviv: Hakibbutz Hameuchad, 1993), 295.

178. Yosl Birshteyn, "Aspektn" [Aspects], *Yung-yisroel* 2 (1956): 56.

179. It is possible that the Kibbutz appears as a theme in one of the *Shund* novels (the sensational serialized novels) published in the Yiddish press in Israel, which have not yet been studied.

180. Louis Wirth, "Urbanism as a Way of Life," *American Journal of Sociology* 44, no. 1 (1938): 1–24.

181. "The city and the country may be regarded as two poles in reference to one or the other of which all human settlements tend to arrange themselves." Wirth, "Urbanism as a Way of Life," 3.

182. On the features of descriptions of the Jewish shtetl in Yiddish literature, see Dan Miron, *Der imazh fun shtetl: Dray literarishe shtudies* [The image of the shtetl: Three literary studies] (Tel Aviv: Y. L. Peretz, 1981).

183. Bina Garncarska-Kadary, *Ḥelqam šel haYehudim beHitpatḥut haTa'aśiya šel warša baŠanim 1816/20–1914* [The role of the Jews in the development of Warsaw's industry 1816/20–1914] (Tel Aviv: Ha-Machon Le-heqer ha-Tfutzot, ha-Merkaz le-Heker toldot ha-Yehudim be-Polin u-Morashtam, 1985).

184. Avraham Novershtern, "Dimuya šel wilna beŠirat yidiš bein štey milḥemot ha'Olam" [The image of Vilna in Yiddish poetry between the two world wars], in *MiWilna leYerušalaim: Meḥqarim beToldoteyhem uVeTarbutam šel yehudei mizraḥ 'eropa mugašim leProfesor Šmu'el Werses* [From Vilna to Jerusalem: Studies in the annals and culture of Eastern European Jews presented to Professor Shmuel Werses], ed. David Assaf et al. (Jerusalem: Magnes, 2002), 488.

185. On the ambivalent descriptions of Tel Aviv in the Hebrew urban novel in Palestine/Eretz Yisrael between the two world wars, see Gershon Shaked, *HaSiporet ha'Ivrit, 1880–1980*, vol. 3 (Tel Aviv: Hakibbutz Hameuchad, 1988), 17–25; 'Oded Menda-Levy, *Liqro' 'et ha'Ir: HaḤawaya ha'Urbanit baSiporet ha'Ivrit me'Emṣ'a haMe'a ha-19 'ad 'emṣ'a haMe'a ha-20* [Reading the city: The urban experience in Hebrew fiction from the mid-nineteenth century to the mid-twentieth century] (Tel Aviv: Hakibbutz Hameuchad, 2010), 176–78. On the nature of Tel Aviv after the establishment of the state, see Hanna Soker-Schwager, *Mek̲ašef haŠeveṭ miMe'onot ha'Ovdim: Ya'aqov Šabt'ai baTarbut haYiśra'elit* [The wizard of the tribe from the worker's housing] (Tel Aviv: Hakibbutz Hameuchad, 2007), 199–252.

186. Shamir, *Hu halak̲ baŚadot*, 198–212.

187. See, for example, Zusman Segalovitsh's description, "Ševa haŠanim šeli beTel-Aviv" [My seven years in Tel Aviv], trans. Gali Drucker Bar-Am, *Ho!* 16 (2018): 348–53.

188. Yablonka, *Survivors of the Holocaust*, 13.

189. The percentage of immigrants with postprimary education, including women, nearly equaled their percentage among the veteran residents: 64.3 percent versus 64.4 percent. Yablonka, *Survivors of the Holocaust*, 13.

190. Yitskhok Perlov, *Flora Ingber: A hoyz in tel-oviv* [Flora Ingber: A house in Tel Aviv] (Buenos Aires: Yidbukh, 1959).

191. This novel began to be published in serialized form in 1929 under the title *Farn mabl* (Before the flood). See Joseph Sherman, "Asch, Sholem," in *YIVO Encyclopedia of Jews in Eastern Europe*, ed. Gershon David Hundert (New Haven, CT: Yale University Press, 2008), 1:74–77.

192. One of the distinctive characteristics of the urban lifestyle is, in Wirth's words, "the substitution of secondary for primary contacts, the weakening of bonds of kinship, and the declining social significance of the family." "Urbanism as a Way of Life," 20–12. For a few of the many examples of the theme of the disintegration of the family in the city, see Dovid Pinski, *Dos hoyz fun noyekh edon* (The house of Noah Edon), 1926; Moyshe Kulbak, *Zalmenyaner* (The Zalmenyaners), 1931–1935; I. J. Singer, *Di brider ashkenazi* (The Brothers Ashkenazi), 1936; and I. J. Singer, *Di mishpokhe karnovski* (The Family Karnowski), 1943.

193. Irving Howe, *Politics and the Novel* (New York: New American Library 1987 [1957]), 254.

194. Moyshe Grosman, *Di vide fun a revolutsyoner: Politisher roman* [Confessions of a revolutionary: A political novel] (Ramat Gan: Mendele moykher sforim, 1956), 191.

195. Grosman, *Di vide fun a revolutsyoner*, 191–93.

196. Yitskhok Perlov, "Der onheyb" [The beginning], in *In eygenem land*, 7–19. The story was first published under this name in the LF 2 (1951): 12–14.

197. Avrom Karpinovitsh, "Di mame vet nokh spondzhe makhn" [Mummy will yet be able to do her floor-washing], in *Der veg keyn sdom*, 51–59. The story was first published under this name in the *LN*, November 5, 1954, 5–7.

198. A description of the "housemaids market" appears also in Mendl Man's *In a farvorloztn dorf.*

199. It is possible that this story reflects echoes of an affair that took place toward the end of 1952: Tsanin published in the *LN* a call to readers to donate money for the purchase of a piano for a musically gifted girl who lived in the Pardes-Hanna Ma'abara and whose family could not afford to pay for an instrument or lessons. According to Tsanin's description, her father worked in Tel Aviv, without a permit, as a horse cart driver and was arrested by the police. After he explained the reasons for his illegal activity, the police officers referred him to the editor of the *LN*. Mordkhe Tsanin, "Undzer hilf tsu a yungn talent in yisroel: Yehudit kern- dos vunderkind" [Our help to a young talent: Yehudit Kern the gifted child], *LN*, December 12, 1952, 2. The *LN* readers responded to the call and donated more than one thousand Palestinian pounds. On July 29, 1953, a festive concert was held at the Ohel Shem hall in Tel Aviv, at which the girl received the piano purchased with the contributions and played for the audience. "Greyt zikh tsu der fayerlekher ibergebung fun dem klavir dem vunderkind Yehudit kern" [Announcing the ceremonial awarding of the piano for the gifted child Yehudit Kern], *LN*, July 19, 1953, 2. So that unlike Karpinovitsh's story, this affair had a positive ending (at least according to the description in the paper).

200. On the construction of this image in the period of the Yishuv, see Tammy Razi, *Yaldey haHefqer: HeḤaṣer ha'Aḥorit šel tel-'aviv haMandaṭorit* [Forsaken children: The backyard of mandatory Tel Aviv] (Tel Aviv: Am-Oved, 2009).

201. Aryeh Tartakower, *HaḤevra haYehudit* [Jewish society] (Tel Aviv: Masada, 1957), 107–18.

202. On the pioneering ethos and the hedonistic ethos in the years of the British mandate, see Anat Helman, *Young Tel Aviv: A Tale of Two Cities*, trans. Haim Watzman (Waltham, MA: Brandeis University Press, 2010), 91–92.

203. Aharon Meged, *Ḥedwa we'Ani uFarašat qoroteynu ba'Ir tel-'aviv* [Hedva and I and the story of what happened to us in the city of Tel Aviv] (Tel Aviv: Hakibbutz Hameuchad, 1955), 354.

204. Y. Burshteyn [M], "'Ariye, der yunger shuster af reḥov bazel" [Arieh, the young shoemaker from Bazel Street], *LN*, December 5, 1952, 2.

205. Burshteyn, "'Ariye, der yunger shuster af reḥov bazel," 2.

206. Dovid Eydlman, "Feyge beyle vil nisht keyn shuster" [Feyge-Beyle does not want a shoemaker], in *Fun gerikht, fun rabinat, fun gas: Reportazhn* [From the courthouse, from the rabbinate, from the street: Reportages] (Tel Aviv: Ha-Menora, 1966), 263. The feuilleton was first published under this name in the *LN*, October 11, 1954, 5.

207. On the humoristic-parodic writing tradition in modern Yiddish literature, see Yechiel Szeintuch, "Introduction," in *Der tunkeler: Sefer haHumoresqot waHaParodyiot haSifrutiyot baYidiš* [The dark one: The book of humoresques and literary parodies in Yiddish] (Jerusalem: Magnes, 1990), 13–68.

208. See Shaked, *HaSiporet ha'Ivrit*, 3:206–15.
The quote is from p. 206.

209. Y. Namdirf [Yankev Fridman], "Dakhloze in tel-oviv" [Homeless in Tel Aviv], *LN*, November 23, 1956, 7.

210. Yiddish, unlike Hebrew, distinguishes between a *shnorer* (a person driven by a psychological complex that causes him to feel a constant sense of lack), a *kabtsn* (a poor person), and a *betler* (a beggar, described in Hebrew as a *Kabtsan*). Bialik was attentive to these nuances and chose to use the Yiddish word *shnor* in order to mark them: "Avaunt ye, beggars [*kabtsanim*], to the charnel-house!. . . . And as you stretched your hand [*pashtetem yad*] so will you stretch it, and as you have been wretched [*shnorartem*] so are you wretched." H. N. Bialik, "The City of Slaughter," trans. Israel Efros, in *Complete Poetic Works of Hayim Nahman Bialik*, ed. Israel Efros (New York: Histadrut 'Ivrit of America, 1948), 1:129–43.

211. Yankev Perlshteyn, "Dalfnike birger" [Poor citizens], *LN*, July 2, 1954, 7.

212. Shloyme Berlinski, "Gasn-shpiler" [Street-musicians], in *Bilder un dertseylungen* [Images and stories] (Tel Aviv: Y. L. Peretz, 1958), 59–61. The story was first published under this name in the *LN*, April 5, 1953, 2.

213. See, for example, Anat Helman's words: "Tel Aviv was built in the Middle East by a population that was mostly Eastern European, with the intent of creating a city according to a modern Western model. . . . It was meant to be a modern alternative not only to Palestine's Arab cities but also to the crowded Jewish urban ghetto and the ramshackle and wretched 'shtetl.'" Helman, *Young Tel Aviv*, 42. It should be noted that up until the Holocaust, Jews in Eastern Europe did not live in ghettos.

214. Magen, "Peysekhdike reportazhn," 2.

215. Yekhiel Granatshteyn, "Mentshn fun undzer land: Tsvey brider" [People from our country: Two brothers], *LN*, February 25, 1955, 5. The same plot, occurring between two sisters instead of two brothers, appears in Levi Papiernikov, "Ir layblekhe shvester" [Her beloved sister], in *In der nayer heym*, 56–60.

216. Eliyezer Rubinshteyn, "Er vart af zey" [He waits for them], *LN*, January 15, 1951, 2.

217. P. Guterman, "Far vos iz zi avek?" [Why did she leave?], *LN*, December 14, 1951, 3.

218. Y. Varanovski, "Dos oysgeloshene lebn" [The extinguished life], *LN*, March 26, 1956, 10.

219. Z"k Lik [M. Zaklik], "A mame" [A mother], *LN*, October 1, 1961, 4.

220. For example, Dovid Eydlman, "Dray sho in burlesk in kafe noga" [Three hours of burlesque in Café Noga], *LN*, March 21, 1955, 3; 'A. HaLevi, "In kafe" [At the café], *LN*, September 1, 1959, 3.

221. Yitskhok Paner, "Er oykh?" [He too?], in *Zun un Shotn*, 111–12.

222. Walter Benjamin, "Šuvo šel haMešoṭeṭ" [Return of the wanderer], in *Mivḥar ktavim*, vol. 1, trans. David Zinger (Tel Aviv: Hakibbutz Hameuchad, 1992), 100–104.

223. Yitskhok Perlov, "In oytobus" [On the bus], in *In eygenem land*, 167–74.

224. Shmaye Avni [Shteynmats], "In oytobus numer 4" [On bus number 4], *LN*, May 26, 1950, 4.

225. A. Narevski [Rives], "Mitn oytobus keyn kiriyat-sholem" [With the bus to Kiryat-Shalom] *LN*, May 5, 1954, 3.

226. Dovid Eydlman, "In Oytobus: Ufgekhapte bildlekh un gasn-stsenes" [On the bus: Captured images and street-scenes], *LN*, August 23, 1954, 3.

227. Yekhiel Granatshteyn, "Ven dos folk fayert" [When the people celebrate], *LN*, May 1, 1953, 5.

228. Yekhiel Granatshteyn, "Khvalyendike likht" [Wavy light], *LN*, May 25, 1955, 5–7.

229. According to Holzman, S. Yizhar rebuked himself and his colleagues in his speech at the 1958 conference of the Writers Association, "for their disconnection from the cultural and spiritual treasures of the Jewish past and for not writing the multiplicity and variety of the country [Israel], and especially for ignoring the new ʿaliya that is changing the country's face." Yizhar, "HeʿAśor laMedina weLaSifrut haʿIwrit, dvarim beWeʿidat haSofrim haI"ḥ" [The state's ten-year anniversary and Hebrew literature, words at the eighteenth writers' conference], *LaMerhav (Masa')*, April 10, 1958, quoted in Holzman, *'Ahavot Ṣion*, 495–96, n. 4.

Conclusion

1. Avrom Sutzkever, "Yidishe gas" [Jewish/Yiddish street], in *Yidishe gas* (New York: Matones, 1948), 11.

2. Y. Artuski, "Tsi darf un tsi muz yidish untergeyn in yisroel?" [Ought and must Yiddish perish in Israel?], *LF* 70–71 (1957): 8–10.

3. M. Shell and W. Sollores (eds.), *The Multilingual Anthology of American Literature* (New York: New York University Press, 2000). On the multilingual literature written in the United States and on earlier attempts to publish anthologies of this kind, see L. A. Rosenwald, *Multicultural America: Language and the Making of American Literature* (Cambridge: Cambridge University Press, 2008).

4. For example, Rubik Rozental, "Ma taʿaśe haIvrit bli lehašviş, lenadned uLeqaṭer?" [What will Hebrew do without "boasting," "nagging," "complaining"? [all words that entered Hebrew from Yiddish]], *Davka* 1 (2006): 4–6; Ghilʿad Zuckermann, *Yiśra'elit śafa yafa* [Israeli—a beautiful language] (Tel Aviv: Am-Oved, 2008).

5. Mordekhe Shekhter, "Dos yidish shebikhtav in erets-yisroel" [The written Yiddish in Israel], *Yidishe shprakh* 37, no. 1–3 (1978/1980): 1–23. In this essay, Shekhter distinguished between works of literature written in Yiddish before the establishment of the state—in what he called "Mandat-yidish" (Mandatory Yiddish)—and those written after its establishment, in "Medine yidish" (Israeli Yiddish). He argued that the latter language was unique not only in its vocabulary (by absorbing into itself new Hebrew words) but also at the level of syntax. According to him, the influence of Hebrew is especially evident in the renewing of the element of "loshn koydesh" (the holy language) in the language and in secularizing it. Thus, in a kind of dialectic process, words of a rabbinical origin returned to the consciousness of those who had long since moved away from the traditional Jewish way of life and from its texts. According to Shekhter, this is one of the significant and blessed influences of the Israeli environment on Yiddish.

Appendix B

1. I thank the team of the Lerner Index to Yiddish Periodicals (IYP) for their important comments.

2. Joseph Fraenkel, ed., *The Jewish Press of the World* (London: Cultural Department of the World Jewish Congress, 1953, 1961, 1967).

Bibliography

Archives

The Gnazim Archive of the Hebrew Writers Association in Israel
The National Library of Israel, Jerusalem, Department of Archives
The Oral History Archives of the Institute of Contemporary Jewry, the Hebrew University of Jerusalem
State Archive, Jerusalem
Yad Vashem Archive, Jerusalem
Yiddish Book Center's Frances Brandt Online Yiddish Audio Library
YIVO Archive, New York

Conversations

Tsvi Ayznman, Kibbutz Alonim
Aviva Halamish, Tel Aviv
Yitskhok and Ester Luden, Giv'atayim
Edna Nahshon, New York
Ester Rozhanski, Ramat Ha-Sharon
Aleksander Shpiglblat, Petah Tikva
Shura Turkov, Holon

Bibliographic Guides and Databases

Altshuler, Mordechai. *Yahadut brit haMo'eṣot ba'Aspaqlaria šel 'etonut yidiš bePolin: Bibliografia, 1945–1970* [Soviet Jewry in the mirror of the Yiddish press in Poland: Bibliography, 1945–1970]. Jerusalem: Hebrew University of Jerusalem, 1975.

Cohen, Berl. *Leksikon fun yidish-shraybers* [Lexicon of Yiddish writers]. New York: R. Ilman-Kohen, 1986.

Fraenkel, Joseph, ed. *The Jewish Press of the World*. London: Cultural Department of the Word Jewish Congress, 1953, 1961, 1967.

The Lerner Index to Yiddish Periodicals (IYP). The Hebrew University of Jerusalem and Beit Sholem Aleykhem.

Niger, Shmuel, and Yankev Shatski, eds. *Leksikon fun der nayer yidisher literatur* [The lexicon of modern Yiddish literature]. New York: Alveltlekhn yidishn kultur-kongres, 1956–1981.

Novershtern, Avraham. *Avrom Sutzkever: Bibliografie* [Avrom Sutzkever: Bibliography]. Tel Aviv: Yisroel-bukh, 1976.

Ramba, Izik. "'Orot uṢlalim baYomonim beYidiš be'Arṣot haBrit" [Lights and shadows in the Yiddish daily press in the United States]. *Qorot ha'Etonayi'm haYehudiyim: Buleṭin šel haLiška ha'Olamit šel ha'Etona'im haYehudiim beYerušalaim* [The annals of Jewish journalists: Bulletin of the World Federation of Jewish Journalists in Jerusalem] 12 (1967): 5–7.

Yediyes fun Y. L. Peretz farlag (1963, 1964, 1966).

Newspapers and Periodicals

Davar: Iton Po'alei Eretz Yisrael [Davar: Newspaper of Eretz Yisrael Workers], 1958.
Di Goldene Keyt: Fertl- yorshrift far literatur un gezelshaftlekhe problemen [The golden chain: A quarterly of literature and social problems], 1949–67.
Di Tsukunft [The future], 1944–68.
Fray-yisroel: Demokratishe vokhnshrift far politik, virtshaft un kultur [Free-Israel: Democratic weekly on politics, economics, and culture], 1948–67.
Heymish: Zhurnal far literatur kritik un sotsiyale problemen [Homey: Journal for literary critique and social problems], 1956–63.
Lebns fragn: Sotsialistishe khoydesh-shrift far politik, virtshaft un kultur [Life questions: A socialist monthly for politics, economics, and culture], 1951–67.
Letste nayes: Umparteyish blat far gezelshaft, politik, virtshaft un kultur [Latest news: A non-partisan daily paper on society, politics, economy, and culture], 1949–67.
Ma'ariv, 1958.
Masa, 1958
Nayvelt: Vokhnshrift far politik un kultur [New world: Weekly writings on politics and culture], 1948–55.
Yung Yisroel: Zamlung far literatur un kritik [Young Israel: A collection of literature and criticism], 1954–56.

Anthologies and Almanacs

Bassok, Moshe. *Mivḥar širei yidiš leMin Y. L. Peretz we'Ad yamenu* [A selection of Yiddish poems from Y. L. Peretz to the present]. Merhavia: Hakibbutz Hameuchad, 1963.
Blumental, Nakhmen. *Verter un vertlekh fun der khurbn-tkufe* [Words and sayings from the Holocaust era]. Tel Aviv: Y. L. Peretz, 1981.
The Editors. *Almanakh fun di Yidishe shrayber in Yisroel* [Almanac of Yiddish writers in Israel]. Tel Aviv: Fareyn fun yidishe shrayber un zshurnalistn in yisroel, 1967.
———. *Almanakh pariz* [Paris almanac]. Paris: Fareyn fun yidishe shrayber un zshurnalistn in frankraykh, 1960.
Halamish, Mordechai, ed. *Mikan uMiqarov: Antologia šel siporei yidiš be'Ereṣ Yiśra'el miRešit haMe'a we'Ad yanenu* [From here and from near: An anthology of Yiddish stories in Eretz Yisrael from the turn of the century to our days]. Tel Aviv: Sifriyat Po'alim, 1966.
———. *Yidiš be Yiśra'el: 'Al sofrim, mešorerim, amanim* [Yiddish in Israel: On writers, poets, artists]. Tel Aviv: Aked, 1990.
Melzer, Shimshon. *'Al neharot: Tiš'a maḥzorei šira miSifrut yidiš* [By the rivers: An anthology of Yiddish poetry]. Jerusalem: Mosad Bialik, 1956.
Rozhanski, Shmuel, ed. *Musterverk fun der Yidisher literatur* [Masterpieces of Yiddish literature], 35, 55. Buenos Aires: Instituto Científico Judío IWO, 1968, 1973.
Shamri, Arie, ed. *Vortslen: Antologye fun yidish-shafn in yisroel, poezye un proze* [Roots: An Anthology of Yiddish Works in Israel, Poetry and Prose]. Tel Aviv: Yisroel-bukh, 1966.
Shell, M., and W. Sollores, eds. *The Multilingual Anthology of American Literature*, 3–14. New York: New York University Press, 2000.
Stern, David. "An Introduction." In *The Anthology in Jewish Literature*, edited by David Stern, 3–14. Oxford: Oxford University Press, 2004.
Sutzkever, Avrom. *A. Sutzkever: Selected Poetry and Prose*. Translated by Barbara Harshav and Benjamin Harshav. Berkeley: University of California Press, 1991.

Yofe, Mordkhe. *Erets-yisroel in der yidisher literatur: Antologye* ['Ereş Yiśra'el in Yiddish literature: Anthology]. Tel Aviv: Y. L. Peretz, 1961.

Yiddish Fiction, Poetry and Translations

Aleichem, Sholem. *Ale verk* [Complete works]. Buenos Aires: Ikuf, 1952.
Ayznman, Tzvi. "Arum beys-haMedresh" [Around the Beit-Midrash]. *DGK* 13 (1952): 221–25.
———. *Di ban: Dertseylungen fun poyln, rusland, yisroel* [The railroad: Stories from Poland, Russia, Israel]. Yagur: Yung-yisroel, 1956.
———. "Dray mayses" [Three tales]. *Yung-yisroel*, vol. 2 (1956): 14–16.
———. *Mazoles* [Zodiac signs]. Tel Aviv: Y. L. Peretz, 1965.
Bergelson, Dovid. *Verk* [Works]. Vol. 5, *Nokh alemen* [When All Is Said and Done]. Berlin: Vostok, 1922.
Berlinski, Shloyme. *Bilder un dertseylungen* [Images and stories]. Tel Aviv: Y. L. Peretz, 1958.
Birshteyn, Yosl. *Af shmole trotuarn* [On narrow sidewalks]. Tel Aviv: Y. L. Peretz, 1958.
Elboym-Dorembus, Khaye. *Af der Arisher Zayt* [On the Aryan side]. Tel Aviv: Letste nayes, 1957.
Eydlman, Dovid. *Fun gerikht, fun rabinat, fun gas: Reportazshn* [From the courthouse, from the rabbinate, from the street: Reportages]. Tel Aviv: Ha-Menora, 1966.
Grosman, Moyshe. *Di vide fun a revolutsyoner: Politisher roman* [Confessions of a revolutionary: A political novel]. Ramat Gan: Mendele moykher sforim, 1956.
Herzl, Theodor. Altnaylend [The Old New Land]. Translated from the German by Isidor [Yisroel] Eliashev [Bal-Makhshoves]. Warsaw: Hatsfire, 1902.
Karpinovitsh, Avrom. *Der veg keyn sdom* [The road to Sodom]. Tel Aviv: Y. L. Peretz, 1959.
Kulbak, Moyshe. *Geklibene verk* [Complete works]. New York: CYCO, 1953.
Kviatkovski-pinkhasik, Rivke. *Fun lager in lager* [From camp to camp]. Buenos Aires: Tsentral farband fun poylishe yidn in argentine in buenos-ayres, 1950.
———. Našim me'Aḥorey haGader [Women behind the fence]. Translated from the Yiddish by K. Shabtai. Tel Aviv: Y. L. Peretz, 1961.
———. *Tsvishn karmel un yam* [Between Carmel and the sea]. Haifa: Aleyn, 1975.
Mali, Malasha. *Tsvey veltn* [Two worlds]. Tel Aviv: Y. L. Peretz, 1965.
Man, Mendl. *Adam ba-Ohel* [A man in a tent]. Translated by Ya'akov Eliav. Tel Aviv: Am-Oved, 1953.
———. *BiKfar naṭuš: Sipur* [In an abandoned village: A story]. Translated from a manuscript by E. D. Shapir. Tel Aviv: Hakibbutz Hameuchad, 1953.
———. *Di gas fun bliendike mandlen* [The street of blooming almonds]. Buenos Aires: Kiem, 1958.
———. *Di shtilkeyt mont: Lider un baladn* [The stillness calls: Poems and ballads]. Lodzh: Borokhov-farlag, 1945.
———. *Fun golan biz sharem a-sheikh* [From the Golan to Sharm El-Sheikh]. Tel Aviv: Y. L. Peretz, 1973.
———. *In a farvorloztn dorf* [In a deserted village]. Buenos Aires: Kiem, 1954.
———. *Kerner in midber: Dertseylungen* [Grains in the desert: Stories]. Paris: Undzer Kiyem, 1965.
———. *Oyfgevakhte erd* [Awakened earth]. Tel Aviv: Di goldene keyt, 1953.
———. *Yerushe: Lider* [Inheritance: Poems]. Regnsburg: Yidishe zester, 1947.
Manger, Itzik. *Lid un balade* [Poem and ballad]. Tel Aviv: Y. L. Peretz, 1976.

———. *Shriftn in proze*. Tel Aviv: Y. L. Peretz, 1980.
Olei, Eliezzer. *Di shtub: Noveln* [The home: Novellas]. Tel Aviv: Eygns, 1959.
Oyerbakh, Rokhl. *In land yisroel: Reportazshn, eseyn, dertseylungen* [In the Land of Israel: Reportages, essays, stories]. Tel Aviv: Y. L. Peretz, 1964.
Paner, Yitskhok. *Zun un shotn: Yisroel-motivn* [Sun and shadows: Israeli motifs]. Tel Aviv: Y. L. Peretz, 1964.
Papiernikov, Levi. *In der nayer heym: Dertseylungen* [In the new home: Stories]. Tel Aviv: Y. L. Peretz, 1960.
Peretz, Y. L. *Ale verk* [Complete works]. New York: CYCO, 1947.
Perlov, Yitskhok. *Dzshebelye* [Jebelye]. Buenos Aires: Yidbukh, 1955.
———. *Flora Ingber: A hoyz in tel-oviv* [Flora Ingber: A house in Tel Aviv]. Buenos Aires: Yidbukh, 1959.
———. *In eygenem land* [In a country of our own]. Buenos Aires: Yidbukh, 1952.
———. *Matilda lebt* [Matilda lives]. Buenos Aires: Farband fun brisk de-lite un umgegnt in argentine, 1954.
Shpigl, Yishaye. *Di brik: Noveln* [The bridge: Stories]. Tel Aviv: Y. L. Peretz, 1963.
Shtshavinski, Yoysef. *Unter eyn dakh* [Under one roof]. Tel Aviv: Me'asef yisroel, 1964.
Slutska-Kestin, Khave. *In undzere teg* [In our days]. Tel Aviv: Meir, 1966.
Sutzkever, Avrom. "Yidishe gas" [Jewish/Yiddish street]. In *Yidishe gas*, 11. New York: Matones, 1948.
Wolf, Leonard. *The World According to Itzik: Selected Poetry and Prose*. New Haven, CT: Yale University Press, 2002.

Short Stories and Feuilletons in Yiddish Not Compiled in Books

Akh [M], Y. "Mizeg-goleyes" [An integration of exiles]. *LN*, December 3, 1954, 7.
Anonymous. "Soydes fun yafo" [Secrets of Jaffa]. *LN*, April 5, 1954, 4.
Avash, Y. [M]. "Di revulutsiye in di 'Amidar *šikunim*" [The revolution in the Amidar public housing projects]. *LN*, January 9, 1953, 4.
Avni [Shteynmats], Shmaye. "A khezhbn" [An account]. In *Almanakh fun di Yidishe shrayber in Yisroel* [Almanac of Yiddish writers in Israel], 281–86. Tel Aviv: Fareyn fun yidishe shrayber un zshurnalistn in yisroel, 1967.
———. "In oytobus numer 4" [On bus number 4]. *LN*, May 26, 1950, 4.
Brat, Yitskhok. "A shmues mit a mistanen" [A conversation with an infiltrator]. *LN*, September 2, 1955, 6.
———. "Kalmens tfile" [Kalman's prayer],) in *Musterverk fun der yidisher literatur* [Masterpieces of Yiddish literature], vol. 55, edited by Shmuel Rozhanski, 149–57. Buenos Aires: Instituto Científico Judío IWO, 1973.
Burshteyn [M], Y. "Ariye, der yunger shuster af reḥov bazel" [Arie, the young shoemaker from Bazel Street]. *LN*, December 5, 1952, 2.
Elboym-Dorembus, Khaye. "Der pomidor" [The tomato]. *LN*, October 23, 1953, 4.
Eydlman, Dovid. "Dos shtetele yazur" [The townlet of Yazur]. *LN*, February 1, 1953, 2.
———. "Dray sho in burlesk in kafe noga" [Three hours of burlesque in Café Noga]. *LN*, March 21, 1955, 3.
———. "In Oytobus: Ufgekhapte bildlekh un gasn-stsenes" [On the bus: Captured images and street-scenes]. *LN*, August 23, 1954, 3.
Granatshteyn, Yekhiel. "A bagegenish af dereḵ petaḥ-tiqwa" [A meeting on Drekh Petah Tikva]. *LN*, September 26, 1956, 5.

———. "A khasene in a ma'abara" [A wedding in the ma'abara]. *LN*, August 8, 1952, 3; *LN*, August 15, 1952, 4.
———. "Aleyn" [Alone]. *LN*, September 9, 1955, 5.
———. "Azoy lebn mir in *šikun*" [Living in the public housing]. *LN*, September 30, 1953, 3.
———. "In blekhenem baydl fun der ma'abara" [In a small tin shack in the ma'abara]. *LN*, September 19, 1952, 5.
———. "Khvalyendike likht" [Wavy light]. *LN*, May 25, 1955, 5–7.
———. "Mentshn fun undzer land: Tsvey brider" [People from our country: Two brothers]. *LN*, February 25, 1955, 5.
———. "Sakh-hakl fun a tog: Fun dem togbikhl fun an arbetslozn" [Summary of a day: From the diary of an unemployed man]. *LN*, October 9, 1953, 3.
———. "Ven dos folk fayert" [When the people celebrate]. *LN*, May 1, 1953, 5.
———. "Zayn ershte freyd" [His first joy]. *LN*, June 20, 1952, 5.
Guterman, P. "Far vos iz zi avek?" [Why did she leave?]. *LN*, December 14, 1951, 3.
HaLevi, A. "In kafe" [At the café]. *LN*, September 1, 1959, 3.
Kants, Shimen. "Šḵunot vos darfn shtern undzer ru" [Neighborhoods that ought to disturb our peace of mind]. *LN*, August 12, 1960, 4.
Lik, Z"k [M. Zaklik]. "A mame" [A mother]. *LN*, October 1, 1961, 4.
Magen, Tsvi. "Peysekhdike reportazhn" [Passover reports]. *LN*, April 5, 1953, 2.
Namdirf, Y. [Yankev Fridman]. "A dkhak-arbeter" [A lowly worker]. *LN*, September 1, 1959, 3.
———. "Dakhloze in tel-oviv" [Homeless in Tel Aviv]. *LN*, November 23, 1956, 7.
Narevski [Rives], A. "Mitn oytobus keyn kiriyat-sholem" [With the bus to Kiryat-Shalom]. *LN*, May 5, 1954, 3.
Noyman, Yoysef. "Yafoer kasba" [Jaffa's casbah]. *LN*, May 14, 1954, 6.
Perlshteyn, Yankev. "A briv fun a mistanen" [A letter from an infiltrator]. *LN*, May 7, 1954, 7.
———. "Dalfnike birger" [Poor citizens]. *LN*, July 2, 1954, 7.
Rubinshteyn, Eliezer. "Er vart af zey" [He waits for them]. *LN*, January 15, 1951, 2.
———. "Zayn ershter tants" [His first dance]. *LN*, August 3, 1951, 4; August 6, 1951, 2; August 13, 1951, 2.
Varanovski, Y. "Dos oysgeloshene lebn" [The extinguished life]. *LN*, March 26, 1956, 10.

Other Primary Sources in Yiddish: Historical Documents, Memoirs, Memorial Books

[The editors]. *Shimen Roznberg gedenkbukh* [Shimon Rozenberg memorial book]. Tel Aviv: Y. L. Peretz, 1966.
———. *Yid, mentsh, sotsialist: Y. Artuski ondenk-bukh* [Jew, human being, socialist: Memory-book for Y. Artuski]. Tel Aviv: Lebns fragn farlag, 1976.
———. *Yosef Rotnberg: Tsu zayn ershter yortsayt* [Yosef Rotnberg: For the first anniversary of his death]. Tel-Aviv: Y. L. Peretz, 1961.
Abramovitsh, Dina. "Dos yidishe bukh in amerike" [The Yiddish book in America]. *Jewish Book Annual* 12 (1953–54): 139–40.
———. "Dos yidishe bukh in amerike." *Jewish Book Annual* 19 (1961–62): 169–71.
———. "Dos yidishe bukh in amerike." *Jewish Book Annual* 19 (1962–63): 18.
Oyerbakh, Rokhl. *BeḤuṣot Warša: 1939–1943* [On the streets of Warsaw). Translated by Mordechai Halamish. Tel Aviv: Am-Oved, 1954.
Goldberg, Avrom. "156 yidishe bikher zenen dershinen in 1963" [156 books in Yiddish were published in 1963]. *LF* 157 (1965): 12.

———. "141 yidishe bikher un broshurn zenen dershinen in 1964" [141 books and brochures in Yiddish were published in 1964]. *LF* 168 (1965): 14.

Grin, M. "Tsen yor yidishe nokhmitog-shul in tel-oviv" [Ten years for the afternoon-school in Tel Aviv]. *LF* 162–63 (1966): 12.

———. "Undzer kinder-kolonye" [Our children's colony]. *LF* 176–77 (1966): 19.

Gris, Noyekh. "Dos ershte yor DGK: Zikhroynes fun a gevezenem redaktsye-sekretar" [The first year of *DGK*: Memories of a former editorial-secretary]. *DGK* 71 (1970): 170–78.

Hertz, J. S., ed. *Ziglboym Bukh*. New York: Undzer Tsayt, 1947.

The Israeli Friends of YIVO Society and the Ganza Museum of Jewish Folk Art, exhibition of memorial books for Jewish communities that were destroyed, Tel Aviv, 1961.

Kazhdan, Kh. Sh. "Der bund biz dem finftn tsuzamenfor" [The Bund up to the fifth convention]. In *Di geshikhte fun bund*, edited by Gregor Aronson et al., vol. 1, 119, 176. New York: Undzer tsayt, 1960.

Lush, Liber. *Landsmanshaftn in Yisroel: Spetsyele oysgabe tsum yelt-ḳongres fun poylishe yidn* [Hometown associations in Israel: Special publication to world-congress of Jews from Poland]. Tel Aviv: Hitahadut ʻolei Polin beYisrael, 1961.

Mayzel, Nakhmen. *Tsurikblikn un perspektivn* [Retrospectives and perspectives]. Tel Aviv: Y. L. Peretz, 1962.

Ravitsh, Meylekh. *Mayn leksikon 3: Yidishe un hebreyishe shraybers in medines Yisroel* [My lexicon vol. 3: Yiddish and Hebrew writers in Israel]. Montreal: A komitet, 1958.

Rotnberg, Yoisef. *Fun Varshe biz shankhay: Notitsn fun a polit* [From Warsaw to Shanghai: Notes of a refugee]. Mexico: Shloyme Mendelson fond bay der gezelshaft far kultur un hilf, 1948.

Roznboym. Mikhl. *Ondenk-bukh fun Yisroel Khadash: Grinder un redaktor fun "Yidishe Tsaytung"* [Memorial book for Yisroel Khadash: Founder and editor of *Yidishe tsaytun*]. Tel Aviv: Nay Lebn, 1973.

Segalovitsh, Zusman. "Ševa haŠanim šeli beTel-Aviv" [My seven years in Tel Aviv]. Translated from the Yiddish by Gali Drucker Bar-Am. *Ho!* 16 (2018): 348–353.

Shamri, Arie. "Fayerung lekoved zekhtsik bend 'di goldene keyt.'" [Celebrating sixty volumes of *DGK*)]. *DGK* 62/63 (1968): 338–39.

———. "Bio-bibliografishe shtrikhn" [Bio-bibliographical characteristics], 1–6. In Aynzamlung [Anthology]. Tel Aviv: Yisroel-bukh, 1982.

Shpiglblat, Aleksander. *Durkh fareykherte shayblekh* [Through a smoked glass panel]. Tel Aviv: H. Leyvik, 2007.

Sutzkever, Avrom. "Briv fun Max Weinreich tsu Avrom Sutzkever (1/30/1947)" [Letter from Max Weinreich to Avrom Sutzkever [1/30/1947]], *DGK* 95–96 (1978): 174–177.

———. *Vilner geto: 1941–1944* [Vilna Ghetto: 1941–1944]. Paris: Farband fun di vilner in frankraykh, 1946.

Temqin-Berman, Batya. *Ir beTok̲ ir* [City within a city]. Translated by Uri Orlev. Tel Aviv: Am-Oved, 2008.

Tsalevitsh, Bentsl. "Mayne 35 yor in yisroel: Mayne ranglenishn far yidish un far bundizm" [My 35 years in Israel: My battles for Yiddish and for Bundism]. *LF* (1957): 14–17.

Studies in Yiddish

Erik, Max. *Di geshikhte fun der yidisher literatur fun di eltste tsaytn biz der haskole-tkufe* [History of Yiddish literature: From earliest times to the Haskalah period]. Varshe: Kultur-Lige, 1928.

Miron, Dan. *Der imazh fun shtetl: Dray literarishe shtudies* [The image of the shtetl: Three literary studies]. Tel Aviv: Y. L. Peretz, 1981.

Niger, Shmuel. *Dertseylers un romanistn* [Story writers and novelists]. New York: CYCO 1946.

———. *Shmuesn vegn bikher* [Conversations on books). New York: Yidish farlag, 1922.

———. *Yitskhok leybush Peretz: Tsu zayn hundertn geboyrntog, 1852–1952* [Yitskhok Leybush Peretz: For his hundredth birthday]. New York: CYCO, 1952.

Pilovski, Arye Leyb. *Tsvishn yo un neyn: Yidish un yidishe literatur in erets- yisroel, 1907–1948* [Between yes and no: Yiddish and its literature in mandate-Palestine, 1907–1948). Tel Aviv: Y. L. Peretz, 1986.

Rozhanski, Shmuel. "Di role fun varshe in der yidisher litertur" [The role of Warsaw in Yiddish literature]. In *Musterverk fun der yidisher literatur* [Masterpieces of Yiddish literature], vol. 80, edited by Shmuel Rozhanski, 5–18. Buenos Aires: Instituto Científico Judío IWO, 1979.

———. *Dos yidishe gedrukte vort un teater in argentine* [The Yiddish printed word and theater in Argentina]. Buenos Aires: A gezelshaftlekher komitet fun yoyvl bukh, 1941.

———. "Medinas yisroel in der yidisher literatur" [Israel in Yiddish literature]. In *Yidishe literatur-yidish lebn: Shraybers, bashraybers un vizyonern in unzer literatur-geshikhte* [Yiddish literature-Jewish/Yiddish life: Writers, describers, and visionaries in our literature-history], 616–19. Buenos Aires: A grupe fraynd fun der literatur gezelshaft baym IWO, 1973.

Shekhter, Mordekhe. "Dos yidish shebikhtav in erets-yisroel" [The written Yiddish in Israel], *Yidishe shprakh* 37, no. 1–3 (1978/1980): 1–23.

Shpiglblat, Aleksander. *Pinot kḥulot: Itzik Manger—ḥaim, šir uBalada* [Blue corners: Itzik Manger—life, poem and ballad]. Translated by Yehuda Gur-Arie. Jerusalem: Carmel, 2009.

Szeintuch, Yechiel. "Introduction." In *Der tunkeler: Sefer haHumoresqot waHaParodyiot haSifrutiyot baYidiš* [The dark one: The book of humoresques and literary parodies in Yiddish]. Jerusalem: Magnes, 1990.

Weinreich, Max. *Geshikhte fun der yidisher shprakh* [History of Yiddish language]. Vol. 1. New York: YIVO, 1973.

———. *Shturemvint: Bilder fun der yidisher geshikhte in zibtsntn yorhundert* [Strom wind: Images from Jewish history in the seventeenth century]. Vilne: Tamar, 1927.

Essays in Yiddish

Artuski, Y. "Der nitsokhn on sholem" [Victory without peace]. *LF* 188–89 (1967): 4.

———. "Di lektsiye fun yidishn khurbn" [The lesson of the Jewish destruction]. *LF* 92 (1959): 4–5.

———. "In an akhrayesfuler tsayt" [In a time filled with responsibility]. *LF* 1 (1951): 1.

———. "Rekht far yidish in shul?" [The right for Yiddish in school?]. *LF* 104 (1960): 11.

———. "Toda'a Yehudit tsi heymland gefil? Oder umvegn fun der yisroelsher yugnt" [Jewish consciousness or nationalism? Or the roundabout ways of the Israeli youth]. *LF* 79 (1958): 7.

———. "Tsi darf un tsi muz yidish untergeyn in yisroel?" [Ought and must Yiddish perish in Israel?]. *LF* 70–71 (1957): 8–10.

———. "Tsvantsik yor lebns-fragn" [Twenty years for *LF*]. *LF* 230–31 (1971): 4.

———. "Val-platform fun bund: Vos vil der bund in yisroel?" [The Bund's election platform: What does the Bund want in Israel?]. *LF* 95 (1959): 2.

Aykhnboym, Yisokher. "Undzer basheydener yubiley: 15 yor bundishe organizatsye un lebns-fragn in Yisroel [Our modest jubilee: 15 years for the Bund organization and *LF* in Israel]. *LF* 173 (1966): 5.
Bal-Makhshoves, "Dray shtetlekh" [Three towns]. In *Geklibene verk* [Collected works], 262–79. New York: Tsiko, 1953.
Bergelson, Dovid. "Dray tsentren" [Three centers]. *In shpan* 1 (1926): 84–96.
Birshteyn, Yosl. "Aspektn" [Aspects]. *Yung-yisroel* 2 (1956): 56.
———. "A yidisher shrayber in Kibbutz" [A Yiddish writer in a Kibbutz]. *DGK* 11 (1952): 165–66.
Drucker Bar-Am, Gali. "Tsvey Yosef Rotnberg" [Two Yosef Rotnberg]. *LF* 701–2 (2011): 19.
———. "Zayn a bundist in Yisroel: An interviyu mitn redaktor" [Being a Bundist in Israel: An interview with the editor]. *LF* 735–36 (2014): 39–41.
Edelman, Marek. "Azoy hobn mir gekemft kegn di daytshn" [How we fought the Germans]. *LN*, April 19, 1954, 3.
Faygnberg, Rokhl. "Berl Katsenelson der grinder fun 'Am 'Oved" [Berl Katznelson the founder of 'Am 'Oved']. *LN*, March 8, 1957, 5.
———. "Der plan fun Berl Katsenelson aroysgebn in hebreyish di yidishe literatur" [Ber Katznelson's plan to publish Yiddish literature in Hebrew]. *LN*, March 29, 1957, 5.
Grosman, Moyshe. "Borekh habo Itzik Manger!" [Welcome, Itzik Manger!]. *Heymish* 24 (1958): 1.
———. "Farlag Y. L. Peretz-bibliyotek in Yisroel" [The Y. L. Peretz Press in Israel]. *Heymish* 18 (1957): 19.
Gros-Tsimerman, Moyshe. "Yisroels-yidish" [Israeli-Yiddish]. In *Intimer videranand: Eseyen* [Intimate contradiction: Essays], 310–20. Tel Aviv: Y. L. Peretz, 1964.
Hayvel, Ben-Tsion. "Literatur, teater un kunst bay der sheyres-hapleyte: Yerlekher iberblik" [Literature, theater and art of the surviving remnants: Yearly review]. *Undzer veg* 129 (1947): 3–4.
Hofer, Yekhiel. "Yosef Rotnberg: Tsu zayn azoy fritsaytikn toyt" [Yosef Rotnberg: For his so-too-early death]. *Di Tsukunft* 65, no. 6–7 (1960): 292.
Kellman, Ellen. "Der groyser kundes un di shund-romanen in dem altn Forverts" [The big mischief and the sensation novels in the old *Forverts*]. *Di Tsukunft* 111 (2008): 10–19.
Kenig, Leo. "Vidergeburt fun folk un shprakh" [Rebirth of the people and their language]. *Di tsukunft* 60, no. 9 (1955): 399.
Kokhav, M. A. [Mordekhe-Arye Shtern]. "Tsi hobn mir take a literarishn nokhvuks?" [Do we indeed have a new literary growth?]. *LF* 1 (1952): 12.
Korn, Yitskhok. *Dos gerangl far yidish: Eseyen* [The struggle for Yiddish: Essays]. Tel Aviv: Veltrat far yidish un yidisher kultur, 1982.
Leshtshinski, Yankev. "A gaystiker denkmol far di khorev gevorene yidishe kehiles in eyrope" [A spiritual monument for the destroyed Jewish communities in Europe]. *LN*, July 13, 1951, 3.
Lev, Avrom. "Avrom Sutskever: A bintl dermonungen tsu zayn yubileum" [Avrom Sutskever: A bundle of memories for his jubilee]. *LF* 143–44 (1963): 15.
Levi, Ruven. "Di bikher produktsye in yisroel" [Book production in Israel]. *DGK* 1 (1949): 239–40.
Leybl, Daniel. "Di goldene keyt." *Neyevelt*, February 11, 1949, 4.
List, Nakhmen. "Af di khurves fun undzer akropol" [On the ruins of our Acropolis]. *LN*, April 22, 1960, 6.

Luden, Yitskhok. *In geyeg nokh momentn: Aktuele publitsistik fun hayntike un fun nekhtike teg* [In pursuit of the moment: Actual publications of todays and of yesterday]. Vol. 1. Tel Aviv: Leyvik, 2009.

———. "In vemens nomen? A por fragn tsum premiyer-minister ben guriyon" [In whose name? Questions for Prime-Minister Ben-Gurion]. *LN*, December 1, 1950, 3.

Mali, Malasha. "In leyter-brand fun gezangen" [The rise of the ignitable poetry]. *Yung-yisroel* 1 (1954): 23–26.

Man, Mendl. "Der yidisher shrayber in yisroel" [The Yiddish writer in Israel]. *Di Tsukunft* 64 (1959): 287.

Manger, Itzik. "Der Litvak un di landshaft" [The Litvak and the landscape], *Di Tsukunft* 59 (1954): 116–17.

Menes, Avrom. "Yidish folk, yidish loshn, yidish gloybn" [Jewish people, Yiddish language, Jewish belief]. *Di Tsukunft* 51 (1946): 423–26.

Niger, Shmuel. "Briv vegn der nayer yidisher literatur." [Letter on the new Yiddish literature]. *Di yudishe velt* 12 (1913): 50–59.

———. "Di goldene keyt." *Di tsukunft* 54 (1949): 310–14.

———. "Di yidishe inteligents un ire naye ufgabn" [The Yiddish intelligentsia and its new tasks]. *Di tsukunft* 50, no. 3 (1945): 141–43.

———. "Premirte dertseylungen," [Award-winning stories]. *Der tog-morgn zshurnal*, August 30, 1953.

Paner, Yitskhok. "Der Kibbutz on shminke" [The Kibbutz with no makeup]. *DGK* 31 (1958): 228–30.

Papiernikov, Levi. "Di shpil fun goyrl" [The game of fate]. *LF* 77 (1958): 11.

Pat, Yankev. "Yidishe un hebreyshe shrayber in medinas Yisroel" [Yiddish and Hebrew writers in Israel]. *Biyuletin fun alveltlekhn yidishn kultur-kongres* 13 (1957): 6.

Perlov, Yitskhok. "Der shrayber antloyft fun zayn dor" [The writer escapes his generation]. *LF* 18–19 (1952): 14.

Rapoport, Shiye. "Di shlikhes fun der yidisher literatur" [The mission of Yiddish literature]. *Di Tsukunft* 53, no. 7 (1948): 484.

Ravitsh, Meylekh. "Erev dem tsentn yortog fun varshever ufshtand" [Tenth memorial evening for the Warsaw uprising]. *LN*, November 14, 1952, 3.

Roskes, Dovid-hersh. "Di shrayber grupe yung-yisroel" [The writers group Young-Israel]. *Yugntruf* 28–29 (1973): 7–12; 33 (1975): 7–8; 34 (1976): 4–7.

Rozhanski, Shmuel. "In keyn land redt men nit azoyfil yidish vi in yisroel" [In no country is Yiddish spoken as much as in Israel]. *Biyuletin fun alveltlekhn yidishn kultur-kongres* [Bulletin of the World Congress for Yiddish/Jewish Culture] 11 (1957): 5.

———. "Yisroel un yidishe literatur" [Israel and Yiddish literature]. Lecture at the Jewish Public Library in Montreal, February 3, 1974.

Shamri, Arie. "Araynfir" [Introduction]. In *Vortslen: Antologye fun yidish-shafn in yisroel*, edited by Arie Shamri, 5–9. Tel Aviv: Yisroel-bukh, 1966.

———. Mi un uftu farn yidishn vort: 5 yor farlag 'yisroel-bukh'" [Toil and accomplishment for the Yiddish word: Five years for the "Israel-book" press]. In *Aynzamlung* [Anthology], 44–48. Tel Aviv: Yisroel-bukh, 1982.

Shpiglblat, Aleksander. "'DGK' un ir melukhishe maymed" [*DGK* and its national status]. *Yidishe Kultur* 1 (1990): 38–43.

Shpizman, Leyb. "Khalutsim far yidish" [Pioneers for Yiddish]. *Biyuletin fun alveltlekhn yidishn kultur-kongres* 16 (1958): 3.

Shtokfish, Dovid. "Landsmanshaftn in yisroel" [Hometown associations in Israel]. *Argentiner Yivo-shriftn* 15 (1989): 56–64.
Shvarts, Pinkhes. "Folkstsaytung" [People's newspaper]. In *Fun noentn over* [From the near past], vol. 2, 303–439. New York: Alveltlekhn yidishn kultur kongres, 1956.
Sutzkever, Avrom. "A por verter vegn unheyb" [A few words on beginning]. *DGK* 100 (1979): 3.
———. "A vort tsum poet" [A word to the poet]. *DGK* 31 (1958): 12–14.
———. "Der mishpet in yerusholoim" [The trial in Jerusalem]. *DGK* 40 (1961): 5.
———. "Fayerung lekoved 50 bend DGK" [Celebration honoring fifty volumes of *DGK*]. *DGK* 51 (1965): 233–36.
———. "Nit nor di yidn" [Not only the Jews]. *DGK* 1 (1949): 9.
———. "Tsum fuftsikstn numer" [For the fiftieth volume]. *DGK* 50 (1964): 4–5.
———. "Tsvey yor di goldene keyt" [Two years of *DGK*]. *DGK* 9 (1951): 214–15.
———. "Yisroel, der yidisher shrayber un di yidishe velt" [Israel, the Yiddish writer and the Jewish world]. *DGK* 19 (1954): 222–24.
Szeintuch, Yechiel. "Yidish limed in yiroelisher mitlshul-dertsiyung" [Yiddish learning in middle-school education in Israel]. *DGK* 91 (1976): 51–60.
Tsanin, Mordkhe. "A heym far yidisher kultur" [A home for Yiddish culture]. *LN*, January 21, 1955, 3.
———. "A sakh nit gemelte kinder ongekumen keyn yisroel" [Many uncircumcised children arrived in Israel]. *Forverts*, November 19, 1949.
———. "Der ufgang un untergang fun der yidisher prese in poyln [The rise and fall of Yiddish press in Poland]. *Kesher* 6 (1989): 112–15.
———. "Di 'aliya un der kultur-krizis" [The 'aliya and the culture crisis]. *LN*, July 13, 1951, 3.
———. "Di yidishe literatur un medinas-yisroel" [Yiddish literature and Israel]. *DGK* 66 (1969): 30–36.
———. "Eyn tog inem lebn fun a froy in Yisroel" [A day in the life of a woman in Israel]. *LN*, December 30, 1949, 4; *LN*, January 6, 1950, 3.
———. "Far vos zeks zaytn letste nayes?" [Why six pages to *Letste nayes*?]. *LN*, June 9, 1950, 3.
———. "Fayerung lekoved zekhtsik bend 'di goldene keyt'" [Celebrating sixty volumes of DGK]. *DGK* 62/63 (1968): 335–37.
———. "Geratevete yidn in yisroel gefinen zeyere payniker fun di lagern" [Jewish survivors in Israel find their torturers from the camps]. *Forverts*, November 19, 1950.
———. "Hefkeyres kegn di Letste nayes" [Wantonness against *Letste nayes*]. *LN*, June 30, 1950, 1.
———. "Hinershe bunkers in tel-oviv" [Bunkers of hen in Tel Aviv]. *LN*, March 3, 1950, 3.
———. "Kibets-golyes mit diskriminatsye: Ofener briv tsum premier-minister [An ingathering of exiles with discrimination: An open letter to the prime minister]. *LN*, July 14, 1950, 3.
———. "Naye imigrantn in di derfer un kolonyes fun yisroel: A nayer tip yishuvnikes—far vos zey viln nisht arayntretn in di kvutsot? Interesante geshprekhn mit yidishe dorfslayt arum Lod" [New immigrants in the villages and settlements in Israel: A new type of *yishuvniks*—why do they not want to join the groups? Interesting conversations with Jewish villagers from around Lod]. *Forverts*, October 9, 1949.
———. "Nisht keyn yom-tovdike shmuesn" [Conversations of an unhappy day]. *LN*, April 6, 1961, 2.
———. *Shabesdike Shmuesn* [Shabbat conversations]. Tel Aviv: Letste Nayes, 1957.
———. "Shikun 'olei Nashelsk" [The housing section of immigrants from Nashelsk]. *LN*, March 24, 1953, 2.

———. "Sholem Asch: A shmues mitn mayster fun der yidisher literatur, an araynfir tsu der parshe Asch" [Sholem Asch: A conversation with the master of Yiddish literature, an introduction to the Asch affair]. *LN*, November 12, 1954, 4.

———. "Sine un tsvies" [Hatred and hypocrisy]. *LN*, October 9, 1952, 2.

———. "Talpiyot" [Talpiyot [the name of a ma'abara in Jerusalem]]. *LN*, November 2, 1952, 2.

———. "Undzer hilf tsu a yungn talent in yisroel: Yehudit kern- dos vunderkind" [Our help to a young talent: Yehudit Kern the gifted child]. *LN*, December 12, 1952, 2.

———. "Unter di khurves fun yafo ligt undzer gevisn!" [Under the ruins of Jaffa lies our conscience!]. *LN*, April 21, 1950, 1.

———. "Vemen iz itst neytik der kamf kegn yidish" [Who needs now the battle against Yiddish?]. *LN*, May 26, 1950, 3.

———. "Yidish un yidishkeyt" [Yiddish and Yiddishkeyt]. *LN*, May 9, 1961, 1.

———. *Zumershney: Noveln, eseyen, reportazhn* [Summer-snow: Novellas, essays, reports], 168–78. Tel Aviv: H. Leyvik, 1992.

Tsharni, Daniel. "Vegn yidish in Yisroel un in der gorer velt" [On Yiddish in Israel and in the whole world]. *LN*, February 26, 1954, 5.

Turkov, Yonas. "Fun funkn—a flam" [From sparks—a flame]. *Folksblat* 2 (1958): 5.

Weichert, Michał. "Der gaystiker qliṭa-protses" [The intellectual absorption process]. *LN*, December 19, 1958, 3.

———. "Yidish-bibliyotekn in tel-oviv" [Yiddish libraries in Tel Aviv]. *LN*, September 25, 1959, 6.

Yasny, A. Volf. "A Byalistoker shtetl af yisroel erd" [A Bialystok-like town on Israeli land]. *LN*, May 10, 1961, 3.

———. "Ershtling verk fun a yungn mekhaber" [The first work of a young author]. *LN*, July 4, 1958, 5.

———. "Rand bamerkungen tsu der for-konferents fun di yidishe zshurnalistn" [Side-remarks for the preliminary conference of Yiddish journalists]. *LN*, December 30, 1960, 6.

———. "Yidish kinstlerishe proze af yisroel-tematik" [Yiddish artistic prose on the Israel-theme]. *Yisroel-shriftn* 1 (1954): 63–78.

———. "Yidish-sektor in der yosroel-kultur" [Yiddish sector in Israeli-culture]. *LN*, May 5, 1957, 6.

———. "Yisroel—der nayster yidish literatue-tsenter" [Israel—the newest Yiddish-literature center]. *LN*, November 6, 1953, 5.

———. "Yung-yisroel zogt zayn Yidish vort" [Young-Israel says its Yiddish word]. *LN*, February 4, 1955, 5.

Yofe, Mordkhe. "Tsen yor yidish-literatur un kultur in yisroel" [Ten years [of] Yiddish literature and culture in Israel]. *Jewish Book Annual* 19 (1958–59): 23–25.

Hebrew Fiction, Poetry, Essays, and Memoir Literature

[Anonymous]. "Yevul haSifrut beTašat tšṭ"w" [The literary yield of 1954–1955]. In *Sefer haŠana šel ha'Itona'im tšṭ"z"* [The 1955–1956 journalists' yearbook]. Tel Aviv: Agudat ha-'Etonaim, 1956, 179.

Balas, Shimon. *HaMa'abara* [The *ma'abara* [emigrant and refugee absorption camp]]. Tel Aviv: Am-Oved, 1964.

Bartov, Hanoch. *Šeš knafaim le'Eḥad* [*Each Had Six Wings*]. Merhavia: Sifriyat haPo'alim, 1954.

Bashan, Refael. *Siḥot ḥulin šel Waiṣman* [Weizmann's casual conversations]. Jerusalem: Mosad Bialik, 1963.

Bialik, H. N. "The City of Slaughter." Translated from the Hebrew by Israel Efros. In Complete Poetic Works of Hayim Nahman Bialik, vol. 1, 129–43, edited by Israel Efros. New York: Histadrut 'Ivrit of America, 1948.

Brenner, Yosef Haim. "HaŽaner ha'Ereṣ-yiśra'eli we'Avizarehu" [The Eretz-Israeli genre and its accoutrements]. In *Kol kitvei Y. H. Brenner* [Complete works of Y. H. Brenner], vol. 8. Tel Aviv: Shtibel, 1937.

Elkoshi, Gedalia. "Yevul sifrutenu biŠnat taši"a" [The yield of our literature in the Hebrew year taši"a [1950–1951]]. *Taw šin yod bet: Šnaton davar* [1951–1952: The Davar annual publication]. Tel Aviv: Davar, 1951.

Feldman, Nira. "Lama we'Eiḥ ḥevra zoḵeret" [Why and how a community remembers]. In *Liqro' qirot: Mismaḵ tarbuti ḥazuti* [Reading walls: A visual cultural document], edited by Ziona Shimshi and Dalit Lahav, 12–14. Ra'anana: Even Hoshen, 2007.

ha-Levi, Judah. "Zion, Won't You Ask." In *Poems from the Diwan*, translated by Gabriel Levin, 100–102. London: Anvil Press Poetry, 2002.

———. "Zion, Won't You Ask." In *Lider fun hurbn un lider fun gloybn* [Poems of the Holocaust and poems of faith], vol. 2., translated by Arn Tseytlin, 349–51. New York: Bergen Belsen Memorial Press, 1970.

Hendel, Yehudit. *'Anašim 'aḥerim hem* [They are different people]. Merhavia: Sifriyat haPo'alim, 1950.

Hirshfeld, Ariel. *Rešimot 'al maqom* [Local notes]. Tel Aviv: Am-Oved, 2000.

Levin, Yisrael, ed. *Yehuda haLewi: Poems*. Tel Aviv: Tel Aviv University Press, 2007.

Margoshes Shmuel. "Tafqida šel ha'Itonut haYidit" [The role of the Yiddish press]. *Korot ha'Itona'im haYehudim* [The annals of Jewish journalists] 6 (1964): 13.

Meged, Aharon. *Ḥedwa we'Ani uFarašat qoroteynu ba'Ir tel-'aviv* [Hedva and I and the story of what happened to us in the city of Tel Aviv]. Tel Aviv: Hakibbutz Hameuchad, 1955.

Mer, Benny. "Kh'hob zikh yorn gevalgert: maqor weTargum" [For Years I Wandered: Original and translation]. *Davke* 3 (2006): 56–57.

Mossinson, Yigal. *Dereḵ Gever* [A man's way]. Tel Aviv: Tberski, 1953.

Oz, Amos. *Elsewhere, Perhaps*. Translated from the Hebrew by Nicholas de Lange in collaboration with the author. New York: Harcourt Brace Jovanovich, 1973.

Pilpel, Shai. "Liṭa' lo reḥoqa miPo" [Lithuania is not far from here]. Accessed March 30, 2024. https://kehilalinks.jewishgen.org/mazeikiai/Lipnitzky2.doc.html. Rozental, Rubik. "Ma ta'aśe haIvrit bli lehašviṣ, lenadned uLeqaṭer?" [What will Hebrew do without "boasting," "nagging," "complaining"?]. *Davka* 1 (2006): 4–6.

Shamir, Moshe. *Hu halaḵ baŚadot* [He walked through the fields]. Merhavia: Sifriyat haPo'alim, 1947.

Shoham, Snunit. "Sifria beLev 'Ir" [A library in the heart of the city]. In *'Ir waSefer: Sifriyat ša'ar ṣion-beit 'ari'ela* [City and book: The Sha'ar Zion-Beit Ariela Library], edited by Ora Ahimeir, 80–95. Jerusalem: Keter, 1987.

Tartakower, Aryeh. *HaḤevra haYehudit* [Jewish society]. Tel Aviv: Masada, 1957.

Temqin-Berman, Batya. "Sifriyot yehudiot beWarša" [Jewish libraries in Warsaw]. *Yad laKore* 3–4 (1953): 145–56.

Yizhar, S. *'Arba'ah Sipurim* [Four stories]. Tel Aviv: Hakibbutz Hameuchad, 1959.

———. *Ḥirbet Ḥiz'eh*. Translated by Nicholas de Lange and Yaacob Dweck. Jerusalem: Ibis, 2008.

———. *Yemei Ṣiqlag* [Days of Ziklag]. Tel Aviv: Am-Oved, 1958.

Academic Studies

In Hebrew or Hebrew Translation

Avital-Florsheim, Ella. "Hanṣaḥa be'Emṣaut te'ud viYeṣira: Ha'Yiton *undzer shtime* miMaḥane ha'Aqira Bergen Belsen, 1945–1947" [Memorialization through documentation and creative production: the paper *undzer shtime* [our voice] from the DP camp Bergen-Belsen, 1945–1947]. Master's thesis, Hebrew University, Jerusalem, 2003.

Azaryahu, Ma'oz. *Tel 'Aviv ha'Ir ha'Amitit: Mitografiya hisṭorit* [Tel Aviv the real city: A historical mythography]. Be'er Sheva: Ben Gurion University Press, 2005.

Baki, Roberto. "Tḥiyat haLašon ha'Ivrit be'Aspaqlariya sṭaṭisṭit" [Revival of the Hebrew language in a statistical view]. *Leshonenu* 21, no. 1 (1958): 10.

Baleslav, Yaron. "He'Aśor haRišon leHitpatḥut śḵunot Tel Aviv šeMe'ever laYarqon 1947–1958" [The first decade of development of the neighborhoods of Tel Aviv beyond the Yarqon stream]. *'Eyunim biTqumat Yisrael* 23 (2013): 252–53.

Bar, Doron. "Le'an nifne beYom haŠoa'? 'Ya'ar haQdošim' weHaHitlabṭut beŠe'elat hanṣaḥat haŠoa'" [Where shall we turn on the Holocaust remembrance day? The "Forest of the Martyrs" and the ambivalence regarding the question of Holocaust commemoration]. *Catedra* 140 (2011): 103–30.

Bartal, Israel. *Qozaq uBedwi* [Cossack and Bedouin]. Tel Aviv: Am-Oved, 2007.

Bassok, Ido. "Tnu'ot haNo'ar haYehudiyot bePolin beyn štey milḥemot ha'Olem" [Jewish youth movements in Poland between the two world wars]. In Novershtern, *'Alilot ne'urim*, 769–792.

Bassok, Ido, and Avraham Novershtern. "Ma'rḵot haḤinuḵ liYehudei Polin beyn štey milḥemot ha'Olem" [The education systems for Polish Jews between world wars]. In Novershtern, *'Alilot ne'urim*, 731–64.

Benjamin, Walter. "Šuvo šel haMešoṭeṭ" [Return of the wanderer]. Translated by David Zinger. In *Mivḥar ktavim*, vol. 1, 100–104. Tel Aviv: Hakibbutz Hameuchad, 1992.

Berzak, Ori. "Nawad Šorši: Tmurot beNof haDqalim beMerḥavei 'Ereṣ Yiśra'el beMahalaḵ haMe'a haEśrim" [A rooted nomad: Changes in the landscape of palm trees in the Land of Israel during the twentieth century]. MA thesis, Haifa University, 2003.

Blatman, Daniel. "HaBund: Mitos haMahapeḵa we'Avodat haYomyom" [The Bund: The myth of revolution and the work of the everyday]. In *Qiyum waŠever: Yehudei polin leDoroteihem* [Exitance and rupture: The Jews of Poland over the generations], vol. 2, edited by Israel Bartal and Israel Gutman, 521–28. Jerusalem: Zalman Shazar, 2001.

Chaver, Yael. *Ma šeḤayavim liškoaḥ: Yidiš baYešuv heḤadaš* [That which must be forgotten: Yiddish in the new Yishuv]. Jerusalem: Yad Ben-Zvi, 2005.

Cohen, Bo'az. *HaDorot haBai'm—eiḵeḵa yed'u? Leidato weHitpatḥuto šel ḥeqer haŠoa' haYiśra'eli* [The next generations—how will they know? The birth and evolution of Israeli Holocaust studies]. Jerusalem: Yad Vashem, 2010.

Cohen, Hagit. *Nifla'ot ba'Olam heḤadaš: Sfarim weQori'm be'Arṣot haBrit, 1890–1940* [Wonders of the New World: Books and readers in Yiddish in the United States, 1890–1940]. Ra'anana: Open University Press, 2016.

Cohen, Nathan. "'Itonut yomit yehudit bePolin" [Daily Jewish press in Poland]. In *Qiyum waŠever: Yehudei polin leDoroteihem* [Exitance and rupture: The Jews of Poland over the generations], vol. 2, edited by Israel Bartal and Israel Gutman, 301–26. Jerusalem: Zalman Shazar, 2001.

———. *Sefer sofer ve'Iton: Merqaz haTarbut haYehudit beVarša, 1918–1942* [Books, writers and newspapers: The Jewish culture center in Warsaw, 1918–1942]. Jerusalem: Magnes, 2003.

———. "Sifriot yehudiot weKor'eyhen bePolin beyn štey milḥamot ha'Olam" [Jewish libraries and their readers between the two world wars]. *Zion* 67 (2002): 163–88.

Drucker Bar-Am, Gali. "BeQolam uVisfatam: Yiśra'el biRe'i śiporet yidiś šeNik̲teva beYiśra'el biYedey oley šeerit haPleṭa" [In their voice and in their language: Israel through the prism of Yiddish fiction written in Israel by members of Sheerit haPleta]. In *Yiśra'el be'Eyney niṣoley hašoa' weŚordea* [Israel in the eyes of the survivors of the Holocaust], edited by Dalia Ofer, 353–81. Jerusalem: Yad Vashem, 2015.

———. "Mas'a bein 'masoes': Diyun hašwa'ati bišloš girsa'ot 'masa'ot binyamin haŠliši' me'et mendele moykher sforim." [Travelling through The Travels: A comparative study of three versions of The Travels of Benjamin III by Mendele Moykher Sforim]. *Jerusalem Studies in Hebrew Literature* 14 (2011): 93–124.

———. "Sifrut yiśra'elit, sifrut Yehudit: HaMenifesṭim šel ḥavurat 'liqra't' veŠel ḥavurat yung yisroel" [Israeli literature, Jewish literature: The manifestos of the Liqrat group and the Young-Israel group]. Seminar paper submitted as part of the MA studies program, Tel Aviv, 2007.

Drucker Bar-Am, Gali, and Yitskhok Luden. "Lebens Fragen: An Introduction." National Library Newspaper Collection, accessed March 29, 2024. http://web.nli.org.il/sites/JPress/Hebrew/Pages/Lebens-Fragen.aspx.

Dubnow, Simon. *Divrey yemei 'am olam: Toldot 'am Yiśra'el miYemei qedem 'ad haYom haZe* [History of the eternal nation: The annals of the Jewish people from antiquity to this day]. Tel Aviv: Dvir, 1958, 1.

Even-Zohar, Itamar. "HaSifrut ha'Ivrit haYiśra'elit: Model hisṭori" [Israeli Hebrew literature: A historical model]. *HaSifrut* 4 (1973): 427–40.

———. "HaṢmiḥa weHaHitgabšut šel tarbut 'ivrit meqomit be'Ereṣ Yiśra'el, 1882–1948" [The growth and establishment of local Hebrew culture in mandatory Palestine, 1882–1948)]. *Katedra* 16 (1980): 165–206.

Florsheim, Ella. *Tarbut yidiś beMaḥanot ha'Aqurim* [Yiddish culture in the DP camps]. Jerusalem: Zalman Shazar and Yad Vashem, 2020.

Friedman Cohen, Carrie. "Rokhl Oyerbakh: Rašey praqim leḤeker ḥayea veYeṣirata" [Rokhl Oyerbakh: Outline of her life and work]. *Huliyot* 9 (2005): 297–304.

Garncarska-Qadary, Bina. *Ḥelqam šel haYehudim beHitpatḥut haTa'aśiya šel warša baŠanim, 1816/20–1914* [The role of the Jews in the development of Warsaw's industry, 1816/20–1914]. Tel Aviv: Ha-Machon le-Heker ha-Tfutsot, ha-Merkaz le-Heker toldot ha-Yehudim be-Polin u-Morashtam, 1985.

Gelbar, Yoav. *Moledet Ḥadaša: 'Aliyat yehudei merkaz 'eropa uQliṭatam, 1933–1948* [A new homeland: The 'aliya and absorption of the Jews of central Europe, 1933–1948]. Jerusalem: Yad Ben-Zvi, 1990.

Govrin, Nurit. *Brenner: 'Oved 'eṣot uMore derek̲* [Brenner: "Nonplussed" and mentor]. Tel Aviv: Misrad Ha-Bitahon, 1991.

Gurevitch, Zali. *'Al haMaqom* [On the place]. Tel Aviv: Am-Oved, 2007.

Gutman, Israel. "HaŠoa' weRišuma beToldot 'am yiśra'el" [The Holocaust and its significance in the history of the Jewish people]. In *Sugiot beḤeqer haŠoa': Biqoret veTruma* [Issues in Holocaust scholarship: Critique and contribution], ed. Israel Gutman, 17–40. Jerusalem: Zalman Shazar, 2008.

———. "Šèerit haPleṭa: Be'ayiot weHavharot" [The surviving remnant: Problems and clarifications]. In *Šèerit haPleṭa, 1944–1948: HaŠiqum weHamàvaq haPoliṭi* [The surviving remnant, 1944–1948: The rehabilitation and political struggle], edited by Israel Gutman et al., 461–79. Jerusalem: Yad Vashem, 1990.

Hacohen, Dvora. *'Olim biSe'ara: Ha'Aliya haGdola uQliṭata beYiśra'el, 1948–1953* [Immigrants in turmoil: The great wave of immigration to Israel and its absorption, 1948–1953]. Jerusalem: Yad Ben-Zvi, 1994.

Halperin, Hagit. *HaMa'esṭro: Ḥayav viYeṣirato šel 'Avraham Šlonsqi* [The maestro: The life and work of Avraham Shlonsky]. Tel Aviv: Sifriyat Po'alim, 2011.

Haršav, Binyamin. *Lašon biYemei mahapeḵa: HaMahapeḵa haYehudit haModernit weTḥiyat haLašon ha'Ivrit.* [Language in revolutionary times: The modern Jewish revolution and the revival of the Hebrew language]. Jerusalem: Carmel, 2008.

Hasan-Rokem, Galit. "HaQrav bein Liviatan veHaYehudi haNoded: Raa'yion haMedina šel Qarl Šmidṭ veHaFolqlor haEropi" [The battle between Leviathan and the wandering Jew: Carl Schmitt's idea of the state and European folklore]. In *Folqlor ve'Idiologia* [Folklore and ideology], edited by Haya Bar-Yitzhak, 91–92. Haifa: Pardes, 2014.

Herman, Shimon. "Ḥaqirot baPsiḵologya haḤevratit šel bḥirat haLašon beYiśrael" [Studies in the social psychology of language choice in Israel]. In *'Olim beYiśrael: Miqra'a* [Newcomers to Israel: A reader], edited by Moshe Lissak et al., 419–36. Jerusalem: Academon, 1969.

Hever, Hannan. *HaSipur weHaLe'om: Qri'ot biqortiyot beQ'anon haSiporet ha'Ivrit* [Narrative and the nation: Critical readings in the canon of Hebrew fiction]. Tel Aviv: Resling, 2007.

Holzman, Avner. *'Ahavot Ṣion: Panim baSifrut ha'Ivrit haḤadaša* [Loves of Zion: Studies in modern Hebrew literature]. Jerusalem: Carmel, 2006.

———. "LiŠe'elat haŠimuš baMunaḥ 'impresionizm beMaḥševet haSifrut" [On the question of the use of the term "impressionism" in literary thought]. In *Mel'eḵet maḥševet tḥiyat ha'Uma: HaSifrut ha'Ivrit leNoḵaḥ ha'Omanut haPlasṭit* [Aesthetics and national revival: Hebrew literature against the visual arts], 280–94. Haifa: Zmora-Bitan and Haifa University Press, 1999.

Laor, Dan. "Bein meṣiut leḤazon: 'Al hištaqfuta šel ha'Aliya haHamonit baRoman haYiśra'eli" [Between reality and vision: Reflections of the massive immigration in the Israeli novel]. In *'Olim uMa'abarot, 1948–1952* ['Olim and ma'abarot, 1948–1952], edited by Mordechai Naor, 205–25. Jerusalem: Yad Ben-Zvi, 1986.

———. "Ha'Aliya haHamonit keToḵen uKeNośe baSifrut ha'Ivrit" [The mass immigration as content and subject in Hebrew literature in the first years of statehood]. *HaZiyonut* 14 (1989): 161–75.

Leshtshinski, Yankev. "HaBehala miSviv leYidiš" [The frenzy around Yiddish-speaking]. *Gesher* 1 (1960):114.

———. *HaPzura haYehudit* [The Jewish Diaspora]. Translated by Moshe Horovitz. Jerusalem: Ha-Mahlaka le-Hinuch u-le-Tarbut ba-Gola shel ha-Histadrut ha-Zionit ha-'Olamit, 1961.

Limor, Yechiel. "'Itonut, radio veṬeleviziya" [Press, Radio and Television]. In *The Hebrew Encyclopedia*, vol. 6, edited by Benzion Netanyahu. Tel Aviv: Encyclopedia Publishing Company, 1970: 1011–15.

Limor, Yechiel, and Dan Caspi. "Ṣmiḥat ha'itonut haLo'zit uDeiḥata" [The rise and the fall of the foreign-language press]. In *HaMetavḵim: 'Emṣaey haTiqšoret beYiśra'el, 1948–1990* [The mediators: Mass media in Israel, 1948–1990], edited by Yechiel Limor and Dan Caspi, 49–51. Tel Aviv: Am-Oved, 1992.

Lissak, Moshe. "'Ereṣ Yiśra'el haRišona' we'Ereṣ Yiśra'el haŠnia': Tahaliḵim mu'aṣim šel qiṭuv ḥevrati-tarbuti biŠnot haḤamišim" [The "first Israel" and the "second Israel": Accelerated processes of social-cultural polarization in the nineteen fifties]. In *Bein 'Olim leWatiqim: Yiśra'el ba'Aliya haGdola, 1948–1953* [Between new immigrants and old-timers: Israel in the great wave of immigration, 1948–1953], edited by Dalia Ofer, 1-8, 83–84. Jerusalem: Yad Ben-Zvi, 1996.

———. *Ha'Aliya haGdola biŠnot haḤamišim: Kišlono šel kur haHituḵ* [The mass immigration of the 1950s: The failure of the melting pot]. Jerusalem: Bialik Institute, 1999.

Manor, Ehud. "Abe Kahan keMetaqen 'olam: 'Eiyun beDarko haPoliṭit waHa'Etonait šel 'oreḵ haForverts" [Abe Kahan as a "perfecter of the world": A study of the political and journalistic vision and activities of the editor of *Forverts*]. *Kesher* 32 (2002): 64–74.

Menahem, Gila, and Efraim Ya'ar. "Mehagrim, pliṭim weNiṣolim beYiśra'el: HaDor haRišon weHašeni" [Immigrants, refugees, and survivors in Israel: The first and second generation]. In *Bein 'Olim leWatiqim: Yiśra'el ba'Aliya haGdola, 1948–1953* [Between new immigrants and old-timers: Israel in the great wave of immigration, 1948–1953], edited by Dalia Ofer, 191–209. Jerusalem: Yad Ben-Zvi, 1996.

Menda-Levy, 'Oded. *Liqro' 'et ha'Ir: HaḤawaya ha'Urbanit baSiporet ha'Ivrit me'Emṣ'a haMe'a ha-19 'ad 'emṣ'a haMe'a ha-20* [Reading the city: The urban experience in Hebrew fiction from the mid-nineteenth century to the mid-twentieth century]. Tel Aviv: Ha-Kibbutz Hameuchad, 2010.

Miron, Dan. *Bein Ḥazon le'Emet: Niṣanei haRoman ha'Ivri veHa'Idi baMe'a haTš'a 'eśre* [From romance to the novel: Studies in the emergence of the Hebrew and Yiddish novel in the nineteenth century]. Jerusalem: Mosad Bialik, 1979.

———. *Bodedim beMo'adam: LiDmuta šel haRepubliqa haSifrutit ha'Ivrit biTḥilat haMea' haEsrim* [When loners come together: A portrait of Hebrew literature at the turn of the twentieth century]. Tel Aviv: Am-Oved, 1987.

Miron, Guy. "Lašon, tarbut uMerḥav: Etgerei haHistoryografia haYehudit be'Edan haTafniyot" [Language, culture and space: The challenges of Jewish historiography in the age of the "turns"]. *Zion* 76 (2011): 63–94.

———. "Legaśer 'al pnei tehom- ḥeqer haŠo'a mul ḥeqer toldot Yiśra'el" [Bridging the divide: Holocaust versus Jewish history research—problems and challenges]. *Yad Vashem Studies* 38, no. 2 (2011): 155–93 (Hebrew version 129–60).

———. *Mi "Šam" le "Kan" beGuf rišon: Ziḵronoteyhem šel ioṣey germania beYiśra'el* [From "there" to "here" in the first person: The memories of Jews of German origin in Israel]. Jerusalem: Magnes, 2004.

Naor, Mordechai. "Ha'Itonut biŠnot haḤamišim" [The press in the fifties]. In *He'Aśor haRišon: 1948–1958* [The first decade: 1948–1958], edited by Zvi Zameret and Hanna Yablonka, 219–20. Jerusalem: Yad Ben-Zvi, 1998.

Neiger, Moti. *Moṣi'im la'Or kiMetavḵei tarbut: Hisṭoria tarbutit šel mea' šnot mol"ut 'ivrit beYiśra'el, 1910–2010* [Publishers as cultural mediators: A cultural history of 100 years of Hebrew publishing, 1910–2010]. Jerusalem: Man, 2017.

Novershtern, Avraham, ed. *'Alilot ne'urim: Oṭobiyografiot šel bnei ne'urim miPolin bein štey milḥemot ha'Olem* [Tales of youth: Autobiographies of youth from Poland between the two world wars]. Jerusalem: Zalman Shazar, 2011.

———. "'Aspeqṭim mivniyim baProza šel dawid bergelson meRešita we'Ad '"midat haDin'" [Structural aspects in Dovid Bergelson's prose from its beginnings to *Midat haDin*]. PhD diss., Hebrew University of Jerusalem, 1981.

———. *'Avraham Sutskever biMl'ot lo šiv'im* [Avraham Sutzkever on his seventieth birthday]. [In Hebrew and Yiddish.] Jerusalem: Beit ha-Sfarim ha-Le'umi ve-ha-Universitai, 1984.

———. "Dimuya šel wilna beŠirat yidiš bein štey milḥemot ha'Olam" [The image of Vilna in Yiddish poetry between the two world wars]. In *MiWilna leYerušalaim: Meḥqarim be-*

Toldoteyhem uVeTarbutam šel yehudei mizraḥ 'eropa mugašim leProfesor Šmu'el Werses [From Vilna to Jerusalem: Studies in the annals and culture of Eastern European Jews presented to Professor Shmuel Werses], edited by David Assaf et al., 505–11. Jerusalem: Magnes, 2002.

———. "HaQolot weHaMaqhela: Širat našim beYidiš beyn štey milḥemot ha'Olam" [The voices and the choir: Women's poetry in Yiddish between two world wars]. *Bikoret Uparshanut* 40 (2008): 61–145.

———. *Kan gar ha'Am haYehudi: Sifrut yidiš beArṣot haBrit* [Here dwells the Jewish people: A century of American Yiddish literature]. Jerusalem: Magnes, 2015.

———. "Meḥolat haMawet" [Dance of death]. *Huliyot* 1 (1993): 93–123.

———. *Qesem haDimdumim: Epoqalipsa uMešiḥiut beSifrut Yidiš* [The lure of twilight: Apocalypse and messianism in Yiddish literature]. Jerusalem: Magnes, 2003.

———. "Sifrut uPolitiqa biYeṣirata šel qvuṣat 'yung-vilne'" [Literature and politics in work of the Young-vilne group]. In *Beyn štey milḥemot 'olam: Praqim beḤayei haTarbut šel yehudei polin liLšonoteyhem* [Between two world wars: Chapters in the cultural life of Jews in Poland in their languages], edited by Khone Shmeruk and Shmuel Werses, 169–81. Jerusalem: Magnes, 1997.

———. "Smiḥatan šel sifrut weTarbut yidiš haModerniot" [The rise of modern Yiddish literature and culture]. In *Toldot yehudei Rusia* [The history of the Jews of Russia], vol. 2, edited by Ilya Luria, 333–63. Jerusalem: Zalman Shazar, 2012.

Ofer, Dalia. "Ma we'Ad kama lizkor meHaŠoa': Zikron haŠoa' biMdinat Yiśra'el ba'Aśor haRišon leQiuma" [What and how much to remember of the Holocaust: Commemorating the Holocaust during the first decade of Israel]. In *Aṣmaut: 50 haŠanin haRišonot* [Independence: The first 50 years], edited by Anita Shapira, 171–93. Jerusalem: Zalman Shazar, 1998.

———. "Niṣolim qe'Olim: HaMiqre šel 'aṣurey qafrisin" [Holocaust survivors as immigrants: The case of Israel and the Cyprus detainees]. In *Briḥim šel štika: Še'erit haPleta ve'Ereṣ Yiśrael* [Bonds of silence: The surviving remnants and mandatory Palestine], edited by Yoel Rappel. *Mesua* 28 (2000): 225.

———. "Watiqim we'Olim ba'Aliya haGdola" [Old-timers and new immigrants in the great wave of immigration]. In *Bein 'Olim leWatiqim: Yiśra'el ba'Aliya haGdola, 1948–1953* [Between new immigrants and old-timers: Israel in the great wave of immigration, 1948–1953], edited by Dalia Ofer, 7–8. Jerusalem: Yad Ben-Zvi, 1996.

Orhan, Nurit. *Yoṣ'ot me'Arba''amot: Našim kotvot baEmperiya haRusit* [Staking a claim: Women writing in the Yiddish press in Tsarist Russia]. Jerusalem: Zalman Shazar, 2013.

Pilovski, Arye Leyb. "Yidiš weSifruta be'Ereṣ Yiśra'el, 1907–1948" [Yiddish and its literature in Eretz Yisrael, 1907–1948]. PhD diss., the Hebrew University, 1980.

Razi, Tammy. *Yaldey haHefqer: HeḤaṣer ha'Aḥorit šel tel-'aviv haMandaṭorit* [Forsaken children: The backyard of mandatory Tel Aviv]. Tel Aviv: Am-Oved, 2009.

Rotman, Diego. *HaBima keVayt 'ar'i: HaTe'aṭron šel Džigan weŠumaker, 1927–1980* [The stage as a temporary home: On Dzhigan and Shumakher's theater, 1927–1980]. Jerusalem: Magness, 2017.

Rojanski, Rachel. "HaOmnam śafa zara weṢoremet'? LiŠe'elat yaḥaso šel Ben-Gurion leYidiś leAḥar haŠoa' [Indeed a "foreign and grating language"? On the question of Ben-Gurion's relationship to Yiddish after the Holocaust]. *Iyunim bi-Tkumat Yisrael* 15 (2005): 463–82.

———. "HaTarbut šelanu hi' haMedina šelanu: Meqoma šel medinat yiśra'el baDiyun 'al 'aṭid haYidiš 'aḥrei haŠoa'" [Our culture is our state: The place of Israel in the debate over the future of Yiddish after the Holocaust]. *Zmanim* 113 (2011): 68–77.

———. "Meruṣa meHaSṭen šela" [Happy with her sten gun]. *Davka* 3 (2007): 44.

Schein, Ada. "Bne beytḵa beQarov: Še'erit haPleṭa baHityašvut haMošavit, 1944–1955" [Build your home soon: The surviving remnant in the Moshavim settlements, 1944–1955]. In *"WeYašavtem beṭaḥ": Niṣoley haŠoa' baHityašvut ha'Ovedet, 1945–1955* ["Dwell in safety": Holocaust survivors in the labor settlement, 1945–1955], edited by Shlomo Bar-Gil and Ada Schein, 143–346. Jerusalem: Yad Vashem, 2010.

Schidorsky, Dov. *Gvilim nisrafim ve'Otiyot porḥot: Toldoteyhem šel osfey sfarim veSifriyot be'Ereṣ yiśrael veNisyonot leHaṣalat śrideyhem le'Aḥar haŠo'a* [Burning scrolls and soaring letters: The history of book collections and libraries in mandatory Palestine and the efforts to save their remnants after the Holocaust]. Jerusalem: Magnes, 2008.

Schirmann, Hayyim. "Targumei Ṣion halo tiš'ali leYehuda haLewi: Rešima bibliografit" [The translations of Judah Ha-Levi's "Zion, Won't You Ask": A bibliography]. *Kiryat Sefer* 15 (1939): 360–67.

Sha'ari, David. "Yiḥuda šel še'erit haPleṭa" [The uniqueness of the surviving remnant]. In *Briḥim šel štiqa: Še'erit haPleṭa we'Ereṣ Yiśra'el* [Bonds of silence: The surviving remnants and mandatory Palestine], edited by Yoel Rappel. *Mesua* 28 (2000): 21–52.

Shaked, Gershon. "Bein haKotel uVein meṣada: HaŠoa' weHatoda'a ha'Aṣmit šel haḤevra haYiśra'elit" [Between the Wailing Wall and Masada: The Holocaust and Israeli society's self-awareness]. In *Tmurot yesod ba'Am haYehudi be'Iqvot haŠoa'* [Major changes within the Jewish people in the wake of the Holocaust], edited by Israel Gutman, 511–23. Jerusalem: Yad Vashem, 1996.

———. *HaSiporet ha'Ivrit, 1880–1980* [Hebrew fiction, 1880–1980]. Vol. 2. Tel Aviv: Hakibbutz Hameuchad, 1977.

———. *HaSiporet ha'Ivrit, 1880–1980* [Hebrew fiction, 1880–1980]. Vol. 3. Tel Aviv: Hakibbutz Hameuchad, 1988.

———. *HaSiporet ha'Ivrit, 1880–1980* [Hebrew fiction, 1880–1980]. Vol. 4. Tel Aviv: Hakibbutz Hameuchad, 1993.

Shapira, Anita. *Yehudim, ṣionim uMa šeBeynehem* [Jews, Zionists, and in-between]. Tel Aviv: Am-Oved, 2007.

Shavit, Ya'akov, and Gid'on Biger. *HaHisṭoria šel Tel 'aviv* [The history of Tel Aviv]. Vol. 2. Tel Aviv: Ramot, 2007.

Shavit, Zohar. *HaḤaim hasifrutiyim be'Ereṣ Yiśra'el, 1910–1933* [The literary life in mandatory Palestine, 1910–1933]. Tel Aviv: Hakibbutz Hameuchad, 1982.

Shmeruk, Khone. *HaQri'a leNavi': Meḥqerey historia weSifrut* [The calling for a prophet: Studies of history and literature]. Jerusalem: Zalman Shazar, 1999.

———. "Ivrit-yidiš-polanit: Tarbut Yehudit tlat-lešonit" [Hebrew-Yiddish-Polish: Tri-lingual Jewish culture]. In *Beyn štey milḥemot 'olam: Praqim beḤayei haTarbut šel yehudei polin liLšonoteyhem* [Between two world wars: Chapters in the cultural life of Jews in Poland in their languages], edited by Khone Shmeruk and Shmuel Werses, 9–33. Jerusalem: Magnes, 1997.

———. "Qawim leToldot haMerkaz šel sifrut yidiš beWarša" [Aspects of the history of Warsaw as a Yiddish literary center]. In *Beyn štey milḥemot 'olam: Praqim beḤayei haTarbut šel yehudei polin liLšonoteyhem* [Between two world wars: Chapters in the

cultural life of Jews in Poland in their languages], edited by Khone Shmeruk and Shmuel Werses, 157–68. Jerusalem: Magnes, 1997.
———. "Yiddish." In *The Hebrew Encyclopedia*, vol. 19, 783–810. edited by Yeshayahu Leibowitz. Tel Aviv: Encyclopedia Publishing Company, 1968.
Slutsky, Yehuda. *Ha'Etonut haYehudit-rusit baMea' haTša'-'esre* [The Jewish-Russian press in the nineteenth century]. Jerusalem: Mosad Bialik, 1975.
Soker-Schwager, Hanna. *Meḵašef haŠeveṭ miMe'onot ha'Ovdim: Ya'aqov Šabt'ai baTarbut haYiśra'elit* [The wizard of the tribe from the worker's housing]. Tel Aviv: Hakibbutz Hameuchad, 2007.
Stauber, Roni. *HaLeqaḥ laDor: Šoa' uGvura baMaḥšava haŞiburit ba'Areş bišnot haḤamišim* [A lesson for this generation: Holocaust and heroism in Israeli public discourse in the 1950s]. Jerusalem: Yad Ben-zvi, 2000.
Szeintuch, Yechiel. *Yišayahu Špigl: Proza sipurit miGeṭo Lodž* [Yišayahu Špigl: Yiddish narrative prose from the Lodzh Ghetto]. Jerusalem: Magnes, 1995.
Tsamriyon, Tsemah. *Ha'Itonut šel Še'erit-haPleṭa beGermanya keVitui leBa'ayoteha* [The surviving remnants' press as an expression of its problems]. Tel Aviv: Irgun Sheerit-haPleta me-ha-Ezor ha-Briti Bergen-Belzen beYisrael, 1970.
Vinitzky-Seroussi, Vered. "Commemorating a Difficult Past: Yitzhak Rabin's Memorials." *American Sociological Review* 67, no. 1 (2002): 30- 51.
Weitz, Yechiam. "'Avi 'avot haQonşenzus: Lewi 'Eškol, ha'Iš weZmano" [The grandfather of the consensus: The life and times of Levi Eshkol]. In *He'Aśor haŠeni: 1958–1968* [The second decade: 1958–1968], edited by Zvi Zameret and Hanna Yablonka, 171–77. Jerusalem: Yad Ben-Zvi, 2000.
———. "'Eşuv ziḵron haŠoa' baḤevra haYiśra'elit bišnot haḤamišim [The shaping of Holocaust memory in Israeli society in the 1950s]. In *Tmurot yesod ba'Am haYehudi* [Major changes within the Jewish people in the wake of the Holocaust], edited by Israel Gutman, 473–93. Jerusalem: Yad Vashem, 1996.
Werses, Shmuel. "Qol haIša baŠvuon beYidiš 'Qol mevaser'" [The woman's voice in the Yiddish weekly "Herald Voice"], *Huliyot* 4 (1997): 53–82.
Yablonka, Hanna. "Ma lizkor weKeişad? Nişolei haŠoa we'Eişuv yedi'ata" [What to remember and how? Survivors of the Holocaust and the shaping of its memory]. In *'Idan ha-Zionut* [The age of Zionism], edited by Anita Shapira et al., 297–316. Jerusalem: Zalman Shazar, 2000.
———. "Qliṭat nişoley haŠoa' biMdinat Yiśrael: Hebeṭim ḥadašim" [The absorption of Holocaust survivors in Israel: New aspects]. *'Eyunim bi-Tqumat Yisrael* 7 (1997): 285–99.
———. "Şayarim nişoley šoa' beYiśrael: Hebet nosaf laŠtika šelo hayta" [Holocaust survivor painters in Israel: Another aspect of the silence that never was]. In *HaŠoa': Historya veZikaron* [The Holocaust: History and memory], edited by Shmuel Almog et al, 207–35. Jerusalem: Yad Vashem, 2002.
Zuckermann, Ghil'ad. *Yiśra'elit śafa yafa* [Israeli—a beautiful language]. Tel Aviv: Am-Oved, 2008.

In English or English Translation

Alexander, J. C. "Toward a Theory of Cultural Trauma." In *Cultural Trauma and Collective Identity*, edited by J. C. Alexander et al, 1–30. Berkeley: University of California Press, 2004.

Almog, Oz. *The Sabra: The Creation of the New Jew*. Translated by Haim Watzman. Berkeley: University of California Press, 2000.

Alter, Robert. "Magic Realism in the Israeli Novel." In *The Boom in Contemporary Israeli Fiction*, edited by Alan Mintz, 17–34. Hanover, NH: Brandeis University Press, 1997.

Anderson, Benedict. *Imagined Communities: Reflections on the Origin and Spread of Nationalism*. London: Verso, 1991.

Assmann, Aleida. "Communicative and Cultural Memory." In *Cultural Memory Studies: An International and Interdisciplinary Handbook*, edited by Astrid Erll and Ansgar Nunning, 97–106. Berlin: Walter de Gruyter, 2008.

Assmann, Jan. *Moses the Egyptian: The Memory of Egypt in Western Monotheism*. Cambridge, MA: Harvard University Press, 1997.

Bakhtin, Mikhail M. *The Dialogic Imagination: Four Essays*. Edited by Michael Holquist. Translated by Caryl Emerson and Michael Holquist. Austin: University of Texas Press, 1981.

Bassok, Ido. "Mapping Reading Culture in Interwar Poland: Secular Literature as a New Marker of Ethnic Belonging among Jewish Youth." *Simon Dubnow Institute Yearbook* 9 (2010): 15–36.

Bauer, Ela. "The Ideological Roots of the Polish Jewish Intelligentsia." *Polin* 24 (2012): 95–109.

Benjamin, Walter. "On the Concept of History." In *Illuminations*, edited by Hannah Arendt, translated by Harry Zohn, 257–58. New York: Schocken, 2007.

Blatman, Daniel. *For Our Freedom and Yours: The Jewish Labor Bund in Poland, 1939–1949*. Translated by Naftali Greenwood. London: Vallentine, Mitchell, 2003.

Brenner, Naomi. "Itzik in Israel: Itzik Manger's Yiddish in Hebrew Translation." *Prooftexts* 28 (2008): 53–84.

Cammy, J. D. "Visions and Redemption: Abraham Sutzkever's Poems of Zion(ism)." In *Yiddish after the Holocaust*, edited by Joseph Sherman, 240–43. Oxford: Boulevard Books, 2004.

Cohen, Boaz. "Rachel Auerbuch, Yad Vashem and Israeli Holocaust Memory." *Polin* 20 (2007): 121–97.

De Certeau, Michel. *The Practices of Everyday Life*. Translated by Steven Rendall. Berkeley: University of California Press, 1984.

Deleuze, Gilles, and Felix Guattari. *Kafka: Toward a Minor Literature*. Minneapolis: University of Minnesota Press, 1986.

Deutsch, Nathaniel. *The Jewish Dark Continent: Life and Death in the Russian Pale of Settlement*. Cambridge, MA: Harvard University Press, 2011.

Diner, Hasia R. *We Remember with Reverence and Love: American Jews and the Myth of Silence after the Holocaust, 1945–1962*. New York: New York University Press, 2009.

Douglas, Mary. *Purity and Danger: An Analysis of Concepts of Pollution and Taboo*. London: Routledge, 1966.

Drucker Bar-Am, Gali. "The Anthological Affect: Memory and Place in Early Post WWII Yiddish Culture." In *Memory, Lament and Endurance in Early Post WWII Yiddish Culture: Yiddish after 1945*, edited by Marion Aptroot, 7–27. Amsterdam: Menasseh ben Israel Institute, 2018.

———. "The Bund in Israel: Searching for Jewish Working Class Secular Brotherhood in Zion." In *"Real" Spaces versus "Displaced" Time? Bundist Legacy after the Second World War*, edited by Vincenzo Pinto, 56–69. Leiden: Brill, 2018.

———. "Gaystike erd by Avrom Sutzkever: Between Personal Mythology and National Ideology." *Journal of Jewish Studies* 67 (2016): 157–81.

———. "The Holy Tongue and the Tongue of the Martyrs: The Eichmann Trial as Reflected in *Letste Nayes.*" *Dapim: Studies on the Holocaust* 28, no. 1 (2014): 17–37.

———. "'Normal People in a Land of Their Own': On Gender and Nationalism in Khaye Elboym-Dorembus's *Af der Arisher Zayt.*" *Nashim: A Journal of Jewish Women's Studies and Gender Issues* 27 (2014): 62–74.

———. "'Record and Lament': Yizker Bikher as History and Literature Conflated." *Yad Vashem Studies* 51, no. 2 (2023): 101–28.

———. "Revenge and Reconciliation: Early Israeli Literature and the Dilemma of Jewish Collaborators with the Nazis." In *Jewish Honor Courts: Revenge, Retribution and Reconciliation in Europe and Israel after the Holocaust*, edited by Laura Jockusch and Gabriel N. Finder, 279–302. Detroit: Wayne State University Press, 2015.

———. "Review of *Jewish People, Yiddish Nation: Noah Prylucki and the Folkists in Poland* by Kalman Weiser." *Studies in Contemporary Jewry* 27 (2015): 296–97.

Estraikh, Gennady. *In Harness: Yiddish Writers' Romance with Communism—Judaic Traditions in Literature, Music, and Art.* Syracuse, NY: Syracuse University Press, 2005.

Fishman, D. E. *The Rise of Modern Yiddish Culture.* Pittsburgh: University of Pittsburgh Press, 2005.

Fishman, Joshua. A., and Dovid E. Fishman. "Yiddish in Israel: The Press, Radio, Theater and Book Publishing." *Yiddish* 1, no. 2 (1973): 4–23.

Frankel, Jonathan. *Prophecy and Politics: Socialism, Nationalism, and the Russian Jews, 1862–1917.* New York: Cambridge University Press, 1981.

Freud, Sigmund. "Mourning and Melancholia" (1917). In *The Standard Edition of the Complete Psychological Works of Sigmund Freud*, vol. 14 (1914–16), *On the History of the Psycho-Analytic Movement, Papers on Metapsychology and Other Works*, translated and edited by James Strachey, Anna Freud, et al., 243–44. London: Hogarth and the Institute of Psycho-Analysis, 1964.

Gellner, Ernest. *Language and Solitude: Wittgenstein, Malinowski and the Habsburg Dilemma.* Cambridge: Cambridge University Press, 1998.

———. *Nations and Nationalism.* Ithaca, NY: Cornell University Press, 1983.

Gorny, Yosef. *Converging Alternatives: The Bund and the Zionist Labor Movement, 1897–1985.* Translated by Naftali Greenwood. New York: State University of New York Press, 2005.

Hacohen, Dvora. *Immigrants in Turmoil: Mass Immigration to Israel and Its Repercussions in the 1950s and After.* Translated by Gila Brand. Syracuse: Syracuse University Press, 2003.

Halbwachs, Maurice. *On Collective Memory.* Translated by L. A. Coser. Chicago: University of Chicago Press, 1992.

Halperin, Liora R. *Babel in Zion: Jews, Nationalism and Language Diversity in Palestine, 1920–1948.* New Haven, CT: Yale University Press, 2015.

Harshav, Benjamin. *The Polyphony of Jewish Culture.* Stanford: Stanford University Press, 2007.

Hasan-Rokem, Galit. "Contemporary Perspectives of Tradition: Moving On with the *Wandering Jew.*" In *Konstellationen Über Geschichte, Erfarung und Erkenntnis*, edited by Nicolas Berg et al., 314–27. Göttingen: Vandenhoeck and Ruprecht, 2011.

Helman, Anat. *Young Tel Aviv: A Tale of Two Cities.* Translated by Haim Watzman. Waltham, MA: Brandeis University Press, 2010.

Hirsch, Marianne. "The Generation of Postmemory." *Poetics Today* 29 (2008): 103–28.

Hobsbawm, Eric. "Introduction: Inventing Traditions." In *The Invention of Tradition*, edited by Eric Hobsbawm and Terence Ranger, 1–14. Cambridge: Cambridge University Press, 1983.

Horowitz, Rosemary, ed. *Memorial Books of Eastern European Jewry: Essays on the History and Meaning of Yizker Volumes.* Jefferson, NC: McFarland, 2011.
Howe, Irving. *Politics and the Novel.* New York: New American Library, 1987. First published 1957.
Huyssen, Andreas. "Nostalgia for Ruins." *Grey Room* 23 (2006): 6–21.
Jacobs, Jack. *Bundist Counterculture in Interwar Poland.* Syracuse: Syracuse University Press, 2009.
Jagendorf, Zvi. "Got fun Avrom: Itzik Manger and Avot Yeshurun Look Homewards." In *Insiders and Outsiders: Dilemmas of East European Jewry,* edited by Richard Cohen, Jonathan Frankel, and Stefani Hofman, 30–39. Oxford: Littman Library of Jewish Civilization, 2010.
Jockusch, Laura. *Collect and Record! Jewish Holocaust Documentation in Early Postwar Europe.* Oxford: Oxford University Press, 2012.
———. "Justice at Nuremberg? Jewish Responses to Nazi War Crime Trials in Allied Occupied Germany." *Jewish Social Studies* 19 (2012): 107–47.
Karlip, J. M. *The Tragedy of a Generation: The Rise and Fall of Jewish Nationalism in Eastern Europe.* Cambridge, MA: Harvard University Press, 2013.
Khazzoom Aziza. "Did the Israeli State Engineer Segregation? On the Placement of Jewish Immigrants in Development Towns in the 1950s." *Social Forces* 84, no. 1 (2005): 115–34.
———. *Shifting Ethnic Boundaries and Inequality in Israel: Or, How the Polish Peddler Became a German Intellectual.* Stanford: Stanford University Press, 2008.
Klein, Melanie. *Love, Guilt, and Reparation: And Other Works, 1921–1945.* London: Virago, 1988.
Kliger, Hanna. *Jewish Hometown Associations and Family Circles in New York.* Bloomington: Indiana University Press, 1992,
Kobrin, Rebecca. *Jewish Bialystok and Its Diaspora.* Bloomington: Indiana University Press, 2010.
Krutikov, Mikhail. *Yiddish Fiction and the Crisis of Modernity, 1905–1914.* Stanford: Stanford University Press, 2001.
———. "Yiddish Literature: Yiddish Literature after 1800." In *YIVO Encyclopedia of Jews in Eastern Europe,* vol. 2, edited by Gershon David Hundert, 2065–84. New Haven, CT: Yale University Press, 2008.
Kugelmass, Jack, and Jonathan Boyarin, eds. *From a Ruined Garden: The Memorial Books of Polish Jewry.* Bloomington: Indiana University Press, 1998.
Kuznitz, Cecile Esther. *YIVO and the Making of Modern Jewish Culture.* New York: Cambridge University Press, 2014.
LaCapra, Dominick. "Trauma, Absence, Loss." *Critical Inquiry* 25 (1999): 696–727.
———. *Writing History, Writing Trauma.* Baltimore: Johns Hopkins University Press, 2014.
Lavsky, Hagit. *New Beginnings: Holocaust Survivors in Bergen-Belsen and the British Zone in Germany, 1945–1950.* Detroit: Wayne State University Press, 2002.
Lederhendler, Eli. "Classless: On the Social Status of Jews in Russia and Eastern Europe in the Late Nineteenth Century." *Comparative Studies in Society and History* 50 (2008): 509–34.
———. *Jewish Responses to Modernity: New Voices in America and East Europe.* New York: New York University Press, 1994.
———. *New York Jews and the Decline of Urban Ethnicity, 1950–1970.* Syracuse: Syracuse University Press, 2001.

Lévi-Strauss, Claude. *Myth and Meaning*. London: Routledge, 1978.
Malia, Martin. "What Is the Intelligentsia?" In *The Russian Intelligentsia*, edited by Richard Pipes, 1–18. New York: Columbia University Press, 1961.
Mankowitz, Ze'ev. *Life between Memory and Hope: The Survivors of the Holocaust in Occupied Germany*. Cambridge: Cambridge University Press, 2002.
Mann, Barbara E. *Space and Place in Jewish Studies*. New Brunswick, NJ.: Rutgers University Press, 2012.
Manna, Adel. *Nakba and Survival: The Story of the Palestinians Who Remained in Haifa and the Galilee, 1948–1956*. Oakland: University of California Press, 2022.
Michmann, Dan. *Holocaust Historiography: A Jewish Perspective—Conceptualizations, Terminology, Approaches, and Fundamental Issues*. London: Vallentine Mitchell, 2003.
Miron, Dan. *A Traveler Disguised: The Rise of Modern Yiddish Fiction in the Nineteenth Century*. Syracuse: Syracuse University Press, 1995.
Morris, Benny. *The Birth of the Palestinian Refugee Problem, 1947–1949*. Cambridge: Cambridge University Press, 1987.
Moss, Kenneth B. *Jewish Renaissance in the Russian Revolution*. Cambridge, MA: Harvard University Press, 2008.
Mosse, George L. *Fallen Soldiers: Reshaping the Memory of the World Wars*. Oxford: Oxford University Press, 1990.
———. *Nationalism and Sexuality: Middle-Class Morality and Sexual Norms in Modern Europe*. Madison: University of Wisconsin Press, 1985.
Nora, Pierre. *Realms of Memory: Rethinking the French Past*. Translated by Arthur Goldhammer. New York: Columbia University Press, 1996–98.
Novershtern, Avraham. "Between Town and Gown: The Institutionalization of Yiddish at Israeli Universities." In *Yiddish in the Contemporary World: Papers of the First Mendel Friedman International Conference on Yiddish*, edited by Gennady Estraikh and Mikhail Krutikov, 1–20. Oxford: Legenda, 1999.
———. "The Multi-colored Patchwork on the Coat of a Prince." *Modern Hebrew Literature* 8–9 (1992): 56–59.
———. "Yiddish Poetry in a New Context." *Prooftexts* 8, no. 3 (1988): 355–63.
Ofer, Dalia. *Escaping the Holocaust: Illegal Immigration to the Land of Israel, 1939–1944*. New York: Oxford University Press, 1990.
Olick, J. K., Vered Vinitzky-Seroussi, and Daniel Levy, eds. *The Collective Memory Reader*. New York: Oxford University Press, 2011.
Peled, Yo'av. *Class and Ethnicity in the Pale: The Political Economy of Jewish Workers' Nationalism in Late Imperial Russia*. New York: St. Martin's, 1989.
Pipes, Richard. "The Historical Evolution of the Russian Intelligentsia." In *The Russian Intelligentsia*, edited by Richard Pipes, 47–62. New York: Columbia University Press, 1961.
Porat, Dina. *Israeli Society, the Holocaust and Its Survivors*. London: Vallentine Mitchell, 2008.
Rojanski, Rachel. "The Final Chapter in the Struggle for Cultural Autonomy: Palestine, Israel and Yiddish Writers in the Diaspora, 1946–1951." *Journal of Modern Jewish Studies* 6 (2007): 185–204.
———. "The Status of Yiddish in Israel, 1948–1958: An Overview." In *Yiddish after the Holocaust*, edited by Joseph Sherman, 46–59. Oxford: Boulevard Books, 2004.
Rosenwald, L. A. *Multicultural America: Language and the Making of American Literature*. Cambridge: Cambridge University Press, 2008.

Roskies, David. *A Bridge of Longing: The Lost Art of Yiddish Storytelling*. Cambridge, MA: Harvard University Press, 1995.

Schein, Ada. "'Everyone Can Hold a Pen': The Documentation Project in the DP Camps in Germany." In *Holocaust Historiography in Context: Emergence, Challenges, Polemics and Achievements*, edited by David Bankier and Dan Michmann, 103–34. Jerusalem: Yad Vashem and Berghahn, 2008.

Schwartz-Seller, Maxine. "Defining Socialist Womanhood: The Women's Page of the *Jewish Daily Forward* in 1919." *American Jewish History* 76 (1987): 416–38.

Shandler, Jefferey. "Anthologizing the Vernacular: Collections of Yiddish Literature in English Translation." In *The Anthology in Jewish Literature*, edited by David Stern, 304–23. Oxford: Oxford University Press, 2004.

Shaul, Michal. *Holocaust Memory in Ultra-Orthodox Society in Israel*. Bloomington: Indiana University Press, 2020.

Shavit, David. *Hunger for the Printed Word: Books and Libraries in the Jewish Ghettos of Nazi-Occupied Europe*. Jefferson, NC: McFarland, 1997.

Sherman, Joseph. "Asch, Sholem." In *YIVO Encyclopedia of Jews in Eastern Europe*, vol. 1, edited by Gershon David Hundert, 74–77. New Haven, CT: Yale University Press, 2008).

Simmel, Georg. "The Metropolis and Mental Life." In *Georg Simmel: On Individuality and Social Forms*, edited by Donald Levine. Chicago: Chicago University Press, 1971. First published 1903. 324–39.

Slucki, David. *The International Jewish Labor Bund after 1945: Toward a Global History*. New Brunswick, NJ: Rutgers University Press, 2012.

Smith, M. L. "No Silence in Yiddish: Popular and Scholarly Writing about the Holocaust in the Early Postwar Years." In *After the Holocaust: Challenging the Myth of Silence*, edited by David Cesarani and Eric J. Sundquist. London: Routledge, 2012, 55–66.

Sollors, Werner. *Ethnic Modernism*. Cambridge, Mass.: Harvard University Press, 2008.

Trachtenberg, Barry. *The Revolutionary Roots of Modern Yiddish, 1903–1917*. Syracuse: Syracuse University Press, 2008.

Veidlinger, Jeffrey. *Jewish Public Culture in the Late Russian Empire*. Bloomington: Indiana University Press, 2009.

Weiser, Kalman. "The Jewel in the Yiddish Crown: Who Will Occupy the Chair in Yiddish at the University of Vilnius?." *Polin: Studies in Polish Jewry* 24 (2012): 223–55.

———. *Jewish People, Yiddish Nation: Noah Prylucki and the Folkists in Poland*. Toronto: University of Toronto Press, 2011.

Wirth, Louis. "Urbanism as a Way of Life." *American Journal of Sociology* 44, no. 1 (1938): 1–24.

Wolff, F. "Revolutionary Identity and Migration: The Commemorative Transnationalism of Bundist Culture." *East European Jewish Affairs* 43, no. 3 (2013): 314–31.

Yablonka, Hanna. *Survivors of the Holocaust: Israel after the War*. Translated by Ora Cummings. London: Palgrave Macmillan, 1999.

Zerubavel, Yael. *Recovered Roots: Collective Memory and the Making of Israeli National Tradition*. Chicago: University of Chicago Press, 1995.

In French

Perego, Simon. "Les commémorations de la destruction des Juifs d'Europe au Mémorial du martyr juif inconnu du milieu des années cinquante à la fin des années soixante." *Revue d'histoire de la Shoah* 193 (2010): 471–507.

Wieviorka, Annette. "Un lieu de mémoire et d'histoire: Le Mémorial du martyr juif inconnu." *Renue de l'université de Bruxelles* 1–2 (1987): 107–132.

In Spanish

Chinski, Milena. "Memorias en plural: Los judíos de Buenos Aires ante el Holocausto, 1945–1955." PhD diss., Universidad Nacional de General Sarmiento, 2017.

Index

Aleichem, Sholem, 9, 11, 45, 72, 100, 162–64, 167–68, 175, 236; Ayznban geshikhte, 261; *Kleyne mentshelekh mit kleyne hasoges*, 233, 240; *Motl Peysi dem khazn's*, 230, 254; Sholem Aleykhem hayzer, 323n86; *Stempenyu*, 163, 230; *Tevye der milkhiker*, 205
Alster, Yisroel, 92, 310n246
Asch, Sholem, 17, 63, 74, 162, 177, 302n144, 312n283, 315nn314–17, 340n191; *Dray shtet*, 249; Sholem Asch street, 267; *A Shtetl*, 193; "A talent tsu erets yisroel," 110–11, 116–17
Ashkenazim, 14–15, 207; East/Eastern European Jews / Eastern European Jewry, 113; Eastern European ghetto, 34, 39, 169, 173, 249, 292n16, 342n213; Eastern European immigrants, 57, 83, 204; Jewish past in Eastern Europe, 128; Jewish small town / Eastern European towns, 32–34, 142, 184, 186, 195, 217, 221, 235, 242, 251, 258–59; Jewish society in Eastern Europe, 7–8; Jews of/from Eastern Europe / Jews of Eastern European origin, 1, 10, 12–15, 17–19, 25, 31, 35, 38, 40, 42, 44–45, 48, 50, 59, 80, 82, 87, 111, 127–29, 135, 141, 143–44, 148, 164, 167, 171–72, 174, 212, 217, 219, 223, 225, 227, 235, 241, 243, 247, 254–56, 259, 261–65, 270, 287n25, 292n23, 323n86, 334n89, 335n110; Nusah Ashkenaz / Poyln, 175, 286n15; Ostjuden / low origin, 225, 245; Shtetl, 3, 31–32, 94–95, 124, 129, 135, 144, 162–65, 169–71, 180, 192, 204–5, 239–40, 243, 247–48, 255, 291n8, 318n22, 319n39, 323n88, 324n91, 340n182
Ayznman, Tzvi, 42, 46–48, 64, 73–74, 78, 100, 106, 159, 170, 175, 217, 241, 245–47, 249, 277, 306nn188–95, 308n214, 313n284, 325n1–2, 335nn108–9, 338n149, 338nn161–62, 339nn163–66; "Arum beys hamedresh," 240; *Di ban: dertseylungen fun poyln, rusland, yisroel*, 174; "A mayse vegn nisim fun har-ṭuv, vegn a varshever hoyf un vegn a shpil-foygl," 215–16; *Mazoles*, 313n290, 331n40; "Mentshelekh," 238–40

Balas, Shimon, 13, 264, 289n51; *HaMa'abara*, 335n88, 338n156
Bartov, Hanoch, 264; *Shesh knafaim le-Ehad*, 199, 332n60, 333n64, 333n66, 334n76
Ben-Gurion, David, 41, 54, 104, 270, 294n51, 304n177, 310n245, 322n71; Ben-Gurion boulevard, 133
Bergelson, Dovid, 74, 168, 230, 291n10, 325n4, 330n32; *Nokh alemen*, 161–65, 187, 326n7
Berlinski, Shloyme, 42, 46, 49, 64, 100, 104, 174, 258, 277, 302n142, 303n150, 342n212
Birshteyn, Yosl, 48, 64, 73–74, 78, 100, 241, 313n285, 338n149, 339n172, 340n178; *Af shmole trotuarn*, 242–47, 249, 339nn167–70, 339n174
Bolel, Nosn, 60–61, 300n124, 311n252
Brat, Yitskhok, 59, 150, 221; "Kalmens tfile," 336n123; "A shmues mit a mistanen," 332n59
Bund, the / Der algemeyner arbeter-bund fun rusland un poyln / Der algemeyner yidisher arbeter-bund in lite, poyln un rusland, 47–48, 80–91; Arbeter-ring (AR), 95–97; Y. Artuski, 42, 46, 79, 82–90, 97, 138, 140, 150, 271, 275–76, 309n226, 309n229, 309n233, 309n236, 310nn239–40, 322n70, 325nn109–10, 343n2; Doikayt (here-ness), 81, 166, 168, 311n247; Israeli Bund party, 83, 88, 309n229; Kurski Library, 91, 95–97, 140, 150, 319n39, 311n259, 324n102; *Lebns-fragn: Sotsialistishe khoydesh-shrift far politik, virtshaft un kultur*, 79, 83–87, 90, 187, 310n234, 310n236; Tsalevitsh, Ben-Zion (Bentsl), 81, 84, 92, 97, 309n224

communism, 47, 84, 86, 186, 190, 219, 251, 234, 251, 275, 277, 280, 282, 289n49, 334n89; *Fray-yisroel: Demokratishe vokhnshrift far politik, virtshaft un kultur*, 79, 308n213, 308n215; Maki (Israeli Communist Party), 79, 231

Eichmann trial, 55–56, 125, 139, 145, 152–55, 227, 299n109, 305n178, 317n14, 319n39, 325n111, 325n112

Elboym-Dorembus, Khaye, 42, 46, 62, 64, 106, 231, 277; *Af der Arisher Zayt*, 104, 301n136, 317n14, 337–338n145; "Der pomidor," 223–24, 337n131

Eydlman, Dovid, 26, 46, 59, 61, 256, 257, 277, 303n151, 332n59, 342n206, 342n220, 343n226

Glatshteyn, Yankev, 101; "A gute nakht, velt," 169, 249, 292n16

Granatshteyn, Yekhiel, 42, 63–64, 209, 220, 248, 301n140; "Aleyn," 223–24, 337n130; "Azoy lebn mir in Shikun," 336n118; "A bagegenish af dereḵpetaḥ-tiqwa," 212, 335n103; "In blekhenem baydl fun der ma'abara," 209–10, 335n96; "A khasene in a ma'abara," 210–12, 335nn99–02; "Khvalyendike likht," 262, 343n228; "Mentshn fun undzer land: tsvey brider," 260, 342n215; "Sakh-hakl fun a tog: fun dem togbikhl fun an arbetslozn," 210, 335n98; "Ven dos folk fayert," 262, 343n227; "Zayn ershte freyd," 210, 335n97

Greenberg, Uri Zvi, 2, 63, 302n148

Gruenbaum, Yitzhak, 54, 60

Grosman, Moyshe, 1, 42, 46, 48, 104, 276, 312n269; *Di vide fun a revolutsyoner: politisher roman*, 106, 313n285, 341nn194–95; *Heymish*, 100, 285n3, 298n101

Gros-Tsimerman, Moyshe, 36, 37, 150, 292n22

Halamish, Mordechai, 36, 150, 275–76, 296n77, 330n28; *Mikan uMiqarov: antologia šel siporei yidiš be'Ereṣ Yiśra'el miRešit haMe'a we'Ad yanenu*, 108, 112–18, 313n283, 315nn319–24, 315n326

Ha-Levi, Judah, 126; Judah ha-Levi's street, 133; "Ṣion halo tiš'ali," 4–8, 286nn14–18

Hendel, Yehudit, 264; *'Anašim 'aḥerim hem*, 202, 242, 334n71

Histadrut ha'Ovdim ha'Ivriim be-Eretz Yisrael / General Organization of Hebrew Workers, 2, 64, 67–68, 71, 84, 92, 95, 151, 303n155, 303n158, 307n209, 308n213

home: big / small home, 188, 190, 214, 221, 240, 245; destruction of the home, 8, 126; family [motif] / disintegration of the Jewish family [motif] / family novel, 159, 162–63, 182–88, 191, 193, 196, 203, 206, 213, 241–47, 249–51, 254–55, 258–63, 301n135, 341n192; family new [motif] / return to a normative family life, 126, 141, 147, 179, 210–11, 216–30, 339n171; home owner / proprietor / ownership of the home, 109, 161, 181, 189, 190, 192, 198, 227, 230–31; Landsmanshaftn / hometown associations, 60, 131–33, 135–37, 140–42, 144–45, 208, 282, 301n129, 317–318n18, 320n41, 323nn80–83; old home, 3, 94, 115, 135, 142–44, 155, 172, 179–80, 185, 208, 224, 232, 258, 267, 308n215, 311n252, 317n16, 333n63; pets [motif], 184, 198–200; refugeehood, return of the refugees [motif], 14, 40, 45, 110, 179, 184–85, 192–94, 196–202, 208–9, 227, 248, 264, 269; root [motif] / rootlessness / uprooting, 1, 3, 7–8, 14, 93, 104, 108–11, 116–17, 126, 145, 170, 179, 184–85, 193–94, 196–98, 200–203, 207, 225–27, 237, 241, 243, 248, 269, 333n63; wedding [motif], 161, 171, 210–11, 224, 245, 249, 258

intelligentsia, 33–35, 42–45, 50, 52, 60, 75, 80, 117–18, 127, 242, 295nn58–59, 296n72, 296n75; elitism, 2, 67–68, 182, 286n12, 334n88; polo intelligentsia, 45, 127

Israel-theme, the, 161, 173, 181, 184, 207, 217–19, 231, 240–41, 253, 263, 270, 327n29, 327n34; housemaids market [motif], 203, 253, 341n198; howling of jackals [motif], 184, 226; independence day celebrations [motif], 60, 237, 261–62; Lot's wife dilemma, 160, 177; *nusah* Israel, 175; Yemenite Jews [motif], 214, 216–17, 335n110

Kants, Shimen, 46, 64, 277; "Shhunot vos darfn shtern undzer ru," 336n121

Karpinovitsh, Avrom, 26, 36, 42, 64, 73, 78, 100, 150, 221, 305n184, 306n193, 330n28; "Di mame vet nokh spondzhe makhn," 253–55, 278, 341n197, 341n199; "Farshpetike blumen," 221, 336n122
Khadash, Yisroel, 53, 55, 276, 299n104
Khave Levkovitsh, 48, 62, 276, 322n74, 339n171
Kishon, Efraim, 257, 265, 289n51
Kulbak, Moyshe, 74, 162, 341n192; "Raysn," 205–6, 334n83
Kviatkovski-pinkhasik, Rivke, 46–48, 62, 64, 85, 100, 106, 231, 278, 296nn78–79, 333n72; "Zamd," 224–28, 337nn133–36

Lavon, Pinhas / Lavon Affair, 2, 55, 304n177
Left Po'ale Zion, 47–48, 50, 53, 67, 71, 79, 92–93, 98, 101, 103, 107, 280, 282; *Nayvelt: Vokhnshrift far politik un kultur*, 50, 71, 79, 103, 282, 308nn213–14
Leshtshinski, Yankev, 36, 292n19, 322n76, 338n154
libraries, public, 32, 43, 50, 81, 91–97, 98, 125, 145, 152, 167, 310n241, 310n243, 311n250, 330n35
List, Nakhmen, 129–30, 300n124, 319n38
Luden, Yitskhok, 26, 42, 47–48, 57, 83, 155, 276, 297n86, 298n100, 300n119, 300n124, 303n151, 307n212, 309n225, 310n245

Mali, Malasha, 46, 48, 100, 109, 230–31, 278, 337nn142–43; "Der forhang," 228–229, 337nn138–140
Man, Mendl, 46, 48, 49, 68, 78, 98, 100, 176, 182, 230, 305n184, 306n188, 327n32, 329n16, 331n45, 331n47, 333n63, 334n87; *Dos hoyz tsvishn derner*, 104; *In a farvorloztn dorf*, 193–207, 296n78, 331n46, 331n48, 334nn77–82, 341n198
Manger, Itzik, 1–3, 17, 26, 39, 74, 111, 206, 273, 285n1–4, 285n7–11, 313n283, 334n84; K'hob zikh yorn gevalgert, 4–9, 126, 149, 285n5, 285nn13–18, 287n20; Manger Prize, 276–77
Mapai party, 55–56, 83, 299n104, 308n213, 322n71
masses, the, 22, 24, 34, 36–50, 52, 60–61, 67, 90, 93, 113, 117, 119, 120, 127, 138, 160, 169, 200, 238, 247, 262–63, 265, 306n199, 323n84; populism, 45, 51, 61, 90, 127, 246, 295n69; Russian populism / Narodism, 44, 171, 233
Meged, Aharon, 264; *Ḥedwa we'Ani uFarašat qoroteynu ba'Ir tel-'aviv*, 245, 249, 341n203
Mendele moykher sforim, 10, 45, 72, 162–63, 166, 167, 185, 291n5, 326n6; *Dos kleyne mentshele*, 240; Mendele Award, 57, 276, 278; Mendele moykher sforim Press, 106, 341n194
Mossinson, Yigal, 305n179; *Dereḵ Gever*, 244, 339n173

Namdirf, Y. [Fridman, Yankev], 61, 257, 278, 342n209; "A dkhak-arbeter," 336n103
Niger, Shmuel, 43, 45, 50, 76, 107, 167, 169, 171–72, 230, 285n4, 295n58, 295n62, 295n69, 296n84, 303n158, 306n199, 307nn209–10, 326n11, 326n14, 327n19, 327n25, 337n143

Oyerbakh, Rokhl, 42–43, 46, 48–49, 100, 120–21, 127, 140, 152–53, 231, 277, 295nn56–57, 296n77, 296n83, 316n3–4, 319n39, 325nn112–13, 325n115, 337n129; "Dos viglid," 223, 337n128; *In land yisroel: reportazshn, eseyn, dertseylungen*, 329n16
Oz, Amos, 305n179, 329n16; *Maqom 'Aḥer*, 254, 339n176

Paner, Yitskhok, 42, 46, 64, 78, 85, 104, 329n16, 339n175, 342n221
Papiernikov, Levi, 46, 100, 174, 278, 329n19, 335n103, 336n116, 342n215; *In der nayer heym: dertseylungen*, 174
Papiernikov, Yosef, 85, 104
Peretz, Y. L., 45, 69, 72, 74, 85, 100, 164–69, 175, 313n283, 315n208, 326n8, 326n11; "Bay nakht afn altn mark," 165; "Bontshe shvayg," 236; Di goldene keyt, 76, 168, 307n207; "Di toyte shtot," 166; "Dray matones," 172; Peretz street, 151; "Tsvishn tsvey berg," 51, 297n90; Y. L. Peretz-farlag, 72, 98–107, 118, 297n86, 312n269, 312nn276–80, 312n282, 313nn286–91; Y. L. Peretz library, 2, 91–95, 140, 285n1, 310n246, 311nn248–49, 311n251, 311n256, 319n39

Perlov, Yitskhok, 46, 49, 63–64, 85, 98, 104, 182, 207, 278, 328n37, 329n12, 329n16, 329nn22–23, 330nn24–25, 334n86; *Dzshebelye*, 133, 179, 182–93, 204–5, 207, 234–35, 248, 321n55, 328n1–3, 330n33, 331nn38–41, 331n44, 338n153, 338n155; *Flora Ingber: a hoyz in tel-oviv*, 249–51, 301n137, 302n146, 330n27, 340n190; *In eygenem land*, 174, 333n74, 337nn126–27, 342n223; "Neqome," 214–15, 302n146, 335n106; "Der onheyb," 252–53, 341n196
Pinski, Dovid, 17, 72, 74, 84, 99, 177, 312n283, 341n192

Rotnberg, Yoisef, 42, 93, 98, 276, 296n78, 310n243, 311n248, 312n276
Rozhanski, Shmuel, 37, 107, 172–73, 265, 292n20, 304n168, 316n2, 326n21, 327n23, 327n28, 336n123
Roznberg, Shimen, 98, 302n141
Rubinshteyn, Eliezer, 26, 150, 236, 239, 241, 249, 260, 277, 302n143; "Er vart af zey," 342n216; "Zayn ershter tants," 338nn157–59
Rubinshteyn, Ruven, 49, 300n124

Sabra, the, 3, 39, 86, 113, 128, 154, 178, 189, 194, 200, 202–3, 220, 223, 235–36, 239, 242–43, 254–57, 268, 270, 319n34, 323n87, 338n146, 338n160, 339n168
Sadan, Dov, 114–15, 302n143, 312n283, 315nn323–24
Shamir, Moshe, 176, 264, 305n179, 327n33; *Hu halak̠ baŚadot*, 188–91, 242, 248, 330n36, 340n186
Shamri, Arie, 169, 276, 326n15, 338n149; *Vortslen: antologye fun yidish-shafn in yisroel, poezye un proze*, 104, 108–12, 114–17, 315nn310–12, 315n318; *Yisroel-bukh*, 98, 104, 106, 313n294
Sheyres-hapleyte / surviving remnant, 1, 3–4, 8–12, 22, 35, 37, 50, 95, 110, 172, 185, 286n18, 287nn25–30, 292nn23–25, 294nn39–41, 300n116, 300n128, 328n8–10; communities of memory, 131, 135–36, 138–39, 144, 147; cultural memory, 148–49, 166, 324n95; displaced persons camps (DP Camps), 12, 49, 63, 109, 132, 167, 182–83, 185, 203, 217, 234, 277, 288n31, 296n80, 296n82, 300n124, 300n126, 304n162, 318n29, 321n52, 326n12, 329n12; empathy [term], 121–22, 134, 192, 199, 214, 264, 269; ghettos, 42, 46, 48, 70, 72, 76, 85, 100, 104, 130, 132–33, 137–38, 145–46, 148, 150–54, 167, 189, 193, 217, 276–78, 296nn76–77, 300n128, 317n15, 318n20, 322n67; Holocaust memorial day, 130, 138–39, 321nn65–66, 322nn68–71; Kdoyshim, 129, 132, 321n56, 324n97; Khurbn, 4, 6–8, 11–12, 36, 58, 68, 120, 125–26, 129, 130, 132, 138, 143, 147, 149, 152, 154–55, 160–61, 165, 170–73, 178, 198, 200, 208, 213, 217, 250, 286n15, 307nn207–8, 322n70, 324n97; khurbn-literatur, 99, 100, 330n29; ruin the [motif], 129–30, 143, 160–61, 164–65, 168, 186, 196, 198, 267, 319n38, 326n9; like sheep to the slaughter, 128, 138; silence-of-the-survivors myth / myth of the silence of [the] survivors, 11, 12, 14, 138, 237, 265, 269–70, 287n30, 292–292n25, 317n13, 318n30; spatial memory, 143, 151; Yizker bikher, 64, 99, 102–3, 109, 312n281, 313n291, 318n19
Shneur, Zalman, 17, 74; Zalman Shneur street, 267
Shpigl, Yishaye, 42, 46, 48, 64, 87, 100, 174, 278, 296n77, 305n184, 313n284, 330n28, 335n103; "A fremde," 222, 337n124; "Di kukavke," 116, 209, 213, 335n94, 335n105, 339n166; "Keter yisroel," 222, 337n125
Shpiglblat, Aleksander, 68–70, 76, 111, 287n20, 304nn164–65, 304n167, 304nn169–70, 304n174, 305n184, 307n205
Singer Isaac, Bashevis, 63, 162; *Di familiye mushkat*, 213
Slutska-Kestin, Khave, 46, 219–20, 231, 278; *In undzere teg*, 219, 336n117
Sprinzak, Yosef, 2, 67, 304n177
Sutzkever, Avrom, 1, 17, 31, 34–36, 42, 46, 48, 51, 67–76, 78–79, 90, 92, 100, 118, 140, 149–52, 154, 161, 168, 174–75, 267, 276, 285n2, 290n1–2, 296n75, 296n77, 303nn155–56, 303n158, 303n161, 304n163, 304n166, 304n168, 304nn172–76, 305nn180–86, 306n192, 306n196, 307nn202–6,

307nn208–9, 307n211, 308n214, 310n246, 324n96, 324n99, 325n108, 325n116, 326n13, 327n31, 334n86, 337n142, 343n1; Yung-yisroel, 73–75, 78, 159, 230, 233, 290n54, 306n187, 306n198, 325n1–2, 331n40, 335n108, 337n142, 338n150, 339n167, 340n178

Temqin-Berman, Batya, 93, 311n250, 311n257, 311n263
Tsanin, Mordkhe, 26, 31, 36, 41–42, 46, 51–59, 61–62, 64–65, 68, 75, 90, 104, 118, 125, 136–37, 140, 145, 150, 153, 234–35, 276, 281, 290n2, 294n51, 297n86, 298nn98–101, 298–299nn103–4, 299n106, 300nn122–23, 300n125, 301nn137–38, 302n142, 303n150, 307n200, 309n232, 310n244, 315n317, 318n23, 321n64, 324n90, 324n100, 325n110, 325n114, 329n22, 330n34, 334n86, 335n91, 337n126, 338n152, 341n199; *Yidishe tsaytung*, 53–55, 276, 282, 298n99, 299nn104–5

Vaysman, Gavriel, 63, 85, 87, 104

wandering Jew, 7–9, 111, 171–72, 193, 287nn21–22
Weichert, Michał, 95, 97, 310nn243–44, 311n255, 311n260, 311n262
Weinreich, Max, 15, 34, 44, 69, 287n23, 288n38, 304n166, 305n182, 318n27, 320n44

Yasny, A. Volf, 26, 42, 48, 56, 64, 75, 95, 97, 100, 103, 145, 276, 297n86, 300n113, 306n198, 311nn253–54, 311n261, 324n91, 328n34, 339n175
Yiddish language, 3, 11, 48, 62, 87, 110, 113, 272, 287n23, 334n88; foreign language, 55–56, 58, 86, 112, 153, 271, 293n31, 298n100, 299n107, 305n180, 310n245; linguistic chauvinism, 20–21, 55; linguistic loyalty, 21–22, 79, 265, 270, 308n215, 324n97; multilingual Jewish culture, 136; war of languages / battle of the tongues, 23, 25, 113, 114, 115, 289n49, 294–295n55; Yiddish in the educational system, 16, 32, 34, 47, 50, 80, 97, 114–15, 125, 129, 141, 152, 167, 222, 271, 310n239
Yiddish literature: children's literature 87, 90, 220; female writers / women's poetry/ women's Yiddish poetry, 62, 219, 223, 231–32, 301n134, 302n135; multilingual literature / multilingual study of Israeli literature, 10, 23–24, 39, 48, 136, 271, 289–290nn52–53, 343n3
Yiddish novel; serial, 53, 62–63, 85, 124, 183, 303n150, 317n14, 340n179, 340n191; immigration, 170–71, 192; local/regional, 172, 193–94
Yiddishland, 31, 35, 42, 50, 52, 119, 263; "affective community," 267–68; centers of Yiddish culture, 31–32, 34–35, 42, 53, 57, 118, 271, 279–84, 290n3; diasporic nationalism, 34, 291n12; synthetic Yiddishism, 256
Yizhar, S., 264, 265, 305n179, 343nn229; "HaŠavuy," 199, 333n61; *Ḥirbet Ḥiz'eh*, 199, 201, 333n61, 333n65; *Yemei Ṣiqlag*, 319n36

Zonshayn, Moyshe, 104, 276; Ha-Menora, 98, 103, 106, 313n293

GALI DRUCKER BAR-AM (PhD, Hebrew University of Jerusalem) is a scholar of modern Yiddish culture and its history. She is a world leading authority on Yiddish literature written in Israel. Her studies focus on the formation of modern and post–World War II Jewish and Israeli (subjective and collective) identities. Her work closely interacts with wider studies of the modern experience, most notably studies of migration and exile cultures, of genocide and trauma, and of the emergence of modern ideologies and political movements and their influence on the collective ethos of place, space, tradition, and memory. She teaches the art of teaching literature at the Levinsky-Wingate Academic Center, Tel Aviv.

For Indiana University Press

Tony Brewer, Artist and Book Designer
Dan Crissman, Editorial Director and Acquisitions Editor
Anna Francis, Assistant Acquisitions Editor
Anna Garnai, Editorial Assistant
Brenna Hosman, Production Coordinator
Katie Huggins, Production Manager
David Miller, Lead Project Manager/Editor
Dan Pyle, Online Publishing Manager
Brandon Spaulding, Journals Production Manager
Stephen Williams, Assistant Director of Marketing
Jennifer Witzke, Senior Artist and Book Designer

www.ingramcontent.com/pod-product-compliance
Lightning Source LLC
Chambersburg PA
CBHW031415230426
43668CB00007B/319
9780253071514